Lecture Notes in Computer Science

AF148087

Lecture Notes in Artificial Intelligence   16122

Founding Editor

Jörg Siekmann

Series Editors

Randy Goebel, *University of Alberta, Edmonton, Canada*
Wolfgang Wahlster, *DFKI, Berlin, Germany*
Zhi-Hua Zhou, *Nanjing University, Nanjing, China*

The series Lecture Notes in Artificial Intelligence (LNAI) was established in 1988 as a topical subseries of LNCS devoted to artificial intelligence.

The series publishes state-of-the-art research results at a high level. As with the LNCS mother series, the mission of the series is to serve the international R & D community by providing an invaluable service, mainly focused on the publication of conference and workshop proceedings and postproceedings.

José Valente de Oliveira · João Leite ·
João Rodrigues · João Dias · Pedro Cardoso
Editors

Progress in Artificial Intelligence

24th EPIA Conference on Artificial Intelligence, EPIA 2025
Faro, Portugal, October 1–3, 2025
Proceedings, Part II

 Springer

Editors
José Valente de Oliveira 🆔
University of Algarve
Faro, Portugal

João Leite 🆔
NOVA University Lisbon
Costa da Caparica, Portugal

João Rodrigues 🆔
University of Algarve
Faro, Portugal

João Dias 🆔
University of Algarve
Faro, Portugal

Pedro Cardoso 🆔
University of Algarve
Faro, Portugal

ISSN 0302-9743   ISSN 1611-3349 (electronic)
Lecture Notes in Artificial Intelligence
ISBN 978-3-032-05178-3   ISBN 978-3-032-05179-0 (eBook)
https://doi.org/10.1007/978-3-032-05179-0

LNCS Sublibrary: SL7 – Artificial Intelligence

This Springer imprint is published by the registered company Springer Nature Switzerland AG
The registered company address is: Gewerbestrasse 11, 6330 Cham, Switzerland

If disposing of this product, please recycle the paper.

Preface

The EPIA Conference on Artificial Intelligence is a well-established conference in the field of Artificial Intelligence (AI). The 24th edition, EPIA 2025, was held in Faro at the University of Algarve, Campus de Gambelas, October 1–3, 2025 (https://epia2025.ual g.pt/).

Faro is the charming capital of the Algarve region in southern Portugal, renowned for its history, picturesque old town, and vibrant culture. The city features cobbled streets, historic landmarks like the Faro Cathedral, and a scenic waterfront along the Ria Formosa lagoon, which is a protected nature reserve teeming with diverse wildlife. Its welcoming atmosphere, combined with lively markets, traditional cuisine, and cultural festivals, makes Faro a captivating destination for travelers seeking both history and relaxation.

The conference was organized with the patronage of the Portuguese Association for Artificial Intelligence (APPIA – http://www.appia.pt). EPIA covers theoretical, fundamental questions, and applications in Artificial Intelligence, allowing scientific exchange between researchers, engineers, and professionals in related disciplines.

The EPIA 2025 program included 15 thematic tracks dedicated to specific areas in AI:

- AI and Creativity (AIC);
- AI for Architecture, Engineering and Conservation (AI4AES);
- Ambient Intelligence and Affective Environments (AmIA);
- Artificial Intelligence and IoT in Agriculture (AIoTA);
- Artificial Intelligence and Law (AIL);
- Artificial Intelligence for Industry and Societies (AI4IS);
- Artificial Intelligence in Medicine (AIM);
- Artificial Intelligence in Power and Energy Systems (AIPES);
- Artificial Intelligence in Transportation Systems (AITS);
- Ethics and Responsibility in AI (ERAI);
- Fuzzy Data Analysis and Applications (FDA);
- Generative AI – Foundations and Applications (GenAI);
- Knowledge Discovery and Business Intelligence (KDBI);
- Natural Language Processing, Text Mining and Applications (NLP-TeMA);
- Artificial Intelligence - Theory, Methods, and Applications (AITMA).

In this edition, EPIA received 158 submissions from 32 different countries. Each submission was reviewed by at least three Program Committee (PC) members of each thematic track. These volumes contain all 76 accepted papers from the thematic tracks.

The conference also featured three distinguished keynote speakers: Paulo Torroni (University of Bologna, Italy) with a talk on "Argument Mining and Reasoning with Large Language Models"; Frans A. Oliehoek (Delft University of Technology, Netherlands) with a talk on "Model-based reinforcement learning and abstraction"; and Mário Figueiredo (Instituto Superior Técnico, University of Lisbon, Portugal) with a talk on

"The Why of AI: Causal Discovery from Observational Data". The invited talks' abstracts are included in these proceedings' front matter.

The EPIA organizers are thankful to our outstanding keynote speakers, to the EPIA 2025 International Steering Committee members for their guidance regarding the scientific organization, and to the Thematic Track Chairs and their respective Program Committee members. Very special thanks are due to all the student volunteers and the Local Organizing Committee, who did a fantastic job, contributing to a very successful conference. The organization would also like to express its gratitude to our sponsors, Empowered Startups (https://empoweredstartups.com/), Dengun (http://dengun.com/) and STAP, SA (http://www.stap.pt/) and Springer (https://www.springer.com) who sponsored the Best Paper Award. To conclude, a word of thanks to our hosts, Câmara Municipal de Faro, the University of Algarve and its Faculty of Sciences and Technology, and the Faculty of Economics.

October 2025

José Valente de Oliveira
João Leite
João Rodrigues
João Dias
Pedro Cardoso

Organization

Event and Program Chairs

José Valente de Oliveira	University of Algarve, Portugal
João Leite	NOVA University Lisbon, Portugal
João Rodrigues	University of Algarve, Portugal
João Dias	University of Algarve, Portugal
Pedro Cardoso	University of Algarve, Portugal

Organization Chairs

Simão Melo de Sousa	University of Algarve, Portugal
Helder Daniel	University of Algarve, Portugal
José Barateiro	University of Algarve, Portugal
Marielba Zacarias	University of Algarve, Portugal
Paula Ventura Martins	University of Algarve, Portugal
Sofia Vairinho	University of Algarve, Portugal

International Steering Committee

Alípio Jorge	University of Porto, Portugal
Ana Bazzan	Federal University of Rio Grande do Sul, Brazil
Bernadete Ribeiro	University of Coimbra, Portugal
Eugénio Oliveira	University of Porto, Portugal
Goreti Marreiros	Polytechnic Institute of Porto, Portugal
Inês Lynce	University of Lisbon, Portugal
José Júlio Alferes	NOVA University Lisbon, Portugal
Juan Pavón	Complutense University of Madrid, Spain
Luís Correia	University of Lisbon, Portugal
Luís Paulo Reis	University of Porto, Portugal
Paulo Novais	University of Minho, Portugal
Virginia Dignum	Umeå University, Sweden

Thematic Track Chairs

AI and Creativity (AIC)

João Miguel Cunha	University of Coimbra, Portugal
Pedro Martins	University of Coimbra, Portugal
Tiago Martins	University of Coimbra, Portugal
Maria Hedblom	Jönköping University, Sweden
Moritz Schwind	Technische Hochschule Nürnberg Georg Simon Ohm, Germany

AI for Architecture, Engineering and Conservation (AI4AES)

Daniele Corradetti	University of Lisbon, Portugal
Nuno Marques	NOVA University Lisbon, Portugal
José Delgado Rodrigues	Consultant in Heritage Conservation, Portugal
Roberta Spallone	Politecnico di Torino, Italia

Ambient Intelligence and Affective Environments (AmIA)

Manuel Rodrigues	Universidade do Minho, Portugal
Luís Conceição	ISEP, Portugal
Sara Rodríguez	University of Salamanca, Spain
Peter Mikulecky	University of Hradec Králové, Czech Republic
Goreti Marreiros	ISEP, Portugal
Paulo Novais	Universidade do Minho, Portugal

Artificial Intelligence and IoT in Agriculture (AIoTA)

Luís Pádua	UTAD, Portugal
Filipe Neves dos Santos	INESC-TEC, Portugal
José Boaventura Cunha	UTAD, Portugal
Paulo Moura Oliveira	UTAD, Portugal
Raul Morais	UTAD, Portugal

Artificial Intelligence and Law (AIL)

Pedro Miguel Freitas   Universidade Católica Portuguesa, Portugal
Ugo Pagallo   University of Torino, Italy
Massimo Durante   University of Torino, Italy
Paulo Novais   Universidade do Minho, Portugal

Artificial Intelligence for Industry and Societies (AI4IS)

Filipe Portela   University of Minho, Portugal
Sherin M. Moussa   Université Française d'Égypte, Egypt
Teresa Guarda   Universidad Estatal Península de Santa Elena,
                            Ecuador
Ioan M. Ciumasu   Paris-Saclay University, France

Artificial Intelligence in Medicine (AIM)

Manuel Filipe Santos   University of Minho, Portugal
Manuel Fernandez Delgado   University of Santiago, Spain
Tiago André Guimarães   University of Minho, Portugal

Artificial Intelligence in Power and Energy Systems (AIPES)

Zita Vale   Polytechnic Institute of Porto, Portugal
Tiago Pinto   UTAD and INESC TEC, Portugal
Pedro Faria   Polytechnic Institute of Porto, Portugal
Bo Norregaard Jorgensen   University of Southern Denmark, Denmark

Artificial Intelligence in Transportation Systems (AITS)

Alberto Fernandez   Universidad Rey Juan Carlos, Spain
Tania Fontes   INESC TEC, Portugal
Zafeiris Kokkinogenis   University of Porto, Portugal
Rosaldo Rossetti   University of Porto, Portugal

Ethics and Responsibility in AI (ERAI)

Tânia Carvalho	University of Porto, Portugal
João Vinagre	European Commission, Joint Research Centre, Spain
Catarina Silva	University of Coimbra, Portugal
Nuno Moniz	Lucy Family Institute for Data & Society, USA

Fuzzy Data Analysis and Applications (FDA)

Susana Nascimento	NOVA University Lisbon, Portugal
Gozde Ulutagay	Ege University, Turkey
João Paulo Carvalho	INESC-ID and University of Lisbon, Portugal

Generative AI – Foundations and Applications (GenAI)

Penousal Machado	University of Coimbra, Portugal
José Machado	University of Minho, Portugal
Paulo Moura Oliveira	UTAD and INESC TEC, Portugal

Knowledge Discovery and Business Intelligence (KDBI)

Paulo Cortez	University of Minho, Portugal
Albert Bifet	Université Paris-Saclay, France
Luís Cavique	Universidade Aberta, Portugal
João Gama	University of Porto, Portugal
Nuno Marques	NOVA University Lisbon, Portugal
Manuel Filipe Santos	University of Minho, Portugal
Rita P. Ribeiro	University of Porto, Portugal

Natural Language Processing, Text Mining and Applications (NLP-TeMA)

Joaquim Silva	NOVA University Lisbon, Portugal
Pablo Gamallo	Universidade de Santiago de Compostela, Spain
Paulo Quaresma	Universidade de Évora, Portugal
Irene Rodrigues	Universidade de Évora, Portugal
Alípio Jorge	University of Porto, Portugal

Artificial Intelligence - Theory, Methods, and Applications (AITMA)

José Valente de Oliveira	University of Algarve, Portugal
João Leite	NOVA University Lisbon, Portugal
João Rodrigues	University of Algarve, Portugal
João Dias	University of Algarve, Portugal
Pedro Cardoso	University of Algarve, Portugal

Program Committee

AI and Creativity (AIC)

Ana Rodrigues	University of Coimbra, Portugal
André Fabiano De Moraes	Instituto Federal Catarinense, Brazil
Brad Spendlove	Randolph College, USA
Carlos León	Universidad Complutense de Madrid, Spain
Caterina Moruzzi	University of Edinburgh, UK
Evana Gizzi	Tufts University, USA
F. Amílcar Cardoso	University of Coimbra, Portugal
Ivan Guerrero	UNAM, Mexico
Ivan Miguel Pires	Universidade de Aveiro, Portugal
João Gonçalves	University of Coimbra, Portugal
Kazjon Grace	University of Sydney, Australia
Ludovica Schaerf	University of Zurich, Switzerland
Manex Agirrezabal	University of Copenhagen, Denmark
Max Peeperkorn	University of Kent, UK
Sara González Gutiérrez	Universidad de Salamanca, Spain
Senja Pollak	Jožef Stefan Institute, Slovenia
Sérgio Rebelo	University of Coimbra, Portugal

AI for Architecture, Engineering and Conservation (AI4AES)

Alberto Pugnale	University of Melbourne, Australia
Amaral Gustavo Garcia Do	University of Kansas, USA
Camilla Pezzica	Cardiff University, UK
David Semedo	NOVA University Lisbon, Portugal
Dominik Lengyel	Brandenburg University of Technology, Germany
Enrico Pupi	Politecnico di Torino, Italy
Fátima Batista	LNEC, Portugal

Francesco Carota	University of Kansas, USA
Gabriele Mirra	Delft University of Technology, Netherlands
João Manso	LNEC, Portugal
João Marcelino	LNEC, Portugal
Michele Russo	Sapienza University of Rome, Italy
Nuno Correia	NOVA University Lisbon, Portugal
Pingbo Tang	Carnegie Mellon University, USA
Rui Nóbrega	NOVA University Lisbon, Portugal
Sarah Fakhreddine	Carnegie Mellon University, USA
Susana Nascimento	NOVA University Lisbon, Portugal
Valerio Palma	Politecnico di Torino, Italy

Ambient Intelligence and Affective Environments (AmIA)

Antonio Fernández-Caballero	Universidad de Castilla-La Mancha, Spain
F. Amílcar Cardoso	University of Coimbra, Portugal
Fábio Silva	University of Minho, Portugal
Fernando De La Prieta	University of Salamanca, Spain
Florentino Fdez-Riverola	University of Vigo, Spain
Hoon Ko	Sunmoon University, South Korea
Ichiro Satoh	National Institute of Informatics, Japan
Javier Jaen	Universitat Politècnica de València, Spain
Jean-Michel Ilié	Sorbonne Université, France
José Machado	University of Minho, Portugal
Jose M. Molina	Universidad Carlos III de Madrid, Spain
Lino Figueiredo	ISEP, Portugal
Luis Macedo	University of Coimbra, Portugal
Miguel J. Hornos	University of Granada, Spain
Ricardo Santos	Polytechnic Institute of Porto, Portugal
Ricardo Costa	Polytechnic Institute of Porto, Portugal
Shinichi Konomi	University of Tokyo, Japan
Tatsuo Nakajima	Waseda University, Japan
Vicente Julian	Universitat Politècnica de València, Spain

Artificial Intelligence and IoT in Agriculture (AIoTA)

Anakkallan Subeesh	ICAR, India
Aneesh Chauhan	Wageningen University and Research, Netherlands
Bruno Tisseyre	Institute Agro Montpellier, France

Carlos Serodio	UTAD, Portugal
Dinos Ferentinos	Hellenic Agricultural Organization (Demeter), Greece
Emanuel Peres	UTAD, Portugal
Javier Sanchis Saez	Universitat Politècnica de València, Spain
João Coelho	Instituto Politécnico de Bragança, Portugal
João Valente	Spanish National Research Council, Spain
Joaquim João Sousa	UTAD, Portugal
José Antonio Sanz Delgado	Universidad Pública de Navarra, Spain
Pedro Couto	UTAD, Portugal
Stef Maree	Wageningen University and Research, Netherlands
Tatiana M. Pinho	INESC TEC, Portugal
Telmo Adão	UTAD, Portugal
Vítor Filipe	UTAD, Portugal

Artificial Intelligence and Law (AIL)

Arlindo Oliveira	INESC-ID and University of Lisbon, Portugal
Carlisle George	Middlesex University London, UK
Cesar Analide	University of Minho, Portugal
Cristina Salgado	Universidad de Santiago de Compostela, Spain
Dalila Durães	Universidade do Minho, Portugal
Daniel Braun	University of Twente, Netherlands
Davide Carneiro	Polytechnic Institute of Porto, Portugal
Enrico Francesconi	IGSG-CNR, Italy
Fábio Silva	University of Minho, Portugal
Francisco Andrade	University of Minho, Portugal
Francisco Marcondes	University of Minho, Portugal
Giovanni De Gregorio	Católica Global School of Law, Portugal
Giovanni Sartor	EUI/CIRSFID, Italy
Goreti Marreiros	Polytechnic Institute of Porto, Portugal
Haihua Chen	University of North Texas, USA
José Machado	University of Minho, Portugal
Luís Conceição	Polytechnic Institute of Porto, Portugal
Luis Mendes Gomes	Universidade dos Açores, Portugal
Lurdes Mesquita	Polytechnic Institute of Porto, Portugal
Manuel Masseno	Polytechnic Institute of Beja, Portugal
Manuel Rodrigues	University of Minho, Portugal
Marco Gomes	University of Minho, Portugal
Marco Gonçalves	University of Minho, Portugal

Pedro Rangel Henriques	University of Minho, Portugal
Sérgio Gonçalves	PHD, Portugal
Teresa Coelho Moreira	University of Minho, Portugal
Tomer Libal	University of Luxembourg, Luxembourg
Vasileios Rovilos	Credo AI, USA
Vicente Julian	Universitat Politècnica de València, Spain

Artificial Intelligence for Industry and Societies (AI4IS)

Alfonso González Briones	University of Salamanca, Spain
Ana Azevedo	CEOS.PP and Polytechnic Institute of Porto, Portugal
Antoni Morell	Universitat Autònoma de Barcelona, Spain
Antonio Moreira	IPCA, Portugal
Cihan Tunc	University of North Texas, USA
Daniel Urda	University of Burgos, Spain
Fabrizio Messina	University of Catania, Italy
George Stalidis	International Hellenic University, Greece
Hanmin Jung	KISTI, South Korea
Hatem Mrad	Université du Québec en Abitibi-Témiscamingue, Canada
Inna Skarga-Bandurova	Oxford Brookes University, UK
Jorge Bernardino	Polytechnic Institute of Coimbra, Portugal
Juan-Ignacio Latorre-Biel	Public University of Navarre, Spain
Mahmoud Mounir	Ain Shams University, Egypt
Marco Alfonse	Université Française d'Egypte, Egypt
Mariam Gawich	Université Française d'Égypte, Egypt
Matsatsinis Nikolaos	Technical University of Crete, Greece
Muhammad Younas	Oxford Brookes University, UK
Omid Fatahi Valilai	Constructor University Bremen, Germany
Panos Fitsilis	University of Thessaly, Greece
Roaa Elghondakly	Ain Shams University, Egypt
Sara Paiva	Instituto Politécnico de Viana do Castelo, Portugal
Sergio Ilarri	University of Zaragoza, Spain
Spyros Panagiotakis	Hellenic Mediterranean University, Greece
Vicente Ferreira Lucena Junior	Federal University of Amazonas, Brazil
Waleed Adel	Université Française d'Egypte, Egypt

Artificial Intelligence in Medicine (AIM)

Ailton Moreira	University of Minho, Portugal
António Abelha	University of Minho, Portugal
Beatriz De La Iglesia	University of East Anglia, UK
Filipe Portela	University of Minho, Portugal
Francini Hak	University of Minho, Portugal
Hugo Peixoto	University of Minho, Portugal
Inna Skarga-Bandurova	Oxford Brookes University, UK
João Lopes	University of Minho, Portugal
José Machado	University of Minho, Portugal
Júlio Duarte	University of Minho, Portugal
Luis Mendes Gomes	Universidade dos Açores, Portugal
Panagiotis Bamidis	Aristotle University of Thessaloniki, Greece
Pedro Gago	Polytechnic Institute of Leiria, Portugal
Regina Sousa	University of Minho, Portugal
Rui Camacho	University of Porto, Portugal
Susana Brás	Universidade de Aveiro, Portugal

Artificial Intelligence in Power and Energy Systems (AIPES)

Alfonso Briones	University of Salamanca, Spain
Ana Estanqueiro	LNEG, Portugal
António Couto	LNEG, Portugal
Brígida Teixeira	GECAD, Portugal
Catia Silva	INESC, Portugal
Fernando Lezama	Polytechnic Institute of Porto, Portugal
Fernando Lopes	LNEG, Portugal
Gabriel Santos	Polytechnic Institute of Porto, Portugal
Germano Lambert-Torres	PS Solutions, USA
Hugo Morais	Universidade de Lisboa, Portugal
John Eugenio Peñaloza Morán	INESC TEC, Portugal
José Baptista	UTAD and INESC TEC, Portugal
Jose L. Rueda	Delft University of Technology, Netherlands
Leonardo Pilarski	UTAD, Portugal
Luis Gomes	Instituto Superior de Engenharia do Porto, Portugal
Mohammad Javadi	INESC-TEC, Portugal
Pedro Salomé	INL, Portugal
Philipp Thunshirn	University of Applied Sciences Technikum Wien, Austria

Ricardo Faia   GECAD, Portugal
Rita Teixeira   UTAD, Portugal
Tiago Soares   INESC TEC, Portugal
Zheng Ma   University of Southern Denmark, Denmark
Zia Ullah   UTAD, Portugal

Artificial Intelligence in Transportation Systems (AITS)

Ana L. C. Bazzan   Universidade Federal do Rio Grande do Sul,
                                        Brazil
António Costa   University Rey Juan Carlos, Spain; University of
                                        Porto, Portugal
António Pedro Aguiar   University of Porto, Portugal
Carlos A. Iglesias   Universidad Politécnica de Madrid, Spain
Cristina Olaverri-Monreal   Johannes Kepler University Linz, Austria
Daniel Castro Silva   University of Porto, Portugal
Davide Carneiro   Polytechnic Institute of Porto, Portugal
Eduardo Camponogara   Federal University of Santa Catarina, Brazil
Fabien Leurent   Université Paris-Est, France
Francesco Renna   University of Porto, Portugal
Gonçalo Correia   Delft University of Technology, Netherlands
Hilmi Berk Celikoglu   Technical University of Istanbul, Turkey
Holger Billhardt   Universidad Rey Juan Carlos, Spain
Joaquín Arias   Universidad Rey Juan Carlos, Spain
Joel Ribeiro   INESC TEC, Portugal
Luís Nunes   University Institute of Lisbon, Portugal
Marin Lujak   Rey Juan Carlos University, Spain
Pedro M. D'Orey   University of Porto, Portugal
Sara Ferreira   Universidade do Porto, Portugal
Sascha Ossowski   Rey Juan Carlos University, Spain

Ethics and Responsibility in AI (ERAI)

Ana Madureira   Departamento de Engenharia Informática,
                                        Portugal
Catarina Barata   Instituto Superior Técnico, Portugal
Jaime Cardoso   University of Porto, Portugal
Joana Costa   Polytechnic Institute of Leiria, Portugal
João Manuel R. S. Tavares   University of Porto and INEGI, Portugal
Joerg Osterrieder   University of Twente, Netherlands

Karla Figueiredo	Rio de Janeiro State University, Brazil
Luis F. Teixeira	Fraunhofer Portugal AICOS, Portugal
Marcelo Graglia	Pontifícia Universidade Católica de São Paulo, Brazil
Mario Figueiredo	Universidade de Lisboa, Portugal
Marley Vellasco	Pontifical Catholic University of Rio de Janeiro, Brazil
Nuno Lourenço	University of Coimbra, Portugal
Petia Georgieva	University of Aveiro, Portugal
Raquel Sebastião	University of Aveiro, Portugal

Fuzzy Data Analysis and Applications (FDA)

Fernando Gomide	University of Campinas, Brazil
João Sousa	University of Lisbon, Portugal
João Moura-Pires	Universidade NOVA de Lisboa, Portugal
Renato Amorim	University of Essex, UK
Rui Jorge Almeida	Maastricht University, Netherlands
Uzay Kaymak	Eindhoven University of Technology, Netherlands
Vitor Lobo	NOVA IMS, Portugal

Generative AI – Foundations and Applications (GenAI)

António Abelha	University of Minho, Portugal
Cristiana Neto	University of Minho, Portugal
Dalila Durães	Universidade do Minho, Portugal
Deden Witarsyah	Universiti Tun Hussein Onn Malaysia, Malasya
Diana Ferreira	University of Minho, Portugal
F. Amílcar Cardoso	University of Coimbra, Portugal
Francisco Marcondes	University of Minho, Portugal
Hugo Peixoto	University of Minho, Portugal
Ichiro Satoh	National Institute of Informatics, Japan
Jaume Jordán	Universitat Politècnica de València, Spain
João Miguel Cunha	University of Coimbra, Portugal
Jose Luis Calvo-Rolle	University of A Coruña, Spain
Júlio Duarte	University of Minho, Portugal
Manuel Filipe Santos	University of Minho, Portugal
Miguel J. Hornos	University of Granada, Spain
Omar D. Castrillon	Universidad Nacional de Colombia, Colombia
Regina Sousa	University of Minho, Portugal

Tatsuo Nakajima   Waseda University, Japan
Vicente Julian   Universitat Politècnica de València, Spain

Knowledge Discovery and Business Intelligence (KDBI)

Agnès Braud   University of Strasbourg, France
Alberto Bugarín-Diz   Universidade de Santiago de Compostela, Spain
Amilcar Oliveira   Universidade Aberta, Portugal
Andre de Carvalho   University of São Paulo, Brazil
Armando Mendes   University of Azores, Portugal
Carlos Ferreira   University of Porto, Portugal
Catarina Moreira   University of Technology Sydney, Australia
Elaine Faria   Federal University of Uberlândia, Brazil
Fátima Rodrigues   Institute of Engineering of Porto, Portugal
Manuel Fernandez Delgado   University of Santiago de Compostela, Spain
Marcos Aurélio Domingues   State University of Maringá, Brazil
Margarida Cardoso   ISCTE, Portugal
Murat Caner Testik   Hacettepe University, Turkey
Nuno Cruz Garcia   University of Lisbon, Portugal
Orlando Belo   Universidade do Minho, Portugal
Paulo Pombinho   Universidade Aberta and Atlântica - Instituto
                                       Universitário, Portugal
Rui Camacho   University of Porto, Portugal
Susana Nascimento   NOVA University Lisbon

Natural Language Processing, Text Mining and Applications (NLP-TeMA)

Bruno Martins   University of Lisbon and INESC-ID, Portugal
Eric De La Clergerie   INRIA, France
Fernando Batista   INESC-ID and ISCTE-IUL, Portugal
Francisco Couto   University of Lisbon, Portugal
Gaël Dias   University of Caen Normandie, France
Hugo Gonçalo Oliveira   University of Coimbra, Portugal
Isabel Trancoso   INESC-ID and University of Lisbon, Portugal
Jesús Vilares   Universidade da Coruña, Spain
João Dias   University of Algarve, Portugal
Manex Agirrezabal   University of Copenhagen, Denmark
Marcos Garcia   Universidade de Santiago de Compostela, Spain
Mário J. Silva   INESC-ID and University of Lisbon, Portugal

Miguel A. Alonso	Universidade da Coruña, Spain
Nuno C. Marques	NOVA University Lisbon, Portugal
Pavel Brazdil	University of Porto, Portugal
Sérgio Nunes	INESC TEC and University of Porto, Portugal

Artificial Intelligence - Theory, Methods, and Applications (AITMA)

Agnès Braud	University of Strasbourg, France
Alberto Bugarín-Diz	Universidade de Santiago de Compostela, Spain
Amilcar Oliveira	Universidade Aberta, Portugal
Ana Azevedo	CEOS.PP and Polytechnic Institute of Porto, Portugal
Andre de Carvalho	University of São Paulo, Brazil
António Abelha	University of Minho, Portugal
António Costa	Rey Juan Carlos University, Spain; University of Porto, Portugal
António Pedro Aguiar	University of Porto, Portugal
Arlindo Oliveira	INESC-ID and University of Lisbon, Portugal
Bruno Martins	University of Lisbon and INESC-ID, Portugal
Carlos Ferreira	University of Porto, Portugal
Carlos A. Iglesias	Universidad Politécnica de Madrid, Spain
Daniel Castro Silva	University of Porto, Portugal
Daniel Urda	University of Burgos, Spain
Daniele Corradetti	University of Lisbon and Universidade do Algarve, Portugal
Davide Carneiro	CIICESI and Polytechnic Institute of Porto, Portugal
Eduardo Camponogara	Federal University of Santa Catarina, Brazil
Enrico Pupi	Politecnico di Torino, Italy
Eric De La Clergerie	INRIA, France
Fabrizio Messina	University of Catania, Italy
Fátima Rodrigues	Institute of Engineering of Porto, Portugal
Francisco Couto	University of Lisbon, Portugal
Gaël Dias	University of Caen Normandie, France
George Stalidis	International Hellenic University, Greece
Giovanni Sartor	EUI/CIRSFID, Italy
Hanmin Jung	KISTI, South Korea
Hilmi Berk Celikoglu	Technical University of Istanbul, Turkey
Holger Billhardt	Universidad Rey Juan Carlos, Spain
Hoon Ko	Sunmoon University, South Korea
Isabel Trancoso	INESC-ID and University of Lisbon, Portugal

Keynotes

Argument Mining and Reasoning with Large Language Models

Paolo Torroni

University of Bologna, Italy

Abstract. The rapid evolution of Large Language Models has sparked discussions about their ability to reason and how they may affect human reasoning. In this talk, we look at LLM reasoning through the lens of argumentation. We will explore how argumentation theories can help investigate the limits of current LLMs and reason about their role in pubic debate.

Model-based Reinforcement Learning and Abstraction

Frans A. Oliehoek

Delft University of Technology, The Netherlands

Abstract. In reinforcement learning (RL), we develop techniques to learn to control complex systems, and over the last decade we have seen impressive successes ranging from beating grandmasters in the game of Go to real-world applications like chip design, power grid control, and drug design. However, nearly all applications of RL require access to an accurate and lightweight simulator from which huge numbers of trials can be sampled. In this talk, I will cover some settings where this is not the case, and where therefore we need to engage in some form of 'model-based RL' to learn an appropriate model. Specifically, I will give an overview of a number of different problem settings (MDPs, POMDPs, and multiagent problems) and various corresponding approaches to learning and using models of the environment (ranging from deep learning, to Bayesian inference, and from planning with MCTS variants to model-free RL), highlighting their strong points as well as limitations. Central to all these approaches is the notion of abstraction: how finely do we represent the world when learning and planning? And what impact might such abstractions actually have on theoretical guarantees of MBRL methods?

The Why of AI: Causal Discovery from Observational Data

Mário Figueiredo

Instituto Superior Técnico, University of Lisbon, Portugal

Abstract. In causal discovery, the aim is to uncover the causal mechanisms that drive the relationships between variables — a critical step beyond the correlational models prevalent in modern machine learning. This pursuit is foundational for the next generation of robust and explainable AI, with applications in most scientific fields. Although, in principle, identifying causal relationships requires interventions (experiments), it is often the case that this is impossible, impractical, or unethical. The challenge of learning cause and effect from purely observational data is therefore central to causal discovery. In this talk, after briefly surveying the field, I will discuss recent advances in causal discovery from data, namely the problem of distinguishing cause from effect on bivariate data.

Contents – Part II

Artificial Intelligence and IoT in Agriculture (AIoTA)

Artificial Intelligence in Transportation Systems (AITS)

**Natural Language Processing, Text Mining and Applications
(NLP-TeMA)**

Ambient Intelligence and Affective Environments (AmIA)

AI and Creativity (AIC)

Artificial Intelligence in Power and Energy Systems (AIPES)

Fuzzy Data Analysis and Applications (FDA)

Contents – Part I

AI for Architecture, Engineering and Conservation (AI4AEC)

Knowledge Discovery and Business Intelligence (KDBI)

Generative AI: Foundations and Applications (GenAI)

Artificial Intelligence: Theory, Methods, and Applications (AITMA)

Ethics and Responsibility in AI (ERAI)

Artificial Intelligence for Industry and Societies (AI4IS)

DLensRisk: A Deep Learning Framework for Financial Risk Analysis in the Oil and Gas Industry

Aguinaldo Júnio Flor$^{(\boxtimes)}$ ⓘ and Adiel T. de Almeida Filho ⓘ

Universidade Federal de Pernambuco, Centro de Informática - CIn, Av. Jorn. Aníbal
Fernandes, s/n - Cidade Universitária, Recife, Brazil
{ajf2,adielfilho}@cin.ufpe.br
https://cin.ufpe.br

Abstract. This research presents DLensRisk, a novel and integrative framework that combines deep learning models with Value-at-Risk (VaR) methodologies to forecast steel price volatility and assess financial risk in offshore oil and gas projects. Steel is a critical input in subsea infrastructure, such as flexible risers, manifolds, and Christmas trees, whose procurement is often affected by global price instability, long lead times, and contract inflexibility. DLensRisk evaluates seven forecasting models across regional datasets (USA, Europe, Asia, and China), including classic methods, ARIMA, Exponential Smoothing, and Linear Regression, and deep learning architectures: Recurrent Neural Networks (RNNs), Transformer, Neural Hierarchical Interpolation for Time Series (N-HiTS), and Temporal Convolutional Network (TCN). Model performance is assessed using SMAPE, MAPE, MASE, and MARRE, with statistical validation via the Friedman and Nemenyi tests. The best-performing model for each region is integrated with four VaR methodologies, Historical Simulation, eGARCH, tGARCH, and Filtered Historical Simulation (FHS), to construct a Financial Risk Index. Results show that deep learning models consistently outperform traditional approaches, with N-HiTS leading in China, RNN in Asia and Europe, and Transformer in the United States. For risk modeling, FHS proved most suitable for stable markets like Asia and China, while tGARCH delivered more conservative estimates for volatile markets like the USA and Europe. By aligning predictive modeling with formal risk metrics, DLensRisk offers a robust, data-driven strategy for mitigating procurement risk in capital-intensive energy projects. This framework enhances scenario planning and supports more accurate, regionally adaptive financial decision-making in the oil and gas industry.

Keywords: Oil and gas industry · Steel price forecasting · Deep learning models · Financial risk

© The Author(s), under exclusive license to Springer Nature Switzerland AG 2026
J. Valente de Oliveira et al. (Eds.): EPIA 2025, LNAI 16122, pp. 3–15, 2026.
https://doi.org/10.1007/978-3-032-05179-0_1

1   Introduction

The advancement of oil exploration technologies in pre-salt reservoirs, such as those in the Gulf of Mexico, Brazil, Guyana, Suriname, and West Africa, has driven increasingly complex, capital-intensive projects in the oil and gas sector. However, these investments carry substantial financial risk due to oil price volatility, which affects stock markets [1] and influences infrastructure decisions. These dynamics directly impact steel, a strategic input for subsea systems, reinforcing the need for advanced financial risk management strategies [2].

Brent crude plays a key role in global pricing and inflationary trends, making its behavior and its relationship with other commodities a central concern for oil companies and suppliers [3]. Recent studies have explored deep learning applications for forecasting oil recovery and metal prices [4], though results vary across commodities [5]. Other research employs spatiotemporal graph neural networks to analyze the relationship between crude oil and precious metals [6], highlighting the growing role of AI in financial modeling and risk management.

This study focuses on flexible pipes for offshore extraction—subsea products with about 40% of their cost in steel [7]. Production typically spans 12–18 months, with projects extending up to 40 months, exposing suppliers to currency variation, inflation, and steel price volatility risks. Due to lean inventories, steel procurement often occurs 6–12 months after contract negotiations, yet prices are rarely adjusted afterward, intensifying financial exposure and demanding robust mitigation strategies.

Recent works have applied CNNs [8], Transformers [9], and RNNs with LSTM/GRU [10] to oil-related data, but many rely on pre-2022 datasets, potentially misaligned with post-pandemic market behavior. Advances in combining Deep Learning with Value-at-Risk (VaR) methodologies [11] have improved volatility forecasting and contributed to domains such as portfolio risk [12], currency prediction [13], and oil market risk assessment [14]. Building on this progress, our research proposes DLensRisk. This integrative framework combines multiple deep learning models with formal financial risk quantification techniques to forecast steel prices critical to offshore oil and gas infrastructure.

DLensRisk stands out by uniting diverse neural architectures, such as RNN, Transformer, N-HiTS, and TCN, within a unified model evaluation and selection environment. The optimal model for each dataset is determined through a rigorous multi-metric scoring system, statistically validated via Friedman and Nemenyi tests. These forecasts are then embedded into four complementary VaR methodologies—Historical, eGARCH, tGARCH, and FHS—to compute a Financial Risk Index. This methodological synthesis addresses a gap in the literature by integrating accurate forecasting with forward-looking risk assessment. Moreover, it offers a replicable and data-driven strategy for mitigating procurement risk in long-term subsea projects, where material cost volatility poses critical financial challenges.

2 The DLensRisk Framework

This paper presents DLensRisk, a multi-model deep learning framework designed explicitly for estimating and interpreting financial risk through Value at Risk (VaR). The name DLensRisk encapsulates the conceptual basis of the framework, serving as a deep learning lens that captures complex, non-linear patterns and tail risk behaviors embedded in financial time series data. The framework integrates a set of heterogeneous deep learning architectures, each contributing distinct modeling capabilities, including sequence modeling, hierarchical decomposition, and temporal convolution.

DLensRisk is designed to support robust and scalable VaR estimation across multiple datasets, enabling comparative analysis and ensemble-based decision strategies. Furthermore, its architecture promotes model transparency and interpretability, allowing for a more granular understanding of risk sources and their temporal evolution. This methodological framework enhances the predictive performance and explanatory power of VaR modeling, making DLensRisk particularly suitable for risk-sensitive sectors such as energy, steel, and oil and gas.

The proposed framework includes classic statistical and deep learning models applied to steel prices. The goal is to compare these models and validate the extent to which deep learning offers superior performance. This comparison seeks to validate the applicability of deep learning models as more advanced tools and explore their capabilities in capturing complex and non-linear patterns in the data that classic statistical models may not be able to identify [15].

As illustrated in Fig. 1, the process begins with collecting steel price datasets from different geographic regions. The preprocessing phase includes quantification, handling of missing values, normalization, the Augmented Dickey-Fuller (ADF) test, and generating descriptive statistics.

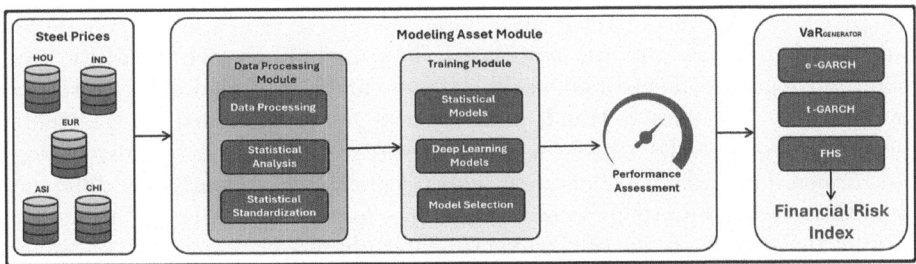

Fig. 1. DLensRisk Framework

During the model training phase, we evaluate the deep learning models with 300 epochs to identify the best fit for each dataset. This evaluation is based on a scoring system, where models are assessed using several performance metrics. The model with the highest aggregate score is then selected as the best predictor for each specific commodity, index, or price. Once all models have been scored, the next step is to construct the Financial Risk Index, primarily based on the $SMAPE$ results, which will quantify the steel price volatility and its financial impact.

In this study, in addition to classic models, ARIMA, Exponential Smoothing, and Linear Regression, deep learning models with distinct architectures were employed to evaluate their suitability for modeling steel price time series. The selected models were Recurrent Neural Networks (RNNs), Transformer, Neural Hierarchical Interpolation for Time Series (N-HiTS), and Temporal Convolutional Network (TCN). The selection of models to compose the Modeling Asset Module was based on the diversity of architectures since the main objective of this research is to evaluate which model presents the most outstanding adherence in capturing the dynamics of the curves, both concerning the type of steel and the production location.

The hyperparameters of deep learning models were optimized through a fine-tuning process to maximize forecasting performance in time series prediction. The Optuna library enabled an efficient automated search in the hyperparameter space. This research conducted ten trials per model, exploring configurations to identify the best results.

After the ranking model performance, statistical tests are applied to verify whether differences in forecasting errors are significant. Depending on the distribution and variance assumptions, using Shapiro-Wilk and Levene tests, either the Friedman test [16,17], or ANOVA [18] is used. Friedman is preferred when normality is not met, with the Nemenyi test [19] identifying pairwise differences, while ANOVA, when applicable, is followed by Tukey's test [20]. This increasingly common practice in AI research ensures that the top-performing model [21], ultimately integrated into the VaR Unit Module, is selected through statistically validated performance metrics.

The experimental phase of this research was conducted using four daily time series of steel price indexes from key procurement regions, Houston (USA), Indiana (USA), Europe, Asia Pacific, and China, selected to represent the geographic diversity of suppliers and the associated risks, including price volatility, taxation, and logistics. These real-world datasets underwent rigorous preprocessing, including seasonality, trend, completeness, and stationarity assessments. The Dickey-Fuller (ADF) test was used to verify stationarity, initially on log-transformed data, which still showed high p-values. Subsequently, log differencing with a twelve-month moving average was applied to achieve stationarity, marking the starting point of the experimental phase.

The greatest challenge for the oil and gas industry is to secure some form of preference from steel producers, as it is not among the top global buyers of this commodity. The dataset has 2,592 weekday prices from June 2015 to March 2025, split into 75% training and 25% testing. The industry needs to carefully plan the procurement of this raw material, as it is not a priority sector for the production industry, making price and delivery negotiations more challenging.

Performance analysis in deep learning is key to evaluating forecasting accuracy. We use four statistical metrics, MAPE, SMAPE, MASE, and MARRE, calculated by the library. A composite score based on these metrics enables automatic model ranking, improving result interpretation, and aiding decision-making.

3   Results and Discussion

The results presented in Table 1 highlight the consistent superiority of deep learning models, particularly RNN, N-HiTS, Transformer, and TCN, over traditional statistical approaches such as linear regression, ARIMA, and exponential smoothing. These neural architectures demonstrated greater ability to capture nonlinear patterns, temporal dependencies, and structural breaks across all evaluated regions, reinforcing their applicability in forecasting steel price volatility in complex markets.

In the United States – Houston dataset, TCN achieved the highest score (26), followed closely by RNN (24) and Transformer (22). These models effectively captured the sequential dependencies and high-frequency fluctuations that characterize the U.S. steel market. N-HiTS also performed competitively, with a score of 16, demonstrating its capacity to handle multiscale signals. On the other hand, classic models such as ARIMA, linear regression, and exponential smoothing presented significantly lower scores, confirming their limitations in modeling dynamic and irregular behaviors in commodity prices. For the United States – Indiana, Transformer achieved the top scorer (28), followed by TCN (23) and N-HiTS (21). The success of Transformer in this dataset is likely related to its strength in modeling long-range dependencies, which appears advantageous in a market marked by moderate volatility and structural complexity. RNN and ARIMA occupied the middle ground, while regression and exponential smoothing again lagged, failing to adapt to the temporal diversity in the data.

In the Europe dataset, RNN stood out as the best-performing model with a perfect score of 28, followed by N-HiTS (24) and Transformer (18). Europe presented smoother fluctuations and more predictable structures, which favored models with strong temporal memory, like RNN. TCN performed comparably (17 points), indicating its robustness even in less volatile markets. Traditional statistical methods struggled to match the performance of deep learning models, especially under seasonality and regime shifts.

The Asia dataset further confirmed the strength of RNN, which once again obtained the highest score (28). TiDE-NHiTS followed closely with 24 points, demonstrating that hybrid models combining frequency decomposition and temporal hierarchies can effectively model volatility in highly dynamic environments. TCN also performed well (19), while Transformer scored 17. classic models, especially exponential smoothing, delivered the weakest results due to their inability to accommodate rapid market shifts.

In China, N-HiTS led with a perfect score of 28, reflecting its proficiency in decomposing multiscale temporal signals in a market characterized by irregular and abrupt variations. TCN and Transformer were followed with scores of 24 and 21, respectively, indicating their capability to model local trends and long-term dependencies. RNN scored slightly lower (20), though it still performed consistently. Once again, the lowest scores were observed in ARIMA, linear regression, and exponential smoothing, which could not capture the complexity and non-linearity inherent to the Chinese steel market.

Table 1. Steel price results

Model	MAPE		SMAPE		MASE		MARRE		Score
	Result	Scr	Result	Scr	Result	Scr	Result	Scr	
United States - Houston									
TCN	13.2291	5	**12.5590**	7	**34.2400**	7	**21.4924**	7	26
RNN	12.8165	6	13.3349	6	35.5532	6	22.3167	6	24
Transformer	**12.6710**	7	13.6488	5	36.8722	5	23.1446	5	22
N-HiTS	14.6841	4	15.3181	4	41.1214	4	25.8118	4	16
Exponential Smoothing	15.6649	3	15.8620	3	42.6993	3	26.8023	3	12
ARIMA	17.1836	2	19.7616	2	51.2980	2	32.1997	2	8
Regression Linear	28.6224	1	26.7641	1	74.8944	1	47.011	1	4
United States - Indiana									
Transformer	**16.3944**	7	**17.3317**	7	**32.5413**	7	**22.1666**	7	28
TCN	17.5972	6	18.5211	5	33.9153	6	23.1025	6	23
N-HiTS	17.9849	5	18.1379	6	34.4726	5	23.4821	5	21
RNN	18.6762	3	19.4559	4	36.2132	4	24.6678	4	15
ARIMA	18.3570	4	21.1994	3	39.1707	3	26.6824	3	13
Regression Linear	22.9608	2	26.2577	2	46.8138	2	31.8888	2	8
Exponential Smoothing	102.1292	1	146.1484	1	185.1648	1	126.1309	1	4
Europe									
RNN	**7.6019**	7	**8.0519**	7	**21.6243**	7	**15.0376**	7	28
N-HiTS	8.3002	6	8.7965	6	24.5805	6	17.0934	6	24
Transformer	10.3310	5	9.9717	5	28.2814	4	19.6670	4	18
TCN	10.8501	3	10.1078	4	28.2626	5	19.6539	5	17
ARIMA	10.6971	4	10.4198	3	28.9574	3	20.1371	3	13
Regression Linear	18.9632	2	21.0358	1	54.3033	2	37.7627	2	7
Exponential Smoothing	22.4738	1	19.5632	2	57.5951	1	40.0519	1	5
Asia									
RNN	**6.9121**	7	**7.2004**	7	**11.3948**	7	**12.6228**	7	28
TiDEN-HiTS	8.4182	6	8.6793	6	13.4583	6	14.9087	6	24
TCN	10.7846	5	11.4860	4	16.2169	5	17.9646	5	19
Transformer	11.5670	4	11.0254	5	17.5935	4	19.4895	4	17
ARIMA	12.0835	3	13.1030	3	20.2346	3	22.4153	3	12
Regression Linear	18.4381	2	17.543	2	27.5658	2	30.5366	2	8
Exponential Smoothing	231.4658	1	176.2975	1	337.2205	1	373.563	1	4
China									
N-HiTS	**6.1595**	7	**6.0999**	7	**11.4450**	7	**12.1231**	7	28
TCN	8.0975	6	7.6849	6	14.4701	6	15.3275	6	24
Transformer	8.5712	5	8.8145	4	15.9585	5	16.9041	5	19
RNN	8.7387	4	8.7293	5	16.3627	4	17.3322	4	17
ARIMA	10.425	3	10.844	3	19.7257	3	20.8945	3	12
Regression Linear	16.9443	2	16.0354	2	29.6303	2	31.3859	2	8
Exponential Smoothing	98.8525	1	140.2708	1	170.8297	1	180.9518	1	4

The results in Table 2 from the Shapiro-Wilk test ($p < 0.05$) indicated non-Gaussian error distributions, while the Levene test ($p < 0.05$) revealed significant variance heterogeneity across models. These violations of normality and homoscedasticity assumptions rendered parametric approaches such as ANOVA unsuitable. As a result, the Friedman test was applied to detect differences among models in this dependent data scenario, yielding statistically significant

Table 2. Statistic Tests

Dataset	Shapiro-Wilk		Levene		Friedman		Result
	Statistic	P-Value	Statistic	P-Value	Statistic	P-Value	
Indiana	0	0	2035.47	0	2292.95	0	Non-nor., non-homog. dist.; models differ greatly
Houston	0	0	375.34	0	2132.83	0	Non-nor., non-homog. dist.; models differ greatly
Europe	0	0	348.99	0	1457.8	0	Non-nor., non-homog. dist.; models differ greatly
Asia	0	0	2145.86	0	2680.46	0	Non-nor., non-homog. dist.; models differ greatly
China	0	0	2137.08	0	2429.45	0	Non-nor., non-homog. dist.; models differ greatly

results ($p < 0.05$). To further identify which model pairs differed meaningfully, we employed the Nemenyi post-hoc test, which confirmed several significant rank disparities.

Across all regions, the results emphasize that no single model dominates universally, but deep learning models consistently outperform traditional approaches. Each neural architecture contributes unique strengths depending on the market's temporal profile, validating the importance of region-specific model selection. These results definitively confirm that the differences in model performance are not due to random variation but rather stem from the intrinsic capabilities of each architecture in capturing patterns, handling volatility, and adapting to the dynamics of steel price forecasting.

4　Performance Assessment

The ClusterMap in Fig. 2 and the violin plot in Fig. 3 clearly illustrate the statistical superiority of deep learning models over traditional statistical methods in

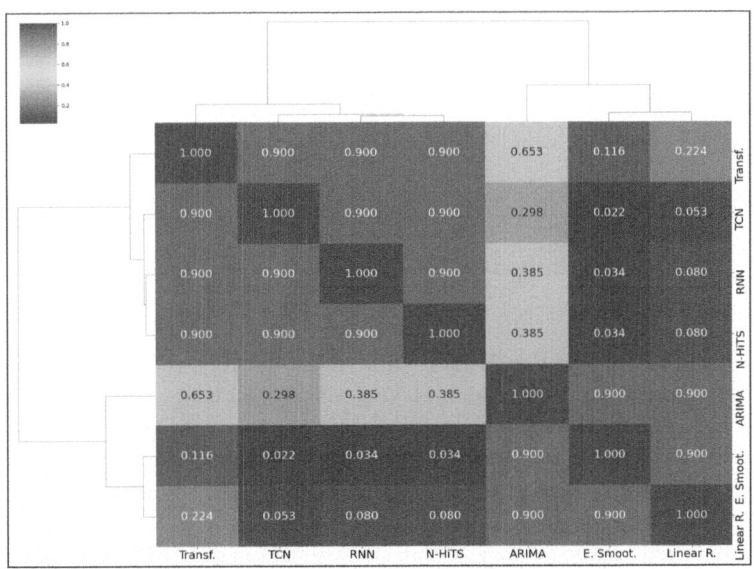

Fig. 2. Post-Hoc Nemenyi Test over SMAPE

forecasting steel prices. Models such as RNN, N-HiTS, Transformer, and TCN consistently cluster with lower SMAPE values and more cohesive error patterns, indicating robust generalization across regions. In contrast, ARIMA, Exponential Smoothing, and Linear Regression form a distinct group with significantly higher error metrics, reinforcing their limited effectiveness in handling complex time series.

The heatmap dendrogram highlights a clear separation between the two model classes. Deep learning models demonstrate substantial mutual similarity, as evidenced by high correlation coefficients near 0.9, and their performance stands in stark contrast to traditional approaches, which exhibit low similarity to neural models and to each other. This clustering validates the hypothesis that neural architectures are better suited for modeling nonlinear and multiscale temporal behaviors in commodity prices.

Figure 3 shows the distribution of model rankings based on MASE, selected for its robustness in multi-scale and volatile financial series. Unlike MAPE or SMAPE, MASE handles zero and extreme values better, making it more suitable for financial forecasting.

The violin plots represent the concentration of ranks across multiple trials. Classic models show higher rank concentrations, indicating weaker performance. In contrast, Deep Learning models, especially TCN, N-HiTS, and Transformer, display distributions skewed toward lower ranks, with TCN achieving the most consistent top performance. This confirms their superior and stable accuracy across datasets.

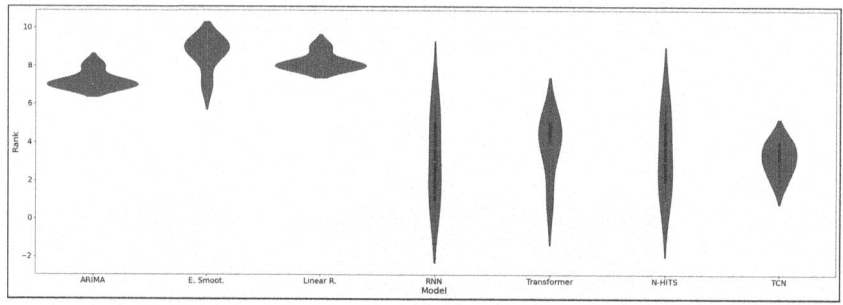

Fig. 3. Post-Hoc Nemenyi Test over MASE

Deep learning models like N-HiTS and RNN exhibit low ranks with narrow, compact distributions, reflecting high forecasting accuracy and consistent performance across datasets. Conversely, classic models display higher and more concentrated ranks around poorer performance scores, particularly evident in Exponential Smoothing and Linear Regression, which consistently underperformed across all regions.

The combined analysis shows that deep learning models outperform traditional approaches in mean accuracy (SMAPE) and offer greater reliability in scaled error (MASE), a critical aspect for decision-making under financial uncertainty. Notably, N-HiTS led performance in China, while RNN and Transformer delivered competitive results across various regions. TCN showed balanced outcomes with a slightly broader rank distribution, indicating occasional variability but strong average performance.

These insights underscore the importance of adopting AI-driven models in financial forecasting tasks. Deep learning architectures provide a resilient and adaptive alternative to outdated statistical methods in sectors like oil and gas, where geopolitical and macroeconomic factors heavily influence price volatility. Their ability to model complex, nonlinear temporal dynamics makes them indispensable tools for risk mitigation, strategic planning, and operational efficiency in the Brazilian energy market.

5   Financial Risk Index

Recent research has combined neural networks with traditional Value at Risk (VaR) models to enhance accuracy in forecasting volatility in financial series [22–24]. In this experiment, a structured framework-based approach was proposed, in which an initial module selects the model that best fits observed volatility curves of steel prices. Subsequently, the forecasts from this chosen model are integrated and hybridized with various VaR methodologies. This combination allows complementary and refined volatility forecasting, resulting in more precise and reliable VaR estimates.

To ensure comprehensive risk assessment, VaR methodologies were applied to the model error distributions: Historical Simulation, eGARCH, tGARCH, and Filtered Historical Simulation (FHS). Each method was chosen for its unique ability to capture different risk dynamics: from empirical distribution perspectives to volatility clustering effects. Table 3 summarizes the risk metrics for each original dataset and the best-performing model, offering a detailed comparison across confidence intervals and VaR methodologies.

Table 3. VaR Results

Dataset	Model	CI	Hist.	eGARCH	tGARCH	FHS	Expected	ES	CVaR Ratio
Houston	TCN	95%	0.1801	0.0669	0.0621	0.0669	0.1678	0.2110	1.2575
Indiana	Transf.	95%	0.2173	0.1419	0.2687	0.1419	0.1946	0.2355	1.2102
Europe	RNN	95%	0.1164	0.0491	0.1451	0.0506	0.1113	0.1289	1.1581
Asia	RNN	95%	0.1721	0.0573	0.0805	0.0215	0.1684	0.1909	1.1334
China	N-HiTS	95%	0.0852	0.0231	0.1356	0.0241	0.0767	0.1138	1.4841

Table 4 presents the Value at Risk (VaR) results using four methodologies across datasets. Historical Simulation (Hist.) revealed significant variability, with

Indiana showing one of the highest VaR (0.2173), while China reported the lowest (0.0852). This contrast suggests greater exposure to extreme deviations in U.S. regional markets compared to more stable dynamics in China. The Filtered Historical Simulation (FHS), on the other hand, consistently produced more conservative and stable estimates. Notably, Asia and China registered the lowest FHS VaR (0.0215), reinforcing this method's suitability in contexts with smoothed volatility.

The eGARCH model effectively captured volatility clustering, showing moderate results for Houston (0.0669) and Europe (0.0491), and the lowest value in China (0.0231). In contrast, the tGARCH model—designed to handle heavy-tailed distributions—returned the highest VaR in Indiana (0.2687), highlighting its sensitivity to extreme market swings. Indiana emerged as the most volatile region, while Asia and China exhibited lower risk levels, especially under volatility-aware models such as FHS. For Houston, Indiana, and Europe, tGARCH is preferred for its ability to model tail risks more conservatively. Houston's VaR was notably updated to 0.0621, in line with the top-performing TCN model (SMAPE: 12.56%). Similarly, tGARCH values of 0.2687 in Indiana and 0.1451 in Europe complement the performance of the Transformer and RNN, reinforcing the method's suitability in more unstable contexts.

Table 4. Recommended VaR per dataset with SMAPE and Expected Shortfall

Dataset	IC	SMAPE (Best Model)	Model	VaR	Expected Shortfall (ES)	Historical VaR
Houston	95%	12.56% (TCN)	tGARCH	0.0621	0.2110	0.1801
Indiana	95%	17.33% (Transformer)	tGARCH	0.2687	0.2355	0.2173
Europe	95%	8.01% (RNN)	tGARCH	0.1451	0.1289	0.1164
Asia	95%	7.20% (RNN)	FHS	0.0215	0.1909	0.1721
China	95%	6.10% (N-HiTS)	FHS	0.0241	0.1138	0.0852

Expected Shortfall (ES) provides a more complete view of risk by estimating the average loss beyond the VaR threshold. While China had the lowest ES (0.1138), Houston and Indiana registered higher values (0.1719 and 0.2355, respectively), signaling greater vulnerability to severe deviations. The CVaR ratio was also highest in China (1.48), indicating that, despite low expected losses, extreme events can have disproportionately large impacts. Although VaR values can be lower than SMAPE, for example, Houston's VaR of 6.21% versus SMAPE of 12.56%, this reflects their differing interpretations. SMAPE considers average symmetric errors, while VaR isolates the upper tail of the error distribution. ES bridges this conceptual gap in Houston, where ES highlights the potential intensity of rare but impactful forecast deviations.

FHS proved to be the most balanced method for Asia and China, providing reliable risk estimates with minimal overstatement. These findings are consistent with the strong forecasting performance of RNN in Asia (SMAPE: 7.20%) and N-HiTS in China (SMAPE: 6.10%). Historical VaR adds further perspective by revealing the effects of past extreme events, such as the 14.72% value observed for Houston, though it may overstate current risks. In contrast, adaptive models like tGARCH and FHS offer estimates better aligned with prevailing market dynamics. Integrating deep learning forecasts with adaptive VaR models thus enhances the robustness and responsiveness of risk management strategies in commodity markets like steel.

6 Conclusion

Steel plays a strategic role in the global energy sector, particularly in offshore oil and gas infrastructure, where components such as flexible risers and manifolds depend heavily on its availability and price stability. However, the inherent volatility of steel prices introduces significant financial risks that can compromise project feasibility, investment outcomes, and procurement planning. This study proposes DLensRisk, a hybrid and adaptive framework integrating deep learning models with Value-at-Risk (VaR) methodologies to forecast steel price behavior and quantify associated financial exposure.

The experimental results confirm that deep learning models—especially N-HiTS, RNN, Transformer, and TCN—consistently outperform traditional statistical approaches across multiple regional datasets. This reinforces the importance of selecting models based on each market's temporal and structural characteristics. Furthermore, by coupling the most accurate forecasting models with adaptive VaR techniques, the framework provides a more precise and interpretable assessment of tail risk. The tGARCH method proved particularly effective in more volatile regions like the United States and Europe. At the same time, FHS delivered conservative and stable estimates in markets with smoother price behavior, such as Asia and China.

DLensRisk offers a scalable, statistically validated, and operationally relevant solution for financial risk assessment in commodity-sensitive industries. By combining predictive accuracy with actionable metrics, it supports informed procurement and enhances resilience in capital-intensive energy projects. The integration of AI with formal risk modeling bridges the gap between data-driven forecasting and strategic planning in the oil and gas sector.

Acknowledgments. This work has been partially supported by Conselho Nacional de Desenvolvimento Científico e Tecnológico (CNPq) (316779/2023-7), and Coordenação de Aperfeiçoamento de Pessoal de Nível Superior (Capes) (001).

Disclosure of Interests. The authors have no competing interests to declare that are relevant to the content of this article.

References

1. Hashmi, S.M., Ahmed, F., Alhayki, Z., Syed, A.A.: The impact of crude oil prices on Chinese stock markets and selected sectors: evidence from the VAR-DCC-GARCH model. Environ. Sci. Pollut. Res. **29**(35), 52560–52573 (2022)

2. Siham, A.K.I.L., Sekkate, S., Abdellah, A.D.I.B.: Multimodal deep learning for oil price forecasting using economic indicators. Procedia Comput. Sci. **236**, 402–409 (2024)
3. Amri-Asrami, M., Jamkhane, E.E.: The effect of oil price on stock market performance and petrochemical stock value using NARDL. J. Ekonomi **6**(1), 25–33 (2024)
4. Asante, J., Ampomah, W., Jiawei, T., Cather, M.: Data-driven modeling for forecasting oil recovery: a timeseries neural network approach for tertiary co2 wag eor. Geoenergy Sci. Eng. **233**, 212555 (2024)
5. Varshini, A., Kayal, P., Maiti, M.: How good are different machine and deep learning models in forecasting the future price of metals? full sample versus sub-sample. Res. Policy **92**, 105040 (2024)
6. Foroutan, P., Lahmiri, S.: Deep learning-based spatial-temporal graph neural networks for price movement classification in crude oil and precious metal markets. Mach. Learn. Appl. **16**, 100552 (2024)
7. Zhang, H., Tong, L., Addo, M.A.: Mechanical analysis of flexible riser with carbon fiber composite tension armor. J. Compos. Sci. **5**(1), 3 (2020)
8. Mohsin, M., Jamaani, F.: A novel deep-learning technique for forecasting oil price volatility using historical prices of five precious metals in context of green financing – a comparison of deep learning, machine learning, and statistical models. Res. Policy **86**, 104216 (2023)
9. He, K., Zheng, L., Yang, Q., Wu, C., Yu, Y., Zou, Y.: Crude oil price prediction using temporal fusion transformer model. Procedia Comput. Sci. **221**, 927–932 (2023)
10. Sen, A., Choudhury, K.D.: Forecasting the Crude Oil prices for last four decades using deep learning approach. Res. Policy **88**, 104438 (2024)
11. Kubo, K., Nakagawa, K.: Portfolio optimization using deep learning with risk aversion utility function. Finan. Res. Lett. **74**, 106761 (2025)
12. Arian, H., Moghimi, M., Tabatabaei, E., Zamani, S.: Encoded value-at-risk: a machine learning approach for portfolio risk measurement. Math. Comput. Simul. **202**, 500–525 (2022)
13. He, K., Ji, L., Tso, G.K., Zhu, B., Zou, Y.: Forecasting exchange rate value at risk using deep belief network ensemble based approach. Procedia Computer Sci. **139**, 25–32 (2018)
14. Kakade, K., Jain, I., Mishra, A.K.: Value-at-Risk forecasting: a hybrid ensemble learning GARCH-LSTM based approach. Resour. Policy **78**, 102903 (2022)
15. Osei-Brefo, E.: Triple discriminator gan and continuous wavelet transform for volatility forecasting. In: 2024 International Joint Conference on Neural Networks (IJCNN), pp. 1–8. IEEE (2024)
16. Friedman, M.: The use of ranks to avoid the assumption of normality implicit in the analysis of variance. J. Am. Stat. Assoc. **32**(200), 675–701 (1937)
17. Demšar, J.: Statistical comparisons of classifiers over multiple data sets. J. Mach. Learn. Res. **7**, 1–30 (2006)
18. Fisher, R.A.: Statistical Methods for Research Workers. Oliver and Boyd, London and Edinburgh (1941)
19. Liu, Y., Chen, W.: A sas macro for testing differences among three or more independent groups using kruskal-wallis and nemenyi tests. J. Huazhong Univ. Sci. Technol. [Med. Sci.] **32**(1), 130–134 (2012)
20. Tukey, J.W.: Comparing individual means in the analysis of variance. In: Biometrics, pp. 99–114 (1949)

21. Rahim, M.A., et al.: An enhanced hybrid model based on CNN and BiLSTM for identifying individuals via handwriting analysis. CMES-Comput. Model. Eng. Sci. **140**(2) (2024)
22. Kristjanpoller, W., Fadic, A., Minutolo, M.C.: Volatility forecast using hybrid neural network models. Expert Syst. Appl. **41**(5), 2437–2442 (2014)
23. Kim, H.Y., Won, C.H.: Forecasting the volatility of stock price index: a hybrid model integrating lstm with multiple garch-type models. Expert Syst. Appl. **103**, 25–37 (2018)
24. Lu, X., Que, D., Cao, G.: Volatility forecast based on the hybrid artificial neural network and GARCH-type models. Procedia Comput. Sci. **91**, 1044–1049 (2016)

LisHAB - A Housing Market Agent-Based Simulation Model

Miguel Alves[1]($\boxtimes$), Pedro A. Santos[1,2] (iD), and João Dias[2,3,4] (iD)

[1] Instituto Superior Técnico, Universidade de Lisboa, Lisbon, Portugal
{miguel.paraiso.alves,pedro.santos}@tecnico.ulisboa.pt
[2] INESC-ID, Lisbon, Portugal
jmdias@ualg.pt
[3] Faculdade de Ciências e Tecnologia, Universidade do Algarve, Faro, Portugal
[4] CISCA, Faro, Portugal

Abstract. With the recent price increases, housing affordability has become a critical issue in Portugal. This situation requires the right policies to be taken. To support informed policymaking, this work presents an agent-based model of the Lisbon Metropolitan Area housing market that simulates interactions between heterogeneous households, a credit system, and a construction sector across rental and ownership markets. The model is grounded in empirical data from 2021 census and it was validated to ensure that it could replicate historical trends, including the 2008 financial crisis and the 2021–2023 period. It was then used to evaluate the potential effects of several policies proposed by the Portuguese political parties regarding the housing market. The model demonstrates how agent-based approaches can capture complex market dynamics and provide a transparent tool for evaluating the impacts of different housing policies.

Keywords: Housing Market · ACE · Agent-based Model · Economical Simulations

1 Introduction

The rapid increase in housing prices has positioned the housing market as a central topic in Portuguese domestic politics, with divergent policy solutions being advocated across the political spectrum. Current real estate values, when contrasted with relatively stagnant wage growth [7], have made homeownership increasingly unattainable—especially for younger individuals seeking to establish independent households.

Such challenges have far-reaching social implications. One consequence has been a notable increase in youth emigration, as well as heightened resentment towards immigrants, who are often perceived as competitors in the already strained housing market [11].

If left unaddressed, these issues may escalate into widespread political and economic crises. Consequently, there is an urgent need for well-informed policy

J. Valente de Oliveira et al. (Eds.): EPIA 2025, LNAI 16122, pp. 16–28, 2026.
https://doi.org/10.1007/978-3-032-05179-0_2

interventions. Developing simulation tools to forecast the outcomes of proposed policies can play a crucial role in supporting policymakers, helping them make evidence-based decisions that address the complexity of the housing market.

1.1 Agent-Based Computational Economics Model

The field of study that utilizes agent-based models to create economic simulations is called Agent-based Computational Economics (ACE). While traditional economic simulation methodologies mostly disregard the interactions between the specific agents of the economy [13], ACE follows a bottom-up approach, where the macroeconomic phenomena are generated by the modeled agents and their interactions.

ACE offers a bottom-up modeling approach in which macroeconomic dynamics emerge from the interactions of simulated agents such as households, firms, and policymakers [14]. Unlike traditional Dynamic Stochastic General Equilibrium (DSGE) models, which rely on aggregate relationships and representative agents [12], ACE captures heterogeneity, bounded rationality, and adaptive behavior, making it well-suited to study complex, real-world economic phenomena.

A key strength of ACE lies in its ability to simulate emergent outcomes like endogenous business cycles without relying on predefined shocks [10], which contrasts with the exogenous disturbances required by DSGE to explain deviations from equilibrium. While ACE models are computationally more demanding due to their granularity, they provide deeper insights into distributional effects and allow the testing of policies at a more detailed, behavioral level.

The agent-based models characteristics allow us to observe fine-grained phenomena that occur within the model, which is ideal considering that our goal is precisely to understand the impacts of certain policies in the housing market.

There has been a lot of relevant work in ACE exploring different sectors such as transport economics, such as ride-pooling simulations [15], which sudied the impact of different service desings. Other studies have tackled sector-specific dynamics, like agricultural land use in the Argentine Pampas [1]. Together, these works underscore the versatility of ACE in capturing emergent behavior across diverse economic contexts. Another good example is the baseline ACE model [6], which uses only households and firms to simulate labor and goods markets while capturing important macroeconomic dynamics through network-based interactions. The AMoSI model [4], which introduced the concept of wealth redistribution in an agent-based simulation, enabling the analysis of how tax-and-transfer policies affect inequality, consumption, and employment in a simplified economic environment, ialso worth mentioning. In the context of housing markets, a notable example is the large-scale, data-driven agent-based model of the Hungarian housing market [9], which integrates regional heterogeneity, evolving housing stock, and a robust credit system. Other studies have also applied agent-based modeling to different housing markets, including the Italian housing market [3] and the UK housing market [2].

We have created an agent-based model to model housing policies, and validated it using the Lisbon Metropolitan Area housing market. In addition to the ability to evaluate proposed housing policies, the model also serves as a valuable baseline for future work, providing a framework that can be enhanced and expanded upon.

The remainder of this paper is organized as follows. Section 2 presents a review of relevant agent-based economic models, covering both general economic simulations and housing market simulations, with a particular emphasis on the latter. Section 3 introduces the model developed for this study, which constitutes the main contribution of the work. Section 4 presents the results obtained from running the model, including both the validation exercises and the policy experiments, which represent the core objective of the research. Finally, Sect. 5 summarizes the key findings and discusses their implications for housing policy in the Lisbon Metropolitan Area.

2   Related Work

Agent-Based Computational Economics (ACE) has produced many contributions over the years. One of the most ambitious was EURACE [5], an EU-funded project that aimed to simulate the European economy in a supercomputer environment. However, it was never fully completed.

This section presents relevant ACE models, starting with general economic simulations, followed by models targeting the housing market.

2.1   Generic Agent-Based Economic Simulations

Agent-based economic modeling has increasingly served as a foundation for simulating core economic dynamics. A good example is the minimal ACE model [6] developed to simulate basic macroeconomic relations using just two types of agents: households and firms. Despite its simplicity, this model reproduces complex labor and goods market interactions, such as job matching processes and wage adjustments. The inclusion of firm-household network ties simulates consumer loyalty and limited information, and the model successfully generates known macroeconomic patterns such as cyclical production, the Phillips Curve, and the Beveridge Curve—illustrating the potential of even minimal agent-based models to replicate economic phenomena endogenously.

Another relevant contribution is the AMoSI model [4], which focuses on analyzing the effects of social policies on inequality. This simulation includes households, firms, and a government agent, and introduces taxation and welfare mechanisms such as unemployment benefits and income support. The model allows for household heterogeneity, including differences in education levels, which affect productivity and employment. Through some experiments, AMoSI demonstrated that tax-and-subsidy schemes not only reduced inequality but also improved overall economic performance by raising consumption and employment. These results highlight how agent-based models can offer important insights into both macroeconomic trends and the distributional impacts of policy choices.

2.2 Heterogeneous Effects and Spillovers of Macroprudential Policy in an Agent-Based Model of the UK Housing Market

The authors of this study [2] developed a sophisticated agent-based model of the UK housing market, with heterogeneous households such as renters, first-time buyers, home owners, and buy-to-let investors. The model simulates both owner-occupier and rental market dynamics and includes a realistic double-auction mechanism for housing transactions. Using real world data from the UK housing market for calibration, the authors assess the impact of two borrower-based macroprudential tools: a hard loan-to-value (LTV) limit and a soft loan-to-income (LTI) cap. The findings show that both instruments reduce credit availability and leverage, thereby moderating house price cycles. However, the effects of policies targeting a single risk metric often spill over into other areas (e.g., LTI limits affecting LTV distributions), underscoring the need for joint calibration. Moreover, lending restrictions disproportionately impact first-time buyers, while BTL investors, less constrained, expand their holdings, contributing to shifts in ownership and measurable spillovers into the rental sector. The analysis highlights the value of ABMs for studying the effects of macroprudential policy, as they capture nonlinear, heterogeneous, and sectoral dynamics often missed by traditional models.

2.3 A Data-Driven Model of the Hungarian Housing Market

A high-resolution, data-driven agent-based model of the Hungarian housing market was recently developed to simulate the market at a national scale, with approximately 4 million households. The model incorporates detailed geographic granularity, dividing the country into 8 regions and 124 neighborhoods, each characterized by quality indicators. Flats are represented by size, state, and location, and housing stock evolves dynamically through deterioration, renovation, and new construction. The construction sector operates based on a "fictive demand" derived from past activity, aiming to anticipate market needs. A sophisticated credit system is also included, featuring housing, bridge, and personal loans, with strict eligibility criteria based on LTV and DSTI rules, income thresholds, and credit history.

The model was calibrated using data from 2018–2019 and achieved strong alignment with empirical indicators such as regional housing prices, number of housing transactions, loan issuance, and share of transactions involving newly built homes. Validation against data that wasn't used during calibration confirmed its ability to reproduce real-world patterns, including transaction volumes by region, loan distributions across income levels, and the relationship between loan characteristics and borrower risk. Despite some underestimation of DSTI values, due to the omission of some loan types, the model proved robust and reliable for experimental applications.

The model was applied to test two specific policy-related scenarios: increasing construction costs and doubling a family support subsidy. Results showed that rising construction costs had a disproportionately negative impact on lower-income regions, where wages were unable to absorb the price increases, leading to a shift toward lower-quality housing. The subsidy experiment revealed that, under fixed supply, increased financial support caused price inflation that counteracted its intended benefits, particularly for lower-income households. In some cases, first-time buyers were effectively priced out of the market. These experiments demonstrate the ability of agent-based models to uncover unintended policy consequences and offer valuable insights into how different segments of the population are affected. This type of modeling serves as a powerful tool for guiding more effective housing policy.

3   LisHAB

Our model, which we called Lisbon Housing Agent-based (LisHAB) is designed to serve as a tool to help policymakers make decisions regarding the housing market, enabling them to anticipate the potential impacts of various housing policies in the Lisbon Metropolitan Area. The model can be tuned to verify specific policies and observe how they influence market outcomes over time.

The most important entities in the model are the households, which drive both demand and supply in the housing market. Households in our model are decision-making entities that interact with our two distinct but interconnected markets: the rental market and the buying-and-selling market. Their behaviors are influenced by their own financial situation, as well as the overall economic state of the model, e.g. interest rates and current houses prices. They also incorporate some stochastic elements into their decisions in an attempt to replicate real-world behavior.

The model incorporates demographic events such as births, deaths, divorces, migrations and children leaving home, to realistically simulate population dynamics and their impact on housing demand and supply. These events are based on empirical data and influence household size, structure, and behavior, such as creating new housing demand after a divorce or when young adults form new households. Together, they ensure that the simulation reflects the demographic forces shaping the Lisbon housing market.

The model features a dynamic construction sector that both builds new houses and renovates existing ones in response to perceived regional demand and housing size preferences. New constructions are guided by market needs, ensuring alignment with buyer affordability and regional housing gaps. Renovations are driven by investor households aiming to enhance property value for resale, reflecting speculative behavior commonly seen in real estate markets. These mechanisms enable the simulation to realistically model fluctuations in housing supply over time.

The model captures two key forms of housing investment behavior: renovation and resale, and buy-to-rent. In the first, households purchase homes to renovate and resell at a profit. In the second, households invest in properties for rental income, reflecting long-term financial planning and contributing to the rental housing supply. These investment dynamics introduce market complexity by influencing both housing prices and the distribution of properties between ownership and rental markets.

To maintain realism, the model includes a variety of taxes that impact household behavior and market conditions. These include income tax and social security contributions, both of which reduce household disposable income. Property transactions are subject to a house transaction tax, while consumption is affected by VAT, applied both to general goods and construction. Investor households are modeled to pay capital gains tax when selling non-primary residences, with renovation costs considered in the calculation. Additionally, a rent tax diverts a portion of tenant payments to the government.

The model includes a simplified representation of non-resident households to reflect their significant role in Lisbon's high-end housing market. Rather than simulating them as agents, their influence is modeled as a virtual demand targeting high-quality properties. To prevent them from permanently occupying a large share of the housing stock, their properties are sold back into the market at a fixed, exogenous rate. This abstraction helps preserve realism while managing complexity and addressing data limitations.

3.1   Model Composition

This section outlines the main components of the model, focusing on the agents and structures that interact within the housing market.

Central to the model are households, which are the only multi-agent of our simulation and serve as both consumers and suppliers of housing. Alongside them, we define the construction sector and the banking system as single entities, and the houses as the main asset the households can own.

Households are the core agents in the simulation, representing both demand and a large share of the supply in the housing market. Each household is characterized by its age, size, economic percentile, and residency zone, which influence its behavior and housing needs. Their actions, buying, renting, selling, or investing, depend on their ownership status and financial condition, reflecting the diverse roles that households play in real-world housing market.

The construction sector in the model builds houses based on expected supply and demand and operates under a debt ceiling tied to Portugal's real GDP per capita, preventing unchecked expansion. It also manages renovation projects initiated by investor households aiming to profit from property resale.

The Bank in the model is a passive entity that issues loans to households and the construction sector, while holding interest rates and macroprudential policy parameters (LTV and DSTI), which are exogenous parameters and not updated by the bank itself.

In the model, houses are the primary assets owned by households and are characterized by their location (municipality), size (in m^2), and quality percentile (1–100), which simplifies various factors affecting value. These attributes directly influence both market price and desirability.

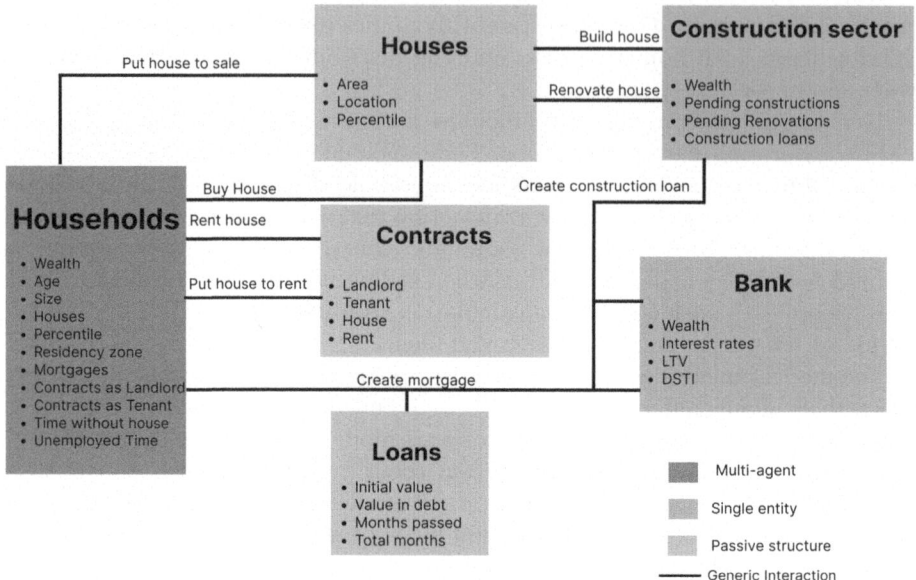

Fig. 1. Model Overview

The simulation also includes two markets, rental and buying/selling, that operate similarly. In each simulation cycle, households post their market intentions, and then the model attempts to match supply with demand by evaluating a subset of available listings for compatibility with each household's needs.

4   Validation and Experiments

This section presents results from two categories of simulation runs: model validation and policy experiments. The validation tests aim to confirm that the model behaves realistically and aligns with observed real-world outcomes. The policy experiments, which were the core objective of the study, evaluate the effects of housing policies proposed by Portuguese political parties by comparing their impacts against a baseline scenario with no policy changes.

4.1   Model Validation

The model was validated using two different approaches. First, it was tested against the housing market fluctuations observed during the 2008 economic crisis, with interest rates and unemployment as inputs. Second, it was evaluated by comparing its simulated housing prices and rents with real-world data from 2021 to 2023, without any inputs besides the empirical data within the model. These validation steps aimed to verify that the model behaves in an economically consistent way and that it reasonably reflects the dynamics of the Lisbon Metropolitan Area housing market, making it a suitable tool for policy analysis.

In the historical validation, the simulation was divided into two periods (2003–2012 and 2012–2019) to capture both the crisis and the recovery. The model successfully mirrored key price trends, such as a temporary price rebound in 2010 and the steady post-crisis growth from 2012 onward. Though absolute price levels were not directly comparable, the relative changes and inflection points aligned well with observed data. This was confirmed by Pearson correlation values of 0.60 for the first period and 0.97 for the second, demonstrating the model's strong ability to replicate historical market shifts, particularly during the recovery years.

The model was further validated by comparing its simulated housing prices and rental values with real-world data from the Lisbon Metropolitan Area, sourced from INE. Median property sale prices (per square meter) were analyzed quarterly, while rental data were evaluated semi-annually. To enable a fair comparison, the empirical data was adjusted for non-housing inflation, which is absent in the simulation. This validation step was essential to confirm that the model could not only reflect economic logic but also closely reproduce actual market trends in both the rental and buying segments.

The validation results show that while the simulation tends to slightly underestimate both housing prices and rents compared to real-world data, it generally follows the observed trends with reasonable accuracy. The rental market, in particular, demonstrates more consistent alignment, with several municipalities showing close matches. Although discrepancies exist up to 21.02% for housing prices and 13.01% for rents, the model exhibits predictable behavior rather than random deviation. This level of accuracy supports the model's use for policy experimentation, acknowledging that it can offer meaningful insights into the possible impacts.

4.2   Policy Experiments

This section describes the policies that will be tested using the developed simulation. Since the model is already validated, it now serves as a testing ground for many different policies. The aim is to assess the potential effects of these policies on the dynamics of the housing market by comparing each scenario to a baseline simulation that assumes no policy intervention. The following subsections describe the policies that will be tested and how they were implemented in the simulation environment. The policies were taken from the 2024 electoral programs of the Portuguese parties except for Ceiling on Rent Increases which was actually implemented by the government in 2023.

A proposed policy by Aliança Democrática and Iniciativa Liberal aims to reduce construction VAT from 23% to 6%, lowering the cost of new housing and potentially influencing market prices. Aliança Democrática, Iniciativa Liberal, and Chega advocate simplifying construction licensing, which is represented in the simulation by reducing the licensing time by half. Iniciativa Liberal also proposes lowering the rental income tax to attract housing supply to the rental market. A Ceiling on Rent Increases policy introduced by Partido Socialista in 2023 is included as a 2% limit on rent increases for second-time leases, consistently applied in the model due to simplifications. Lastly, Bloco de Esquerda's proposal to ban non-resident property purchases is implemented by fully excluding non-resident demand, enabling the analysis of its impact on speculative pressure in the housing market.

The impacts of the VAT reduction policy were minimal in the simulation, largely due to two factors: first, in the simulation, the construction sector does not actually pay VAT during construction, instead applying it only to calculate the cost-driven sale price (mirroring real-world VAT reimbursement mechanisms), and second, this cost-driven price is only used when it exceeds the market value, meaning that in most cases, houses are sold at prevailing market prices regardless of VAT. As a result, when market values already exceed construction costs (plus VAT), the VAT reduction has no meaningful effect on either construction volume or housing prices.

The construction licensing simplification policy had a limited effect on overall housing prices, showing modest price changes that varied by municipality. However, it had a significant impact on market activity, notably increasing the number of transactions, especially in smaller municipalities like Barreiro and Moita. The lack of substantial price reductions can be attributed to the structural imbalance between supply and demand in the housing market, where demand remains so strong that additional supply is quickly absorbed without downward pressure on prices. Additionally, the introduction of newer, higher-quality housing increased the average quality of transacted properties, which in turn pushed prices upward due to the model's price-setting mechanism based on transaction averages within quality quartiles. This dynamic disproportionately inflated prices for top-tier houses, while prices for lower-quality homes did experience some decline, as can be seen in Fig. 2b, indicating that the policy was more effective at improving affordability in the lower segments of the market.

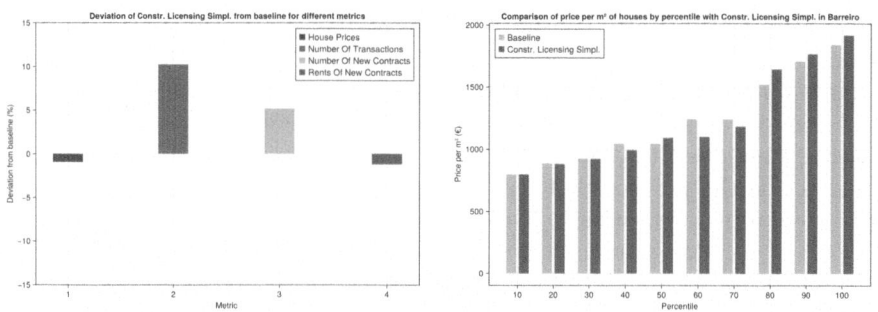

(a) Effects of Construction licensing simplification in different metrics (Deviation in % from baseline)

(b) Effects of Construction licensing simplification in Houses prices by percentile of houses in Barreiro

Fig. 2. Construction Licensing Simplification Results

The Reduced Rent Tax policy, while designed to strengthen the rental market, produced unintended consequences in the housing market by encouraging households to shift houses from the buying and selling market to the rental market, thereby tightening supply and driving up prices, as shown in Fig. 3. This effect was observed across all municipalities, with Amadora experiencing the highest average price increase of 20%. The simulation may have amplified this effect due to the absence of idle housing behavior, where households hold properties without renting or selling, which is common behavior in real-world markets [8]. This policy also led to a decrease in the number of house purchases, while having limited impact on rent values. However, it significantly increased rental activity, particularly in municipalities like Sesimbra, Sintra, and Lisboa, suggesting its effectiveness in boosting rental supply even if it negatively affects affordability in the ownership market.

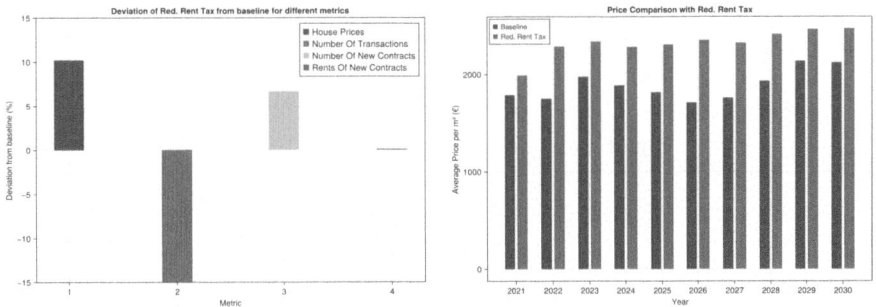

(a) Effects of Reduced Rent Tax in different metrics (Deviation in % from baseline)

(b) Effects of Reduced Rent tax in Amadora Houses prices

Fig. 3. Reduced Rent Tax Results

The Rents Increase Ceiling policy had minimal effects across all evaluated metrics. Rent values showed a slight downward trend, with the largest average decrease being just 1%, observed in Cascais, Setúbal, and Vila Franca de Xira. Similarly, the number of new rental contracts experienced only marginal growth, with the most notable increase occurring in Vila Franca de Xira, where contract volume rose by just 3% compared to the baseline.

The Non-Residents Prohibition policy produced the most significant reduction in housing prices among all tested measures, with a maximum decrease of 7.5% in Mafra and notable drops of around 5% in larger municipalities like Oeiras and Odivelas. As expected for a demand-reduction policy, it also led to fewer overall transactions, reflecting the absence of non-resident buyers. In contrast to the construction licensing simplification policy, this measure resulted in a slight decline in the average quality of houses sold, as shown in Fig. 4b, since non-residents in the simulation were modeled to primarily target high-end properties. This shift in transaction quality likely contributed to the observed price reductions. Given that non-residents are not represented in the rental market within the simulation, the policy had no meaningful impact on rental prices or contract volumes.

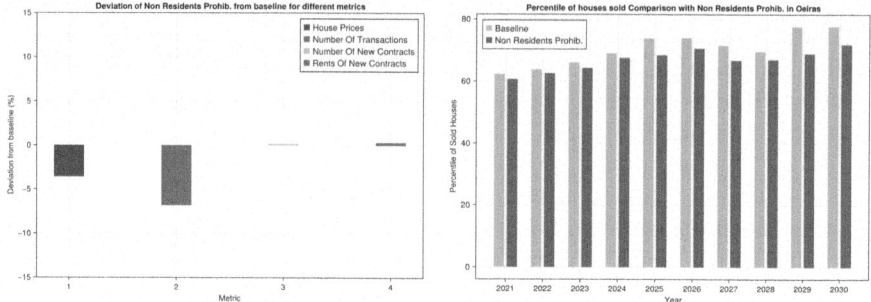

(a) Effects of Non Residents prohibition (b) Effects of Non Residents Prohibition in different metrics (Deviation in % from in sold houses percentile in Oeiras baseline)

Fig. 4. Non Residents Prohibition Results

5   Conclusions

This paper presented the development and application of an agent-based model tailored to simulate housing market dynamics across the 18 municipalities of the Lisbon Metropolitan Area. The model represents diverse household behaviors and investment strategies, enabling the analysis of property transactions, pricing, and policy interventions.

The simulation was used to evaluate the effects of several housing policy proposals. The Construction VAT Reduction policy had negligible effects due to model assumptions about VAT refundability and the already high market prices. Construction Licensing Simplification, while not significantly lowering prices, greatly increased transaction volumes, especially in smaller municipalities. The Reduced Rent Tax policy led to a marked increase in house prices as investor focus shifted from ownership to rental markets, though its effect on actual rents was modest. The Rent Increase Ceiling policy produced only minor effects, but its small positive impact could be seen as encouraging, given that it is the only measure that has been implemented in practice. Finally, the Non-Residents Purchase Prohibition policy was the only one that reduced housing prices, suggesting that supply-side measures might not be sufficiently effective on their own, at least in overheated markets.

Together, these findings illustrate the value of agent-based modeling as a tool for understanding and anticipating the effects of housing policies. While the model has limitations and would benefit from further refinement—particularly in areas such as space constraints and landlord behavior—it lays the groundwork for more sophisticated simulations that can support data-informed policymaking in complex urban markets.

Acknowledgements. This work was supported by national funds through Fundação para a Ciência e a Tecnologia (FCT) with reference UIDB/50021/2020.

Disclosure of Interests. The authors have no competing interests to declare that are relevant to the content of this article.

References

1. Bert, F.E., et al.: An agent based model to simulate structural and land use changes in agricultural systems of the argentine pampas. Ecol. Model. **222**(19), 3486–3499 (2011)
2. Carro, A., Hinterschweiger, M., Uluc, A., Farmer, J.D.: Heterogeneous effects and spillovers of macroprudential policy in an agent-based model of the UK housing market. Ind. Corp. Change **32**(2), 386–432 (2022). https://doi.org/10.1093/icc/dtac030
3. Catapano, G., Franceschi, F., Michelangeli, V., Loberto, M.: Macroprudential Policy Analysis via an Agent Based Model of the Real Estate Sector. Temi di discussione (Economic working papers) 1338, Bank of Italy, Economic Research and International Relations Area (2021). https://ideas.repec.org/p/bdi/wptemi/td_1338_21.html
4. Costa, D., Soares, J., Santos, P.A.: Rich and poor: simulating social policies to build a fairer society. In: Verhagen, H., Borit, M., Bravo, G., Wijermans, N. (eds.) Advances in Social Simulation. SPC, pp. 117–134. Springer, Cham (2020). https://doi.org/10.1007/978-3-030-34127-5_11
5. Deissenberg, C., van der Hoog, S., Dawid, H.: Eurace: a massively parallel agent-based model of the european economy. Appl. Math. Comput. **204**(2), 541–552 (2008). https://doi.org/10.1016/j.amc.2008.05.116
6. Lengnick, M.: Agent-based macroeconomics: a baseline model. J. Econ. Behav. Organ. **86** (2011). https://doi.org/10.1016/j.jebo.2012.12.021
7. Lorga, M., Januário, J.F., Cruz, C.O.: Housing affordability, public policy and economic dynamics: an analysis of the city of Lisbon. J. Risk Finan. Manag. **15**(12) (2022). https://doi.org/10.3390/jrfm15120560
8. Mendes, L.: The dysfunctional rental market in Portugal: a policy review. Land **11**(4), 566 (2022)
9. Mérő, B., Borsos, A., Hosszú, Z., Oláh, Z., Vágó, N.: A high-resolution, data-driven agent-based model of the housing market. J. Econ. Dyn. Control **155**, 104738 (2023). https://doi.org/10.1016/j.jedc.2023.104738
10. Napoletano, M.: A short walk on the wild side: agent based models and their implications for macroeconomic analysis. Sciences po publications, Sciences Po (2018)
11. Salomon, K.: Dynamics of immigrant resentment in Europe. Technical report, WZB Discussion Paper (2020)
12. Sbordone, A.M., Tambalotti, A., Rao, K., Walsh, K.J.: In: Policy analysis using DSGE models: an introduction, pp. 24–26 (2010)

13. Tesfatsion, L.: Agent-based computational economics: growing economies from the bottom up. Artif. Life **8**(1), 55–82 (2002)
14. Tesfatsion, L.: Agent-based computational economics: a constructive approach to economic theory. Handb. Comput. Econ. **2**, 831–880 (2006)
15. Zwick, F., Kuehnel, N., Moeckel, R., Axhausen, K.W.: Agent-based simulation of city-wide autonomous ride-pooling and the impact on traffic noise. Transp. Res. Part D: Transp. Environ. **90**, 102673 (2021). https://doi.org/10.1016/j.trd.2020.102673

Food Waste Detection in Canteen Plates with Visual Large Language Models

Raffaele Calì[1] 📷, João Ferreira[2] 📷, Paulino Cerqueira[2] 📷, and Jorge Ribeiro[2,3](✉) 📷

[1] Università di Catania, 95131 Catania, Italy
`clarfl00t07b202x@studium.unict.it`
[2] Instituto Politécnico de Viana do Castelo, 4900-347 Viana do Castelo, Portugal
`{j.pedro.ferreira,paulinoc}@ipvc.pt, jrbeiro@estg.ipvc.pt`
[3] ADiT-Lab, Instituto Politécnico de Viana do Castelo, 4900-347 Viana do Castelo, Portugal

Abstract. This work addresses a research gap in the automated detection of Food Waste (FW) on canteen plates by presenting an innovative system that combines Computer Vision (CV) and Visual Large Language Models (VLLMs) in a hybrid Artificial Intelligence approach. The system uses a pretrained CV model to identify and differentiate between food and garbage, quantify waste, and recognize food items within the plate area. In the CV approach the percentage of food waste is calculated by analyzing segmented regions, measuring the food and garbage areas in pixels, and accounting for possible variations in food density. Since most VLLMs rely on vision encoders pretrained on loosely aligned image-text pairs often resulting in limited visual reasoning capabilities we incorporate Dual-Level Visual Knowledge (DLVK) extracted from a pretrained CV model to enhance understanding. The system is evaluated using a real-world dataset and three benchmarking datasets featuring food on plates. To evaluate the effectiveness of VLLMs in estimating FW from plate images, we designed and tested four prompting strategies of increasing complexity and visual guidance. These strategies were applied across three VLLMs, Gemini 2.5 Pro, GPT-4o, GPT-o3, and LLaVA 1.6 (7b Q:4). Gemini 2.5 Pro, when combined with the refined DLVK, delivers the lowest error and the highest share of explained variance reaching an MSE of 84.69 and an R2 of 0.88, outperforming all other configurations. We conclude that pure segmentation signals whether delivered to a model (ex. LLaVA 1.6) or used in the YOLOv11 baseline were insufficient, confirming that structured priors and explicit reasoning are essential once visual noise, occlusion and class imbalance enter the scene.

Keywords: Artificial intelligence · Food Waste · Food Waste detection · Instance Segmentation · Computer Vision · Visual Large Language Models

1 Introduction

Food Waste (FW) can be considered one of humanity's greatest unsolved problems, affecting not only developed countries but developing countries as well. Most of the FW is generated during the consumption stage, at which it has already reached the final consumer, while most of the FW in developing countries is generated at the production and post-harvest stages, due to the lack of modern technology [1]. Schools can also benefit from reducing FW, as it will consequently reduce the costs to produce that food and serve it to their consumers [2]. However, accurately and efficiently measuring FW in a school canteen can be challenging.

In recent years, there has been a significant rise in Artificial Intelligence (AI), particularly in Computer Vision (CV) through open-source frameworks for object detection. YOLO [3] is one such framework and has been applied and explored in numerous food detection [4, 5], food waste [6, 7], as well as food detection in plates [8, 9].

Also, in the last years, there has been a revolution in AI technology, particularly with the rise of Large Language Models (LLMs) [10] which have fundamentally changed how people perceive and utilize AI. The large applicability and exploration success in several areas of the society of the LLMS [11], Multimodal Large Language Models (MMLLM) [12], Vison Large Models (VLMs) [13, 14] and Visual Question Answering (VQA) [15] and potentiate their complementarity to the traditional Deep Learning Techniques, in particular the CV approaches [9, 16, 17]. In fact, Multimodal Large Language Models and Visual Large Language Models (VLLMs) are remarkable in vision-language tasks, such as image captioning and question answering, but lack essential perception ability and in some situations, present hallucinations that have been studied [18] and mitigated with some approaches such as Chain-of-Thought [19] or Retrieved Augmented Generation (RAG) [20].

In this sense, in the field of food detection and food waste detection, some works have been presented using CV [4–9] and exploring the LLMs (Visual and Multimodal) for food image classification [21, 22].

The motivation of this work arises from the gap identified in the literature review and the lack of real implementations in FW reduction systems. In this sense, we are not only interested in the simple identification of items in food plates but also in quantifying the food waste and the waste trends in plates in canteens using a CV model and LLMs. Thus, based on the creation of a CV model to detect food waste in canteens, this work explores the performance of the CV model as well as the performance of three LLMs platforms, namely LLaVa, GPT, and Gemini. We followed the idea of [16] and [23] for the integration with the VLLMs and [9] for the CV model creation.

The document is organized as follows. Section 2 presents the related work of the last research in computer vision for food detection, FW detection and FW detection in plates as well as VLLMs for Food Detection. Section 3 presents the methods, namely the context and architecture, the computer vision model creation, and the VLLMs prompting setup. Then we present the results achieved and finally the conclusions and future work as well as the references.

2   Related Work

2.1   Computer Vision for Food Detection, Food Waste Detection and Food Waste Detection in Plates

Food detection, Food Waste (FW) detection and FW detection in plates using Deep Learning (DL) approaches and CV have been an important field of research, especially for applications in dietary monitoring [4, 5]. Martinel et al. (2016) [24], proposed an architecture for food recognition using residual networks and slice convolution layers to address food structure, such as the layered appearance of some dishes. This method has significantly improved the accuracy of food recognition, outperforming other approaches. Goswami et al. (2017) [25] applied Deep Neural Networks (DNN) to classify food dishes. The study showed that DNN outperformed traditional machine learning methods, offering better performance in identifying food dishes, considering the unique visual characteristics of each dish, such as shape, colour and texture.

Ciocca et al. (2020) [26] focused on detecting the state of food (such as raw, processed, cut, or mixed food). The use of features extracted by DNN, combined with support vector machines, showed that the detection of food states, in addition to food categories, is a feasible and efficient task, outperforming manually made features. Sousa et al. (2019) [27] proposed a DL approach for detecting FW and automatically sorting waste from food trays. Using the Faster R-CNN model, the results showed a significant improvement in the accuracy of FW detection, which can be applied in industrial processes to optimize recycling and reduce waste. Dhelia et al. (2024) [7] used YOLOv8 to detect damaged food in the food industry concluding that their integration can help quickly identify damaged or unfit-to-eat food, which can optimize quality control processes and reduce waste on production lines.

Fan et al. (2023) [6] focused on FW detection using data augmentation techniques and YOLOv4. They used generative adversarial networks to generate FW images, which helped to improve the performance of the YOLO model to detect waste more efficiently and accurately. Ciocca et al. (2015) [28] has developed a system for estimating leftover food on plates. Using food detection and analysis of remaining portions, the system was able to help estimate the amount of food left on the plate, providing useful information for users in dietary monitoring applications. The research demonstrated that accurate detection of food on plates is crucial for estimating calories and portions. Ciocca et al. (2016) [29] introduced a new dataset containing images of canteen trays, with multiple foods arranged in various ways. These studies used convolutional neural networks to identify foods on the trays and classify the foods. The results showed good accuracy in identifying food and trays, with a focus on dynamic environments such as canteens. Pouladzadeh et al. (2017) [8] proposed a mobile food recognition system capable of identifying multiple foods in a meal. The solution uses deep learning to extract features from food images and identify the food in question, allowing users to monitor their food intake and estimate their calories accurately.

These works reinforce the importance of having an efficient recognition system to detect FW on plates, whether for dietary monitoring or portion control purposes, with promising results in terms of accuracy and applicability in real-world environments.

2.2 Multimodal and Visual Large Language Models for Food Detection

In the last years the exploration of LLMS for food detection have been presented [21–23]. Ma et al. (2023) [22] presented a food caption dataset (Food-500 Cap), which contains 24,700 food images with 494 categories. Experiments using MLLM (including VLLMS) demonstrate an underperform in the food domain compared with the performance in the general domain, and the research reveals severe bias in MLLMs' ability to handle food items from different geographic regions. Ma et al. (2024) [22] exploring the innovations and applications with LLMs models in food science concluding the LLMs hold significant potential in automating processes and improving accuracy and efficiency in the global food system and successful implementations require continuous updates and ethical considerations. Jun-Hwa et al. (2024) [21] explored Multimodal Food Image Classification with Large Language Models for fine-grained food image classification employing a cross-attention mechanism to effectively fuse visual and textual modalities, enhancing the model's ability to extract discriminative features beyond what can be achieved with visual features alone. According to the actual literature several works explore VLLMS to detect contextual information in images, for example [23, 30]. However, it is evidenced a lack in studies applied to the food sector and in waste detection and quantification, and more specifically in food waste detection in plates, which is the context of the applicability of this work.

3 Methods

3.1 Context and Architecture

In the context of sustainability and nutrition, allied to AI capabilities, this work explores a research gap in automated food waste detection on canteen plates in particular the percentage of waste and the waste items in plates after a dinner or a lunch. The implementation of this work is separated in two main components: the first using a CV model following the work [9] allows the recognition of food items and categorize the items in categories and then, with new images after detecting the plate, the segmentation and identification of the food items are carried out using the model. At the same time the model identifies and classifies food items in the plate (garbage, food, or waste) with high precision, providing a confidence score for each detected item. In this work, we consider the following items and objects as garbage: forks, knifes, spoons, cups, chips, bread, board and garbage (generic class, which contains for example napkins and bones). To determine the FW on plates, we first consider the area of the plate and detect the area of each individual item. With this model and submitting another image of a plate after a dinner or a meal and to determine the percentage (%) of FW and the food items we analyse its area in pixels and return a percentage. We consider the *FoodArea* refers to the area occupied by leftover food, *PlateArea* is the total area of the plate, and *WasteArea* represents the space occupied by inedible or discarded items. The calculation of the percentage of FW, using the following formula [61]:

$$\text{Waste}(\%) = \frac{FoodArea}{PlateArea - GarbageArea} \times 100 \qquad (1)$$

The second component is the use of a LLM with or without the integration of the CV model (YOLOv11, specifically the YOLOv11 l-seg variant) [9] in order to compare the performance of the waste detection between YOLOv11 and VLLMs (GPT, Gemini and LLaVA). The integration of the CV Model and LLM is to text the performance of VLLMs with Dual-Level Visual Knowledge [23] (information obtained by the CV Model) or by the traditional existing VLLMs simply submitting a prompt with zero-shot approach. Figure 1 presents the architecture of the system.

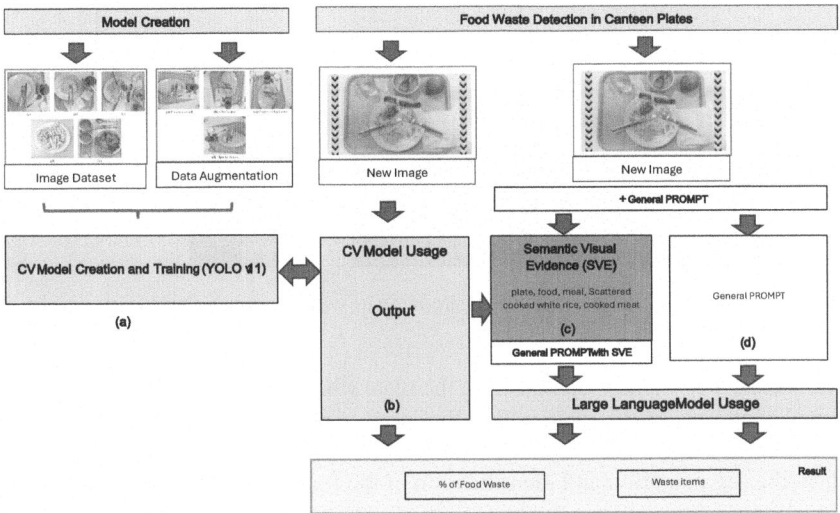

Fig. 1. Architecture of the System.

The architecture is divided into four main components and is illustrated in Fig. 1. The first component (Fig. 1 (a)) is responsible for the model creation and training process using (YOLO v11) to create a model to categorize the items in each image in two categories (garbage or not garbage), the component (b) corresponds to the CV model usage and the components (c) and (d) are related to the integration with Visual LLM. The components are more detailed described in the next sections.

3.2   Computer Vision Model Creation

The CV model was created using the YOLOv11 version and with more details in the work [9] and all the information provided in the opensource GitHub repository. The Fig. 2 illustrates more clearly the CV Model's usage, demonstrating the step-by-step process from image acquisition to waste calculation. The process begins with the input image of a tray containing food. This image is captured by a camera positioned above the plate to provide a clear view of the meal, including the plate and its contents.

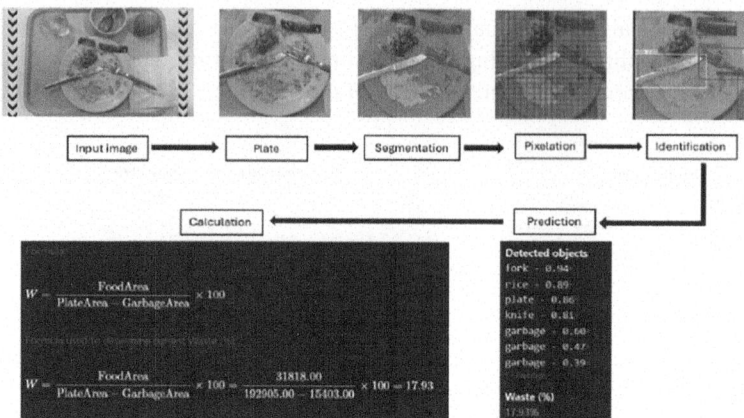

Fig. 2. System flow to calculate the percentage of waste using the YOLOv11 model.

The second step focuses on detecting the plate where the system automatically identifies the boundaries of the plate within the input image to isolate the food items from the surrounding elements, such as the tray or other objects on the table. After detecting the plate, the segmentation and identification of the food items are carried out using the YOLO v11 model to segment the image, efficiently separating the different food items on the plate. Segmentation helps distinguish leftover food from consumed food. At the same time, YOLO v11 identifies and classifies food items with high Precision, providing a confidence score for each detected item. In the context of waste calculation, to determine the FW on plates, we consider the area of the plate and detect the area of each individual item. Then, for each item, the category of the item (garbage, food, or waste) is detected and analyse its area in pixels with the formula (1) and return a percentage of food waste.

3.3 Prompting Setup for Visual Large Language Models

The exploration of VLLMs, particularly GPT (gpt-4o and gpt-o3), Gemini (gemini-2.5-pro), and LLaVa 1.6 7B. Using an image of a plate after dinner or lunch we used VLLMS's submitting the image to VLLM using zero-shot prompting approach. The other uses the concept of Dual-Level Visual Knowledge (DLVK) [23]. Considering that typically existing VLLM generates a vague and inaccurate response, the objective of DLVK is to enrich the visual information in VLLMs in two levels: progressive incorporation of fine-grained spatial-aware visual knowledge and soft prompting of high-level semantic visual evidence. With this we try to provide a more precise and contextually accurate description by incorporating softly prompting semantic visual evidence [23].

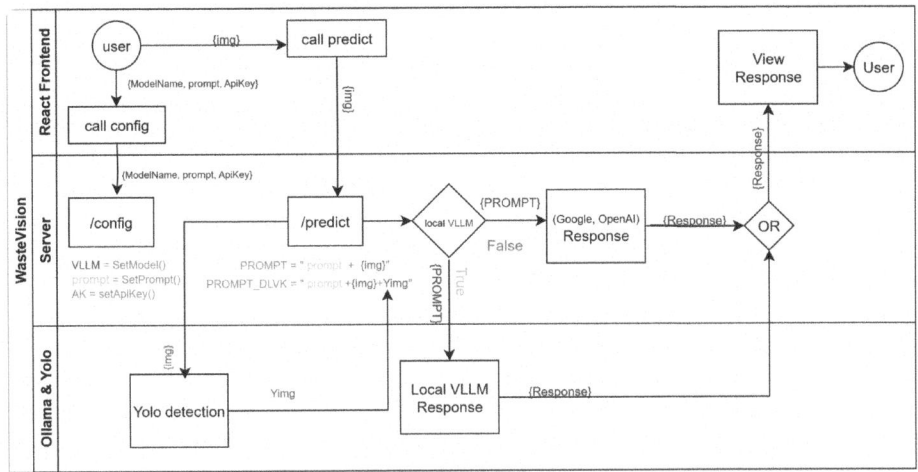

Fig. 3. LLMs Architecture Overview.

Figure 3 describes the system architecture, designed for an image-based analysis, featuring a react frontend and a python backend server that interacts with VLLMs. Users on the react frontend can either configure the VLLM, setting parameters like the model's name, a default prompt, and an API key, or initiate a prediction by uploading an image.

When a prediction is requested, the server constructs a complete prompt by combining the predefined text prompt with the uploaded image data. The system then makes a crucial decision: it can send this combined prompt to a local VLLM, such as one managed by Ollama, or, if a local option isn't chosen, forward it to an external cloud-based VLLM service like those offered by Google or OpenAI. Regardless of the VLLM chosen, it processes the prompt and image to generate a response, which is then sent back to the server. Finally, the server relays this response to the React frontend, allowing the user to view the analysis or prediction. This setup provides flexibility, enabling the system to leverage either local or external VLLM capabilities based on specific needs for performance, data privacy, or operational costs.

To evaluate the effectiveness of VLLMs in estimating FW from plate images, we designed and tested four prompting strategies of increasing complexity and visual guidance. These strategies were applied across three Vision-Language Models: Gemini 2.5 Pro, GPT-4o, GPT-o3 and LLaVA 1.6 (7b Q:4).

All experiments were conducted on a common test set obtained by merging the test splits of four publicly available datasets [9]: Custom, Tossit, Seoyoung, and Koo. This unified test-mix consists of 2,147 images and includes a manually validated subset of images with known food waste percentages to support fine-grained evaluation.

Each prompt was submitted along with one or more images showing a canteen plate after a meal. In specific conditions, additional detection data were injected using our DLVK mechanism, everything in zero-shot setting. We defined and tested four prompts:

- **Prompt 1 – Zero-shot baseline (P1):** This minimal configuration relies solely on the image and a brief task description, asking the model to estimate the percentage of leftover food after a meal. No formulas or object lists are provided. The objective is to assess the model's native visual reasoning capabilities in an unconstrained zero-shot setting.

- **Prompt 2 – Formula-based guidance (P2):** This setup introduces the definition of a mathematical formula for food waste percentage, based on pixel area ratios between food, garbage, and the total plate. Although numerical values are not supplied, the formula (1) guides the model's internal reasoning and encourages more structured estimations. In combination with the image, it represents a mid-level prompting approach, situated between zero-shot and fully assisted inference.
- **Prompt 3 – DLVK baseline (P3):** image with segmentation mask and detection list (P3): In this strategy, the model receives the original image (Image A) along with its segmented counterpart (Image B), annotated with bounding boxes and class labels generated by the YOLOv11 l-seg model. A detection list containing object names, confidence scores, and pixel areas is also included. However, the prompt remains general and does not explicitly encourage the model to challenge, correct, or reinterpret this information. The intent is to observe how the model integrates structured visual priors when no critical reasoning is prompted, relying primarily on the supplied annotations rather than its own perceptual analysis.
- **Prompt 4 – DLVK refined (P4):** active reasoning beyond YOLOv11 l-seg output. Prompt 4 uses the same input image A, annotated image B, and the detection list but introduces a role-specific, structured prompt designed to fully engage the model's visual reasoning. The model is explicitly assigned the role of an "Expert Multimodal Analyst" and instructed to transcend the limitations of the YOLOv11 l-seg output. Unlike Prompt 3, the model is not expected to passively interpret the detections but rather to: identify missing food items not boxed in the YOLOv11 l-seg annotation, such as crumbs, sauces, or liquids; Infer occluded regions, such as food partially covered by cutlery or napkins; Correct possible misclassifications, e.g., bones labelled as edible items or discarded lemon wedges counted as food. In this sense the prompt 4, simulates a more human-like analysis process, pushing the model to reassess the evidence and refine the estimate through critical, context-aware reasoning. By design, it fosters a more robust and accurate evaluation of the true food waste on the plate.

4   Results and Discussion

To evaluate the effectiveness of VLMs in estimating FW from plate images, we tested four prompting strategies of increasing complexity and visual guidance, as described in Sect. 3.3. These strategies were applied across three Vision-Language Models: Gemini 2.5 Pro, GPT-4o, GPT-o3 and LLaVA 1.6 (7b Q:4).

All experiments were conducted on a common test set obtained by merging the test splits of four publicly available datasets [9]: Custom, Tossit, Seoyoung, and Koo. This unified test-mix consists of 2,147 images and includes a manually validated subset of images with known food waste percentages to support fine-grained evaluation. Each prompt was submitted along with one or more images showing a canteen plate after a meal. In specific conditions, additional detection data were injected using our DLVK mechanism, everything in zero-shot setting.

Table 1. VLLMs and CV model evaluation.

Model	Prompt	MSE	MAE	R^2
Gemini 2.5 Pro	P1	143.86	7.67	0.80
	P2	197.26	9.75	0.72
	P3	423.00	10.67	0.40
	P4	**84.69**	**5.93**	**0.88**
GPT-4o	P1	639.81	12.77	0.09
	P2	381.21	9.99	0.46
	P3	501.63	14.17	0.29
	P4	479.31	15.53	0.32
o3	P1	104.20	6.87	0.85
	P2	130.01	7.81	0.81
	P3	516.33	12.14	0.26
	P4	134.40	7.61	0.81
LLaVA 1.6	P2	2061.00	38.26	−1.94
	P3	1353.30	30.49	−0.93
YOLO		952.71	16.47	−0.36

Table 1 presents the achieved results, for each model and prompts analysing the metrics Mean Absolute Error (MAE), Mean Square Error (MSE) and R-squared (R^2).

The experimental campaign shows a clear hierarchy among the tested systems. Gemini 2.5 Pro, when combined with the refined DLVK, delivers the lowest error and the highest share of explained variance: its mean squared error drops to 84.69, the mean absolute error to 5.93, and the coefficient of determination rises to 0.88. Removing the refined reasoning layer weakens the same backbone and replacing it with a purely formulaic prompt degrades performance still further, indicating that Gemini benefits only from structured priors that it is explicitly invited to critique.

The o3 family follows a different trend. Its zero-shot baseline (P1) remains strong, posting an MSE of 104.20, an MAE of 6.87 and an R2 of 0.85. Adding only the algebraic definition of the food-waste ratio (P2) nudges those numbers downward but not disastrously, raising the squared error to 130.01 and trimming R2 to 0.81.

By contrast, the unrefined DLVK prompt (P3) overwhelms the model with unfiltered detections: the MSE quintuples to 516.33, the MAE climbs to 12.14 and R2 collapses to 0.26, showing that o3 will over-trust noisy visual priors if it is not explicitly told to question them. The refined DLVK variant (P4) largely repairs the damage (MSE 134.40, MAE 7.61, R2 0.81), yet it still cannot beat the original zero-shot pass. In short, o3 extracts most of what it needs directly from the image; active reasoning helps it recover from bad external hints but does not deliver a net gain over its own baseline performance.

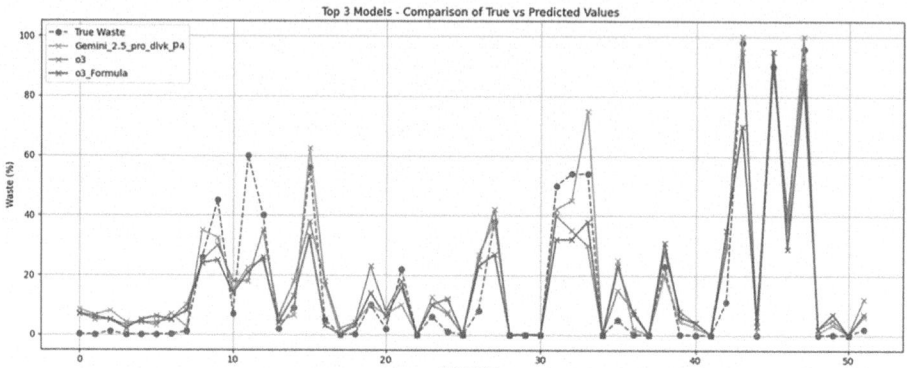

Fig. 4. Best VLLMs evaluation performance.

Analysing the Table 1, Fig. 4 present the best VLLMS evaluation performance, given special attention to the three best models, namely the Gemini_2.5_pro with the DLVK P4, o3 and o3 with the formula (1) and analysing the mean difference between predicted and ground-truth values (True waste in Fig. 4). We consider that MAE, MSE, R^2 and better reflect model performance for the task of estimating FW from plate images.

GPT-4o behaves very differently. In the absence of any prompt engineering, it is the weakest of the large models, but when a definition of the food-waste ratio is provided its error is almost halved, lifting R2 to 0.46. Adding segmentation masks and detection lists does not help; indeed, the refined DLVK prompt pushes the squared error back up toward five hundred. Evidently, GPT-4o is sensitive to noisy visual priors and prefers the clarity of an algebraic framing over additional, fallible annotations.

LLaVA 1.6 never escapes negative R2 values, even when assisted, exposing a persistent confusion between edible leftovers and inedible refuse. The YOLOv11 l-seg area-ratio baseline is similarly unreliable, confirming that segmentation masks alone cannot capture occluded or misclassified food items. We believe that this performance is a direct consequence of the small size of the model, meaning that the task is not easily solvable without higher computational capabilities or different priors.

Qualitative inspection of representative images explains these quantitative trends. When residual sauces or crumbs are too small to trigger a YOLO bounding box, Gemini and o3 under the DLVK P4 prompt consistently add them back into the estimate, whereas GPT-4o accepts the mask at face value and thus underestimates waste. Both GPT-4o and LLaVA tend to amplify segmentation artefacts (bones read as meat, plate patterns read as food), while Gemini and o3 usually flag and correct such anomalies.

5 Conclusions and Future Work

This study closes a persistent gap in automated plate-waste assessment by demonstrating that a hybrid approach, pairing a segmentation-based computer-vision backbone with reasoning-capable multimodal language models can achieve high performances on canteen imagery. Across a custom dataset and three public benchmarks, the refined

Dual-Level Visual Knowledge prompt enabled Gemini 2.5 Pro to reach an MSE of 84.69 and an R2 of 0.88, outperforming all other configurations. The o3 model proved that strong zero-shot baselines can be eroded by indiscriminate visual hints yet substantially restored when the same hints are supplied in a form that invites critique. GPT-4o, conversely, benefited most from an explicit algebraic definition of the food-waste ratio and showed marked sensitivity to noisy segmentation artefacts. Pure segmentation signals whether delivered to LLaVA 1.6 or used in the YOLOv11 baseline were insufficient, confirming that structured priors and explicit reasoning are essential once visual noise, occlusion and class imbalance enter the scene.

Several avenues emerge for future exploration. First, replacing YOLOv11 with more recent transformer-based detectors or self-supervised masked-autoencoder backbones may raise the ceiling on segmentation fidelity, especially for fine-grained leftovers. Second, fine-tuning the VLMs on domain-specific captions could make the system robust to noisy priors. Third, volumetric or mass-based waste metrics, derived from depth cameras or stereo pairs, would bring the estimates closer to nutritional reality than the current two-dimensional area ratios. Finally, on-device optimisation and incremental learning could pave the way for real-time deployment in commercial kitchens, we consider that nutritionists can gain insights into waste patterns for specific food groups, enabling data-driven meal planning to improve student nutrition.

Acknowledgments. This work is financed by National Funds through the Portuguese funding agency, FCT - Fundação para a Ciência e a Tecnologia within project: UID/06121/2023.

Disclosure of Interests. The authors have no competing interests.

References

1. Commission, E.; for Environment, D.G. Preparatory study on food waste across EU 27 - Final report; Publications Office (2011)
2. Belot, M., James, J.: Healthy school meals and educational outcomes. J. Health Econ. **30**, 489–504 (2011). https://doi.org/10.1016/j.jhealeco.2011.02.003
3. Redmon, J., et al.: You Only Look Once: Unified, Real-Time Object Detection (2016)
4. Zhang, Y., et al.: Deep learning in food category recognition. Inf. Fusion **98**, 101859 (2023). https://doi.org/10.1016/j.inffus.2023.101859
5. Lan, X., et al.: FoodSAM: any food segmentation. IEEE Trans. Multimed. **2024**, 1–14 (2024). https://doi.org/10.1109/tmm.2023.3330047
6. Fan, J., Cui, L., Fei, S.: Waste detection system based on data augmentation and YOLO_EC. Sensors **23** (2023). https://doi.org/10.3390/s23073646
7. Dhelia, A., Chordia, S.: YOLO-based Food Damage Detection: An Automated Approach for Quality Control in Food Industry (2024). https://doi.org/10.1109/I-SMAC61858.2024.10714664
8. Pouladzadeh, P., Shirmohammadi, S.: Mobile Multi-Food Recognition Using Deep Learning (2017). https://doi.org/10.1109/ICAC3N56670.2022.10074297
9. Ferreira, J., Cerqueira, P., Ribeiro, J.: Food waste detection in canteen plates using YOLOv11. Appl. Sci. **15**(13), 7137 (2025). https://doi.org/10.3390/app15137137
10. Xiao, T., Zhu, J.: Foundations of Large Language Models (2025). arXiv:2501.09223, https://doi.org/10.48550/arXiv.2501.09223

11. Smith, B., et al.: A Comprehensive Analysis of Large Language Model Outputs: Similarity, Diversity, and Bias (2025). https://doi.org/10.48550/arXiv.2505.09056
12. Huang, D., et al.: From large language models to large multimodal models: a literature review. Appl. Sci. **14**, 5068 (2024). https://doi.org/10.3390/app14125068
13. Li, Z., et al.: A Survey of State of the Art Large Vision Language Models: Alignment, Benchmark, Evaluations and Challenges (2025). https://doi.org/10.13140/RG.2.2.14334.91209
14. Li, Y., et al.: Visual Large Language Models for Generalized and Specialized Applications (2025). https://doi.org/10.48550/arXiv.2501.02765
15. Xue, J., et al.: Enhanced Multimodal RAG-LLM for Accurate Visual Question Answering (2024). https://doi.org/10.48550/arXiv.2412.20927
16. Zang, Y., et al.: Contextual object detection with multimodal large language models. Int. J. Comput. Vis. **133**(2), 825–843 (2025). https://doi.org/10.1007/s11263-024-02214-4
17. Limberg, C., et al.: Leveraging YOLO-World and GPT-4V LMMs for Zero-Shot Person Detection and Action Recognition in Drone Imagery (2024). ArXiv, abs/2404.01571
18. Lee, J., et al.: Exploring Multimodal Perception in Large Language Models through Perceptual Strength Ratings (2025). https://doi.org/10.48550/arXiv.2503.06980
19. Wei, J., et al.: Chain-of-thought prompting elicits reasoning in large language models. Adv. Neural Inf. Process. Syst. **35**, 2482
20. Long, X., et al.: Retrieval-Augmented Visual Question Answering via Built-in Autoregressive Search Engines (2025). 2502.16641v1
21. Jun-Hwa, K., et al.: Multimodal food image classification with large language models. Electronics (2024). https://doi.org/10.3390/electronics13224552
22. Ma, P., et al.: Large language models in food science: Innovations, applications, and future. Trends Food Sci. Technol. (2024). https://doi.org/10.1016/j.tifs.2024.104488
23. Chen, G., et al.: LION: Empowering Multimodal Large Language Model with Dual-Level Visual Knowledge (2024). https://doi.org/10.1109/CVPR52733.2024.02506
24. Martinel, N., Foresti, G., Micheloni, C.: Wide-Slice Residual Networks for Food Recognition (2016). https://doi.org/10.48550/arXiv.1612.06543
25. Goswami, A.: Deep Dish: Deep Learning for Classifying Food Dishes (2017)
26. Ciocca, G., Micali, G., Napoletano, P.: State recognition of food images using deep features. IEEE Access **8**, 32003–32017 (2020). https://doi.org/10.1109/ACCESS.2020.2973704
27. Sousa, J., Rebelo, A., Cardoso, J.: Automation of Waste Sorting with Deep Learning (2019). https://doi.org/10.1109/WVC.2019.8876924
28. Ciocca, G., Napoletano, P., Schettini, R.: Food Recognition and Leftover Estimation for Daily Diet Monitoring (2015). https://doi.org/10.1007/978-3-319-23222-5_41
29. Ciocca, G., Napoletano, P., Schettini, R.: Food Recognition: A New Dataset, Experiments, and Results (2016). https://doi.org/10.1109/JBHI.2016.2636441
30. Ma, C., et al.: Groma: Localized Visual Tokenization for Grounding Multimodal Large Language Models (2025). https://doi.org/10.1007/978-3-031-72658-3_24

Optimizing 2D Packing Strategies for Autoclave Loading Using Deep Reinforcement Learning

Victor U. Pugliese[1,2,3]([⊠]) [iD], Diogo S. Carvalho[2,3] [iD], Oseias F. Ferreira[4] [iD], Fabio A. Faria[1,2,3] [iD], and Francisco S. Melo[2,3] [iD]

[1] Universidade Federal de São Paulo, São José dos Campos, São Paulo, Brazil
pugliese@unifesp.br
[2] Instituto Superior Técnico, Universidade de Lisboa, Lisbon, Portugal
diogo.s.carvalho@tecnico.ulisboa.pt
[3] INESC-ID, Lisbon, Portugal
{fabio.faria,fmelo}@inesc-id.pt
[4] EMBRAER SA, São José dos Campos, São Paulo, Brazil
oseias.ferreira@embraer.br

Abstract. Optimizing the loading of autoclaves is a critical 2D packing problem in aerospace manufacturing. This paper investigates using deep reinforcement learning (DRL), specifically the proximal policy optimization (PPO) algorithm, to learn effective packing strategies. We developed a custom OpenAI Gym environment that simulates the process, with an observation space that details three matrices representing the initial and final states of the board, the shape of the item and the quantities of the remaining items, a multidiscrete action space to select and place the items, and a reward function that incorporates item profit and invalid action penalties. We evaluated our PPO-based agent against a genetic algorithm (GA) across scenarios involving regular items, mixed regular/irregular items, and item prioritization based on size. In the simplest case with only regular items, PPO achieved a high fill rate (99.37%), slightly surpassing GA (97.50%). In more complex scenarios involving mixed shapes and item prioritization, the GA achieved board fill rates of 94.57% and 96.57%, while PPO reached only 90.00% and 93.75%. However, in our experiments, PPO correctly move a greater number of the prioritized items in total. Prioritizing specific items is a critical task in the autoclave context, and highlighting PPO is more capable of learning value-driven allocation strategies.

Keywords: 2D Packing · Reinforcement Learning · Autoclave

1 Introduction

The aerospace industry continually seeks advancements in materials and manufacturing processes to produce lighter, stronger, and more fuel-efficient aircraft.

J. Valente de Oliveira et al. (Eds.): EPIA 2025, LNAI 16122, pp. 41–53, 2026.
https://doi.org/10.1007/978-3-032-05179-0_4

Composite materials, consisting of a matrix reinforced with fibers such as carbon, glass, or Kevlar, offer an exceptional strength-to-weight ratio, making them critical not only in aerospace but also in sectors like automotive, construction, and shipbuilding [1]. This demand has driven widespread adoption, with some manufacturers incorporating composites in over 50% of their aircraft structures [2].

Aerospace composite manufacturing typically involves a two-stage hybrid flow-shop process. The initial stage focuses on the fabrication of preforms, typically accomplished through cutting operations. Then these preforms are carefully placed and stacked on or within tools, such as molds, where layers of fibers are meticulously stacked according to the part design specifications. Lamination techniques can vary, including laser-assisted and conventional methods. Once in-tool lamination is complete; the assembly is prepared for curing, often involving vacuum bagging to consolidate the plies and remove trapped air and volatiles. To optimize the subsequent autoclave process (a chamber used for curing composite materials under heat and pressure), the tool packages containing the composite lamination are grouped based on their specific curing requirements. This grouping strategy, as described by Azami et al. [3], aims to minimize curing cycles and maximize utilization of autoclave resources, like a bin packing problem. The assembled tooling packages are then inserted into the autoclave to begin the curing cycle. After the curing cycle is complete and the composite material has solidified, the cured parts are demolded and the molds returned to begin the next cycle.

The autoclave scheduling problem has been studied over the years. Zheng et al. [4] investigated a single batch machine scheduling problem for autoclave molding, in which two-dimensional rectangular bin packing (2DRBP) plays a central role by directly affecting dual setup times and the makespan objective. They proposed a two-stage metaheuristic: an initial greedy packing algorithm, followed by a local search incorporating metaheuristic elements to refine the solution while accounting for all setup costs. In a related study on batch processing and resource allocation, Xie et al. [5] modeled the spatial and type constraints of autoclave scheduling as a 2DRBP, developing a tailored heuristic aimed at minimizing makespan and enhancing production efficiency in composite material manufacturing. Similarly, Dios et al. [6] addressed the problem through a 2DRBP formulation using mixed integer linear programming (MILP) to determine the precise position (cart, deck, tray, coordinates) and orientation of each part, with the goal of reducing maximum curing delay. Other works have also proposed solutions for autoclave scheduling; however, they do not determine exact (x, y) coordinates. Instead, they model the problem more abstractly using constraints related to the total volume of the item or autoclave capacity and the number of tools required, such as the work in [7] and [1]. However, these solutions typically perform well only in static, batch-based scenarios, whereas real-world production scheduling often involves stochastic and dynamic behaviors, such as fluctuations in worker productivity and random job arrivals [8]. Furthermore, system components may exhibit both explicit interdependencies, such as those between machines and tools, and implicit ones, such as the influence of weather on process parameters, thus increasing the complexity of manually constructing an accurate mathematical model of the system [9].

In contrast, reinforcement learning (RL) offers the advantage of not requiring an exact mathematical model of the system. This makes it especially well-suited for scenarios where system dynamics are too complex to model accurately. While no studies have yet applied RL directly to the autoclave packing problem, several works show promising results in other contexts. For example, Li et al. [10] investigated soft actor-critic (SAC) to 2D and 3D strip packing problems, modeling the action as a sequence of sub-actions (item selection, rotation, and positioning), so each one uses the output of the previous one as input, avoiding the combinatorial complexity of generating actions as a cartesian product, Kundu et al. [11] used double deep q-network (DDQN) to predict the location of the next box from image inputs in regular and online instances of bin packing problems, Fang et al. [12] combined REINFORCE with maxrect bottom-left heuristic to guide board filling in regular strip packing. Beyond regular shapes, Feng et al. [13] explored monte carlo, q-learning, and SARSA with bottom-left and no fit polygon heuristics for 2D irregular packing, and Crescitelli et al. [14] and Yang et al. [15] applied DDQN to this kind of problem. In general, these works compared RL with metaheuristics such as genetic algorithms (GA) and simulated annealing, or with traditional heuristics, and do not explore non-spatial reward functions.

This paper explores RL to develop strategies for solving the 2D packing problem, including prioritization of items directly integrated into the spatial reward function. The state of the RL environment is defined by the board, the shape of the last item, and the quantities of available items, while its multi-discrete actions involve selecting an item and specifying its coordinates ($Length \times Width$). Unlike other authors, we used the Stable Baselines library [16] to implement PPO, a state-of-the-art model-free RL algorithm [17] that supports multi-discrete action spaces. Standard implementations such as DQN and SAC are not directly applicable to these action spaces. Thus, we developed a custom OpenAI Gym [18] environment that simulates the autoclave loading process, and evaluated the performance of the PPO agent against GA in various scenarios such as regular items, a mix of regular and irregular items, and situations that require explicit prioritization based on the type of the item. The experimental results highlight the relative strengths and limitations of the DRL approach in handling varying levels.

2   Background

This section briefly introduces the key concepts relevant to this work.

2.1   Knapsack Problem

The packing problem is a well-known combinatorial optimization task that focuses on efficiently arranging items within a container to minimize wasted space [10]. It can involve both regular (e.g., rectangular) [11] and irregular [19] shapes, and is typically approached in either streaming (online) or batching (offline) settings.

One well-known variant is the knapsack problem. Given a set of n items, each with an associated profit p_j and weight w_j ($j = 1, \ldots, n$), and a container (knapsack) with capacity $C_{\max}$, the objective is to select a subset of items such that the total weight does not exceed the capacity while maximizing the total profit [20].

2.2   Deep Reinforcement Learning

DRL combines reinforcement learning principles with deep neural networks to learn decision-making policies through trial and error [21]. Unlike supervised learning, DRL does not rely on labeled data; instead, it uses a reward signal and delayed feedback to guide learning. At each time step t, an agent observes a state s_t, selects an action a_t, receives a reward r_{t+1}, and transitions to a new state s_{t+1} [22]. The agent's behavior is governed by a policy $\pi_t(s, a)$, which maps states to action probabilities. Over time, the agent updates this policy to maximize the expected cumulative reward, using experience gathered through interaction with the environment.

PPO is an on-policy algorithm based on the actor-critic framework. It employs two neural networks: an actor, which learns the policy (i.e., how to act), and a critic, which estimates the value function to guide the actor's updates [23]. PPO improves the current policy using data collected from its own interactions with the environment, and as training progresses, the policy exhibits less variability. The algorithm optimizes a clipped surrogate objective function based on advantage estimates, which helps to limit large policy updates and ensure training stability [23].

2.3   Metaheuristic

Metaheuristics are optimization strategies designed to find near-optimal solutions to complex and computationally difficult problems where exact methods are impractical. Unlike traditional heuristics, which are tailored to specific problems, metaheuristics are problem-independent and often inspired by natural processes such as evolution, swarm behavior, or physical annealing [24].

GA is a population-based optimization technique inspired by the principles of natural selection. They maintain a population of candidate solutions that evolve over generations through selection, crossover, and mutation. The selection process favors individuals with higher fitness, while crossover and mutation introduce variation to explore the solution space. A fitness function evaluates the quality of each solution, guiding the algorithm toward regions of higher performance [25].

3   DRL Approach for 2D Knapsack Problem

In this section, we present our DRL approach to the 2D packing problem. Developed with the OpenAI Gym framework, the environment simulates the efficient placement of items on a board and models the packing task using the following core components:

1. **State Space** (S): The state consists of three matrices: two represent the initial and final states of the boards, with dimensions $L_1 \times W_1$, and one represents the shape of the item, with dimensions $L_2 \times W_2$. In addition, there are N integer values that indicate the available quantity of each type of item.
2. **Action Space** ($A(s_t)$): The action space is defined as a multi-discrete space. Each action specifies the (x, y) coordinates where the top-left corner of an item is placed, along with an index indicating which item type is placed at each time step.
3. **Reward** (R): The learning algorithm is designed to reward the agent for actions that effectively utilize the available space on the boards, with the item's profit serving as a positive reward per time step. We introduce a dynamic profit system based on piece prioritization. When the agent prioritizes Item 4 (size 1×4) and Item 5 (T-shaped, size 3×3), their respective profits are doubled to 8 and 10. Similarly, if the agent prioritizes Item 2 (size 1×2) and Item 3 (size 2×1), their profit increases to 8. However, if an Item is not prioritized, its profit remains equal to its original size. Penalties, set at -8, are still applied for invalid actions, such as selecting an item with a quantity of zero remaining or placing an item in an already occupied region. Upon the episode's conclusion, the RL agent also receives a score based on how much space on the board was filled.
4. **Algorithm:** During each episode, the agent and the simulator interact in a discrete time sequence $t = 0, 1, 2, 3, \ldots$. At each time step t, the agent receives the current state $s_t \in S$, which includes the representation of the three matrices and the remaining quantities of items. The agent then selects an action $a_t \in A(s_t)$, consisting of the placement coordinates (x, y), and the item index. As a result, at time step $t+1$, the agent receives a reward $r_{t+1} \in R$ and transitions to the next state s_{t+1}, as illustrated in Fig. 1. Episodes end when the available area is fully utilized (100% coverage) or when the agent attempts to place more than 15% beyond the total number of available items, preventing unrealistic or invalid packing behavior.
5. **Training and Testing:** The PPO agent was trained in a 2D packing environment for 5 million episodes. Evaluations were performed every 25 episodes under deterministic conditions.

4   Experiments

This section presents the experimental protocol and results achieved by DRL methods.

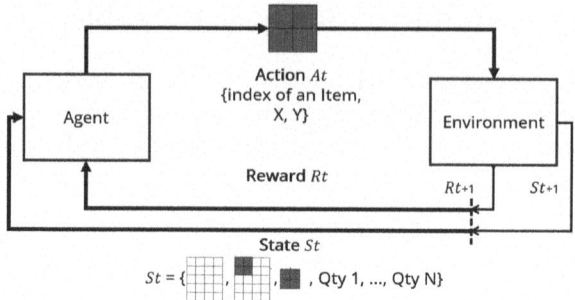

Fig. 1. Our OpenAI Gym Environment to 2D Packing Problem

4.1 Experimental Methodology

In real-world aerospace manufacturing, the number of parts placed in an autoclave can vary significantly depending on the available volume and batch size. Typically, each curing cycle contains around 30 to 50 parts, but this number may be lower in specific cases, such as when processing large components like aircraft fairings. It is important to note that the packing phase does not involve irregularly shaped parts, due to the constraints imposed by the mold, tooling cart, and required safety margins to ensure the desired product properties.

We designed four distinct experiments based on abstract scenarios to evaluate the performance of our packing strategy under different conditions: (1) packing only regular-shaped items; (2) packing both regular and irregular-shaped items; (3) packing items with priority given to those with the largest individual size; and (4) packing items with priority given to those with the smallest individual size. The criteria adopted in experiments (3) and (4) are intended to simulate the prioritization of parts for delivery, a common practice in the aerospace industry. Thus, the algorithm must prioritize specific items during the packing process.

Although real-world autoclave scenarios do not involve irregular shapes, modeling the problem as a knapsack with irregular items allows to evaluate the agent in a more complex environments. Furthermore, the profit value associated with each item can be interpreted either as a priority score (representing delivery urgency) or simply as the item's size, thereby enabling different prioritization strategies.

To evaluate the effectiveness of our proposed approach, we compared the performance of PPO (with a linear learning rate of 0.0005 and a discount factor γ of 0.95 as hyperparameters) against a GA (with a population size of 100, mutation rate of 0.05, crossover rate of 0.9, and 500 generations). Crucially, the GA's fitness function was identical to the reward function used by PPO. Both experiments were repeated five times to ensure a robust evaluation.

Throughout the experiments, we used various types of items that were placed within a board that defines the boundaries of our packing environment. Figure 2 illustrates the shapes of these items and Table 1 shows the amount of items used per experiment.

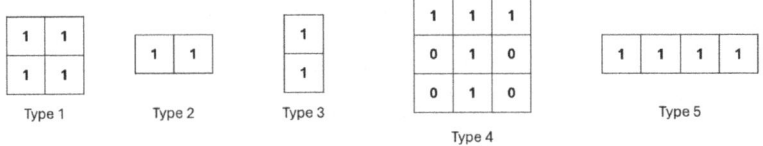

Fig. 2. The types of item available to be placed into the board.

Table 1. The sets of the board and items used for each experiment.

Experiment	L_1	W_1	Qty Item 1	Qty Item 2	Qty Item 3	Qty Item 4	Qty Item 5
1	8	8	8	16	0	0	0
2	8	8	5	4	8	4	0
3	8	8	5	4	8	4	4
4	8	8	5	8	8	4	4

4.2 Packing Items with Regular Shapes Only

We packed all regular items available, such as 8 items of type 1 (2×2) and 16 items of type 2 (1×2), in a predefined area 8×8. This simplification enabled a more controlled evaluation of the packing strategies themselves, rather than the algorithms ability to handle geometric variability. PPO outperformed GA, achieving a higher average performance ($99.37\% \pm 1.00\%$) compared to GA's ($97.50\% \pm 3.00\%$), but both are effective in maximizing board utilization, when the environment does not involve extreme geometric complexity.

Figure 3 shows the mean reward for the evaluation during the reinforcement learning process. Performance starts low but quickly rises within the first few hundred thousand timesteps, surpassing 100 rewards. The agent then maintains a high reward level with some fluctuations up to around 5M timesteps. These results indicate that PPO quickly learns an effective packing strategy.

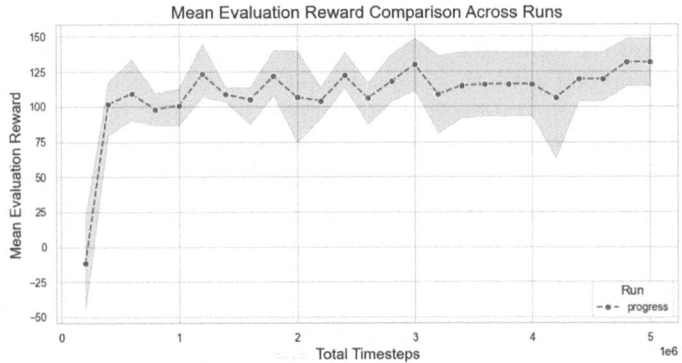

Fig. 3. PPO learning curves in the Experiment 1

4.3 Packing a Mixture of Regular and Irregular-Shaped Items

We packed a complete combination of regular and irregular items in a predefined 8×8 area. The instance included 5 regular items of type 1 (2×2), 4 of type 2 (1×2), 8 of type 3 (2×1), and 4 irregular items of type 4, each with a T-shaped layout occupying a 3×3 area. This setup allows for the evaluation of the algorithms' ability to handle geometric variability without prioritization order. As a result, if regular items are placed first, it may become difficult to fit the irregular ones. Under these conditions, PPO reached an average performance of $86.25\%(\pm 3.00\%)$, while GA achieved $90.93\%(\pm 1.50\%)$. This difference may be attributed to a limitation of the model-free architecture. Without an explicit model of the environment, PPO may struggle to reason about complex geometries and the long-term implications of each placement, such as creating gaps that hinder future insertions. Although PPO learns from rewards, it lacks an explicit mechanism to represent spatial structure, which can be more naturally handled by search-based approaches like GA. Table 2 presents the results of these experiments.

Table 2. A comparative analysis between PPO and GA for the Experiment 2.

Experiment 2									
	PPO					GA			
	% Fill	Type 1	Type 2	Type 3	Type 4	% Fill	Type 1	Type 2	Type 3	Type 4
#1	84,37	5/5	4/4	8/8	2/4	**92,18**	5/5	4/4	8/8	3/4
#2	84,37	5/5	4/4	8/8	2/4	**89,06**	5/5	4/4	7/8	3/4
#3	84,37	5/5	4/4	8/8	2/4	**92,18**	5/5	4/4	8/8	3/4
#4	**93,75**	5/5	2/4	8/8	4/4	92,18	5/5	4/4	8/8	3/4
#5	84,37	5/5	4/4	8/8	2/4	**89,06**	5/5	4/4	7/8	3/4
% Mean	86,25					**90,93**				
% Std	3,00					**1,50**				

Figure 4 shows a rapid early improvement from negative values to positive rewards by around 600–800k timesteps. Despite fluctuations between 1M and 3M timesteps, performance stabilizes around 90–95 after 3M, remaining consistent until the end of training.

4.4 Packing Items in a Priorization Order

Two approaches were defined to assign profits to items: the first prioritized items of types 4 and 5, while the second prioritized types 2 and 3. In both experiments, a combination of regular and irregular items was packed in a predefined 8×8 area. The experiments included item of the 5 types, and the total number of items exceeded the area capacity, thus some items had to be excluded from the final solution.

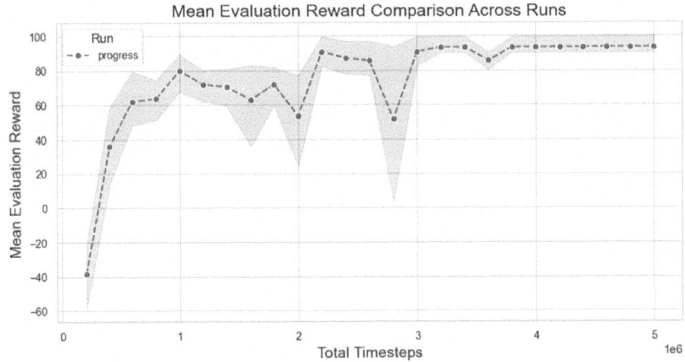

Fig. 4. PPO learning curves in the Experiment 2

Prioritizing the Types 4 and 5. This configuration is designed to evaluate the ability of algorithms to deal with geometric variability, especially in scenarios where type 4 and 5 items are prioritized. As a result, it was easier to accommodate the irregular items first, followed by the minors. PPO achieved a mean performance of 93.75%($\pm$0.63%), whereas GA reached 96.57%($\pm$1.50%). Despite achieving a lower fill rate, PPO demonstrated superior prioritization of item types 4 and 5 compared to GA. This behavior can be attributed to PPO's reward-driven learning process, which enables the agent to internalize the relative value of different items. When the reward function assigns higher weights to priority items, PPO learns to consistently favor their placement. Table 3 presents the results of these experiments.

Table 3. A comparative analysis between PPO and GA for the Experiment 3.

Experiment 3											
	PPO						GA				
	% Fill	Type 1	Type 2	Type 3	Type 4	Type 5	% Fill	Type 1	Type 2	Type 3	Type 4	Type 5
#1	93,75	2/5	4/4	4/8	**4/4**	**4/4**	**100**	5/5	4/4	7/8	2/4	3/4
#2	95,32	2/5	4/4	7/8	3/4	**4/4**	95,32	3/5	2/4	8/8	3/4	3/4
#3	93,75	2/5	2/4	8/8	4/4	3/4	**96,87**	2/5	4/4	7/8	4/4	3/4
#4	93,75	1/5	2/4	8/8	**4/4**	4/4	**95,32**	4/5	4/4	8/8	1/4	4/4
#5	92,18	1/5	4/4	8/8	**3/4**	4/4	**95,32**	4/5	4/4	8/8	1/4	4/4
% Mean	93,75						**96,57**					
% Std	**0,63**						1,50					

Figure 5 shows a sharp initial improvement from negative values, with rewards reaching 80 to 90 despite early fluctuations, and stabilizing around 100 to 105 after 2.5M timesteps through to the end of training.

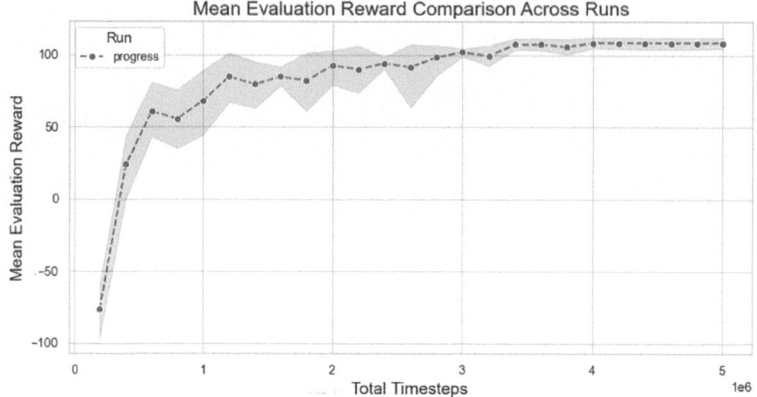

Fig. 5. PPO learning curves in the Experiment 3

Prioritizing the Types 2 and 3. This setup aimed to evaluate the algorithms' performance when types 2 and 3 are prioritized. In this scenario, the algorithms tended to place the smaller regular items first, which made it more difficult to fit the irregular ones later. PPO achieved a mean performance of 90.00%($\pm$1.75%), while GA obtained a mean of 94.57%($\pm$2.87%). Although the PPO filled less the board, the algorithm prioritized items type 2 and 3 better than GA likely due to the PPO's reward-driven learning process, as previously discussed. Table 4 shows the performance of these experiments.

Table 4. A comparative analysis between PPO and GA for the Experiment 4.

Experiment 4											
	PPO						GA				
	% Fill	Type 1	Type 2	Type 3	Type 4	Type 5	% Fill	Type 1	Type 2	Type 3	Type 4	Type 5
#1	89,06	1/5	8/8	8/8	1/4	4/4	**96,32**	5/5	8/8	8/8	1/4	1/4
#2	87,5	3/5	**8/8**	**8/8**	0/4	3/4	**100**	5/5	7/8	6/8	2/4	2/4
#3	89,06	4/5	8/8	8/8	1/4	1/4	**92,18**	1/5	8/8	8/8	3/4	2/4
#4	93,75	4/5	7/8	8/8	0/4	3/4	93,75	2/5	**8/8**	8/8	4/4	0/4
#5	90,62	3/5	8/8	8/8	2/4	1/4	90,62	2/5	8/8	8/8	2/4	2/4
% Mean	90,00						**94,57**					
% Std	**1,75**						2,87					

Figure 6 shows a sharp initial improvement in performance, with rewards rising from below –50 to above 100 by around 1M timesteps. Despite some mid-training fluctuations, the mean reward stabilizes around 140–150 from 3M timesteps onward, maintaining high performance until the end of training.

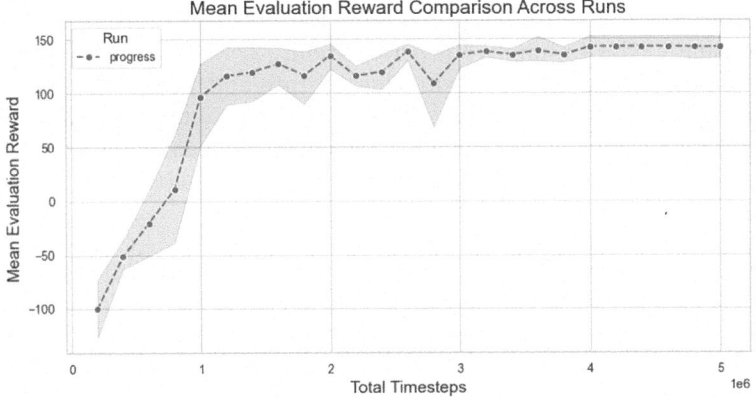

Fig. 6. PPO learning curves in the Experiment 4

5   Conclusion

This work address a 2D knapsack problem, formulated as an abstraction of the autoclave loading process in the aerospace industry, using a reinforcement learning approach based on the PPO algorithm. We developed a customized OpenAI Gym environment with an observation space composed of three matrices representing the initial and final states of the board, the shape of the item to be placed, and the remaining quantities of items. The environment presents a multi-discrete action space that allows the agent to choose the type of item and its placement coordinates. Additionally, we incorporated item prioritization through the reward mechanism.

We conducted a series of experiments comparing the performance of our PPO agent against a GA, a well-established metaheuristic for packing problems. The experiments evaluated performance in different scenarios: packing only regular items, packing a mixture of regular and irregular items, and packing with priority given to specific item types based on size.

In the simplest scenario with only regular items, PPO achieved a board fill rate of 99.37%, slightly surpassing the GA (97.50%). However, in more complex situations involving mixed items and prioritization of smaller ones, GA proved superior to the DRL approach, maximizing overall area utilization. Despite this, Experiments 3 and 4 indicate that PPO was more effective in placing prioritized items, suggesting its ability to learn value-driven allocation strategies.

These findings indicate that PPO is a promising approach for 2D packing problems, capable of learning effective policies and handling prioritization. While GA might currently outperform DRL in maximizing space in complex, static offline instances, DRL's learning ability offers advantages in more dynamic, uncertain, or constrained real-world autoclave loading scenarios where complex, non-explicit rules or objectives extend beyond simple area maximization.

For future work, we propose: (1) training the DRL agent on a wider range of instances using CNNs to improve generalization; (2) reformulating the problem as a multiobjective task (e.g., maximizing fill rate and profit while minimizing invalid actions) using multi-objective DRL to approximate the Pareto front; (3) adapting the environment for dynamic scenarios like sequential item arrivals; and (4) incorporating autoclave-specific constraints to better reflect real-world conditions.

Acknowledgments. The authors would like to thank the National Council for Scientific and Technological Development (CNPq) for granting a scholarship to Victor Pugliese through the Academic Master's and Doctorate Program in Innovation (MAI/DAI) in collaboration with the EMBRAER S.A. company. This project was also funded by Portuguese national funds through Fundação para a Ciência e a Tecnologia (FCT), under projects UIDB/50021/2020 (INESCID multi-annual funding), PTDC/CCI-COM/5060/2021 (RELEvaNT), and AI-PackBot (project number 14935, LISBOA2030-FEDER-00854700). Diogo S. Carvalho also acknowledges his FCT PhD grand 2020.05360.BD.

Disclosure of Interests. The authors have no competing interests to declare that are relevant to the content of this article.

References

1. Haskilic, V., Ulucan, A., Atici, K.B., Sarac, S.B.: A real-world case of autoclave loading and scheduling problems in aerospace composite material production. Omega **120**, 102918 (2023)
2. Kırdar, G.: Optimization of composite parts placement in autoclave (2020)
3. Azami, A.: Scheduling Hybrid Flow Lines of Aerospace Composite Manufacturing Systems. PhD thesis, Concordia University (2016)
4. Zheng, S., Xie, N., Qiao, W.: Single batch machine scheduling with dual setup times for autoclave molding manufacturing. Comput. Oper. Res. **133**, 105381 (2021)
5. Xie, N., Zheng, S., Qiao, W.: Two-dimensional packing algorithm for autoclave molding scheduling of aeronautical composite materials production. Comput. Ind. Eng. **146**, 106599 (2020)
6. Dios, M., Gonzalez-R, P.L., Dios, D., Maffezzoli, A.: A mathematical modeling approach to optimize composite parts placement in autoclave. Int. Trans. Oper. Res. **24**(1–2), 115–141 (2017)
7. Tang, T.Y.: Exact and Heuristic Approaches to Batching-and-Scheduling for the Composites Manufacturing Problem. University of Toronto (Canada) (2020)
8. Waubert de Puiseau, C., Meyes, R., Meisen, T.: On reliability of reinforcement learning based production scheduling systems: a comparative survey. J. Intell. Manuf. **33**(4), 911–927 (2022). https://doi.org/10.1007/s10845-022-01915-2
9. Chang, J., Dong, Yu., Yi, H., He, W., Haoyu, Yu.: Deep reinforcement learning for dynamic flexible job shop scheduling with random job arrival. Processes **10**(4), 760 (2022)
10. Li, D., Gu, Z., Wang, Y., Ren, C., Lau, F.C.: One model packs thousands of items with recurrent conditional query learning. Knowl.-Based Syst. **235**, 107683 (2022)

11. Kundu, O., Dutta, S., Kumar, S.: Deep-pack: a vision-based 2d online bin packing algorithm with deep reinforcement learning. In: 2019 28th IEEE International Conference on Robot and Human Interactive Communication (RO-MAN), pp. 1–7. IEEE (2019)
12. Fang, J., Rao, Y., Shi, M.: A deep reinforcement learning algorithm for the rectangular strip packing problem. PLoS ONE **18**(3), e0282598 (2023)
13. Fang, J., Rao, Y., Zhao, X., Bing, D.: A hybrid reinforcement learning algorithm for 2d irregular packing problems. Mathematics **11**(2), 327 (2023)
14. Crescitelli, V., Oshima, T.: Optimization of 2D irregular packing: deep reinforcement learning with dense reward. Int. J. Semant. Comput. **18**(03), 405–416 (2024)
15. Yang, Z., Pan, Z., Li, M., Kui, W., Gao, X.: Learning based 2d irregular shape packing. ACM Trans. Graph. (TOG) **42**(6), 1–16 (2023)
16. Hill, A., et al.: Stable baselines (2018). https://github.com/hill-a/stable-baselines
17. Sun, Y., Yuan, X., Liu, W., Sun, C.: Model-based reinforcement learning via proximal policy optimization. In: 2019 Chinese Automation Congress (CAC), pp. 4736–4740. IEEE (2019)
18. Brockman, G., et al.: Openai gym (2016)
19. Crescitelli, V., Oshima, T.: A deep reinforcement learning method for 2d irregular packing with dense reward. In: 2023 Fifth International Conference on Transdisciplinary AI (TransAI), pp. 270–271. IEEE (2023)
20. Cacchiani, V., Iori, M., Locatelli, A., Martello, S.: Knapsack problems–an overview of recent advances. part ii: Multiple, multidimensional, and quadratic knapsack problems. Comput. Oper. Res. **143**, 105693 (2022)
21. Kaelbling, L.P., Littman, M.L., Moore, A.W.: Reinforcement learning: a survey. J. Artif. Intell. Res. **4**, 237–285 (1996)
22. Sutton, R.S., Barto, A.G.: Reinforcement Learning: An Introduction. MIT press, Cambridge (2018)
23. FrameWork Keras. PPO proximal policy optimization (2022)
24. Bandaru, S., Deb, K.: Metaheuristic techniques. In: Decision Sciences, pp. 709–766. CRC Press (2016)
25. Sastry, K., Goldberg, D., Kendall, G.: Genetic algorithms. In: Search Methodologies: Introductory Tutorials in Optimization and Decision Support Techniques, pp. 97–125 (2005)

Intelligent Models for Predicting Water Quality in the Textile Processes

Maria Inês Lima[1], Rita Miranda[2], and Filipe Portela[1,2](✉) (iD)

[1] Algoritmi Centre, University of Minho, Guimarães, Portugal
cfp@dsi.uminho.pt
[2] IOTech-Innovation on Technology, Trofa, Portugal

Abstract. The textile industry is essential to the global economy but poses environmental challenges, particularly regarding water use and pollution. Sustainable production necessitates improved water management and reuse. This study forecasts water quality for reuse using data collected from twelve Portuguese textile companies over two months. To achieve this, the CRISP-DM methodology was adhered to, monitoring key water quality factors such as pH and turbidity. The data were cleaned, features selected, normalized, and class imbalance addressed using SMOTE. Five machine learning models were assessed: Decision Trees, Random Forest, Logistic Regression, Support Vector Machines, and XGBoost. The best results were obtained from XGBoost, Random Forest, and Logistic Regression, particularly in scenario 2. In Company 11, Random Forest achieved 98% sensitivity and a 97% F1-score, whereas XGBoost exhibited 98% sensitivity and 94% accuracy. These models demonstrated high accuracy and sensitivity in classifying water quality. The findings indicate that machine learning can assist in enhancing water reuse decisions in the textile industry and mitigating environmental impact.

Keywords: Textile Industry · Water Quality Prediction · Machine Learning

1 Introduction

Worldwide freshwater and net water resources, key for biological processes and productive industry processes, are highly exposed to anthropogenic pressures [1]. Reports have indicated that the textile industry is responsible for one-fifth of global freshwater pollution due to its water consumption practices of dyeing and finishing textiles [2]. To contribute to sustainability in the textile industry, this study will analyze and predict water quality, with the emphasis on advanced classification algorithms. In conducting this research, it is anticipated finding predictive models that can classify water quality as either satisfactory or unsatisfactory quality using reference parameters, in this instance, pH and turbidity. When the pH and turbidity values are within and conform to the permissible environmental limits, in such case the water sample is deemed good, if not, it is considered poor. The proposed study intends to employ operational records collected from twelve textile companies to improve quality control, environmental compliance and improve informed decision making with regards to industry practices.

J. Valente de Oliveira et al. (Eds.): EPIA 2025, LNAI 16122, pp. 54–66, 2026.
https://doi.org/10.1007/978-3-032-05179-0_5

The data used in this research is derived from the GIATEX: Intelligent Water Management for the Textile and Clothing Industry, coordinated by *Estamparia Adalberto Pinto da Silva*, and originally a consortium of 27 partners with 12 textile manufacturers, the purpose of the project was to determine reduction of water consumption in the textile finishing processes by employing robust monitoring systems, water recycling measures and waste treatment measures allowing for industrial use of finite resources to be effective and efficient [3]. Reduce consumption of water in textile finishing processes, which applies strong monitoring, recycling and waste treatment strategies to promote industry measures for effective and resource efficient use of water [4]. Water use in finishing processes can be improved as mentioned and similar measures are used for several processes throughout the fabric supplier industry and textile finishing process. This paper is organized into five sections: the first introduces the research aims and key concepts, the second reviews relevant literature and background, the third describes materials, data sources, and methods, the fourth explains the CRISP-DM methodology and its application, and the fifth discusses the findings and future work.

2 Background

This section aims to consolidate and critically review the existing literature and practical advances on this topic to provide a basis for the present study.

2.1 Water Quality in Textile Industry

In the textile industry, the lack of regular monitoring of effluent discharge means that contaminated wastewater is released, leading not only to loss of valuable water resources but the erosion of the environment [2]. This has devastating implications when taking into account that the sector is responsible for nearly 20% of global freshwater pollution [2]. The amount of chemicals used in the dyeing and finishing process contributes a considerable amount of contaminants into aquatic systems, and this is a major contributor to the degradation of freshwater quality and ecosystem health [5]. Water quality is an essential factor in effective textile processing as it directly influences the final performance of finishing processes. When water parameters are not within the right limits none of the aspects of textile treatment will work well, cleaning effectiveness will be poor, successful whiteness will not be achieved, the dye will not dissolve properly, the color will not distribute evenly and the colorfastness developed in the finish will be ineffective [6]. The interdependence between water quality and processing outcomes creates cascading effects that can compromise entire production runs, necessitating rigorous quality control measures throughout manufacturing operations [7].

Inefficient use of water in textile manufacturing results in significant costs in terms of chemical usage, energy costs, and equipment wear and tear [8]. Inefficient water management will incur capital cost expenditure on wastewater treatment equipment whilst exposing manufacturers to regulatory compliance risk and loss of productivity from quality issues [8]. Water optimization programmers can achieve operational cost savings estimated between 15–30%, which highlights the need for valid water conservation practices within textile operations for legitimate economic reasons [8].

2.2 Machine Learning for Water Quality Classification

Artificial Intelligence (AI) is being increasingly identified as a disruptive technology across industries that can provide solutions to real sustainability, cost, and efficiency issues. AI is defined as the emergence of computational systems that are capable of performing tasks that are associated with human intelligence, including reasoning, learning, and decision making [9].

There has been substantial interest recently in Machine Learning (ML), a prominent subfield of AI for its ability to automate complex decision-making processes that traditionally required interaction from people, such as monitoring water quality [10]. Compared to rules-based approaches, where rules are pre-defined before events occur, ML approaches make decisions based on historical data to understand non-linear relationships and relationships that are not evident in the data, leading to more precise water state classifications [11]. The ability of ML classification to handle high-dimensional data without sacrificing predictive performance is a key concern. To curtail computational cost and enhance the models' generalization capability, strategies such as dimensionality reduction and feature selection are standardly used to identify the most predictive variables [11, 12]. Moreover, supervised machine learning algorithms known to yield high accuracy and flexibility in a wide range of environmental conditions are extensively applied to binary and multiclass classification issues [13]. For this study, five algorithms were selected based on their complementary strengths and proven effectiveness in environmental monitoring: Logistic Regression (LR), Decision Trees (DT), Random Forest (RF), XGBoost, and Support Vector Machines (SVM). This selection encompasses linear and non-linear approaches, individual and ensemble methods, ensuring comprehensive comparison across different modeling paradigms. The technical characteristics and specific advantages of each algorithm for water quality classification are detailed in Sect. 3.3.

2.3 Related Work

Predicting water quality in the textile industry is difficult for various reasons, which include effluents that vary daily, the complicated processes of textile, and environmental constraints. However, traditional statistical methods are now being combined with ML methods, and ML research has followed the traditional data mining models, such as CRISP-DM. Rustam et al. [13] applied artificial neural networks (ANN) for water safety classification, achieving 96% accuracy and outperforming DT, RF, and SVM despite limited data availability. A related study [14] evaluated over 650 regression models for pH prediction, reporting optimal results when models were trained per company, underscoring process variability and data constraints. More recently, Mahanna et al. [15] demonstrated the efficacy of ML algorithms in forecasting wastewater treatment plant performance, highlighting their utility in real-time monitoring and control. Existing literature predominantly addresses general water quality assessment, with limited focus on textile-specific reuse applications and class imbalance mitigation in industrial datasets. This study addresses these limitations through targeted classification models for textile water reuse, incorporating SMOTE-based class balancing and company-specific validation methodologies.

3 Material and Methods

This research is part of the GIATEX project, coordinated by CITEVE and led by Estamparia Adalberto Pinto da Silva. It focuses on the textile finishing stage, addressing the critical challenge of high water consumption in the industry.

3.1 Methodology

The present study employs the Design Science Research (DSR) paradigm, which is concerned with creating new artefacts for solving practical problems and improving existing solutions [16]. The DSR process consists of six stages including problem identification and motivation, defining the objectives of a solution, designing and developing the artefact, demonstrating the use of the artefact, evaluating the artefact, and communicating the research results. In this paper, the introduction and literature review sections align with the initial two stages of the DSR approach. The methodological components, comprising materials, methods, and CRISP-DM implementation, correspond to the third and fourth stages. The concluding component addresses the fifth methodological stage, while this article serves as the sixth phase of the DSR methodology. In addition, the work of developing the data mining models within this study was guided by the CRISP-DM methodology. The CRISP-DM methodology consists of six iterative and interrelated phases, and in this study these phases include business understanding, data understanding, data preparation, modeling, evaluation and deployment [17]. In this paper, the implementation of each of these phases was described based on the adopted CRISP-DM structure.

3.2 Technologies and Tools

The research employed various technologies and tools for data processing and model development, as outlined in Table 1.

Table 1. Technologies and Tools employed

Technology	Type	Description
Python	Programming Language	Use for data preparation, analysis, and building machine learning models
Pandas	Library	Used for data manipulation, cleaning, and storage in DataFrame structures
Scikit-learn	Library	Provided tools for data preprocessing, model training, validation and evaluation
Matplotlib & Seaborn	Visualization Libraries	Used for generating plots and visualizing data distributions and results

3.3 Classification Algorithms and Evaluation Metrics

To meet the aims of this study, several classification algorithms were used: LR, DT, RF, XGBoost, SVM.

- **Logistic Regression:** A probabilistic classification model that estimates class probabilities conditional on input features. It is computationally efficient, suitable for both binary and multinomial classification, and provides interpretable outputs that facilitate decision-making in industrial water monitoring systems [18].
- **Decision Trees:** A rule-based, hierarchical classification approach that captures non-linear relationships without requiring data normalization. Its high interpretability and ability to process both categorical and numerical features make it particularly appropriate for industrial process data [19].
- **Random Forest:** An ensemble learning method that aggregates predictions from multiple DT through majority voting. It enhances predictive performance, reduces overfitting, and performs reliably on imbalanced datasets [20].
- **XGBoost:** A gradient boosting algorithm that sequentially builds DT, where each new model corrects the residual errors of its predecessor. It offers high predictive accuracy, incorporates regularization to prevent overfitting, and handles missing or noisy data effectively, making it suitable for complex industrial datasets [21].
- **Support Vector Machine:** A supervised learning algorithm that constructs an optimal hyperplane to separate classes. Through kernel functions, it models non-linear relationships and is particularly effective in high-dimensional settings typical of industrial process monitoring [22].

Although accuracy measures overall correct classifications, it can be misleading with class imbalance or differing error costs. Therefore, a multi-metric approach was adopted, focusing on accuracy, sensitivity (recall), specificity, and F1-score, all derived from confusion matrix analysis and defined as follows [23]:

- $Accuracy = (TP + TN)/(\text{TP+FP+TN+FN})$ (1)
- $Sensitivity = TP/(TP + FN)$ (2)
- $\text{Specificity} = \text{TN/(TN+FP)}$ (3)
- $F1 - score = 2 \times (Precision \times$ (4)
  $Sensitivity)/Precision + Sensitivity)$

The confusion matrix consists of four classification outcomes: True Positives (TP), False Positives (FP), True Negatives (TN), and False Negatives (FN). Python's scikit-learn library was used to compute the confusion matrices and their metric values. Specific threshold requirements were established to ensure the models' practical applicability in water quality monitoring: accuracy must exceed 80%, sensitivity must exceed 90%, and F1-score must exceed 85%. This balanced approach is crucial as misclassifying poor water quality is more severe than the opposite error.

4   CRISP-DM Methodology

This section outlines the methodological framework adopted in this study, detailing the analytical techniques applied and summarizing the results derived from each phase of the CRISP-DM methodology. An overview of the full process is provided in Fig. 1.

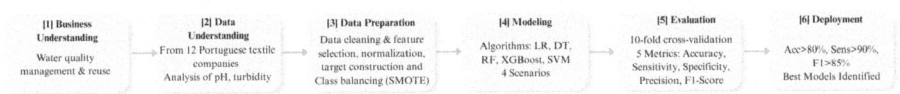

Fig. 1. Methodological flowchart for water quality prediction model development

4.1   Business Understanding

The primary business objective of this study is to support decision making related to water management and reuse in the textile production process. By accurately predicting water quality at each stage, the project aims to enable more sustainable and efficient use of this critical resource. Therefore, the objective of data mining is to create strong predictive models that can classify water quality according to physicochemical parameters like pH and turbidity for determining compliance with regard to set reuse standards. The predictions are used to decide on reuse, additional treatment, or disposal, hence optimizing the use of resources and reducing environmental impact.

4.2   Data Understanding

The data were provided by CITEVE, a consortium partner in the project, comprising measurements collected from 12 textile companies. The dataset covers a period of approximately two months, from October to December 2023. However, some companies provided data for shorter timeframes. Given the limited duration and variability across the data, the time-related variable was excluded from the analysis. All data was manually acquired and recorded by analyzing water samples before and after each process. Table 2 provides descriptive statistics for the quantitative variables in the dataset.

Table 2. Dataset Variables Description

Column	Data Type	Description
R:B	Quantitative	Ratio between the volume of processing liquid and the weight of textile material
Id_company	Categoric	Unique numeric identifier corresponding to the company where the data was collected
Bath Number	Categoric	Bath number in the process
Order	Categoric	Step order in the production workflow

(continued)

Table 2. (*continued*)

Column	Data Type	Description
OF	Categoric	Production order reference
Product	Categoric	Type of textile substrate being processed
Quantity	Quantitative	Total amount of textile material processed
Fibre	Categoric	Main fiber composition of the textile substrate
Color	Categoric	Describes the color of the material
Dye	Categoric	Indicates the dye used in the process
Tag	Categoric	Equipment or machine identifier used during the process
Type of Process	Categoric	Describes the operational mode of the process
Process	Categoric	Denotes the specific textile processing method applied
Substep	Categoric	Sub-step within the process
General Process	Categoric	Broad classification of the process stag

Table 3 presents descriptive statistics for the quantitative and categorical variables in the dataset.

Table 3. Descriptive Analysis of Dataset Variables

Variables	Mean	Median	Mode	stdev	Minimum	Maximum
R:B	−14.18	7.0	−99.0	44.07	−99.0	22.9
Bath number	−	−	1.0	−	1.0	23.0

4.3 Data Preparation

The data preparation phase aimed to transform raw industrial and environmental datasets into a structured format suitable for predictive modeling. It included:

- **Dataset cleaning and dimensionality reduction:** Two datasets were loaded: fact_gia_v3.csv, containing process information, and recommended_value.csv, with reference parameter values. After inspecting the data structure, numerous irrelevant or redundant columns were removed to reduce dimensionality. All time-related columns (e.g., id_calendar, id_time, timestamp) were removed from the dataset. The dataset sampling period was relatively short limited to a maximum of 57 days, with some companies contributing data for only one or two days. This pruning reduced noise and improved computational efficiency.
- **Construction of the Target Variable:** The target variable was constructed by defining minimum and maximum acceptable thresholds for pH and turbidity based on recommended values. Binary indicators were created to show whether each measurement fell within these limits. Combining these checks produced a single binary

target variable, where 1 indicates both parameters are within acceptable ranges and 0 indicates at least one exceeds the threshold.

- **Feature Encoding and Normalization:** Categorical features are represented as one-hot indicators, dropping the first level to avoid multicollinearity. Numerical features are normalized to have zero mean and unit variance so that each input has the same contribution when training the model.
- **Class Imbalance:** This research reveals a significant class imbalance, with a limited number of minority class examples. This results in underrepresentation of minority class samples in model training, leading to biased predictions. To address this, the Synthetic Minority Over-sampling Technique (SMOTE) was used to generate synthetic minority class samples and balance the data [24]. Additional bias mitigation was implemented through stratified sampling across 12 companies to reduce selection bias and feature selection across multiple scenarios to prevent feature bias. The distribution of the target variable before and after SMOTE application is illustrated in Fig. 2. Initial trials with various classification approaches yielded suboptimal outcomes, prompting the application of SMOTE prior to dividing data into training and testing sets. This approach ensures both sets exhibit balanced class distributions, enhancing model generalization. Various settings of SMOTE parameter k_neighbors were tried to determine the best setting, and the performance of the model was evaluated using stratified 10-fold cross-validation.

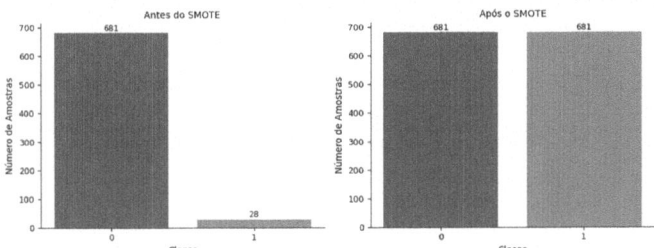

Fig. 2. Target Distribution before and after SMOTE

4.4 Modelling

Subsequent to data preparation, the modelling process was conducted using Python. Given the classification nature of the problem and the pronounced class imbalance within the target variable, a diverse set of algorithms was employed to balance model robustness with interpretability. The selected classifiers comprised DT, RF, SVM, LR and XGBoost. To mitigate the effects of class imbalance, the SMOTE was applied to the training data within each fold of the stratified 10-fold cross-validation. This approach ensured a balanced class distribution during model training.

To investigate the influence of varying feature subsets on predictive performance, four distinct modelling scenarios were devised:

- S1: {R:B, id_company, bath number, order, OF, product, fibre, color, dye, tag, type of process, process, substep, general process, target}

- S2: S1 enhanced with variable quantity
- S3: Reduced set excluding dye, type of process, and quantity
- S4: S3 with quantity reintegrated

4.5 Evaluation

In this evaluation stage, the performance of several machine learning models was analyzed across four distinct scenarios. For testing purposes, data from Company 10 and Company 11 were used, allowing a focused assessment of model behavior under different conditions. This assessment considered five ML models: DT, LR, RF, SVM, and XGBoost. The evaluation was based on five key metrics: accuracy, precision, sensitivity, specificity, and F1-score. All evaluations were conducted using 10-fold cross-validation to reduce the risk of overfitting and ensure consistent results.

Company 10: Table 4 presents the results for company 10 (78 rows). Overall, XGBoost, RF and LR performed best. Notably, XGBoost reach sensitivity (1.00) in Scenario 1 and maintained high values across all metrics and scenarios. Scenario 2 consistently produced the most balanced results. LR reached a sensitivity of 0.99 and F1-score of 0.91, while XGBoost had a precision of 0.91 and F1-score of 0.92. This indicates that feature selection improved model effectiveness and generalization. In contrast, DT underperformed in all scenarios, with lower accuracy and F1-scores than other models.

Table 4. Performance metrics for Company 10 across four scenarios

Scenario	ML Models	Accuracy	Precision	Sensitivity	Specificity	F1-Score
1	DT	0.88	0.86	0.94	0.82	0.89
	LR	**0.96**	**0.97**	0.96	**0.97**	0.96
	RF	0.95	**0.97**	0.93	**0.97**	0.94
	SVM	0.93	0.94	0.94	0.93	0.93
	XGBoost	**0.96**	0.92	**1.00**	0.94	**0.95**
2	DT	0.92	0.92	0.93	0.91	0.92
	LR	**0.96**	0.95	**0.99**	0.94	0.91
	RF	**0.96**	**0.97**	0.96	**0.97**	**0.96**
	SVM	0.94	0.95	0.94	0.94	0.94
	XGBoost	0.94	0.91	0.94	0.94	0.92
3	DT	0.87	0.86	0.91	0.82	0.88
	LR	**0.96**	**0.97**	0.96	**0.97**	**0.96**
	RF	**0.96**	**0.97**	0.94	**0.97**	0.95
	SVM	0.93	0.94	0.94	0.93	0.93
	XGBoost	0.95	0.94	**0.95**	0.96	0.94
4	DT	0.91	0.92	0.91	0.91	0.91
	LR	**0.96**	0.95	**0.99**	0.94	**0.97**

(continued)

Table 4. (*continued*)

Scenario	ML Models	Accuracy	Precision	Sensitivity	Specificity	F1-Score
	RF	**0.96**	0.07	0.96	**0.97**	0.96
	SVM	0.94	0.95	0.94	0.94	0.94
	XGBoost	0.94	**0.95**	0.91	0.96	0.91

Company 11: Table 5 presents the results for company 11 (103 rows). Overall, all models performed increase compared to company 10. LR, RF, and XGBoost achieved accuracy above 0.96, with similarly strong results across other metrics. Scenario 2 again yielded the best outcomes. RF achieved an F1-score of 0.98, and LR and XGBoost also performed consistently well. SVM showed slightly lower precision and specificity but kept competitive accuracy. DT improved compared to Company 10 but remained the weakest model.

Table 5. Classification performance metrics for Company 11 across four scenarios

Scenario	Models	Accuracy	Precision	Sensitivity	Specificity	F1-Score
1	DT	0.96	0.93	**1.00**	0.92	0.97
	LR	**0.97**	**0.97**	0.99	**0.96**	**0.98**
	RF	**0.97**	0.96	0.99	0.95	0.97
	SVM	0.91	0.9	0.95	0.88	0.92
	XGBoost	**0.97**	0.93	0.98	**0.96**	0.95
2	DT	0.96	0.93	**1.00**	0.92	0.97
	LR	**0.97**	**0.96**	0.99	**0.96**	0.97
	RF	**0.97**	**0.96**	**1.00**	0.95	**0.98**
	SVM	0.92	0.9	0.96	0.9	0.93
	XGBoost	0.94	0.93	0.94	0.95	0.92
3	DT	0.97	0.95	1	0.95	0.97
	LR	**0.98**	**0.97**	0.99	**0.96**	**0.98**
	RF	0.96	0.95	0.99	0.94	0.96
	SVM	0.91	0.9	0.95	0.88	0.92
	XGBoost	0.95	0.93	0.92	**0.96**	0.92
4	DT	0.96	0.94	**1.00**	0.92	**0.97**
	LR	**0.97**	**0.96**	0.99	**0.95**	**0.97**
	RF	0.96	0.94	**1.00**	0.93	**0.97**
	SVM	0.92	0.9	0.96	0.89	0.93
	XGBoost	0,96	0.92	0.98	**0.95**	0.94

Table 6 presents average performance metrics for the three best-performing models across both companies. All algorithms achieved accuracy exceeding 95% while maintaining balanced sensitivity and specificity performance.

Table 6. Average Classification Metrics for Top 3 Models Across Company 10 and 11

Model	Accuracy	Precision	Sensitivity	Specificity	F1-Score
LR	0.97	0.96	0.98	0.96	0.96
RF	0.96	0.96	0.97	0.96	0.96
XGBoost	0.95	0.93	0.95	0.95	0.93

5 Conclusion

This study used the CRISP-DM framework to analyze water quality compliance in the textile sector utilizing data from 12 companies to develop classification models based on pH and turbidity compliance thresholds. The study included comprehensive and investigative data preparation, feature selection and addressed class imbalance with SMOTE data augmentation. Five classification algorithms, DT, RF, SVM, LR and XGBoost, were applied and compared across four modeling scenarios. While existing studies achieve 70–75% accuracy with traditional methods and Rustam et al. [14] reached 96% accuracy using ANNs, these approaches focus on general applications rather than industry-specific complexities. The present study advances these methodologies by combining pH and turbidity classification with textile-specific process variables, achieving 97% accuracy and 98% sensitivity through XGBoost and RF models. This represents significant improvement over existing approaches while addressing stringent requirements of industrial water reuse decisions in textile manufacturing. The study found that Scenario 2 outperformed other models in terms of accuracy, with XGBoost, RF, and LR showing the highest levels of accuracy. In Company 11 data, RF achieved a 100% sensitivity, with an F1-score of 98%, LR achieved a 99% sensitivity level and 97% F1-score, while XGBoost had a precision level of 93% with 92% F1-score. These results suggest that the models are well-trained and perform well in classifying water quality to support reuse decisions. The predictive models are based on laboratory measurements, ensuring strong validity and reliability. This is particularly important for practical applications, where decisions can impact resource use and environmental standards.

The predictive models have demonstrated a solid basis built on objective and validated industrial data, which is critical for practical applications where organizational decision-making could impact resource usage and compliance with standards for the environment. The predictive models hold significant importance for the textile industry, as they enable more accurate and timely identification of water quality compliance that leads to improved water reuse, lessens freshwater use and wastewater volume, reduces operation costs, and ultimately decreases the risks for environmental penalties. There are possibilities respectively related to sustainability and resource efficiency towards textiles and textile production processes.

Despite the promising early findings, it should be noted that there is a need for validation of the model's advantageously overstretched timeliness across various datasets. As the current dataset is bounded by time and volume, it inhibits the identification of the generalizability and robustness of the predictive algorithms for potential use within other textile industrial contexts. Future data collection should address this issue by collecting more comprehensive datasets that include forms of temporal dynamics and higher discrepancies in production contexts to develop a more reliable model and extend usage. In conclusion, the research represents a strong methodology and initial findings with reasonable functionality toward real-world applications in sustainable water management systems for the textile industry.

Acknowledgements. This work is supported by the PRR – Recovery and Resilience Plan – Mobilizing Agendas under the project GIATEX (02/C05-i01.01/2022.PC644943052-00000050).

Disclosure of Interests. The authors have no competing interests to declare that are relevant to the content of this article.

References

1. Vörösmarty, C.J., et al.: Global threats to human water security and river biodiversity. Nature **467**(7315), 555–561 (2010)
2. Parliament, E.: The Impact of Textile Production and Waste on the Environment (infographics). European Parliament, Brussels (2020)
3. GIATEX , CITEVE. (2023, maio 29). Gestão Inteligente da Água na ITV. https://www.citeve.pt/inteligencia_tecnologica/projetos/giatex_2-dffadbca
4. Baloyi, R., et al.: Recent advances in recycling technologies for waste textile fabrics: a review. Text. Res. J. **94**(3–4), 210–239 (2023)
5. Dutta, S., et al.: Contamination of textile dyes in aquatic environment: adverse impacts on aquatic ecosystem and human health, and its management using bioremediation. J. Environ. Manag. **353**, 120103 (2024)
6. Rabbi, M.A., et al.: Investigation of waste water quality parameters discharged from textile manufacturing industries of Bangladesh. Curr. World Environ. **13**(2), 206–214 (2018)
7. Niinimäki, K., et al.: The environmental price of fast fashion. Nat. Rev. Earth Environ. **1**, 189–200 (2020)
8. Kumar, P., Basu, A.: Case Studies on Reducing Water and Chemical Consumption in Textile Processing. Industrial Press, New York (2024)
9. Malik, S., Muhammad, K., Waheed, Y.: Artificial intelligence and industrial applications—a revolution in modern industries. Ain Shams Eng. J. **15**(9), 102886 (2024)
10. Zou, S., Ju, H., Zhang, J.: Water quality management in the age of AI: applications, challenges, and prospects. Water **17**(11), 1641 (2025)
11. Zhu, M., et al.: A review of the application of machine learning in water quality evaluation. Environ. Ecol. Health **1**(1), 100003 (2022)
12. Guyon, I., Elisseeff, A.: An introduction to variable and feature selection. J. Mach. Learn. Res. **3**, 1157–1182 (2003)

13. Rustam, F., et al.: An artificial neural network model for water quality and water consumption prediction. Water **14**(21), 3359 (2022)
14. Silva, A.R., Miranda, R., Portela, F.: Preliminary study about water quality prediction models: a textile case study. In: Guarda, T., Portela, F., Augusto, M.F. (eds.) Advanced Research in Technologies, Information, Innovation and Sustainability. ARTIIS 2024. CCIS, vol. 2349, pp. 37–51. Springer, Cham (2025). https://doi.org/10.1007/978-3-031-83432-5_3
15. Mahanna, H., et al.: Prediction of wastewater treatment plant performance through machine learning techniques. Desalin. Water Treat. **14**, 100524 (2024)
16. Peffers, K., et al.: A design science research methodology for information systems research. J. Manag. Inf. Syst. **24**(3), 45–77 (2007)
17. Chapman, P., Clinton, J., Kerber, R.: CRISP-DM 1.0: Step-by-Step Data Mining Guide. SPSS Inc., Chicago (2000)
18. Peng, C.Y.J., Lee, K.L., Ingersoll, G.M.: An introduction to logistic regression analysis and reporting. J. Educ. Res. **96**(1), 3–14 (2002)
19. Song, Y.-Y., Lu, Y.: Decision tree methods: applications for classification and prediction. Shanghai Arch. Psychiatry **27**(2), 130–135 (2015)
20. Breiman, L.: Random forests. Mach. Learn. **45**(1), 5–32 (2001)
21. Osman, A.I.A., et al.: Extreme gradient boosting (Xgboost) model to predict the groundwater levels in Selangor Malaysia. Ain Shams Eng. J. **12**(2), 1545–1556 (2021)
22. Mamat, N., Razali, S.F.M., Hamzah, F.B.: Enhancement of water quality index prediction using support vector machine with sensitivity analysis. Front. Environ. Sci. **10**, 1061835 (2023)
23. Sokolova, M., Lapalme, G.: A systematic analysis of performance measures for classification tasks. Inf. Process. Manag. **45**(4), 427–437 (2009)
24. Elreedy, D., Atiya, A.F.: A comprehensive analysis of Synthetic Minority Oversampling Technique (SMOTE) for handling class imbalance. Inf. Sci. **505**, 32–64 (2019)

Artificial Intelligence and Law (AIL)

The Dawn of a XAI Road
to Humachinal-Centric Justifications
in EU Consumer Credit Denials

Diogo Morgado Rebelo[1,2](✉) (iD), Francisco Pacheco de Andrade[2](iD),
and Paulo Novais[3](iD)

[1] School of Law, University of Minho (FCT Grant 2023.01496.BD), Braga, Portugal
djmr1995@gmail.com
[2] JusGov R&D Unity, School of Law, University of Minho, Braga, Portugal
[3] ALGORITMI Research Center/LASI, School of Engineering, University of Minho,
Braga, Portugal

Abstract. Today, personal data and cutting-edge AI-based scoring
models play an ever-increasing role in determining who is accepted or
rejected for consumer credit. This process is becoming more automated
than ever before. Determining whether consumers are creditworthy or
not is often obscured within a maze of tenuous transparency. Black Box
models pose a serious threat, particularly when a credit applicant is
categorized as 'bad' payer. This study employs the Diverse Counterfactual Explanations (DiCE) technique in three Use Cases through a
Multi-Layer Perceptron (MLP) embedded with the separated combination of J48 Algorithm and Random Forest (RF) for feature selection.
The classifier was deliberately pre-processed on the UCI German Credit
Dataset (GCD) to clarify the negative impact software engineers have on
both scoring and post-hoc explanations. Our findings indicate that while
Counterfactuals (CFs) can, in some circumstances, help consumers whose
credit was denied, they are often incomplete for providing legally and
reasonably grounded explanations of why and how. So, besides imposing a 'de-individualized' identity on consumers, CFs do not fulfill all
criteria to achieve a grounded right to ex-post justification. We thus
inferred that the field of eXplainable AI (XAI) has yet a long path to
deliver reasonable solutions to address the challenges posed by EU Law.
To date, justifications should be provided through Machine-Scoring-to-
Human-Justifications (MS2HJ) Interaction. However, as XAI becomes
more and more trustworthy, we do not deny fully automated justifications, embedding legal values and norms (i.e., Humanichal). Until now,
DiCE shortcomings suggest that the Portuguese legislator, when trans-
posing Art. 18 of the Directive (EU) 2023,2225, of October 18, should
enshrine the right to Human-Centric justifiability based on proportional
and legally grounded or actionable alternatives.

Keywords: AI-based Scoring · Consumer Creditworthiness
Assessment · Counterfactual Explanations · Humanichal-Centric
Justifications

© The Author(s), under exclusive license to Springer Nature Switzerland AG 2026
J. Valente de Oliveira et al. (Eds.): EPIA 2025, LNAI 16122, pp. 69–82, 2026.
https://doi.org/10.1007/978-3-032-05179-0_6

1 Introduction

The automation of consumer credit decisions through AI predictive models is revolutionizing the European consumer lending landscape. Algorithmic scoring systems, driven by diverse data sources, are taking the place of traditional credit risk analysis, significantly improving efficiency, consistency, and scalability in evaluating creditworthiness. [12] This transformation is occurring within a complex regulatory framework: AI-driven credit assessments must comply with legal requirements including the General Data Protection Regulation (GDPR) [5], the Artificial Intelligence Act [7], and especially the Consumer Credit Directive 2023/2025, of October 18 (CCD2). [6] The EU is committed to ensuring consumers can inquire how creditors evaluate their creditworthiness, including the rationale and risks associated with Automated Decision-Making (ADM) and its implications. However, despite stringent regulations, the opacity of algorithms continues to pose a real challenge. Black Box models obscure the reasoning behind ADM, complicating the understanding of credit denials.

Continuing the tradition of "Law in Books", the Court of Justice of the European Union (CJEU) has recently clarified the normative essence of providing a comprehensible and clear explanation in automated decision-making through its ruling in the case of *CK v. Magistrat der Stadt Wien and Dun & Bradstreet Austria GmbH*, Case C-203/22, on February 27, 2025. [3] Under Arts. 15(1)(h) and 22 of the GDPR, the Court recognized that a meaningful explanation can be achieved by informing individuals about how variations in their personal data might lead to different results. While DiCE approach appears sound in theory, it encounters both technical and legal challenges. Some scholars propose CFs as a promising way to tackle the issue of opacity [14–16]. In fact, these clarifications create avenues to inform, challenge, and modify outcomes without exposing the internal mechanisms of the black box. Nonetheless, research focusing on operational aspects of their limitations—especially concerning the application of DiCE at the intersection of AI and Law—is notably scarce. Thus, despite advancements in XAI, a critical gap persists: existing counterfactual explanations frequently lack realism, proportionality, and normative alignment. Therefore, forthcoming XAI techniques must ensure compliance with the European right to explanation while promoting responsible lending practices.

This is precisely where our paper comes into play. We present a pipeline that incorporates feature selection using the J48 algorithm, followed by modeling with an 18-3-1 MLP. Though the model is trained, validated, and tested, it currently fails to produce realistic or legally sound CFS based on the GCD.

Our primary research questions focus on how effectively DiCE's counterfactual explanations align with EU law. Additionally, we examined three Use Cases in an effort to propose a mixed approach that balances technological enthusiasm with human considerations. The main contribution of this study lies in its critical integration of normative and technically sound explanatory requirements. Most importantly, it tackles pressing challenges and offers guidelines for the Portuguese legislature to implement Art. 18(8)(a) of the CCD2 by November 20, 2026, as mandated by its Art. 48.

The structure of our investigation is as follows: Sect. 2 reviews existing literature; Sect. 3 elaborates on our methodology; Sect. 4 outlines our results; and Sect. 5 provides conclusions and forward-looking perspectives.

Overall, this research seeks to demonstrate the conflict between the feasibility of counterfactual explanations and the principles of Consumer Law.

2 Literature Review

2.1 EU Law-Powered Explainability

The ongoing legal debates surrounding AI-driven consumer credit decisions are heavily shaped by the ambiguity and extent of the right to ex-post explanation, especially as the GDPR, the AI Act, and soon, CCD2, come into effect.

Art. 22(3) of the GDPR does not explicitly grant data subjects such protection. Only Recital 71 suggests that the term "explanation" implies some level of ex-post understanding.[1]. A ruling on the contentious issue regarding the right to ex-post explanation was made by February 27, 2025. Paragraph 62 of the C-203/22 judgment highlights the necessity for "meaningful information," interpreting Art. 15(1)(h) of the GDPR as imposing a duty on controllers to elucidate the reasoning behind their decisions. While there is no obligation to disclose the algorithm itself, safeguarded as a trade secret (Recital 63), the process must facilitate fair proceedings and protect the rights of individuals

The AI Act categorizes credit scoring systems as high-risk systems (Art. 6(2)(b), *ex vi* Annex III, 5(b)), which imposes enhanced transparency and explainability requirements as outlined in Art. 13. This encompasses the provision of clear, understandable information regarding the system's operation, risks, and limitations. Additionally, the standard for explanations demands more than vague information: it should be auditable, meaningful, interpretable, and importantly, practical and actionable to foster accountability and effective management of Machine Learning models.

Moreover, CCD2, in Art. 18(8)(a), aligns with this rationale by mandating a clear statement of reasons for credit decisions. It stresses the importance of explaining the logic and factors at play, which promotes a responsible credit evaluation and ensures that information provided to consumers is comprehensible.

This regulatory evolution signifies a trend towards increasing explainability requirements, striving to strike a balance between automation and the protection of fundamental rights in Creditworthiness Assessment (CWA). Nevertheless, while the European regulatory framework for algorithms is theoretically robust, it simultaneously highlights the immediate need to legally validate the DiCE method.

One thing in clear, the triangular regime does not yet addressed the criteria for what should be understood as legally grounded justifications. Indeed, justifying a denial goes beyond mere explanation; it uncovers the underlying reasons,

---

[1] The CJEU's Schufa judgment—Case C-634/21, *OQ v. Land Hessen*, of 7 December 2023—clarifies that a "solely based decision" occurs when credit is granted based on scoring output, even if some human oversight is involved [2].

particularly when that decision adversely affects someone. The effectiveness of a justification hinges on the social and legal context, including the authority of the decision-maker, alongside solid evidence and the applicable legal framework [10].

2.2 Post-Hoc Explanations for Credit Denials with DiCE

In recent years, XAI has emerged as a significant player in AI-driven credit scoring, enhancing transparency and accountability. Notably, various post-hoc inductive methods, including Local Interpretable Model-Agnostic Explanations (LIME), SHapley Additive eXplanations (SHAP), and the DiCE approach, are critical in improving clarity in decision-making processes.

Local Interpretable Model-Agnostic Explanations (LIME) works by simplifying intricate models through local linear approximations. It generates explanations for credit decisions by constructing model-agnostic local models that prioritize both local fidelity and interpretative lucidity. SHAP utilizes additive attribution techniques grounded in game theory to evaluate the marginal contribution of each feature. This method can yield reasonable global and local explanations, making it robust and consistent in its assessments, sometimes serving a dual purpose in feature selection [1].

However, these techniques are not without their pitfalls. Both LIME and SHAP exhibit notable limitations that can undermine their effectiveness in high-stakes environments like consumer credit risk assessments. For instance, LIME encounters challenges with inconsistent explanations due to random sample generation, diminished fidelity in nonlinear contexts, and poor local consistency in its attributions. Conversely, while SHAP offers greater robustness, it typically incurs significant computational costs and often struggles with complex variable interactions, leading to oversimplifications and misrepresentations of sparse data regions. Most critically, neither LIME nor SHAP offers actionable recommendations—an essential requirement for consumers seeking justifications that are both user-friendly and legally compliant [11].

These considerations substantiate the relevance of DiCE. Such an innovative approach is distinguished by its unique ability to generate multiple counterexamples through optimization. DiCE is specifically crafted to identify minimal alterations that can reverse a model's decision, all while adhering to the principles of diversity, proximity, sparsity, plausibility, and feasibility. Unlike LIME and SHAP, which focus on local or attributive explanations by assessing variable importance, DiCE tackles the pivotal question: "What must change to achieve a different outcome?" This counterfactual methodology proves invaluable in consumer credit denials, as it elucidates alternative actions that can lead to overrides. Furthermore, DiCE seamlessly integrates with black box models, avoiding assumptions of linearity or additivity, thus making it particularly suitable for neural network-based scoring systems [8].

From the outset, it appears now evident that selecting DiCE as the cornerstone XAI technique is not only scientifically somewhat feasible but also essential for further legally validating its purported effectiveness in addressing consumer credit challenges. This necessity becomes even more pronounced when examining the reasoning behind a candidacy's rejection and identifying avenues for improving one's score. DiCE's has the ability to simulate various alternative scenarios, providing individuals with clearer insights into their profiles and potential modifications.

Nonetheless, certain drawbacks may accompany its implementation. As clarified in Sect. 4, DiCE can produce counterexamples that are unrealistic and contravene EU Consumer Credit Law, exhibit explanatory instability due to fluctuating output probability scores, and pose challenges in assessing plausibility.

3 Methodology

3.1 Database Selection

The German Credit Data (GCD) from the UCI Machine Learning Repository is chosen for its significant scientific and regulatory relevance. It comprises 1,000 instances and 20 diverse predictor variables (refer to Table 1), establishing it as a benchmark for the development and validation of binary classification models in consumer credit. This dataset effectively embodies authentic credit scenarios [4].

Table 1. List of Predictors

No.	Variable	Description
1	Account Status	Status of the checking account
2	Duration	Duration of the credit in months
3	Credit History	Past credit history
4	Purpose	Purpose of the credit
5	Credit Amount	Total amount of credit requested
6	Savings	Amount saved
7	Employment Duration	Years at current employment
8	Installment Rate	Percentage of disposable income
9	Other Debtors	Presence of other debtors/guarantors
10	Residence	Years at current residence
11	Property	Type of property owned
12	Age	Age of the applicant (in years)
13	Other Installments	Other installment plans
14	Housing	Housing type
15	No. of Credits	Existing credits at other institutions
16	Job	Job type
17	No. of Dependents	Number of dependents
18	Telephone	Telephone line registered

3.2   Pre-processing

At the outset, the authors opted to remove sensitive variables, specifically those associated with nationality and gender, referred to as "Personal Status" and "Foreign Worker." This decision is in accordance with Art. 18(3) of the CCD2, which follows the prohibition in Art. 9(1) and its applicability due to Art. 22(4), as outlined in the GDPR.

To improve transparency and facilitate auditing, all categorical variables that were coded were carefully aligned with their semantic definitions according to the official UCI glossary. This ensures that each transformation is traceable and comprehensible, aiding validation efforts by experts and auditors.

The choice to use LabelEncoder over alternative methods like one-hot encoding proved particularly beneficial for variables demonstrating an implicit hierarchy (for example, savings and length of employment). This approach preserved ordinal relationships, reduced dataset dimensionality, and ensured compatibility with the dense layers of neural networks.

Variables were categorized based on their informational weight into three distinct feature selection groups: highest, intermediate, and lowest. Each category underwent specific normalization processes using MinMaxScaler with tailored intervals of (0.2), (0.1), and (0.01). This method regulates the influence of each variable within the model, enhances training stability, and contributes to explanations that more accurately reflect the operational realities of credit.

3.3   Feature Selection: J48 and CfsSubsetEval

The features were selected using the J48 algorithm, an implementation of C4.5, via the python-weka-wrapper3 setup within the Conda environment with Zulu 17 JVM. We applied the CfsSubsetEval method to assess the relevance of the attributes by analyzing their correlation with the target variable and accounting for internal redundancy. [4] In a distinct Jupyter Notebook, employing the same pipeline, we utilized a RF model to pinpoint the two variables that received the lowest weights in the results. The search was further refined with the BestFirst heuristic.

This Data Mining framework led to the identification of four key attributes: "Account Status", "Duration", "Credit History", and "Savings". Through Random Forest (RF) analysis, we found that the variables "No. of Dependents" and "Telephone" were of minimal relevance to the outcome. All remaining variables were categorized as intermediate. This meticulous selection process helped reduce the risk of overfitting, improved interpretability, and bolstered the robustness of the model, allowing for more accurate and legally sound explanations.

3.4   Modeling MLP Classifier

Data modeling for credit risk evaluation is a vital step in developing machine learning systems, requiring methodological choices that go beyond merely optimizing performance metrics. When using an MLP for assessing creditworthiness, selecting data splits and neural network architectures is essential. This section discusses the reasons for choosing the 60/20/20 split and the 18-3-1 MLP architecture.

On the one hand, the 60/20/20 split, rooted in a multidimensional analysis, emphasizes performance metrics, statistical reliability, and assessment robustness. As shown in Table 2, below, our partitioning, which has 1000 parameters: (a) finds that allocating 60% of the data to training offers an adequate sample size for effective generalization; (b) suggests that a dedicated 20% validation set is essential for early stopping, hyperparameter tuning, and avoiding overfitting; and (c) the final 20% reserved for testing allows for a statistically reliable assessment of the model's generalization ability.

Table 2. Comparative analysis of splitting strategies

	Split 60/20/20	Split 70/15/15	Split 80/10/10
Partitioning			
Training Set	600 instances	700 instances	800 instances
Validation Set	200 instances	150 instances	100 instances
Test Set Size	200 instances	150 instances	100 instances
Performance			
Training Accuracy	0.7383	0.7443	0.7538
Training AUC	0.7676	0.7788	0.7789
Validation Accuracy	0.7750	0.7867	0.8300
Validation AUC	0.8217	0.7598	0.8314
Test Accuracy	*0.7900*	0.7933	0.8300
Test AUC	*0.8023*	0.8180	0.8314
Statistical Reliability			
Standard Error (σ)	*0.029*	0.033	0.041
Model Robustness			
Overfitting (Accuracy)	*−0.0367*	−0.0424	−0.0762
Generalization Gap |Val-Test|	*0.0150*	0.0066	0.0000
Explainability			
No. of Cfs | Quality (Paper's Purpose)	*38 Optimal*	32 Moderate	19 Limited

The 60/20/20 split strikes the best balance, minimizing trade-offs between accuracy and explanatory power [9]. Although the 70/15/15 split adds 100 training instances, it cuts the evaluation set by 25%, increasing the standard error from 0.029 to 0.033 and raising instability. The validation-test AUC gap is 5.82%, indicating less reliable generalization, compared to just 1.94% for 60/20/20. The 80/10/10 split performs worse for the paper's purpose by drastically reducing its explanatory power. With only 100 validation and testing instances, respectively, it shows higher error (0.041) and fewer counterfactuals (19 vs. 38).

Table 3. MLP Performance Comparison

Metric	2 Hidden	3 Hidden	4 Hidden
Training Accuracy	0.7450	0.7383	0.7400
Training AUC	0.7613	0.7676	0.7670
Validation Accuracy	0.7450	0.7750	0.7750
Validation AUC	0.8212	0.8217	0.8190
Test Accuracy	0.7850	0.7900	0.7850
Test AUC	0.7940	0.8023	0.8013

On the other hand, as depicted in Table 3, above, 18-3-1 architecture consistently outperforms others, achieving the highest test accuracy (79%) and AUC (80.23%). Conversely, the 2-neurons hidden setup is too simplistic to effectively model credit risk patterns, whereas incorporating a 4-neurons hidden layer adds unnecessary complexity without yielding any significant improvement. Consequently, the stability observed during training of the 18-3-1 architecture becomes a crucial factor (Fig. 1).

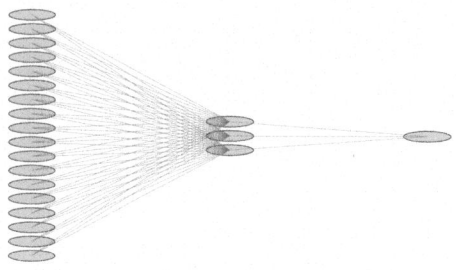

Fig. 1. 18-3-1 MLP with Sigmoid activation Function and 5000 iterations

3.5   Our Approach to DiCE

To hypothesize unsuitable CFs within EU Law, we utilized the Dice-ML library. Specifically, we focused on the test subset of the MLP incorporating attribute selection. This methodology enhances both the generalization and robustness of our findings. Additionally, we opted for the sigmoid activation function due to its aptitude for continuous differentiation of probabilities. This selection also aids in avoiding irreversible coding, thereby promoting the generation of coherent and mathematically differentiable counterfactual instances. As a result, the explanatory process became more nuanced, ensuring that each counterfactual exemplified was tailored to the unique profiles of specific users and subjected to thorough auditing. Importantly, this approach aligns with Art. 15(1)(h) of the GDPR, as interpreted by the Court of Justice of the European Union on February 27, 2025, which underscores the right to an automated explanation characterized by transparency and accountability.

We generated three counterfactual explanations for each of the 30 instances that the model rejected. This sampling confirmed the inherent imbalance present in the German Credit Data, a well-documented phenomenon noted in the literature for the predominance of negative instances over positive ones. Subsequently, we systematically produced these CFs and employed a mining technique to select the instances with the highest probability scores for counterfactual validation.

Ultimately, a structured prompt was utilized to underscore three real cases among the analyzed CFS. In these scenarios, despite considerable scores indicating a possible reversal of the initial decision, the explanations were found to be impractical and potentially inconsistent with Art. 18 of the CCD2.

4 Discussion of the Results on Case Studies

Table 4. Selected CFs

Inputs	Case 1	Case 2	Case 3
Account Status	$0.000 \rightarrow 0.667$	—	—
Duration	—	$1.206 \rightarrow 0.267$	—
Credit History	—	—	$1.000 \rightarrow 2.000$
Savings	$0.000 \rightarrow 2.000$	$0.000 \rightarrow 2.000$	—
Credit Amount	—	—	—
Age	—	—	—
Purpose	—	—	—
Employment	—	—	—
Property	—	—	$0.667 \rightarrow 0.000$
Installment Rate	—	— X > IR	—
Other Debts	—	—	—
Residence	—	—	—
Other Installment Plans	—	—	—
Housing	—	—	—
No. of Existing Credits	—	—	—
Job	—	—	—
No. of Dependents	—	—	—
Telephone	—	—	—

Table 5. Comparison – Original Scores *vs* Counterfactual Scores

Case	Original Score	Counterfactual Score
1	0.2781	0.7382
2	0.4375	0.6618
3	0.2979	0.6374

Analysis of three counterfactual creditworthiness assessment scenarios reveals concerning patterns. We observed artificial changes in key variables that significantly inflate credit scores (165%, 51%, 114%), without reflecting actual improvements in consumers' financial capacity. These practices violate CCD2's fundamental principles, namely, the promotion of responsible credit practices. The manipulation of variables such as account status, savings, credit duration, credit history, and property highlights areas where AI systems may be susceptible to unintended influences. Tables 4 and 5, below, encapsulate the most pertinent outcomes from the analysis of 30 rejection cases.

4.1   Case 1 - The Illusion Of Financial Miracle

The first scenario shows a miraculous transformation in the consumer's finances, changing the account status from negative (< 0 Deutsche Mark(DM))[2] to positive (0-200 DM) and savings from less than 100 DM to 500-1000 DM. Legally, this manipulation violates Art 18(3) of the CCD2, which calls for assessment based on necessary, sufficient, and proportionate information" about the consumer's financial state. The sudden account improvement and substantial savings increase, without verifiable justification, distort financial reality and contradict the principle of transparency in solvency assessment.

Economically, this scenario creates an illusion of solvency that is completely disconnected from reality. The 165% increase in the credit score (from 0.2781 to 0.7382) through these artificial manipulations demonstrates the fragility of the evaluation system. A consumer who suddenly goes from a negative balance and minimal savings to an apparently stable position, without any real basis, represents a significant risk of default. This practice not only increases the consumer's risk of over-indebtedness, but also contributes to the instability of the financial system by basing credit decisions on unrealistic and unfounded assumptions.

4.2   Case 2 - The Ambushed Shortened Term

The second scenario presents a significant reduction in credit duration combined with a substantial increase in savings, from less than DM 100 to between DM 500 and DM 1,000. From a legal point of view, this manipulation violates the principle of realistic and proportionate assessment of creditworthiness, enshrined

---

[2] DM refers to "Deutsche Mark", the old German currency used before the introduction of the Euro, and is the original monetary unit in the dataset.

in Art. 18(4) of the CCD2. The drastic reduction in the duration of the credit, without a corresponding assessment of the consumer's ability to bear higher installments (unavoidable in a shorter term), constitutes a breach of the duty of diligence in assessing creditworthiness. This practice is particularly serious when we consider that Art. 18(1) of the CCD2 states that creditors must rigorously assess the creditworthiness of the consumer.

In the economic dimension, this scenario poses significant risks for both the consumer and the stability of the financial market. A loan with a shorter duration necessarily implies higher monthly installments, requiring greater financial capacity on the part of the consumer. The manipulation of this variable, without properly assessing whether the consumer can afford this increase in installments, creates a false perception of lower risk. The 51% increase in the credit score (from 0.4375 to 0.6618) through these manipulations demonstrates how the system overvalues the reduction in the term, ignoring the increase in monthly financial pressure on the consumer, boosting situations of default and over-indebtedness.

4.3   Case 3 - The Overvalued Collateral Paradox

The third scenario presents a paradoxical situation: a deterioration in credit history (from all duly paid loans to late payments) combined with an improvement in the type of guarantee (from life insurance to real estate). From a legal point of view, this manipulation creates a legally untenable scenario, violating the principle of holistic and balanced assessment of creditworthiness enshrined in the CCD2. Overvaluing the guarantee to the detriment of payment history goes against the fundamental logic of credit risk assessment, where past behavior is generally considered a strong predictor of future behavior. This practice may also constitute a violation of the principle of non-discrimination by creating potential biases against consumers without real estate.

From an economic perspective, this scenario reveals a serious distortion in risk assessment. The 114% increase in the credit score (from 0.2979 to 0.6374) despite the deterioration in payment history demonstrates a dangerous overvaluation of material guarantees. This practice ignores the fact that the ability and willingness to pay (reflected in the track record) are fundamental to preventing default. Enforcing collateral is always a costly and inefficient process for all parties. By giving excessive priority to the existence of a property as collateral, the system encourages irresponsible lending practices, increasing systemic risk in the financial market and boosting over-indebtedness crises.

5   Humachinal Justifiability: a Call for Reflection

This research investigates the role of DiCE in AI-driven consumer credit decisions, employing an 18-3-1 MLP model alongside feature selection techniques such as J48 and Random Forest DM. The findings highlight significant obstacles in generating legally valid and realistic counterfactuals, revealing a disconnection between technical capabilities and European regulatory standards. An analysis of the GCD indicates that, although counterfactuals can aid consumers, they do not offer legally sound justifications.

We also recognized that the adjustment of feature normalization and the streamlined MLP architecture could not guarantee coherent explanations, which resulted in output score instability and challenges in determining counterfactual plausibility. Nevertheless, our main aim was to demonstrate the importance of human pre-processing and fine-tuning of models, and how these factors influence both outputs and explanations. This gap between algorithmic optimization and legal compliance reveals a fundamental flaw in the current development of XAI: the faulty belief that technical explainability automatically equals normative justification. Our findings show that DiCE, by focusing on the easiest mathematical route to change a classification, produces solutions that are not only financially impractical but also violate key principles of responsible credit evaluation, such as proportionality and truthful information, as outlined in Art. 18 of the CCD2. Therefore, justifying a credit denial involves more than simply reversing variables; it is an essential communicative act meant to empower consumers with a credible and legally defensible option. Without this, XAI systems like DiCE risk turning into tools of transparent obfuscation, where the appearance of explanation masks the lack of real remedies or fair guidance, ultimately maintaining the power imbalance between creditors and consumers.

Indeed, issues with data management led to a de-individualized consumer identity [13], failing to meet the necessary requirements for post-hoc explanations. Also, the legal framework in the EU necessitates justifications that extend beyond mere technical explanations, underscoring the necessity for economic and normative foundations that are currently lacking in XAI systems.

Future research should focus on developing both hybrid human-machine and humanichal credit justification methods that incorporate legal perspectives into XAI systems, explore complex network architectures, impose legal constraints on algorithms, and establish metrics for legal plausibility. Furthermore, it would be beneficial to create datasets annotated by legal professionals and investigate approaches to tailor explanations based on individual consumer profiles. In conclusion, when implementing Art. 18 of CCD2, Portuguese legislators should prioritize, at least for now, a justification right designed to be human-centered.

Disclosure of Interests. This research was funded by FCT – Fundação para a Ciência e a Tecnologia, I.P., under project reference 2023.01496.BD with DOI 10.54499/2023.01496.BD.

References

1. Arrieta, A.B., et al.: Explainable artificial intelligence (XAI): concepts, taxonomies, opportunities and challenges toward responsible AI. Inf. Fusion **58**, 82–115 (2020). https://doi.org/10.1016/j.inffus.2019.12.012
2. Court of Justice of the European Union: Judgment of the Court (First Chamber) of 7 December 2023, OQ v Land Hessen, Case C-634/21 (2023). https://

eur-lex.europa.eu/legal-content/EN/TXT/?uri=CELEX%3A62021CJ0634.
eCLI:EU:C:2023:957

3. Court of Justice of the European Union: Judgment of the Court (First Chamber) of 27 February 2025, CK v Dun & Bradstreet Austria GmbH and Magistrat der Stadt Wien, Case C-203/22 (2025). https://eur-lex.europa.eu/legal-content/EN/TXT/?uri=celex:62022CJ0203. eCLI:EU:C:2025:117

4. Dastile, X., Celik, T., Potsane, M.: Statistical and machine learning models in credit scoring: a systematic literature survey. Appl. Soft Comput. **91**, 106263 (2020). https://doi.org/10.1016/j.asoc.2020.106263

5. European Parliament and Council: Regulation (EU) 2016/679 of the European parliament and of the council of 27 April 2016 on the protection of natural persons with regard to the processing of personal data and on the free movement of such data, and repealing directive 95/46/EC (general data protection regulation) (2016). https://eur-lex.europa.eu/eli/reg/2016/679/oj/eng, oJ L 119, 4.5.2016, p. 1–88

6. European Parliament and Council: Directive (EU) 2023/2225 of the European Parliament and of the Council of 18 October 2023 on credit agreements for consumers and repealing Directive 2008/48/EC (2023). https://eur-lex.europa.eu/eli/dir/2023/2225/oj/eng, oJ L, 30.10.2023

7. European Parliament and Council: Regulation (EU) 2024/1689 of the European Parliament and of the Council of 13 June 2024 laying down hamonised rules on artificial intelligence and amending certain Union legislative acts (Artificial Intelligence Act) (2024). https://eur-lex.europa.eu/eli/reg/2024/1689/oj/eng, oJ L, 12.7.2024

8. Guidotti, R.: Counterfactual explanations and how to find them: literature review and benchmarking. Data Mining Knowl. Discov. **38**(9), 2770–2824 (2024). https://doi.org/10.1007/s10618-022-00831-6

9. Gunning, D., Aha, D.: Darpa's explainable artificial intelligence (XAI) program. AI Mag. **40**(2), 44–58 (2019). https://doi.org/10.1609/aimag.v40i2.2850

10. Hulstijn, J.: Computational accountability. In: Proceedings of the 19th International Conference on Artificial Intelligence and Law (ICAIL 2023), pp. 121–130. Association for Computing Machinery, New York (2023). https://doi.org/10.1145/3594536.3595122

11. Kedar, M.M., Mhatre, G.N.: Exploring the effectiveness of shap over other explainable AI methods. Int. J. Sci. Res. Eng. Manag. (IJSREM) **06**(06), 1–7 (2024). https://ijsrem.com/download/exploring-the-effectiveness-of-shap-over-other-explainable-ai-methods/

12. Langenbucher, K.: Responsible A.I.-based credit scoring – a legal framework. Eur. Bus. Law Rev. **31**(4), 527–572 (2020). https://doi.org/10.54648/eulr2020022

13. Magrani, E., de Miranda, P.R.: The right to reasonable inferences in automated decision systems as an unfolding of the fundamental right to the protection of personal data in brazil and beyond. Int. Rev. Law Comput. Technol. **39**(1), 75–94 (2025). https://doi.org/10.1080/13600869.2024.2351676

14. Morgado Rebelo, D., Andrade, F.P.D., Novais, P.: AI-based consumers' creditworthiness fate needs EU lawgorithmics to innovate. In: Proceedings of the Twentieth International Conference on Artificial Intelligence and Law (ICAIL 2025), Chicago, IL, USA, pp. 12–21. ACM (2025). https://doi.org/10.1145/nnnnnnn.nnnnnnn, presented and accepted for publication in camera-ready version

15. Mothilal, R.K., Sharma, A., Tan, C.: Explaining machine learning classifiers through diverse counterfactual explanations. In: Proceedings of the 2020 Conference on Fairness, Accountability, and Transparency (FAT*), pp. 607–617. Association for Computing Machinery, New York (2020). https://doi.org/10.1145/3351095.3372850
16. Wachter, S., Mittelstadt, B., Russell, C.: Counterfactual explanations without opening the black box: automated decisions and the GDPR. Harvard J. Law Technol. **31**(2), 841–887 (2018). https://ora.ox.ac.uk/objects/uuid:86dfcdac-10b5-4314-bbd1-08e6e78b9094

Autonomous Systems are Mere Tools: Legal Fiction or Reality?

Xiaoshui Zhai(✉) 🆔

University of Warwick, Coventry CV4 7AL, UK
Xiaoshui.Zhai@warwick.ac.uk

Abstract. This article examines the debate surrounding the classification of autonomous systems as mere tools within the legal framework. Critics argue that this classification represents a "legal fiction," failing to reflect the autonomous and decision-making capabilities of such systems in practice. By contrast, this paper defends the Mere Tools perspective, contending that it aligns with technological realities and preserves the foundational principles of accountability. The analysis begins by exploring the origins of the "legal fiction" critique, highlighting concerns about responsibility attribution and the evolving role of autonomous systems. It then addresses these critiques, demonstrating that autonomous systems, despite their advanced capabilities, remain extensions of human agency and operate within the parameters established by their designers and users. The paper concludes by affirming that the Mere Tools theory offers a realistic and justifiable framework for integrating autonomous systems into existing legal structures without compromising accountability or predictability. This discussion contributes to the broader discourse on how the law should adapt to emerging technologies.

Keywords: Autonomous Systems · Mere Tools Theory · Legal Fiction · Attribution Rules

1 Introduction

The rapid evolution of autonomous systems has transformed the landscape of technology and law, prompting critical questions about how such systems should be conceptualized and regulated. One of the most debated perspectives in this discourse is the notion that autonomous systems are mere tools. This Mere Tools theory frames autonomous systems as extensions of their human users, attributing actions and outputs of the systems to the individuals or entities behind them, and not to the system itself.

This perspective has gained support in some recent institutional frameworks dealing with automated contracting. For instance, the United Nations Commission on International Trade Law (UNCITRAL), in its *Model Law on Automated Contracting* (MLAC), endowered the view that AI systems are tools whose outputs should be attributed to persons.[1] It explicitly rejected any notion that such systems possess legal personality or

---

[1] See [1], Article 7(2).

independent will [2]. Likewise, the European Law Institute (ELI), in its *Guiding Principles and Model Rules on Digital Assistants for Consumer Contracts*, clearly states that the digital assistant used for contractual relations is treated as a tool, as opposed to being considered as separate from the user [3].

While the simplicity of this theory has made it appealing to legal theorists and practitioners, its adequacy is challenged. Critics argue that the theory constitutes a "legal fiction," an artificial construct that overlooks the reality of autonomous systems' operational complexity, learning capabilities, and decision-making autonomy [4–10]. These critics contend that treating autonomous systems as mere tools fails to reflect their unique characteristics, potentially leading to gaps in accountability and fairness in legal regimes.

This paper argues against such criticisms and defends the position that autonomous systems, despite their complexity and autonomy, should be understood as mere tools. It demonstrates that this legal nature aligns with both technological realities and legal attribution rules. The paper begins by analysing the critiques that label the Mere Tools theory as a legal fiction, exploring why such arguments arise in the context of autonomous systems. It then refutes these critiques, highlighting how the Mere Tools perspective accommodates the technological and legal realities of these systems.

2   Viewing Autonomous Systems as Mere Tools: A Legal Fiction?

The applicability of the Mere Tools theory to autonomous systems has faced criticism, particularly due to its perceived inconsistency with the reality of how these systems function. It is argued that characterizing autonomous systems as Mere Tools creates a form of legal fiction [4–10], insofar as it assumes as true something that is clearly false [11]. This approach is seen as overlooking the defining technical characteristic of these systems—autonomy—rendering this approach apparently artificial [4, 12, 13].

Under their understanding or presumption, a system is the mere tool of its user only when it passively transmits the already given declaration or intention to others [14]. In other words, a system is regarded as a mere tool if it functions in ways that can be traced directly back to the programming and knowledge humans embedded in the system [15]. In such circumstances, anything that issues from the system actually issues directly from its user.

This is obviously true for traditional automatic systems, which operate by strictly following specific pre-set instructions and parameters defined by their users. Consequently, when a user sets up and deploys an automatic system to automate contractual processes—such as contract formation or performance—all relevant contractual decisions are pre-determined by the user and encapsulated within the system's programming. Automatic systems are unable to independently determine the contractual content and, thus, the legal rights and obligations of their users. Rather, they function as 'servants' to the deploying party, passively transmitting the decisions or representations that have been pre-determined and agreed upon by their user without altering them in any way [10]. In such cases, the user decides and controls, in advance, the conditions under which the automatic system will issue certain statements to other counteracting parties [16]. As a result, automatic systems are considered mere tools, passively transmitting statements that are directly determined by the user. Such systems are simply taken as an extension of their users.

However, the technical characteristics of autonomous systems are perceived as making them beyond the status of a mere tool. The main reason is that autonomous systems are considered to induce a significant shift in the source of decision-making. Unlike automatic systems, which adhere rigidly to human directives, autonomous systems possess the capability to independently make contractual decisions based on information they collect and analyse themselves, such as whether, when, and under what terms to enter into a contract. Instead of just following the user's instructions, these systems are endowed with a certain degree of discretion to actively shape the contractual content [4, 8, 10]. This means that the specific contractual content is no longer directly determined by the user and passively transmitted by the system. In this context, the role of users in autonomous systems is limited to stipulating the logical rules or goals that guide the systems in the process of contracting, rather than specifying operational instructions as with automatic systems. As a result, it is considered that human users effectively transfer (at least a portion of) control over the contractual decision to the autonomous systems. The source of contractual decision-making is transferred from human users to autonomous systems, thereby differentiating them from the passive tool paradigm typically associated with traditional automatic systems.

Given these technical characteristics, the application of the mere tools approach to autonomous systems is the subject of critique on account of its deliberate oversight of the autonomy of these systems. Treating autonomous systems as mere tools of their users indicates that all actions or outputs generated by these systems are considered directly coming from their users, according to their understanding of the Mere Tools theory [7, 9]. This is inconsistent with the technical reality where the autonomy enables these systems to decide the courses of actions independently. As Sommer puts it, it is not a plausible argument to characterize electronic agents in a similar fashion to these passive devices [17]. Essentially, critics think that the disparate technical characteristics between automatic and autonomous systems should result in divergent legal treatment. In the case of automatic systems, the decision is clearly made and controlled by the human user, whereas in the case of autonomous systems, the decision is considered to be made by the systems themselves. In this view, critics give a conclusion that autonomous systems cannot be seen as a mere tool since the user's intentions are not just transmitted by it, but given its autonomous character, determined and declared to the other party with almost no involvement from the user [14].

However, this research argues that the criticisms leveled against the application of the Mere Tools theory to autonomous systems stem from either a misinterpretation of the theory itself or a misunderstanding of the technical characteristics of autonomy in such systems. When correctly interpreted, the Mere Tools theory remains compatible with the technical realities of autonomous systems. By acknowledging both the scope of the theory and the specific nature of autonomy in these systems, we can effectively apply the Mere Tools framework to autonomous decision-making processes without contradicting the underlying technological principles.

3   Reassessing the Narrative: Towards a Realistic Understanding

3.1   What is the Mere Tools Theory?

Many argue that attributing the actions of autonomous systems to their users constitutes legal fiction, on the grounds that it seems to pretend that the system's actions are the user's own, in order to allocate responsibility where none otherwise exists. If one interprets this attribution rule in this incorrect way, it might be easy to object to the application of the Mere Tools theory to autonomous systems, or to argue that such an application is fictional, especially given that autonomous systems are able to act independently rather than strictly following the user's specific instructions.

However, this critique stems, at least in part, from a misinterpretation of the nature and function of attribution rules. A legal fiction, properly understood, involves a conscious departure from known facts, whereby the law deliberately treats something false as if it were true for institutional purposes [11]. Classic examples include the treatment of corporations as "persons" or the assumption that an unborn child is "already born" for inheritance purposes. These fictions are explicitly constructed to override factual reality.

In contrast, attribution rules are not based on fiction but rather grounded in the factual premise that autonomous systems are not legal agents. Attribution does not purport to describe who "actually" performed a given action. While autonomous systems may participate directly in the causal chain producing certain outcomes—thereby functioning as proximate causes—the theory explicitly denies that such systems possess the ontological status of legal agents endowed with intentions, understanding, or normative capacities [18–20]. As such, they cannot be primary bearers of legal responsibility, so the attribution of behavior should naturally fall on humans. The attribution of autonomous systems' behavior to human users is therefore not a fiction, but a necessary normative allocation of responsibility to someone within the human control structure. Thus, attributing actions of autonomous systems to users does not involve pretending the user 'did' what the AI did; it simply reflects the reality that legal systems must assign responsibility to actors with agency. In this sense, the Mere Tools theory is about rejecting fiction, not assuming it.

Additionally, another potential misunderstanding among critics of the Mere Tools theory is the belief that applying this attribution rule to both automatic systems and autonomous systems equates them in terms of their technical capabilities. Such critics may argue that the Mere Tools theory simplifies the reality of how these systems operate, suggesting that the rule assumes all systems, from fax machines to highly sophisticated autonomous systems, are technically identical. This is because, historically, the Mere Tools theory has been applied to automatic systems or some simple devices characterised by the mere tools technical attribute—that is, systems whose actions are passively, fully controlled, and predictable by their users.[2] These systems, characterised by their shared technical attribute, are subject to the same attribution rule as Mere Tools. Consequently, extending the Mere Tools theory to autonomous systems might prompt some to view it as categorizing autonomous systems as mere tools in a technical sense. Thus, they

---

[2] This paper uses uppercase (Mere Tools) and lowercase (mere tools) letters to distinguish between the Mere Tools theory as an attribution rule and the technical attribute of mere tools.

purport that this approach is different from reality and ignores the autonomy of these advanced systems.

However, as a rule of attribution, the Mere Tools theory simply posits that the actions of both autonomous and automatic systems should be attributed to their users, or that users should bear the consequences of these actions. It is essential to recognize that equally applying the Mere Tools theory to autonomous systems, automatic systems, and even very simple devices like fax machines, merely standardizes the attribution rule across them. In other words, this approach signifies only that the same attribution rule—assigning the actions of these systems to their users—is applied consistently to all of them. Extending the Mere Tools theory to include autonomous systems does not imply that these systems are identical to traditional, automatic systems in terms of their technical attributes and complexity. Instead, it suggests that differences in their technical attributes do not necessitate different attribution rules.

The technical discrepancy between the various systems would only have an impact on the different justifications for the application of the attribution rule, rather than the application itself. In the case of automatic systems, the justification for the attribution rule is relatively straightforward. These systems operate under the full control of the user, performing tasks that are strictly pre-programmed or predetermined by the user. The user has direct control over every action taken by the system, and, as such, the responsibility for any outcomes produced by the system naturally falls to the user. In contrast, the justification for applying the Mere Tools theory to autonomous systems introduces additional complexity that will be examined subsequently.

3.2 Why Autonomous Systems can be Regarded as Mere Tools?

With a proper understanding of the Mere Tools theory, it becomes essential to critically evaluate its suitability for application to autonomous systems. One significant advantage of adopting the Mere Tools theory is that it preserves technical neutrality and maintains the legal status quo. This approach ensures that attribution rules remain consistent across varying types of algorithmic systems, regardless of their level of complexity or autonomy. As such, the Mere Tools theory offers a means of integrating advanced autonomous systems into existing legal frameworks without necessitating radical legal reforms, thereby minimizing disruption to established legal framework.

In contrast, alternative proposals—such as analogizing to the law of agency [9] or granting legal personality to these systems [4, 8]—would require far-reaching changes to substantive law. For instance, if autonomous systems were to be recognized as legal persons, this may necessitate significant reform of contract law to accommodate them as contracting parties. This is because many foundational concepts and doctrines in contract law—such as legal capacity, intention, knowledge, and mistake— are deeply rooted in human attributes and do not easily map onto algorithmic decision-making processes.

To fully justify the continued application of the Mere Tools theory in the context of autonomous systems, this research will address three key areas of concern that form the foundation of most criticisms: the control condition, the instrumentality nature of technology and the fairness of the risk allocation. These three aspects represent the most significant points of contention in the debate surrounding the application of the Mere Tools theory to autonomous systems. By addressing these concerns in detail, this research aims to demonstrate that the theory remains a viable and fair framework for assigning responsibility in the age of autonomous technology.

Control Condition

From the perspective of the control condition, the attribution logic of the Mere Tools theory rests on a factual foundation rather than on any legal fiction. In legal and moral responsibility theory, control is widely recognized as a necessary precondition for attributing responsibility: one cannot be held responsible for outcomes over which they had no relevant control [21, 22].

In discussions surrounding the attribution of actions performed by autonomous systems, critics of the Mere Tools theory frequently appeal to the control condition. A common argument holds that such systems have become so autonomous that neither designers nor users retain the degree of control or understanding necessary to support attribution [23, 24]. As the system's autonomy increases, the control initially exercised by human users is seen to shift gradually to the system itself [22]. This perceived shift appears to disrupt the normative link between human input and system output. Accordingly, critics argue that attributing the actions of autonomous systems to human operators is both inappropriate and artificial. Thus, some scholars go further to argue that, in such cases, legal personality should be conferred upon the system itself, allowing actions to be attributed to the system as an independent legal subject [4, 8].

This agreement, however, tends to overestimate the autonomy of such systems and underappreciate the nuanced structure of human control. While it is true that the specific outputs of autonomous systems may not be directly determined—or even foreseen—by their human operators, this does not amount to full independence from human control. Human control is not exercised continuously or reactively but rather takes a pre-configurative and structural form. It manifests through the design of the system's architecture, the programming of its operational parameters, and the specification of its ultimate objectives.

Human developers retain decisive control during the "getting ready" stage, in which they design, train, and configure the system to perform specific functions within defined parameters and environmental constraints [25, 26]. Although autonomous systems may exhibit adaptive capabilities, including the ability to respond dynamically to changing inputs or contexts, such behaviour is always bounded by predefined principles and embedded constraints. These structural features—set in advance by human agents—determine the scope of the system's behavioural repertoire and ensure that its operations remain aligned with the purposes of its creators. Crucially, autonomous systems lack the capacity to redefine their ultimate goals or operate entirely outside the boundaries established by their programming. The autonomy demonstrated by such systems must be carefully distinguished from human autonomy, which entails self-determination and the ability to choose one's own ends [19, 20]. AI systems do not possess such agency; rather, they function within the constraints and objectives imposed by their human designers and operators. As such, the proposal to grant legal personality to autonomous systems constitutes a legal fiction in the true sense: it artificially constructs a subject of law that is misaligned with the underlying technological reality.

In addition, some critics challenge the fairness of the Mere Tools theory by drawing a comparison between the attribution rules applicable to human agents and their principals, and those applied to autonomous systems and their users. They argue that the scope of a user's liability under the Mere Tools theory could even be broader than in traditional agency relationships involving human agents [9]. In human agency relationships, the doctrine of authority limits the principal's responsibility to only those actions taken by their human agent that fall within the scope of their authority. If the human agent acts outside of this scope, these actions are not attributed to the principal. Consequently, the principal is shielded from the responsibility associated with unauthorized acts of the agent, such as unauthorized agreements or unexpected contracts. However, under the Mere Tools theory, critics argue that all actions carried out by autonomous systems are attributed to their users, even those that may not have been anticipated or authorized. This seemingly broader scope of responsibility leads to a question about the fairness of this attribution rule.

This critique, however, again reveals a misunderstanding of the autonomy of algorithmic systems. Critics appear to conflate the autonomy of human agents with that of algorithmic systems. The autonomy possessed by human agent enables them to make decisions and act beyond their authorization. In contrast, the autonomy of algorithmic systems does not give them such an ability. These systems follow pre-programmed rules, which dictate the scope of their actions and ensure that their outputs remain within the operational boundaries set by the user or designer. Every action they take is a result of the configuration, logic, and algorithms embedded within them at the outset. They do not possess the ability to override the boundaries of their programming. As such, autonomous systems do not have the capacity to exceed their authorization in the same way that human agents do.

Given this fundamental difference between the two types of autonomy, it is inappropriate to criticize the fairness of the attribution rule of the Mere Tools theory in comparison to human agency relationships. Unlike human agents, autonomous systems operate within the scope of their programming, meaning they cannot exceed the authority given to them. Holding users responsible for the actions of their autonomous systems is fair and justified, all their actions are essentially 'authorized' by the user through the initial programming and configuration.

Attributing the actions of AI systems to human users, therefore, is not an act of legal fiction or a mere artificial construct. Rather, it reflects the concrete reality that human actors possess the necessary control and oversight to be held accountable. This attribution respects the factual circumstances and aligns with foundational principles in legal and moral philosophy that tie responsibility to control and agency.

Instrumentality of Technology

Across the spectrum of technological artefacts—from simple hand tools to complex autonomous systems—there exists a vast range of technical complexity and operational sophistication. Despite these differences, all technologies share a fundamental feature: instrumentality [27]. As a universal attribute, it signifies that technologies, irrespective of their complexity, serve as means used by humans for specific ends. This instrumental view is widely accepted as the common-sense view of technology [28].

Understood in this way, instrumentality implies both value-neutrality and the absence of moral agency in the technology itself. Its evaluation is contingent upon the specific applications as determined by its human operators. As a means to an end, technology is not valued independently but in light of its application and outcomes, as decided by human intentions. As Deborah Johnson [29] notes, "Computer systems are produced, distributed, and used by people engaged in social practices and meaningful pursuits. This is as true of current computer systems as it will be of future computer systems. No matter how independently, automatic, and interactive computer systems of the future behave, they will be the products (direct or indirect) of human behaviour, human social institutions, and human decision."

In this sense, the emergence of advanced autonomous system does not mark a departure from the instrumental nature of technology, but rather a continuation of it. These systems may operate with a degree of independence or unpredictability, but their design, objectives, and parameters are set by human agents. They are not capable of self-determining their use or moral purpose. The power to decide how such systems function and to what ends they are applied remains decisively human.

This continuity in instrumentality provides a compelling basis for maintaining existing rules of attribution. Even when systems exhibit adaptive, emergent, or seemingly independent behaviours, such actions should be understood as extensions of their human designers and operators, rather than as independent acts separable from human agency. Whether the object in question is a hammer or a highly-autonomous AI system, the principle of instrumentality provides a coherent basis for attributing responsibility to the human behind it. As J. Storrs Hall [30] aptly remarks, "If machines changed the ease with which things were done, they did not change the responsibilities for doing them. People have always been the only 'moral agents.'".

Accordingly, the instrumental perspective supports a consistent and technologically neutral attribution framework, one that applies uniformly across the full range of technological systems. From basic tools to advanced autonomous systems, each technological object embodies instrumentality as a foundational attribute. This universal feature transcends variations in technological sophistication, enabling the rule of attribution to remain stable and uniformly applicable across all technological forms. Consequently, even in the face of rapid technological advancement, the enduring instrumentality of technology grounds a robust and justified model of human-centred attribution.

Moreover, the persistent instrumentality of autonomous systems presents a fundamental obstacle to granting them legal personality. Although these systems can produce complex outputs and even exhibit adaptive behaviors, they do so without any internal awareness, normative understanding, or intentionality. Their outputs are generated through statistical pattern recognition and optimization algorithms, rather than through deliberative processes informed by evaluative reasoning. In essence, they function as non-subjective mechanisms, entirely lacking the capacity for moral or legal self-reflection.

Although corporations are recognized as artificial legal persons, they are fundamentally grounded in the subjectivity and agency of natural persons [31]. Corporate actions are not directly performed by the corporation itself; rather, they are carried out by human agents such as directors, managers, and shareholders, who possess agency and act intentionally within the organizational framework. In other words, the actual legal actors behind corporate decisions are natural persons endowed with agency, not the corporation as a separate entity. The corporation has a governance structure, internal norms, decision-making procedures, and legal representation, all of which presuppose human agency embedded within the artificial entity. Conversely, if legal personality were attributed to autonomous systems, the actual legal actor would be the system itself—an entity lacking agency and subjectivity—which conflicts with fundamental principles of legal responsibility.

Fairness Considerations: Attribution Without Automatic Liability

It is necessary to clarify that the application of the Mere Tools theory does not entail that users are automatically liable for all actions undertaken by their algorithmic systems. Attribution rules function as a preliminary mechanism to identify the relevant legal actor—that is, the person to whom the system's actions is ascribed—but they do not in themselves establish liability. Whether a particular attributed action ultimately gives rise to legal responsibility depends on the applicable substantive rules, such as those of contract or tort law.

Importantly, attribution encompasses not only expected or intended outputs but also unexpected or even irrational ones. For instance, in the context of automated contracting, an autonomous system might generate offers or acceptances that significantly deviate from market norms due to malfunction or unforeseen input combinations. Under the Mere Tools framework, such an action should be still attributed to the user.

Some critics argue that such attribution would impose an unfair and overly harsh burden on users [4, 7, 32]. Ooi, for instance, suggests that this approach imposes an extremely heavy burden on users by legally binding them to the actions of an autonomous system, even in cases where the system produces outputs that are so irrational that no reasonable counterparty could possibly believe it to be functioning properly. This critique is based on the assumption that the Mere Tools theory would hold users responsible for all actions or outputs produced by the system they employ. In other words, they assume that all outputs of the system would result in legally binding contracts under this theory, thus holding the users responsible for them.

However, this assumption is flawed. This assumption is based on a misunderstanding of the consequence of the attribution rule. The application of Mere Tools theory does not mean that all statements sent by an algorithmic system will bind its user without further inquiry, as is mistakenly assumed. In fact, the consequence of the application of this rule is to determine that the user will bear the contractual responsibility if there is a valid contract. If no valid contract is created, then naturally, then the user is not held responsible for the corresponding statement generated by the system, as there would be no legal responsibility at all. It is not the task of the attribution rule to assess whether a legal consequence has arisen from the actions or outputs of an algorithmic system. Instead, the rule operates to assign responsibility in situations where a legally valid contract is formed. Therefore, even under the Mere Tools theory, users are not bound by every output generated by their systems, but only by those outputs that lead to a valid and enforceable contract.

Determining whether a statement generated by an autonomous system constitutes a legally binding contract requires recourse to the relevant rules of contract law, rather than relying solely on the attribution rule. In contract law, a statement generated by an autonomous system will only bind the user if it satisfies the doctrinal requirements for contract formation—such as offer, acceptance, consideration and intention to create legal relations. If those requirements are not met, no contract is formed, and no liability arises, despite the attribution of the conduct to the user.

It is important to recognise that contract law could function as a safeguard to prevent users from being overburdened by some absurd outputs of autonomous systems. For example, if an "offer" issued by an autonomous system is so implausible or absurd that no reasonable counterparty could have believed it to reflect an intention to contract, then such an offer may not be treated as legally binding [33].

Moreover, under contract law, if—based on the evaluation of relevant normative considerations—it would be unjust or unreasonable to bind the user to certain unexpected outputs, the legal system may interpret or adapt contractual rules to prevent those outputs from giving rise to legal obligations, or allocate relevant risks in an balance way from the perspective of contract law and their priority considerations. In other words, concerns about potential unfairness in attributing the actions of autonomous systems to users can be effectively addressed through the lens of substantive legal doctrines, rather than through a rejection of attribution rule itself.

4   Conclusion

This article has critically examined the application of the Mere Tools Theory as an attribution rule in the context of autonomous systems. By offering a thorough clarification of the theory itself and its legal implications, this research establishes a comprehensive and nuanced understanding of the Mere Tools Theory. The theory posits that the actions of an algorithmic system are attributed to their users rather than to the systems themselves. This attribution does not imply that the actions undertaken by the system are directly performed by the user; instead, it just signifies that the consequences or legal responsibilities arising from these actions are to be assigned to the user. It is important to note that applying the Mere Tools Theory to both automatic and autonomous systems does not equate them in terms of their complexity or technical attributes. Instead, it merely standardizes the attribution rule across diverse technologies. This research highlights that the application of the Mere Tools Theory acknowledges the technical autonomy of sophisticated systems while maintaining that such autonomy does not alter the attribution rule: users are accountable for the actions of their systems.

Under the Mere Tools Theory, in the context of automated contracting, statements or actions generated by autonomous systems are attributed to their users who deploy these systems for the purpose of transactions. Users bear contractual obligations when such statements or actions lead to valid contracts. Importantly, the Mere Tools Theory serves solely as an attribution rule, determining the responsible party when there is a valid contract generated by autonomous systems as for the assessment of whether a legal consequence arises from the system's actions still needs to further inquire the relevant rules in contract law.

When aligned with the technological characteristics and operational realities of autonomous systems, the analysis demonstrates that the application of the Mere Tools Theory is not only consistent with the technological landscape but also well-justifiable. Far from being a legal fiction, the Mere Tools theory provides a robust and adaptable framework for attributing responsibility in a manner consistent with both technological realities and fundamental principles of justice. By recognizing the unique characteristics of autonomous systems while maintaining a consistent attribution rule, the theory ensures that legal responsibility keeps pace with technological advancements, providing clarity and fairness in the rapidly evolving landscape of autonomous technology.

Disclosure of Interests. The authors have no competing interests to declare that are relevant to the content of this article.

References

1. UNCITRAL Model Law on Automated Contracting. https://uncitral.un.org/sites/uncitral.un.org/files/mlac_en.pdf. Accessed 03 June 2025
2. UNCITRAL Model Law on Automated Contracting with Guide to Enactment, p. 27. https://uncitral.un.org/sites/uncitral.un.org/files/2424674e-mlautomatedcontracting-ebook.pdf. Accessed 08 July 2025
3. ELI Guiding Principles and Model Rules on Digital Assistants for Consumer Contracts, p. 10. https://www.europeanlawinstitute.eu/fileadmin/user_upload/p_eli/Projects/Algorithmic_Contracts/Guiding_Principles_and_Model_Rules_on_Digital_Assistants_for_Consumer_Contracts.pdf. Accessed 02 July 2025
4. Widdison, R., Allen, T.: Can computers make contracts? Harv. J. Law Technol. **9**(1), 25–52 (1996)
5. Kerr, I.R.: Spirits in the material world: intelligent agents as intermediaries in electronic commerce. Dalhousie Law J. **22**(2), 190–249 (1999)
6. Bellia, A.J.: Contracting with electronic agents. Emory Law J. **50**(4), 1047–1092 (2001)
7. Weitzenboeck, E.M.: Electronic agents and the formation of contracts. Int. J. Law Inf. Technol. **9**(3), 204–234 (2001). https://doi.org/10.1093/ijlit/9.3.204
8. Andrade, F., Novais, P., Machado, J., Neves, J.: Contracting agents: legal personality and representation. Artif. Intell. Law **15**(4), 357–373 (2007). https://doi.org/10.1007/s10506-007-9046-0
9. Chopra, S., White, L.: Artificial agents and the contracting problem: a solution via an agency analysis. Univ. Ill. J. Law Technol. Policy 363–403 (2009)
10. Scholz, L.H.: Algorithmic contracts. Stanf. Technol. Law Rev. **20**(2), 128–169 (2016)
11. Fuller, L.L.: Legal Fictions. Stanford University Press, Stanford (1967)
12. Bashayreh, M., Sibai, F.N., Tabbara, A.: Artificial intelligence and legal liability: towards an international approach of proportional liability based on risk sharing. Inf. Commun. Technol. Law **30**(2), 169–192 (2021). https://doi.org/10.1080/13600834.2020.1856025
13. Księżak, P., Wojtczak, S.: Toward a Conceptual Network for the Private Law of Artificial Intelligence, pp.77–107,1st edn. Springer, Cham (2023). https://doi.org/10.1007/978-3-031-19447-4
14. Ismayilzada, T.: Technical overview of AI and its participation in the contract formation. In: A Framework for AI-Made Mistakes in German and English Contract Law, pp.115–185. 1st edn. Springer, Cham (2024). https://doi.org/10.1007/978-3-031-61999-1_4
15. Vladeck, D.C.: Machines without principals: liability rules and artificial intelligence. Wash. Law Rev. **89**(1), 117–150 (2014)
16. Cross, S.R.: Agency, contract and intelligent software agents. International Rev. Law Comput. Technol. **17**(2), 175–189 (2003). https://doi.org/10.1080/1360086032000122556
17. Sommer, J.H.: Against cyberlaw. Berkeley Technol. Law J. **15**(3), 1145–1232 (2000)
18. McFarland, T.: The Concept of Autonomy. OSF Preprints (2020). https://doi.org/10.31228/osf.io/bac5w

19. Chia, H., Beck, D., Paterson, J.M., Savulescu, J.: Autonomous AI: what does autonomy mean in relation to persons or machines? Law Innov. Technol. **15**(2), 390–410 (2023). https://doi.org/10.1080/17579961.2023.2245679

20. Santoni de Sio, F., Mecacci, G.: Four responsibility gaps with artificial intelligence: why they matter and how to address them. Philos. Technol. **34**(4), 1057–1084 (2021). https://doi.org/10.1007/s13347-021-00450-x

21. Johnson, D.G., Verdicchio, M.: Reframing AI discourse. Mind. Mach. **27**(4), 575–590 (2017). https://doi.org/10.1007/s11023-017-9417-6

22. Matthias, A.: The responsibility gap: ascribing responsibility for the actions of learning automata. Ethics Inf. Technol. **6**(3), 175–183 (2004). https://doi.org/10.1007/s10676-004-3422-1

23. Sparrow, R.: Killer robots. J. Appl. Philos. **24**(1), 62–77 (2007). https://doi.org/10.1111/j.1468-5930.2007.00346.x

24. Berber, A., Srećković, S.: When something goes wrong: who is responsible for errors in ML decision-making? AI Soc. **39**(4), 1891–1903 (2024). https://doi.org/10.1007/s00146-023-01640-1

25. Haselager, W.F.G.: Robotics, philosophy and the problems of autonomy. Pragmat. Cogn. **13**(3), 515–532 (2005). https://doi.org/10.1075/pc.13.3.07has

26. Asada, M.: Rethinking autonomy of humans and robots. J. Artif. Intell. Consciousness **7**(2), 141–154 (2020). https://doi.org/10.1142/S2705078520500083

27. Heidegger, M.: The Question Concerning Technology, and Other Essays, 1st edn., pp. 4–5. Harper & Row, New York (1977)

28. Gunkel, D.J.: Perspectives on ethics of AI: philosophy. In: Dubber, M.D., Pasquale, F., Das, S. (eds.) The Oxford Handbook of Ethics of AI. Oxford University Press, Oxford (2020). https://doi.org/10.1093/oxfordhb/9780190067397.013.35

29. Johnson, D.G.: Computer systems: moral entities but not moral agents. Ethics Inf. Technol. **8**(4), 195–204 (2006). https://doi.org/10.1007/s10676-006-9111-5

30. Hall, J.S.: Ethics for Machines. In: Anderson, M., Anderson, S.L. (eds.) Machine Ethics, pp. 28–44. Cambridge University Press, Cambridge (2011). https://doi.org/10.1017/CBO9780511978036.005

31. Solaiman, S.M.: Legal personality of robots, corporations, idols and chimpanzees: a quest for legitimacy. Artif. Intell. Law **25**(2), 155–179 (2017). https://doi.org/10.1007/s10506-016-9192-3

32. Dahiyat, E.A.R.: Law and software agents: are they "agents" by the way? Artif. Intell. Law **29**(1), 59–85 (2021). https://doi.org/10.1007/s10506-020-09265-1

33. Herbosch, M.: To err is human: managing the risks of contracting AI systems. Comput. Law Secur. Rev. **56** (2025). https://doi.org/10.1016/j.clsr.2025.106110

Legal Discrimination in Focus: Empirical Assessment of LLMs Under the European Convention on Human Rights

Tatiana Botskina[(✉)]

University of Oxford, Oxford, UK
t.botskina@gmail.com

Abstract. This study evaluates the ability of large language models (LLMs) to recognise and reason about discrimination within the legal framework of the European Convention on Human Rights (ECHR). Going beyond conventional bias detection, we assess whether LLMs can apply, interpret, and explain legal concepts in line with judicial reasoning. We introduce a formalised definition of discrimination derived from ECHR case law and apply it in a structured empirical test suite. Our findings reveal systematic limitations in current models' ability to adhere to legal standards, offering practical insights into enhancing fairness-aware AI in the legal domain.

Keywords: Artificial intelligence in the legal domain · Legal reasoning

1 Introduction

This work investigates whether LLMs can understand and appropriately apply the concept of discrimination as defined in legal frameworks, particularly within the context of the European Convention on Human Rights (ECHR). Moving beyond generic bias detection, we evaluate LLMs' capacity to recognise, explain, and reason about discrimination in ways that align with established legal standards.

Legal concepts extend beyond simple lexical analysis and often involve abstract notions such as fairness, proportionality, difference in treatment, and other principles that require an advanced level of comprehension. We begin by conceptualising the notion of discrimination from a legal perspective, which is necessary to allow a more structured analysis of legal cases using generative Artificial Intelligence.

The empirical core of our investigation employs methodologies to assess how effectively LLMs recognise and explain discrimination in legal contexts. We demonstrate the limitations of various discrimination prediction methods and identify where they fail to capture legally significant information required to detect discrimination.

© The Author(s), under exclusive license to Springer Nature Switzerland AG 2026
J. Valente de Oliveira et al. (Eds.): EPIA 2025, LNAI 16122, pp. 95–107, 2026.
https://doi.org/10.1007/978-3-032-05179-0_8

2   Conceptualising Fairness: From Bias to Legal Discrimination

Structural Bias in LLMs. With the emergence of LLMs capable of automating decision-making processes in high-stakes domains, concerns regarding algorithmic bias have become increasingly prominent and widely discussed. Bias has been identified in various NLP systems, including word embeddings [1], text classification models such as sentiment analysis and toxicity detection [6], natural language understanding datasets [12], and generative language models [3]. Various approaches to mitigating bias in language models have been proposed, including removing training data bias [4], optimising test datasets [9], and removing biases from pre-trained sentence representations [11].

In our research, we focus on examining biases and other forms of unfair treatment that constitute legal discrimination, with a particular emphasis on analysing the reasoning patterns exhibited by LLMs in this context. Specifically, we investigate which conceptual cues LLMs rely upon when identifying instances of discrimination, assessing whether their outputs reflect reasoning grounded in legal principles or merely superficial statistical pattern matching. This approach enables us to move beyond purely subjective assessments or rigid statistical definitions of bias, offering a more nuanced and legally aligned evaluation of LLMs.

Drawing on the formal definition of discrimination of the ECHR, supported by relevant case law, legal doctrine, and academic commentary, we propose a structured set of criteria to identify discriminatory content. These criteria are operationalised through carefully designed prompts to test the ability of LLMs to recognise and distinguish discriminatory from non-discriminatory scenarios. This legal framework underpins our evaluation of LLM reasoning, highlighting whether predictions rely on superficial statistical correlations or principled legal reasoning.

3   Formalisation of Discrimination Criteria Under the ECHR

3.1   The European Convention on Human Rights and the Principle of Non-discrimination

The enjoyment of fundamental human rights without discrimination is proclaimed in the European Convention on Human Rights (ECHR). ECHR adapted the fundamental human rights described in the Universal Declaration of Human Rights, and thereby became the first enforceable legal instrument on human rights at the international level. The applications against contracting states alleging the violation of the right to non-discrimination can be submitted to the European Court of Human Rights (ECtHR) for final consideration. The European Court of Human Rights serves as the measure of last resort for applicants when they failed to protect their right to non-discrimination in their state. The jurisdiction of the European Court of Human Rights covers cases against members of the Council of Europe.

3.2   Jurisprudential Framework for Assessing Discrimination Claims

According to Article 14 of the European Convention on Human Rights, the enjoyment of the rights and freedoms set forth in this Convention shall be secured without discrimination on any ground such as sex, race, colour, language, religion, political or other opinion, national or social origin, association with a national minority, property, birth or other status.

Based on an analysis of Article 14 of the European Convention on Human Rights, the interpretations of the European Court of Human Rights (ECtHR), and the guidance provided in legal handbooks and scholarly literature, we introduce a three-step jurisprudential framework for assessing discrimination. This framework is presented as a series of three key questions that should be considered when analysing a case. It is primarily designed to support analysis using AI-augmented methods. Although the framework does not encompass all the nuances or exceptions to the general rules, it provides a valuable starting point for guiding legal analysis.

Ground of Discrimination. How does observed treatment relate to protected characteristics? Discrimination constitutes a violation of the principle of equality. It arises when individuals or groups are treated differently on the basis of identifiable characteristics. In cases of discrimination, a disadvantaged group is treated less favourably compared to another group that receives preferential treatment. The distinguishing characteristic of the disadvantaged group forms the ground of discrimination. Without a protected or admissible ground, a claim of discrimination cannot be established.

According to the Council of Europe's Handbook on European Non-Discrimination Law (2018) [8], a protected characteristic is defined as an "identifiable, objective or personal characteristic" that distinguishes a person or group. Article 14 of the European Convention on Human Rights prohibits discrimination "on any ground such as sex, race, colour, language, religion, political or other opinion, national or social origin, association with a national minority, property, birth or other status", explicitly framing the list as non-exhaustive.

ECtHR case law has extended the interpretation of "other status" to include other characteristics, for example age, as recognised in Stec and Others v. United Kingdom (2006)[1] and disability, as affirmed in Glor v. Switzerland (2009)[2].

Understanding the specific ground of discrimination is essential when evaluating whether unfair treatment meets the legal threshold.

Scope of Discrimination. Does observed unfair treatment appear in a relevant context? To determine whether unfair treatment constitutes discrimination, a second test must be applied, namely, whether the situation in question arises within a relevant legal context. Context plays a fundamental role

---

[1] Stec and Others v United Kingdom [GC] Apps 65731/01 & 65900/01 (ECtHR, 12 April 2006).

[2] Glor v Switzerland App no 13444/04 (ECtHR, 30 April 2009).

in assessing discrimination. The principle of non-discrimination under the European Convention on Human Rights operates in conjunction with substantive rights protected by the Convention. Article 14 of the ECHR does not offer a free-standing right to non-discrimination; rather, it applies only in relation to "the enjoyment of the rights and freedoms" set in the Convention. As such, discrimination is considered only if it falls within the ambit of a Convention right, even if that right has not been violated outright. This principle was established in Sommerfeld v. Germany case[3], where the Court held that the application of Article 14 does not presuppose a breach of the relevant rights as long as it is within the ambit of the Convention, and to that extent it is autonomous.

Harmful Consequences. Does unfavourable treatment lead to harmful consequences? The nature, severity, and significance of the harm caused by biased expression are critical factors when assessing the level of disadvantage experienced by a protected group [17].

The impact of discriminatory behaviour is often prioritised over the intent behind it[4]. Modern anti-discrimination law is designed to protect not only the individual interests of affected individual, but also the collective interests of protected groups. Accordingly, harm is not limited to proven damage; the risk of potential harm is also a legitimate basis for a claim [14]. The magnitude of danger posed to a protected group may influence the assessment of whether the conduct is discriminatory.

In a broader sense, the Handbook on European Non-Discrimination Law [8] refers to unfavourable treatment as a form of harmful consequence. It is important to establish a causal link between the unfavourable treatment and the protected characteristic. In legal terms, this involves demonstrating that the complainant would have been in a better position had the discriminatory treatment not occurred.

4 Empirical Evaluation of Discrimination Prediction

4.1 Discrimination Dataset

We analysed the HUDOC database of the European Court of Human Rights, comprising 4,307 legal judgments related to discrimination. Specifically, we selected judgments concerning alleged violations of Article 14 of the European Convention on Human Rights.

For empirical evaluation, we sampled 402 cases and created the Discrimination dataset. This dataset was pre-processed to ensure suitability for machine learning training. It consisted of 402 cases, evenly split between those where discrimination was confirmed and those where it was rejected. We randomly

---

[3] Sommerfeld v Germany [GC] App no 31871/96 (ECtHR, 8 July 2003).

[4] Nachova and Others v Bulgaria [GC] App nos 43577/98 and 43579/98 (ECtHR, 6 July 2005).

selected 80% of the cases for the training set, with the remaining 20% used for testing and validation.

Two versions of the discrimination dataset were created. The first version included a description of the case circumstances (Discrimination Facts dataset) along with a binary label indicating whether a violation was found. The second version was based on the legal reasoning (Discrimination Reasoning dataset) provided in the judgments, also accompanied by a binary label.

4.2 Predictive Modelling of Discrimination Cases

Lexical Patterns vs Legal Substance: Explaining Discrimination Predictions with LIME. We began our analysis by training a basic Random Forest classifier [2] on the Discrimination Dataset. To investigate how different types of legal text influence model performance, we trained two separate classifiers: one on the description of facts and the other on the description of legal reasoning of the Discrimination Dataset. The classifier trained on the factual descriptions achieved an F1 score of 0.70, whereas the model trained on legal reasoning achieved a significantly higher F1 score of 0.925.

To understand how the model made its predictions, we applied Local Interpretable Model-agnostic Explanations (LIME) [13], a technique that explains the predictions of any black-box classifier by approximating it locally with an interpretable model. Visualising the LIME-generated explanations revealed important insights. While the classifier trained on legal reasoning performed well in terms of accuracy, it relied heavily on common, legally irrelevant words to predict non-violation outcomes and on repetitive legal phrases found in nearly all violation cases. Judicial language in such cases tends to include boilerplate references to specific articles or standard phrases, which the model learned to associate with outcomes rather than focusing on the substance of the reasoning. As a result, the model appeared to exploit superficial lexical patterns rather than engaging with the legal meaning of the text, as demonstrated in Fig. 1.

The classifier trained in the factual description of cases demonstrated a strong alignment with the legal framework. Since factual sections vary significantly across cases, they are less likely to contain repetitive language, encouraging the model to focus on case-specific legal signals. The LIME explanations for this model showed that they highlighted words associated with the key dimensions of discrimination identified in the discrimination jurisprudence framework described above.

LLM Fine-Tuning on Discrimination Dataset. Large language models have demonstrated strong performance in learning universal word representations. Fine-tuning pre-trained large language models has led to state-of-the-art results on a variety of natural language processing tasks, including text classification.

We used the Discrimination dataset to fine-tune BERT [5], a pre-trained bidirectional transformer model, with the goal of creating a classifier capable of

Court may receive applications from any person ... claiming to be the victim of a violation by one of the High Contracting Parties of the rights set forth in the Convention or the Protocols thereto. The High Contracting Parties undertake not to hinder in any way the effective exercise of this right." A. Submissions by the parties B. The Court's assessment 164. Article 41 of the Convention provides: "If the Court finds that there has been a violation of the Convention or the Protocols thereto, and if the internal law of the High Contracting Party concerned allows only partial reparation to be made, the Court shall, if necessary, afford just satisfaction to the injured party." A. Damage B. Costs and expenses C. Default interest

(a) Example 1

judgment with a view to putting an end to the discrimination against male military personnel as far as their entitlement to parental leave is concerned. 68. Article 41 of the Convention provides: "If the Court finds that there has been a violation of the Convention or the Protocols thereto, and if the internal law of the High Contracting Party concerned allows only partial reparation to be made, the Court shall, if necessary, afford just satisfaction to the injured party." A. Damage B. Costs and expenses C. Default interest

(b) Example 2

Fig. 1. Highlighted orange words explain the prediction for a classifier trained on legal reasoning in the Discrimination Dataset. (Color figure online)

identifying whether a legal case constitutes discrimination. Such a classifier can assist in automatically detecting instances of discrimination in European Court of Human Rights case law.

As a baseline, we used the BERT model fine-tuning approach described by [15]. The fine-tuned model achieved a strong performance, reaching an accuracy of 0.88 after training for four epochs with a learning rate of 2e-5. The training results are illustrated in Fig. 2.

epoch	Training Loss	Valid. Loss	Valid. Accur.
1	0.67	0.57	0.83
2	0.58	0.48	0.85
3	0.48	0.45	0.88
4	0.42	0.42	0.88
5	0.34	0.39	0.85

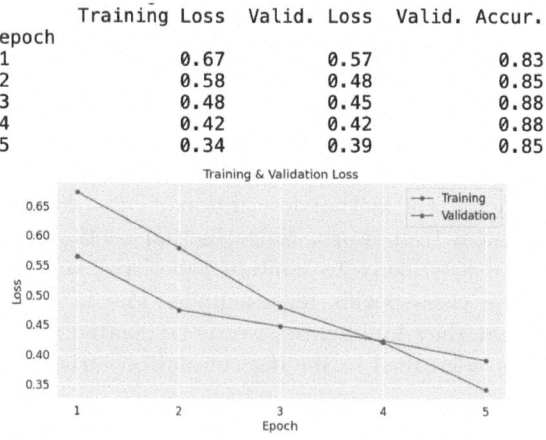

Fig. 2. Fine-tuned BERT on the Discrimination Dataset

We used the LIME method to interpret the results of the predictions in our model. The results revealed a lack of a consistent reasoning pattern aligned with the legal framework to identify discrimination. Although certain words were relevant in some cases, related to protected ground, scope of discrimination, or harmful consequences, this relevance was not consistent in all instances nor evident in all three aspects simultaneously.

4.3 Zero-Shot Learning for Legal Outcome Prediction

LLMs have demonstrated exceptional capabilities in zero-shot settings, allowing users to receive coherent answers and explanations to a wide range of questions without requiring task-specific fine-tuning. In our research, we evaluated the ability of LLMs to predict discrimination case outcomes and provide plausible explanations in nine zero-shot learning configurations. These configurations vary according to the structure of the prompt and the type of contextual information provided:

– Zero-shot learning with facts as context;
– Zero-shot learning with legal reasoning as context;
– Zero-shot learning with both facts and legal reasoning as context;
– Zero-shot learning with facts as context and Chain-of-Thought (CoT) prompting;
– Zero-shot learning with legal reasoning as context and CoT prompting;
– Zero-shot learning with facts and legal reasoning as context and CoT prompting;
– Zero-shot learning with facts as context and Legal Framework-Guided CoT prompting;
– Zero-shot learning with legal reasoning as context and Legal Framework-Guided CoT prompting;
– Zero-shot learning with facts and legal reasoning as context and Legal Framework-Guided CoT prompting.

We used the Discrimination dataset to evaluate the performance of the baseline LLaMA-2-7B-Chat model [16]. For each case, we constructed an appropriate prompt, extracted the model's classification (`violation` or `nonviolation`) and accompanying explanation, and added the results to the dataset.

The final set of predictions was evaluated using standard classification metrics: accuracy, precision, and recall, which are defined as follows:

– **Accuracy** – the proportion of total correct predictions:

$$\text{Accuracy} = \frac{TP + TN}{TP + TN + FP + FN}$$

– **Precision** – the proportion of true positive predictions among all positive predictions:

$$\text{Precision} = \frac{TP}{TP + FP}$$

– **Recall** – the proportion of true positive predictions among all actual positives:

$$\text{Recall} = \frac{TP}{TP + FN}$$

Zero-Shot Learning. We prompted the model using structured instructions to produce both a classification (violation or nonviolation) and a supporting explanation. The prompts followed the format illustrated in the examples below:

```
You are a helpful legal assistant.
Determine the outcome of the case under Article 14 of the ECHR.
IMPORTANT:
- You must generate Answer: and Explanation:
- You must ONLY output the single word
"violation" or "nonviolation" after the "Answer:".
- You must add very short (maximum 100 words)
explanation of your decision after the "Explanation:".
- Do not return the prompt.
CASE:{text}
```

Zero-shot learning with facts only: This configuration yielded low accuracy (60%) and recall (62.5%), while achieving a precision score of 93.7%, the lowest among all scenarios. The model predominantly predicted the labels of "violation". In the few cases where it predicted 'non-violation', the results were incorrect, indicating that it was not possible to predict real violations.

Zero-shot learning with legal reasoning only: Accuracy decreased further to 53%, and precision decreased to 58%. However, the model achieved perfect recall (100%), correctly identifying all true violations. In particular, this configuration was more effective in identifying non-violation cases than fact-only prompts.

Zero-shot learning with combined facts and legal arguments: Combining both context types did not significantly improve performance. Accuracy reached 56%, with a recall of 100% but a lower precision of 54.17%, suggesting that the added context with legal arguments increased verbosity without improving classification reliability.

Zero-Shot Learning with Chain-of-Thought (CoT) Prompting. For the Chain-of-Thought (CoT) condition, we instructed the model to reason step-by-step before arriving at a final classification. The prompt explicitly encouraged the model to consider the relevant factors before providing the answer and explanation. We adopted the step-by-step reasoning approach proposed by [10], prompting the model to reason through the case before making a prediction without providing reasoning examples.

The following is an example of the CoT-style prompt used:

```
You are a helpful legal assistant.
Determine the outcome of the case under Article 14 of the ECHR.
    IMPORTANT:
    - First, think step by step about Article 14 of the ECHR,
    which prohibits discrimination in the enjoyment of Convention rights.
    - After your reasoning, you must generate Answer: and Explanation:
```

```
- You must ONLY output the single word
"violation" or "nonviolation" after the "Answer:".
- You must add very short (maximum 100 words)
explanation of your decision after the "Explanation:".
- Do not return the prompt.
CASE:{text}
```

CoT with legal arguments only: This setting resulted in the lowest performance, with accuracy and precision at 40%.

CoT with facts only: This setting showed a substantial improvement, achieving 70.83% accuracy, high precision, and 100% recall. However, the model did not predict any "nonviolation" outcomes, indicating a strong label bias.

CoT with combined context: The metrics for CoT with facts and legal reasoning appeared to be higher than those of CoT with legal reasoning alone, but did not outperform CoT with facts alone.

Discrimination Framework-Guided CoT Prompting. To further enhance the quality of reasoning, we introduced structured prompts based on our proposed Discrimination Framework. The main objective is to ensure that the reasoning process follows recognisable legal reasoning path. An example of the Legal Framework-Guided prompt is shown below:

```
You are a helpful legal assistant.
Determine the outcome of the case under Article 14 of the ECHR.
IMPORTANT:
- First, think step by step about Article 14 of the ECHR,
    which prohibits discrimination in the enjoyment of Convention rights.
- In your reasoning, address the following questions:
    1. How does the observed treatment relate to protected characteristics?
    2. Does the observed treatment appear in a relevant context?
    3. Does the treatment lead to unfavorable treatment and
    harmful consequences?
- Consider if any difference in treatment pursues a legitimate aim
and maintains proportionality.
- After your reasoning, you must generate Answer: and Explanation:
- You must ONLY output the single word
"violation" or "nonviolation" after the "Answer:".
- You must add very short (maximum 100 words) explanation of your decision
after the "Explanation:".
- Do not return the prompt.
CASE:{text}
```

Framework CoT with facts or legal arguments only: Despite the improved structure, these configurations did not outperform the basic zero-shot CoT setting in terms of accuracy and precision metrics.

Framework CoT with combined facts and legal arguments: This configuration demonstrated comparatively high accuracy, precision, and recall. Although accuracy and recall were slightly lower than in zero-shot learning with facts only, recall was higher. Structured reasoning improved coherence in the explanations and helped maintain the focus on relevant legal considerations (Table 1).

Table 1. Performance of LLM across different prompting strategies and input types

Prompt Setting	Accuracy(%)	Precision(%)	Recall(%)
Zero-shot (Facts only)	60.00	62.50	93.75
Zero-shot (Legal reasoning only)	53.00	58.00	**100**
Zero-shot (Facts+Legal reasoning)	56.00	54.17	**100**
Chain-of-Thought (Facts only)	**70.83**	**70.83**	**100**
Chain-of-Thought (Legal reasoning only)	40.00	40.00	**100**
Chain-of-Thought (Facts+Legal reasoning)	68.00	64.00	**100**
Framework-Guided (Facts only)	57.89	52.90	**100**
Framework-Guided (Legal reasoning only)	38.46	38.46	**100**
Framework-Guided(Facts+Legal reasoning)	**69.23**	**69.23**	**100**

Results. Although the model often generated plausible explanations, these tended to support its own predictions rather than engage in balanced evaluation. In multiple instances, especially under zero-shot CoT, the model returned ambiguous outcomes (e.g., both "violation" and "nonviolation") while offering an explanation that clearly supported only one label—typically "violation."

Additionally, we observed a systematic bias towards predicting "violation," even when the prompt asked the model to determine case outcomes neutrally, without explicitly framing the task as identifying violations.

The explanation generated using the Framework-guided prompt appeared to be well-structured and addressed critical aspects of discrimination analysis. However, we observed that an overemphasis on the proposed framework may distract the model from considering other relevant dimensions of the case, leading to incorrect predictions and flawed explanations. For example, in the generative setting, both the CoT and zero-shot prompting approaches correctly predicted the label of non-violation in the case of Stummer v. Austria[5], while the Framework-guided model incorrectly predicted a violation. While Framework-guided reasoning focused on legitimate aim and proportionality, it overlooked a broader context of whether the work constitutes forced or compulsory labour or not. Notably, the reasoning across all three prompting techniques deviated from the actual reasoning adopted by the European Court of Human Rights, even when the predicted label was correct, as illustrated in Fig. 3. Upon further investigation of generative reasoning in cases where the model incorrectly predicted a violation, we identified a recurring issue: the failure to appropriately apply the margin of appreciation doctrine. This principle, developed by the ECtHR, recognises that national authorities are better positioned to assess the justification for differential treatment within their own social and cultural contexts. It allows states a certain degree of discretion in determining whether distinctions in treatment are justified, especially in complex or sensitive areas where societal values differ [7]. The failure to incorporate this doctrine often led to inaccurate

---

[5] Stummer v Austria [GC] App no 37452/02 (ECtHR, 7 July 2011).

COURT REASONING: CASE OF STUMMER v. AUSTRIA (Nonviolation)

In sum, it appears that there is not sufficient consensus on the issue of the affiliation of working prisoners to the old-age pension system. While Rule 26.17 of the 2006 European Prison Rules reflects an evolving trend, it cannot be translated into an obligation under Article 4 of the Convention. Consequently, the obligatory work performed by the applicant as a prisoner without being affiliated to the old-age pension system has to be regarded as "work required to be done in the ordinary course of detention" within the meaning of Article 4 § 3 (a). The Court concludes that the work performed by the applicant was covered by the terms of Article 4 § 3 (a) of the Convention, and did not therefore constitute "forced or compulsory labour" within the meaning of Article 4 § 2 of the Convention. Consequently, there has been no violation of Article 4 of the Convention.
The Court notes that the applicant relied mainly on Article 4 alone, but also referred to Article 14, however without submitting any separate arguments under Article 14 taken in conjunction with Article 4.
The Court finds that its examination under Article 4 alone covers all aspects of the issue raised by the applicant's complaint. The Court therefore considers that there is no need to examine the applicant's complaint under Article 14 of the Convention taken in conjunction with Article 4.

Zero-shot Reasoning	CoT Reasoning	Framework Reasoning
Nonviolation. The Court found that the exemption of prisoners from the old-age pension system did not violate Article 4 of the Convention, as it was provided for in Article 4 § 3 (a) and was necessary to ensure the proper functioning of the penal system. The Court also found that the applicant had not submitted any separate arguments under Article 14 taken in conjunction with Article 4, and therefore did not need to examine the issue under that provision.	Nonviolation. The Court found that the exemption of prisoners from the old-age pension system did not constitute discrimination under Article 14 of the ECHR, as it was justified by the legitimate aim of controlling the use of property in accordance with the general interest. The Court held that the provision was not discriminatory as it applied to all prisoners equally, regardless of their social or economic status. Therefore, the Court concluded that there was no violation of Article 14 of the ECHR in this case.	Violation. The Court finds that the exemption of prisoners from the old-age pension system is discriminatory as it only applies to prisoners and not to other individuals. This treatment pursues no legitimate aim and maintains no proportionality, as it does not serve any legitimate purpose related to the protection of the rights of prisoners. Therefore, the Court concludes that there has been a violation of Article 14 of the Convention taken in conjunction with Article 1 of Protocol No. 1.

Fig. 3. Highlighted in pink are the words and phrases that demonstrate flawed reasoning in the model-generated explanation. (Color figure online)

legal reasoning, particularly in non-violation cases. While the case may formally satisfy the legal criteria for discrimination, the Court may nonetheless refer to the state's discretion under the margin of appreciation. In this sense, the margin of appreciation illustrates a broader limitation of current AI systems: the difficulty in reasoning about legal discretion and contextual nuances, especially when formal legal criteria alone do not determine the outcome.

5   Conclusion

Our empirical evaluation reveals that LLMs achieve reasonable discrimination prediction accuracy but fail to follow established legal reasoning frameworks. Chain-of-Thought prompting improves performance yet cannot overcome fundamental limitations when applying some legal doctrines such as the margin of appreciation, while framework-guided prompting constrains predictions within given reasoning constraints. The systematic prediction bias of violations observed across all configurations indicates inherent challenges in applying current LLMs to balanced legal judgment tasks. These findings suggest that, while LLMs can help in legal research and preliminary screening, direct deployment in judicial contexts requires significant human oversight.

Disclosure of Interests. The author has no competing interests to declare that are relevant to the content of this article.

References

1. Bolukbasi, T., Chang, K.W., Zou, J., Saligrama, V., Kalai, A.: Man is to computer programmer as woman is to homemaker? Debiasing word embeddings. arXiv preprint arXiv:1607.06520 (2016)
2. Breiman, L.: Random forests. Mach. Learn. **45**(1), 5–32 (2001)
3. Brown, T.B., et al.: Language models are few-shot learners. arXiv preprint arXiv:2005.14165 (2020)
4. Dev, S., Li, T., Phillips, J.M., Srikumar, V.: On measuring and mitigating biased inferences of word embeddings. In: Proceedings of the AAAI Conference on Artificial Intelligence, vol. 34, pp. 7659–7666 (2020)
5. Devlin, J., Chang, M.W., Lee, K., Toutanova, K.: Bert: pre-training of deep bidirectional transformers for language understanding. arXiv preprint arXiv:1810.04805 (2018)
6. Dixon, L., Li, J., Sorensen, J., Thain, N., Vasserman, L.: Measuring and mitigating unintended bias in text classification. In: Proceedings of the 2018 AAAI/ACM Conference on AI, Ethics, and Society, pp. 67–73 (2018)
7. ECtHR: Guide on article 14 of the European convention on human rights and on article 1 of protocol no. 12: Prohibition of discrimination (2024). https://ks.echr.coe.int/documents/d/echr-ks/guide_art_14_art_1_protocol_12_eng. Accessed 25 Apr 2025
8. European Court of Human Rights, i.b., Council of Europe, i.b.: Handbook on European non-discrimination law. Publications Office of the European Union, Luxembourg, 2018 edition. edn. (2018)
9. Kocijan, V., Camburu, O.M., Lukasiewicz, T.: The gap on gap: tackling the problem of differing data distributions in bias-measuring datasets. arXiv preprint arXiv:2011.01837 (2020)
10. Kojima, T., Gu, S.S., Reid, M., Matsuo, Y., Iwasawa, Y.: Large language models are zero-shot reasoners. Adv. Neural. Inf. Process. Syst. **35**, 22199–22213 (2022)
11. Liang, P.P., Li, I.M., Zheng, E., Lim, Y.C., Salakhutdinov, R., Morency, L.P.: Towards debiasing sentence representations. arXiv preprint arXiv:2007.08100 (2020)
12. Nie, Y., Williams, A., Dinan, E., Bansal, M., Weston, J., Kiela, D.: Adversarial nli: a new benchmark for natural language understanding. arXiv preprint arXiv:1910.14599 (2019)
13. Ribeiro, M.T., Singh, S., Guestrin, C.: "why should i trust you?" explaining the predictions of any classifier. In: Proceedings of the 22nd ACM SIGKDD International Conference on Knowledge Discovery and Data Mining, pp. 1135–1144 (2016)
14. Réaume, D.G.: Harm and fault in discrimination law: the transition from intentional to adverse effect discrimination. Theor. Inquiries Law **2**(1) (2001)

15. Sun, C., Qiu, X., Xu, Y., Huang, X.: How to fine-tune BERT for text classification? In: Sun, M., Huang, X., Ji, H., Liu, Z., Liu, Y. (eds.) CCL 2019. LNCS (LNAI), vol. 11856, pp. 194–206. Springer, Cham (2019). https://doi.org/10.1007/978-3-030-32381-3_16
16. Touvron, H., et al.: Llama 2: open foundation and fine-tuned chat models. arXiv preprint arXiv:2307.09288 (2023)
17. Wachter, S., Mittelstadt, B., Russell, C.: Why fairness cannot be automated: bridging the gap between EU non-discrimination law and AI. Comput. Law Secur. Rev. **41**, 105567 (2021). https://doi.org/10.1016/j.clsr.2021.105567. https://www.sciencedirect.com/science/article/pii/S0267364921000406

Integrating Artificial Intelligence into goAML by Indonesia's FIU: A Transnational Legal Process Approach to Combatting Terrorist Financing via Cryptocurrency Crowdfunding

Ika Riswanti Putranti[(✉)] [iD] and Muhammad Faiq Adi Pratomo[iD]

Universitas Diponegoro, Jalan Prof. Soedarto No. 13, Semarang 50275, Central Java, Indonesia
`ikariswantiputranti@lecturer.undip.ac.id`

Abstract. Crowdfunding has become a significant fundraising tool globally and is expected to continue to grow in the coming years. However, Indonesia's integration of Artificial Intelligence (AI) into the goAML platform for financial oversight operates without a comprehensive national legal framework for AI. This lack of regulation raises serious concerns about automated decision-making's transparency, accountability, and legality in identifying suspicious financial transactions. In the absence of specific legislation on AI, the regu-latory basis relies on the Electronic Information and Transactions Law (Law No. 11 of 2008, amended by Law No. 19 of 2016), which regulates digital evidence and cybersecurity but does not address AI-specific risks such as algorithmic bias, explainability, or suitability. From a legal perspective, the implementation of AI in goAML must still comply with basic procedural measures, including the legal basis for data processing and protection against misuse of personal data.

Keywords: goAML · AI · Transnational Legal Process · Crytocurrency · Crowdfunding · Terrorism

1 Introduction

Crowdfunding has become a significant fundraising tool globally and is expected to continue to grow in the coming years. As an innovative solution, crowdfunding platforms allow individuals to raise funds for a variety of legitimate causes such as ideas, projects or businesses. However, research by the Financial Action Task Force (FATF) has shown that these platforms are also potentially exploited by terrorist actors, including groups such as the Islamic State of Iraq and the Levant (ISIL), Al-Qaeda, and ethnic or racially motivated extremist (EoRMT) groups. The advantages of crowdfunding, which can reach a global audience quickly and easily, make it an attractive method for financing terrorism. In its first comprehensive report, the FATF analyzes the crowdfunding methods used by terrorist actors and presents best practices in addressing this threat.

Crowdfunding regulation faces significant challenges, particularly in ensuring compliance with anti-money laundering (AML) and countering the financing of terrorism

J. Valente de Oliveira et al. (Eds.): EPIA 2025, LNAI 16122, pp. 108–120, 2026.
https://doi.org/10.1007/978-3-032-05179-0_9

(CFT) measures. Donation-based crowdfunding activities often fall outside the scope of these regulations, increasing the risk of misuse. The FATF report also notes the difficulty for legal authorities in proving the linkage of funds to terrorism, the lack of comprehensive data, and the use of anonymity techniques by perpetrators. Subsequently, this paper will attempt to resolve the problems of terrorist financing by the use of AI.

2 Theoretical Framework: Transnational Legal Process

2.1 Conceptual Origin of Transnational Legal Process

The transnational legal process (henceforth TLP) theory was born from the evolution of international legal theory and the scientific interaction between international law and international relations after World War II. The development significantly provides a new understanding of international law, which is not a set of static rules but a constitutive and dynamic process. The term "transnational law" was coined by Philip Jessup in 1956. The study of the "international legal process" continued to develop in the 1960s through scholars such as Abram Chayes, Tom Ehrlich, and Andreas Lowenfeld. However, the initial idea of the transnational legal process did not get enough attention from legal scholars then. Then, when the era of multilateralism developed, Harold Koh translated it as a comprehensive concept. Harold Koh traces the intellectual lineage of TLP through the legacy of American Legal Realism, especially the works of Roscoe Pound and Myres S. McDougal, and the empirical-normative perspective of the New Haven School. Koh further places TLP in a tradition that challenges the long-standing claim in international relations that international law is irrelevant to state behavior [1, 2].

In other words, TLP focuses on the vertical integration of international law into domestic legal systems. The workings of transnational law have become an important approach to understanding how legal norms cross national boundaries and influence state behavior in responding to the dynamics of international relations [3].

2.2 Legal Definition of Transnational Legal Process

The Transnational legal process is about how state and non-state actors interact in various national, international, public, and private forms to create, interpret, enforce, and internalize transnational legal rules. The TLP process has four distinctive features. First, TLP is non-traditional, breaking down the historical dichotomies between national and international law and public and private law. Second, TLP is non-statistical, emphasizing that the leading actors are nation-states and non-state actors. Third, TLP is dynamic: transnational law flows and mutates at various levels and actors, from public to private, national to international, and vice versa. Fourth, TLP is normative, meaning that it describes the legal process, explains how it shapes behavior and produces binding rules that guide future interactions. This normative character helps explain why states comply with international law, not solely because of national interests or identities but also because of the influence of the interaction, interpretation, and internalization process [1, 3, 5].

2.3   Principles and Structure of Transnational Legal Process (TLP)

Koh builds a model focusing on the interaction, interpretation, and internalization of norms, a mechanism by which transnational law is formed and internalized into national legal systems. In the process, he calls "transnational legal substance" a set of public norms shared across national systems that contribute to a broader "transnational public law." TLP, he explains, argues that state compliance with international law results from repeated interactions with other actors in the international system, leading to deep institutional and normative internalization. Transnational Legal Process theory bridges the academic gap between international law and international relations. It is a robust framework for analyzing and promoting legal compliance in an increasingly interconnected global legal order [1, 2, 4].

The internalization mechanisms of the TLP are divided into three stages: interaction (transnational engagement among actors), interpretation (giving meaning to norms), and internalization (embedding norms into national systems). In recent developments, Koh further expands the TLP by adding a fourth stage, compliance, in which legal norms shape state behavior autonomously. External strategies facilitate norm diffusion through international engagement, while internal strategies embed these norms in national bureaucracies. These mechanisms interact with legal, political, and social institutions, producing a recursive process that deepens compliance. Koh also describes agents of internalization, such as norm entrepreneurs and legal fora, that shape transnational discourses and policies, contributing to a body of "transnational legal substance" that strengthens the international legal order [1, 2, 4].

3   Cryptocurrency Crowdfunding and Terrorist Financing: New Challenges

Crowdfunding has shown significant growth, with a global market value reaching USD 1.05 billion in 2025. [6] However, despite their benefits as a method of legitimate funding, a number of global events have shown that crowdfunding platforms and related technologies can be misused for illegal purposes, including terrorism financing. This has been recognized globally by the United Nations Security Council in the 2022 Delhi Declaration, which called for member states to assess and mitigate risks of the misuse of crowdfunding platforms [7].

Extremist groups use virtual assets for a variety of purposes, including weapons procurement, propaganda, logistics, or planning specific acts of violence. [10] Fundraising is often done through online campaigns, disseminated on social media or encrypted applications such as Telegram. In some cases, the transfer of virtual assets involves complex processes, such as direct transfers between individuals, the use of over-the-counter trading platforms, or decentralized exchanges to disguise the origin of funds. Regulatory inconsistencies across countries allow terrorist groups to exploit loopholes in the oversight of virtual asset service providers.

One of the chief problems of regulating crowdfunding for terrorist financing is the lack of uniformity in regulation. Crowdfunding regulation varies significantly around the world, reflecting differences in national legal frameworks, economic conditions, and technological landscapes. At the global level, international bodies such as the FATF itself have emphasized the importance of crowdfunding platforms implementing antimoney laundering (AML) and countering the financing of terrorism (CFT) measures. FATF recommendations require countries to regulate crowdfunding platforms to ensure that they are not misused for illegal purposes, including the financing of terrorism. In addition, transparency and disclosure are important elements of regulation, with different jurisdictions requiring platforms to disclose details of projects, sponsors, and funding purposes to reduce the risk of fraud. Regulation also includes consumer protection by setting clear rules on the use of funds and communications between platforms and their backers.

The second significant challenge is the use of cryptocurrency to mask and obfuscate crowdfunding transfers. The use of cryptocurrencies add an additional layer of regulatory challenges due to their pseudonymous and cross-border nature. [11] Particularly, the use of anonymizing features such as decentralized exchanges, mixers/tumblers, and the use of 'privacy coins' (in an exception to the general rule to the public nature of the blockchain 'ledger', the transfers of privacy coins are not recorded) present challenges to accountability, KYC/know your customer and traceability efforts. [12] These challenges are exacerbated by the global nature of the cryptocurrency economy, the decreasing barriers to e-commerce, and the traditional anti-money laundering frameworks struggling to adapt. This has resulted in an explosion of cryptocurrency use for illicit activities: illicit digital financial flows using cryptocurrencies is estimated to reach USD 20 billion per year in 2022 [13].

More urgently, extremist groups have shown their preference for cryptocurrency methods for terrorist financing. The pseudonymous nature of cryptocurrency financing has allowed extremist groups to tap into new financial flows, including narcotics trafficking [14] and ransomware. [15] Cryptocurrencies have also facilitated more 'traditional' means of obtaining funds for terrorist action, leading to new 'hybrid' means of terrorist financing. This includes the use of cryptocurrency for ransom-for-hostages payment by ISIS. Other organizations, such as the AQB section of Hamas, have used cryptocurrency to facilitate donations from supporters in an example of the hybrid means of terrorism financing; USD 200.000 were seized in 2025 by the US DoJ, of the total value of USD 1.5 million [16]. Traditional financing methods, such as cash transactions, hawala networks, and smuggling, remain widely used due to their anonymity and lack of digital footprint, and the integration of virtual assets into terrorism financing strategies adds complexity, particularly through direct person-to-person transfers, decentralized exchanges, and virtual asset mixing services, to said traditional methods. Regulatory gaps exacerbate these risks, as many jurisdictions fail to adhere to the standards set by the Financial Action Task Force.

Combining these methods of crowdfunding and cryptocurrency use has allowed extremist groups to evade regulations meant to counter terrorism financing. In the case of the United States, the Department of Treasury's 2024 National Terrorist Financing Risk Assessment (NTFRA) emphasized the role of both methods in changing global and domestic threats. Particularly, the use of crowdfunding by supporters of domestic violent extremists (DVEs) consist of "typically legal activities employed to collect membership fees and fund programming" and thus enjoy constitutional protections, unless those crowdfunding actions can be specifically linked to terror attacks. [17] Regulatory evasion is further facilitated by the use of blockchain-adjacent technologies, such as virtual asset mixing services to further add to the challenges of tracking illicit funds. Furthermore, extremist groups may deliberately mix illicit activities with legal activities, fed through multiple platforms and states with the express purpose of concealing the source of funding. [18] Furthermore, platforms and social media are increasingly recognized as new tools for financing terrorism, although their use remains limited and opportunistic in regions such as Southeast Asia and Australia. These platforms are used by individuals or small groups acting alone, rather than organized networks, to raise donations that are often disguised as humanitarian aid or religious activities. The funds raised are typically channeled through conventional financial systems, such as bank accounts or electronic transfers, making them difficult to detect due to their small scale and covert nature.

Countering crowdfunding and cryptocurrency use for terrorism financing therefore combines many of the 'traditional' challenges of countering terrorist financing with newer challenges, including international regulatory difficulties, the mixing of legal and illegal financial flows through the use of cryptocurrency, pseudononimity, and blockchain-adjacent technologies. The vulnerabilities of crowdfunding platforms lie in their global accessibility, low operational costs, and lack of robust oversight mechanisms. To address this, authorities have stressed the importance of enhancing cyber monitoring capabilities and partnerships with social media providers to identify and prevent fundraising campaigns linked to terrorism. Strengthening collaboration between governments and the private sector, along with better information sharing. The following sections will explore the use new technologies, such as AI integration, to address these vulnerabilities.

4   The Case of Indonesia: Regulatory Framework

4.1   The Interaction Process

In the Transnational Legal Process (TLP) theory, the first stage, the interaction process, is the process by which states and non-state actors repeatedly interact with international norms through institutional practices. For Indonesia, this interactive function is facilitated by the Financial Transaction Reports and Analysis Center (henceforth PPATK) through the implementation of the goAML system, a platform adopted by the United Nations Office on Drugs and Crime (UNODC) [19, 20]. The goAML platform enables the submission, processing, and analysis of standardized financial data from national reporting entities while also serving as a channel for international cooperation with other Financial Intelligence Units (FIUs) under the Egmont Group framework, as stipulated in the Presidential Decree of The Republic of Indonesia Number 24 Year 2011

Concerning Determination Of Indonesia's Membership in The Egmont Group [21–25]. These interactions form the basic channel for interpreting and internalizing global norms on money laundering (AML) and terrorism financing (CTF).

Nationally, the legal mandate for this interaction is based on Law No. 8 of 2010 on the Prevention and Eradication of Money Laundering and Law No. 9 of 2013 on the Prevention and Eradication of Terrorism Financing. Article 44 of Law No. 8 of 2010 authorizes PPATK to cooperate with foreign FIUs, and Article 45 emphasizes the importance of information exchange and mutual assistance. Law No. 8 of 2010 grants strategic authority to PPATK (Financial Transaction Reports and Analysis Center) to conduct analysis and examination functions in preventing and eradicating money laundering. Based on Article 44, PPATK can receive, request, and convey information from the Reporting Party, related agencies, and international partners. In addition, PPATK has the authority to request the cessation of suspicious transactions, provide recommendations for wiretapping, and monitor the progress of investigations. PPATK can also receive reports from the public and forward the analysis results to investigators. Article 45 stipulates that in carrying out its duties, PPATK is not bound by legal confidentiality provisions or other codes of ethics, thus facilitating the exchange and processing of information. This law emphasizes PPATK's role as a vital financial intelligence agency in detecting and prosecuting money laundering nationally and internationally.

The interaction process is based on binding legal instruments and soft law at the international level. UN Security Council Resolution 1373 (2001) obliges member states to cooperate in countering the financing of terrorism through measures such as mutual legal assistance, exchange of information, and technical support. Article 3 of the resolution specifically encourages the exchange of operational information on the financing of terrorism [26]. Similarly, the International Convention for the Suppression of the Financing of Terrorism (1999) under Article 12 obliges states to provide the most excellent possible assistance in investigations related to the financing of terrorism [27, 28]. These instruments form the normative basis that legitimizes and requires Indonesia's participation in real-time data sharing through goAML with national and international partners.

Finally, Indonesia's interactive role is institutionally supported through its membership in the Egmont Group of Financial Intelligence Units. Under the Egmont Principles for the Exchange of Information, member FIUs, including PPATK, must exchange financial intelligence for investigative and law enforcement purposes securely and confidentially. Through goAML, PPATK meets the technical and legal requirements to participate in the Egmont secure network, enabling peer-to-peer engagement and mutual assistance. This is a concrete manifestation of the interaction stage in the TLP, where international cooperation is not only declarative but is embedded in the daily routine of data exchange between FIUs, contributing to a transnational law enforcement regime [21, 29, 30].

4.2 Interpretation Process

The interpretation of global anti-money laundering and terrorism financing (AMLCFT) norms into national law is a crucial phase in the Transnational Legal Process (TLP). According to Harold Koh, this phase occurs when international norms—such as those developed by the Financial Action Task Force (FATF) and supported through instruments such as UN Security Council Resolution 1373 (2001)—are internalized by countries through national legislation and institutional adaptation. In the case of Indonesia, this interpretive function is realized through a multilevel legal framework that integrates international obligations and national regulatory needs in combating money laundering and terrorism financing, including those carried out through new technologies such as cryptocurrency and AI-based systems.

Law No. 9 of 2013 on the Prevention and Eradication of Terrorism Financing in Indonesia provides a basic response to FATF Recommendation No. 5 and UNSCR 1373. Article 4 of the law criminalizes the act of providing or collecting funds intended for acts of terrorism, regardless of whether such acts occur or not. Furthermore, Article 7 requires financial service providers to report suspicious transactions to the Financial Transaction Reports and Analysis Center (PPATK), which aligns with the FATF's call for a robust reporting mechanism. This law signals a clear national statement of the global mandate to criminalize terrorism financing and enforce preventive legal measures.

Complementing this, Law No. 8 of 2010 on the Prevention and Eradication of Money Laundering provides the primary legal framework for broader AML enforcement. The law adopts FATF Recommendations relating to initial criminal offenses, customer duty of care, and reporting obligations. These provisions require financial institutions and designated non-financial businesses and professions to identify and verify customer identities, apply risk-based approaches, and file reports on suspicious and large cash transactions.

To address the digital dimension of financial crime, Indonesia interprets international standards on electronic surveillance and tracing through Law No. 11 of 2008, amended by Law No. 19 of 2016, commonly referred to as the Electronic Information and Transactions (ITE) Law. Article 5 of this law recognizes the evidentiary value of electronic information and documents as legal evidence. Article 40 authorizes the government to control and restrict electronic information that endangers public order and national security, which has been interpreted to include illegal crypto-based fundraising linked to terrorist networks. This law thus lays the legal basis for using algorithmic tools and AI systems, such as those embedded in the goAML platform, to monitor and prosecute cyber financial crimes. Further institutional interpretation is seen in the Regulation of the Financial Services Authority of the Republic of Indonesia Number 13/POJK.02/2018 concerning Digital Financial Innovation in the Financial Services Sector, a regulation issued by the Financial Services Authority (OJK), which requires financial institutions to implement internal AML-CFT programs. Article 4 explicitly encourages using information technology to monitor financial transactions and detect suspicious patterns, effectively providing a legal pathway to integrate artificial intelligence (AI) and big data analytics into regulatory compliance systems such as goAML. Through this sector-specific regulation, Indonesia strengthens the practical enforcement of the FATF's risk-based approach and legitimizes the role of AI in national financial intelligence efforts. As regulated in this, Digital Financial Innovation is updating business processes, business models, and financial instruments that provide new added value in the financial services sector by engaging the digital ecosystem.

In short, Indonesia's interpretation of the global AML-CFT standards is expressed through a coordinated legal framework consisting of substantive laws, sector-specific regulations, and executive directives. Each of these instruments reflects an effort to institutionalize international norms into national practice—ensuring that global obligations are translated into applicable and context-sensitive national regulations. The integration of AI tools such as goAML into this legal framework underscores Indonesia's commitment not only to interpreting global standards but also to implementing them through mechanisms that are technologically adaptive and normatively robust.

4.3   Internalization Process

In the Transnational Legal Process (TLP) theory explained by Harold Koh, internalization refers to the stage at which international norms are absorbed into national legal systems and institutions through an iterative process of internal interaction, interpretation, and acceptance. In the Indonesian context, the integration of Artificial Intelligence (AI) into the goAML system—developed by the United Nations Office on Drugs and Crime (UNODC)—is a substantial example of normative internalization in the money laundering and terrorist financing (AML/CTF) regime. Indonesia, as a member of the Asia/Pacific Group on Money Laundering (APG) and the Egmont Group, has legal and policy obligations to implement FATF Recommendations, such as Recommendation 29 on financial intelligence units, Recommendation 15 on emerging technologies, and UN Security Council Resolution 1373 (2001) on terrorist financing. These global instruments encourage risk-based surveillance and technology-assisted analysis, which are now embedded in Indonesia's national operational procedures through AI-powered modules in goAML. This institutional adaptation marks a shift from formal compliance to the practice of internalization, where AI becomes a normative tool aligned with global standards.

The legal insertion of AI into goAML is facilitated through Indonesia's national legal architecture. Law No. 8 of 2010 authorizes the Financial Transaction Reports and Analysis Center (PPATK) to collect, process, and analyze financial data. Law No. 9 of 2013 on the Eradication of Terrorism Funding imposes a binding obligation on financial service providers to report suspicious activity. These legal provisions are complemented by a series of PPATK implementing regulations that set out technical and procedural requirements for Suspicious Transaction Reports (STR) and Cash Transaction Reports (CTR), operationalizing Indonesia's AML/CTF framework in line with global expectations. From a TLP perspective, this represents the instrumentalization of law: a process by which global norms are nationalized and institutionalized through national lawmaking and bureaucratic practices. Rather than treating AI as a mere technological add-on, the Indonesian legal system uses it as an operational extension of its international obligations, transforming abstract global standards into enforceable national mechanisms. At the operational level, AI tools embedded in goAML enable PPATK to perform automated risk assessments, pattern recognition, cross-matching with sanctions lists, and predictive analytics. These algorithmic processes reflect a deep internalization of the FATF's risk-based approach and typologies developed under the UN framework. As a result, AI is used for efficiency and serves as a norm enforcement mechanism—triggering legal investigations, supporting prosecution processes, and influencing judicial outcomes through evidence collection. However, several critical legal challenges remain: Indonesia lacks specific AI regulations, a comprehensive data protection law specific to financial oversight, and the evidentiary status of AI-generated reports remains legally ambiguous under the Criminal Procedure Code (KUHAP). Furthermore, the lack of robust oversight and procedural measures raises concerns about due process and rights protection. These shortcomings suggest that while Indonesia has made progress in internalizing global norms behaviorally and institutionally, it must further develop its normative and procedural framework to ensure full compliance with the principles of legality, accountability, and human rights in enforcing its AI-driven AML/CTF obligations.

5   The Role of FIUs and the Benefits of goAML and AI Integration

The task of analyzing suspicious financial flows for signs of terrorist financing often falls to each state's Financial Intelligence Unit (FIU). FIUs receive, analyze, and transmit reports of suspicious financial transfers turned in by the private and public sector, acting as an intermediary between entities subject to anti-money laundering and counter-terrorist financing (AML/CTF) regulations and the law enforcement sector. [31] In the case of Indonesia, this is filled by The Indonesian Financial Services Authority and the Indonesian Financial Intelligence Unit (INTRAC), otherwise referred to as the PPATK. In the case of Indonesia, the compliance of the banking sector to AML/CTF regulations has been adequate. In accordance with local Financial Services Authority (Otoritas Jasa Keuangan) law, namely POJK No. 12/2017 and POJK No. 23/2019, banks have a responsibility to turn in Suspicious Activity Reports (SAR) to the Financial Services Authority, more specifically to INTRAC. Banks receive an 'adequate' rating when they receive a 4 out of 5 rating in compliance, and reports have shown that most banks comply. [32] However, many challenges remain. First, Indonesian compliance to FATF regulations is still notably lacking, compared to neighboring states as Singapore and Malaysia. Second, banks in Indonesia have been dogged by the problem of fake identities used to create accounts, which have resulted in doubts to Indonesia's Know Your Customer regimes [32].

goAML is an application designed by the UNODC to be used by various states' FIU (Financial Intelligence Units) to prevent money laundering in service of terrorist financing, or anti-money laundering and counter-terrorist financing (AML/CTF). goAML acts as a central database of reports on suspicious financial transactions, as reported by various financial institutions including banks. Furthermore, goAML is an intelligent analysis system capable of analyzing said suspicious financial transactions. The four stages of goAML use include: (a) Collection of suspicious financial data, including Cash Transaction Reports (CTR), Suspicious Transaction Reports (STR), Electronic Funds Transfer Reports (EFT) and List-based reports, such as reports generated from lists of known terrorist identities, (b) Analysis of said reports to find patterns, (c) Dissemination of findings to relevant national authorities including law enforcement officials and financial regulatory entities, (d) Interface with regional and national systems used by FIU to reduce the challenge of inter-agency and inter-state cooperation.[34] However, challenges remain, and the following is an attempt to categorize the effects (Table 1).

Table 1. Illicit Financial Flows (IFFs) and Their Associated Activities ([35])

Types	Activities	Blockchain Impact	Blockchain Layers/Features
Trade-Related	Trade mis-invoicing, Abu- sive transfer pricing, Other base-erosion and profit-shifting practices	Deterrent (transparency, auditability)	Smart Contracts, Public Ledgers, Timestamping
Corrup- tion & Gov- ernance	Bribery- and theft-related, Stolen asset recovery, Anti- money-laundering	Deterrent (tracea- bility), Enabler (se- cure transfers)	Public Ledgers, Tokenization, Ora- cles
Orga- nized Crime	Drug trafficking, Human traffick- ing, Kidnapping, Cy- bercrime	Enabler (anony- mous coins), Both (depends on use case)	Privacy Coins, Zero-Knowledge Proofs, Tumblers
Orga- nized Crime	Counterfeit medications, Il- licit controlled substances	Deterrent (supply chain transparency)	Public Ledgers, Tokenization
Orga- nized Crime	Illicit firearms and ammuni- tion	Enabler (obfus- cated transfers)	Privacy Coins, Tumblers
Orga- nized Crime	Other counterfeit goods	Deterrent (prove- nance tracking)	Public Ledgers, Tokenization
Resource Ex- ploitation	Oil thefts, Conflict com- modities, Illegal artisanal min- ing	Deterrent (supply chain tracking)	Public Ledgers, Tokenization
Resource Ex- ploitation	Illegal fishing and logging, Wild- life poaching	Deterrent (prove- nance tracking)	Public Ledgers, Tokenization
Security & Conflict	Terrorism financing, Anti- money-laundering	Potential Enabler (if obfuscated)	Privacy Coins, Tumblers

6   Implications of Using Artificial Intelligence in the Criminal Law

Law enforcement in the investigation process related to money laundering crimes still refers to the Criminal Procedure Code if no specific method is stipulated in the lex specialis, this is in line with Article 68 and Article 69 of Law Number 8 of 2010. For several cyber issues, legislation still refers to several laws, such as Law Number 1 of 2024 concerning the Second Amendment to Law Number 11 of 2008 concerning Electronic Information and Transactions and Law Number 27 of 2022 concerning Personal Data Protection in Indonesia. Existing laws do not explicitly regulate the validity of data or evidence generated by AI systems, so the use of AI should be viewed as a tool in law enforcement processes, including the detection and prevention of money laundering, rather than as the sole determinant of criminal evidence.

As part of a law enforcement tool, AI must adhere to the principles of due process of law, non-discrimination, and protection of human rights. First, the principle of non-discrimination is regulated in Article 3, paragraph 2, and Article 4, letter d of Law No. 39 of 1999 concerning Human Rights. Applying AI systems that contain algorithmic bias can create a form of systemic discrimination in the law enforcement process. Second, the provisions of Law No. 27 of 2022 concerning Personal Data Protection (PDP Law) provide an important legal basis for criticizing the use of AI for automated decision-making. Article 20 paragraphs (1) and (2) provide data subjects with the right to object to decisions based solely on automated processing, including profiling that has a legally significant impact. In the context of the principle of due process of law, Article 183 of the Criminal Procedure Code (Law No. 8 of 1981) regulates the evidentiary system in

Indonesian criminal procedure law. AI processing results cannot be considered stand-alone evidence because they lack explicit legal standing in criminal procedure law.

7 Conclusion

Indonesia's integration of Artificial Intelligence (AI) into the goAML platform for financial oversight operates without a comprehensive national legal framework for AI.. In the absence of specific legislation on AI, the regulatory basis relies on the Electronic Information and Transactions Law, which regulates digital evidence and cybersecurity but does not address AI-specific risks such as algorithmic bias, explainability, or suitability. From a legal perspective, the implementation of AI in goAML must still comply with basic procedural measures, including the legal basis for data processing and protection against misuse of personal data.

From TLP approach has successfully explained the process of legal transnationalization in several legal areas, this success does not automatically guarantee the effectiveness of the TLP in the realm of regulating new technologies such as AI. The consequences of the legal vacuum governing the use of AI in the monitoring and enforcement of money laundering crimes present challenges in asset tracing, asset confiscation, evidence in court, and asset recovery.

Acknowledgments. This study was funded by a grant from Universitas Diponegoro.

Disclosure of Interests. The authors have no competing interests to declare that are relevant to the content of this article.

References

1. Jefferies, R.: Transnational legal process: an evolving theory and methodology. SSRN Electron. J. (2021). https://doi.org/10.2139/ssrn.3990378
2. Koh, H.H.: Transnational Legal Process, in Routledge eBooks, Informa, 2017, pp. 311–338. https://doi.org/10.4324/9781315202006-11
3. Koh, H.H.: The 1994 roscoe pound lecture: transnational legal process. Neb. Law Rev. **75**(1), 181–208 (1996)
4. Shen, W.-M.: The role of transnational legal process in enforcing WTO law and competition policy. SSRN Electron. J. (2020)
5. Schaffer, G.: Transnational Legal Process and State Change: Opportunities and Constraints, pp. 1–43, 2010
6. Statista, "Reward-Based Crowdfunding - Worldwide | Market Forecast," Statista. http://frontend.xmo.prod.aws.statista.com/out-look/fmo/capital-raising/digital-capital-raising/reward-based-crowdfunding/world-wide?currency=USD. Accessed 22 May 2025
7. United Nations Security Council - Counter-Terrorism Committee (CTC), "Delhi Declaration on countering the use of new and emerging technologies for terrorist purposes." https://www.un.org/securitycoun-cil/ctc/news/delhi-declaration-countering-use-new-and-emerging-technologies-terrorist-purposes-now-available. Accessed 22 May 2025
8. Europol, "The Internet Organised Crime Threat Assessment (IOCTA) 2015," Europol, 2015

9. European Union Agency for Law Enforcement Cooperation., European Union terror-ism situation and trend report 2024. LU: Publications Office, 2024. Accessed 22 May 2025
10. Bauer, K., Levitt, M.: Funding in Place: Local Financing Trends Behind Today's Global Terrorist Threat, Int. Cent. Count.-Terror. – Hague ICCT Evol. Count.-Terror., vol. 2, November 2020
11. Ahari, A., Duong, J., Hanzl, J., Lichtenegger, E.M., Lobnik, L., Timel, A.: Is it easy to hide money in the crypto economy? The case of Russia. Focus Eur. Econ. Integr. (Q4) (2022)
12. Dupuis, D., Gleason, K.: Money laundering with cryptocurrency: open doors and the regulatory dialectic. J. Financ. Crime **28**(1), 60–74 (2020). https://doi.org/10.1108/jfc-06-2020-0113
13. Padalkar, N.R.: Unveiling the Digital Shadows: Exploring the Role of Technology in Illicit Financial Flows, 11th IMF Stat. Forum, 2023
14. Misra, S., Kashyap, V., Poonacha, K.B., Mukund, A., Parameshwar, H.S.: Crypto-currency: a black and white analysis. Int. J. Inf. Syst. Soc. Change **11**(2), 24–40 (2020). https://doi.org/10.4018/ijissc.2020040103
15. Alfieri, C.: Cryptocurrency and national security. Int. J. Criminol. **9**(1) (2022). https://doi.org/10.18278/ijc.9.1.3
16. Office of Public Affairs, United States Department of Justice, "Justice Department Disrupts Hamas Terrorist Financing Scheme Through Seizure of Cryptocurrency". https://www.justice.gov/opa/pr/justice-department-disrupts-hamas-terrorist-financing-scheme-through-seizure-cryptocurrency. Accessed 23 May 2025
17. United States, Department of Treasury, "2024 National Terrorist Financing Risk Assessment (NTFRA)," 2024
18. Al-Suwaidi, N.A., Nobanee, H.: Anti-money laundering and anti-terrorism financing: a survey of the existing literature and a future research agenda. J. Money Laund. Control **24**(2), 396–426 (2021). https://doi.org/10.1108/jmlc-03-2020-0029
19. PPATK, "PPATK | Pusat Pelaporan dan Analisis Transaksi Keuangan". https://www.ppatk.go.id/siaran_pers/read/1229/ppatk-gelar-goaml-interregional-meeting.html. Accessed 27 May 2025
20. PPATK, "Sistem Anti Pecucian Uang goAML". https://goaml.ppatk.go.id/Home. Accessed 27 May 2025
21. FATF - Egmont Group, "EG Member FIU Information - Egmont Group". https://egmontgroup.org/members-by-region/eg-mem-ber-fiu-information/. Accessed 27 May 2025
22. FATF - Egmont Group, "Members by Region - Egmont Group". https://egmontgroup.org/members-by-region/. Accessed 27 May 2025
23. OJK, "OJK". https://ojk.go.id/en/kanal/perbankan/Pages/Prinsip-Mengenal-Nasabah-dan-Anti-Pencucian-Uang.aspx. Accessed 27 May 2025
24. Korupsi, K.P.: Indonesia'S Money Laundering Risk Assessment on Corruption, 2017. ojk.go.id
25. Kemenko Polkam R.I., "Egmont Group - Kemenko Polkam R.I". https://polkam.go.id/tag/egmont-group/. Accessed 27 May 2025
26. United Nations Security Council, "Security Council Resolution 1373 (2001)," vol. 1373, no. September, pp. 348–350, 2001. https://doi.org/10.4324/9781315170657-71
27. UNODC, "International Convention for the Suppression of the Financing of Terrorism," vol. 1–2, 1999
28. UNODC, United Nations Convention Against Transnational Organized Crime and the Protocols Thereto. New York: United Nations on Drugs and Crime, 2004, p. 92
29. F. A. T. F. (FATF), "International Standards on Combating Money Laundering and The Financing of Terrorism & Proliferation," FATF Recomm., pp. 1–148, 2012
30. F. A. T. F. (FATF), "International Standards on Combating Money Laundering and The Financing of Terrorism & Proliferation," FATF Recomm., pp. 1–148, 2025

31. Council of Europe, "Financial Intelligence Units - Committee of Experts on the Evaluation of Anti-Money Laundering Measures and the Financing of Terrorism - www.coe.int," Committee of Experts on the Evaluation of Anti-Money Laundering Measures and the Financing of Terrorism. https://www.coe.int/en/web/moneyval/implementation/fiu. Accessed 26 May 2025
32. Rengganis, F.D., Susanto, D.S.: Evaluation of the anti-money laundering programs implementation in Indonesia. Integritas J. Antikorupsi **9**(2), 229–240 (2023). https://doi.org/10.32697/integritas.v9i2.973
33. Gilmour, N., Hicks, T., Mason, P.: The War on Dirty Money. Policy Press, Bristol, 2023. https://doi.org/10.51952/9781447365143
34. United Nations, "Description - About goAML". https://unite.un.org/goaml/content/description. Accessed 23 May 2025
35. Padalkar, N.R.: Unveiling the digital shadows: exploring the role of technology in illicit financial flows. IMF Stat. Forum **11**(ChainAnalysis 2022), 1–17 (2023)

Retrieval-Augmented Generation for Addressing Consumer Complaints

David Lima[1,2(✉)], Pedro A. Santos[1,2] (ID), and João Dias[2,3,4] (ID)

[1] Instituto Superior Técnico, Universidade de Lisboa, Lisbon, Portugal
{davidazevedolima,pedro.santos}@tecnico.ulisboa.pt
[2] INESC-ID, Lisbon, Portugal
[3] Faculdade de Ciências e Tecnologia, Universidade do Algarve, Faro, Portugal
jmdias@ualg.pt
[4] CISCA, Faro, Portugal

Abstract. Consumers in Portugal often encounter challenges when seeking resolutions to their complaints, as information regarding consumers' rights may be inaccessible or hard to understand. In this work, we focus on this gap, introducing a system that responds to consumer complaints with legally grounded, understandable explanations based on Portuguese consumer law. To achieve this, a Retrieval-Augmented Generation architecture was implemented, combining information retrieval with natural language generation. The system consists of two main components: a Retriever and a Generator. The Retriever was built by fine-tuning Albertina, a BERT-family model for European Portuguese, to identify the most semantically relevant legal segments for a given complaint. To support this, a new dataset was created, consisting of Portuguese consumer complaints paired with legislative excerpts, an essential contribution given the absence of existing resources of this kind. The Generator component then produces a response using the retrieved legal information, presenting it in a simplified and user-friendly manner. The system was evaluated through both quantitative and qualitative methods. The retriever showed significant gains in accuracy compared to a traditional BM25 baseline, demonstrating improved ability to match complaints with relevant legal content. To assess the generator's effectiveness, a user study was conducted in which participants compared full system responses to a baseline consisting only of retrieved legal segments. In this evaluation, 78.67% of participants preferred the generated responses, indicating the potential of the RAG architecture to provide clearer and more helpful legal guidance to consumers.

Keywords: Retrieval Augmented Generation · Legal Information Retrieval · Large Language Models

1 Introduction

Portuguese consumers often struggle to understand their rights due to the complex and technical nature of legal language. This challenge is even greater due the lack of accessible legal resources. Without clear guidance, many consumers are unable to act confidently when facing unfair practices or resolving disputes.

This work lies in the field of Legal Information Retrieval (LIR), which focuses on extracting and organizing legal information from unstructured text. However, it also aims to prioritize accessibility and user-friendliness, answering the users' questions in a more comprehensible and intuitive manner. To do this, we developed a Retrieval-Augmented Generation (RAG) system that combines legal text retrieval with natural language generation, to create clear, legally grounded responses to consumer complaints.

To support this, we built a new dataset that links real consumer complaints to relevant legal segments. The system consists of a Retriever, which finds the most relevant law excerpts, and a Generator, which transforms them into assistance for the consumers.

2   Related Work

Legal Information Retrieval (LIR) is a subfield of Information Retrieval that focuses on retrieving legal documents, such as legislation and case law. Traditional methods, e.g. Boolean search, manual classification, and ranking algorithms like BM25 [4], help organize and locate relevant documents. More recent approaches use deep learning techniques and language models such as BERT [2], which enable a better understanding of context and semantics within legal texts. The rise of conversational models like ChatGPT [7] has also opened new possibilities in LIR by enabling more accessible and natural interactions with legal information.

Albertina [9] is a family of encoder models specifically developed to address the lack of high-quality language models for Portuguese, particularly the European variant (PT-PT). It offers two model sizes, 100M, designed for efficiency, and 1.5B, larger and higher-performance, each available in both PT-PT and PT-BR, and trained exclusively on Portuguese corpora. Albertina showed strong results in several benchmarks, including STS tasks, highlighting its capacity for semantic understanding in Portuguese.

Llama 3.1 represents the latest generation of the Llama family of language models, with a focus on multilingual understanding, reasoning, and tool usage. Among its variants is Llama 3.1 Instruct, an instruction-tuned model optimized to follow instructions, align with human preferences and improve various capabilities, like reasoning. Llama 3.1 Instruct is openly available to the public, facilitating its integration into research and practical applications.

The Legal Semantic Search Engine (LeSSE) [1] is a system developed as an alternative to the official search engine of Diário da República Eletrónico (DRE), the official online portal for Portuguese legislation. LeSSE combines syntactic and semantic search algorithms for retrieving information, allowing users to search for both literal terms and synonymous words and expressions without having to understand legal jargon.

Retrieval-Augmented Generation (RAG) [6] is a framework that addresses limitations of Pre-trained Language Models, particularly how they struggle to retrieve and use external knowledge effectively, which makes them less effective in tasks that require domain-specific knowledge. It consists of two components: a Retriever, which searches an external knowledge source for relevant documents, and a Generator, which produces responses conditioned on the retrieved information and the original query. This architecture grounds generated answers in real data, reducing the risk of producing factually incorrect information. Furthermore, the external memory can be easily updated without retraining the models, which allows it to adapt to changes in the knowledge base.

CBR-RAG [10] is a recent RAG-based system that modifies the retrieval stage of RAG pipelines by integrating principles from Case-Based Reasoning (CBR) to enhance legal question answering. Evaluated on the ALQA dataset, CBR-RAG uses a hybrid retrieval strategy, matching both legal questions and contextual elements like supporting texts and named entities to find relevant past cases. It uses AnglEBERT, a contrastively trained encoder, to improve semantic comparison, which was shown to outperform general-purpose and legal-domain models like BERT and LegalBERT. By providing the Generator with full structured cases rather than isolated text excerpts, CBR-RAG produces more factually grounded and interpretable generated responses. This system illustrates the importance of a strong Retriever in legal RAG systems.

3   Creating a Consumer Complaints Dataset

At the start of this work, there was no publicly available dataset of Portuguese consumer complaints, nor one that linked those complaints to relevant segments of Consumers' Rights legislation, which we needed in order to train our system. To address this gap, we collected real consumer complaints.

Data Source. Portal da Queixa is a widely used Portuguese platform where consumers can voice their discontent with products or services, providing valuable insights for other consumers. It not only helps other consumers make more informed decisions but also puts pressure on businesses to improve customer service. For this work, 62900 complaints were collected from the platform. This equals to 50 complaints from each company with more than 50 complaints - to ensure equal representation across companies and focus on ones with significant consumer interaction. The data covers a wide range of topics, organized by the platform's category and subcategory structure (e.g. Health or Water, Gas and Electricity).

Preprocessing. Several preprocessing steps were applied to the raw complaints for effective use in the dataset. Basic preprocessing included removing duplicates, filtering out very short or very long complaints and erasing irrelevant content such as greetings and closings. Beyond these, two additional preprocessing techniques, summarization and segmentation, were applied to generate four versions of the dataset: (1) summarized complaints, (2) segmented complaints, (3) summarized then segmented, and (4) original complaints. Summarization aimed to reduce the length of the complaints and retaining only essential details, bringing them closer to the language and conciseness of legal texts. Segmentation split complaints into individual sentences to focus on specific parts instead of the whole complaint. This allows us to select law segments that are most similar to one of the segments of the complaint.

Embeddings. To enable semantic comparison between consumer complaints and relevant law segments, embeddings were generated using OpenAI's embedding models. By mapping complaints and law segments into the same vector space, these embeddings enable the computation of cosine similarity to identify the most relevant law segments for a given complaint. For each complaint, the top 3 most relevant segments are selected. Two embedding models were used: *text-embedding-3-small* and *text-embedding-3-large* [8]. Given the absence of human-supervised labels for training, our goal was to utilize these models' capabilities to generate more reliable training data without expert annotations and to assess the impact of embedding quality on performance. By combining the two embedding models with the previously mentioned four preprocessing configurations, a total of eight versions of the dataset were created.

Semantic Pairs. To train the Retriever, semantic pairs were created by matching each consumer complaint with relevant segments of Portuguese consumer law based on cosine similarity between their embeddings. For each complaint, the top three most similar law segments were selected, after being filtered by a heuristic threshold that excludes weaker matches. Specifically, only those with similarity above the mean cosine similarity minus one standard deviation were kept as positive pairs. This approach was preferred over a standard percentile-based threshold, which consistently worse results during testing.

To support contrastive learning, negative pairs were also generated. These negative pairs are used as a signal for the model to distinguish between relevant and irrelevant legal segments for each complaint. These were selected with a lower threshold, similarity scores below the mean minus two standard deviations. Additionally, hard negatives were included. These are pairs that fall between the positive and regular negative thresholds. Being closer to the boundary between positive and negative pairs makes them more challenging for the model to classify, forcing it to learn more nuanced distinctions between relevant and seemingly similar but irrelevant segments.

Train, Validation and Test Sets. For training and validation, each of the eight dataset versions was split using a standard 80/20 ratio.

To evaluate the accuracy of the Retriever model, a manually curated test dataset of 100 complaint-segment pairs was created. Pairs were selected by reviewing automated matches and extracting those that appeared to be relevant. These examples were then excluded from the training and validation sets. Balancing the dataset was a priority to ensure representativeness across categories (taken from Portal da Queixa) and laws: at least two complaints per category were included, with the rest distributed proportionally, and 32 of the 66 laws present in the full consumer law dataset were included.

4   Solution Architecture

Our solution follows a Retrieval-Augmented Generation (RAG) architecture, which integrates an information retrieval component with a generative language model. The primary goal of this approach is to provide user-friendly responses to consumer complaints, while being grounded on relevant excerpts from the Portuguese "Consumers' Rights" legislation.

This architecture consists of two main components: a Retriever, which is used to search and identify the most relevant legal segments from the legal corpus, given a consumer complaint; a Generator, which produces a response by combining the retrieved legal segments and the original complaint and using the as input.

An overview diagram of our solution architecture can be seen in Fig. 1.

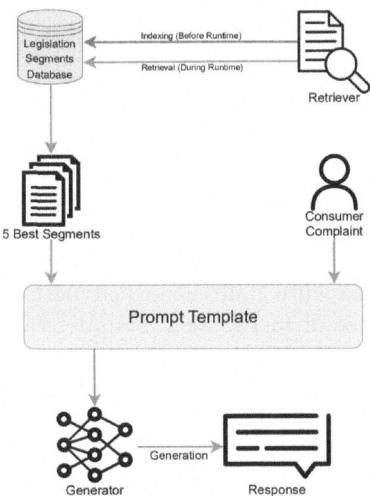

Fig. 1. Overview of our RAG system.

4.1   Retriever

The Retriever is the first component of the RAG architecture, responsible for identifying the most relevant segments of Portuguese Consumers' Rights legislation given a consumer complaint. uses dense vector representations, i.e. embeddings, of both complaints and legal segments, comparing them based on semantic similarity. The legal database is embedded and indexed beforehand using a

FAISS [5] index, allowing the system to perform efficient retrieval at runtime. When creating a response, the Retriever computes an embedding of the complaint and compares it with the previously created index to identify the most relevant legal segments.

To train the Retriever, the Albertina 100M PT-PT model was fine-tuned using hyperparameter optimization on a dataset of complaint–segment pairs. The 100M PTPT version, with 100 million parameters, was chosen for our task, as it still offers strong performance and requires less extensive fine-tuning.

The loss function that was used for fine-tuning was a Cosine Contrastive Loss function, defined as:

$$\mathcal{L} = \sum_{i=1}^{N} y_i \cdot (1 - \cos(\mathbf{u_i}, \mathbf{v_i})) + (1 - y_i) \cdot \max(0, \cos(\mathbf{u_i}, \mathbf{v_i}) - m)$$

where u_i and v_i are the embedding vectors of a complaint and a legal segment, $\cos(\mathbf{u_i}, \mathbf{v_i})$ is the cosine similarity between the two vectors, y_i is the relevance label (1 for positive pairs and 0 for negative pairs) and m is a margin hyperparameter. This loss function maximizes similarity between positive pairs while minimizing similarity between negative pairs. It directly optimizes the embedding space, ensuring that legal segments are closely mapped to complaints to which they are relevant.

4.2   Generator

The Generator component is responsible for producing text based on a prompt and the output from the Retriever. For this component, the LLaMA-3.1-8B-Instruct model was selected. This model was chosen for its ability to handle structured prompts and execute multi-step instructions, which is essential for following a logical sequence of tasks, such as understanding a consumer's complaint, interpreting relevant legislation, and offering actionable advice. The 8B variant was chosen as it offers a balanced compromise between performance and computational efficiency.

To generate accurate, informative, and context-sensitive responses, the Generator must combine three elements into a single input: the original consumer complaint, the relevant retrieved legal segments and a clear set of instructions on how to process this information. For this reason, a structured prompt template was created, which serves not only as a tool for merging all necessary content into one input but also as a way to guide the model's response. The full prompt template is shown next.

```
<|begin_of_text|><|start_header_id|>system<|end_header_id|>

You are an assistant specialized in helping consumers in Portugal
understand their rights based on excerpts from provided Decree-Laws.
Your role is to explain, in a clear and neutral way, how the decree-laws
presented may (or may not) be relevant to the situation described.
```

```
**Instructions:**
- Only include decree-laws with a clear link to the complaint.
If a passage is not relevant, ignore it completely.
- Use neutral and cautious language, without definitive judgments.
- Be impartial - don't assume the consumer is right.
- Never recommend contacting associations, external entities or
regulatory bodies.

**Mandatory structure for the answer:**

**Key parts of the complaint:**
- [Clear and objective summary of the main elements of the complaint]

If no decree-law is relevant:
"Based on available information, and taking into account the legal
passages retrieved, it was not possible to identify a clear link
between the described situation and the retrieved legislation."

**Conclusion:**
Based on the presented legislation, [neutral answer on possible legal
implications, mentioning and citing decree-laws when possible].

**Reformulation of your complaint with relevant legislation:**
"[Reformulated text of the complaint, from the consumer's perspective,
with clear language and focus on the most relevant legal aspects,
citing decree-laws where possible]"

Decree-laws:
{joined_legislation}

<|eot_id|><|start_header_id|>user<|end_header_id|>

Complaint: {complaint}
<|eot_id|><|start_header_id|>assistant<|end_header_id|>
```

The instructions present in the template don't only provide a format for the
response, as they are also designed to mitigate certain risks. For instance, by
instructing the model to disregard irrelevant decree-laws, it acts as a secondary
filter when the Retriever includes irrelevant results. Additionally, prohibiting
the recommendation of external institutions is done due to the model's lack of
access to up-to-date or verified information about Portuguese consumer support
services, helping to prevent the spread of outdated or misleading guidance.

The fixed structure helps control variability in the model's output and makes
responses easier to interpret and evaluate. The initial "Key parts of the complaint" section serves to focus the model but also to show the user whether
it understood their complaint, adding a layer of transparency to the system's
reasoning process.

Finally, the inclusion of a dedicated reformulation section aids the user in rewriting their complaint in a more legally grounded way. This reinforces the consumer's understanding of how the legal references apply, and it helps them to articulate their issue better. Lastly, attached to the response, we also include links to official PDF files for each decree-law, allowing the user to independently verify the legal references and compare the original texts with the content of the response.

5   Evaluation

5.1   Retriever

To evaluate the effectiveness of the retrieval component in the RAG system, two metrics were defined: Top x (Segment) and Top x (Ato). These metrics measure how well the Retriever identifies relevant legal text for a given consumer complaint, with different levels of granularity.

The Top x (Segment) metric checks whether the exact legal segment designated as relevant in the test dataset appears within the top x retrieved results. The Top 5 (Segment) is particularly important, as the system is configured to retrieve the top five segments at runtime.

The Top x (Ato) metric evaluates whether the Retriever identifies a segment from the same Decreto-Lei (Decree-Law) as the expected relevant segment within the top x retrieved results, even if it does not retrieve the exact segment found in the test dataset. Since legal texts are often structured with related provisions grouped within the same decree-law, retrieving from the correct ato can still be useful for providing relevant legal context. As with the segment-level metric, Top 5 (Ato) is particularly important due to the system's retrieval configuration. If one of the retrieved segments comes from the same decree-law as the expected reference, it may still hold relevance for that complaint, even if it is not the exact segment found in the test set.

Result	BM25	Small				Large			
		Segmented		Unsegmented		Segmented		Unsegmented	
		Sum.	N/Sum.	Sum.	N/Sum.	Sum.	N/Sum.	Sum.	N/Sum.
Top 1 (Ato)	24	40	38	42	**48**	37	40	39	42
Top 3 (Ato)	33	57	58	61	**67**	55	59	55	64
Top 5 (Ato)	44	67	68	73	**77**	63	67	65	75
Top 10 (Ato)	53	75	81	85	**89**	74	83	76	85
Top 1 (Seg)	6	12	16	**19**	18	14	14	16	**19**
Top 3 (Seg)	9	19	27	31	**36**	26	25	31	33
Top 5 (Seg)	13	26	32	**44**	41	30	30	37	41
Top 10 (Seg)	17	39	44	55	**56**	46	41	50	**56**

Fig. 2. Performance Comparison of Different Retrieval Configurations and a BM25 baseline on our Test Set.

The results presented in Fig. 2 illustrate the retrieval performance across different configurations after fine-tuning. The best-performing setup was the non-segmented, non-summarized dataset generated using small embeddings, which achieved the highest score in Top 5 (Ato) at 77%, and the second highest in Top 5 (Segment) at 41%, as well as the highest score in several other of the performance metrics. These results suggest that using the full, unsegmented, and non-summarized complaints may allow the Retriever to better capture contextual information that improves accuracy.

Datasets created using larger embeddings generally underperformed compared to those generated with smaller embeddings, despite the expectation that larger models would offer more detailed text representations. One possible explanation is that the smaller model was better at capturing essential semantic information while avoiding unnecessary complexity. In the context of matching consumer complaints with legal text using cosine similarity, this additional complexity may have lead to prioritizing less relevant aspects of the text.

Datasets that used segmentation and summarization generally performed worse than those based on full, unaltered complaints. Although these preprocessing steps were initially intended to improve data quality by reducing noise and focusing on essential information, they appear to have had a negative effect. Segmenting and summarizing can result in the loss of valuable contextual information, making it more difficult to establish strong semantic similarities between complaints and legal provisions. In particular, summarization tends to make complaints more condensed and generic, reducing their distinctiveness. Since the Retriever relies on semantic embeddings to differentiate complaints, this loss of variation may have caused different complaints to become more similar in the embedding space.

Furthermore, the segmentation process may have disrupted the overall meaning of the complaints by isolating segments. When a complaint was split into segments, each segment was independently compared to a legal provision. This process may have put too much emphasis on isolated parts of the complaint while disregarding the overall context. Additionally, different segments of the same complaint can vary significantly in relevance in regards to a certain legal provision, making similarity scores less representative of the full complaint's legal connection.

5.2   Generator

To illustrate how the Generator functions, Fig. 3 presents an example of a response (translated from Portuguese) to a real consumer complaint taken from Portal da Queixa, generated by the system.

Evaluating the Generator required a different approach from the Retriever, as its output is meant to communicate legal information in a structured and user-friendly manner. Instead of relying on quantitative metrics, a small-scale human evaluation was conducted to assess the quality of the generated responses. The study was built around a set of five real consumer complaints, collected from Portal da Queixa. For each complaint, participants were shown two responses: one

---

Key parts of the complaint:

– The consumer is complaining about receiving value-added SMS messages from a company, even though he is not their client and has not given permission to receive advertising campaign messages.
– He is abroad, in the United Arab Emirates, and is being charged for incoming and outgoing SMS, in addition to the daily rate of his MEO plan.
– He tried to contact the company by phone, but was unable to get through.

Conclusion: Based on the presented legislation, the consumer has the right not to receive value-added messages without having given permission. In addition, the consumer has the right not to be charged for SMS received, in accordance with Decree-Law 63/2009. The consumer also has the right not to be charged for waiting minutes in the event of non-answering, in accordance with Decree-Law 134/2009.

Reformulation of your complaint with relevant legislation: "I'm complaining because I'm receiving value-added messages from you without having given permission. In addition, I am being charged for SMS received and sent, which is not correct according to Decree-Law 63/2009. In addition, I tried to contact the company by phone, but I couldn't get through, so I was charged for minutes on hold, which is also not correct according to Decree-Law 134/2009. Please remove my number from the mailing lists and send me an email confirming the removal."

Legal references:
[1]: Decree-Law no. 63/2009: `https://dre.pt/application/conteudo/604820`
[2]: Decree-Law no. 134/2009: `https://dre.pt/application/conteudo/494477`
[3]: Decree-Law no. 199/2012: `https://dre.pt/application/conteudo/174544`

Fig. 3. Example of a response from the system to a complaint (translation).

with only the retrieved decree-laws (representing a traditional retrieval-based approach), and the other generated by our RAG system. This side-by-side comparison was meant to allow participants to assess whether the generated response offered added value over simply reading the raw legal text.

To evaluate these responses, participants were first asked which of the two they preferred overall, as a direct preference indicator. They then assessed the RAG-generated response using four qualitative criteria: relevance, correctness, clarity, and usefulness. These criteria were chosen to evaluate both the legal grounding and communicative quality of the answers. Relevance and correctness captured how well the responses aligned with the complaint and legal content, respectively. Clarity and usefulness reflected the consumer's ability to understand clearly and apply the information, respectively. Each of these was rated on a 5-point Likert scale. Before beginning, participants were given a short preamble explaining the survey's purpose and methodology, clarifying that one response was purely retrieved text while the other was generated, and noting the estimated time to complete the study was 10–15 min.

5.3   Results

In terms of overall preference, participants strongly favored the RAG-generated responses. Out of the 30 evaluations, 78.67% preferred the generated response, while only 21.33% favored the retrieval-only version. This preference was consistent across all five complaints, with individual complaint scores ranging from 76.67% to 86.67%. These results indicate that participants generally valued the added structure, clarity, and explanation provided by the generator compared to simply reading the legal text alone.

Looking at the relevance and correctness of the RAG-generated responses, relevance received the highest overall rating, with a mean score of 4.05 out of 5. This suggests that participants found the generated answers well-aligned with the content of the original complaints. Correctness, while slightly lower with an average score of 3.90, was the lowest-scoring dimension in three of the five complaints. This indicates that, although participants generally considered the legal interpretations accurate, some uncertainty in the legal interpretation remained, possibly a result of occasional mismatches in retrieved legal segments due to the limitations of the Retriever.

In terms of clarity and usefulness, clarity was the lowest-rated dimension overall, with a mean score of 3.88, suggesting that some responses may have been difficult to follow. This may reflect limitations of the LLaMA 3.1 8B Instruct model, which, while effective, struggles with consistently adhering to stylistic guidelines and generating clearer, more human-like responses. Usefulness scored 3.97, making it the second-highest rated dimension. Despite occasional issues with clarity or precision, participants generally found the responses helpful. The explicit references to legislation, and the reformulation of the complaint may have contributed to the perceived usefulness.

5.4   Expert Analysis

In addition to the user study, feedback was obtained from a legal expert who reviewed several system-generated responses and provided insights from a professional legal perspective. One of the key points raised was the importance of ensuring that the legal references are up to date.

The expert also noted certain limitations in content coverage and contextual understanding. In some responses, they observed that key sanctioning provisions, such as articles detailing penalties or fines, were missing, even though they could be important to the case.

Additionally, while some retrieved segments were considered appropriate, they were not always directly applicable to the situation. For example, one decree-law cited would only apply if the consumer had filed a formal complaint through official channels. Another observation highlighted the system's current lack of broader legal reasoning, such as recognizing that price discrepancies between a brand and a reseller might be legally acceptable, depending on the contractual relationship. Addressing these gaps would require not only more refined retrieval but also deeper legal domain reasoning.

6   Conclusion and Future Work

This project aimed to help Portuguese consumers better understand their rights by providing responses to complaints grounded in real legislation. The system follows a Retrieval-Augmented Generation (RAG) architecture, combining a Retriever that identifies relevant legal segments with a Generator that transforms these segments, along with the original complaint, into clear and accessible explanations.

To train the retriever, we fine-tuned Albertina, a BERT-based model built for European Portuguese. We created multiple dataset configurations using different preprocessing techniques and matching methods to pair complaints with relevant legal segments. These datasets supported fine-tuning experiments to find the best-performing setup. A manually curated test set of 100 complaint–segment pairs was used for evaluation. While improvements over a BM25 baseline were modest, they still outperformed a traditional BM25 baseline and provided valuable insights into how the embedding spaces of consumer complaints and legal texts can be more effectively aligned.

For the generator, we used LLaMA 3.1-Instruct, guided by a structured prompt to ensure responses were neutral, legally grounded, and easy to understand. A user study showed that 78.67% of participants preferred the system's responses over simply viewing retrieved legal texts. Participants also rated responses on relevance, correctness, clarity, and usefulness. Expert analysis was also obtained, which generally found the system's outputs well-structured and helpful, though it also pointed out specific flaws, gaps in legal completeness, and important considerations for future enhancements.

Regarding future improvements, they could be focused on both the Retriever and Generator components. Adding expert-annotated pairs to the training data could increase retrieval accuracy and legal reliability. Expert feedback also suggested improving the detection of sanctioning articles, such as fines, which are sometimes missed. This could be addressed with a post-retrieval mechanism to append relevant sanction articles from the same decree-law. On the generation side, using larger models like LLaMA 3.1 70B or 405B could overall quality of the responses.

Acknowledgements. This work was supported by national funds through Fundação para a Ciência e a Tecnologia (FCT) with reference UIDB/50021/2020 and FCT project AILA with reference 2024.07657. IACDC supported by the measure "RE-C05-i08.m04 – Apoiar o lançamento de um programa de projetos de I&D orientado para o desenvolvimento e implementação de sistemas avançados de cibersegurança, inteligência artificial e ciência de dados na administração pública, bem como de um programa de capacitação científica", under the Recovery and Resilience Plan (PRR), as part of the funding agreement signed between a Estrutura de Missão Recuperar Portugal (EMRP) and FCT, acting as an intermediate beneficiary.

Disclosure of Interests. The authors have no competing interests to declare that are relevant to the content of this article.

References

1. Cordeiro, N.P., Dias, J., Santos, P.A.: LeSSE—a semantic search engine applied to portuguese consumer law. In: Progress in Artificial Intelligence: 22nd EPIA Conference on Artificial Intelligence, EPIA 2023, Faial Island, Azores, 5–8 September 2023, Proceedings, Part II. LNCS, vol. 14285, pp. 118–130. Springer, Heidelberg (2023). https://doi.org/10.1007/978-3-031-49011-8_10

2. Devlin, J., Chang, M.-W., Lee, K., Toutanova, K.: BERT: pre-training of deep bidirectional transformers for language understanding. In: Proceedings of the 2019 Conference of the North American Chapter of the ACL: Human Language Technologies, Minnesota, vol. 1, pp. 4171–4186. ACL (2019)

3. Dubey, A., Jauhri, A., Pandey, A., Kadian, A., Al-Dahle, A., et al.: The Llama 3 Herd of Models. CoRR (2024). arxiv.org/abs/2407.21783

4. Gain, B., Bandyopadhyay, D., Saikh, T., Ekbal, A.: IITP@ COLIEE 2019: legal information retrieval using BM25 and BERT. In: Proceedings of the 6th Competition on Legal Information Extraction/Entailment. COLIEE (2019)

5. Johnson, J., Douze, M., Jégou, H.: Billion-scale similarity search with GPUs. IEEE Trans. Big Data **7** (2017). https://doi.org/10.1109/TBDATA.2019.2921572

6. Lewis, P., et al.: Retrieval-augmented generation for knowledge-intensive NLP tasks. In: Proceedings of the 34th International Conference on Neural Information Processing Systems (NeurIPS 2020), pp. 793–808. Curran Associates Inc., Red Hook (2020)

7. OpenAI Blog. https://openai.com/blog/chatgpt. Accessed 12 Oct 2024

8. OpenAI Blog. https://openai.com/index/new-embedding-models-and-api-updates/. Accessed 23 Nov 2024

9. Santos, R., et al.: Fostering the ecosystem of open neural encoders for Portuguese with Albertina PT* family. In: Proceedings of the 3rd Annual Meeting of the Special Interest Group on Under-Resourced Languages @ LREC-COLING 2024, pp. 105–114. ELRA and ICCL, Torino, Italia (2024)

10. Wiratunga, N., et al.: CBR-RAG: case-based reasoning for retrieval augmented generation in LLMs for legal question answering. In: Case-Based Reasoning Research and Development: 32nd International Conference, ICCBR 2024, Merida, Mexico, 1–4 July 2024, Proceedings. LNCS, vol. 14561, pp. 445–460. Springer, Heidelberg (2024). https://doi.org/10.1007/978-3-031-63646-2_29

Benefit-Harm Assessment of AI in the Justice System

Inesa Stolper[1,2](✉) 🔟

[1] Mykolas Romeris University, Vilnius, Lithuania
inesa.stolper@ehu.lt
[2] European Humanities University, Vilnius, Lithuania

Abstract. This article explores the topic of the efficient use of Artificial Intelligence by judicial bodies. Beginning with the evolution from early digital tools to AI systems, it examines existing European assessment instruments, including frameworks developed by CEPEJ, the Council of Europe Committee on Artificial Intelligence's HUDERIA methodology, and the fundamental rights impact assessment envisaged by Article 27 of the EU Artificial Intelligence Act. Current frameworks recognise that the use of AI as an element of justice system modernisation can bring benefits but also risks that require mitigation. Grounded in the principle of proportionality, the article suggests a more balanced assessment of the utility of AI linked to the justice system's objectives. It advocates for context-sensitive evaluation and proposes a benefit-harm assessment framework to guide responsible and justified use of AI in the justice system.

Keywords: AI & Justice · Assessment · Proportionality

1 Introduction

The evolution of technology in the justice system has been a story of transition from digitising isolated tasks to deploying complex systems that support the court in various ways. This transformation reflects an ongoing effort to modernise judicial administration, improve procedural efficiency, and safeguard core values and fundamental rights. The integration of technology in courts has not followed a linear path but has evolved in overlapping and iterative stages. What began as the computerization of registers has developed into a complex digital ecosystem, with Artificial Intelligence (AI) now at the center of attention as a technology that could shape the future of the court. Unlike earlier tools, AI systems offer capabilities such as reasoning, natural language processing, and predictive analytics. These developments require a rethinking of how courts assess the use of technology.

This article aims to formulate a more comprehensive approach to the assessment of the use of AI in court and tribunals. To attain this aim, it provides a summary of the evolution of the use of digital technology in the justice system, an overview of the methodology of assessment of digital technologies in Europe, which developed in parallel to the progressive integration of technologies and argues for the adoption of a benefit-harm assessment framework. To preserve analytical clarity and coherence with established assessment methodologies, this article limits its scope to the European context.

2   From ICTs to AI Systems

The starting point of the use of technology in the court can be traced down to around the 1980s-1990s, when computers were introduced. Early computerisation enabled a shift from paper-based working to digital data management. Most of these technologies allowed the creation, storage, and editing of documents and the execution of specific tasks [1]. For example, an automated court register helped to record information [2], track, store, and reference various documents when necessary, providing access to multiple users [1]. Keeping various documents and data in electronic format enabled quicker information retrieval from the system. During the initial phase of automation, many judicial systems implemented standalone systems. These systems worked independently within the court's local infrastructure. As technology advanced, courts began to integrate more sophisticated systems.

The subsequent emergence of the internet was a catalyst that accelerated the development of various court tools. From the mid-1990s to the 2000s, the use of technologies expanded beyond internal digital tools to systems that facilitate communication across court participants. Information and communication technologies (ICTs) made it possible to share legal documents electronically, host public information portals, and develop tools that supported broader court functions.

Three main categories of tools emerged: (1) those supporting the administration of justice, such as electronic case management systems [2]; (2) those enhancing access to justice through online portals and remote proceedings [2]; and (3) those supporting judges directly, including legal research databases and document drafting tools [1, 2]. Many of these tools evolved incrementally, some through national court modernisation strategies, others as innovation projects within specific jurisdictions or court levels [3]. While the internet enabled greater accessibility, it also raised new concerns about digital vulnerabilities and the unequal ability of users to interact with online systems [4].

In recent years, advancements in AI could be considered a new phase in the evolution of court technologies. AI-based systems are evolving to support legal research and assist decision-making in varying contexts. AI systems have been developing, in a way, in parallel to ICTs. The main difference between ICTs and AI systems is that the latter focuses on processing, analyzing, summarizing, and, recently, interpreting information in the form of text or image. The AI systems are interactive, autonomous, and self-learning agencies. They engage users in interactive dialogue and allow them to pose natural language queries. They exhibit a degree of autonomy by generating outputs without requiring line-by-line instructions and can sometimes suggest legal arguments. Moreover, some of these tools employ self-learning mechanisms, improving their performance through interactions with users, databases, and feedback [5]. These features distinguish AI systems from computers and the internet, and hence, AI could be grouped in a separate cluster of technologies. However, it is important to note that ICTs made the development of AI systems possible. The creation and development of computers, especially improvements in computing power and the internet, contributed greatly to the development of AI.

While many AI applications remain in the experimental or pilot phase, their presence is expanding. Nowadays, around 125 different AI-based and digital tools are deployed in European justice systems [6, 7]. These tools have a varying degree of autonomy and assist with tasks ranging from document organisation and translation to analysis and decision support [7]. For example, in Germany, an AI system called *OberLandesGerichts-Assistent* was introduced to help categorize and manage the very large number of case files concerning diesel emissions [7]. Another German pilot system, Frankfurt Judgement Configurator ("Frauke"), was tested at the Frankfurt District Court to assist in drafting judgements for routine air-passenger compensation cases. Frauke automatically extracts case-specific data, such as flight numbers and delay durations, from litigants' submissions, and uses pre-approved text templates to generate draft judgements once the judge inputs the ruling [7]. In France, the Court of Cassation has experimented with an AI system to detect inconsistencies in jurisprudence [7]. In Switzerland, the judiciary implemented an AI-based anonymization tool to prepare judgements for publication [7]. These examples demonstrate how AI can support the work of the court by sorting files, drafting routine text, or synthesising information.

3   Overview of Existing Evaluation Frameworks

The use of technologies in the court should enhance the administration and quality of justice. It is possible to measure the actual use of technology. Still, it is challenging to quantify the impact of technology on the quality of justice and its contribution to achieving justice objectives. To address this challenge, evaluation frameworks for the quality of justice have emerged. At the European level, the Council of Europe and the European Union (EU) have each developed mechanisms to track the integration and performance of technological tools.

3.1   CEPEJ's Assessment of ICTs and AI in the Justice System

The Council of Europe's primary mechanism for assessing the justice system is through the European Commission for Efficiency of Justice (CEPEJ), launched in 2002. Since 2004, CEPEJ has conducted regular assessments of Council of Europe member states' judicial systems [8]. The CEPEJ has advocated for a multidimensional framework to assess the quality of justice. This is done in two ways: a) through measuring the number of features and pre-defined indicators that a service has, and b) through measuring the gap between users' expectations before using the service and after [9]. This theoretical framework was translated later into practice through the development of composite indicators and instruments [9].

With the gradual digitalization of the justice system, the quality of justice evaluation has increasingly incorporated metrics assessing the use of digital technologies in courts. This evaluation initially was limited and fragmented. For example, the 2008 CEPEJ checklist for promoting the quality of justice and the courts included assessment of the tools related to access to justice and communication with the public [10]. It focused on the existence of court websites and the availability of court decisions [10]. The reason for the limited assessment reflects the level of use of these tools in European courts in that period. However, the expansion of technology in the judiciary eventually necessitated a separate area of assessment within the quality of justice frameworks.

In 2016, CEPEJ adopted Guidelines on how to drive change towards cyberjustice. The Guidelines documented the experience of the Council of Europe member states with implementing projects on the integration of technology in courts up to that point in time, accompanied by a self-assessment checklist for cyberjustice projects [11] and an ICT questionnaire [8, section V.2]. It outlined principles for planning, implementing, and managing the use of digital technologies in courts and introduced a framework for assessment [11]. This framework analysed the benefits expected by using the digital tools, long-term developments, essential aspects for successful innovation, and potential risks [11]. It focuses on the idea that the use of technology in the justice system brings about benefits, but at the same time incorporates essential requirements concerning safety and protection of personal data. By 2024, CEPEJ developed a comprehensive ICT Index methodology to quantitatively score and compare countries' technology implementation [12]. The questionnaire includes 38 questions related to ICT and covers such areas as ICT organization, electronic case processing tools, and other digital tools.

While AI in courts is a form of digital technology, it is assessed through a distinct set of metrics. In 2018, CEPEJ adopted Ethical Guidelines on the use of AI in judicial systems [13], accompanied by an operationalization tool [14]. This instrument focuses primarily on risk mitigation and emphasizes data audit procedures, the detection of biases, and the principle of explainability, especially the obligation to inform users that an AI system was used to produce the decision [13]. While these are important steps, they do not assess whether an AI contributes to the broader objectives of justice, such as improving access to justice or the quality of the justice system.

In parallel to CEPEJ's work, the Committee on AI (CAI) set up by the Council of Europe has advanced a broader conceptual model for assessing AI systems. The Human Rights, Democracy and Rule of Law Assessment (HUDERIA) methodology seeks to provide a structured approach to AI risk and impact assessment, complementing existing assessment tools [15]. The HUDERIA methodology draws inspiration from established human rights due diligence processes, such as those set out in the UN Guiding Principles on Business and Human Rights and the OECD Guidelines for Multinational Enterprises [15]. It proposes that the assessment of AI should comprise the following methodology: identifying potential adverse impacts, consulting relevant stakeholders, implementing mitigation measures, and reassessing outcomes over time [15].

One of the HUDERIA methodology's notable contributions is its commitment to including democratic and rule of law dimensions in the assessment. While data protection and anti-discrimination remain central, the model also draws attention to more systematic risks. Although not specific to the judiciary, CAI's work provides a conceptual foundation for evaluating how AI tools affect rights, institutions, and public interests.

3.2 The EU Assessment of Technology in the Justice System

Within the EU, the assessment framework of the justice system since 2013 has been the EU Justice Scoreboard. The EU Scoreboard uses data from various sources. It relies mostly on quantitative data collected by the Council of Europe's CEPEJ, with which the EU Commission has concluded an agreement for data collection [16]. It incorporates input data from bodies such as the European Network of Councils for the Judiciary, the Network of the Presidents of the Supreme Judicial Courts of the EU, Eurostat, the European Judicial Training Network, and others [16]. Over time, the European Commission has developed its own questionnaire for Member States' justice authorities [16]. It covers information on digitalization, access, and other quality aspects that might not be fully represented in the CEPEJ's assessment.

The EU Justice Scoreboard monitors certain indicators of the development of e-justice. Recently, special emphasis has been placed on the use of digital tools in courts. Notably, the 2024 Scoreboard highlighted how digital technologies kept courts functional during the COVID-19 pandemic lockdowns and underscored "the need for an acceleration of the digitalisation of justice systems" [16], indicating that this acceleration should contribute positively to the justice system. It has also included in the assessment AI and other advanced analytical tools used in the justice system [16].

The recently adopted EU Artificial Intelligence Act (AIA) also envisages the assessment of the use of AI by public authorities, if an AI system is classified as a "high-risk" system [17]. The AIA groups all AI systems into four categories: 1) prohibited practices, [17, Art. 5], 2) high-risk AI systems [17, Art. 6], 3) AI systems with limited risk [17, Art. 51], and 4) systems with minimal risks, which are, generally, outside the scope of this legal act. It is important to point out that this classification does not depend on the type of AI system. Most AI systems, such as ChatGPT, Co-Pilot, and Claude, constitute general-purpose artificial intelligence [17, Art. 3]. General-purpose AI can be used for various purposes, both directly and as integrated into another AI system. It is considered to be an AI system with systematic but limited risks. However, the AI model or AI system can be used in a way that its use can be classified as prohibited or high-risk.

It rather classifies how, the locations where, and the types of activities and tasks for which the system is used. Therefore, the same AI system used differently may fall into one or another category depending on the context of use.

It is unlikely that the application of an AI system by the judicial bodies will fall under the definition of prohibited practices unless it is used in a way to manipulate or deceit, used for social scoring or emotion recognition, or is used to infer, for example, political views or determine sex life [17, Art. 5]. However, depending on the context, it can fall under the definition of high risk.

The use of an AI system in the court can fall into the category of high risk when several conditions are fulfilled: a) it is listed as a high-risk system in Annex I or Annex III of the AIA; b) an AI system can cause significant harm; c) the use of AI system does not fall under one of the exceptions listed in Art. 6, par. 3. In other words, integration and use of AI systems in the justice system do not *per se* fall into the category of a high-risk system. The latter is limited to researching the law, interpreting the law and facts, and applying the law to facts, according to Annex III of the AIA, which is classified as high-risk [17, Annex III, par. 8(a)]. The use of an AI system for court administration, which does not directly relate to the decision-making in the case, is outside the scope of this definition. Hence, the high-risk use is limited mostly to the work of the judge.

The AI system can be classified as a high-risk system if it poses a significant risk of harm to the fundamental rights of a natural person [17, Art. 6, par. 3]. Significant harm can occur if the AI system is used to 'materially influence the outcome of decision-making' [17, Art. 6, par. 3]. The significant harm is a context-specific concept and has to be assessed on a case-by-case basis [18, pars. 91–92].

Article 6, par. 3, of the AIA also provides four exceptions when the use of AI systems, even if listed in Annex III, will not constitute a high risk, meaning that it is unlikely to produce significant harm since it does not materially impact the outcome of the case [17, recit. 53]. First, if the AI system is used to perform narrow procedural tasks [17, Art. 6, par. 3(1)]. For example, the AI system is used to structure information, group documents, and detect duplicates of documents [17, recit. 53]. Second, an AI system is used to improve activities previously completed by humans. In this case, it won't pose a high risk to the fundamental rights of a litigant since AI supplements the work of a person rather than being involved in the decision-making process [17, Art. 6, par. 3(2)]. For example, the AI system can be used to improve the draft of a document created by a human [17, recit. 53]. Third, an AI system that is used to detect decision-making patterns or deviations from prior decision-making for informative purposes is not considered an AI system that poses significant risks [17, Art. 6, par.3]. It can help identify relevant case-law, provide analytical information about the pattern of decisions, and recommend a course of action. Fourth, an AI system is used to assist with preparatory tasks when it is applied as a supplementary tool [17, Art 6, par.4].

It can be concluded from reading Annex III and the exceptions cumulatively that an AI system can be considered a high-risk system only if it is used to analyse the facts and the law and draft a decision by applying the law to the facts. In such circumstances, an AI system no longer serves as a tool that '*improves* activities *completed* by humans' and no longer acts as an information-providing tool. It becomes a part of the decision-making process, which can influence the outcome of a case.

If the AI system is classified as a high-risk system, under AIA, the public authorities are required to undertake a fundamental rights impact assessment (FRIA) before the high-risk AI system is put into service or use [17, Art. 27]. The FRIA can also be considered as an *ex ante* assessment framework of the use of technology in the justice system.

The FRIA aims to identify specific risks to the rights of individuals and the measures to be taken to mitigate these risks [17, recit. 96]. The EU Guidelines on Trustworthy AI refer to "mitigation of risks" in the form of "trade-offs" [19]. If identified, a risk has to be acknowledged and evaluated [19]. The CAI report echoes the same idea that "in almost all technical decisions there is always a trade-off between the values that the technical system gives and the damage that a concrete system may produce" [15].

In the context of judicial proceedings, this problem requires a balancing between the use of technology and the protection of the right to a fair trial. FRIA is meant to systematically identify how AI might affect human rights and integrate safeguards. The assessment should describe the process, where and how the AI tool will be used in court [17, Art. 27, par.1]. For example, whether the system will be used to research the law and recommend specific case-law as the basis of the decision, or whether some of the procedural steps will be automated. The intended purpose and functionality of the AI system also have to be defined. FRIA can include such information, namely, whether the AI tool directly assists in drafting decisions or only makes recommendations. This step of the impact assessment defines the scope of the assessment for further evaluation. The FRIA has certain similarities with the HUDERIA methodology.

However, the AIA does not provide step-by-step guidance on the content of the FRIA. Moreover, a technology's place on the risk spectrum does not necessarily correlate directly with its institutional legitimacy or contribution to justice. Therefore, there should be a broader evaluative lens.

To sum up, the existing approaches to the assessment of technology focus on two broad areas of assessment. One area is assessing the level of digitalization of the justice system and the use of technologies. The second, more recent area concerns the assessment of risks of using AI systems in courts. Few indicators in these frameworks envisage instruments to assess potential benefits. However, considering the benefits of AI is important to ensure that, in the assessment of the risks and drafting a mitigation plan, the actual contribution to the core objectives of the justice system is not lost. If this aspect is not taken into account, the legal system may end up either over-relying on technological tools of limited value or failing to critically examine the conditions under which technological benefits can justify institutional change.

4   Aligning AI Assessment with Justice System Objectives

Excluding issues related to financial viability, the purpose of the benefit-harm evaluation is to assess whether AI systems contribute to the objectives of the justice system without infringing individual rights and to determine whether their deployment is justifiable at all. If the risks are significant and the necessary mitigation measures would undermine the advantages of using AI, then the system may become inefficient, redundant, or even counterproductive. Given the high cost and complexity of integrating AI technologies into the justice system, this evaluation serves as a critical tool for deciding whether the use of a particular AI system is truly necessary or whether its risks and required safeguards outweigh its potential value.

Benefit-harm evaluation of the use of AI in the justice system can be composed of three components: 1) the use of AI helps achieve justice system objectives (benefit); 2) the risks of using AI are identified (harm); 3) if the risks are not unacceptable as such, a mitigation plan whose burden is commensurate with the benefits can help reduce them (balance). The frameworks summarised earlier in this article address the identification of the risk of harm. Hence, the following section focuses on the two other components of the benefit-harm evaluation: contribution to the objectives of the justice system (benefit) and the assessment of the balance between benefit and harm.

The justice system in a democratic society upholds the rule of law, protects individual rights, and ensures fair dispute resolution. The use of technology in the courts should support the protection of fundamental rights, improve the administration of justice, and facilitate access to justice [20–22]. This support is evaluated within the broader assessment of the quality of justice. Efficiency has become a central concern in the discussion on the digitalisation of justice [1, 3, 23]. For instance, making digital justice more efficient is listed as one of four strategic objectives for EU e-justice 2024–2028

[24, par. 43]. This focus is not only driven by practical demands for faster proceedings but is also encompassed by legal standards such as Art. 6 of the ECHR (hearing within a reasonable time) [21]. In the words of the ECtHR, Art. 6 requires and allows the judicial system to be organised in a manner enabling expeditious and efficient judicial proceedings [25]. The use of technology should be guided by these goals of the justice system and can be incorporated into the benefit-harm assessment.

Once the benefits and harms are identified, it is important to find the balance between them. It is suggested to apply the principle of proportionality as an instrument for assessing the benefits and risks for the use of an AI system in court.

In legal decision-making, the principle of proportionality is often invoked as an instrument to find the balance between competing interests. It is used to assess whether the reasons given by authorities justify the benefits to the public interest.

Analogously, the principle of proportionality is included as one of the ethical principles in several ethical guidelines related to AI. [13, 19, 26, 27]. According to Section III.2 of the UNESCO Guidelines on Ethics of AI, the use of AI must be proportionate to achieving legitimate objectives and should not exceed what is necessary. It is emphasized that the intensity of use of AI tools should be appropriate and balanced to the purpose they serve [26]. The EU Guidelines for Trustworthy AI incorporate proportionality as a substantive aspect of fairness [19]. The principle serves as a safeguard to ensure that AI systems do not create imbalances or inequalities in decision-making. To summarize, AI should be used in a way that is justified by its intended goals and does not exceed what is necessary to achieve them. Proportionality pertains to whether the value of using the system is justifiable. In other words, this principle helps to ensure that the use of AI remains reasonable. By articulating the relationship between benefits and harm, it can be assessed the use of AI more comprehensively.

A similar approach is also adopted in interdisciplinary studies. In the field of information systems evaluation, the model developed by DeLone and McLean [28] introduced the concept of "net benefit" to assess digital tools. The net benefit reflects the overall impact of introducing technology, taking into account both positive and negative effects on individuals and organizations. This concept has since been applied in various public sector contexts, including the justice system. Giampiero Lupo, building on the concept of net benefit, has proposed adapting the model to the assessment of technology in the justice system [29]. To assess the benefit, it is also important to establish a benchmark of what kind of benefit the use of technology seeks to achieve. Lupo suggested linking it to values such as transparency, accessibility, and impartiality, thereby shifting the focus from operational success to institutional relevance and justice-system alignment [29]. The objectives of the justice system can provide the context on how the principle of proportionality functions in practice. Eventually, benefit-harm analysis and finding the balance between the two would require a set of clear metrics. A few examples below demonstrate the overall logic of this assessment.

When an AI system is used, whether to manage case files, analyse parties' submissions, or suggest relevant legal sources, it must not intrude more than necessary upon the privacy and procedural rights of the parties. For instance, an AI system might help a court registry and a judge to organize written submissions and evidence to speed up the proceedings. The AI system may also check for missing documents or inconsistencies.

In this example, the proportionality principle ensures that the system strictly focuses on what is needed to assess the case without intruding on the rights of parties, for instance, by considering elements irrelevant to the case. The AI system can be used to create a "profile" of a person based on the documents submitted and information available on the internet and social media platforms. This profile can assess personal characteristics. However, such information is irrelevant to the hearing of the case, and processing it is not proportional to the legitimate aim.

AI systems can help courts work more efficiently. It can support case management or assist with preliminary analysis of the case. However, the use of AI systems to achieve efficiency should be proportional and should not undermine fundamental procedural rights, such as the right to a fair hearing, the right to adversarial proceedings, and judicial independence and impartiality. For instance, the AI system can be used to determine legal issues in the case and suggest relevant legal provisions and case law. The proportionality principle requires the court to retain control of the legal qualification in the case and allows both parties to present their arguments (equality of arms).

AI can help handle large sets of information or recurring disputes more effectively. For example, in cases concerning environmental regulation, AI might process large datasets, such as pollution records, to confirm compliance or violations. To use the AI system proportionately means it is used to analyze the data insofar as it helps to clarify factual or legal questions, rather than to produce an outcome that will be the basis for the decision in the case.

The benefit-harm assessment is also relevant when applied to the mitigation of risk strategies. When the implementation of mitigation measures significantly reduces the value an AI system is intended to deliver, the overall utility of its deployment becomes questionable. For example, if an AI system used in judicial drafting persistently references non-existent case-law, the necessity of human verification becomes unavoidable. The oversight measures may reduce the expected efficiency gains and require additional resources. At the same time, the system may introduce secondary benefits, such as promoting greater uniformity in citation practices, which could justify the continued use of the technology despite the need for manual review. These trade-offs must be critically examined when assessing the actual contribution of AI systems to the functioning of the judiciary.

The proposed framework of benefit-harm assessment constitutes a theoretical model. Subsequent steps involve testing this model under real-world conditions to gather empirical evidence regarding its robustness and to identify potential challenges related to its practical implementation. The proposed model may be applied to AI systems already in use to assess their benefits, risks, and overall utility. This approach could involve the collection of both quantitative and qualitative data regarding the functioning and impact of AI systems in judicial bodies. Where such systems enhance efficiency, the findings can provide valuable insights for other courts and judicial bodies considering the adoption of similar tools.

It is important to note that the proposed model of evaluation applies only to AI systems that fall within an acceptable range of risks. It is not intended to justify or assess technologies that give rise to unacceptable risks, which should be excluded from deployment in the justice system altogether [17]. These types of systems pose fundamental risks to human rights and therefore lie beyond the scope of the proposed analysis. Their use would be incompatible with core legal standards underpinning the justice system.

Some systems pose substantial risks that could be remedied by envisaging a mitigation plan [17, Art. 6, Art. 9, Art. 15, Art. 57]. Such risks include, but are not limited to, the use of AI systems that produce binding decisions that require human oversight [17, Art. 6, Art. 14, Annex III]; systems that can reinforce or amplify discrimination patterns and require data audit [17, Art. 6, Art.10, Annex III,]; and an automated processing and decision-making system where an individual has a right to information [17, 30, 31]. In such instances, the benefit-harm assessment could be conducted, including the impact of mitigation measures on the use of the system.

The following graph (Fig. 1) presents a conceptual illustration of how the proposed model could be applied in future evaluations of AI systems in the justice sector. It visualizes the relationship between benefits and risks and indicates the perceived utility of each system through the marker. The present graph serves as a modeling example and does not reflect the actual utility of each AI tool. The benefit-harm assessment framework requires a more nuanced assessment of AI tools by developing concrete metrics and collecting empirical data.

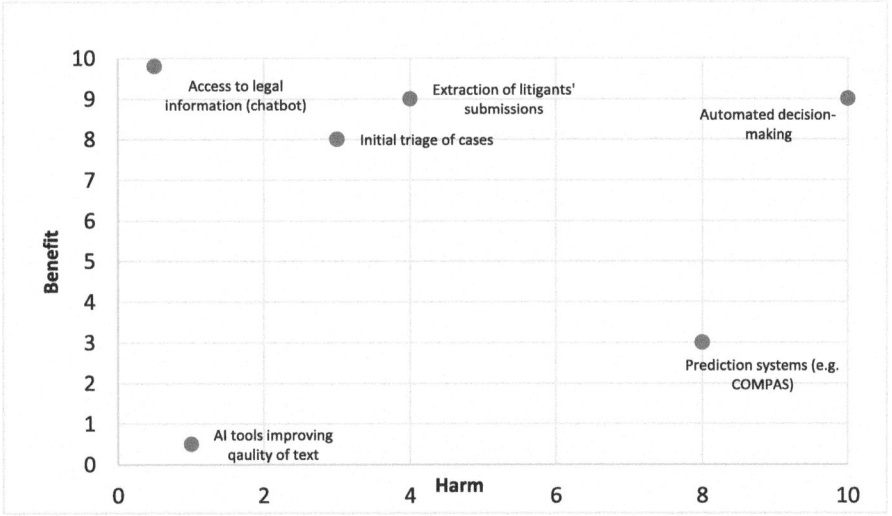

Fig. 1. Benefit-harm assessment of AI tools in the justice system.

5 Conclusion

The use of AI in the justice system represents both a continuation of digitalisation efforts and an incremental change in how justice is administered. While earlier technologies primarily enhanced procedural efficiency and access to legal information, AI systems introduced capabilities such as autonomous reasoning, text interpretation, and self-learning, which raise new challenges for institutional legitimacy.

To date, AI assessment frameworks, such as those developed by the EU and the Council of Europe, have primarily focused on risk mitigation. Despite the increased sophistication of these methodologies, several challenges persist. Most frameworks are still skewed toward quantifiable metrics, such as system availability and functionality, underemphasizing more qualitative aspects such as user trust and adaptability. In practice, digital tools may be available but underused, or worse, misused in ways that introduce new vulnerabilities into the justice system.

To address this gap, the article proposes a benefit-harm assessment grounded in the principle of proportionality. This approach introduces three key considerations: (1) whether the AI system supports justice system objectives, (2) whether risks are adequately identified and mitigated, and (3) whether the mitigation efforts preserve the intended benefits of the system. Proportionality implies that the greater the potential for harm, the stronger the justification required for the AI system's use. AI tools that are deeply embedded in legal reasoning that affect the outcome of decisions, or that operate in sensitive areas such as asylum or criminal law, must be subject to fundamental rights impact assessment and especially stringent evaluation. By contrast, some tools may be of limited complexity or impact and do not require the same level of scrutiny.

As a theoretical model, the proposed framework invites further empirical research. Its application to existing AI tools could support evidence-based analysis of both utility and risk. Collecting empirical data, both quantitative and qualitative, will be essential to assess system performance. This evaluation can inform procurement decisions based on evidence of system performance and may lead to the development of an index reflecting the global rationale of the system, thereby providing a structured basis for extending its application to comparable judicial and court administration functions.

This approach is relevant in light of emerging practices in courts where AI is used for a variety of tasks, ranging from administrative support to those that involve the interpretation and application of law. If risks of AI are identified and the mitigation measures are so burdensome that they significantly reduce the system's added value, their deployment may be unjustified. The benefit-harm assessment provides insight that the use of AI in the justice system is meaningful, proportionate, safe, and aligned with the justice system's objectives.

Disclosure of Interests. The authors have no competing interests to declare that are relevant to the content of this article.

References

1. Velicogna, M.: Justice systems and ICT: what can be learned from Europe? Utrecht Law Rev. **3**(1), 129–147 (2007)
2. Velicogna, M.: Use of information and communication technologies (ICT) in European judicial systems. CEPEJ Studies No. 7 (2007)
3. Fabri, M.: From court automation to e-justice and beyond in Europe. Int. J. Court Adm. **15**(3), 7 (2024)
4. Gomes, A., Dias, J.G.: Digital divide in the European Union: a typology of EU Citizens. Soc. Indic. Res. **176**, 149–172 (2025)
5. Michalski, R.S., Carbonell, J.G., Mitchell, T.M: Machine Learning: An Artificial Intelligence Approach, Springer, Berlin, Heidelberg (1983). https://doi.org/10.1007/978-3-662-12405-5

6. CEPEJ Resource Center on Cyberjustice and Artificial Intelligence. https://www.coe.int/en/web/cepej/resource-centre-on-cyberjustice-and-ai
7. CEPEJ: 1st AIAB Report on the use of Artificial Intelligence (AI) in the judiciary, CEPEJ-AIAB(2024)4Rev5, Council of Europe, Strasbourg (2025)
8. CEPEJ: European judicial systems: efficiency and quality of justice, Studies No. 23, Council of Europe (2016)
9. CEPEJ: Measuring the quality of justice. CEPEJ(2016)12, Council of Europe, Strasbourg (2016)
10. CEPEJ: Checklist for promoting the quality of justice and the courts, Section III. Council of Europe, Strasbourg (2008)
11. CEPEJ: Guidelines on how to drive change towards cyberjustice. Council of Europe, Strasbourg (2016)
12. CEPEJ: Methodology for the calculation of the CEPEJ Information and Communication Technologies (ICT) indices, CEPEJ-GT-EVAL (2024)20, Council of Europe, Strasbourg (2024)
13. CEPEJ: European Ethical Charter on the Use of Artificial Intelligence (AI) in Judicial Systems and their Environment. Council of Europe, Strasbourg (2018)
14. CEPEJ: Assessment Tool for the Operationalisation of the European Ethical Charter on the Use of Artificial Intelligence in Judicial Systems and Their Environment. CEPEJ(2023)16final, Council of Europe, Strasbourg (2023)
15. Committee on Artificial Intelligence: HUDERIA Methodology – Methodology for the risk and impact assessment of artificial intelligence systems. CAI(2024)16rev2, Council of Europe, Strasbourg (2024)
16. European Commission: 2024 EU Justice Scoreboard. COM (2024)950 Brussels (2024)
17. EU: Regulation (EU) 2024/1689 of the European Parliament and of the Council of 13 June 2024 laying down harmonised rules on artificial intelligence and amending Regulations (EC) No 300/2008, (EU) No 167/2013, (EU) No 168/2013, (EU) 2018/858, (EU) 2018/1139 and (EU) 2019/2144 and Directives 2014/90/EU, (EU) 2016/797 and (EU) 2020/1828 (EU Artificial Intelligence Act), OJ L 2024/1689 (2024)
18. European Commission: Annex to the Communication to the Commission: Approval of the content of the draft Communication from the Commission – Commission Guidelines on prohibited artificial intelligence practices established by Regulation (EU) 2024/1689, C (2025)884, Brussels (2025)
19. European Union: High-level Expert Group on Artificial Intelligence, Ethics Guidelines for Trustworthy AI, European Commission (2019)
20. CEPEJ: Opinion No. 14 on justice and information technologies. Council of Europe, Strasbourg (2011)
21. Council of Europe: European Convention on Human Rights (1950)
22. European Union: Charter of Fundamental Rights of the European Union, OJ C 326 (2012)
23. Reiling, D.: Technology for Justice: How Information Technology can Support Judicial Reform. Leiden University Press, Leiden (2009)
24. Council of the European Union: European e-Justice Strategy 2024–2028. 15509/23, Brussels (2023)
25. European Court of Human Rights: Case Zavodnik v. Slovenia, no. 53723/13, Strasbourg (2015)
26. UNESCO: Recommendation on the Ethics of Artificial Intelligence, SHS/BIO/PI/2021/1, (2022)
27. UNESCO: Draft UNESCO Guidelines for the Use of AI Systems in Courts and Tribunals (2024)
28. DeLone, W.H., McLean, E.R.: The DeLone and McLean model of information systems success: a ten-year update. J. Manag. Inf. Syst. **19**(4), 9–30 (2003)

29. Lupo, G.: Assessing e-Justice smartness: a new framework for e-justice evaluation through public values. In: Setting Foundations for the Creation of Public Values in Smart Cities (2019)
30. Court of Justice of the European Union: Case C-817/19 Ligue des droits humains v. Conseil des ministres, ECLI:EU:C:2022:491 (2022)
31. Court of Justice of the European Union: Case C-203/22 Dun & Bradstreet Austria, ECLI:EU:C:2025:117 (2025)

Not Knowing, Yet Living: AI and the Modern Legal Trial of Prometheus in Medicine

Uchenna Nnawuchi and Carlisle George[✉]

ALERT Research Group, Department of Computer Science, Faculty of Science and Technology,
Middlesex University, London, UK
uchennannawuchi@gmail.com, UN055@live.mdx.ac.uk,
c.george@mdx.ac.uk

Abstract. This paper explores the paradox of Artificial Intelligence (AI), particularly Machine Learning (ML), in modern medicine, promising enhanced diagnostics and treatment while in many instances also leading to a profound loss of transparency and interpretability. Complex AI systems such as Automated Decision-Making Systems (ADMS) increasingly guide critical clinical decisions; however, their opaque "black box" nature challenges traditional medical ethics centred on transparency, due process, accountability, and patient autonomy. ADMs often make recommendations that cannot be fully understood or explained due to the system's opacity. This raises both legal and ethical concerns. For example, the ability of clinicians to justify clinical decisions informed by AI when they themselves lack insight into its reasoning raises concerns about clinical legal liability. This, in turn, raises ethical concerns regarding patient autonomy if patients are unable to meaningfully make informed choices on treatments due to the opacity of decisions made by AI. The extent to which patients should consent to and place their trust in life-saving technologies whose inner workings remain opaque remains an open debate. These technologies, arguably, can diminish patients' rights to knowledge, autonomy, and dignity. Such concerns underscore the fragility of trust within clinical relationships and expose the limitations of prevailing frameworks for medical explanation (MedX) and informed consent. This paper examines the role of explainability in AI-driven medicine, arguing that while explanation is essential, it must be balanced against the clinical utility of high-performing, opaque systems. To address this tension, the paper proposes the Promethean Threshold Heuristic (PTH)—a normative framework designed to reconcile the need for explanation with clinical efficacy. Drawing on Promethean myth, it frames the ethical dilemma posed by AI as one of balancing risk, knowledge, and human dignity. Ultimately, it calls for principled AI governance in healthcare—one that preserves trust, prioritises transparency where feasible, and recognises the trade-offs inherent in deploying powerful but opaque technologies.

Keywords: Artificial Intelligence · Machine Learning · Medicine · Healthcare · transparency · explanation · opacity · black box

© The Author(s), under exclusive license to Springer Nature Switzerland AG 2026
J. Valente de Oliveira et al. (Eds.): EPIA 2025, LNAI 16122, pp. 147–159, 2026.
https://doi.org/10.1007/978-3-032-05179-0_12

1 Introduction

> "Prometheus gave man fire and was punished
> for it. Maybe that is the price of progress."
>
> by *Mary Shelley*[1].

Prometheus's gift of fire to humanity, a symbol of knowledge and power, came with unintended consequences—a dual legacy of advancement and suffering. Similarly, the advent of Artificial Intelligence (AI), specifically Machine Learning (ML) in medicine, represents a profound leap forward, promising to revolutionise healthcare through improved diagnostics, treatment precision, and patient outcomes. However, this progress is accompanied by a form of punishment: a loss of transparency and autonomy over the knowledge or reasoning that may inform life-saving decisions. The fire of AI brings about new possibilities but also casts shadows of uncertainty and ethical complexity.

At Duke University Hospital, Nurse Dina Sarro struggled to explain alerts from an AI system, Sepsis Watch, which flagged sepsis risks using vast data [2]. Physicians were sceptical, and Sarro admitted she could not justify the algorithm's output. This reflects a broader shift in medicine, where AI-based recommendations often lack transparency [3], leaving clinicians caught between black-box systems and sceptical colleagues. ADMs are now widespread across domains like healthcare, finance, and justice [4, 5], aiding diagnosis through analysis of clinical data [6]. While they improve efficiency and access [7, 8], their opacity raises serious ethical concerns, compromising informed consent, clinical accountability, and potentially embedding bias [9, 10]. Cases like the failed 2018 sepsis detection highlight the stakes [11]. This paper explores the tension between explainability and performance in clinical AI, proposing the Promethean Threshold Heuristic (PTH) as a framework to balance trust, dignity, and patient survival.

2 Automated Decision-Making and Application in Medicine

The COVID-19 pandemic rapidly accelerated digital transformation in healthcare, specifically in medicine and clinical practice [12]. Traditional care models gave way to telemedicine, which became a cornerstone of health delivery across Europe and beyond. Tools like remote monitoring, AI-assisted diagnostics, and virtual consultations proliferated [13–16]. This shift laid the groundwork for the widespread integration of ML into clinical practice [3], forming what is termed Medical Artificial Intelligence (MAI). MAI encompasses a broad spectrum of AI technologies used in medicine, including ML, natural language processing, and expert systems [3]. These tools support or replace clinician decision-making in diagnosis, treatment planning, and patient monitoring [17]. Related concepts—Machine Learning in Medicine (MLM) [18] and Medical Augmented Intelligence [19]—focus on data-driven care [18] and human-AI collaboration, respectively [19]. Though nuanced in focus, all share a central challenge: algorithmic opacity and bias in their recommendation [9]. This paper uses the term MAI to collectively refer to these related paradigms, focusing on their shared reliance on opaque, high-performing systems and their impact on clinical reasoning and patient care. As AI systems become more embedded in healthcare, they raise urgent ethical, legal, and practical concerns about explainability, autonomy, trust, and accountability. Despite their promise, these systems are often obscured not only to patients but also to clinicians and even to the developers of these systems [9]. Consequently, clinicians may struggle to explain AI-informed decisions, complicating informed consent, patient autonomy and dignity, and human rights. This issue is particularly pronounced with a subset of MAI, *id est* ADMs, which are increasingly responsible for critical tasks such as disease prediction, diagnosis, and treatment [18]. The application of ADMs has raised critical ethical and legal questions about explainability, accountability [20], and the thresholds of trust in AI-driven medicine [3]. Consequently, regulation is playing catch-up, and this has led to several recent enactments, including the Artificial Intelligence Act (AIA) 2021 [21] and the European Health Data Space Regulation (EHDS) [22]. However, existing regulations already in place include the General Data Protection Regulation (GDPR) 2016 [23], the Medical Device Regulation (MDR) 2017 [24], and the Vitro Diagnostic Regulation (IVDR) [25].

2.1 Application of Automated Decision-Making (ADMs)

The zeitgeist suggests that ADMs are increasingly seen as a solution to many challenges in medicine, specifically clinical practice, promising greater speed, accuracy, and efficiency [26]. ADMs used prediction, assessing patient deterioration risks by integrating behavioural and physiological data—often from wearables or external sources—to detect early warning signs [5, 27]. However, the reasoning behind these predictions is frequently opaque, raising issues of privacy, dignity, and autonomy. Furthermore, in diagnosis, particularly in fields like radiology, ADMs such as IDx-DR detect complex patterns that may elude human perception [8]. These systems rely on processing data at scales beyond human capability. Yet, the lack of transparency often leads clinicians to accept decisions they cannot fully interpret, weakening shared decision-making and introducing automation bias [28].

Additionally, ADMs draw on large datasets—including patient histories, biomarkers, and past outcomes—to suggest interventions [29]. In fields like oncology [30] and sepsis care [31], they increasingly shape clinical decisions, guiding therapeutic strategies and influencing whether aggressive or conservative approaches are pursued. Beyond the sepsis case, numerous examples illustrate the challenges clinicians face in fully trusting algorithmic outputs within clinical practice, largely due to understandable scepticism arising from the potential for false positives and false negatives. For instance, a deep learning model assessing mortality risk from pneumonia categorised patients with asthma as low risk [32]. This counterintuitive outcome stemmed from the model's reliance on a training dataset in which asthmatic patients had benefited from proactive clinical interventions, thereby skewing the risk profile. Similarly, another deep learning system designed to screen chest X-rays for pneumonia inadvertently exploited confounding variables such as the geographic location of the imaging scanner, rather than the clinical features of the X-rays themselves [32]. In a further case, a model aimed at stratifying patients by risk level based on radiographic data relied on hardware-specific metadata, rather than pathophysiological indicators, to generate its predictions [32]. More so, IBM Watson used for oncology received serious widespread criticism because its treatment recommendations were sometimes inconsistent or insufficiently explainable, leading to concerns about reliability and clinical trust [33]. Reports indicated that Watson occasionally provided unsafe or irrelevant advice due to limitations in its training data and opaque decision processes [33]. Collectively, these examples underscore the compounding systemic issues of opacity, trust, and accountability that continue to confound the integration of AI into clinical practice. They highlight the urgent need for greater transparency and explainability to support clinician confidence and ensure the safe, ethical deployment of such systems. When clinicians are unable to comprehend or interrogate the decision-making processes of AI models, this not only undermines patients' rights to informed consent and autonomous decision-making but also raises serious legal concerns. Particularly, clinical reliance on opaque algorithmic outputs may give rise to liability and causation disputes should patient harm occur, further eroding the trust that is foundational to both ethical medicine and effective AI governance.

These issues associated with these ADM tools require their role to be examined within ethical and legal frameworks that prioritise transparency, accountability, and the patient's right to understand and consent.

2.2   Challenges of Applying Automated Decision-Making

While ADMs have enhanced efficiency and precision in healthcare, their growing role as quasi-clinicians poses serious ethical and legal challenges. They shift traditional roles, raise accountability questions, and disrupt foundational principles such as shared decision-making (SDM), data privacy, informed consent, and transparency.

2.2.1   Shared Decision-Making (SDM)

SDM relies on a dialogic relationship between patients and clinicians, grounded in mutual respect and autonomy [34]. The integration of opaque ADMs threatens this balance [34]. When patients cannot understand or challenge algorithmic recommendations, consent becomes symbolic rather than substantive. ADM systems, especially black-box models, risk making patients passive recipients of decisions they neither shape nor fully grasp [35]. This undermines agency, reducing humans to data points and clinicians to intermediaries between patients and machines [36]. Further complicating matters, there is no clear consensus on how AI should function within SDM frameworks—should it guide, assist, or override decisions? Without transparency, AI risks substituting probabilistic logic for principled judgment, introducing automation bias and diminishing ethical integrity. If clinicians defer to systems they do not understand or cannot explain, the clinician-patient alliance is eroded, and accountability becomes murky.

2.2.2   Legal and Ethical Challenges

A. *Data Protection and Privacy*
   ADMs depend on large datasets from EHRs, wearables, and apps, raising risks of re-identification, discrimination, and data misuse [5]. While models like federated learning enhance privacy [37], tension persists between the need for long-term data and GDPR principles like minimisation [23]. Particularly in imaging [38], vast

identifiable data are needed to train accurate systems, making robust anonymisation and public trust essential. Compliance with GDPR remains difficult, especially for predictive ADMs that require data persistence.

B. *Autonomy and Informed Consent*

Meaningful consent is increasingly difficult in AI-driven care ecosystems [36]. Patients often lack awareness of how their data is processed or how algorithms influence their care [39]. Opaque ADM reasoning challenges both patient and surrogate decision-making, making informed consent fragile at best [40]. When neither the patient nor clinician can explain or contest a system's output, consent becomes procedural theatre [36]. This not only undermines the patient's moral agency but also compromises the clinician's ethical obligations under medical codes that prioritise autonomy and informed decision-making [41]. Clinicians risk being reduced to conduits of algorithmic authority, their fiduciary role diluted. To preserve the integrity of informed consent, investments in interpretability, communication tools, and clinician training are essential.

C. *Transparency*

Transparency (the degree to which the *inner workings* of an AI system, including its structure, data sources, design, and decision-making processes, are open and accessible for scrutiny) —closely tied to explainability and interpretability —is vital for trust in AI healthcare [42]. However, most ADMs function as black boxes, even to developers. Unlike some traditional medical uncertainties, algorithmic opacity is systemic and scalable, making it harder to justify or contest outcomes [42]. This creates a troubling scenario: patients denied care by opaque ADMs cannot understand or challenge the decision, stripping them of agency. The ethical and legal implications are profound—when harm results, who is accountable? Existing legal safeguards, such as the GDPR's right to contest [23] and the AI Act's right to explanation [21], are difficult to implement in practice but increasingly necessary. Without them, trust in AI-driven medicine will erode. Upholding the right to explanation reasserts the patient's autonomy, dignity, and moral standing and ensures ADM systems support, rather than replace, ethical clinical judgment.

3   The Right to Explanation

3.1   Proposed Solutions to ML Opacity in Medical AI

Some scholars argue that the right to explanation offers limited value, warning it may become "meaningless" in practice [36]. They favour architectural regulation and tools like DPIAs over enforceable rights to build trust [36]. Ghassemi et al. [43] also question current explainability methods, calling them inadequate for patient-level decision-making. Others defend black-box models for their diagnostic accuracy, suggesting that proven outcomes matter more than transparency, especially since human reasoning is not always explainable either [44]. A more nuanced scholarly position proposes the ethical governance of opacity [45]. As opposed to viewing opacity as an inherent flaw, this perspective reframes it as a manageable condition—one that, when accompanied by institutional trust and role-sensitive justification, can coexist with the responsible deployment of AI. This approach explicitly moves away from epistemic idealism—the belief that full transparency is always desirable or achievable—toward epistemic realism, which recognises that explanations must be contextually calibrated. Trust, in this view (epistemic realism), is not produced by making all internal workings visible, but by ensuring that decisions are justifiable to stakeholders in ways that are meaningful for their specific roles and risks [45]. This proposition, though arguable, makes these systems more responsible, trustworthy, and ethical. However, this view does not overlook ethical duties like informed consent under the WMA Code, but supports it. More so, clinical scholars such as Mehlus and her group argued that AI offers significant benefits in clinical practice, but its adoption hinges on calibrated trust [46]. Clinicians must rely on AI without deferring to it uncritically, especially when its outputs contradict clinical judgment. Explainable AI (XAI) addresses this by clarifying how decisions are made, supporting both trust and accountability. Even ethicists like Grote and Berens contended that the absence of reliable, meaningful explanations can erode the clinician–patient relationship and distort shared decision-making [47]. Thus, the Sepsis Watch example paragraph 1 and other examples in paragraph 2.1 exemplify this broader phenomenon: opacity without compensatory frameworks for explanation amounts to a structural ethical risk in AI-assisted medicine. Ultimately, without explainability, patient autonomy, trust, and accountability suffer, making it not just a technical concern, but a moral imperative.

3.2   Meaning and Justification of the Right to Explanation in Clinical Practice

The right to explanation in the context of medical or clinical practice refers to a patient's ability to understand why an MAI, specifically ADMs, made a particular recommendation [48]. In this context, *explanation* means providing understandable reasons for a decision [49]; *explainability* means the system itself can generate such reasons in a human-comprehensible way [50]. This right affirms patient autonomy and dignity. It has both intrinsic value (respecting individuals as rational agents) and instrumental value (helping them make informed choices, challenge decisions, or seek redress). Explanations must serve a purpose: enabling understanding and informed decision-making, especially when decisions affect health or legal status [51]. An explanation is very important because opaque decisions risk eroding trust, harming patients, and weakening professional accountability [52]. Explanations are necessary to detect errors, address bias, ensure fairness [20], and uphold the clinician's duty of care. Without explanation, patients become passive recipients of black-box outputs, undermining informed consent [52]. As stated above (*paragraph 3.1*), some scholars argue that performance alone justifies trust (epistemic realism), while we insist on transparency as a moral obligation (epistemic idealism). Ultimately, the right to explanation is not a technical luxury but a safeguard for safety, dignity, and ethical medical practice. However, the right to explanation and explainability is not without its challenges, especially when considered against the trade-off with model performance.

4 Trade-off Between Performance and Explainability

As AI becomes more integrated, particularly in high-stakes fields like medicine, where decisions impact life, autonomy, and legal rights, the demand for XAI grows exponentially [53]. Explainability is essential for accountability, trust, and informed consent. A patient cannot make an informed choice on different procedures, whether it is immunotherapy or chemotherapy, when diagnosed with cancer. This undermines dignity and could violate the right to life, Article 8 ECHR and 6 ICCPR; this right to life is not just a right to live [54, 55] but includes the right to choose how you want to live, the way you want to live, if you want to live [56], and a quality end to life [57]. This right to life, in medical or clinical practice, is protected, supported, and valued by the right to explanation. However, the most accurate AI systems (like deep neural networks) are often the least transparent [58]. This creates a trade-off: performance vs explainability. More explainable models can lack diagnostic power, while high-performing models can be "black boxes" which are incomprehensible to the clinicians, the patients and even to their developers [58]. However, explanation is not just about understanding—it supports ethical practice, respects patient choice, and fulfils legal obligations under frameworks like Articles 9, 12,15, 22 GDPR, Article 86 EU AI Act, and Article 26 WMA. Clinical AI decisions, like recommending cancer treatments or life-saving surgeries, must be explainable to preserve patient autonomy. Without clear reasoning, patients are denied the chance to consent meaningfully or understand the risks involved. Some studies [59] also show that poor-quality or misleading explanations can confuse clinicians or lead to over-reliance, often referred to as automation bias [5]. But this highlights the need for better explainability, not abandoning it. Properly designed, explainable AI supports trust, reduces bias, and promotes accountability. This issue is even more dire in and compounded during a medical emergency. For instance, the Sepsis case of 2018 given above, where the nurse stated that she would not have a good reason for the algorithm's decision. In such situations, perhaps where the case is one of emergency, explanation will give way. The challenge with this is one of legal liability and causation, where the treatment goes wrong. One is uncertain where to attribute responsibility, whether it is the clinicians who adopted the algorithm's recommendation or the developers of the algorithm. The position of the law is still unclear in this area. However, where it is not an emergency, and the patient's life is not hanging by a thread, then performance should give way to explanation. The patient or their surrogates or representatives would require an explanation to make an informed decision. Ultimately, balancing accuracy with patient autonomy and safety is not optional—it's a moral and legal imperative.

5 The Promethean Threshold Heuristic: Balancing Explanation and Survival in AI-Driven Healthcare

The proposed Promethean Threshold Heuristic (PTH) is designed to help healthcare professionals, AI developers, and policymakers navigate the ethical dilemmas posed by Automated Decision-Making Systems (ADMs). It seeks to balance life-saving interventions with the patient's right to meaningful explanation, upholding autonomy, beneficence, and legal accountability. PTH is rooted in internationally recognised ethical and legal standards, including the UNESCO Declaration on Bioethics and Human Rights (2005) [60], WMA International Code of Medical Ethics (2022) [41], OECD AI Principles (2019) [61], Oviedo Convention (1997) [62], Declaration of Helsinki (2013) [63], GDPR (2016) [23], and the EU AI Act (2021) [21]. These frameworks provide a strong ethical and legal foundation, ensuring that PTH reflects global norms and is adaptable across healthcare contexts. Additionally, it is structured around four core medical scenarios— life-threatening emergencies, emergencies with available surrogates, non-emergencies, and cases involving unknown patient status. PTH engages with the principles of autonomy, non-maleficence, beneficence, justice, and accountability [41]. It offers a novel and principled approach to reconciling medical necessity with the ethical demand for explanation in the age of AI.

5.1 The Promethean Threshold Heuristic (PTH)

Heuristic Statement: *In Automated Decision-making systems and AI-assisted medical decision-making, the importance of saving life may at times be justifiably overridden by the demand for patient-centred explanation. However, where explanation is to be deferred, it must be provided as soon as practicable to the patient or their designated surrogate family member/representative, balancing respect for human rights, dignity, and autonomy with clinical urgency.*

Table 1 below outlines the PTH components and how they are applied in the context of the four scenarios identified.

Table 1. The PTH Components and Application

No	Scenario	Priority	Action	Post-emergency
1	Life-Threatening Emergency	Save the patient's life with the most effective means available, even if, at the given time, the AI decision-making processes are not fully explainable	If the patient is incapacitated and no surrogate or family member/representative is available to receive an explanation and make an informed decision, the decision to prioritise saving the patient's life over explanation is justified	Provide a detailed explanation to the patient once stabilised or to family/surrogates/representatives as soon as possible
2	Emergency with Available Surrogate or Family Member	Save the patient's life while initiating real-time explanation to the surrogate/family/representatives to respect patient autonomy	The involvement of family members/representatives/surrogates should be leveraged to maintain transparency and trust, even during urgent care	Follow-up explanations to the patient and surrogates for full disclosure
3	Non-Emergency/Elective Care	Explanation and informed consent take precedence; AI decisions should be fully explainable to the patient prior to treatment	Patients have the right to understand the extent of AI involvement and its recommendations in their care before treatment begins	Ongoing consent and shared decision-making should be ensured throughout the care process
4	Unknown Patient Status or Absence of Surrogates	Follow the principle of beneficence—act to preserve the patient's life and wellbeing while documenting all AI decisions carefully	Action: Efforts must be made to identify surrogates or legal guardians for subsequent explanation and consent	Provide explanation to any identified representatives or to the patient upon regaining capacity

5.2 Justification of the PTH

The PTH aligns with core ethical principles in healthcare: autonomy, beneficence, non-maleficence, justice, and accountability [41].

1. **Respect for patient autonomy**
   The PTH defers explanation only in urgent care scenarios, reaffirming the obligation to inform patients as soon as possible. This mirrors international standards:

   - *UNESCO Declaration* (Arts. 5–6) emphasises autonomy and informed consent, allowing exceptions in emergencies.
   - *WMA Code of Ethics* (Arts. 13, 15, 17) supports patient autonomy and permits treatment without prior consent only when the patient is incapacitated and no surrogate is available. Thus, the heuristic safeguards autonomy while balancing clinical necessity.

2. **Beneficence and non-maleficence**
   The PTH prioritises life-saving intervention while minimising harm, justifying temporary non-disclosure only when delay could endanger life. This principle is supported by:

   - WMA *WMA Article 14* and *Declaration of Helsinki* (paragraphs 18, 30) stress prioritising patient welfare and minimising risk.
   - *OECD AI Principles* advocate for human-centric, transparent AI systems that avoid harm. The heuristic reflects this by ensuring deferred explanation is ethically justified, time-limited, and subject to oversight.

3. **Justice**
   The PTH affirms the legitimacy of surrogates or proxies in safeguarding patient rights when direct consent is not possible. This is consistent with:

   - *WMA Code* (Arts. 16, 19) endorses involving trusted representatives for patients with impaired capacity and stresses respect for patient preferences while preserving confidentiality.
   - Oviedo *Oviedo Convention* (Arts. 6, 9) mandates proxy consent and equitable access to care without discrimination. By incorporating surrogates in decision-making, the heuristic promotes fairness and continuity of care, ensuring patient rights are upheld in vulnerable scenarios.

4. **Accountability**
   PTH requires timely documentation and disclosure to preserve trust and professional responsibility. This aligns with:

   - *WMA Code* (Arts. 21, 23) emphasises transparency, including disclosure of third-party involvement and maintaining accurate records.
   - *GDPR* (Arts. 5, 12, 15) supports transparency in automated decision-making and grants patients access to data and explanations.
   - *IMIA Code of Ethics* highlights integrity, confidentiality, and clear communication in digital health. Together, these frameworks support the heuristic's demand for AI systems that combine rapid clinical response with post-event explainability and traceability.

Thus, the PTH encourages that AI systems should be designed to enable rapid and accurate decision-making for emergencies and transparent, explainable outputs for their decisions.

6   Conclusion

As Artificial Intelligence continues to transform the clinical landscape, the tension between algorithmic performance in decision-making and the ethical and legal imperative for explainability has become increasingly pronounced. This paper argued that while the right to explanation remains a fundamental concept for patient autonomy, informed consent, and trust, it must sometimes kowtow —temporarily and proportionally— in situations where a patient's survival and life are at stake. The Promethean Threshold Heuristic (PTH) responds to this challenge by offering a normative framework that is both context-sensitive and ethically grounded. Drawing on foundational principles peculiar to medical practice, such as autonomy, beneficence, and accountability, the PTH delineates clear conditions under which explanation may be deferred and when it must be promptly restored.

By acknowledging the moral complexity and ethical quagmire of AI in medicine, the PTH contributes meaningfully to the ongoing debate over the trade-off between explainability and performance. Opposed to framing the two in zero-sum opposition, the PTH proposes a structured reconciliation based on urgency, human dignity, and proportionality. This heuristic offers a flexible, rights-conscious model adaptable to real-world practice, capable of guiding clinicians, designers, and regulators.

Looking forward, further empirical work is needed to test and refine the heuristic across diverse healthcare settings, and policy frameworks must evolve to support systems capable of both high clinical performance and post hoc transparency. In this way, the PTH helps pave the way for AI systems that are not only powerful but also principled and patient-centred.

Disclosure of Interests.   The authors have no competing interests to declare that are relevant to the content of this article.

References

1. Shelley, M.: Frankenstein; or, The Modern Prometheus (Penguin Classics 2003) 84
2. Upson, S.: 'AI Is Helping Patients—but Doctors Still Need to Understand It' Wired (9 March 2020). https://www.wired.com/story/ai-help-patients-doctors-understand. Accessed 21 May 2025
3. Solaiman, B.: 'From "AI to Law" in healthcare: the proliferation of global guidelines in a void of legal uncertainty'. Med. Law **42**(2), 391–406 (2023)
4. Dormehl, L.: Thinking machines: the quest for artificial intelligence—and where it's taking us next. Penguin–TarcherPerigee, New York (2017)
5. Pierce, R.: 'AI in healthcare: solutions, challenges, and dilemmas in medical decision-making' (2019). https://ssrn.com/abstract=3806767. Accessed 21 May 2025
6. Susskind, J.: Future politics: 'living together in a world transformed by tech' (2020)

7. Esteva, A., et al.: Dermatologist-level classification of skin cancer with deep neural networks. Nature **542**, 115–118 (2017). https://doi.org/10.1038/nature21056
8. Gulshan, et al.: Development and validation of a deep learning algorithm for detection of diabetic retinopathy in retinal fundus photographs. JAMA **316**(22), 2402–2410 (2016)
9. Pazzanese, C.: "Great promise but potential for peril" (The Harvard Gazette) (2020). https://news.harvard.edu/gazette/story/2020/10/ethical-concerns-mount-as-ai-takes-bigger-decision-making-role/. Accessed 06 Feb 2023
10. Buolamwini, J., Gebru, T.: Gender shades: intersectional accuracy disparities in commercial gender classification. Proc. Mach. Learn. Res. **81**, 1–15 (2018)
11. Widely used AI tool for early sepsis detection may be cribbing doctors' suspicions. University of Michigan News (2024). https://news.umich.edu/widely-used-ai-tool-for-early-sepsis-detection-may-be-cribbing-doctors-suspicions/. Accessed 01 May 2025
12. Cheshmehzangi, et al.: Space and social distancing in managing and preventing COVID-19 community spread: an overview. Heliyon **9**(3), e13879 (2023). https://doi.org/10.1016/j.heliyon.2023.e13879
13. Marr, B.: 'Amazing Possibilities of Healthcare in the Metaverse' Forbes (2022). https://www.forbes.com/sites/bernardmarr/2022/02/23/the-amazing-possibilities-of-healthcare-in-themetaverse/?sh=72fe5fc19e5c. Accessed 10 May 2023
14. Mueller, B.: "Telemedicine Arrives in the U.K.: 10 Years of Change in One Week", New York Times (2020). https://www.nytimes.com/2020/04/04/world/europe/telemedicine-uk-coronavirus.html. Accessed 10 May 2023
15. Negreiro, M.: The rise of digital health technologies during the pandemic (EPRS, PE 690.548) (2021). https://www.europarl.europa.eu/RegData/etudes/BRIE/2021/690548/EPRS_BRI(2021)690548_EN.pdf
16. Bestsennyy, et al.: 'Telehealth: A Quarter-Trillion-Dollar Post-COVID-19 Reality? McKinsey & Company (2021). https://www.mckinsey.com/industries/healthcare-systems-and-services/our-insights/telehealth-a-quarter-trillion-dollar-post-covid-19-reality
17. Price, W.N., II.: Medical AI and contextual bias. Harvard J. Law Technol. **33**(1), 65–116 (2019)
18. Rajkomar, A., Dean J., Kohane I.: 'Machine learning in medicine.' New England J. Med. 380(25), 1347 (2019)
19. Liew, C.: 'The future of radiology augmented with artificial intelligence: a strategy for success.' Eur. J. Radiol. Open **15**(3), 298 (2018)
20. Nnawuchi, U., George, C.: Orwellian odyssey: Smart borders and the imperative for explainability. In: Farhaoui, Y., Herawan, T., Imoize, A.L. and El Allaoui, A. (eds.) Intersection of Artificial Intelligence, Data Science, and Cutting-Edge Technologies: From Concepts to Applications in Smart Environment. ICAISE 2024. Lecture Notes in Networks and Systems series Vol 2 LNNS 1397. Springer (2025). https://link.springer.com/book/9783031909207
21. European Commission. Proposal for a Regulation of the European Parliament and of the Council laying down harmonised rules on artificial intelligence and amending certain Union legislative acts. COM(2021) 206 final (2021). https://eur-lex.europa.eu/legal-content/EN/TXT/?uri=CELEX%3A52021PC0206
22. European Commission. Proposal for a Regulation on the European Health Data Space. COM(2022) 197 final (2022). https://eur-lex.europa.eu/legal-content/EN/TXT/?uri=CELEX%3A52022PC0197. Accessed 21 May 2025
23. Regulation (EU) 2016/679 of the European Parliament and of the Council of 27 April 2016 on the protection of natural persons with regard to the processing of personal data and on the free movement of such data, and repealing Directive 95/46/EC

24. Regulation (EU) 2017/745 of the European Parliament and of the Council of 5 April 2017 on medical devices, amending Directive 2001/83/EC, Regulation (EC) No 178/2002 and Regulation (EC) No 1223/2009 and repealing Council Directives 90/385/EEC and 93/42/EEC

25. Regulation (EU) 2017/746 of the European Parliament and of the Council of 5 April 2017 on in vitro diagnostic medical devices. Official Journal of the European Union. https://eur-lex. europa.eu/eli/reg/2017/746/oj. Accessed 01 May 2025

26. Emmanuel, E., Wachter, R.: Artificial intelligence in healthcare: will the value match the hype? JAMA (2019). https://doi.org/10.1001/jama.2019.4914

27. Harvey, et al.: The future of technologies for personalised medicine. N Biotechnol. **29**(6), 625–33 (2012). https://doi.org/10.1016/j.nbt.2012.03.009. PMID: 23091837

28. Article 29 Working Party. Guidelines on Automated Individual Decision-Making and Profiling for the purposes of Regulation 2016/679 (WP251rev.01). European Commission (2017)

29. Malone, E.R., et al.: Molecular profiling for precision cancer therapies. Genome Med. **12**, 8 (2020). https://doi.org/10.1186/s13073-019-0703-1

30. Zhou, et al.: Concordance study between IBM Watson for Oncology and clinical practice for patients with cancer in China. Oncol. **24**(3), e196-e204. (2019). https://doi.org/10.1634/the oncologist.2018-0255

31. Henry, et al.: 'A Targeted Real-Time Early Warning Score (TREWScore) for Septic Shock.' Sci. Transl. Med. (2015). https://doi.org/10.1126/scitranslmed.aab3719

32. Sandeep, R.: Explainability and artificial intelligence in medicine. Lancet Dig. Health **4**(4), e214-e215 (2015)

33. Ross, C., Swetlitz I.: 'IBM's Watson Supercomputer Recommended "Unsafe and Incorrect" Cancer Treatments, Internal Documents Show' Stat (2018)

34. Barry, M.J., Edgman-Levitan, S.: Shared decision making–pinnacle of patient-centred care. Engl. J. Med. **366**, 780–781 (2012)

35. Pierce, R.: Machine learning for diagnosis and treatment: gymnastics for the GDPR. Eur. Data Prot. Law Rev. **3**, 333–343 (2018)

36. Edwards, L., Veale, M.: 'Enslaving the algorithm: from a "right to an explanation" to a "right to better decisions"?' IEEE Secur. Priv. **16**(3) 46–54 (2018)

37. Kohli, M., Geis, R.: Ethics, artificial intelligence, and radiology. J. Am. Coll. Radiol. **15**(9), 1317–1319 (2018)

38. European Society of Radiology. What the radiologist should know about artificial intelligence an ESR white paper. Insights into Imaging 10 (2019). https://doi.org/10.1186/s13244-019-0738-2

39. Price, W.N., Cohen I.G.: 'Privacy in the age of medical big data.' Nat. Med. **105**, 117–119 (2019). https://doi.org/10.1038/s41591-018-0272-7

40. Beauchamp, T.L.: Principles of Biomedical Ethics, 8th edn. Oxford University Press (2019)

41. World Medical Association. International Code of Medical Ethics. https://www.wma.net/pol icies-post/wma-international-code-of-medical-ethics/. Accessed 01 May 2025

42. Hosny, et al.: Artificial intelligence in radiology. Nat. Rev. Cancer **18**(8), 500–510 (2018)

43. Ghassemi, M., Oakden-Rayner, L., Beam, A.L.: The false hope of current approaches to explainable artificial intelligence in health care. Lancet Digit. Health **3**(11), e745–e750 (2021)

44. McDougall, R.J.: Computer knows best? The need for value-flexibility in medical. AI J. Med. Ethics **45**(3), 156-160 (2019). https://doi.org/10.1136/medethics-2018-105118

45. Herrera, F, Calderón, R.: Opacity as a Feature, Not a Flaw: The LoBOX Governance Ethic for Role-Sensitive Explainability and Institutional Trust in AI (2025). https://arxiv.org/html/2505.20304v1

46. Rosenbacke, et al.: 'How explainable artificial intelligence can increase or decrease clinicians' trust in AI applications in health care: systematic review. JMIR AI (2024). https://ai.jmir.org/2024/1/e5320710.2196/53207

47. Grote, T., Berens, P.: On the ethics of algorithmic decision-making in healthcare. J. Med. Ethics **46**(3), 205–211 (2020). https://doi.org/10.1136/medethics-2019-105586
48. Arrieta, et al.: 'Explainable Artificial Intelligence (XAI): Concepts, taxonomies, opportunities and challenges towards responsible AI', Elsevier Information Fusion Vol. 58, pp. 82–115. https://dictionary.cambridge.org/dictionary/english/explanation. Accessed 21 Oct 2021
49. Inam, et al.: Explainable AI: How humans can trust AI', Ericsson White Paper GFTL-21:000529Uen (2021)
50. Nnawuchi, U., George, C.: A grand entrance without a blueprint. J. AI Law Regul. **1**(4), 402–419 (2024). https://doi.org/10.21552/aire/2024/4/6
51. Barocas, S., Selbst, A.D.: Big data's disparate impact. Calif. L. Rev. **104**, 671 (2016)
52. Pavlidis, G.: Unlocking the black box: analysing the EU artificial intelligence act's framework for explainability in AI. Law Innov. Technol. **16**(1), 293–308 (2024). https://doi.org/10.1080/17579961.2024.2313795
53. Convention for the Protection of Human Rights and Fundamental Freedoms (ECHR as amended), adopted 4 November 1950, entered into force 3 September 1953, ETS No. 5
54. International Covenant on Civil and Political Rights, adopted 16 December 1966, entered into force 23 March 1976, 999 UNTS 171
55. Roberts, A.: 'Portuguese parliament votes to allow limited euthanasia' (BBC News) (2023). https://www.bbc.co.uk/news/world-europe-65574311. Accessed 29 May 2025
56. Citizens Advice. Your right to life (2025). https://www.citizensadvice.org.uk/law-and-courts/civil-rights/human-rights/what-rights-are-protected-under-the-human-rights-act/your-right-to-life/. Accessed 29 May 2025
57. Doshi-Velez, F., Kim, B.: Towards a rigorous science of interpretable machine learning (2017). arXiv:1702.08608 https://arxiv.org/abs/1702.08608
58. Gunning, D.: 'Explainable Artificial Intelligence (XAI)' (Defence Advanced Research Projects Agency (DARPA) (2017). https://www.darpa.mil/program/explainable-artificial-intelligence
59. UNESCO.: Universal Declaration on Bioethics and Human Rights. https://unesdoc.unesco.org/ark:/48223/pf0000146180
60. OECD Principles on Artificial Intelligence. https://www.oecd.org/going-digital/ai/principles/. Accessed 01 May 2025
61. Council of Europe. Convention for the Protection of Human Rights and Dignity of the Human Being with regard to the Application of Biology and Medicine: Convention on Human Rights and Biomedicine (Oviedo Convention). CETS No.: 164 (1997)
62. Declaration of Helsinki – Ethical Principles for Medical Research Involving Human Subjects (WMA). (2013). https://www.wma.net/policies-post/wma-declaration-of-helsinki-ethical-principles-for-medical-research-involving-human-subjects/. Accessed 10 May 2025

Artificial Intelligence and IoT in Agriculture (AIoTA)

CVVEFM Layer: An Edge Detection Inspired Layer for Image Segmentation Tasks

Khalid El Amraoui[1]([✉]) [ID], Mustapha El Alaoui[1] [ID], Aziz Amari[1],
Hassane Roukhe[1] [ID], Mohamed El Ansari[2] [ID], Lhoussaine Masmoudi[1] [ID],
and José Valente de Oliveira[3,4] [ID]

[1] LCS Laboratory, Physics Department, Faculty of Science, Mohammed V University, Rabat, Morocco
`Khalid.elamraoui@um5r.ac.ma`
[2] Informatics and Applications Laboratory, Faculty of Science, Moulay Ismail University, Meknes, Morocco
[3] University of Algarve, Faro, Portugal
[4] NOVA-LINCS, Lisbon, Portugal

Abstract. The advancement of image segmentation models has been significantly driven by the development of convolutional neural networks (CNNs). These homogeneous architectures demonstrate strong performance in feature extraction through the use of convolutional operations applied via a sliding window mechanism. However, their effectiveness tends to diminish when training data is limited, often resulting in overfitting. In this study, we propose a novel regularization method inspired by the electric force model for edge detection. A custom layer, referred to as the CVVEFM layer, is developed and integrated into a U-Net architecture for the segmentation of agricultural aerial imagery. To evaluate the effectiveness of the proposed method, comparisons were conducted against conventional regularization techniques, such as Dropout and ReLU. Experimental results demonstrate that the CVVEFM layer outperforms existing methods in terms of evaluation metrics: accuracy, precision, recall, and f1-score, as well as training stability. These findings highlight the potential of physics-inspired regularization approaches to enhance model generalization in data constrained environments.

Keywords: CNN · Image segmentation · Regularization

1 Introduction

Image segmentation is a vital tool across various fields, as it enables the identification and analysis of different components within an image [1]. It supports a deeper understanding of objects, leading to more accurate and informed detection or localization. The impact of this technique in the agricultural field is evident in applications such as disease detection [2], vegetation zone classification [3], and fruit localization [4]. These applications contribute to more efficient crop monitoring, resource management, and automation of harvesting processes [5].

© The Author(s), under exclusive license to Springer Nature Switzerland AG 2026
J. Valente de Oliveira et al. (Eds.): EPIA 2025, LNAI 16122, pp. 163–175, 2026.
https://doi.org/10.1007/978-3-032-05179-0_13

With the emergence of deep learning models, more robust and adaptive segmentation solutions have been developed. A major advantage of these models, is their capacity to automatically learn complex features from data, thereby enabling more precise and context-aware segmentation across diverse applications [6].

Convolutional Neural Networks (CNNs) have become the most widely used models for image segmentation due to their ability to automatically extract relevant features at multiple spatial scales. By applying convolutional kernels to input data, CNNs can capture spatial patterns, such as edges, textures, and shapes, that are essential for both semantic and instance segmentation [7]. Architectures such as U-Net [8] and SegNet [9] leverage this capability by combining progressive spatial encoding with symmetric decoding, resulting in accurate segmentation maps.

However, one of the major limitations of CNN-based models is their susceptibility to overfitting, particularly when trained on limited imbalanced datasets [10]. This often leads the model to perform well on the training data but fail to generalize to unseen samples, thereby reducing its effectiveness in real-world applications. To mitigate this issue, researchers proposed a wide range of techniques, that can be broadly categorized into two main categories. The first one focuses on data strategies, aiming to enhance the diversity and robustness of the training dataset. Data augmentation, for example, expands the training set by applying random transformations such as cropping, rotation, flipping, and noise addition [11–13], helping models generalize better to unseen data.

The second one involves architectural and training-level regularization techniques. These include early stopping [14], where training is halted before convergence to prevent overfitting, and weight decay. Another method is l2-regularization method that constrains parameter growth [15]. More recent methods such as Dropout[16] and DropConnect [17] randomly deactivate neuron outputs or weights during training, reducing reliance on specific features. Additionally, techniques like Stochastic Pooling and Probabilistic Maxout [18] introduce randomness into pooling and activation functions, promoting model robustness by preventing deterministic overfitting. Collectively, these strategies contribute to building more generalizable and stable CNN-based segmentation models.

The motivation of this paper is to propose a new regularization method for image segmentation tasks. The methodology is inspired from an edge detection model in color images using Cubical Voxels and Virtual Electric Field Model(CVVEFM) [19]. It was first introduced by Bouda et al. [19, 20], and it has demonstrated that electrostatic forces can effectively enhance edge detection by treating pixels as charged elements within a virtual electric field. Extending these concepts into artificial neural networks offer an innovative perspective on feature extraction by capturing interactions at a finer spatial granularity.

To assess the effectiveness of this approach, experiments were performed on an aerial images dataset of an avocado farm located in Morocco [21]. The main goal is to segment the images into regions based on tree sizes. Comparisons between different regularization methods, including the proposed one, were evaluated using a simple U-Net model, focusing on evaluation metrics, and training stability. Qualitative visualizations demonstrated the proposed method's capability in accurately classifying different regions within the images.

The main goals of this paper are;

- Propose a novel regularization method inspired from Cubical Voxels and Virtual Electric Field Model (CVVEFM) to eliminate overfitting and enhance segmentation task.
- Evaluate the performance of the proposed method in terms of evaluation metrics: accuracy, precision, recall, and f1-score.
- Compare its performances with other regularization methods: Dropout and ReLU activation.

The rest of the paper is organized as follows: Sect. 2 describes the methodology and its integration into the model architecture. Section 3 presents the results obtained using the proposed method, along with comparisons to other regularization techniques. Finally, a conclusion summarizing the main contributions and outlining directions for future research.

2 Methodology and Implementation

2.1 Cubical Voxels and Virtual Electric Field Model (CVVEFM)

The motivation for this work is grounded in the studies by Bouda et al. [19, 20]. They demonstrated that electrostatic forces can effectively enhance edge detection in color images by modeling pixels as charged elements within a virtual electric field. In three-dimensional space, the volumetric equivalent of a pixel is referred to as a voxel. Among the regular polyhedron, the cube is uniquely suited for regular tiling of 3D space, making it an appropriate structural element for image representation. Using a cubical tiling scheme, the image volume can be modeled as a structured mesh of voxels, each defined by its three spatial coordinates $(\vec{e_x}, \vec{e_y}, \vec{e_z})$.

Each voxel in this configuration is surrounded by 26 neighbors, which can be categorized into three types as illustrated in Fig. 1: eight diametric neighbors (connected via cube vertices, (Blue)), six axial neighbors (connected via faces (Green)), and twelve diagonal neighbors (aligned along edges in orthogonal planes (Orange)). This structured voxel arrangement supports the simulation of virtual electric field interactions across the image volume.

To compute the gradients while preserving maximal color information, the authors selected the twelve diagonal neighbors within the voxel structure. This configuration corresponds to four voxels per color component (Red, Green, Blue) along the z-axis, enabling a more comprehensive capture of spatial and chromatic variations.

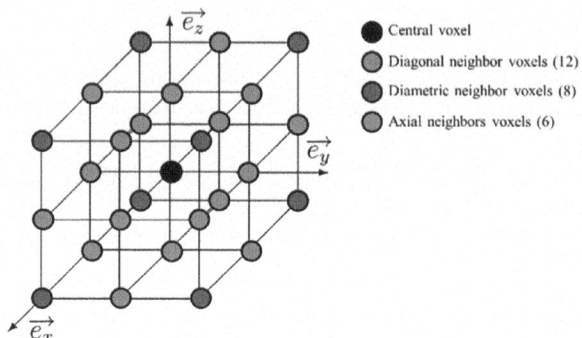

Fig. 1. The three possible distributions of the voxels in a cube.

In the context of electrostatic, each voxel is considered as a charge exerting and attractive, or repulsive force on the central voxel (Fig. 2). The electrostatic field generated by each charge in a position $M(x_M, y_M, z_M)$ is giving by (1)

$$\overrightarrow{E_{q1}} = \frac{K.q_1}{d^2}\left[\frac{2(x_M - x_m)}{d}\overrightarrow{e_x} + \frac{2(y_M - y_m)}{d}\overrightarrow{e_y} + \frac{2(z_M - z_m)}{d}\overrightarrow{e_z}\right] \quad (1)$$

where $d = \sqrt{(x_M - x_m)^2 + (y_M - y_m)^2 + (z_M - z_m)^2}$ represents the Euclidean distance between the charge located at position M and a nearby point m. $K = \frac{1}{8\pi\varepsilon_0}$ is a constant.

By considering that each neighboring voxel exert an electric force $\overrightarrow{F}$ on the central voxel, the total force applied on the central voxel by the 12 neighbors is giving by (2).

$$\vec{F}_{tot} = \sum_{i=1}^{12}\overrightarrow{F_{I/0}} = \sum_{i=1}^{12}\frac{Kq_0q_i}{d^2}\left[\frac{2(x_M - x_m)}{d}\overrightarrow{e_x} + \frac{2(y_M - y_m)}{d}\overrightarrow{e_y} + \frac{2(z_M - z_m)}{d}\overrightarrow{e_z}\right]$$

$$\quad (2)$$

After projections the forces along each axis are giving by (3), (4), (5). The calculation are detailed in [19]

$$\vec{F}_{e_x} = \frac{KP_0}{r^2}\sqrt{2}[q_3 + q_6 - q_7 - q_8 + q_9 + q_{10} - q_{11} - q_{12}]\overrightarrow{e_x} \quad (3)$$

$$\vec{F}_{e_y} = \frac{KP_0}{r^2}\sqrt{2}[-q_1 - q_2 + q_4 + q_5 - q_9 + q_{10} + q_{11} - q_{12}]\overrightarrow{e_y} \quad (4)$$

$$\vec{F}_{e_z} = \frac{KP_0}{r^2}\sqrt{2}[-q_1 + q_2 - q_3 + q_4 - q_5 + q_6 - q_7 - q_8]\overrightarrow{e_y} \quad (5)$$

Using these equations along with the projections illustrated in Fig. 2, the authors of the paper generate 3 unique kernels for edge detection (Fig. 3). An example of edge detection in aerial images using the obtained kernels is given in Fig. 5.

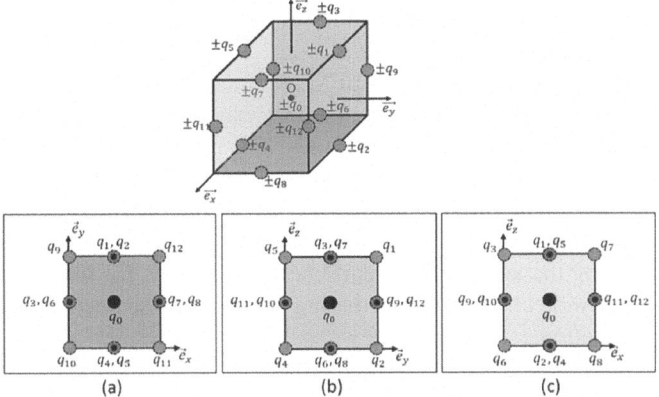

Fig. 2. The projection of the charges onto planes: (a) (x, y); (b) (y, z); (c) (x, z).

$\sqrt{2}$	$2\sqrt{2}$	$\sqrt{2}$	$\sqrt{2}$	0	$-\sqrt{2}$	$-\sqrt{2}$	$-2\sqrt{2}$	$-\sqrt{2}$
0	0	0	$2\sqrt{2}$	0	$-2\sqrt{2}$	0	0	0
$-\sqrt{2}$	$-2\sqrt{2}$	$-\sqrt{2}$	$\sqrt{2}$	0	$-\sqrt{2}$	$\sqrt{2}$	$2\sqrt{2}$	$\sqrt{2}$
(a)			(b)			(c)		

Fig. 3. Corresponding masks obtained from the projections. (a): (x, y) filtre; (b): (y, z) filtre; (c): (x, z) filtre.

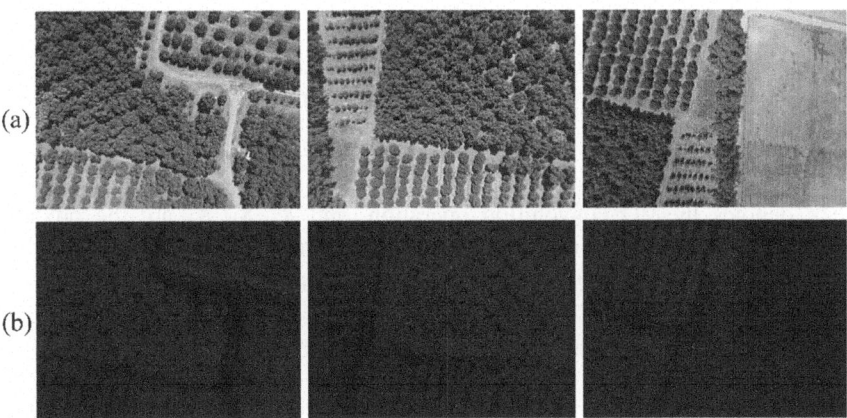

Fig. 4. Visualization of CVVEFM outputs on color agricultural aerial images, (a) original image, (b) its corresponding CVVEFM outputs.

Figure 4 presents visualizations results of the CVVEFM algorithm for edge detection applied on agricultural aerial images. As illustrated, for the first image, correspond to a drone-captured view of a tree plantation, the CVVEFM method reveals distinct circular textures, highlighting the canopies of individual trees. The clarity of these circles suggest that the method is effective in detecting vegetation patterns in structured environments.

Additionally, the foliage and branches in the second image of the tree are accentuated indicating accurate edge detection.

Overall, by integrating the three CVVEFM obtained kernels, the approach improves edge retention and reduces the tendency toward excessive segmentation, a frequent issue with conventional gradient-based methods. The presence of a darker background and sharply defined edges reflects strong noise reduction capabilities, which the study identifies as a significant strength. Furthermore, the technique leverages multi-channel dynamics to enhance the reliability of feature extraction. These promising results suggest potential for adapting the kernels into neural network models for image segmentation, positioning it as a new mechanism for mediating interactions between inputs and kernels during feature extraction.

2.2 Implementation

To assess the effectiveness of the CVVEFM-inspired edge-aware mechanism, the kernels mentioned in Fig. 3 were incorporated to build a custom layer and integrate it within a simplified U-Net architecture designed for aerial image segmentation. The dataset used, which is publicly available[4], consists of aerial top-view images of an avocado farm with their corresponding labels. The objective is to segment each image into distinct regions based on tree sizes (small, medium, and large).

Mathematically, the proposed CVVEFM layer takes a 4D input tensor denoted by $X \in \mathbb{R}^{B \times H \times W \times C}$, where B is the batch size, H and W are the spatial dimensions, and C is the number of channels. The layer operates by convolving each input channel separately with the three fixed kernels obtained by CVVEFM designed to capture gradient information along virtual x, y, and z directions. These kernels, approximate electric field interactions across neighboring voxels.

For a given input channel Xc, the directional gradients are computed as:

$$G_c^x = X_c * K_x, \; G_c^y = X_c * K_y, \; G_c^z = X_c * K_z \tag{6}$$

where $*$ denotes the 2D convolution operation, and K_x, K_y, K_z are the predefined CVVEFM kernels in the x, y, and z directions respectively.

The gradient magnitude for each channel is then computed using the Euclidean norm:

$$M_c = \sqrt{(G_c^x)^2 + (G_c^y)^2 + (G_c^z)^2} \tag{7}$$

The final edge-enhanced map is obtained by averaging over all channel-wise gradients:

$$M = \frac{1}{C} \sum_{c=1}^{C} M_c \tag{8}$$

The output $M \in \mathbb{R}^{B \times H \times W \times 1}$ is a single-channel edge map summarizing edge intensity derived from all input channels. This edge-aware activation map highlights directional discontinuities and structural features in the input image, enhancing the model's ability to distinguish fine-grained regions during segmentation.

The U-Net architecture employed for evaluating the proposed integration comprises four Conv2D-MaxPooling blocks in the encoder, paired with corresponding upsampling and skip connection layers in the decoder. To investigate the effectiveness of the CVVEFM-based edge-aware filter, it was incorporated as a custom component within the model's feature extraction pipeline, with the objective of improving segmentation performance in complex and heterogeneous aerial imagery while mitigating overfitting. As shown in Fig. 5, the CVVEFM layer is applied in a parallel path within the encoder: each input is first processed by the CVVEFM layer and then concatenated with the original input before being passed to the subsequent convolutional block. The output of each encoder block is further concatenated with the corresponding CVVEFM-enhanced features before being passed forward. This mechanism preserves essential spatial features while reinforcing them with edge-based activations, enabling more robust representation learning. Comparative evaluations against conventional regularization methods were conducted to demonstrate the advantages of the proposed integration.

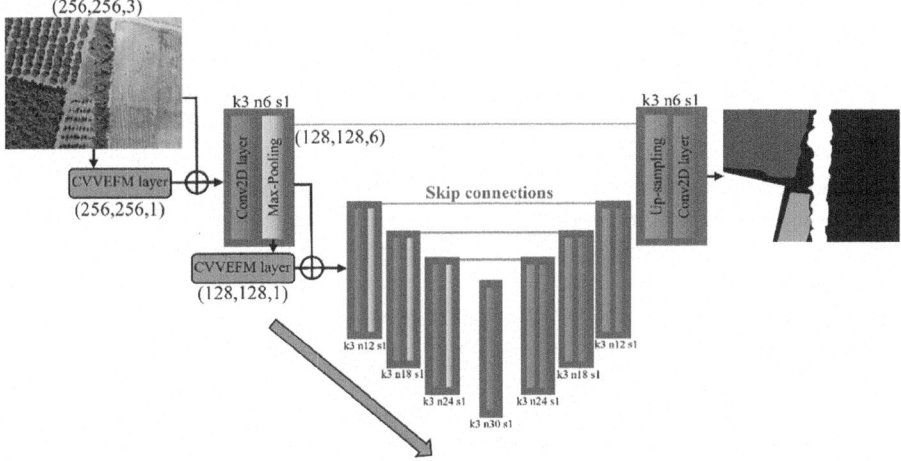

Fig. 5. The proposed U-net model architecture integrating the CVVEFM layer for aerial image segmentation.

3   Results and Discussion

3.1   Experimental Setup

To ensure a robust and fair evaluation, the training was conducted from scratch on a small set of 560 images and their corresponding masks from the aerial dataset described earlier. To ensure consistent evaluation of model performance, training was carried out 30 times using different random seeds for initializing weights. The experiments were run on a desktop system equipped with an Intel i7 8th generation CPU, 16 GB of DDR4 RAM operating at 2666 MHz, and an Nvidia GeForce GTX 1070 graphics card with 8 GB of video memory. The software stack consisted of Python version 3.8.8, TensorFlow 2.7.0, CUDA 11.2 for GPU-accelerated computations, and CUDNN 8.1 to optimize deep learning operations. Each training session lasted for a maximum of 500 epochs, with early stopping triggered if validation accuracy showed no improvement over five successive epochs.

The experiments were designed to evaluate six different scenarios. The first scenario (S1) employed a baseline U-Net model without any regularization. The second scenario (S2) introduced ReLU activation functions after each Conv2D layer in the encoder. In the third scenario (S3), a dropout layer with a rate of 0.3 was added instead of ReLU activations after each Conv2D layer. The fourth scenario (S4) is a model with both ReLU and Dropout. The fifth scenario (S5) implemented the proposed CVVEFM layer in a parallel path to the encoder, aiming to enhance edge-awareness and spatial feature preservation. Finally, the sixth scenario (S6) combined the CVVEFM layer with ReLU activations following each Conv2D layer.

3.2 Results

The primary objective of these comparisons was to assess the impact of the CVVEFM layer on model performance, particularly in terms of evaluation metrics (accuracy, precision, recall, and f1-score), the consistency of these metrics across epochs, and training stability. Consistency among evaluation metrics typically indicates a well-balanced model that maintains a stable trade-off between sensitivity (recall) and specificity (precision), without disproportionately favoring one at the expense of the other. Balanced metrics reflects strong generalization ability and minimal bias in prediction.

To assess segmentation performance across six experimental scenarios (S1–S6), boxplots were used to visualize key evaluation metrics, highlighting both accuracy and consistency (Fig. 6). Scenarios S5 and S6 consistently outperformed others across all metrics. They achieved the highest median accuracy (~85–86%) and f1-scores (~85–85.3%) with minimal variability, indicating robust and stable segmentation. Precision was highest in S4 (~90%), though S5 and S6 also showed strong and reliable precision above 88%. In terms of recall, S5 and S6 again led with median values above 81%, whereas S2 showed high recall (~72.4%) but with significant variability. Scenarios S1, S3, and S4 generally underperformed in recall and f1-scores, despite some showing tighter distributions. Overall, S5 and S6 emerged as the most effective and reliable configurations across all evaluation criteria.

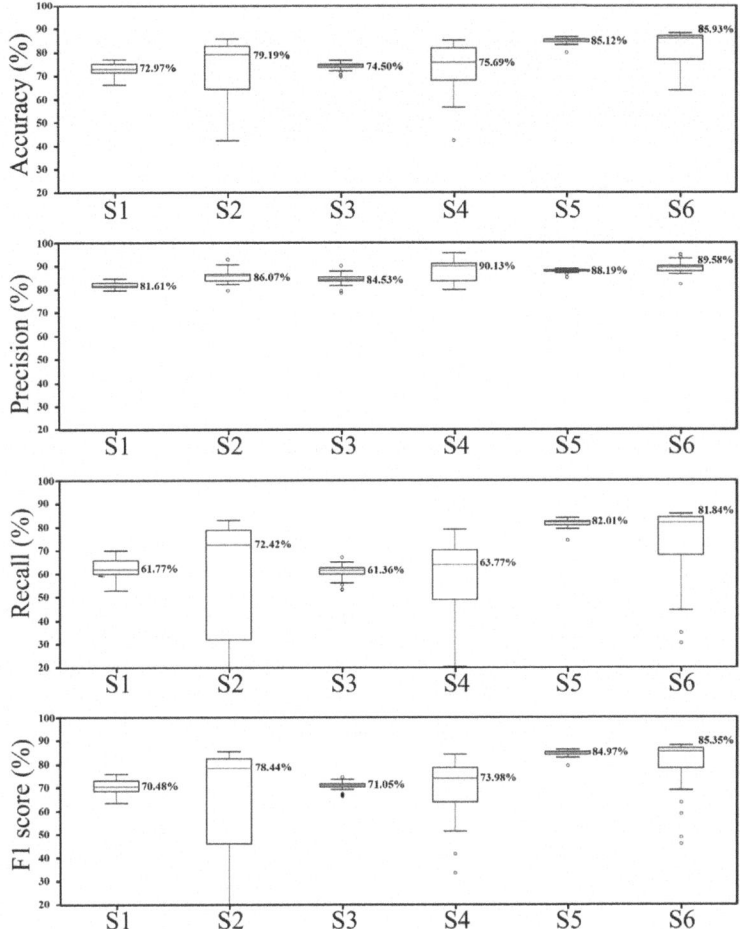

Fig. 6. Boxplot showing the variation of evaluation metrics along the 30 seeds.

Overall, the comparative analysis of the six scenarios reveals that scenarios S5 and S6 that includes the CVVEFM layer consistently outperform the others across all evaluation metrics, demonstrating high segmentation quality with minimal variability. These two configurations exhibit a strong balance between precision and recall, as reflected in their superior f1-scores, and maintain excellent accuracy with stable behavior across trials.

These quantitative findings are further supported by a qualitative assessment of the prediction results obtained using the best-performing seed for each scenario. As illustrated in Fig. 7, the predicted segmentations closely align with the training performance trends. Scenarios S5 and S6, both incorporating the CVVEFM layer, produce notably superior segmentation outputs compared to other scenarios, particularly in accurately delineating tree sizes. This visual confirmation reinforces the effectiveness and consistency of these configurations across both numerical evaluation and practical application.

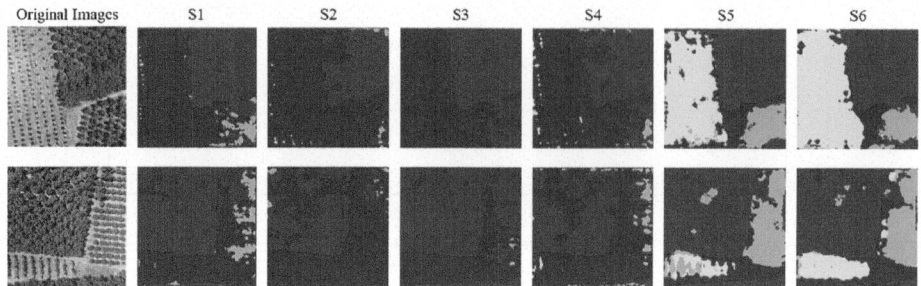

Fig. 7. Prediction of the best seed of each scenario on random aerial image.

3.3 Discussion

To validate the generalizability of the proposed layer, another test was performed on a publicly available aerial imagery dataset from Kaggle: the "Semantic Segmentation of Aerial Imagery" dataset [22]. It includes high-resolution aerial tiles of various urban and semi-urban landscapes with corresponding pixel-wise annotations for buildings, roads, trees, crops, and water bodies, offering diverse scenes and lighting conditions. With a total of 72 annotated images, this dataset presents a challenging benchmark for evaluating the robustness of the proposed layer. The evaluation focuses on scenarios S2 and S6, which respectively represent the best-performing configurations with and without the proposed layer. The same data preprocessing steps, model architectures, and training procedures were applied to this dataset, leading to the results illustrated by the boxplots in Fig. 8.

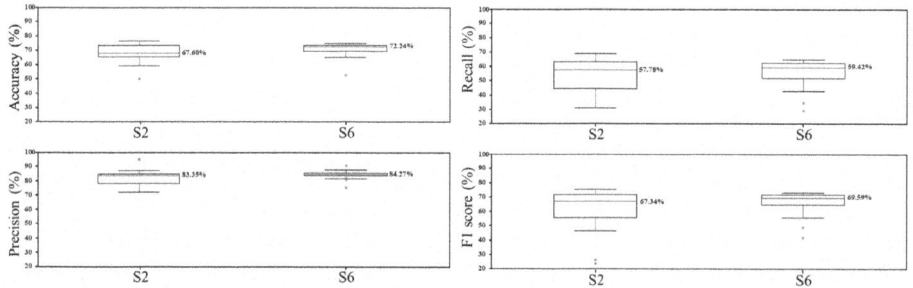

Fig. 8. Quantitative comparison between scenarios with and without the proposed layer.

The figure demonstrates that the scenario incorporating the proposed layer (S6) consistently outperforms the alternative, showing a 1–5% advantage across all evaluation metrics. Furthermore, it exhibits greater stability across multiple runs, as indicated by the smaller interquartile ranges in the box plots. To support these quantitative findings, the qualitative results presented in Fig. 9 further highlight the superior performance of the proposed layer.

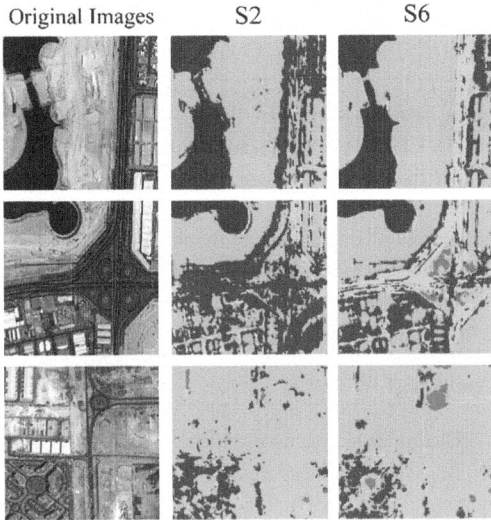

Original Images   S2   S6

Fig. 9. Different scenarios predictions. (S2) without the custom layer, (S6) with the custom layer.

Visually, the S6 predictions demonstrate more coherent and sharper delineation of structures such as roads, buildings, and boundaries, particularly in challenging regions characterized by low contrast or complex textures. In contrast, the S2 predictions are less precise and tend to misclassify features. For example, in the first and second images, S2 misclassifies roads (depicted in yellow) as buildings (depicted in blue). These qualitative results support the effectiveness of the CVVEFM layer in enhancing edge definition and semantic consistency, further reinforcing the quantitative improvements reported earlier.

These observations highlight the potential of the CVVEFM layer as a lightweight, generalizable, and scalable component for enhancing segmentation performance across various visual domains. Its ability to improve spatial precision without introducing significant computational overhead makes it suitable for integration into diverse architectures and deployment in resource-constrained environments.

Beyond its current integration into a conventional CNN, future work will focus on designing a complete architecture inspired by the electric force model. This direction aims to more deeply embed the principles of spatial field interaction into the network's core structure, potentially unlocking further gains in boundary preservation and contextual awareness.

4 Conclusion

This paper introduces a novel custom layer inspired by an edge detection approach based on the electric force model. The proposed layer was integrated into a segmentation model and evaluated under constrained conditions, including limited training data and a reduced number of kernels. Its performance was benchmarked against conventional regularization techniques such as the ReLU activation function and dropout layer. Experimental results demonstrate that models incorporating the CVVEFM layer significantly outperform those using ReLU or dropout in terms of key evaluation metrics. In addition, the CVVEFM-based models exhibited greater stability across runs, as indicated by lower variability in metric distributions. Qualitative assessments further support these findings, showing more precise and consistent segmentations when the proposed layer is employed. Overall, the results highlight the effectiveness, adaptability, and potential scalability of the CVVEFM layer for enhancing segmentation performance, with promising implications for broader computer vision applications.

Acknowledgments. The authors of this paper are thankful to the Ministry of Higher Education and Scientific Research of Morocco (MESRSFC), the National Centre of Scientific and Technical Research of Morocco (CNRST) and Digital Development Agency of Morocco (ADD) for funding this project through AL-KHAWARIZMI program of Morocco. This work is also supported by NOVA LINCS ref. UIDB/04516/2020 (https://doi.org/https://doi.org/10.54499/UIDB/04516/2020) with the financial support of FCT.IP.

Disclosure of Interests. The authors have no competing interests to declare that are relevant to the content of this article.

References

1. El Joumani, S., El Amraoui, K., Mechkouri, S.E., Zennouhi, R., Masmoudi, L.: Segmentation of satellite image based on quantum approach and the Havrda-Charvat entropy. Multimed. Tools Appl. (2023). https://doi.org/10.1007/s11042-023-17299-1
2. Singh, V., Misra, A.K.: Detection of plant leaf diseases using image segmentation and soft computing techniques. Inf. Process. Agric. **4**(1), 41–49 (2017). https://doi.org/10.1016/j.inpa.2016.10.005
3. El Amraoui, K., et al.: An algorithm for crops segmentation in UAV images based on U-Net CNN model: Application to Sugarbeets plants. ITM Web Conf. **46**, 05002 (2022). https://doi.org/10.1051/itmconf/20224605002
4. El Amraoui, K., et al.: Machine learning algorithm for avocado image segmentation based on quantum enhancement and random forest. In: 2022 2nd International Conference on Innovative Research in Applied Science, Engineering and Technology (IRASET), pp. 1–7 (2022). https://doi.org/10.1109/IRASET52964.2022.9738360
5. Alaoui, M.E., Amraoui, K.E., Masmoudi, L., Ettouhami, A., Rouchdi, M.: Unleashing the potential of IoT, Artificial Intelligence, and UAVs in contemporary agriculture: a comprehensive review. J. Terramech. **115**, 100986 (2024). https://doi.org/10.1016/j.jterra.2024.100986
6. Hamuda, E., Glavin, M., Jones, E.: A survey of image processing techniques for plant extraction and segmentation in the field. Comput. Electron. Agric. **125**, 184–199 (2016). https://doi.org/10.1016/j.compag.2016.04.024
7. Bargoti, S., Underwood, J.P.: Image segmentation for fruit detection and yield estimation in apple orchards. J. Field Robot. **34**(6), 1039–1060 (2017). https://doi.org/10.1002/rob.21699
8. Ronneberger, O., Fischer, P., Brox, T.: U-Net: convolutional networks for biomedical image segmentation (2015). arXiv: arXiv:1505.04597. https://doi.org/10.48550/arXiv.1505.04597
9. Badrinarayanan, V., Kendall, A., Cipolla, R.: SegNet: a deep convolutional encoder-decoder architecture for image segmentation. IEEE Trans. Pattern Anal. Mach. Intell. **39**(12), 2481–2495 (2017). https://doi.org/10.1109/TPAMI.2016.2644615
10. Ying, X.: An overview of overfitting and its solutions. J. Phys. Conf. Ser. **1168**(2), 022022 (2019). https://doi.org/10.1088/1742-6596/1168/2/022022

11. Cireşan, D.C., Meier, U., Gambardella, L.M., Schmidhuber, J.: Deep, big, simple neural nets for handwritten digit recognition. Neural Comput. **22**(12), 3207–3220 (2010). https://doi.org/10.1162/NECO_a_00052

12. Krizhevsky, A., Sutskever, I., Hinton, G.E.: ImageNet classification with deep convolutional neural networks. In: Advances in Neural Information Processing Systems, Curran Associates, Inc. (2012). https://proceedings.neurips.cc/paper/2012/hash/c399862d3b9d6b76c8436e924a68c45b-Abstract.html. Accessed 25 Sep 2024

13. Reed, R., Oh, S., Marks, R.J.: Regularization using jittered training data. In: [Proceedings 1992] IJCNN International Joint Conference on Neural Networks, vol.3, pp. 147–152 (1992). https://doi.org/10.1109/IJCNN.1992.227178

14. Vilares Ferro, M., Doval Mosquera, Y., Ribadas Pena, F.J., Darriba Bilbao, V.M.: Early stopping by correlating online indicators in neural networks. Neural Netw. **159**, 109–124 (2023). https://doi.org/10.1016/j.neunet.2022.11.035

15. Demir-Kavuk, O., Kamada, M., Akutsu, T., Knapp, E.-W.: Prediction using step-wise L1, L2 regularization and feature selection for small data sets with large number of features. BMC Bioinform. **12**(1), 412 (2011). https://doi.org/10.1186/1471-2105-12-412

16. Wu, H., Gu, X.: Towards dropout training for convolutional neural networks. Neural Netw. **71**, 1–10 (2015). https://doi.org/10.1016/j.neunet.2015.07.007

17. Mobiny, A., Yuan, P., Moulik, S.K., Garg, N., Wu, C.C., Van Nguyen, H.: DropConnect is effective in modeling uncertainty of Bayesian deep networks. Sci. Rep. **11**(1), 5458 (2021). https://doi.org/10.1038/s41598-021-84854-x

18. Ait Skourt, B., El Hassani, A., Majda, A.: Mixed-pooling-dropout for convolutional neural network regularization. J. King Saud Univ. - Comput. Inf. Sci. **34**(8), Part A, 4756–4762 (2022). https://doi.org/10.1016/j.jksuci.2021.05.001

19. Bouda, B., Masmoudi, L., Aboutajdine, D.: CVVEFM: cubical voxels and virtual electric field model for edge detection in color images. Signal Process. **88**(4), 905–915 (2008). https://doi.org/10.1016/j.sigpro.2007.10.006

20. Bouda, B., Masmoudi, L.: Electrostatic forces approach to color edge detection based on cubical voxel adjacencies. Int. J. Imaging Robot. **19**(2), 2 (2019)

21. el Amraoui, K., et al.: Avo-AirDB: an avocado UAV Database for agricultural image segmentation and classification. Data Brief **45**, 108738 (2022). https://doi.org/10.1016/j.dib.2022.108738

22. Semantic segmentation of aerial imagery. https://www.kaggle.com/datasets/humansintheloop/semantic-segmentation-of-aerial-imagery. Accessed 11 Jul 2025

Artificial Intelligence in Transportation Systems (AITS)

A MaxSAT Approach for the Train Timetabling Problem with Route Choice and Other Features

Filipe Gouveia[ID], Luís Albino[ID], and Ricardo L. Saldanha[✉][ID]

SISCOG - Sistemas Cognitivos, SA, Lisbon, Portugal
{filipe.gouveia,lmalbino,rsaldanha}@siscog.pt
http://www.siscog.pt/

Abstract. We address a variant of the train timetabling problem where choices involve not only defining the schedules of trains but also their routes (among a given set of alternatives) as well as which trains to plan, and where the goal is to obtain a conflict-free timetable as close as possible to a given ideal timetable. To our knowledge, such variant of the problem has not yet been fully addressed in the literature. We propose a MaxSAT approach using order encoding to solve this NP-hard problem. We evaluate the approach with real-world problem instances from Swiss Federal Railways and with realistic problem instances from Washington Metro. Results, presented for different time granularities, show that instances with more than 2000 trains can be solved efficiently.

Keywords: Train scheduling · MaxSAT · Constraint optimisation

1 Introduction

We address the Train Timetabling Problem with Route Choice and Other Features (TTPwRCOF), which can be defined in the following way. Given a set of service intentions and a railway network, we want to obtain a feasible minimum-cost train schedule. A service intention specifies a draft train trip that may or not be scheduled, depending on whether there is enough track capacity. It defines a sequence of stations where the first (last) is the trip origin (destination) and the remaining intermediate stations. It also defines alternative routes between each pair of consecutive stations as well as minimum, maximum and ideal times for the departure event at the origin station, for the arrival and departure event at each intermediate station and for the arrival event at the destination station. Minimum and maximum travelling times for each section track and service are also supplied.

In terms of cost structure, we have the following. Each service intention is associated with a cancellation cost, which works as a penalty for leaving that service intention unscheduled. Each alternative route of a service intention is

© The Author(s), under exclusive license to Springer Nature Switzerland AG 2026
J. Valente de Oliveira et al. (Eds.): EPIA 2025, LNAI 16122, pp. 179–191, 2026.
https://doi.org/10.1007/978-3-032-05179-0_14

associated with a cost, which is typically zero for the preferred route. Each event of a service intention is associated with a cost measuring the deviation from the ideal time. With this cost structure, we can conclude that, in an ideal situation, if there is enough track capacity, all service intentions will be scheduled with the ideal times and preferred routes, which is often not the case.

Because the given service intentions do not necessarily follow a regular pattern, this problem can be regarded as a non-periodic train timetabling problem. Because it is a planning problem, it is regarded as a strategic-level or tactical-level problem. This is why in this paper "cancellation" refers to the inability to schedule a service intention and not to the suppression of a scheduled service.

In short, the TTPwRCOF is a train timetabling problem that combines multiple features, namely the possibility of choosing among multiple routes, cancelling trains and penalising the differences with respect to an ideal timetable. As it will be shown in the next section, this variant of train timetabling problems, which together with other variants was shown to be NP-hard [3], has not yet been fully addressed.

All these features concern important real-life aspects of timetable generation. Having to consider multiple routes is of paramount importance in complex networks where there are junctions, sidings and stations with multiple platforms. Addressing train cancellations is also required in the context of train path allocation from the perspective of the infrastructure manager or in what-if scenario analysis. The concept of ideal timetable is also important because it relates with commercial requirements such as desired arrival times and connection times for passengers.

The main contributions of this work are the following: the formal definition of a new variant of the train timetabling problem, the TTPwRCOF; and a Maximum Boolean Satisfiability (MaxSAT) approach to solve this problem exactly, being evaluated with a set of problem instances from Swiss Federal Railways (SBB) and Washington Metro (WM).

2   Previous Work

As we can see in a recent survey [4], the train timetabling problem has received considerable attention during the last 50 years. Several variants of the problem were addressed with different methods.

Variants of this NP-hard problem [3] can be found across different dimensions, for example: periodic and non-periodic timetables, problems where the route of each train is fixed or problems where the route of each train has multiple choices [2,5,10,12,17,18], problems that allow train cancellations [2] and problems that don't, problems that include the concept of ideal timetable [2,5,10] and problems that don't.

Besides Boolean Satisfiability (SAT) and MaxSAT, this problem has been addressed with methods such as Mixed-Integer Linear Programming (MILP), local search, genetic algorithms, simulated annealing, constraint programming, reinforcement learning, and with a combination of them [4].

Works based on Boolean Satisfiability combine SAT with binary search or other optimisation methods to solve periodic [7,8,14,15] or non-periodic [12] timetabling problems.

Works based on Maximum Boolean Satisfiability (MaxSAT) address scheduling both periodic [11,14], and non-periodic [11] timetables.

The only work on non-periodic timetables that addresses simultaneously multiple routes, the concept of ideal timetable and the possibility of cancelling trains is [2], but it does so only in the specific case of inserting new trains in an existing timetable, which is a problem with a much more restricted solution space when compared with the problem of producing a complete timetable from scratch.

3   Problem Formulation

Next, we formalise the definition of the TTPwRCOF, providing a clear separation between the problem definition and the proposed method to solve it. With such separation, the problem definition presented in this work can promote the development of new approaches.

Formally, the TTPwRCOF can be defined by a railway network $\mathcal{N}$ and a set of service intentions $\mathcal{T}$. The railway network $\mathcal{N}$ is represented by a directed graph (V, E), where V is the set of nodes representing station entry and exit points, and junctions, *i.e.*, points where the network joins or splits, or where the track changes quality. The set of edges E represents sections of the network tracks $e = (v, u)$ where $v, u \in V$.

A section track can have one or more resources associated with it, and each resource can be used by multiple section tracks. A resource can represent the physical track or other elements, such as railway switches. If a resource is used by a service intention at a given time, no other service intention can use the same resource. A minimum release time can be set for a given resource, representing the minimum time required for a service intention to use the resource after another intention stops using it. Let $\mathcal{R}$ be the set of resources ρ in the railway network $\mathcal{N}$. Each edge $e \in E$ can have one or more resources associated, represented by the set $\mathcal{R}_e \subseteq \mathcal{R}$. The minimum release time of each resource $\rho \in \mathcal{R}$ is denoted by t_ρ^{rel}.

Each service intention $\tau \in \mathcal{T}$, has an associated set of section tracks that it can use, therefore can be represented by a railway network $\mathcal{N}_\tau = (V_\tau, E_\tau)$, where $V_\tau \subseteq V$ and $E_\tau \subseteq E$. Each section track $e_\tau = (v, u) \in E_\tau$, $v, u \in V_\tau$, has a minimum travel time $t_{\tau,e}^{min}$ representing the minimum time that intention τ takes traversing track e_τ. There can be a penalty $p_{\tau,e}$ associated with each section track e_τ, representing the cost of intention τ using section track e_τ. Moreover, each track e_τ can have entry (exit) earliest and latest time requirements denoted by $t_{\tau,e}^{entryEar}$ and $t_{\tau,e}^{entryLat}$ ($t_{\tau,e}^{exitEar}$ and $t_{\tau,e}^{exitLat}$) respectively, representing the time interval allowed for the intention to enter (exit) the corresponding section track. We denote the entry (exit) time interval of track e_τ by $\gamma_{\tau,e}^{entry} = [t_{\tau,e}^{entryEar}, t_{\tau,e}^{entryLat}]$ ($\gamma_{\tau,e}^{exit} = [t_{\tau,e}^{exitEar}, t_{\tau,e}^{exitLat}]$).

For each node $v_\tau \in V_\tau$ the allowed time interval $\gamma_{\tau,v} = [t^{ear}_{\tau,v}, t^{lat}_{\tau,v}]$ can be defined, where:

$$t^{ear}_{\tau,v} = \max\{ \min_{e_\tau=(u,v)} \{t^{exitEar}_{\tau,e}\}, \min_{e_\tau=(v,u)} \{t^{entryEar}_{\tau,e}\} \}$$

$$t^{lat}_{\tau,v} = \min\{ \max_{e_\tau=(u,v)} \{t^{exitLat}_{\tau,e}\}, \max_{e_\tau=(v,u)} \{t^{entryLat}_{\tau,e}\} \}$$

The time interval $\gamma_{\tau,v}$ takes into account the earliest and latest that a service intention can exit an incoming track (edge) and enter an outgoing track (edge).

In this work, a station platform, where a service intention stops, is represented by a section track $e_\tau = (u, v)$, where u (v) is the entry (exit) point of the station. Each section track e_τ can have a minimum stopping time denoted by $t^{stop}_{\tau,e}$.

Ideal Time Requirements

Besides the earliest and latest time requirements, we allow the definition of ideal times, representing the desired time for a service intention to enter or exit a given route track. Each e_τ can have an associated ideal entry (exit) time denoted by $t^{entryIdeal}_{\tau,e}$ ($t^{exitIdeal}_{\tau,e}$). Moreover, considering deviations from the ideal time, a penalty can be associated with such deviations, denoted by $p^{ideal}_{\tau,e}$.

Service Connections

In this work, we consider that two service intentions can have a connection, where passengers from one intention are transferred to another. Let $\mathcal{C}$ be the set of defined connections. A connection $c = (\tau, \tau') \in \mathcal{C}$ represents that intention τ will transfer to intention τ'. Each connection $c \in \mathcal{C}$ has an associated minimum connection time represented by t^{conn}_c. Let $c = (\tau, \tau') \in \mathcal{C}$ be a connection between service intention τ and τ'. We denote by $\mathcal{E}_{c,\tau}$ and $\mathcal{E}_{c,\tau'}$ the sets of section tracks $e \in E$, where connection c can occur for intentions τ and τ', respectively.

Service Cancellations

Furthermore, we consider that a service intention can be cancelled, resulting in having no schedule or route. Let $\mathcal{S}$ be the set of service intentions $\tau \in \mathcal{T}$ that can be cancelled (suppressed). Each intention $\tau \in \mathcal{S}$ has an associated penalty denoted by p_τ, representing the cost of cancelling the corresponding intention.

Service Delays

Considering entry and exit time requirements, when such requirements are too restrictive, the TTPwRCOF may become infeasible, i.e., no solution satisfies all the requirements. Often, it is desirable to allow some margin in time requirements, enabling a service intention to be scheduled to arrive or depart with a delay. Ideally, such delay is the minimum possible. To support the existence of delays, we consider the definition of a time buffer tb, extending each time interval. In this work, the time buffer only extends the upper limit of each time interval, allowing delays. However, it can similarly extend the lower limit, allowing an intention to arrive earlier than required. This extension is parametrizable. Considering a time buffer tb, time intervals are relaxed such that:

$$\gamma^{entry}_{\tau,e} = [t^{entryEar}_{\tau,e}, t^{entryLat}_{\tau,e} + tb], \forall \tau \in \mathcal{T}, \forall e_\tau \in E_\tau$$

$$\gamma_{\tau,e}^{exit} = [t_{\tau,e}^{exitEar}, t_{\tau,e}^{exitLat} + tb], \forall \tau \in \mathcal{T}, \forall e_\tau \in E_\tau$$

For each track $e_\tau \in E_\tau$ of each intention $\tau \in \mathcal{T}$, considering possible time delays, a penalty is associated. We denote the corresponding penalty by $p_{\tau,e}^{delay}$.

TTPwRCOF Solution

The goal of the TTPwRCOF is to find, for each service intention τ, a sequence of section tracks in E_τ forming a route, and associate with each chosen track e_τ an entry time $t_{\tau,e}^{entry}$ and exit time $t_{\tau,e}^{exit}$, such that:

- Each entry (exit) time $t_{\tau,e}^{entry} \in \gamma_{\tau,e}^{entry}$ ($t_{\tau,e}^{exit} \in \gamma_{\tau,e}^{exit}$);
- The minimum travel time of each track is respected, *i.e.*, $t_{\tau,e}^{exit} - t_{\tau,e}^{entry} \geq t_{\tau,e}^{min}$;
- For each e_τ with a minimum stopping time: $t_{\tau,e}^{exit} - t_{\tau,e}^{entry} \geq t_{\tau,e}^{min} + t_{\tau,e}^{stop}$;
- No two intentions are using the same resource $r \in \mathcal{R}$ at the same time, and the minimum release time t_r^{rel} is respected;
- For each connection $c \in \mathcal{C}$ the minimum connection time t_c^{conn} is respected.

Let the 4-tuple $X = (\Phi, \Theta^{entry}, \Theta^{exit}, \Psi)$ be a solution for TTPwRCOF where Φ is the set of chosen section tracks $e \in E$ for the scheduled service intentions, Θ^{entry} (Θ^{exit}) is the set of scheduled time events $t_{\tau,e}^{entry}$ ($t_{\tau,e}^{exit}$) for the corresponding service intentions and chosen section tracks $e_\tau \in \Phi$, and Ψ is the set of service intentions $\tau \in \mathcal{T}$ that are unscheduled, *i.e.*, cancelled. The cost of a solution $X = (\Phi, \Theta^{entry}, \Theta^{exit}, \Psi)$ is given by the sum of penalties ($p_{\tau,e}$) of each chosen section track $e_\tau \in \Phi$, plus the sum of associated time penalties ($p_{\tau,e}^{ideal}$ or $p_{\tau,e}^{delay}$) considering the scheduled time events Θ^{entry} and Θ^{exit} and the corresponding time requirements, plus the sum of penalties (p_τ) of each cancelled service intention $\tau \in \Psi$. Formally, we can define the cost function as:

$$\sum_{e_\tau \in \Phi} p_{\tau,e} + \sum_{t_{\tau,e}^{entry} \in \Theta^{entry}} f_{entry}(t_{\tau,e}^{entry}) + \sum_{t_{\tau,e}^{exit} \in \Theta^{exit}} f_{exit}(t_{\tau,e}^{exit}) + \sum_{\tau \in \Psi} p_\tau \quad (1)$$

where f_{entry} and f_{exit} are time cost functions. Function f_{entry} is defined as:

$$f_{entry}(t_{\tau,e}^{entry}) = \begin{cases} p_{\tau,e}^{ideal} \times |t_{\tau,e}^{entry} - t_{\tau,e}^{entryIdeal}| & \text{if } t_{\tau,e}^{entryIdeal} \text{ is defined} \\ p_{\tau,e}^{delay} \times (t_{\tau,e}^{entry} - t_{\tau,e}^{entryLat}) & \text{if } t_{\tau,e}^{entry} \geq t_{\tau,e}^{entryLat} \\ & \text{and } t_{\tau,e}^{entryIdeal} \text{ is not defined} \\ 0 & \text{otherwise} \end{cases}$$

The time function f_{exit} is defined similarly to f_{entry}.

The goal of the TTPwRCOF is to find the optimal solution, *i.e.*, the solution with minimum cost, given by Eq. (1).

4   Solution Method

We address the TTPwRCOF using Maximum Boolean Satisfiability (MaxSAT), an optimisation version of Boolean Satisfiability (SAT) [1]. We encode the TTP-wRCOF in a propositional formula using conjunctive normal form (CNF). A

CNF formula is a conjunction ($\wedge$) of clauses, where a clause is a disjunction ($\vee$) of literals, and a literal is a Boolean variable (positive literal) or its negation (negative literal). A formula is said to be satisfied if all its clauses are satisfied. A clause is satisfied if at least one of its literals is assigned value `true`. A positive (negative) literal is assigned value `true` if the corresponding variable is assigned value `true` (`false`); otherwise it is assigned value `false`. The SAT problem is to decide whether there exists an assignment to the variables of a CNF formula that satisfies the formula. The MaxSAT problem is an optimisation version of SAT, where the objective is to find an assignment that maximises the number of satisfied clauses. In this work, we consider the partial and weighted version of MaxSAT, where a formula $\varphi = \varphi_h \cup \varphi_s$ consists of a set of hard clauses φ_h and a set of soft clauses φ_s, where each soft clause has a weight associated. The goal is to find an assignment such that all hard clauses in φ_h are satisfied, while maximising the total weight of the satisfied soft clauses in φ_s.

4.1 Variables

To model TTPwRCOF using SAT, we define Boolean variables to represent the possible route paths used by each service intention, and time events of entry and exit of each section track. Since each intention $\tau \in \mathcal{T}$ has its own railway network $\mathcal{N}_\tau = (V_\tau, E_\tau)$, we can precompute the set of all possible paths (or routes) for each intention. Note that, usually, each railway network of a service intention has a limited number of alternative routes, having one preferred path, *i.e.*, a sequence section tracks without penalties associated. Let $\mathcal{P}_\tau$ be the set of possible paths for intention τ, where each $P_\tau^i \in \mathcal{P}_\tau$ is the set of section tracks $e_\tau \in E_\tau$ forming the corresponding path.

For the routing part of the problem, we define the following Boolean variables:

- q_τ^i: intention $\tau \in \mathcal{T}$ goes through path $P_\tau^i \in \mathcal{P}_\tau$;
- $r_{\tau,e}$: intention $\tau \in \mathcal{T}$ uses section track $e_\tau \in E_\tau$.

To model the scheduling part of the problem, to assign time values to each event, we consider the order encoding [16] that has been used in train timetabling problems [8,14] to efficiently represent time with Boolean variables. Therefore, to represent time events, we define the following Boolean variables:

- $s_{\tau,v}^t$: intention $\tau \in \mathcal{T}$ goes through node $v \in V_\tau$ at time $t \in \gamma_{\tau,v}$;
- $o_{\tau,v}^t$: intention $\tau \in \mathcal{T}$ goes through node $v \in V_\tau$ at time **less than or equal to** $t \in \gamma_{\tau,v}$;

For the sake of readability and to simplify some constraints, we define exact time variables s. However, they are inferred from the order time variables o. If the time assigned to a node v is less than or equal to t ($o_{\tau,v}^t$), and is not less than or equal to $t-1$ ($\neg o_{\tau,v}^{t-1}$), then we know that the time assigned is t ($s_{\tau,v}^t$).

Note that we assign time values to nodes in the network. This considers that the exit time of a section track is the same as the entry time in the following track. Moreover, time intervals at each node are propagated throughout the network to the minimum possible. For example, if an intention τ can go through node v_τ at time t as its earliest and the following section track has a minimum travel time of m, then the earliest that intention τ can arrive at the next node is $t+m$. The same reasoning can be applied to propagate time intervals backwards.

In this work, the problem can be defined with different time granularities, *e.g.* a time variable for each second, each two seconds, each 6 seconds, or each minute. The granularity is parametrizable to any positive integer value in seconds, and the time values and intervals are adjusted accordingly. Without loss of generality, assume that all variables are defined for a granularity of one second, *i.e.*, a variable for each second.

4.2 Constraints

In our approach, all formulas are encoded into CNF. However, for the sake of readability, we will write some constraints as logic implications, or in pseudo-Boolean (PB) form, that can be easily translated into CNF [6]. Moreover, we consider the integer variables 1 as `true` and 0 as `false`.

Here, we will not show the constraints defining the order encoding (see [16] for details), and focus on the constraints modelling the TTPwRCOF.

Route and Path Constraints

For an intention to go through a valid sequence of section tracks, we define routing constraints in a recursive way. Let $E_\tau^{end} \subseteq E_\tau$ be the set of section tracks e_τ that are the last tracks of the railway network N_τ, *i.e.*, for which there is no following track. Each service intention must have at most one last track selected. This is represented by the following constraint:

$$\sum_{e\in E_\tau^{end}} r_{\tau,e} \leq 1 \quad \forall_{\tau\in\mathcal{T}} \tag{2}$$

If a section track is selected, at least one of its predecessors must be selected if it exists. This is represented by the following constraint:

$$r_{\tau,e} \implies \bigvee_{e'=(u,v)\in E_\tau} r_{\tau,e'} \quad \forall_{\tau\in\mathcal{T},e=(v,x)\in E_\tau}$$

To ensure that at most one path is chosen, we first define the equivalence between a path and the corresponding sequence of section tracks:

$$q_\tau^i \iff \bigwedge_{e\in P_\tau^i} r_{\tau,e} \quad \forall_{\tau\in\mathcal{T},P_\tau^i\in\mathcal{P}_\tau}$$

Finally, for the definition of the routing part of the problem, we define that each service intention must have at most one path:

$$\sum_{P_\tau^i\in\mathcal{P}_\tau} q_\tau^i \leq 1 \quad \forall_{\tau\in\mathcal{T}} \tag{3}$$

For the service intentions that cannot be cancelled, *i.e.*, intentions $\tau \notin \mathcal{S}$, the constraints (2) and (3) becomes an *exactly one* constraints, replacing the $\leq$ operator by $=$.

Time Constraints

To correctly assign a valid time to a network node, we must ensure that the chosen time falls within the exit time interval of the incoming section track and within the entry time interval of the outgoing section track. For the incoming case, we define the following set of constraints:

$$r_{\tau,e} \implies \neg o_{\tau,v}^{t-1} \quad \forall_{\tau \in T, e_\tau = (x,v) \in E_\tau} : \gamma_{\tau,e}^{exit} = [l_e, u_e], \gamma_{\tau,v} = [l_v, u_v], t = \max\{l_e, l_v\}$$

$$r_{\tau,e} \implies o_{\tau,v}^{t} \quad \forall_{\tau \in T, e_\tau = (x,v) \in E_\tau} : \gamma_{\tau,e}^{exit} = [l_e, u_e], \gamma_{\tau,v} = [l_v, u_v], t = \min\{u_e, u_v\}$$

The above constraints represent that if an incoming edge $r_{\tau,e}$ is chosen, then the assigned time cannot be lower than the most restrictive lower bound of the corresponding intervals $(\neg o_{\tau,v}^{t-1})$ and must be lower than the most restrictive upper bound $(o_{\tau,v}^{t})$. A similar set of constraints is defined for the outgoing tracks.

The difference between entering and exiting a section track must respect the minimum travel time plus the minimum stopping time if it exists. In other words, if a section track e_τ is selected and the exit time is less than or equal to time x, then the corresponding entry time must be less than or equal to $x' = x - t_{\tau,e}^{min} - t_{\tau,e}^{stop}$. This is defined by the following constraint:

$$(r_{\tau,e} \wedge o_{\tau,v}^{x}) \implies o_{\tau,u}^{x'} \quad \forall_{\tau \in T, e=(u,v) \in E_\tau, x \in \gamma_{\tau,e}^{exit}} : x' = x - t_{\tau,e}^{min} - t_{\tau,e}^{stop}, x' \in \gamma_{\tau,e}^{entry}$$

Two service intentions cannot occupy the same resource at the same time. After a resource is released, there is a minimum release time during which no intention can use the resource. Given two section tracks from different intention networks ($e_\tau = (u,v)$ and $e'_{\tau'} = (u',v')$) that share a resource (ρ), if one starts being used at a given time (x), either: the other is not used (by the other intention); or the other starts using it at least after the resource is released and the minimum released time has passed; or the other used the same resource previously and already released it. Note that two section tracks can correspond physically to the same track, however, they are modelled as two different tracks if used by different intentions. This constraint is defined as:

$$(r_{\tau,e} \wedge s_{\tau,u}^{x}) \implies (\neg r_{\tau',e'} \vee \neg o_{\tau',u'}^{x'} \vee o_{\tau',v'}^{x''})$$

$$\forall_{\tau,\tau' \in T, e=(u,v) \in E_\tau, e'=(u',v') \in E_{\tau'}, \rho \in \mathcal{R}_e \cap \mathcal{R}_{e'}, x \in \gamma_{\tau,e}^{entry}} :$$

$$\tau \neq \tau', x' = x + t_{\tau,e}^{min} + t_{\tau,e}^{stop} + t_{\rho}^{rel} - 1, x'' = x - t_{\rho}^{rel}$$

To model connections between two service intentions, the service receiving a connection can only depart at least a given connection time after the giving service arrives, considering the section tracks where the connection occurs. Considering a connection $c = (\tau, \tau') \in \mathcal{C}$, the minimum connection time t_c^{conn}, and $\mathcal{E}_{c,\tau}$ and $\mathcal{E}_{c,\tau'}$ the sets of section tracks $e \in E$, where connection c can occur, we define the following constraint:

$$(r_{\tau,e} \land s_{\tau,u}^{x}) \implies (\neg r_{\tau',e'} \lor \neg o_{\tau',v'}^{x'})$$

$$\forall_{c=(\tau,\tau')\in\mathcal{C},e=(u,v)\in\mathcal{E}_{c,\tau},e'=(u',v')\in\mathcal{E}_{c,\tau'},x\in\gamma_{\tau,e}^{entry}} : x' = x + t_{c}^{conn} - 1$$

This constraint means that if the connection occurs in track e_τ at time x for the giving intention τ, then either: the connection does not occur in track $e'_{\tau'}$ for intention τ' (it occurs in a different track); or intention τ' cannot leave track $e'_{\tau'}$ at time $x' = x + t_c^{conn} - 1$ or before.

Soft Constraints

The constraints presented so far are considered hard constraints, *i.e.*, must be satisfied. The goal of this work is to minimise the cost of a TTPwRCOF solution, given by Eq. 1. Remember that the goal of a MaxSAT approach is to maximise the total weight of the satisfied soft clauses, which is equivalent to minimising the total weight of the unsatisfied ones.

To take into account the route penalty associated with the use of the corresponding section track, we add the following soft constraint:

$$\neg r_{\tau,e} \text{ with weight } p_{\tau,e} \quad \forall_{\tau\in\mathcal{T},e_\tau in E_\tau}$$

The above constraint means that we prefer not to use section track e_τ, and if we use it (the clause is unsatisfied), we "pay" the cost of $p_{\tau,e}$.

To minimise the deviation from an ideal time, we define the following set of soft constraints if the ideal time is defined:

$$\neg o_{\tau,u}^{t} \text{ with weight } p_{\tau,e}^{ideal} \quad \forall_{\tau\in\mathcal{T},e_\tau=(u,v)\in E_\tau,t\in\gamma_{\tau,e}^{entry}} : t < t_{\tau,e}^{entryIdeal} \quad (4)$$

$$o_{\tau,u}^{t} \text{ with weight } p_{\tau,e}^{ideal} \quad \forall_{\tau\in\mathcal{T},e_\tau=(u,v)\in E_\tau,t\in\gamma_{\tau,e}^{entry}} : t \geq t_{\tau,e}^{entryIdeal} \quad (5)$$

The above constraints penalise each time unit that the solution deviates from the given ideal time. Equation (4) penalises each time before the ideal time, while Eq. (5) penalises each time after the ideal time. A similar set of constraints is defined for the exit events as well, considering the node of arrival instead of the node of departure of a section track.

When the ideal time is not defined, we want to minimise allowed delays (see Sect. 3, Service Delays). For that, we add the following constraint:

$$o_{\tau,u}^{t} \text{ with weight } p_{\tau,e}^{delay} \quad \forall_{\tau\in\mathcal{T},e_\tau=(u,v)\in E_\tau,t\in\gamma_{\tau,e}^{entry}} : t \geq t_{\tau,e}^{entryLat}$$

A similar constraint is added for the exit event (exit latest). Note that if arriving earlier than required is allowed, we can add similar constraints penalising time events occurring before the required time interval.

To penalise unscheduled services, for each service $\tau \in \mathcal{S}$ that can be cancelled, we add the following soft constraint, meaning that each intention τ should have at least one path chosen, and if not, we incur a penalty of p_τ:

$$\sum_{P_\tau^i\in\mathcal{P}_\tau} q_\tau^i \geq 1 \text{ with weight } p_\tau \quad \forall_{\tau\in\mathcal{S}}$$

Table 1. Time granularity (Gr.), time buffer (T.B.), number of intentions (Trains), variables, clauses, average solving time in seconds, and cost for each instance (Inst.).

Inst.	Gr. (s)	T.B. (s)	Trains	Variables	Clauses	Time (s)	Cost
P01	1	120	4	146 474	219 155	0.644	0
P02	1	120	58	3 096 193	7 667 390	24.379	0
P03	1	120	143	5 649 879	15 446 228	57.356	0
P04	1	120	148	8 062 317	30 958 872	152.675	0.083
P05	1	120	149	8 085 574	31 396 938	103.335	UNSAT
P06	1	120	365	26 523 694	226 344 430	1 424.192	0
P07	1	120	467	36 399 205	391 155 925	–	–
P08	1	120	133	14 310 140	197 911 769	1 115.118	0
P05	1	360	149	12 611 974	63 459 070	18 766.520	32.983
P07	2	120	467	18 116 009	193 146 572	1 882.506	0.367

5   Computational Results

To evaluate our approach, assessing whether we can successfully schedule a set of service intentions considering multiple alternative routes, service cancellations, and ideal time preferences, we considered real-world problem instances from SBB and realistic ones from WM.

From SBB, we use SBB Challenge instances [9] comprising between 4 and 467 intentions, and between 318 and 51 807 section tracks[1].

From WM, we use instances with different amounts of service intentions produced by us in a realistic way, in the sense that we took in consideration the real network at macro level and real running times. In order to be able to run these instances, we converted the macro representation into a micro representation considering two minutes as the minimum allowed time space between trains.

To our knowledge, the presented variation of the train timetabling problem, TTPwRCOF, has not yet been fully addressed in the literature. Therefore, no fair comparison can be made with other state-of-the-art approaches.

The experiments were conducted on a machine with Intel(R) Core(TM) i9-9980XE 3.00 GHz CPU and 64 GB of RAM, in a single-thread scenario. We ran every experiment 5 times to take into account possible computational time variations, showing the average time results. The time results shown here include the processing of the instances, creation of the MaxSAT model, and the solving time using the MaxSAT solver Open-WBO [13].

Table 1 shows the results for the SBB instances used, considering a granularity of one second and a time buffer of 120 seconds. Instance P05 has no feasible solution using a time buffer of 120 seconds, because it requires higher delays. By

---

[1] https://github.com/crowdAI/train-schedule-optimisation-challenge-starter-kit/ blob/master/documentation/instance_description.md.

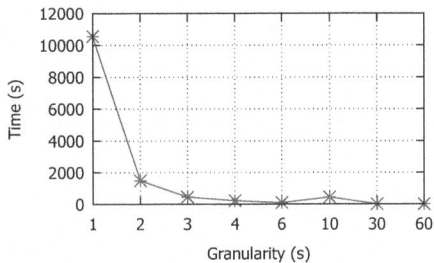
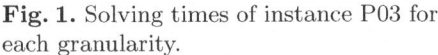

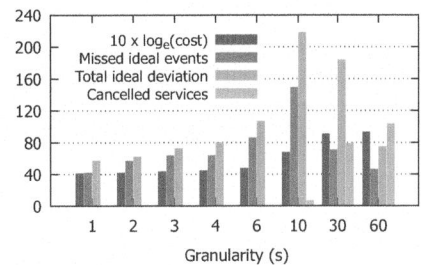

Fig. 1. Solving times of instance P03 for each granularity.

Fig. 2. Logarithm of solution cost, number of missed ideal events, total deviation of ideal times in minutes, and number of cancelled services for each granularity.

increasing the time buffer to 360 seconds, an optimal solution is found, having a lower cost than previously reported by non-optimal approaches [9], as shown at the end of Table 1. Instance P07 ran out of memory due to the high number of clauses. When solving with a granularity of 2 seconds, a solution can be found.

Although our approach can solve SBB instances, they do not consider service cancellations or ideal time requirements. We conducted experiments to explore such features using instance P03, which has a considerable number of intentions (143) and a feasible solution without delays (cost 0). We changed the original instance by allowing service cancellations, with a penalty of 100, and by considering that the original latest time requirements are ideal time requirements, with a penalty of 1 per minute. The penalties were chosen to illustrate the capabilities of the proposed approach. Different penalties can be used. We analysed the impact of different time granularities, considering a time buffer of 360 seconds. Note that by using different granularities, time values need to be adjusted, where minimum travel times or release times have to be rounded up to the closest value within the time granularity, *e.g.*, for a granularity of 30 seconds, a release time of 10 seconds is rounded to 30 seconds. This can lead to greater solution costs due to rounded values. Figure 1 shows that the solving time decreases with the increase of granularity. This is expected since with higher granularities there are fewer time variables and constraints. Figure 2 shows that with the increase of granularity, both the number of missed ideal events and the corresponding total ideal time deviation increase, up to the point when service cancellations begin to compensate (granularity of 10 seconds). These results confirm the expected behaviour, due to the degradation of the time precision with the increase of the granularity.

The WM instances were generated considering two minutes as the minimum time space between trains, and we computed a feasible schedule to use as an ideal timetable. To evaluate the capability of our approach to find an optimal schedule when the ideal timetable is not feasible, we changed the instances by increasing the minimum time space between trains from two to three minutes. This is done

Table 2. Number of intentions (Trains), variables, clauses, average solving time in seconds, cost, average deviation from ideal time (Dev.), and number of cancelled intentions for each instance (Inst.). Granularity of 60 seconds. Time buffer of 360 seconds.

Inst.	Trains	Variables	Clauses	Time(s)	Cost	Dev.(s)	Cancelled
WM01	616	3 613 148	11 467 435	110.154	110	60.0	0
WM02	1 232	4 407 656	15 981 181	387.509	436	60.0	0
WM03	1 848	4 866 444	19 339 625	1 308.620	1 314	69.4	0
WM04	2 024	5 331 788	21 382 627	1 528.970	1 452	80.0	0

by increasing each resource release time accordingly. Experiments were made with a granularity of 60 seconds, a time buffer of 360 seconds, an ideal time penalisation of 1 per minute, and a service cancellation penalisation of 100. Our approach was able to find optimal solutions, with minimum deviations from the ideal timetable of around one minute per track, which is expected, and without cancelling services, as shown in Table 2.

6   Conclusions

In this work, we used a MaxSAT approach to the Train Timetabling Problem with Route Choice and Other Features, whose goal is to find a minimum-cost schedule for a set of service intentions and determine the corresponding routes. We allow service intentions to be cancelled, *i.e.*, remain unscheduled, and for the scheduled services, we want to obtain a conflict-free timetable as close as possible to a given ideal timetable. To the best of our knowledge, such combination of features of the train timetabling problem, for which we presented a formal definition, has not been fully addressed before.

Our approach is able to find routes and schedules in real-world scenarios, being able to consider up to 2024 service intentions, and finding an optimal solution. As expected, results show that as time granularities increase, the running times decrease significantly, the MaxSAT model decreases in size, and the cost of the optimal solution tends to increase. Considering a granularity of 2 seconds revealed a good compromise between solution quality and running time.

As future work, we intend to explore the use of different granularities by solving a problem with a higher granularity, and then solving a portion of the problem with lower granularity using information from the initial solution.

Moreover, different methods, such as MILP, can be explored to address the presented variation of train timetabling problem.

Acknowledgments. This study was funded by under grant LISBOA2030-FEDER-01057000 (project n.° 17222).

Disclosure of Interests. The authors have no competing interests to declare that are relevant to the content of this article.

References

1. Biere, A., Heule, M., van Maaren, H.: Handbook of Satisfiability, vol. 185. IOS press (2009)
2. Cacchiani, V., Caprara, A., Toth, P.: Scheduling extra freight trains on railway networks. Transp. Res. Part B: Methodol. **44**(2), 215–231 (2010)
3. Caprara, A., Fischetti, M., Toth, P.: Modeling and solving the train timetabling problem. Oper. Res. **50**(5), 851–861 (2002)
4. Correia Duarte, P.J., et al.: 50 years of or in railway timetabling and rolling stock planning. EURO J. Transp. Logist. **14**, 100155 (2025)
5. Danavulapadu, V.P., Singamsetty, P.: Trains scheduling problem with multiple lines. Sci. Rep. **14**(1) (2024)
6. Eén, N., Sörensson, N.: Translating pseudo-Boolean constraints into SAT. J. Satisf. Boolean Model. Comput. **2**(1–4), 1–26 (2006)
7. Gattermann, P., Großmann, P., Nachtigall, K., Schöbel, A.: Integrating passengers' routes in periodic timetabling: a SAT approach. Schloss Dagstuhl – Leibniz-Zentrum für Informatik (2016)
8. Großmann, P., Hölldobler, S., Manthey, N., Nachtigall, K., Opitz, J., Steinke, P.: Solving periodic event scheduling problems with SAT. In: Jiang, H., Ding, W., Ali, M., Wu, X. (eds.) IEA/AIE 2012. LNCS (LNAI), vol. 7345, pp. 166–175. Springer, Heidelberg (2012). https://doi.org/10.1007/978-3-642-31087-4_18
9. Jordi, J., Toletti, A., Caimi, G., Schüpbach, K.: Applied timetabling for railways: experiences with several solution approaches (2019)
10. Lamorgese, L., Mannino, C., Natvig, E.: An exact micro–macro approach to cyclic and non-cyclic train timetabling. Omega **72**, 59–70 (2017)
11. Lemos, A., Gouveia, F., Monteiro, P.T., Lynce, I.: Iterative train scheduling under disruption with maximum satisfiability. J. Artif. Intell. Res. **79**, 1047–1090 (2024)
12. Leutwiler, F., Corman, F.: A logic-based benders decomposition for microscopic railway timetable planning. Eur. J. Oper. Res. **303**(2), 525–540 (2022)
13. Martins, R., Manquinho, V., Lynce, I.: Open-WBO: a modular MaxSAT solver'. In: Sinz, C., Egly, U. (eds.) SAT 2014. LNCS, vol. 8561, pp. 438–445. Springer, Cham (2014). https://doi.org/10.1007/978-3-319-09284-3_33
14. Matos, G.P., Albino, L., Saldanha, R.L., Morgado, E.M.: Optimising cyclic timetables with a SAT approach. In: Oliveira, E., Gama, J., Vale, Z., Lopes Cardoso, H. (eds.) EPIA 2017. LNCS (LNAI), vol. 10423, pp. 343–354. Springer, Cham (2017). https://doi.org/10.1007/978-3-319-65340-2_29
15. Matos, G.P., Albino, L.M., Saldanha, R.L., Morgado, E.M.: Solving periodic timetabling problems with sat and machine learning. Public Transp. **13**(3), 625–648 (2020)
16. Tamura, N., Taga, A., Kitagawa, S., Banbara, M.: Compiling finite linear CSP into sat. Constraints **14**(2), 254–272 (2008)
17. Wang, E., Yang, L., Li, P., Zhang, C., Gao, Z.: Joint optimization of train scheduling and routing in a coupled multi-resolution space–time railway network. Transp. Res. Part C: Emerg. Technol. **147**, 103994 (2023)
18. Zhou, W., Teng, H.: Simultaneous passenger train routing and timetabling using an efficient train-based Lagrangian relaxation decomposition. Transp. Res. Part B: Methodol. **94**, 409–439 (2016)

Driving Scene Context-Augmented Trajectory Prediction with Risk-Aware Decision Reasoning Using Multimodal LLM

Sunghun Kim[1] , Seokjun Hong[2] , Joobin Jin[2] ,
and Byeongjoon Noh[1,2(✉)]

[1] Department of AI and Big Data, Soonchunhyang University, 22 Soonchunhyang-ro,
Asan 31538, South Korea
{ksh0816,powernoh}@sch.ac.kr
[2] Department of Future Convergence Technology, Soonchunhyang University,
22 Soonchunhyang-ro, Asan 31538, South Korea
{hongsj,jjb0821}@sch.ac.kr

Abstract. In complex urban environments, autonomous driving systems face persistent challenges due to unpredictable behaviors such as jaywalking and sudden lane changes, necessitating integrated approaches capable of accurate trajectory prediction and interpretable risk reasoning. This study proposes a multimodal framework that jointly performs trajectory prediction and explainable risk-aware decision reasoning by combining dynamic states of objects and contextual visual information extracted from vehicle-mounted imagery. The proposed framework comprises four modules: object behavior feature extraction, scene context feature extraction, driving scene context-augmented trajectory prediction, and risk-aware decision reasoning. Specifically, the model integrates behavioral features modeled through long-short term memory (LSTM)-based gated units and transformer encoders with visual context features to enhance trajectory forecasting. Furthermore, the DeepSeek-based multimodal large language model (MLLM) generates interpretable explanations by identifying critical risk objects, describing potential risks, and recommending vehicle actions. In our experiment, we confirm the feasibility and applicability of the proposed framework by implementing and applying it to Rank2Tell open dataset, achieving significant performance improvements (ADE: 10.972, FDE: 13.701, RMSE: 8.782) compared to baseline models, and qualitative comparisons across multiple language models, including DeepSeek (ours), LLaMA, Mistral based model, demonstrated superior reasoning capability and interpretability of the proposed multimodal approach.

Keywords: Trajectory Prediction · Driving Scene Context · Risk-aware Reasoning · Multimodal LLM · Autonomous Driving System

J. Valente de Oliveira et al. (Eds.): EPIA 2025, LNAI 16122, pp. 192–204, 2026.
https://doi.org/10.1007/978-3-032-05179-0_15

1   Introduction

In recent years, autonomous driving technologies have made remarkable progress; however, numerous technical challenges remain to be resolved to achieve stable and reliable vehicle operation in complex urban environments [1]. Urban driving scenarios, in particular, frequently involve unexpected situations such as jaywalking pedestrians, sudden lane changes, and illegally parked vehicles, requiring the autonomous driving system to quickly perceive and respond effectively to these abnormal and emergency conditions [2].

One of the critical technologies for addressing these requirements is accurate trajectory prediction of surrounding objects, including vehicles and pedestrians [3,4]. However, most existing trajectory prediction studies focus primarily on historical trajectories or positions without considering the broader visual context of the driving scene [5,6]. In real urban environments, diverse visual factors such as interactions between nearby objects significantly influence object trajectories; thus, integrating these factors into prediction models is indispensable.

Moreover, existing approaches often lack sufficient interpretability, despite the safety-critical nature of autonomous driving, where both passenger and pedestrian safety must be ensured. In this context, models must not only predict future trajectories, but also explain their rationale, identify potential risks, and suggest appropriate driving responses [7]. Recently, approaches leveraging large language models (LLMs), such as video-language models (VLM), have emerged to qualitatively evaluate traffic scenarios by providing natural language descriptions of visual scenes and associated risks [8,9]. However, the majority of existing studies still treat trajectory prediction and risk explanation as separate tasks, with few attempts made to integrate these tasks into a coherent framework capable of supporting autonomous decision-making.

To overcome these limitations, this study proposes a multimodal framework that simultaneously performs trajectory prediction and explainable risk-aware decision reasoning by jointly utilizing the dynamic states of objects and contextual visual information extracted from driving scenes. The proposed framework consists of four main modules: 1) object behavior feature extraction, 2) scene context feature extraction, 3) driving scene context-augmented trajectory prediction, and 4) risk-aware decision reasoning. Each module extracts distinct information from forward-facing vehicle imagery and performs complementary functions based on this information.

First, the object behavior feature extraction module processes behavioral information in sequences-such as trajectories, velocities, yaw angles, and dynamic status of surrounding objects-to extract behavioral features required for trajectory prediction. These features are initially modeled using a long short-term memory (LSTM)-based gated architecture [10] to capture long-term dependencies in sequential data, followed by a Transformer-based model to effectively identify global temporal relationships.

In parallel, the scene context feature extraction module processes the forward-facing vehicle imagery to extract visual features of the driving scene, which are then combined with object behavior features into a unified representation-termed the "driving scene context"-to support trajectory prediction. Through this process, trajectory prediction transcends the conventional approach of merely predicting positional changes, advancing toward contextually-informed, precise, and adaptive predictions.

Furthermore, to ensure interpretability in risk perception and decision making, the proposed framework combines a risk-aware decision reasoning module. This module is based on a multimodal large language model (MLLM), receiving multimodal input composed of driving scene imagery and user-defined textual prompts, and produces advanced interpretative outputs. Specifically, it: 1) identifies the most critical risk-related object within the current driving scene, 2) provides natural language explanations clarifying why the identified object is considered risky, and 3) suggests appropriate actions for autonomous vehicles to undertake in response to the identified risk. Consequently, this enables users to clearly understand the rationale behind autonomous system decisions.

In the proposed framework, the object behavior feature extraction and scene context feature extraction modules operate in parallel on the same input imagery and share extracted information, forming an integrated structure capable of simultaneously achieving accurate trajectory prediction and explainable risk-aware decision reasoning. This study demonstrates the strong potential for real-world application of autonomous driving systems in urban environments by relying solely on imagery and fundamental object state data, without the need for expensive sensors such as LiDAR, while achieving both high predictive performance and interpretability.

2   Related Work

2.1   Trajectory Prediction

Trajectory prediction is essential for autonomous driving systems, particularly in urban environments where accurately predicting future movements of vehicles and pedestrians is critical for ensuring safety. In this study, all vehicles and pedestrians within the autonomous vehicle's forward field of view are considered as prediction targets.

Traditionally, trajectory prediction has been defined as a time-series forecasting problem that estimates future positions based on historical data, and numerous studies have been conducted across various fields [5]. Early models, such as bidirectional LSTM (Bi-LSTM) networks, which captured temporal dependencies from historical data [11,12]. Subsequently, graph neural network (GNN)-based approaches were introduced to model spatial relationships between agents and capture multi-agent interactions [13].

Recently, transformer-based architectures have gained attention due to their ability to model long-range temporal dependencies. For example, LTSF-NLinear demonstrates robust accuracy over extended prediction horizons, proving particularly effective in long-term forecasting tasks [14]. In addition, semantic lane-level data from LiDAR-based HD maps improve trajectory prediction accuracy and support direction-aware predictions aligned with road structures [15].

Moreover, recent advancements have extended trajectory prediction beyond positional forecasting to anticipating social behaviors and latent intentions of surrounding objects. Notably, multimodal approaches leveraging LLMs have been proposed to generate natural language descriptions of object states or scene context, enhancing interpretability and prediction diversity [16,17]. For example, LG-Traj [18] combines Transformers with LLMs to model pedestrian behaviors and social interactions for context-aware trajectory predictions.

Building upon these recent research trends, this study proposes a framework intergrating dynamic object behavior features and scene contextual information, simultaneously achieving precise trajectory prediction and situational awareness.

2.2   Scene Understanding in Autonomous Driving Systems

With the advancements of LLMs, numerous studies have focused on improving the interpretability and scene understanding capabilities of autonomous driving systems. In particular, elucidating the decision-making processes of autonomous driving systems in a human-understandable manner has become increasingly prominent [19,20]. While previous autonomous driving studies often treated the decision-making process as a black-box, recent approaches have emphasized enhancing system transparency and user trust through natural-language explanations [21].

A representative research trend involves converting structured numerical data, such as object velocity, position, and yaw angle, into natural-language descriptions, which are subsequently aligned with language representations within LLMs to explicitly convey the underlying rationale for decisions [22]. Examples of this approach include pairing simulation-generated autonomous driving data with natural-language explanations and fine-tuning LLMs using question-and-answer formats tailored specifically for driving scenarios [23].

Additionally, recent methodologies have advanced beyond simple numeric-to-language translations, incorporating transformer-based modules (e.g., VectorFormer) to efficiently model interactions between structured vector representations and linguistic information [24]. Furthermore, lightweight adaptation techniques such as low-rank adaptation (LoRA) have been increasingly employed within LLMs to enhance training efficiency and inference speed [25]. Such multimodal approaches integrate object-centric quantitative data with scene-centric qualitative descriptions to yield interpretable decision outputs [26].

Collectively, these emerging studies indicate a paradigm shift in autonomous driving research from focusing on accurate predictions to models that articulate reasoning, identify risk factors, and recommend appropriate actions for autonomous vehicles in urban driving scenes.

However, most existing studies still address trajectory prediction and risk-aware decision reasoning as separate tasks. Unified frameworks supporting both functionalities in real-time autonomous driving remain relatively scarce. To bridge this gap, the current study proposes an integrated autonomous driving framework that simultaneously provides accurate trajectory predictions and risk-aware decision reasoning.

3 Methodology

In this section, we describe the proposed framework in Fig. 1 that integrates driving scene context with MLLM-based reasoning to predict object trajectories and provide explainable risk-aware decisions. The proposed framework mainly consists of four modules: 1) object behavior feature extraction 2) scene context feature extraction 3) driving scene context-augmented trajectory prediction 4) risk-aware decision reasoning.

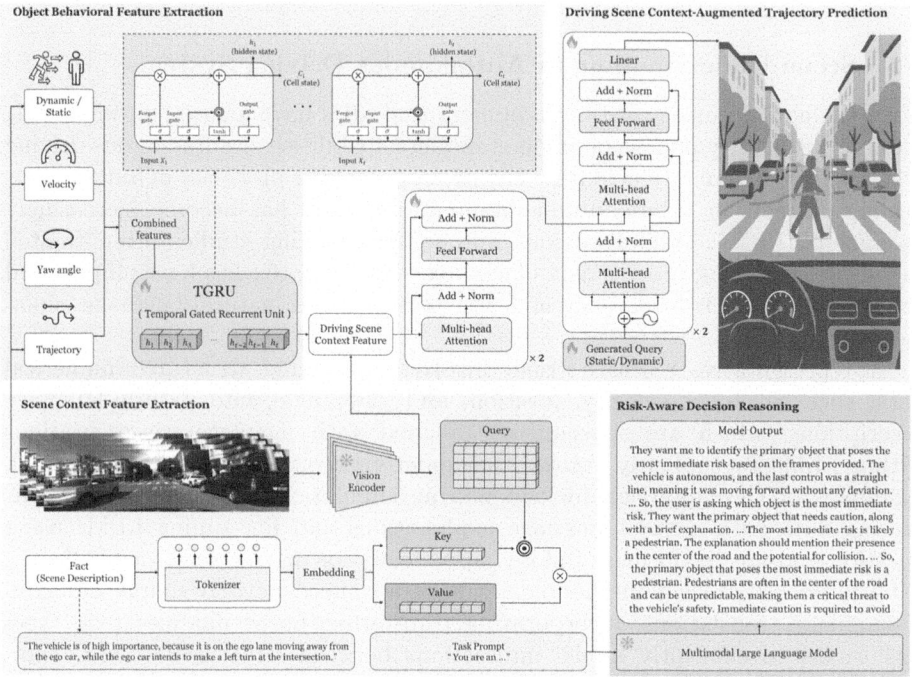

Fig. 1. Overall architecture of the proposed method

3.1 Object Behavior Feature Extraction

This object behavior feature extraction module captures behavioral patterns of surrounding objects by encoding sequential motion data, including trajectories, velocities, yaw angles, and dynamic states. Specifically, trajectories provide historical positional sequences; velocities quantify motion intensity derived from positional displacements between consecutive frames; yaw angles represent the object's heading direction; and dynamic states indicates whether objects are stationary or in motion.

These multidimensional features are combined into temporally aligned, unified state representations. The resulting state sequences are processed through a temporal gated recurrent unit (TGRU), an advanced recurrent neural network that maintains the long-term dependency capturing capacities of traditional LSTM models while utilizing simplified gating mechanisms for improved computational efficiency and stability. Unlike conventional recurrent models, which output only a final hidden state, the TGRU employed in this study generates an accumulated state representation at each time step. These outputs, incorporating cumulative temporal context, subsequently serve as structured inputs for visual context fusion and global temporal modeling.

3.2   Scene Context Feature Extraction

This module analyzes global visual information from the driving environment, providing essential spatial context for interpreting object behaviors. Given that trajectories are inherently influenced by the surrounding visual context, incorporating such visual cues significantly improves trajectory prediction accuracy and risk-aware decision reasoning.

This module processes imagery from onboard vehicle cameras using a contrastive language-image pre-training (CLIP) model-based vision encoder [27], extracting high-dimensional visual features. These features are then fused with the temporal motion representations generated from the object behavior feature extraction module, forming a coherent "driving scene context" representation. This integration facilitates clearer interpretation of complex motion patterns, significantly improving adaptability to dynamic urban scenarios.

Concurrently, the module encodes natural language descriptions of the driving scenes into linguistic embeddings. We first tokenize the textual data using a pretrained LLM, then fuse the resulting embeddings with visual features using a cross-attention mechanism—where visual features serve as queries and textual embeddings act as keys and values—to form multimodal representations that emphasize image regions aligned with the linguistic context. These multimodal embeddings are then forwarded to the risk-aware decision reasoning module, enabling nuanced interpretation of potential risks and facilitating the suggestion of appropriate driving actions.

3.3   Driving Scene Context-Augmented Trajectory Prediction

This module employs a non-autoregressive approach to predict future trajectories, utilizing a global behavior context derived from fused temporal motion and visual scene features. These features are processed through a transformer-based encoder-decoder architecture, enabling accurate position predictions and consideration environmental interactions.

The transformer encoder aggregates global behavior contexts across all time steps, generating a comprehensive contextual representation of object motions and scene information. This encoded output is utilized in two primary ways. First, a global behavioral context vector is computed by average pooling across all encoder outputs, providing a compact representation of long-term behavioral trends. Second, a classifier implemented as a multi-layer perceptron (MLP) predicts future object dynamic states. These predictions, combined with positional encodings and the global behavioral context vector, formulate input queries for the transformer decoder.

The transformer decoder integrates contextual information into each query through multi-head attention mechanisms over encoder outputs. Utilizing a non-autoregressive decoding strategy, this decoder simultaneously generates future trajectory positions, significantly reducing inference latency and avoiding error accumulation typically observed in autoregressive models [28].

3.4   Risk-Aware Decision Reasoning

This module aims to identify critical objects within the driving scene, elucidate the reasons for identified risks, and propose suitable responses for autonomous vehicles through natural language outputs. It leverages the multimodal embeddings produced by the scene context feature extraction module, combined with user-defined textual prompts, to guided the reasoning process within an MLLM.

Specifically, given multimodal input representations and targeted prompts, the MLLM executes step-by-step reasoning, generating natural language outputs that: 1) pinpoint the most critical risky object in the given scene; 2) provide detailed explainations of why this object poses a risk; and 3) recommend appropriate vehicle responses.

To ensure efficient processing and sophisticated reasoning capabilities, we adopt the DeepSeek-R1-Distill-QWEN-7B [29] as the MLLM, leveraging its lightweight architecture, effective chain-of-thought (CoT) reasoning capability, and proficient handling of zero-shot instructions.

4   Results

4.1   Experimental Details

Dataset. The experiments were conducted using the Rank2Tell dataset [30], consisting of 116 video clips (an average 20 s per clip) recorded from vehicle-mounted cameras positioned at the left, center, and right viewpoints. All videos were captured at 10 frames per second, with annotations provided every five frames. Each annotated frame includes object bounding boxes, trajectories, yaw angles, dynamic status information, and corresponding natural language descriptions of the driving scene.

Training Setup. The proposed framework was trained to forecast object positions over a 5-second horizon based on a 5-second observation window. The model operates non-autoregressively, predicting all future positions simultaneously. The loss functions is a combination of mean squared error (MSE) for coordinate prediction and a cross-entropy for dynamic state classification, weighted at 0.1 to balance contributions. The dataset was divided into training and test sets in an 8:2 ratio. The pretrained vision encoder and MLLM components were frozen during training and activated only during training.

4.2   Evaluation Metrics

Trajectory prediction performance was evaluated using three standard metrics: average displacement error (ADE) [31], final displacement error (FDE) [31], and root mean squared error (RMSE). ADE measures the average euclidean distance between predicted and ground-truth trajectories, while FDE focuses only on the final predicted position. Due to the generative nature of risk-aware decision reasoning outputs, qualitative evaluation was performed using three criteria: contextual plausibility, scene understanding accuracy, and relevance and practicality of recommended actions.

4.3   Quantitative Evaluation for Trajectory Prediction

Baseline Experiment. A comparative experiment was conducted against a baseline "standard transformer [32]" model, which implements a vanilla autoregressive encoder-decoder architecture. At each prediction step, the transformer concatenates linearly projected motion features and CLIP-based image embeddings with positional encodings and employs causal self-attention to generate the next position conditioned on all previous outputs, without any mechanism for temporal context accumulation. Both models were trained and evaluated under identical conditions. Table 1 summarizes the results. The proposed model outperformed the baseline across all metrics, achieving reductions of 34.0% in ADE, 28.7% in FDE, and 30.9% in RMSE. These findings indicate that incorporating temporally accumulated context significantly improves trajectory prediction accuracy and stability by better capturing object motion dynamics and mitigating the error accumulation characteristic of autoregressive decoding.

Table 1. Performance evaluation

Model	ADE	FDE	RMSE
Transformer	16.631	19.218	12.712
Ours	**10.972**	**13.701**	**8.782**

Ablation Study. An ablation study was conducted to quantitatively evaluate the contribution of each input feature, including visual features (image), dynamic status, velocity, and yaw angle. Table 2 summarizes the results, showing that the model utilizing all features achieved the highest performance. Excluding velocity resulted in the largest performance decline, emphasizing its importance in capturing motion dynamics beyond positional data alone. Visual features significantly contributed by providing spatial constraints such as road geometry and obstacle positions. Conversely, yaw angles and dynamic statuses showed minor individual impacts but potentially enhanced performance when combined with other features. These results underscore the importance of integrating both temporal and spatial features for precise trajectory prediction.

Table 2. Ablation studies by input features

Image	Dynamic Static	Velocity	Yaw	ADE	FDE	RMSE
✓	✓	✓	✓	**10.972**	**13.701**	**8.782**
✓	✓	✓	–	11.570	14.079	9.193
✓	✓	–	✓	13.874	16.481	10.571
✓	–	✓	✓	12.055	14.791	9.517
–	✓	✓	✓	14.622	17.351	11.317

4.4   Qualitative Evaluation for Risk-Aware Decision Reasoning

To assess the impact of reinforcement learning training and chain-of-thought (CoT) optimization on interpretability in risk-aware decision reasoning, we conducted a comparative qualitative evaluation against two widely adopted baseline models with different training piplines. LLaMA3.1-8B [33] undergoes autoregressive next-token pretraining only, without any subsequent fine-tuning. Mistral-7B-Instruct-v0.3 [34] builds upon the same autoregressive pretraining and then receives supervised instruction fine-tuning on publicly available promptâĂŞresponse datasets, but does not employ reinforcement learning or CoT optimization. DeepSeek-R1-Distill-QWEN-7B inherits the QWEN-7B pretrained and instruction-tuned weights and further integrates a reinforcement-learning objective together with CoT optimization within its training framework. All models received the same multimodal input-comprising visual features and language prompts-and were guided to identify potential risks, explain their causes, and suggest appropriate driving responses.

The response generated by DeepSeek-R1-Distill-QWEN-7B (proposed) were analyzed based on its ability to 1) correctly identify the primary risk-related object, 2) provide contextually grounded reasoning, and 3) generate coherent and plausible behavioral suggestions. As depicted in Fig. 2, the model successfully pinpointed the most critical object-typically a pedestrian exhibiting risk behavior-and justified its decision by referencing a combination of contextual elements such as pedestrian orientation, spatial layout of the road, and traffic signal states.

Notably, the model exhibited strong alignment between perception and action by recommending that the vehicle maintain a stop position until the pedestrian

You are the real-time control module of an autonomous vehicle.
Given a sequence of fused image–text features, identify
1. Which object poses the most immediate risk while driving,
2. The reason of risk object
3. What driving action you recommend to avoid it.
Please format your output exactly as follows:
Risky Object: <Type of the object and location of the object>
Reason of the Risk Object: <concise rationale>
Risk-aware Driving Decision Recommendation: <action-oriented instruction>

∞ Meta

Risky Object: Pedestrian in the middle of the lane
Reason of the Risk Object: The pedestrian is in a risky spot and may not be visible to other drivers.
Risk-aware Driving Decision Recommendation: Yield

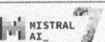

Risky Object: A pedestrian crossing the road diagonally in front of the vehicle.
Reason of the Risk Object: The pedestrian's unpredictable crossing path
Risk-aware Driving Decision Recommendation: Slow down and prepare to stop if necessary,
yielding to the pedestrian

🐋 deepseek R1 Distill Qwen

Risky Object: Pedestrians crossing from the left side of the intersection
Reason of the Risk Object: The pedestrians are jaywalking across the intersection from left to
right, disregarding the traffic signal. While they are not directly blocking the right-turn path,
their unpredictable movement near the front of the vehicle introduces a high risk.
Risk-aware Driving Decision Recommendation: Yield and remain fully stopped until the
pedestrians have cleared the entire front field of view. Do not begin the right turn until both
individuals are visibly outside of the ego lane and crossing path.

Fig. 2. Qualitative Evaluation: Risk-aware Decision Reasoning

had fully cleared the path, demonstrating a consistent semantic flow between situation understanding and behavioral recommendation.

In comparison, LLaMA3.1-8B and Mistral-7B-Instruct-v0.3 were also capable of identifying the correct risk object in most scenarios. However, their reasoning often lacked depth and occasionally included fragmented or overly generic content. Moreover, these models frequently expressed uncertainty in their suggested actions, reducing the clarity and confidence of their guidance. In contrast, DeepSeek-R1-Distill-QWEN-7B consistently produced structured and interpretable outputs, a result attributed to its CoT-based reasoning strategy and alignment.

These findings highlight that, in addition to structured multimodal representation and CoT-based instruction alignment, the reinforcement-learning training of DeepSeek-R1-Distill-QWEN-7B further contributes to its robust and explainable decision reasoning in autonomous driving systems.

5 Conclusion

This study proposed a multimodal framework that jointly performs trajectory prediction and risk-aware decision reasoning for urban autonomous driving scenarios. The proposed framework integrates dynamic behavioral states of surrounding objects with visual scene context to improve the performance and contextual relevance of trajectory prediction. In addition, it combines natural language descriptions with visual features to generate interpretable risk assessments and action recommendations. Quantitative experiments demonstrate that the model consistently outperforms a transformer-based baseline across multiple evaluation metrics, confirming the effectiveness of temporal and contextual integration. The ablation analysis further reveals the individual and complementary contributions of input features such as velocity, yaw, and visual cues. Qualitative evaluation results indicate that the structured multimodal input generated by the scene context extraction enhances the consistency and interpretability of reasoning across different language models.

In future work, we will extend the framework to integrate risk-aware decision reasoning with trajectory prediction into a single safe-path planning module. This unified module will dynamically generate and adapt driving paths that proactively avoid detected hazards while preserving real-time responsiveness.

Acknowledgments. This research was supported by the MSIT (Ministry of Science, ICT), Korea, under the National Program for Excellence in SW, supervised by the IITP (Institute of Information & communications Technology Planning & Evaluation) in 2025" (2021-0-01399).

Disclosure of Interests. The authors have no competing interests to declare that are relevant to the content of this article.

References

1. Chen, Z., et al.: MineSim: a scenario-based simulation test system and benchmark for autonomous trucks in open-pit mines. Accid. Anal. Prevent. **213**, 107938 (2025)
2. Abdel-Aty, M., Ding, S.: A matched case-control analysis of autonomous vs human-driven vehicle accidents. Nat. Commun. **15**(1), 4931 (2024)
3. Zhang, Z., Ding, Z., Tian, R.: Decouple ego-view motions for predicting pedestrian trajectory and intention. IEEE Trans. Image Process. (2024)
4. Wang, C., Liao, H., Li, Z., Xu, C.: WAKE: towards robust and physically feasible trajectory prediction for autonomous vehicles with wavelet and kinematics synergy. IEEE Trans. Pattern Anal. Mach. Intell. (2025)

5. Tang, R., Ng, K.K., Li, L., Yang, Z.: A learning-based interacting multiple model filter for trajectory prediction of small multirotor drones considering differential sequences. Transp. Res. Part C: Emerg. Technol. **174**, 105115 (2025)
6. Jiang, T., Dong, Q., Ma, Y., Ji, X., Liu, Y.: Customizable multimodal trajectory prediction via nodes of interest selection for autonomous vehicles. Expert Syst. Appl. 128222 (2025)
7. Atakishiyev, S., Salameh, M., Yao, H., Goebel, R.: Explainable artificial intelligence for autonomous driving: a comprehensive overview and field guide for future research directions. IEEE Access (2024)
8. Rivera, E., Lübberstedt, J., Uhlemann, N., Lienkamp, M.: Scenario understanding of traffic scenes through large visual language models. In: Proceedings of the Winter Conference on Applications of Computer Vision, pp. 1037–1045 (2025)
9. Xiao, D., Dianati, M., Jennings, P., Woodman, R.: Hazardvlm: A video language model for real-time hazard description in automated driving systems. IEEE Trans. Intell. Veh. (2024)
10. Hochreiter, S., Schmidhuber, J.: Long short-term memory. Neural Comput. **9**(8), 1735–1780 (1997)
11. Guan, L., Shi, J., Wang, D., Shao, H., Chen, Z., Chu, D.: A trajectory prediction method based on bayonet importance encoding and bidirectional LSTM. Expert Syst. Appl. **223**, 119888 (2023)
12. Huang, Z., Xu, W., Yu, K.: Bidirectional LSTM-CRF models for sequence tagging. arXiv preprint arXiv:1508.01991 (2015)
13. Du, Q., Wang, X., Yin, S., Li, L., Ning, H.: Social force embedded mixed graph convolutional network for multi-class trajectory prediction. IEEE Trans. Intell. Veh. (2024)
14. Cyranka, J., Haponiuk, S.: Unified long-term time-series forecasting benchmark. arXiv preprint arXiv:2309.15946 (2023)
15. Tang, X., Kan, M., Shan, S., Ji, Z., Bai, J., Chen, X.: HPNet: dynamic trajectory forecasting with historical prediction attention. In: Proceedings of the IEEE/CVF Conference on Computer Vision and Pattern Recognition, pp. 15261–15270 (2024)
16. Gruver, N., Finzi, M., Qiu, S., Wilson, A.G.: Large language models are zero-shot time series forecasters. Adv. Neural. Inf. Process. Syst. **36**, 19622–19635 (2023)
17. Chen, L., et al.: Driving with LLMs: fusing object-level vector modality for explainable autonomous driving. In: 2024 IEEE International Conference on Robotics and Automation (ICRA), pp. 14093–14100. IEEE (2024)
18. Chib, P.S., Singh, P.: LG-Traj: LLM guided pedestrian trajectory prediction. arXiv preprint arXiv:2403.08032 (2024)
19. Zhang, H., Zhang, W., Qu, H., Liu, J.: Enhancing human-centered dynamic scene understanding via multiple LLMs collaborated reasoning. Vis. Intell. **3**(1), 3 (2025)
20. Xu, Z., et al.: DriveGPT4: interpretable end-to-end autonomous driving via large language model. IEEE Robot. Autom. Lett. (2024)
21. Luo, X., Ding, F., Panda, R., Chen, R., Loo, J., Zhang, S.: "What's happening"- a human-centered multimodal interpreter explaining the actions of autonomous vehicles. In: Proceedings of the Winter Conference on Applications of Computer Vision, pp. 1163–1170 (2025)
22. Feng, Y., Hua, W., Sun, Y.: NLE-DM: natural-language explanations for decision making of autonomous driving based on semantic scene understanding. IEEE Trans. Intell. Transp. Syst. **24**(9), 9780–9791 (2023)
23. Peng, M., et al.: LC-LLM: explainable lane-change intention and trajectory predictions with large language models. Commun. Transp. Res. **5**, 100170 (2025)

24. Chen, Z., et al.: Learning high-resolution vector representation from multi-camera images for 3d object detection. In: Leonardis, A., Ricci, E., Roth, S., Russakovsky, O., Sattler, T., Varol, G. (eds.) ECCV 2024. LNCS, vol. 15093, pp. 385–403. Springer, Cham (2024). https://doi.org/10.1007/978-3-031-72761-0_22

25. Hu, E.J., Shen, Y., Wallis, P., Allen-Zhu, Z., Li, Y., Wang, S., Wang, L., Chen, W., et al.: LoRA: low-rank adaptation of large language models. In: ICLR, vol. 1, no. 2, p. 3 (2022)

26. Tian, R., et al.: Tokenize the world into object-level knowledge to address long-tail events in autonomous driving. arXiv preprint arXiv:2407.00959 (2024)

27. Radford, A., et al.: Learning transferable visual models from natural language supervision. In: International Conference on Machine Learning, pp. 8748–8763. PMLR (2021)

28. Chen, X., Zhang, H., Zhao, F., Cai, Y., Wang, H., Ye, Q.: Vehicle trajectory prediction based on intention-aware non-autoregressive transformer with multi-attention learning for internet of vehicles. IEEE Trans. Instrum. Meas. **71**, 1–12 (2022)

29. Guo, D., et al.: DeepSeek-R1: incentivizing reasoning capability in LLMs via reinforcement learning. arXiv preprint arXiv:2501.12948 (2025)

30. Sachdeva, E., et al.: Rank2Tell: a multimodal driving dataset for joint importance ranking and reasoning. In: Proceedings of the IEEE/CVF Winter Conference on Applications of Computer Vision, pp. 7513–7522 (2024)

31. Alahi, A., Goel, K., Ramanathan, V., Robicquet, A., Fei-Fei, L., Savarese, S.: Social LSTM: human trajectory prediction in crowded spaces. In: Proceedings of the IEEE Conference on Computer Vision and Pattern Recognition, pp. 961–971 (2016)

32. Vaswani, A., et al.: Attention is all you need. Adv. Neural Inf. Process. Syst. **30** (2017)

33. Grattafiori, A., et al.: The LLaMA 3 herd of models. arXiv preprint arXiv:2407.21783 (2024)

34. Jiang, A.Q., et al.: Mistral 7B (2023). https://arxiv.org/abs/2310.06825

RailSafeNet: Visual Scene Understanding for Tram Safety

Ondřej Valach$^{(\boxtimes)}$ ⓘ and Ivan Gruber ⓘ

Department of Cybernetics, University of West Bohemia, Pilsen, Czechia
valacho@kky.zcu.cz, grubiv@ntis.zcu.cz

Abstract. Tram-human interaction safety is an important challenge, given that trams frequently operate in densely populated areas, where collisions can range from minor injuries to fatal outcomes. This paper addresses the issue from the perspective of designing a solution leveraging digital image processing, deep learning, and artificial intelligence to improve the safety of pedestrians, drivers, cyclists, pets, and tram passengers. We present RailSafeNet, a real-time framework that fuses semantic segmentation, object detection and a rule-based Distance Assessor to highlight track intrusions. Using only monocular video, the system identifies rails, localises nearby objects and classifies their risk by comparing projected distances with the standard 1435 mm rail gauge. Experiments on the diverse RailSem19 dataset show that a class-filtered SegFormer B3 model achieves 65% intersection-over-union (IoU), while a fine-tuned YOLOv8 attains 75.6% mean average precision (mAP) calculated at an intersection over union (IoU) threshold of 0.50. RailSafeNet therefore delivers accurate, annotation-light scene understanding that can warn drivers before dangerous situations escalate. Code available at https://github.com/oValach/RailSafeNet.

Keywords: tram · rails · pedestrian safety · artificial intelligence · computer vision · deep learning · image segmentation · object detection · distance estimation

1 Introduction

Urban tram networks remain prone to severe conflicts with other road users. A recent study of 7,535 incidents across Germany, Austria, Switzerland and Sweden recorded 8,802 injuries; although only 3% proved fatal, almost one-quarter were classified as serious [15]. Most crashes involve pedestrians or cyclists who share the track corridor, and the typical impact pattern—head, chest and lower-limb trauma—points to the limited protection these users enjoy. Reducing such harm therefore demands not only better infrastructure and traffic rules [11] but also on-board assistance able to warn drivers before a collision happens.

Recent progress in computer vision makes that goal realistic. Real-time semantic segmentation can now delineate rail geometry, while lightweight detectors localize people, cars and other critical objects in the same frame. What

© The Author(s), under exclusive license to Springer Nature Switzerland AG 2026
J. Valente de Oliveira et al. (Eds.): EPIA 2025, LNAI 16122, pp. 205–218, 2026.
https://doi.org/10.1007/978-3-032-05179-0_16

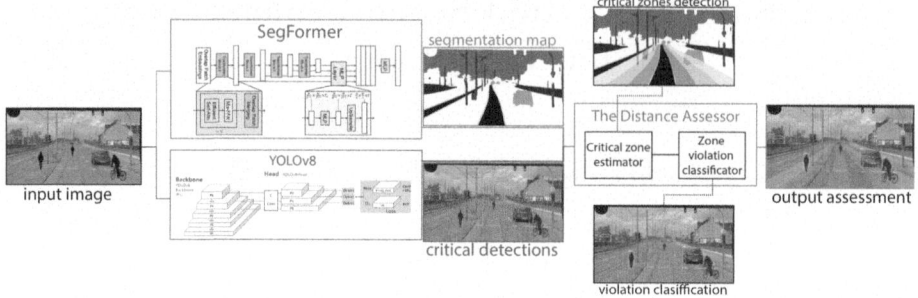

Fig. 1. The system pipeline visualization, starting with the system input data sample on the left, continuing to the parallel segmentation and detection, entering The Distance Assessor and ultimately coming out of the system as an output visualization.

is still missing is a monocular method that converts those predictions into an accurate, camera-agnostic estimate of an object's distance from the track. We solve this problem with a pipeline (see Fig. 1) that: (i) segments rails, (ii) detects surrounding objects, and (iii) infers distance via rule described in Sect. 4.3. By fusing these steps in a rule-based *Distance Assessor*, our system turns the driver's forward view into a continuously updated "criticality map" highlighting objects that could intrude into the tram path.

The proposed approach requires no camera calibration, depth sensor or LiDAR, and it runs fast enough for in-cab deployment. Ultimately, it provides tram operators with a low-cost means to mitigate collisions with pedestrians, cyclists, vehicles, animals or debris before they become unavoidable.

The three main contributions of this paper are as follows: (i) we introduce an approach for the task of **distance to rail estimation** in images without any knowledge of the capture, camera or setup parameters from **single image input,** (ii) we utilize a **custom segmentation processing** approach using data class filtering and mask post-processing, achieving superior results compared to the original RailSem19 dataset paper, (iii) we propose a **Distance Assessor system** which processes outputs from scene segmentation and object detection to accurately estimate distances from track and classify object criticality.

2   Related Work

Interactions between trams, pedestrians and vehicles still generate disproportionate numbers of serious pedestrian injuries and fatalities [12,15,17,22]. Collision analyses further show that tram-front design and risky pedestrian behavior amplify trauma severity [12,16,19].

Onboard perception has advanced with computer-vision progress. FCN and U-Net pioneered dense prediction [23]; DeepLabv3+ added multi-scale atrous pooling [7]; transformer models Mask2Former and SegFormer give lightweight real-time masks [8,27]. Foundation-level SAM further boosts cross-domain accuracy [13]. Object localization evolved from successive YOLO releases to transformer-based DETR [4,26].

Monocular distance estimation exploits rail geometry, linear cues or depth networks such as HybridDepth and UniDepthV2 [1,18]. These cues feed prototype warning systems that issue real-time alerts [2,9,14,24]. Our study unifies these strands in a class-filtered SegFormer, fine-tuned YOLOv8 and gauge-guided Distance Assessor specialized for tram scenes.

3   Data

Before detailing the methods, we first describe the RailSem19 dataset [29] used to train and evaluate our models. This dataset was selected for its large size and high variability in rail scene-related situations. It consists of 8,500 unique images extracted from 350 h of video captured from the ego-perspective of trains and trams across 58 different countries, thereby encompassing diverse sceneries—from wilderness areas with meadows, forests, and mountains to urban environments. Unlike other available datasets such as Rail-5k [30], and RailVID [28] or a synthetic approach for simulating real world data [10], which either lack tram data, overly segment track details, or have issues with public availability, RailSem19 provides segmented classes and combined train/tram scenarios along with annotations, including semantic segmentation dense label masks and JSON files containing rail-relevant polygons and rails as polylines. This dataset also includes bounding box annotations, these are further utilized for fine-tuning, see more in Sect. 5.2.

The dataset features 20 annotated classes, with five predominant ones, these are: *construction* (8250), *pole* (8200), *vegetation* (8250), *sky* (8150) and *rail-track* (7800), its approximate occurence frequencies are in parentheses. Dataset examples showcasing environmental variability are shown in Fig. 2. It is essential to points out that segmentation maps were generated using a state-of-the-art semantic segmentation solution from year 2019. According to the authors of the RailSem19 paper, most of these labels are well above 90% of intersection over union. However, after manual inspection, many misleading annotations and objects not detected or partially detected were found.

This data were split between train, test and evaluation subsets with ratio of 80/10/10 where the distribution of each subset aligns with the distribution of the whole dataset. Due to the fact of not ideally segmented ground truth segmentation masks, hand inspection of classes was performed to exclude classes with poor ground truth accuracy. This way the number of classes was reduced from twenty to eleven maintaining important classes for this project such as tram-track, rail-track and rail-raised and filtering out classes such as vegetation, terrain or road. This approach significantly increased the quality of our training data and cleaned the segmentation masks, removing the seemingly arbitrary edges in between not ideally segmented classes.

Fig. 2. RailSem19 [29] dataset examples, eight different data samples showing diversity in different ways (a), example segmentation mask in a photo overlay (b), example segmentation mask (c)

4   Methods

RailSafeNet consists of three main stages: rail segmentation to identify track area, object detection for critical objects localization, and distance estimation from tram to obstacle. This section describes each stage in detail. Both image segmentation and object detection are essential for the usability of the whole system, however, both of these tasks operate independently. That can not be said about the Distance Assessor end system which relies solely on the outputs from these two models. This overall system architecture is shown in Fig. 1.

The image segmentation is to be used mainly for the localization of rail related classes and scene understanding where the output segmentation mask should include information about the rail location, shape, direction etc. The task of the object detection executed in parallel with the segmentation, is to detect and provide accurate information about location and number of any objects that appeared to be around the railway. This is the fundamental information to work with in the following rule-based Distance Assessor system which should estimate the distance of detected objects from the track. By combination with the information from the detection system, there is enough information for the distance approximation.

4.1   Image Segmentation

The image segmentation task provides information about the rail position in the image, based on that, the following Distance Assessor estimates zones around rails in which the tram passage could be critical to the entity present.

For this task, the chosen model is a SegFormer with tested versions B2 and B3. This model provides great trade-off between accuracy and speed, with an ability to provide real-time inference [6,27]. This high inference speed is essential for our use case. For training these SegFormer models, a class filtration and mask postprocessing (more about that in Sect. 4.4) was applied,

For better model generalization, extensive image augmentations using the Albumentations [3] library were applied with a respect to the environment structure. We evaluated three augmentation tiers: Tier 1 used the raw images with no modifications; Tier 2 introduced moderate transformations, combining geometric shifts, scaling, rotations, flips, color adjustments (brightness, contrast, jitter), blur, and coarse dropout; and Tier 3 applied the full Tier 2 with simulated weather effects (rain, fog, snow, sun flare) and extra noise effects as ISO and Gaussian noise. Augmentation Level 1 retains the original image with a probability of 12.3%. When using Augmentation Level 2, this probability further decreases to 6.1%.

4.2 Object Detection

Due to the lack of data annotations for instance segmentation in rail scene understanding, the model's performance suffers because it is trained on multiple classes with imbalanced frequencies. Classes, such as "human" and "car", are underrepresented compared to "rail-track" resulting in lower accuracy for critical objects. Such reduced performance was be observed, for example, by merging of heterogeneous regions, regions being incomplete or completely missing. This led to the decision of employing a separate object detection algorithm, which offers faster and more accurate object localization. A YOLOv8 model was chosen for object detection mostly because of its competitive trade-off between speed and performance [25]. Further, it was finetuned on RailSem19 filtered classes bounding box annotations, see more in Sect. 5.

4.3 Distance Assessor

After the segmentation mask from the SegFormer block and bounding-box predictions from the YOLOv8 block are obtained, the next step is to extract the needed information from both of these outputs. That is done in the following The Distance Assessor block which processes the segmentation mask and bounding-boxes individually. The segmentation mask is utilized to obtain estimations of the distance to rail, that happens in the Critical zones estimator sub-block. That is followed by the processing of output bounding-boxes, these are used for extraction of object locations and labeling, which happens in the sub-block Zone violation classificator. This block also evaluates the object to rail criticality based on its distance from rail utilizing the output from the Critical zone estimator. The background of The Distance Assessor block is going to be described in detail in the following paragraphs. The Distance Assessor block output should look like in Fig. 3.

A subsystem denoted as **Critical zones estimator** leverages a key aspect of the system, that is the use of the standardized rail gauge, which measures 1435 mm across much of Europe [5]. That is a reliable reference for distance

Fig. 3. Visualization of the expected output from the system: each level of borders marked with different color represents different areas of the so-called "distance criticality". From yellow being the least critical to orange marking the moderately critical zone to red, which is the most critical zone, also including the whole rail tracks.

estimation. By detecting the rail in each image, the algorithm determines the number of pixels in width (d_{px}^{in}) that represent this known dimension (d_{real}^{in}). This comparison allows for the computation of a conversion factor (p_d) for each depth level affected by perspective distortion. Using this factor, the system converts distance estimations to pixel measurements following the formula

$$D_{depth} = p_d \ d_{real}^{out}; \quad p_d = \frac{d_{px}^{in}}{d_{real}^{in}}, \tag{1}$$

where d_{real}^{out} is the real-world distance that we need to estimate the number of pixels for. This approach enables precise distance estimation by using the rail gauge as a reference point. After the distance derivation for the given depth from each rail class mask edge point, the border between the estimated critical zone edge points is an interpolation. That way, the more depth levels are included, the more precise the final estimation will be. This way the final trio of critical zones is derived in specific distances as discussed further in Sect. 5.3.

Following is the classification of the objects close to the tram. The **Zone Violation Classifier** evaluates detected objects by checking whether specific border points of their bounding boxes intrude into predefined critical zones surrounding the railway. The system systematically analyzes 12 equidistant points along each bounding box - covering the corners and sides - and classifies objects based on the presence of any intrusion. Detected objects are divided into two categories: movable objects (such as persons, cars, and bicycles), which are prioritized due to their immediate life risk, and stationary objects (like backpacks and umbrellas), which are considered lower-level hazards. A color coding further helps to easily differentiate the level of criticality among the detected intrusions, using green, yellow, orange and red color in this given order starting from no risk to the highest.

Table 1. Hyper-parameter ranges and settings.

Model	SegFormerB2, SegFormerB3
Learning rate	1e-2–1e-6
Batch size	2–32
No. of epochs	50–200
Scheduler	LinearLR, ReduceLROnPlateau [20]
Optimizer	SGD, Adagrad, Adam, AdamW
Augmentation levels	0, 1, 2
Input resolution	224×224, 480×480, 512×512, 550×550, 700×700, 1024×1024 (adapted to GPU VRAM limitations along with batch size)

4.4 Evaluation

Intersection over Union and Mean Average Precision are used for the segmentation and detection evaluation. Segmentation evaluation takes into account every class in the mask, including small meaningless patches resulting from imprecise training data (even though the class filtration). Classes representing amorphous objects like grass or terrain lack clearly defined boundaries, making precise segmentation challenging. These artifacts can be suppressed through postprocessing techniques like morphological operations or rule-based filtering.

We use one technique to post-process the predicted segmentation masks, that is a morphological operation of closing (a dilation followed by an erosion), aimed to remove small meaningless patches. Because this post-processing is never flawless, we also utilize a custom modification to the IoU and mAP metrics to ignore small patches of a specific size. This patch size L was experimentally tested to be the most effective at 12×12 pixels and was utilized in our final solutions.

5 Experiments and Results

This section describes the training setup and follows with training results. All models were trained using a single NVIDIA A40 GPU setup with varying learning rate and batch size, schedulers, optimizers, augmentation levels, input image sizes and number of training epochs. All of the hyperparameters and their experimented options are listed in Table 1. Different combinations were deeply explored with a Wandb Sweep tool to search the hyper-parameter space, see Sect. 5.1. Results of individual subsystems are described in following sections.

5.1 Segmentation Experimental Evaluation

The original RailSem19 paper used the FRRNB model [21] for segmentation task, which serves as our baseline. However, as introduced in Sect. 4.1, we decided to explore the SegFormer architecture instead, testing different different model sizes: SegFormer B2 and SegFormer B3. Specifically, we evaluated multiple pre-trained SegFormer variants to determine the most promising starting point. These models differed in their pre-training configurations, including input resolution and dataset. We tested SegFormer B2 trained on ADE20k (512×512 input), SegFormer B2 trained on Cityscapes (1024×1024), and SegFormer B3 trained on Cityscapes (1024×1024). Without any data augmentation and using a constant learning rate with the Adam optimizer, SegFormer B2 reached the best IoU of 0.58, while B3 achieved 0.56—both pretrained for 50 epochs on Cityscapes with 1024×1024 inputs. Based on these results, these two models were selected for further tuning using the WanDB Sweep tool. The best resulting checkpoints were then compared to the baseline model, as shown in Table 2.

Table 2. Comparison of results for best performing SegFormer setups on RailSem19 segmentation with FRRNB baseline model trained by RailSem19 paper authors [29]. mAP and IoU metrics are reported with IoU representing evaluation with utilizing our best postprocessing approach.

Model	Setup						mAP	IoU
	B	classes	epochs	optim.	sched.	aug.		
FRRNB [21]	–	21	60	–	–	–	–	0.576
SegFormer	2	11	80	Adam	LRS*	2	0.629	0.641
	3	11	90	Adam	RLROP	2	0.634	0.646
	3	11	80	Adam	LRS*	2	**0.638**	**0.650**
	3	21	50	Adam	LRS*	2	0.587	0.598

The original semantic segmentation FRRNB model achieved IoU of 0.576, our training run on all 21 classes achieved 0.563 IoU without any postprocessing and 0.598 after applying the mask postprocessing techniques (morphological operation of closing and small patches filtration). With this we surpass the baseline model by 0.022 IoU score. With training on the filtrated 11 classes, the IoU score further moves up on average by 0.047. This improvements indicates that the transformer-based model architecture in combination with our mask postprocessing techniques and extensive image augmentations, significantly contributes to superior performance in rail-track scene segmentation tasks. The best achieved IoU score with employing all techniques and picking the best found hyperparameter combination is 0.65 with the SegFormer B3. Hyperparameter searches can be accessed from following links: 0, 1, 2, 3, 4, 5, 6, 7.

To gain deeper insights into models performance, class-wise IoU scores were evaluated and compared against a model trained on all 21 classes. As supposed, IoU scores for retained classes decrease when the model is fine-tuned even on those remaining ten classes. This indicates that the filtering strategy was effective—it didn't just eliminate classes with low performance that were dragging down the overall IoU, but it also led to better segmentation results for the retained classes, with an average IoU improvement of 8.8% per class.

5.2   Object Detection Experimental Evaluation

The detection model was fine-tuned using bounding-box annotations from the RailSem19 dataset. While the dataset contains a relatively high total number of class annotations, only three classes are applicable for our project's purposes: 'person' with 234 annotations, 'car' with 172 annotations, and 'truck' with 11 annotations. The majority of the remaining annotations belong to traffic signs and traffic lights, which do not carry any use for us at all. Comparison of YoloV8 baseline and fine-tuned model performance is in Table 3. See also the fine-tuned model detections in the overall system output visualizations in Fig. 5.

Table 3. Comparison of detection results from baseline and fine-tuned YoloV8, evaluated with mAP_{50} and IoU.

Class	Baseline		Fine-tuned	
	mAP_{50}	IoU	mAP_{50}	IoU
Person	0.723	0.707	0.814	0.789
Car	0.683	0.655	0.805	0.766
Truck	0.600	0.577	0.651	0.609
Mean	0.667	0.644	0.756	0.721

5.3   Distance Assessor

Because the final results rely heavily on the accuracy of the detected critical areas, this aspect was subjected to further analysis. To validate the distance estimation experimentally, real-world measurements were conducted and compared with algorithmically identified zones. This required direct access to a stationary tram, which was made possible through collaboration with Public Transport in Pilsen. With their support, a tram was made available at the depot. Three critical zones at distances of 60, 100, and 200 cm were defined based on recommendations from the head of ED-provoz. These zones were visually marked using orange and black tape. To closely replicate actual camera input, photographs were taken from the tram driver's point of view. In post-processing, all other tracks in the image were masked to ensure that the segmentation focused solely on the track occupied by the reference tram (in a real world scenario, we do not focus on just the given trams track, but on the whole track bed even in the opposite direction).

Estimations shown in Fig. 4 is highly precise from a perpendicular view (a), with little variations at distant and lateral points. The second image, captured from an angle simulating a tram arriving from a turn (b), confirms the method's capability without relying strictly on straight rails, although slight deviations occur due to imperfect track segmentation. The third example, involving curved tracks (c), introduces greater complexity. Using horizontal cross-sectional measurements causes angled tracks to appear wider, slightly enlarging distance estimates. This effect is noticeable on the right side of the image, where the estimated area overlaps the actual boundary. Furthermore, narrower segmentation on the left side shifts the critical area inward, causing deviations of approximately 3–4 cm at the widest points. Despite minor accuracy reductions with sharper angles, deviations remain minimal, preserving the practical usability of the system.

Fig. 4. Examples of critical zones estimations under different simulated conditions: perpendicular view (a), oblique view (b), curved rail track (c)

5.4   Output Visualizations

This study prioritized improving safety for the most frequent tram-surrounding entities—particularly pedestrians, cyclists and vehicles. Figure 5 includes few end system outputs.

5.5   Additional Material

As a final demonstration of system functionality, two visualizations are provided. The first is a processed video showing frame-by-frame system inference (video). The second is an interactive Hugging Face Space that lets users upload images and see risk overlays (online demo).

6   Conclusion

This paper addressed the critical issue of tram-human interaction safety by developing a comprehensive framework that integrates automatic scene segmentation, object detection, and accurate estimation of object-to-rail distances. Leveraging advanced deep learning architectures, specifically the SegFormer model, we

input   system output   output overlayed

Fig. 5. The final outputs from the system, cases of people crossing and surrounding the track to show the potential critical situations and cases of a typical traffic situations with cars surrounding tram tracks.

implemented class-specific data filtration and sophisticated mask postprocessing strategies, which significantly enhanced segmentation performance. The resulting model achieved an Intersection-over-Union (IoU) score of 65.0%, exceeding previously established benchmarks on the RailSem19 dataset. Concurrently, the object detection task was addressed by fine-tuning the YOLOv8 model on relevant classes, effectively improving its localization performance, with a mean Average Precision (mAP$_{50}$) of 75.6% and an IoU of 72.1%.

A key innovation of this research is the introduction of the Distance Assessor system, designed to integrate segmentation and detection outputs effectively. This system classifies detected objects according to their criticality based on proximity to tram tracks, without the need for explicit depth data or camera parameters. Practical validation was conducted through collaborative experiments with Public Transport in Pilsen, demonstrating that the system accurately estimates distances even under challenging conditions, such as curved tracks or angled camera perspectives, with deviations limited to just a few centimeters.

Overall, this work provides robust evidence supporting the potential of combining digital image processing and artificial intelligence to significantly enhance tram safety. Further improvements will be realized through enhancements in training datasets, particularly in terms of more precise rail and rail-bed annotations. Such advancements will position the proposed framework as a practical, everyday tool for tram operators, offering the possibility to integrate this solution into some automatic breaking system etc., substantially reducing the risk and severity of accidents involving pedestrians, cyclists, and vehicles in dense urban environments.

Acknowledgments. The work has been supported by the grant of the University of West Bohemia, project No. SGS-2025-011. Computational resources were provided by the e-INFRA CZ project (ID:90254), supported by the Ministry of Education, Youth and Sports of the Czech Republic.

Disclosure of Interests. The authors have no competing interests to declare that are relevant to the content of this article.

References

1. Al-Hasanat, M., Alsafasfeh, M., Alhasanat, A., Althunibat, S.: Retinanet-based approach for object detection and distance estimation in an image. Int. J. Commun. Antenna Propagat. **11**, 19–25 (2021). https://api.semanticscholar.org/CorpusID: 233845065
2. Bidve, V., et al.: Pothole detection model for road safety using computer vision and machine learning. IAES Int. J. Artif. Intell. (IJ-AI) (2024). https://api. semanticscholar.org/CorpusID:273263637
3. Buslaev, A., Parinov, A., Khvedchenya, E., Iglovikov, V.I., Kalinin, A.A.: Albumentations: fast and flexible image augmentations. ArXiv e-prints (2018)
4. Carion, N., Massa, F., Synnaeve, G., Usunier, N., Kirillov, A., Zagoruyko, S.: End-to-End object detection with transformers. In: Vedaldi, A., Bischof, H., Brox, T., Frahm, J.-M. (eds.) ECCV 2020. LNCS, vol. 12346, pp. 213–229. Springer, Cham (2020). https://doi.org/10.1007/978-3-030-58452-8_13
5. Central Intelligence Agency: Railways – the world factbook (2024). https://www. cia.gov/the-world-factbook/field/railways. Accessed 17 Apr 2024
6. Chen, L.C., Papandreou, G., Kokkinos, I., Murphy, K., Yuille, A.L.: Semantic image segmentation with deep convolutional nets and fully connected crfs. arXiv preprint arXiv:1412.7062 (2014)
7. Chen, L.C., Papandreou, G., Kokkinos, I., Murphy, K., Yuille, A.L.: Deeplab: semantic image segmentation with deep convolutional nets, atrous convolution, and fully connected crfs. IEEE Trans. Pattern Anal. Mach. Intell. **40**(4), 834–848 (2017)
8. Cheng, B., Misra, I., Schwing, A.G., Kirillov, A., Girdhar, R.: Masked-attention mask transformer for universal image segmentation. In: Proceedings of the IEEE/CVF Conference on Computer Vision and Pattern Recognition, pp. 1290–1299 (2022)
9. Ferrer, B., Pomares, J.C., Irles, R., Espinosa, J., Mas, D.: Image processing for safety assessment in civil engineering. Appl. Optics **52 18**, 4385–90 (2013). https:// api.semanticscholar.org/CorpusID:28825832
10. de Gordoa, J.A.I., García, S., Urbieta, I., Aranjuelo, N., Nieto, M., de Eribe, D.O., et al.: Scenario-based validation of automated train systems using a 3d virtual railway environment. In: 2023 IEEE 26th International Conference on Intelligent Transportation Systems (ITSC), pp. 5072–5077. IEEE (2023)

11. Guerrieri, M.: Tramways in urban areas: an overview on safety at road intersections. Urban Rail Transit **4**(4), 223–233 (2018)
12. Ježdík, R., Kemka, V., Kovanda, J., Lopot, F., Purs, H., Hájková, B.: Various approaches to reduce consequences of pedestrian-tram front end collision. Promet - Traffic&Transportation (2023). https://api.semanticscholar.org/CorpusID:258365169
13. Kirillov, A., et al.: Segment anything. In: Proceedings of the IEEE/CVF International Conference on Computer Vision, pp. 4015–4026 (2023)
14. Kozlov, E., Gibadullin, R.: Prerequisites for developing the computer vision system for drowning detection. In: E3S Web of Conferences (2024). https://api.semanticscholar.org/CorpusID:266876763
15. Lackner, C., et al.: Tram to pedestrian collisions–priorities and potentials. Front. Future Transport. **3**, 15 (2022)
16. Lackner, C., Heinzl, P., Leo, C., Klug, C.: Investigations on tram-pedestrian impacts by application of virtual testing with human body models. Eur. Transp. Res. Rev. **15**, 1–13 (2023). https://api.semanticscholar.org/CorpusID:260321751
17. Lackner, C., .: Tram to pedestrian collisions—priorities and potentials. Front. Future Transport. (2022). https://api.semanticscholar.org/CorpusID:249975455
18. Lee, S., Han, K.B., Park, S., Yang, X.: Vehicle distance estimation from a monocular camera for advanced driver assistance systems. Symmetry **14**, 2657 (2022). https://api.semanticscholar.org/CorpusID:254807430
19. Lopot, F., et al.: Pedestrian safety in frontal tram collision, part 1: Historical overview and experimental-data-based biomechanical study of head clashing in frontal and side impacts. Sensors (Basel, Switzerland) **23** (2023). https://api.semanticscholar.org/CorpusID:264817472
20. Paszke, A., et al.: Automatic differentiation in pytorch (2017)
21. Pohlen, T., Hermans, A., Mathias, M., Leibe, B.: Full-resolution residual networks for semantic segmentation in street scenes. In: Proceedings of the IEEE Conference on Computer Vision and Pattern Recognition, pp. 4151–4160 (2017)
22. Purs, H., et al.: Tram-pedestrian collision modeling using experimental data—its validation, repeatability, and challenges: a pilot study. Transport. Res. Rec. J. Transport. Res. Board (2024). https://api.semanticscholar.org/CorpusID:267595102
23. Ronneberger, O., Fischer, P., Brox, T.: U-net: convolutional networks for biomedical image segmentation. In: Navab, N., Hornegger, J., Wells, W.M., Frangi, A.F. (eds.) MICCAI 2015. LNCS, vol. 9351, pp. 234–241. Springer, Cham (2015). https://doi.org/10.1007/978-3-319-24574-4_28
24. Shetye, S., Shetty, S., Shinde, S., Madhu, C., Mathur, A.: Computer vision for industrial safety and productivity. 2023 International Conference on Communication System, Computing and IT Applications (CSCITA), pp. 117–120 (2023). https://api.semanticscholar.org/CorpusID:258260530
25. Ultralytics: Yolov8 (2022). https://github.com/ultralytics/yolov8
26. Wang, C.Y., Yeh, I.H., Liao, H.Y.M.: Yolov9: Learning what you want to learn using programmable gradient information. arXiv preprint arXiv:2402.13616 (2024)
27. Xie, E., Wang, W., Yu, Z., Anandkumar, A., Alvarez, J.M., Luo, P.: Segformer: simple and efficient design for semantic segmentation with transformers. Adv. Neural. Inf. Process. Syst. **34**, 12077–12090 (2021)
28. Yuan, H., Mei, Z., Chen, Y., Niu, W., Wu, C.: Railvid: a dataset for rail environment semantic. In: ICONS 2022, 17th (2022)

29. Zendel, O., Murschitz, M., Zeilinger, M., Steininger, D., Abbasi, S., Beleznai, C.: Railsem19: a dataset for semantic rail scene understanding. In: Proceedings of the IEEE/CVF Conference on Computer Vision and Pattern Recognition Workshops, pp. 0–0 (2019)
30. Zhang, Z., Yu, S., Yang, S., Zhou, Y., Zhao, B.: Rail-5k: a real-world dataset for rail surface defects detection. arXiv preprint arXiv:2106.14366 (2021)

Deep Reinforcement Learning for the Berth Allocation Problem with Inventory Control: A DQN-LSTM Approach

Victor Hugo Barros[1]([✉]) [iD] and Alexandre César Muniz de Oliveira[2][iD]

[1] Instituto Federal do Maranhão, Pinheiro, MA, Brazil
victor.silva@ifma.edu.br
[2] Universidade Federal do Maranhão, São Luís, Brazil
alexandre.cesar@ufma.br

Abstract. Given the current scenario of uncertainty in port operations, the berth allocation problem remains a crucial issue in port operations. This work presents a method that combines the Deep Q-Network (DQN) algorithm with the Long Short-Term Memory (LSTM) neural network architecture within a reinforcement learning framework applied to berth allocation under inventory constraints. The results are promising and indicate that the approach can respect inventory limits while producing quality solutions comparable to those obtained by a commercial solver, thereby offering support for informed decision-making.

Keywords: Berth Allocation Problem · Inventory Control · Deep Q-Network · Long Short-Term Memory

1 Introduction

Researchers have addressed various problems in port operations, notably the Berth Allocation Problem (BAP) and the Quay Crane Allocation Problem (QCAP), often combining the two. The importance of BAP and QCAP stems from their impact on port productivity and service quality, both of which are closely tied to the terminal's handling system [1]. [2] and [3] extensively investigated both problems, classifying problem types and the methods used to solve them.

In this work, we are interested in a specific case of the berth allocation problem, presented by [4], where inventory levels influence the ship berthing decision process. At each unit of time (discretized berthing windows determined by tides), port inventory levels must be at safe thresholds. This situation is more common in bulk ports, which are often linked to the production or consumption of the cargo being handled.

J. Valente de Oliveira et al. (Eds.): EPIA 2025, LNAI 16122, pp. 219–231, 2026.
https://doi.org/10.1007/978-3-032-05179-0_17

Several studies in the literature address the issue of inventory management in conjunction with BAP. [5] consider using a replenishment and inventory management performance measure in the decision-making process at a container terminal. [6] discuss how product perishability in inventories affects customer satisfaction, demanding greater port efficiency. Recently, [7] modeled a global supply chain integrating BAP, inventory management, and production scheduling. Inventory management is done at stocking points along the chain. [8] addresses a complex problem involving coal supply from various sources with differing qualities. They must perform blending to ensure the minimum quality required by the client. These and many other works demonstrate how inventory management, among other elements in port operations, has demanded greater efforts from port administrators regarding the ship allocation process.

In recent years, the COVID-19 pandemic and geopolitical crises have significantly impacted maritime trade. In 2022, maritime trade volume decreased by 0.4%, continuing a trend established in 2021. Congestion from sustained high demand and the Ukraine war caused losses in port efficiency. From the second half of 2022, supply and demand dynamics normalized as pandemic-related lockdowns were relaxed and companies regularized their inventories, particularly in the United States and Europe. As a result, the projection for 2023 is growth [9]. However, this entire situation has heightened the sense of uncertainty among various agents in maritime trade. The outcome is increased efforts to make the entire supply chain more resilient to new configurations and, consequently, a greater use of machine learning techniques, which effectively handle uncertainties.

The objective of this work is to develop a method based on the deep reinforcement learning technique, specifically the Deep Q-Network (DQN), combined with a Long Short-Term Memory (LSTM) recurrent neural network architecture, for the berth allocation problem in bulk port terminals with inventory control. The method should be able to find quality solutions comparable to those obtained by the Gurobi solver that do not violate the problem's constraints from the port operators' perspective.

This work is structured as follows: Sect. 2 reviews the applications of reinforcement learning to berth allocation. Section 3 presents the integer linear programming model. Section 4 formulates the problem under reinforcement learning. Section 5 details the DQN-LSTM architecture. Section 6 describes the methodology. Section 7 presents the results, and Sect. 8 concludes and suggests future work.

2   Related Work

Reinforcement learning is already used in the port context, as presented in [10] to solve the quay crane allocation problem. However, few works have explored the direct use of deep reinforcement learning techniques in berth allocation problems. In [11], the Berth Allocation Problem (BAP) is addressed indirectly through intelligent scheduling of cargo routes from storage yards to ships. In this work, an agent's action corresponds to selecting a path between a yard and a vessel, and the Double DQN technique was used to train the agent. More recently, [12] proposed a method based on deep reinforcement learning for this combination of berth allocation and crane assignment in a bulk terminal. The problem is considered multi-objective, aiming to improve ship service times and reduce total transportation costs. [13] also addressed the BAP combined with crane assignment using reinforcement learning. The goal is to minimize the total waiting time of vessels. The authors use reinforcement learning in the online case, where the statuses of ships and berths are precisely known at the moment ships arrive at the port.

The use of reinforcement learning to handle uncertainties has recently been applied to a discrete and dynamic berth allocation problem at a container terminal in [14]. The work focuses on the unpredictability of arrival and service times, which are modeled as an exponential distribution and a stochastic probability distribution, respectively. The objective is to minimize the average waiting time of vessels and make the port more resilient—that is, able to recover more quickly in disruptive event scenarios.

[15] address the dynamic and continuous berth allocation problem across multiple integrated terminals using reinforcement learning. The goal is to minimize vessel dwell time at ports using the Dueling Double DQN (D3QN) algorithm. Initially, the problem is represented by a mixed-integer programming model and then reformulated as a Markov Decision Process. The results obtained by training the D3QN algorithm are compared with those from DQN, Dueling DQN, and PPO, as well as with results from the mathematical model solved via the commercial solver CPLEX.

3   Mathematical Formulation

The berth allocation problem with inventory control addressed in this work was modeled as an Integer Linear Programming (ILP) problem [16]. The model's input parameters are defined as follows: a set of ships, N; a set of tidal time windows, M; a set of berths, L; set of handled cargo types, K; expected time of arrival of ship i, a_i (ETA); service rate of berth l, v_l; initial stock of cargo k, e_k; consumption rate of cargo k, c_k; service time of ship i at berth l, h_{il}, given by $h_{il} = \frac{\sum_{k \in K} q_{ik}}{v_l}$; and amount of cargo k carried by ship i, q_{ik}.

The solution to the problem consists of sequencing ships at each berth over the tidal time windows (TTW). Thus, y_{ijl} is a binary decision variable defined over the sets N, M, and L, which indicates whether ship i will be assigned to TTW j and berth l ($y_{ijl} = 1$) or not ($y_{ijl} = 0$).

$$y_{ijl} = \begin{cases} 1, & \text{if ship } i \text{ is allocated to TTW } j \text{ and berth } l \\ 0, & \text{otherwise} \end{cases}$$

The decision criterion adopted in this model is the total service time, defined as the sum of the service times of all ships. The service time of each vessel corresponds to the sum of the waiting time and the handling time. Therefore, the goal is to minimize this sum, as represented by the objective function defined in Eq. 1.

$$\min \sum_{i=1}^{|N|} \sum_{j=1}^{|M|} \sum_{l=1}^{|L|} (j + h_{il} - a_i) \times y_{ijl} \tag{1}$$

The set of problem constraints is defined in the mathematical model through Eqs. 2, 3, 4, and 5.

$$\sum_{j=1}^{a_i-1} \sum_{l=1}^{|L|} y_{ijl} = 0, \quad \forall i \in N \tag{2}$$

$$\sum_{j=a_i}^{|M|} \sum_{l=1}^{|L|} y_{ijl} = 1, \quad \forall i \in N \tag{3}$$

$$\sum_{n=1, n\neq i}^{|N|} \sum_{m=j, m\leq |M|}^{j+h_{il}-1} y_{nml} \leq (1 - y_{ijl})|N||M|, \quad \forall i \in N, j \in M, l \in L \tag{4}$$

$$\sum_{i=1}^{|N|} \sum_{l=1}^{|L|} \sum_{z=a_i}^{j} \frac{\min(j - a_i + 1, h_{il})}{h_{il}} q_{ik} \times y_{izl} \leq j \times c_k + e_k, \quad \forall j \in M, k \in K \tag{5}$$

Equation 2 ensures that ships cannot berth before their expected arrival time. For this reason, allocations at those times are set to zero. Equation 3 ensures that each ship is assigned to exactly one berth and one-time window starting from its expected arrival time. Equation 4 prevents two ships from occupying the same berth in overlapping time windows. Equation 5 ensures that stockouts are avoided. This constraint maintains a balance between the cargo consumption at the port (or industrial facility) and the unloading by ships combined with the initial inventory. In each time window, inventory levels must remain above the minimum threshold, here assumed to be zero.

4   BAP with Inventory Control as an MDP

We can easily visualize the BAP as a sequential decision-making problem and a Markov Decision Process (MDP). In this section, we develop the MDP formulation, which is equivalent to the ILP formulation (1)–(5), hereafter referred to as BAP-RLIM, defining the environment, agent, actions, states, and rewards.

4.1 Environment and Agent

Typically, the online BAP presents partial information about demanding ships. As decisions evolve, we define information that was previously absent or imprecise. Here, we use a look-ahead mechanism, which contains the ϵ observed ships with the closest estimated arrival times. We disregard other ships scheduled for service but outside the look-ahead in the current time's decision process. Figure 1 illustrates the look-ahead structure.

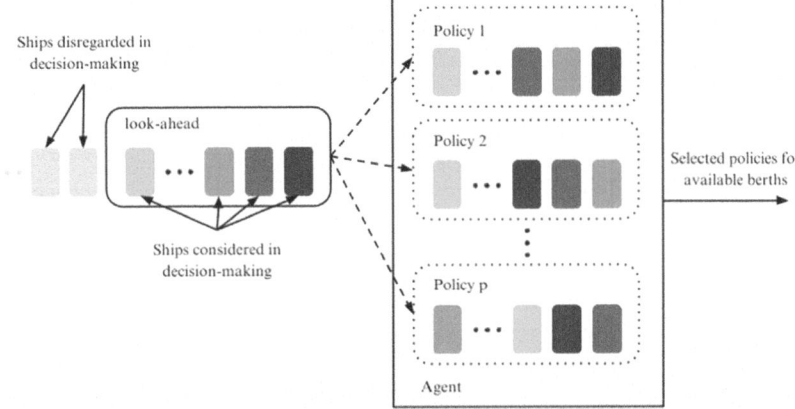

Fig. 1. Simplified scheme of policy selection with look-ahead.

At each decision point, the agent selects one or more ships from the look-ahead for berthing, and it automatically removes them. The agent then adds the same number of ships from those previously disregarded, using the shortest expected arrival time as the criterion. The general parameters of the environment include the set of berths, L, the set of handled cargo types, K, and the size of the planning horizon window (look-ahead), ϵ.

The process of allocating a ship to a berth occurs when a berth is available, meaning no other ship is currently being serviced there. In this context, the agent is responsible for the ultimate decision of which ship to berth at which berth. However, in BAP-RLIM, the agent does not select the ship directly. The agent selects a policy that represents a rule for choosing the ship.

When two or more berths are simultaneously available, the berthing decision will involve the same number of policies as the number of available berths. This approach aims to give the agent autonomous decision-making power. On the other hand, this choice leads to a set of invalid actions that require careful handling to ensure the non-overlap constraint for ships is met.

4.2 State Space

We must model the state space to be representative enough to provide relevant information to the agent for decision-making while also maintaining a correlation with the reward function to ensure a connection between the two. In BAP-RLIM, we divide the state space into information about the status of ships in the look-ahead, berth service, and inventory levels. We summarize the state space configuration in Table 1.

Table 1. State space configuration.

Description	Component
Remaining service time at each berth	Berth
Remaining time each berth must wait until selected ship berths	Berth
Throughput of each berth	Berth
Consumption rate of each cargo type	Inventory
Current inventory level of each cargo type	Inventory
Time until depletion of each cargo	Inventory
Remaining time until arrival of each ship in the lookahead window	Ship
Service time of each ship in the lookahead window at each berth	Ship × Berth
Quantity of each cargo type per ship in the lookahead window	Ship × Inventory

Each state is associated with a unit of time (a tide j), where at least one berth is available for service. The state changes as follows: (i) the berthing decision assigns (through policies) ships to all available berths, (ii) we recalculate environment updates at each unit of time, representing the evolution of port operations, until another berth becomes available again.

4.3   Action Space

In this work, the actions do not directly indicate ships for berthing. We propose a strategy for creating ship selection policies, where each policy aims to obtain a ship, according to a specific criterion, from the queue of ships present in the look-ahead.

Ship Selection Policies. The agent's role in this proposal is to select one of the implemented policies, which determines which ship to allocate to the berth. For each berth, the number of policies to implement, along with an additional "no-operation" policy, defines the set of possible actions.

An action taken is represented in Fig. 2. We adopt a policy $p \in P$ for all $l \in L$. The agent can assign the same policy to multiple berths in a single action. We can conclude that in every decision-making step, the agent selects one policy for each berth. If a berth is occupied, the agent cannot berth any ship, thus necessitating the "no-operation" policy.

Service Time Policy. This policy orders the ships by shortest service time and selects the first available one for the berth.

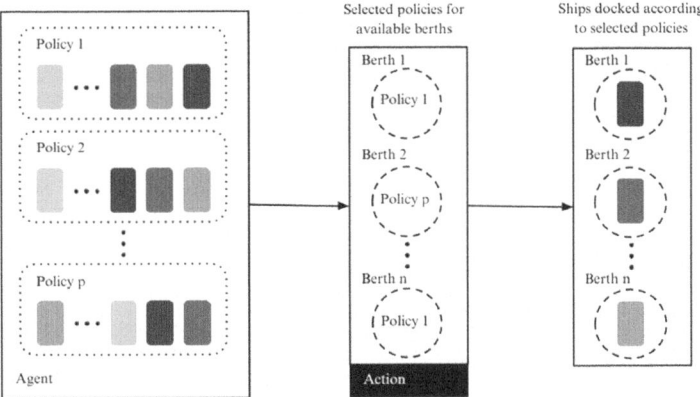

Fig. 2. Representation of an action taken.

Completion Time Policy. This policy is a strategy where the agent chooses the ship that, if serviced, will undock first.

Inventory Priority Policy. This measure gauges each ship's priority based on its inventory levels. Each ship receives a score. The agent chooses the ship with the highest score under this policy.

4.4 Reward

We may divide the reward into two parts: (i) the average service time of the vessels selected in the action and (ii) a non-linear function that measures the criticality of inventory levels.

The first component is normalized by a sigmoid function, as defined in Eq. 6, where $\bar{T}$ is the average service time, r is the inflection point, and η is the growth rate.

$$\mathcal{T} = \frac{1}{1 + e^{-\eta(\bar{T}-r)}} \tag{6}$$

Inventory criticality, $\mathcal{C}_{\max}$, depends on the current inventory levels, $e_k(t)$, and the negative variation concerning the previous action, $\Delta_k(t) = e_k(t) - e_k(t-1)$. From the current levels, we compute the criticality as shown in Eq. 7. When the variation is negative, we aggregate the term described in Eq. 8.

$$\mathcal{C}_{\text{level}} = \frac{1}{1 + e_k(t)} \tag{7}$$

$$\mathcal{C}_{\text{variation}} = \frac{1}{1 + e^{R \cdot \left(\frac{\Delta_k(t)}{-\Delta_k(t)+\kappa}+\xi\right)}} \cdot \mathcal{C}_{\text{level}} \tag{8}$$

where R, κ, and ξ are parameters of $\mathcal{C}_{\text{variation}}$ that adjust the steepness, smoothness, and offset of the curve, respectively.

The combined criticality for each item is:

$$\mathcal{C} = \alpha_{\text{level}} \cdot \mathcal{C}_{\text{level}} + \beta_{\text{variation}} \cdot \mathcal{C}_{\text{variation}}$$

The maximum criticality across inventory levels is then given by:

$$\mathcal{C}_{\text{max}} = \max_{j=1}(\mathcal{C}_j)$$

Finally, the overall reward function is defined in Eq. 9:

$$\mathcal{R} = 1 - \alpha \cdot \mathcal{T} - \beta \cdot \mathcal{C}_{\text{max}} \tag{9}$$

where $\alpha_{\text{level}} + \beta_{\text{variation}} = 1$ and $\alpha + \beta = 1$.

5   Architecture

5.1   Deep Q-Network

Nonlinear function approximators are known to be unstable and may even diverge when used to approximate an action-value function Q. The Deep Q-Network (DQN) algorithm addresses these issues using several mechanisms. First, it employs a technique known as experience replay, which mitigates correlations between observations by storing the experiences collected during training in a buffer and randomly reusing them as inputs to the neural network. This strategy also helps to smooth changes in the policy. Second, the update of Q-values is performed towards target Q-values, which are updated periodically. The last one reduces the correlation between the current and target Q-values.

5.2   LSTM

The Long Short-Term Memory (LSTM) neural network architecture is a type of recurrent neural network (RNN) designed to model long-term dependencies in sequential data. It uses input, forget, and output gates that regulate the flow of information over time. This mechanism can selectively preserve and forget information over long time intervals, unlike traditional recurrent networks, and thus avoids the vanishing gradient problem in sequential tasks [19].

5.3   Network Architecture

To leverage the LSTM's ability to process sequences, we employ a scheme in this work that combines it with the DQN framework. Figure 3 illustrates the basic scheme of DQN with LSTM used for the BAP-RLIM. The replay buffer stores the experiences collected during training as fragments of 10-step episodes. From this buffer, it selects batches of 32 samples as inputs. These batches are passed through the LSTM at each step. Each input is composed of the state information of the ships, berths, and inventories, as described in Sect. 4.2.

At each time step, the observation vector is processed by two fully connected layers with 75 and 40 units, respectively, both of which use the hyperbolic tangent activation function. The output is then passed through a stacked LSTM with two layers of 64 units each, followed by an additional fully connected layer with hyperbolic tangent activation. A final fully connected layer outputs the Q-values, with dimensionality equal to the number of available actions.

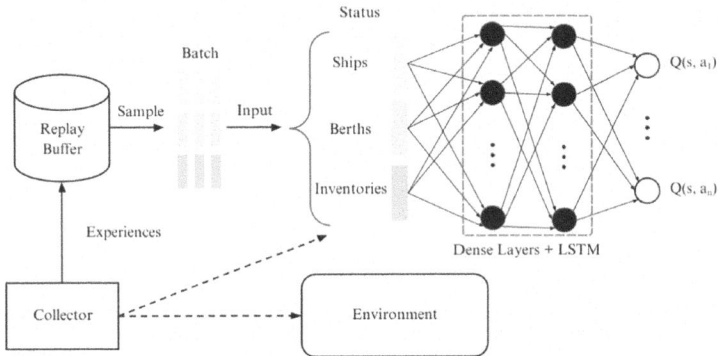

Fig. 3. Basic scheme of DQN+LSTM integrated with BAP-RLIM

6   Instances and Training

The instances are based on the mathematical model presented in Sect. 3, organized with 35, 40, 45, and 50 ships; 4 and 5 berths; and 4, 5, and 6 cargo types, resulting in a total of 20 instances. All instances used in this work are available in [20].

For training, one reference instance is selected for each combination of the number of berths and cargo types, resulting in 6 training processes. All reference instances consist of 30 ships. We use other instances with 35, 40, 45, and 50 ships to evaluate the trained agents. Its performance is compared to the optimal solutions obtained by the integer linear programming model.

During training, each reference instance is repeated after the last ship twice to form an episode containing 90 ships, with the arrival times of additional ships adjusted accordingly. However, the ship attributes listed in Table 2 are subject to uniformly distributed noise within the specified intervals. Table 3 summarizes the general parameters used in the training process.

Table 2. Intervals for arrival times, initial inventory levels, and cargo quantities.

Attribute	Interval
Arrival times	$(-10, +10)$
Initial inventory levels	$(-20, +20)$
Cargo quantities transported by ships	$(-10, +10)$

Table 3. General training and port environment parameters.

Parameter	Value
Training	
Number of iterations	10,000
Initial collection steps	2,000
Batch size	32
Sequence length (LSTM)	10
Replay buffer capacity	2,000
Target update interval	2,000 steps
Hyperparameters	
Learning rate	0.04 to 0,026
Discount factor (γ)	0.99
ϵ-greedy	1.0 to 0.05
Network Architecture	
LSTM layers	(64, 64)
Final fully connected layer size	number of actions
Port Environment	
Look-ahead size	10

7   Computational Results

Throughout the training, the 20 instances shown in Table 4 were solved by the corresponding agents to evaluate their ability to obtain feasible solutions that respect the inventory constraints while also achieving good performance in terms of total service time.

Table 4 presents the computational results, where the best total service times obtained during training are compared to those produced by the Gurobi solver, version 9.5.1. The table also reports the solver execution times, limited to 4,800 s, and highlights the best solution found for each instance across both approaches.

All instances were solved by the BAP-RLIM approach without inventory violations, thus fulfilling the feasibility objective. It can be observed that the results obtained by BAP-RLIM outperformed those obtained by Gurobi in several instances. The best-performing approach for each instance is marked with (**). It is worth noting that in all six cases where the solver finished before the

Table 4. Resultados computacionais

Instance	BAP-RLIM	Gurobi v 9.5.1		Best
	Solution	Solution	Time (s)	Solution
35N.4B.5P	1.098,0	**1.086,0	1.273,3	1.086,0
35N.4B.6P	1.239,0	**1.234,0	2.114,7	1.234,0
35N.5B.4P	1.224,0	**1.210,0	508,5	1.210,0
35N.5B.6P	1.606,0	**1.597,0	1.555,2	1.597,0
40N.4B.4P	1.805,0	**1.664,0	4.800,5	1.664,0
40N.4B.5P	2.223,0	**2.181,0	4.800,5	2.181,0
40N.4B.6P	2.183,0	**2.151,0	4.804,6	2.114,0
40N.5B.4P	2.035,0	**2.015,0	4.800,4	2.015,0
40N.5B.5P	2.357,0	**2.272,0	4.804,6	2.272,0
40N.5B.6P	**2.603,0	2.661,0	4.808,7	2.603,0
45N.4B.4P	1.748,0	**1.699,0	1.493,5	1.699,0
45N.4B.5P	**1.588,0	1.590,0	4.800,8	1.588,0
45N.4B.6P	**2.199,0	2.246,0	4.800,9	2.199,0
45N.5B.5P	**2.136,0	2.101,0	4.800,6	2.136,0
45N.5B.6P	**2.545,0	2.661,0	4.800,6	2.545,0
50N.4B.4P	2.013,0	**1.987,0	3.024,0	1.987,0
50N.4B.5P	**2.194,0	2.413,0	4.891,5	2.194,0
50N.4B.6P	**2.726,0	2.755,0	4.812,6	2.726,0
50N.5B.5P	2.703,0	**2.685,0	4.800,9	2.685,0
50N.5B.6P	**3.349,0	3.526,0	4.800,9	3.349,0

time limit, Gurobi provided better solutions, as expected. In contrast, for the remaining 14 instances, eight were better solved by BAP-RLIM.

8   Conclusions

The objective of this work is to develop a method based on the DQN technique combined with the LSTM neural network architecture to solve the berth allocation problem in a scenario with inventory control. In addition to the challenge of minimizing total service times, the approach must address the complex problem of verifying, at each time unit, whether inventory levels have been violated, which would otherwise result in infeasible solutions.

LSTM is employed as it is well-suited to sequential decision-making processes, where the sequence of past inputs influences future decisions. The trained agents aim to indicate ship selection policies. The results presented indicate that the BAP-RLIM combined with LSTM is capable of obtaining high-quality solutions that respect inventory constraints. Therefore, researchers can apply the reinforcement learning framework with LSTM to the berth allocation problem with inventory control. In future work, the proposed approach could be enhanced to incorporate uncertainties throughout the decision-making process, thereby leveraging the reinforcement learning capability to handle uncertainties, bringing the solution to the berth allocation problem closer to addressing new real-world operational challenges.

Disclosure of interests. The authors have no competing interests to declare that are relevant to the content of this article.

References

1. Chang, S.-C., Lin, M.-H., Tsai, J.-F.: An optimization approach to berth allocation problems. Mathematics **12**(5), 753 (2024)
2. Bierwirth, C., Meisel, F.: A survey of berth allocation and quay crane scheduling problems in container terminals. Eur. J. Oper. Res. **202**(3), 615–627 (2010)
3. Bierwirth, C., Meisel, F.: A follow-up survey of berth allocation and quay crane scheduling problems in container terminals. Eur. J. Oper. Res. **244**(3), 675–689 (2015)
4. Barros, V.H., Costa, T.S., Oliveira, A.C.M., Lorena, L.A.N.: Model and heuristic for berth allocation in tidal bulk ports with stock level constraints. Comput. Ind. Eng. **60**(4), 606–613 (2011)
5. Liu, C., Xiang, X., Zhang, C., Zheng, L.: A decision model for berth allocation under uncertainty considering service level using an adaptive differential evolution algorithm. Asia-Pacific J. Oper. Res. **33**(06), 1650049 (2016)
6. Aghalari, A., Nur, F., Marufuzzaman, M.: A bender's based nested decomposition algorithm to solve a stochastic inland waterway port management problem considering perishable product. Int. J. Prod. Econ. **229**, 107863 (2020)
7. El Mehdi, E.R., Ilyas, H., François, S., et al.: Incremental lns framework for integrated production, inventory, and vessel scheduling: application to a global supply chain. Omega **116**, 102821 (2023)
8. Belov, G., Boland, N.L., Savelsbergh, M.W.P., Stuckey, P.J.: Logistics optimization for a coal supply chain. J. Heurist. **26**(2), 269–300 (2020). https://doi.org/10.1007/s10732-019-09435-8
9. Secretariat, W.T.O.: World Trade Report 2023. World Trade Organization, Genève, Switzerland (2023)
10. Zhang, Y., Bai, R., Qu, R., Tu, C., Jin, J.: A deep reinforcement learning based hyper-heuristic for combinatorial optimisation with uncertainties. Eur. J. Oper. Res. **300**(2), 418–427 (2022)
11. Li, C., Wu, S., Li, Z., Zhang, Y., Zhang, L., Gomes, L.: Intelligent scheduling method for bulk cargo terminal loading process based on deep reinforcement learning. Electronics **11**(9), 1390 (2022)
12. Ai, T., Huang, L., Song, R.J., Huang, H.F., Jiao, F., Ma, W.G.: An improved deep reinforcement learning approach: a case study for optimisation of berth and yard scheduling for bulk cargo terminal. Adv. Prod. Eng. Manag. **18**(3), 1–14 (2023)
13. Dai, Y., Li, Z., Wang, B.: Optimizing berth allocation in maritime transportation with quay crane setup times using reinforcement learning. J. Mar. Sci. Eng. **11**(5), 1025 (2023)

14. Lv, Y., Zou, M., Li, J., Liu, J.: Dynamic berth allocation under uncertainties based on deep reinforcement learning towards resilient ports. Ocean Coastal Manag. **252**, 107113 (2024)

15. Li, B., Yang, C., Yang, Z.: Multiple container terminal berth allocation and joint operation based on dueling double deep q-network. J. Mar. Sci. Eng. **11**(12), 2240 (2023)

16. Silva, J.R.S.: Dynamic berth allocation problem for tidal bulk ports with inventory level constraints. Master's thesis, Universidade Federal do Maranhão, São Luís (2021). https://tedebc.ufma.br/jspui/handle/tede/3995. Accessed 10 Nov 2024

17. Mnih, V., et al.: Playing Atari with Deep Reinforcement Learning. arXiv preprint arXiv:1312.5602 (2013)

18. Mnih, V., et al.: Human-level control through deep reinforcement learning. Nature **518**(7540), 529–533 (2015)

19. Hochreiter, S., Schmidhuber, J.: Long short-term memory. Neural Comput. **9**(8), 1735–1780 (1997)

20. e Silva, J.R.S., de Oliveira, A.C.M.: Instances for the berth allocation problem in tidal bulk ports with inventory control (BAPTBI). Mendeley Data **3** (2022). https://data.mendeley.com/datasets/58ph43s6h4/3. https://doi.org/10.17632/58ph43s6h4.3

Interpretable Predictive Maintenance: Combining Anomaly Detection with Quantitative Root Cause Analysis

Inês Barbosa[1,2]($\boxtimes$), João Gama[1,2], and Bruno Veloso[1,2]

[1] Faculty of Economics, University of Porto, 4200-464 Porto, Portugal
{up202004910,jgama,bveloso}@fep.up.pt
[2] INESC TEC, 4200-465 Porto, Portugal

Abstract. Predictive Maintenance (PdM) aims to prevent failures through early detection, yet lacks explainability to support decision-making. Current PdM models often identify failures, but fail to explain their root causes, especially in real-world scenarios, with complex and limited labeled data. This study proposes an interpretable framework that combines LSTM-based Anomaly Detection with a dual-layered Root Cause Analysis (RCA) based on SHAP attributions. Applied to a real-world dataset, the method detects degradation transitions, tracks failure patterns over time, and provides interpretable information without explicit root cause labels.

Keywords: Predictive Maintenance · Anomaly Detection · Root Cause Analysis · Explainability

1 Introduction

In high-stakes industrial environments, unexpected equipment failures result in considerable safety hazards, productivity losses, and maintenance costs. Consequently, many organizations are adopting Predictive Maintenance (PdM) strategies that monitor multivariate sensor data to detect early signs of degradation and allow timely interventions [6,8].

While many PdM approaches predict *whether* a failure might occur, they often stop short of explaining *why*. Without interpretable information into root causes, maintenance teams must rely on manual diagnostics that are slow and do not scale, especially when causal labels are missing. To overcome these limitations, this study introduces a quantitative Root Cause Analysis (RCA) pipeline, designed to operate without ground-truth failure labels. This makes it especially suitable for real-world settings where only coarse degradation stage labels are known. The pipeline begins with an Anomaly Detection (AD) phase, where multivariate time-series data are segmented as healthy and degraded states using a supervised Long Short-Term Memory (LSTM) model, trained on available stage labels. Rare failure transition events are oversampled to improve the detection

J. Valente de Oliveira et al. (Eds.): EPIA 2025, LNAI 16122, pp. 232–245, 2026.
https://doi.org/10.1007/978-3-032-05179-0_18

of degradation onsets. In the RCA phase, transitions are explained using SHAP (SHapley Additive exPlanations) values, which are analyzed via a dual strategy: (i) clustering feature-attribution vectors to identify recurring failure patterns; and (ii) applying sequential pattern mining to assess whether the same root-cause signals persist throughout the degradation trajectory.

The main contributions of this work are: (i) a label-free RCA methodology that provides interpretable fault explanations using SHAP, without requiring labeled failure causes; (ii) a novel application of SHAP analysis across temporal degradation transitions, enabling dynamic feature-level insights; (iii) validation on the real-world SCANIA Component X dataset [7], from the 22nd IDA Industrial Challenge 2024, demonstrating that this approach can detect and explain evolving failure signatures in complex, label-scarce industrial scenarios. Unlike prior studies that rely on reconstruction errors or isolated anomaly points, this method captures recurring and evolving failure patterns both within degradation transitions and across full vehicle trajectories.

The remainder of this paper is structured as follows: Sect. 2 discusses related work in PdM and RCA. Section 3 describes the methodology, including data pre-processing, AD, and the dual RCA strategy. Section 4 presents the experimental results, and Sect. 5 discusses the implications and limitations of the findings. Finally, Sect. 6 concludes the paper and outlines directions for future work.

Finally, to ensure reproducibility, an anonymous repository containing the full implementation, data preprocessing steps, and experimental results is provided.[1]

2   Related Work

This section reviews recent developments in PdM, especially those combining Anomaly Detection with interpretability or Root Cause Analysis. Deep learning methods have become prominent due to their ability to capture temporal patterns in sensor data [8,12].

Several hybrid approaches combine temporal models with interpretable classifiers. For example, Chatterjee and Dethlefs [2] proposed an LSTM-XGBoost system enhanced by SMOTE and PCA for fault detection in wind turbines. Roelofs et al. [11] introduced ARCANA, which uses autoencoder reconstruction with sparse optimization for interpretable RCA. Gama et al. [4] combined LSTM-AE with AMRules to enable both detection and symbolic RCA, assisted by SHAP values and oversampling.

Recent PdM research has shifted to using event-based diagnostic data, like Diagnostic Trouble Codes (DTCs) from vehicle On-Board Diagnostics (DTCs) from vehicle On-Board Diagnostics (OBD) systems. [5] reframed fault prediction as next-event prediction using DTC sequences, proposing a hybrid Transformer-GRU model that improves top-5 accuracy. Similarly, [9] applied causal Transformers, drawing analogies to language processing, to predict the timing and

---

[1] Anonymous code repository:
   https://anonymous.4open.science/r/InterpretablePredictiveMaintenance-39E1.

type of failure vehicle errors. These methods handle high event cardinality and imbalanced data, showing strong predictive performance for maintenance.

However, many studies use synthetic or idealized datasets, limiting real-world applicability [3]. To address this, the SCANIA Component X dataset was introduced in the IDA Industrial Challenge 2024 [7]. Several teams proposed solutions: Zhong and Wang [13] tested MLP, CNN, and Bi-LSTM with feature selection and sampling; Parton et al. [10] applied graph-based methods using visibility graphs and GNNs; Carpentier et al. [1] explored survival analysis with feature extraction via tsfresh, a Python library that computes statistical characteristics from time-series data. These works show strong results under noisy and imbalanced data, but focus primarily on classification or forecasting, without detailing why or how degradation occurs. While some include feature-based explanations, few offer sequential interpretability, tracking how root causes evolve across degradation phases.

In contrast to prior efforts, which detected anomalies with limited interpretability, this study introduces a quantitative, label-free RCA framework integrated with AD, capable of operating without causal fault labels. By leveraging sequential SHAP analyses on detected transitions, it provides interpretable, time-evolving explanations of failures. To our knowledge, this is the first work to apply unsupervised RCA on the SCANIA dataset with temporal SHAP clustering and pattern mining.

3 Methodology

This section describes the proposed framework, illustrated in Fig. 1, which consists of two main phases: Anomaly Detection and Root Cause Analysis. It begins by presenting the characteristics and challenges of the used dataset, followed by preprocessing techniques applied to prepare the data. The AD phase formulates degradation prediction as a supervised learning task using LSTM networks, while the RCA introduces an interpretability pipeline based on SHAP attributions.

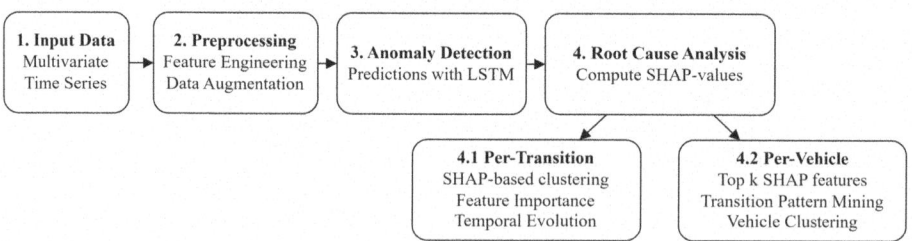

Fig. 1. Schematic Overview of the proposed framework.

3.1   Data Understanding

Data for Component X are sourced from three distinct sources: operational time series, repair records, and vehicle specifications metadata. Each of these sources is provided in non-overlapping training, validation, and test splits, with 23 550, 5 046, and 5 045 vehicles, respectively. As a result, no vehicle appears in more than one subset, allowing for an assessment of out-of-fleet generalization. The operational series includes up to 107 anonymized variables per vehicle, incorporating cumulative counters, as well as histogram-based features. The vehicles' sequence lengths span from approximately 50 to over 1 000 time steps; the actual sampling frequency is unspecified due to anonymization, and the time steps represent relative (not absolute) time intervals. Validation and test set trajectories are randomly truncated to simulate live monitoring. Repair records in the training set include exact Time-to-Event and failure flags, whereas validation and test sets present only discretized proximity-to-failure labels (0-4), corresponding to time windows of more than 48, 48-24, 24-12, 12-6, and 6–0 time steps before failure, respectively. Vehicle specifications include eight categorical attributes, the marginal frequencies of which remain stable across splits, despite the occasional near-perfect redundancy among certain feature pairs.

These data present a series of modeling challenges. First, the extensive dimensionality and deliberate anonymization of sensor channels limit both explainability and root-cause analysis. In addition, the presence of heterogeneous variable types and considerable variation in sequence lengths requires both careful preprocessing and flexible architectures. The pronounced class imbalance (9.7% training failures, less than 3% non-zero proximity classes in validation/test) complicates the multi-class anomaly detection task. Finally, the presence of weak associations between the specifications and failure outcomes suggests that simple feature correlations will be insufficient.

3.2   Data Preprocessing

A preprocessing workflow was implemented to transform raw vehicle data into features suitable for predictive modeling. The time-series counters were first cleaned by imputing missing values using forward and backward filling within each vehicle, preserving their cumulative nature. These counters were then differentiated and normalized by elapsed time to obtain rate-of-change indicators. Counter resets were corrected via preceding-value imputation and temporal recalibration. Histogram variables underwent similar imputation, followed by dimensionality reduction into three fixed bins to improve interpretability and reduce sparsity – drawing inspiration from semantic groupings (e.g., cold, mild, hot for temperature). The resulting distributions were normalized into frequencies and summarized via Shannon entropy to capture behavioral diversity. This multi-step process ensured a temporally consistent, compact, and informative dataset for modeling degradation patterns.

In the operational readouts train set, class labels were created by comparing each observation's timestamp to the recorded time-to-event (TTE) information, assigning classes based on predefined degradation thresholds. To avoid any ambiguity that might arise due to censorship near the conclusion of the observational period of healthy trucks, the data from the final forty-eight time steps were excluded. In addition, to address class imbalance, vehicles that transitioned to the most severe degradation class were used to generate augmented sequences by extracting earlier time segments that reflected milder degradation states. This strategy improved representation across failure classes, increasing the model's sensitivity to transitional patterns.

3.3   Anomaly Detection Phase

In the first phase of the proposed framework, anomaly detection is formulated as a supervised, multiclass classification of degradation stages. Motivated by the proven capacity of deep learning architectures to model complex, temporal dependencies in PdM applications [8,12], and following the preprocessing applied, an LSTM network is trained to classify degradation stages.

Hyperparameter optimization was performed via Keras-Tuner's Hyperband search. The tuning process targeted important parameters, including the number and size of LSTM layers, dropout rates, optional dense layers, and the learning rate. Validation loss was used as the objective function to promote generalization, and early-stopping and learning-rate-reduction callbacks were used to prevent overfitting. The tuned LSTM is trained to discriminate among healthy, holding, and failing stages, using the balanced sliding-window dataset. To assess the model's ability to detect degradation both within and beyond the training distribution, a two-stage evaluation strategy was adopted. First, a stratified 80–20 split was applied to the training dataset at the vehicle level, creating a hold-out partition that preserves intra-vehicle temporal coherence. This assesses how well the model detects transitions in familiar vehicles using unseen time windows. Second, performance is evaluated on completely unseen assets in the validation and test sets, allowing the measurement of true generalization across the fleet. With reliable proximity-to-failure estimates produced by the LSTM, the framework can proceed to a quantitative RCA phase that leverages these detected transitions.

3.4   Root Cause Analysis Phase

The proposed framework consists of a dual-approach pipeline to perform quantitative RCA without ground-truth causal labels. After the LSTM classifier was fitted and validated, the training dataset was filtered to retain only those vehicles that exhibit at least one true degradation transition (from class 0 to class 1–4). From the set of vehicles that experienced at least one true degradation transition, two levels of filtering were applied. At the transition level, transitions that were correctly predicted by the LSTM model – determined by comparing true and predicted transition labels – were identified. These transitions, regardless of their vehicle of origin, were used in the *per-transition SHAP (SHapley Additive exPlanations) analysis*. At the vehicle level, only those vehicles for which all degradation transitions were predicted correctly across the entire timeline were retained. This more stringent subset was used in the *per-vehicle top-3 feature analysis*, allowing for a longitudinal evaluation of feature consistency throughout the degradation process. SHAP was applied to decompose each predicted transition score into mean per-feature contributions. These SHAP values are the basis of both approaches to the RCA pipeline.

Per-Transition SHAP Analysis. To analyze the temporal dynamics of feature attributions across system degradation stages, a transition-level clustering framework applied to SHAP values is proposed. This approach examines the four consecutive state changes ($0\rightarrow1$, $1\rightarrow2$, $2\rightarrow3$, $3\rightarrow4$) to identify and track distinct failure trajectories over time. Without ground truth root causes, each cluster serves as a hypothesis for a distinct failure mode or severity stage, enabling monitoring of cluster coherence and evolution of failure approaches. Clusters are obtained by applying k-Means to the absolute SHAP value matrices for each transition, selecting the number of clusters, k, from 2 to 10, by maximizing the Calinski-Harabasz Index (CHI), which favors compact and well-separated groups. k-Means was chosen for its simplicity, scalability, hard cluster assignments, consistent outputs, clear centroids (useful for SHAP interpretation), and direct control over cluster number, despite alternatives like HDBSCAN potentially capturing more complex shapes. Within each cluster, top driver features are defined as those whose mean absolute SHAP Values exceed the 95th Percentile threshold, identifying the most influential feature prefixes that characterize each cluster's failure pattern by aggregating these drivers across clusters and transitions. A "prefix" refers to the central source variable from which a feature was derived – whether from histogram-based attributes (split into multiple bins or suffixes) or numerical time-series variables. Only the main variable prefix is retained in the SHAP analysis, focusing on the signal origin rather than its directionality. The sign and magnitude of the SHAP indicate whether that variable contributes positively or negatively to degradation prediction. Therefore, the framework allows temporal monitoring of feature importance evolution. A Sankey diagram is used to visualize cluster flows over consecutive transitions, providing interpretable information about the progression and recurrence of failure drivers.

Per-Vehicle Top-3 Feature Analysis. To analyze the main feature contributions at the vehicle level across state transitions, SHAP values are computed for sliding windows surrounding each transition for each vehicle. For every vehicle and transition, the top three features are identified by selecting those exceeding the 95th percentile of mean absolute SHAP values. While choosing only the top 3 features may oversimplify complex degradation behaviors, it provides consistent, high-salience signalings, balancing complexity and interpretability. Feature prefixes are extracted, and only vehicles with complete data across all transitions are retained. Sequences of consecutive transition features per vehicle are constructed and analyzed using the PrefixSpan. This algorithm, used to efficiently discover sequential patterns in sequence data, was applied to identify frequent two-step transition patterns. Support, confidence, and lift metrics are computed to evaluate these patterns. In addition, UMAP embedding combined with HDBSCAN clustering is applied to the vehicle-level feature sequences to identify distinct failure trajectory groups for each cluster, dominant feature prefixes, and vehicle counts are summarized to provide interpretable information about different vehicle degradation behaviors. On the one hand, UMAP was used to reduce dimensionality while preserving the local structure of SHAP sequences. HDBSCAN, on the other hand, was chosen for its ability to identify clusters of varying density and to detect noise, supporting the hypothesis that not all vehicles follow consistent degradation patterns.

4   Results

4.1   Anomaly Detection Results

Compared to baseline models (XGBoost, LightGBM, AE, and LSTM-AE), the LSTM consistently outperformed others, particularly on the training hold-out fold (lowest cost, higher AUC, and F_2. Therefore, it was selected as the final model (see Table 1). The F2-score (Eq. 1), which weights recall more heavily than precision, making it particularly relevant in PdM, where minimizing false negatives (missed failures) is often a priority.

$$F_2 = \frac{5 \times Precision \times Recall}{4 \times Precision + Recall} \qquad (1)$$

Table 1. Comparison of anomaly scoring metrics across models (no clustering). Best results per metric and scenario are in bold. The final row (LSTM, tuned) presents results obtained after hyperparameter optimization.

Model	Train			Validation			Test		
	Mean Cost	F_2	AUC	Mean Cost	F_2	AUC	Mean Cost	F_2	AUC
XGB	12.853	0.230	0.912	**11.193**	0.203	0.621	11.127	0.197	**0.654**
LGBM	12.994	0.219	0.869	11.285	0.201	0.612	11.554	0.183	0.646
RF	11.136	0.313	0.912	11.356	0.199	0.539	11.120	0.199	0.547
LSTM	**5.910**	**0.462**	**0.980**	11.255	**0.205**	0.631	**10.683**	**0.214**	0.617
AE	13.289	0.206	0.766	11.383	0.198	**0.645**	11.047	0.206	0.629
LSTM-AE	9.669	0.317	0.954	11.416	0.205	0.608	11.065	0.201	0.625
LSTM (tuned)	3.440	0.640	0.988	10.930	0.198	0.660	10.930	0.205	0.627

Although a cluster-based approach was explored, where models were trained per vehicle group, it did not lead to consistent improvements and was, therefore, not adopted.

Table 1 shows that the LSTM model achieves low cost and high discriminative power (AUC = 0.988) on the hold-out fold, indicating strong performance on familiar vehicles. This high AUC reflects the model's performance on unseen time windows from previously unseen vehicles (intra-fleet hold-out), which complements – but is distinct from – the validation and test evaluations that assess inter-fleet generalization. On unseen trucks (validation and test sets), however, performance declined, but maintained moderate anomaly separability ($F_2 \approx 0.20$), in particular through improved detection of rare events compared to the baselines. The confusion matrices in Table 2 show that most errors occur between adjacent severity levels, which suggests that the model still captures the relative risk of anomalies, even under domain shift.

Table 2. Confusion matrices for the tuned LSTM in the three evaluation scenarios. Each matrix shows the distribution of true labels (T) versus predicted labels (P). Most errors occur between adjacent classes, suggesting the model preserves the ordinal structure of anomaly severity, even under domain shift.

(a) Train Hold-out					(b) Validation Last-Window					(c) Test Last-Window				
	P0	P1	P2	P3	P4	P0	P1	P2	P3	P4	P0	P1	P2	P3	P4
T0	73 530	235	24	13	27	4 709	85	40	28	48	4 755	53	34	13	48
T1	351	1 076	179	5	5	16	0	0	0	0	24	0	1	0	1
T2	65	144	549	87	17	13	1	0	0	0	15	0	0	0	0
T3	37	6	147	175	91	27	0	0	0	3	34	4	1	2	0
T4	101	19	48	121	271	65	4	3	2	2	58	2	0	0	0

4.2 Root Cause Analysis Results

Only 201 out of the 2.262 failed vehicles (8.9%) had all transitions predicted correctly. Individual transitions were predicted with varying accuracy, with correct predictions ranging from 556 to 747. These results demonstrate the challenge of capturing full degradation pathways and justify focusing the explainability analysis on more reliably predicted segments.

Transition-Level Analysis. Each cluster represents a distinct SHAP attribution profile, identified by a subset of dominant histogram prefixes – these can correspond to different failure types. For instance, Cluster C0 in the $0 \to 1$ transitions is primarily driven by variables (prefixes) 291, 272, and 427, while Cluster C1 highlights 272, 158, and 459. These prefixes suggest variations in early failure symptoms across the fleet. Although the features are anonymized, their recurrence across transitions provides insights into the evolving nature of degradation signatures (Table 3).

Table 3. Top SHAP-driver prefixes per cluster, by transition

Transition	Cluster (size)	Top drivers (prefixes)
0 → 1	C0 (107)	291, 272, 427
	C1 (221)	272, 158, 459
	C2 (255)	309, 167
1 → 2	C0 (101)	427, 272, 167
	C1 (92)	291, 666, 309
	C2 (179)	459, 171, 397
	C3 (211)	167, 158
	C4 (78)	459
	C5 (85)	459
	C6 (1)	397, 167, 837
2 → 3	C0 (310)	100, 272, 158
	C1 (321)	309, 158, 291
3 → 4	C0 (555)	666, 100, 167
	C1 (1)	459, 291, 158

Initially, three relatively balanced profiles emerge from 0→1, each characterized by distinct top drivers. However, by the subsequent step, the system abruptly fragments into seven smaller clusters, including two clusters exclusively defined by feature 459 and one isolated outlier whose extreme SHAP magnitude marks it as qualitatively different. This divergence of modes then converges: by transition 2→3, the majority of the seven clusters converge, resulting in two distinct clusters, whose driver sets remain consistent into the final 3→ stage.

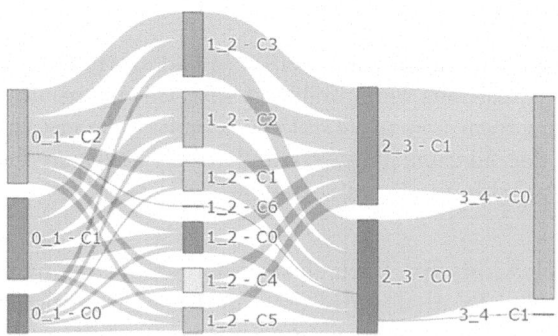

Fig. 2. Cluster Flow Across Transitions.

Figure 2 traces sample flows between these clusters across transitions, allowing to test two main hypotheses: first, that each cluster represents a distinct failure type; and second, that samples of the same type will remain in the same cluster as they approach failure. At 0→1, three distinct early-warning profiles can be observed. If these were true, persistent failure types, it would be expected that their SHAP signatures to endure. Instead, at 1→2, they split into seven smaller clusters – including two small 459-only groups and a singleton outlier – only to converge by 2→3 into two mid-stage modes; and finally, funnel almost entirely into one imminent-failure cluster, with just that lone outlier remaining. This pattern suggests that, absent labels, the SHAP-based clusters are tracking a continuum of severity rather than discrete failure types. That said, the Sankey could support either interpretation. On the one hand, genuine failure modes might briefly diverge into subtypes before converging under shared end-stage dynamics. On the other hand, the anonymized data may simply encode a single underlying failure process expressed through varying signal combinations.

Vehicle-Level Analysis. The sequential pattern mining revealed a small set of transition rules across consecutive transitions, using a minimum support of 2 to ensure non-empty results. Despite their limited number, the rules presented high confidence (up to 1.0) and strong lift (often > 20), indicating that some transitions occur more than expected by chance. While stable progression paths are rare, these results emphasize temporal dependencies in failure evolution, reinforcing the view that degradation is gradual and heterogeneous.

The clustering analysis identified five distinct groups of vehicles and a noise cluster, reflecting both shared and divergent early failure signatures. By focusing on initial failure signals, this framework aligns with PdM objectives of early detection. Prefix (variables) 397 emerged consistently across all clusters, suggesting it as a global degradation indicator; prefixes like 271, 298, and 158 appeared only in specific subgroups, indicating variation in failure expression. These findings extend the transition-level analysis, showing how different combinations of symptoms manifest across vehicle groups, supporting interpretable monitoring of failure progression. Figure 3 and Table 4 summarize the visual and quantitative characteristics of the clusters, including symptom prevalence and spatial separation.

Table 4. Summary of vehicle clusters identified by HDBSCAN on UMAP embeddings (for early failure symptoms).

Cluster	Num. Vehicles	Percentage (%)	Top Prefixes
−1	21	22.11	397, 291, 459, 167, 158
0	23	24.21	397, 158, 167, 459, 272
1	14	14.74	397, 459, 291, 158, 272
2	19	20.00	397, 291, 459, 272, 158
3	10	10.53	397, 167, 459, 272, 291
4	8	8.42	397, 272, 291, 459, 167

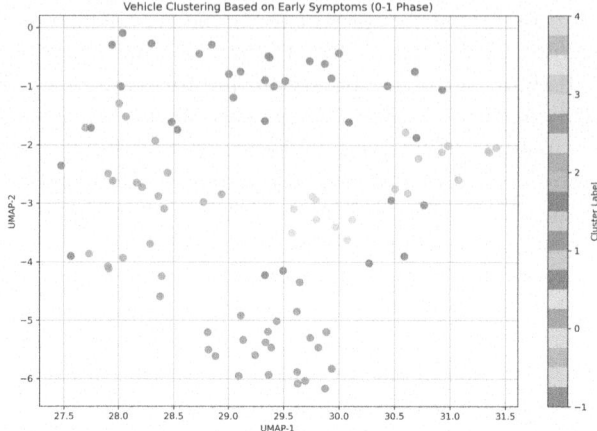

Fig. 3. UMAP visualization of vehicle early failure symptom profiles with HDBSCAN clustering.

The noise cluster in the HDBSCAN output reflects degradation heterogeneity across the fleet, likely due to varying operational conditions and usage patterns, which can partly explain reduced AD performance on unseen vehicles. Rather than being discarded, such clusters reveal that degradation does not follow a single path, and that methods like HDBSCAN are well-suited to capturing this structure. Variables relevant in the noise cluster also appear in other groups. The recurrence of specific drivers, such as prefix 397, suggests the presence of global degradation indicators. Although anonymized, its consistent contribution across failure transitions points to a potentially reliable, system-wide signal.

4.3   Discussion

The experimental results show that the framework achieves competitive detection performance while offering interpretable insights into degradation dynamics. It captures evolving patterns and influential features using SHAP, revealing variations across vehicle trajectories. The dual evaluation strategy – combining a train hold-out partition and out-of-sample fleet testing – clarifies how well the model detects degradation in known versus unseen vehicles.

While the high AUC on the hold-out set confirms strong detection within known assets, performance on unseen trucks declines, particularly due to the model's tendency to favor the dominant healthy class. This is expected given the severe class imbalance and limited representation of failure transitions in the validation and test sets. In addition, the common failure symptomatology experienced by trucks limits the anomaly prediction task (it becomes harder to distinguish between failure classes as all present the same symptoms). Despite this, the SHAP-based RCA remains effective even under weak anomaly detection, offering structured feature-level explanations for transitions that were correctly identified. This supports the use of interpretability techniques even in low-signal or imbalanced regimes. Some limitations emerged. The RCA step relies on degradation-stage labels during training, which may not always be available. The k-Means clustering used for SHAP attributions favors simplicity, but may miss irregular structures that density-based methods like HDBSCAN can detect. The emergence of a noise cluster reflects behavioral heterogeneity across the fleet and highlights the need for models that can capture more diverse degradation trajectories. As the dataset is anonymized and lacks explicit root-cause labels, it is not possible to directly validate whether each cluster corresponds to a specific failure type. Instead, the clusters are interpreted as hypothetical degradation pathways, inferred from unsupervised SHAP analysis. This label-free approach is intended for exploratory diagnostics, especially in real-world systems, where failure modes are unknown, evolving, or undocumented.

5   Conclusion

This study proposes a novel, domain-agnostic framework for RCA in PdM, designed to operate without labeled failure data or prior knowledge of root causes. By integrating LSTM-based AD with transition-level filtering and SHAP-based feature attribution, the framework identifies and tracks the main drivers of system degradation over time, bridging the gap between AD and explainable RCA. The framework was applied to an anonymized real-world vehicle dataset, demonstrating its ability to identify evolving failure behaviors and providing interpretable explanations of system behaviors that support early warning and informed maintenance decisions. Future work will explore alternative AD baselines and improve adaptability through transfer and online learning to support dynamic conditions and unseen systems. Expanding the RCA process to include vehicle-specific context is also expected to improve the explanations. Finally, evaluation on datasets from other domains will help determine the framework's generalizability.

Acknowledgments. This work was realised within the scope of the project EnSafe, with reference 2024.07677.IACDC, co-funded by Component 5 - Capitalization and Business Innovation, integrated in the Resilience Dimension of the Recovery and Resilience Plan within the scope of the Recovery and Resilience Mechanism (MRR) of the European Union (EU), framed in the Next Generation EU, for the period 2021–2026, measure "RE-C05-i08.M04 - "To support the launch of a programme of R&D projects geared towards the development and implementation of advanced cybersecurity, artificial intelligence and data science systems in public administration, as well as a scientific training programme", as part of the funding contract signed between the Recovering Portugal Mission Structure (EMRP) and the FCT - Fundação para a Ciência e a Tecnologia, I.P. (Portuguese Foundation for Science and Technology), as intermediary beneficiary. (https://doi.org/10.54499/2024.07677.IACDC

Disclosure of Interests. The authors declare no relevant competing interests regarding this article.

References

1. Carpentier, L., Temmerman, A.D., Verbeke, M.: Towards contextual, cost-efficient predictive maintenance in heavy-duty trucks. In: Lecture Notes in Computer Science (including subseries Lecture Notes in Artificial Intelligence and Lecture Notes in Bioinformatics), vol. 14642 LNCS, pp. 260–267. Springer, Heidelberg (2024). https://doi.org/10.1007/978-3-031-58553-1_21
2. Chatterjee, J., Dethlefs, N.: Deep learning with knowledge transfer for explainable anomaly prediction in wind turbines. Wind Energy **23**(8), 1693–1710 (2020). https://doi.org/10.1002/we.2510. https://onlinelibrary.wiley.com/doi/abs/10.1002/we.2510
3. Fernandes, M., Corchado, J.M., Marreiros, G.: Machine learning techniques applied to mechanical fault diagnosis and fault prognosis in the context of real industrial manufacturing use-cases: a systematic literature review. Appl. Intell. **52**, 14246–14280 (2022). https://doi.org/10.1007/S10489-022-03344-3/FIGURES/9. https://link.springer.com/article/10.1007/s10489-022-03344-3
4. Gama, J., Ribeiro, R.P., Mastelini, S., Davari, N., Veloso, B.: From fault detection to anomaly explanation: a case study on predictive maintenance. J. Web Semant. **81**, 100821 (2024). https://doi.org/10.1016/j.websem.2024.100821
5. Hafeez, A.B., Alonso, E., Riaz, A.: Dtc-trangru: improving the performance of the next-dtc prediction model with transformer and gru. In: Proceedings of the ACM Symposium on Applied Computing, pp. 927–934 (2024). https://doi.org/10.1145/3605098.3635962. https://dl.acm.org/doi/pdf/10.1145/3605098.3635962
6. Katreddi, S., Kasani, S., Thiruvengadam, A.: A Review of Applications of Artificial Intelligence in Heavy Duty Trucks (2022). https://doi.org/10.3390/en15207457. https://192.147.130.58/chcservices/services/redirect?u=http://help.adobe.com&p=Reader&l=en_US&id=InternetAccess_TrustManager
7. Kharazian, Z., Lindgren, T., Magnússon, S., Steinert, O., Reyna, O.A.: Scania component x dataset: a real-world multivariate time series dataset for predictive maintenance (2024). https://arxiv.org/abs/2401.15199
8. Lee, J., Kao, H.A., Yang, S.: Service innovation and smart analytics for industry 4.0 and big data environment. Procedia CIRP **16**, 3–8 (2014). https://doi.org/10.1016/J.PROCIR.2014.02.001
9. Math, H., Lienhart, R., Schön, R.: Harnessing event sensory data for error pattern prediction in vehicles: a language model approach. In: Proceedings of the AAAI Conference on Artificial Intelligence, vol. 39, 19423–19431 (2025). https://doi.org/10.1609/AAAI.V39I18.34138. https://ojs.aaai.org/index.php/AAAI/article/view/34138
10. Parton, M., Fois, A., Vegliò, M., Metta, C., Gregnanin, M.: Predicting the failure of component x in the scania dataset with graph neural networks. In: Lecture Notes in Computer Science (including subseries Lecture Notes in Artificial Intelligence and Lecture Notes in Bioinformatics), vol. 14642 LNCS, pp. 251–259. Springer, Heidelberg (2024). https://doi.org/10.1007/978-3-031-58553-1_20
11. Roelofs, C.M., Lutz, M.A., Faulstich, S., Vogt, S.: Autoencoder-based anomaly root cause analysis for wind turbines. Energy AI **4**, 100065 (2021). https://doi.org/10.1016/j.egyai.2021.100065. https://www.sciencedirect.com/science/article/pii/S2666546821000197

12. Serradilla, O., Zugasti, E., Rodriguez, J., Zurutuza, U.: Deep learning models for predictive maintenance: a survey, comparison, challenges and prospects. Appl. Intell. **52**(10), 10934–10964 (2022). https://doi.org/10.1007/s10489-021-03004-y

13. Zhong, J., Wang, Z.: Implementing deep learning models for imminent component x failures prediction in heavy-duty scania trucks. In: Lecture Notes in Computer Science (including subseries Lecture Notes in Artificial Intelligence and Lecture Notes in Bioinformatics), vol. 14642 LNCS, pp. 268–276. Springer, Heidelberg (2024). https://doi.org/10.1007/978-3-031-58553-1_22

Natural Language Processing, Text Mining and Applications (NLP-TeMA)

Prompting LLMs for Relation Classification in Portuguese: Is It Worth It?

Tomás Pinto[✉], Bruno Ferreira, Catarina Silva, and Hugo Gonçalo Oliveira

University of Coimbra, CISUC/LASI, DEI, Coimbra, Portugal
tomaspinto@student.dei.uc.pt, {brunof,catarina,hroliv}@dei.uc.pt

Abstract. This paper explores relation classification as a step toward extracting structured information from unstructured Portuguese text. We evaluate prompt-based approaches using generative large language models and compare them with fine-tuned BERT and DeBERTa models, which serve as the baselines in this study. Experiments are conducted on two Portuguese-language datasets: RelEx-PT, a custom sentence-level dataset created by aligning Wikidata triples with Wikipedia sentences, and a second consisting of multi-sentence texts annotated with multiple triples. Results show that, while prompt-based methods offer flexibility and solid performance, they are still not sufficient to overtake fine-tuning, as the latter yields significantly better results in identifying relation types, even widening the gap in more complex task settings.

Keywords: Relation Classification · Large Language Models · Prompting Strategies · Fine-Tuning · Portuguese-Language

1 Introduction

Relation Classification (RC) is a fundamental subtask of Relation Extraction (RE), concerned with identifying the semantic relationship between two entities in a text. As a key step in transforming unstructured text into structured representations, RC plays a vital role in multiple areas, such as the construction and enrichment of Knowledge Graphs (KGs). Correctly identifying the relation between entity pairs directly impacts the accuracy and utility of the resulting data in downstream applications such as information retrieval, question answering, and recommender systems [29].

In recent years, the emergence of generative Large Language Models (LLMs), such as GPT-4 and Llama 3 [1,7], reshaped the landscape of Natural Language Processing tasks, including RC [24]. Their ability to generalize and perform well in zero-shot (without any task-specific examples) or few-shot (with only a handful of examples) settings makes them attractive candidates for a wide range of tasks, from text classification and translation to content generation [25].

Prompting LLMs comes as an alternative to traditional methods, offering flexibility. Nevertheless, encoder-based models, such as BERT [6], are generally

J. Valente de Oliveira et al. (Eds.): EPIA 2025, LNAI 16122, pp. 249–261, 2026.
https://doi.org/10.1007/978-3-032-05179-0_19

smaller, more resource-efficient, and should not be disregarded when labeled data is available, particularly in scenarios requiring high precision. Supervised fine-tuning involves adapting a pretrained model to a specific task by further training it on labeled data, allowing the model to specialize in recognizing particular patterns relevant to the task at hand. Fine-tuned models are known to perform well in scenarios where sufficient labeled data is available for training [28].

Although extensively studied for English, research in RE and RC for other languages, particularly Portuguese, is still limited. This is largely due to the scarcity of annotated datasets, adapted models, and language-specific tools [28]. To address this gap, our study systematically investigates RC in Portuguese using both prompting strategies with generative LLMs and supervised fine-tuning. We evaluate five distinct prompting formulations across open and proprietary models, comparing them to fine-tuned encoder-only baselines. Experiments are conducted on two datasets with differing levels of complexity, allowing us to assess the behavior of each approach under varied conditions. This comprehensive comparison aims at studying the performance of these methods and models, contributing to a clearer understanding of their strengths and limitations.

This study makes three key contributions: experimenting with different LLMs (open and proprietary, of varying sizes) and prompting techniques for RC in Portuguese; analyzing their performance across two datasets with a range of relations and comparing them to fine-tuned models; introducing RelEx-PT, a new, balanced, and simplified sentence-level dataset for RE/RC in Portuguese.

2 Related Work

The RE and RC tasks have traditionally been addressed using supervised learning approaches, where labeled datasets and dedicated classifiers were central to performance [27]. With the advent of pretrained transformer models, particularly BERT [6] and its variants, supervised fine-tuning has continued the dominant paradigm for improving RC accuracy [30].

In parallel, recent studies explored alternative methods to enhance model performance, particularly through various prompting strategies aimed at generative LLMs for RE and RC tasks. These include prompting with task demonstrations [22], question-answering (QA) formats that frame relation prediction as a multiple-choice task [26], and chain-of-thought (CoT) prompting, which encourages step-by-step reasoning before producing a final answer [13]. More advanced techniques such as reflexive prompting have also emerged, where models iteratively critique and revise their own outputs to improve reliability [23].

Despite these advancements, the application of generative LLMs in RE tasks for Portuguese remains limited. A few prior efforts have explored Portuguese RE using BERT-based models [12,15], but the use of generative LLMs in this context remains largely unexplored.

In contrast, work in Open Information Extraction, a related area that focuses on extracting structured information from unstructured text without predefined relation types, has seen more dedicated exploration for the Portuguese language.

For example, Cabral et al. introduced PortOIELlama, a fine-tuned Llama-2 model tailored specifically for Portuguese [4]. Similarly, Silva et al. combined Graph Machine Learning (Graph ML) with LLMs to develop a multilingual Open IE model capable of handling both English and Portuguese [17].

3   Methodology

This section describes the core methodologies employed in this work, focusing on the prompting strategies explored and presenting the fine-tuning setup.

3.1   Prompting Strategies

Five prompting strategies were designed for the study, drawing inspiration from existing approaches in the literature:

- **Instruct**:
  A direct instruction-based prompt that asks the model to identify the relation between entities using only the given sentence or text. No examples are provided. The model must choose from the list and respond with relation names only, without explanations.
- **Descriptive**: Extends the Instruct prompt by appending brief definitions for each relation, helping the model better understand the label space. This added context aims to reduce ambiguity in relation selection while maintaining a zero-shot setting.
- **Few-shot**: Presents the model with three randomly selected annotated examples from the training set to demonstrate the task format and expected output. This approach aims to guide the model's prediction by providing concrete illustrations of subject–object–relation mappings.
- **QA-style**: Directly inspired by Zhang et al. [26], we recast the task as a multiple-choice question. Each possible relation is phrased as a declarative sentence involving the entity pair. The model selects the one option that best aligns with the input text, evaluating its ability to reason over natural language rather than predict labels directly.
- **CoT-style**: Implements a chain-of-thought inspired approach by prompting the model to reason through intermediate steps, from identifying entities to selecting the appropriate relation.

Since the task is performed in Portuguese text, the prompts are written in Portuguese. For complete prompt templates, including both the original Portuguese versions and their English translations, please check: https://github.com/TomasCCPinto/EPIA25_Prompts.

3.2 Model Fine-Tuning

For the supervised learning setup, BERTimbau and Albertina were adapted for RC by adding a linear classification head on top of the encoder, predicting one of the predefined relation types. The input to the model consisted of the original sentence with the two target entities explicitly marked using XML-style tags ([SUBJ]entity[/SUBJ] and [OBJ]entity[/OBJ]), enabling the model to localize the relevant context. The model was trained using cross-entropy loss and evaluated using standard classification metrics. For the RelEx-PT dataset, which is balanced across relation types, we used macro-averaged F1 as the primary evaluation metric to give equal importance to each class. In contrast, for the SRED^{FM} dataset, which exhibits class imbalance, we report the weighted-averaged F1 score. This approach accounts for the relative frequency of each relation in the test set, providing a more accurate evaluation by giving higher importance to the more frequent classes.

The training process used the train/test split indicated, for each dataset, in Sect. 4.1, with hyperparameters set according to standard BERT fine-tuning practices: a learning rate of 2e-5, 5 epochs, and a train batch size of 8.

4 Experimentation

This section describes the experimental setup, including the datasets and models used to evaluate the performance of both prompting techniques and fine-tuning.

4.1 Datasets

This work uses two datasets for evaluating RC in Portuguese: RelEx-PT, a custom sentence-level dataset constructed via distant supervision, and an adapted version of an existing dataset, the Portuguese part of SRED^{FM} [3], originally developed for multiple languages and that is composed of multi-sentence texts.

The motivation for using both datasets is to analyze performance differences between sentence-level and multi-sentence setups. This allows us to explore how well LLMs capture relations that can possibly be spread across sentences, how they benefit (or suffer) from additional context, and what is gained or lost when moving from simpler conditions to more complex, real-world scenarios.

The SRED^{FM} dataset was created by automatically aligning Wikidata triples with text extracted from Wikipedia dumps. Notably, this dataset covers 18 languages (including Portuguese) and encompasses over 400 distinct relation types. It consists of texts of varying lengths, with each instance potentially containing one or more triples, where relations may span entities across different sentences. The dataset is highly unbalanced, with a few relation types dominating the majority of the entries. An example instance is shown in Table 1.

While SRED^{FM} presents a complex environment, there was a need for an easier, more controlled dataset to evaluate the methods. Lower complexity settings, such as RelEx-PT, our sentence-level dataset, are crucial as they allow for a

Table 1. Example instance from the SRED^{FM} dataset

Text: Sekai-ichi Hatsukoi é um mangá "yaoi" escrito e ilustrado por Shungiku Nakamura. Em 2011 o mangá ganhou uma adaptação em anime com o título Sekai-ichi Hatsukoi. Produzido pelo Studio Deen com a direção de Chiaki Kon, a primeira temporada foi ao ar em 8 de Abril de 2011. Um OVA de DVD foi empacotado com o quinto volume da série de mangá, lançado em março de 2011. A segunda temporada foi exibida entre 7 de outubro Āă 23 de dezembro de 2011.[a]

Triples: ["Sekai-ichi Hatsukoi", "género/genre", "yaoi"], ["Sekai-ichi Hatsukoi", "empresa de produção/production company", "Studio Deen"]

---

[a]Sekai-ichi Hatsukoi is a yaoi manga written and illustrated by Shungiku Nakamura. In 2011, the manga received an anime adaptation under the title Sekai-ichi Hatsukoi. Produced by Studio Deen and directed by Chiaki Kon, the first season aired on April 8, 2011. A DVD OVA was bundled with the fifth volume of the manga series, released in March 2011. The second season was broadcast from October 7 to December 23, 2011.

more manageable environment to first test the models. By focusing on sentence-level, instances have reduced context complexity and we can more effectively identify potential difficulties and limitations of the methods before advancing to more challenging settings. Additionally, RelEx-PT is perfectly balanced across relation types, eliminating any imbalance issues.

The **RelEx-PT dataset** was created using a distant supervision approach, where Wikidata[1] triples were aligned with Portuguese Wikipedia[2] sentences that contain both the subject and object entities. For each instance, the sentence, subject, object, and corresponding relation label are included, as shown in Table 2. The dataset covers 18 distinct Wikidata relation types: *author, composer, director, developer, father, genre, headquarters location, instance of, located in or next to body of water, main subject, occupation, place of birth, producer, production company, religion, sport, subclass of,* and *taxon rank.* These were selected based on their frequency in the Wikidata triples dump and the number of valid instances generated by our pipeline. The data is divided into 70 training instances and 30 testing instances for each relation type, totaling 1,260 training and 540 testing instances overall.

To reduce distant supervision noise, we applied a Natural Language Inference (NLI) filtering step, inspired by Cabot et al. [3]. A Portuguese NLI model[3] was used to verify the entailment between the Wikidata triple (expressed textually) and the corresponding sentence [5]. Only instances with an entailment probability higher than or equal to 95% were retained, ensuring high semantic consistency in the dataset.

---

[1] https://www.wikidata.org/.

[2] https://pt.wikipedia.org/.

[3] https://huggingface.co/ruanchaves/mdeberta-v3-base-assin2-entailment.

Table 2. Example instance from the RelEx-PT dataset.

Sentence: "Na mitologia nórdica, Bestla era uma antiga jotun (mulher gigante), filha de Bolthorn e irmã de Mímir."[a]

Subject: Bestla / **Object:** Bolthorn / **Relation:** pai (father)

---

[a]"In Norse mythology, Bestla was an ancient jotun (giantess), daughter of Bolthorn and sister of Mímir."

To adapt SRED^{FM}, we retained only the relation types present in the RelEx-PT dataset and restricted instances to texts with 4–10 sentences, to ensure contextual depth without excessive length. To address data imbalance, we capped the number of examples for high-frequency relations while preserving all examples of rarer ones, which helped improve the balance, though the dataset remains imbalanced. The most common relation is *country* (433 training, 58 testing triples), while the least is *production company* (21 training, 7 testing). Additionally, we divided the data into a 70/30 instance split, resulting in 2,100 training and 410 testing triples. After filtering, 16 of the original 18 relations remained, excluding *father* and *composer*, as they did not appear in any instance meeting the selection criteria. Finally, we removed duplicate triples within instances.

A broader concern in LLM-based evaluation is the potential for prior exposure to evaluation data, particularly when using publicly available datasets like SRED^{FM}. While we cannot confirm whether the dataset was included in any model's pretraining corpus, and it is difficult to estimate the actual impact of such exposure, it remains a possibility, especially given the broad, often opaque training data of large models. This limitation is acknowledged, and it highlights a key factor that is challenging to fully control in LLM research.

All five prompting strategies were initially evaluated on the RelEx-PT dataset. Based on their performance, the most effective prompts were then selected and applied to the SRED^{FM} dataset for further experimentation. This choice was motivated by the need to reduce computational cost and shorten the overall runtime, while focusing on the most promising strategies.

Whenever logically possible in the SRED^{FM} dataset, which can contain more than one triple per instance, we include multiple entity pairs within a single prompt and instruct the model to return one relation per line, preserving the order. This strategy avoids splitting instances into separate prompts, minimizing token repetition and reducing the number of API calls, thereby reducing costs both in terms of time and monetary resources. However, it is not applicable to all prompting formats, particularly QA-style prompts, without substantially altering their structure.

4.2 Models

The primary focus is on experimenting with a diverse group of generative LLMs, exploring how well the presented prompting techniques can be applied to RC in Portuguese. In contrast, we use BERTimbau base [18] and Albertina 100M

PTPT [16], Portuguese pretrained encoders based on BERT [6] and DeBERTa [8], respectively. These models serve as the reference baselines in this study, as we fine-tuned them on the datasets in a supervised setting.

Table 3 lists the models used, along with their number of parameters, versions and sources. For OpenAI's proprietary models, parameter counts are not publicly disclosed, but since GPT-4o is ChatGPTn's[4] main backend and a GPT-4 successor, we assume it to be among the largest LLMs. Meanwhile, GPT-4o-mini is likely a much more compressed version in terms of scale.

Table 3. Generative LLMs used in prompt-based inference.

Model	Parameters	Version	Source
gemma-2-2b-it [21]	2B	Full	Hugging Face[a] (Local)
Mistral-7B-Instruct-v0.3 [10]	7B	Full	OpenRouter[b] (API)
gemma-2-9b-it [21]	9B	Full	OpenRouter (API)
gemma-3-27b-it [20]	27B	Quantized (Q4)	Ollama[c] (Local)
Llama-3.3-70B-Instruct [14]	70B	Quantized (Q4)	Ollama (Local)
DeepSeek-V3-0324 [11]	685B	Full	OpenRouter (API)
GPT-4o [9]	N/A	Full	OpenAI[d] (API)
GPT-4o-mini [9]	N/A	Full	OpenAI (API)
BERTimbau Base [18]	110M	Full	Hugging Face (Local)
Albertina PTPT [16]	100M	Full	Hugging Face (Local)

[a]https://huggingface.co.
[b]https://openrouter.ai/.
[c]https://ollama.com/.
[d]https://platform.openai.com/.

The selected models represent a range of parameter sizes, enabling both a comparison between prompt-based and fine-tuned approaches, as well as an investigation into how model scale impacts performance. We also compare the effectiveness of open LLMs with that of proprietary, closed-source models.

5 Results and Discussion

We now present the results for both datasets, comparing prompting strategies across models and contrasting them with fine-tuned baselines. Key trends and differences are discussed below.

5.1 Results on the RelEx-PT Dataset

Table 4 presents the macro F1 scores obtained by each model using the five prompting strategies on the RelEx-PT dataset. We also report the results of fine-tuned BERTimbau and Albertina models for comparison.

---

[4] https://chatgpt.com/.

Table 4. Macro F1 Scores by Model and Method for the RelEx-PT dataset

Prompting Strategies

Model	Instruct	Descriptive	CoT	QA	Few-shot	Mean/Std
Gemma2-2B	0.63	0.46	0.19	0.64	0.39	0.46/0.17
Mistral-7B	0.71	0.80	0.06	0.74	0.58	0.58/0.27
Gemma2-9B	0.82	0.85	0.76	0.82	0.46	0.74/0.14
Gemma3-27B	0.82	**0.89**	0.86	0.76	0.86	0.84/0.04
Llama3.3-70B	0.83	0.82	0.84	0.81	0.68	0.80/0.06
DeepSeekV3	0.81	0.83	0.83	0.86	0.47	0.76/0.15
GPT-4o	0.77	0.87	0.82	**0.92**	0.82	0.84/0.05
GPT-4o-mini	0.77	**0.90**	0.75	0.78	0.72	0.78/0.06
Mean/Std	0.77/0.06	0.80/0.13	0.64/0.30	0.79/0.08	0.62/0.15	

Fine-tuning

BERTimbau	0.96					
Albertina	0.94					

Among open-source models, Gemma3 achieves the highest overall mean score, followed by Llama3.3 and DeepSeekV3, suggesting an interesting trend for this group, where larger models did not perform better. Gemma2-2B and Mistral have lower mean scores, with higher variance across prompting strategies, indicating that smaller models are more sensitive to prompt design. Notably, despite not being significantly larger than the two smallest models, Gemma2-9B performs much closer to the larger ones, with a mean score of 0.75. This highlights the role of architecture, training, and other improvements in the robustness of LLMs.

The proprietary GPT-4o and GPT-4o-mini perform competitively with or slightly better than the strongest open models. GPT-4o achieves the best single result (0.92) under the QA-style prompt, and GPT-4o-mini obtains the highest score under the Descriptive prompt (0.90). However, Gemma3, an open model, matches this overall performance, indicating that strong open LLMs can rival proprietary ones when sufficiently scaled and well-prompted.

Fine-tuned BERTimbau and Albertina outperform all prompt-based methods, reaching macro F1 scores of 0.96 and 0.94, respectively. This confirms the effectiveness of supervised learning when sufficient labeled data is available. It also highlights the potential of domain-specific fine-tuning for achieving high-accuracy RC in low-resource languages like Portuguese.

When averaging across models, the Descriptive prompt achieves the highest mean score, followed closely by QA-style and Instruct. These methods showed a significant gap in performance compared to the remaining two, which led to their selection for the experiments on the SRED^{FM} dataset. The distinction of the two best prompts suggests that instruction-tuned models can benefit from more descriptive prompting, potentially leveraging the added context to disambiguate fine-grained relations. CoT-style prompting, while beneficial for larger models, is less effective overall, likely due to increased complexity and verbosity. Few-shot prompting shows moderate results, with more stable performance in models like GPT-4o and Gemma3, though adding demonstrations is not always beneficial and can sometimes lead to diminishing returns.

5.2 Results on the SRED^{FM} Dataset

Table 5 presents the performance of the evaluated models, reporting weighted average F1 scores for both prompting and fine-tuning on the SRED^{FM} dataset.

Table 5. Weighted average F1 Scores by Model and Method for the SRED^{FM} dataset

Prompting Strategies				
Model	Instruct	Descriptive	QA	Mean/Std
Gemma2-2B	0.29	0.20	0.26	0.25/0.04
Mistral-7B	0.43	0.64	0.69	0.59/0.13
Gemma2-9B	0.38	0.45	0.77	0.53/0.19
Gemma3-27B	0.71	0.78	0.78	0.76/0.04
Llama3-70B	0.72	0.72	**0.83**	0.76/0.06
DeepSeekV3	0.63	0.73	0.80	0.72/0.08
GPT-4o	0.62	0.73	**0.82**	0.72/0.10
GPT-4o-mini	0.56	0.75	0.67	0.66/0.09
Mean/Std	0.54/0.16	0.63/0.20	0.70/0.18	
Fine-tuning				
BERTimbau	0.94			
Albertina	0.93			

Prompting performance did not scale linearly with model size. While larger models generally outperformed the smaller ones, the trend was not absolute. Gemma3 is mid-range in our size spectrum yet proves to be the most consistent performer, even on the challenging SRED^{FM} data. It outperformed the proprietary GPT-4o and the much larger DeepSeekV3 in some settings, indicating that defaulting to the largest models is not always the most effective strategy.

While the Descriptive prompt achieved the highest mean score on the RelEx-PT dataset, QA-style prompting performed better on SRED^{FM}, suggesting that more structured and constrained formulations are better suited to handling longer inputs. However, it is worth noting that the QA prompt could not be adapted to classify multiple triples per instance, requiring those cases to be split and processed separately, potentially affecting overall performance.

However, mean scores of the models are generally lower on this data, reflecting the increased difficulty posed by multi-sentence inputs and multiple relation candidates per instance, where more context must be tracked and disambiguated. For example, Gemma2-9B drops from 0.75 to 0.53 across datasets. Despite this, the top-performing models on RelEx-PT maintain robustness across both settings, reinforcing the importance of model selection and effective prompt design in consistently handling more complex RC tasks.

It is important to note that as generative LLMs increase in size, operating them demands high-end hardware or access to paid APIs, whereas fine-tuning compact encoder models such as our baselines is far more affordable. Our results show that these smaller, fine-tuned models consistently outperform all prompt-based approaches, and the gap becomes more evident on the noisier, multi-sentence SRED^{FM} dataset. This underscores the continued advantage of explicitly training models on labeled data for RE tasks. Recent studies have reached the same conclusion, highlighting that prompting strategies still do not match the capabilities of fine-tuning, not only in RE but also in other text classification tasks [2,19]. Meanwhile, prompt-based generative approaches, despite slightly lower overall accuracy, offer a simpler and adaptable alternative, especially in scenarios where annotated data is scarce.

5.3   Relation-Wise Performance Comparison

Table 6 presents a comparative analysis of F1 scores per relation between one of the most consistent prompting configurations (GPT-4o with QA prompt) and the best fine-tuned model, BERTimbau.

Table 6. F1 scores per relation for GPT-4o with the QA prompt and fine-tuned BERTimbau across both datasets used.

Relation	GPT-4o		BERTimbau	
	RelEx-PT	SRED^{FM}	RelEx-PT	SRED^{FM}
author	0.81	0.96	0.97	0.93
composer	0.72	–	0.98	–
country	1.00	0.86	0.97	0.97
developer	0.93	0.88	0.90	0.96
director	0.98	0.91	0.98	0.98
father	1.00	–	1.00	–
genre	0.87	0.72	0.94	0.96
headquarters location	1.00	0.76	0.98	0.95
instance of	0.78	0.56	0.89	0.85
located in or next to body of water	1.00	1.00	0.95	0.97
main subject	0.91	0.69	0.89	0.74
occupation	0.98	0.98	1.00	1.00
place of birth	1.00	0.93	1.00	0.98
production company	0.94	0.60	0.98	1.00
religion	1.00	0.95	0.98	0.92
sport	1.00	0.98	0.98	0.95
subclass of	0.68	0.17	0.84	0.86
taxon rank	0.98	0.92	0.95	1.00

The fine-tuned model demonstrates more consistent performance across relation types, particularly excelling in cases where precise semantic disambiguation is required, such as *subclass of* and *instance of.*

Notably, on the RelEx-PT dataset, GPT-4o shows a drop in performance for *author* and *composer*, which can be attributed to confusion between the two relations, likely due to their semantic proximity and overlapping usage in natural text. However, prompting remains competitive, especially for relations with more direct lexical cues, such as *occupation, located in or next to body of water*, and *sport*, where both methods perform equally well or with minimal differences.

The differences between prompting and fine-tuning become much more pronounced on the SRED^{FM} dataset, where the gap in performance is visible across most relations. While results were closer on RelEx-PT, the longer texts and denser relational structure of SRED^{FM} pose greater challenges for prompting, highlighting the robustness of fine-tuned models in more complex settings.

Nevertheless, these results achieved by GPT-4o reinforce the notion that prompting with large generative models can also yield impressive results when guided by well-structured prompts like QA formulations, especially considering that the model is not exposed to any training data.

6   Conclusion and Future Work

In this work, we explored RC using prompting techniques with generative LLMs, aiming to extract structured information from Portuguese text. We evaluated a variety of prompting strategies using both open and closed generative LLMs, ranging from the smaller Gemma2 model with 2 billion parameters to the larger DeepSeekV3 model with 685 billion parameters. As a baseline, we also fine-tuned two Portuguese encoder-only models, BERTimbau and Albertina, on the datasets used in this study.

Despite having only around 100 million parameters, the fine-tuned models outperformed the larger generative ones, confirming the strength of supervised adaptation when labeled data is available. This was particularly noteworthy as prompting-based models experienced a significant drop in performance with the increased complexity of the SRED^{FM} dataset, while fine-tuned models maintained consistently high scores. We highlight a practical trade-off: fine-tuning delivers superior accuracy and robustness, making it highly suitable for RC tasks, whereas prompting enables competitive performance without the need for a dedicated training process, relying solely on inference.

In the future, we plan to publicly release the RelEx-PT dataset and integrate RC with entity recognition for a complete triple extraction process. We then intend to create KGs with the extracted triples, enabling a fully automated end-to-end pipeline from Portuguese text to structured human-interpretable knowledge.

Acknowledgments. This work is financed through national funds by FCT - Fundação para a Ciência e a Tecnologia, I.P., in the framework of the Project UIDB/00326/2025 and UIDP/00326/2025; and by the Portuguese Recovery and Resilience Plan (PRR) through project C645008882-00000055, Center for Responsible AI.

Disclosure of Interests. The authors have no competing interests to declare that are relevant to the content of this article.

References

1. Achiam, J., et al.: GPT-4 technical report. arXiv preprint arXiv:2303.08774 (2023)
2. Bucher, M.J.J., Martini, M.: Fine-tuned 'small' LLMs (still) significantly outperform zero-shot generative AI models in text classification. arXiv preprint arXiv:2406.08660 (2024)
3. Cabot, P.L.H., Tedeschi, S., Ngomo, A.C.N., Navigli, R.: RED FM: a filtered and multilingual relation extraction dataset. arXiv preprint arXiv:2306.09802 (2023)
4. Cabral, B., Claro, D., Souza, M.: Exploring open information extraction for Portuguese using large language models. In: Proceedings of 16th International Conference on Computational Processing of Portuguese (PROPOR), pp. 127–136 (2024)
5. Chaves Rodrigues, R.: Lessons learned from the evaluation of Portuguese language models. Master's thesis, University of Malta (2023)
6. Devlin, J., Chang, M.W., Lee, K., Toutanova, K.: BERT: pre-training of deep bidirectional transformers for language understanding. In: Proceedings of 2019 Conference of the North American Chapter of the Association for Computational Linguistics: Human Language Technologies, pp. 4171–4186. ACL (2019)
7. Dubey, A., et al.: The Llama 3 herd of models. arXiv preprint arXiv:2407.21783 (2024)
8. He, P., Liu, X., Gao, J., Chen, W.: DeBERTa: decoding-enhanced bert with disentangled attention. arXiv preprint arXiv:2006.03654 (2020)
9. Hurst, A., et al.: GPT-4o system card. arXiv preprint arXiv:2410.21276 (2024)
10. Jiang, A.Q., et al.: Mistral 7b (2023). https://arxiv.org/abs/2310.06825
11. Liu, A., et al.: DeepSeek-V3 technical report. arXiv preprint arXiv:2412.19437 (2024)
12. Lucena, A.D.L.: Utilizando extração de relação entre entidades para detecção de informações pessoais sensíveis em português. Trabalho de conclusão de curso (bacharelado), Universidade Federal de Campina Grande (2024)
13. Ma, X., Li, J., Zhang, M.: Chain of thought with explicit evidence reasoning for few-shot relation extraction. arXiv preprint arXiv:2311.05922 (2023)
14. Meta: Llama 3.3 Model Card. https://github.com/meta-llama/llama-models/blob/main/models/llama3_3/MODEL_CARD.md (2024)
15. Rodrigues, F.B., Giozza, W.F., de Oliveira Albuquerque, R., Villalba, L.J.G.: Natural language processing applied to forensics information extraction with transformers and graph visualization. IEEE Trans. Comput. Social Syst. (2022)
16. Santos, R., et al.: Fostering the ecosystem of open neural encoders for Portuguese with Albertina PT* family (2024)
17. Silva, G., Rodrigues, M., Teixeira, A., Amorim, M.: Advancing open information extraction for Portuguese by leveraging graph structures and large language models. In: IberSPEECH 2024, pp. 61–65 (2024)

18. Souza, F., Nogueira, R., Lotufo, R.: BERTimbau: pretrained BERT models for Brazilian Portuguese. In: 9th Brazilian Conference on Intelligent Systems, BRACIS, Rio Grande do Sul, Brazil, October 20-23 (to appear) (2020)
19. Susanti, Y., Holsmoelle, N.: Prompting or fine-tuning? exploring large language models for causal graph validation (2025). https://arxiv.org/abs/2406.16899
20. Team, G., et al.: Gemma 3 technical report. arXiv preprint arXiv:2503.19786 (2025)
21. Team, G., et al.: Gemma 2: improving open language models at a practical size. arXiv preprint arXiv:2408.00118 (2024)
22. Wan, Z., et al.: GPT-RE: In-context learning for relation extraction using large language models. arXiv preprint arXiv:2305.02105 (2023)
23. Wang, Y., Zhao, Y.: Metacognitive prompting improves understanding in large language models. arXiv preprint arXiv:2308.05342 (2023)
24. Xu, D., et al.: Large language models for generative information extraction: a survey. Front. Comp. Sci. **18**(6), 186357 (2024)
25. Yang, J., et al.: Harnessing the power of LLMs in practice: a survey on chatgpt and beyond. ACM Trans. Knowl. Discov. Data **18**(6), 1–32 (2024)
26. Zhang, K., Gutiérrez, B.J., Su, Y.: Aligning instruction tasks unlocks large language models as zero-shot relation extractors. arXiv preprint arXiv:2305.11159 (2023)
27. Zhang, Q., Chen, M., Liu, L.: A review on entity relation extraction. In: 2017 2nd International Conference on Mechanical, Control and Computer Engineering (ICMCCE), pp. 178–183. IEEE (2017)
28. Zhao, X., et al.: A comprehensive survey on relation extraction: recent advances and new frontiers. ACM Comput. Surv. **56**(11), 1–39 (2024)
29. Zhong, L., Wu, J., Li, Q., Peng, H., Wu, X.: A comprehensive survey on automatic knowledge graph construction. ACM Comput. Surv. **56**(4), 1–62 (2023)
30. Zhong, Z., Chen, D.: A frustratingly easy approach for entity and relation extraction. arXiv preprint arXiv:2010.12812 (2020)

Cross-Lingual Information Retrieval in Tetun for Ad-Hoc Search

Altedio Araújo[1] , Gabriel de Jesus[2]([✉]) , and Sérgio Nunes[2]

[1] School of Management and Technology, Polytechnic of Porto (ESTG),
Felgueiras, Portugal
8220759@estg.ipp.pt
[2] INESC TEC/Faculty of Engineering, University of Porto (FEUP), Porto, Portugal
gabriel.jesus@inesctec.pt, sergio.nunes@fe.up.pt

Abstract. Developing information retrieval (IR) systems that enable access across multiple languages is crucial in multilingual contexts. In Timor-Leste, where Tetun, Portuguese, English, and Indonesian are official and working languages, no cross-lingual information retrieval (CLIR) solutions currently exist to support information access across these languages. This study addresses that gap by investigating CLIR approaches tailored to the linguistic landscape of Timor-Leste. Leveraging an existing monolingual Tetun document collection and ad-hoc text retrieval baselines, we explore the feasibility of CLIR for Tetun. Queries were manually translated into Portuguese, English, and Indonesian to create a multilingual query set. These were then automatically translated back into Tetun using Google Translate and several large language models, and used to retrieve documents in Tetun. Results show that Google Translate is the most reliable tool for Tetun CLIR overall, and the Hiemstra LM consistently outperforms BM25 and DFR BM25 in cross-lingual retrieval performance. However, overall effectiveness remains up to 26.95% points lower than that of the monolingual baseline, underscoring the limitations of current translation tools and the challenges of developing an effective CLIR for Tetun. Despite these challenges, this work establishes the first CLIR baseline for Tetun ad-hoc text retrieval, providing a foundation for future research in this under-resourced setting.

Keywords: Cross-lingual information retrieval · Tetun · Ad-hoc text retrieval · Low-resource language

1 Introduction

Cross-lingual information retrieval (CLIR) systems are essential for enabling users to submit queries in one language and retrieve relevant documents written in another. Such systems are particularly valuable in linguistically diverse contexts, such as Timor-Leste. As a multilingual country, Timor-Leste designates Tetun and Portuguese as its official languages, and English and Indonesian as working languages [27], with over 30 dialects spoken across the territory [7].

© The Author(s), under exclusive license to Springer Nature Switzerland AG 2026
J. Valente de Oliveira et al. (Eds.): EPIA 2025, LNAI 16122, pp. 262–275, 2026.
https://doi.org/10.1007/978-3-032-05179-0_20

Within this complex linguistic landscape, CLIR becomes a crucial tool for facilitating access to information across these languages.

A classical CLIR system typically consists of a translation step followed by monolingual retrieval [29]. Two primary translation strategies are commonly employed: **query translation**, where the user's query is translated into the language of the documents, and **document translation**, where documents are translated into the language of the query [18,30]. Query translation is generally more efficient and conducive to rapid experimentation, whereas document translation can be computationally expensive and time-intensive, especially when translating an entire corpus [16,24].

Tetun, a dialect that became one of the official languages following the country's restoration of independence from Indonesia in 2002, remains under-resourced, with few algorithms and tools available to support the language. Notably, the first initiative focused on Tetun text information retrieval (IR) began in 2022 [7,8], leading to the creation of foundational resources for IR and natural language processing (NLP) [10–12], including a test collection and baselines for the ad-hoc text retrieval task [9].

Building on these efforts, and given the lack of existing CLIR for Tetun, this study explores the effectiveness of CLIR for retrieving Tetun documents using queries in Portuguese, English, and Indonesian. Results from this study are compared against existing monolingual Tetun ad-hoc text retrieval baselines [9] to evaluate the performance of CLIR for Tetun. This study is guided by the following research questions (RQs):

RQ1: How does the quality of query translation influence the effectiveness of Tetun ad-hoc text retrieval?
RQ2: How does the effectiveness of CLIR compare to that of monolingual retrieval in Tetun?

To address these RQs, we first manually translated the original Tetun queries from *Labadain-Avaliadór* [12] into Portuguese, English, and Indonesian, resulting in a multilingual query set. These translated queries served as input to the CLIR system for retrieving documents in Tetun. To enable retrieval, the multilingual queries were automatically translated back into Tetun using both Google Translate and large language models (LLMs) before being submitted to the Tetun monolingual retrieval system.

To respond to RQ1, we evaluate the quality of the translated queries using the BLEU metric [20], with the original Tetun queries serving as reference texts. This RQ aims to examine whether translation quality directly influences the effectiveness of the CLIR system. For RQ2, we compare the retrieval performance of the CLIR system to the established monolingual baselines, evaluating effectiveness using P@10, MAP@10, and NDCG@10 for each source language.

The findings provide initial insights into the feasibility of CLIR for Tetun, demonstrating the impact of translation quality on retrieval effectiveness. This highlights the potential of machine translation-based query methods to enhance the performance of Tetun ad-hoc text retrieval.

The remainder of this paper is organized as follows. Section 2 reviews the background and related work. Section 3 presents the methodology, followed by the CLIR experimental setup in Sect. 4. Section 5 reports the evaluation and results, which are further discussed in Sect. 6. Finally, Sect. 7 summarizes the main conclusion and outlines directions for future work.

2   Background and Related Work

Tetun is an Austronesian language spoken in Timor-Leste, an island country in Southeast Asia. Historically used as a lingua franca in trade and religious activities, Tetun became one of Timor-Leste's official languages when the country restored its independence in May 2002. It is a low-resource language spoken by approximately 79% of the country's 1.18 million population, according to the 2015 census [6,10]. The development of Tetun IR and NLP algorithms and tools began in 2022 [8], leading to the creation of key resources, including a text dataset [11] and a test collection with baselines for the ad-hoc text retrieval task [9]. These tools and resources provide the essential foundation for investigating CLIR in Tetun.

CLIR has been extensively studied, with several works exploring its application to low-resource languages (LRLs). Adeyemi et al. [2] conducted CLIR experiments covering several African languages, including Hausa, Somali, Swahili, and Yoruba, using English queries. Their study investigated both manual and automatic query translation from English into the target languages, and automatic translation of documents into English. For query translation, they used Google Translate, and reported that human-translated queries retrieved using BM25 outperformed automatically translated ones by 5.78% points in NDCG@20. In the CLEF 2009 track [4], the use of Google Translate for query translation significantly improved cross-lingual retrieval performance. Similarly, a study focusing on English to Chinese retrieval showed that translating queries using Google Translate could achieve performance comparable to monolingual baselines, particularly when queries are longer [28].

Several studies have explored the use of LLMs for query translation in CLIR. Adeyemi et al. [1] investigated the effectiveness of LLMs for query translation by adopting zero-shot prompting with GPT-3.5 and GPT-4 to translate English queries into Hausa, Somali, Swahili, and Yoruba. The translation quality was evaluated using BLEU [20], and GPT-4 achieved the highest scores for all languages. Similarly, Valentini et al. [26] translated both queries and documents from English to French using zero-shot prompting with GPT-4o-mini and LLaMA-3.2, evaluating translation quality using several metrics, including BLEU. For document translation, GPT-4o-mini achieved a higher BLEU score than LLaMA-3.2 and was subsequently used for query translation. For retrieval, BM25 was used, and document translation with GPT-4o-mini achieved better performance than LLaMA-3.2 in terms of Recall@100 and NDCG@10.

Pecina et al. [21] investigated CLIR in the medical domain, focusing on improving query translation quality and examining its impact on retrieval effectiveness. They used Moses [13], a phrase-based statistical machine translation system trained on medical domain data, and compared its performance with Google Translate and Microsoft Bing Translator. Retrieval was conducted in English using the CLEF eHealth 2013 collection, while the original queries (written in Czech, German, and French) were translated into English. In terms of translation quality, Moses outperformed both Google Translate and Microsoft Bing Translator. For retrieval, Moses maintained superior performance compared to Bing Translator in Czech to English translation at P@10, but it did not consistently outperform Google Translate across all input languages. Overall, the authors reported that higher BLEU scores in translation did not lead to improved retrieval effectiveness.

Likewise, Lignos et al. [15] examined the relationship between machine translation quality and retrieval effectiveness in CLIR for Czech and German, focusing on document translation. In their study, queries were written in English, and documents in Czech and German were translated into English. In line with the findings of Pecina et al. [21], higher BLEU scores in document translation did not enhance retrieval performance.

Building on this foundation, and given recent advancements in LLMs and the inclusion of Tetun to Google Translate,[1] new opportunities have emerged to explore the applicability of these approaches to Tetun. In this study, we evaluate the application of Google Translate alongside several LLMs to assess their effectiveness in translating queries into Tetun and compare their performance against established monolingual Tetun IR baselines.

3 Methodology

To investigate CLIR for Tetun, we use *Labadain-Avaliadór* [12], a Tetun test collection for the ad-hoc text retrieval task, which contains 33,500 documents, 59 queries, and 5,900 relevance judgments (qrels) [9]. The study began by manually translating Tetun queries into Portuguese, English, and Indonesian. The translations were conducted by three native Tetun-speaking volunteer students, each responsible for a single target language in which they are fluent. The process followed established guidelines, including specific instructions to preserve abbreviations and named entities, resulting in a multilingual query set.

These multilingual queries are subsequently used as input for retrieval. During the query processing phase, the input queries are automatically translated back into Tetun using Google Translate and LLMs, including GPT-4.5, DeepSeek-Chat, Claude 3.7 Sonnet, and LLaMA 3.3 70B. To assess translation quality, the outputs are evaluated using the BLEU metric [20], with the original Tetun queries serving as reference texts.

The translated queries are then used for retrieval. To enable performance comparison, we adopt the best-performing retrieval strategy previously reported in monolingual Tetun ad-hoc text retrieval. The retrieval and ranking models used in the experiments are BM25 [23], DFR BM25 [3], and the Hiemstra language model (LM) [22]. These models are evaluated using Precision, MAP, and

---

[1] https://blog.google/products/translate/google-translate-new-languages-2024/.

NDCG at rank ten ($k = 10$) for each input query in English, Portuguese, and Indonesian. Results from CLIR are compared to the monolingual Tetun ad-hoc text retrieval baselines [9] to assess their relative performance.

4   Experimental Setup

The experiments are organized into two parts: query translation and cross-lingual retrieval. Three query translation strategies were evaluated: Google Translate, LLMs with zero-shot prompting, and LLMs with few-shot prompting using one example. The experimental setup for each configuration is described below.

4.1   Query Translations

Query translation using Google Translate follows the official documentation and default settings of the basic translation endpoint[2] provided by the Google Translate API. For LLM-based translations, the same prompt is used across all models, with the temperature set to zero to ensure deterministic outputs.

The prompt used to instruct the LLMs was compiled based on best practices for prompting translation models [1,5,25].[3] Details of the zero-shot prompting are presented in Prompt 4.1.

Prompt 4.1. Zero-shot prompt used for query translation with LLMs

You are an expert translator. Your task is to translate the following user search query from *{source_ lang}* into Tetun.

Query: *{query}*

Translate the query accurately, using the official grammar of Tetun and correct vocabulary. Return only the translation and do not include any additional text.

For few-shot prompting, we used the same base prompt as in the zero-shot setting, with one example query and its corresponding translation in each target language included in the prompt for each LLM call. The additional instruction appended to the base prompt is shown below:

Refer to the example below to guide your translation:

{source_ lang} query: *{example_ query}*
Tetun translation: *{example_ translation}*

---

[2] https://cloud.google.com/translate/docs/reference/rest/v2/translate.
[3] https://docs.anthropic.com/en/resources/prompt-library/polyglot-superpowers.

4.2   Cross-Lingual Retrieval

For retrieval, we employed the monolingual Tetun ad-hoc text retrieval framework adopted by de Jesus and Nunes [9]. We used PyTerrier [17], a Python API for the Terrier IR platform [19], for indexing, retrieval, and ranking, using the default settings for each retrieval model. This setup indexes only the document titles and applies uniform preprocessing to both queries and titles, including lowercasing and the removal of punctuation, special characters, apostrophes, and hyphens. All queries translated from Portuguese, English, and Indonesian into Tetun, using each of the translation techniques described in Subsect. 4.1, were employed for retrieval and evaluated using *Labadain-Avaliadór* [12].

5   Evaluation and Results

The evaluation focuses on the quality of query translations and the effectiveness of CLIR compared to monolingual Tetun ad-hoc text retrieval. Translation quality was measured using BLEU [20], while retrieval effectiveness was assessed at P@10, MAP@10, and NDCG@10. The evaluation results are shown in Table 1.

Table 1. BLEU scores for translation quality from Portuguese (Pt), English (En), and Indonesian (Id) into Tetun (Tdt).

Model	Zero-Shot			Few-Shot		
	PT-Tdt	En-Tdt	Id-Tdt	Pt-Tdt	En-Tdt	Id-Tdt
Google Translate	**0.4659**	0.4530	0.5636	-	-	-
GPT-4.5-preview	0.4156	**0.4882**	0.6038	0.4215	0.4156	0.4616
DeepSeek-Chat	0.3655	0.3762	0.5091	0.4634	0.4183	0.4994
Claude-3.7 Sonnet	0.4602	0.4649	**0.6256**	**0.5378**	**0.5412**	**0.6425**
LLaMA-3.3 70B	0.3566	0.3184	0.4172	0.3704	0.3122	0.4033

As observed, under the zero-shot setting, BLEU scores varied across source languages and models. Google Translate achieved the highest score for Portuguese-to-Tetun translation, GPT-4.5 performed best for English-to-Tetun, and Claude 3.7 Sonnet achieved the highest score for Indonesian-to-Tetun. In the few-shot setting, Claude 3.7 Sonnet recorded the highest BLEU scores for all languages.

When comparing BLEU scores from few-shot and zero-shot LLM-based translations, the following results are observed: (1) **Portuguese-to-Tetun:** translation quality improved across all models in the few-shot setting, with gains of up to +9.79% points; (2) **English-to-Tetun:** results varied by model, performance dropped for GPT-4.5-preview and LLaMA-3.3 70B by up to -7.25% points, while DeepSeek-Chat and Claude 3.7 Sonnet showed improvements of up to +7.63% points; and (3) **Indonesian-to-Tetun:** only Claude 3.7 Sonnet showed an improvement (+1.69% points), while the other models experienced performance drops of up to -14.22% points.

Regarding the evaluation of retrieval performance, results using zero-shot query translations are presented in Table 2. The findings show that translating input queries with Google Translate, followed by retrieval and ranking using the Hiemstra LM, generally outperformed the LLM-based approaches. An exception was observed in Portuguese-to-Tetun translation, where LLMs achieved higher scores at P@10 and MAP@10. Nevertheless, all CLIR results remained significantly below the performance of the monolingual Tetun IR baselines, by up to -26.95% points for Portuguese-to-Tetun translation, -25.93 for English-to-Tetun, and -23.22 for Indonesian-to-Tetun.

Evaluating the retrieval performance for few-shot prompting with one example per language, Claude 3.7 Sonnet outperformed all other models across all languages and metrics, as shown in Table 3. Compared to the zero-shot results, providing one example per LLM call for Portuguese-to-Tetun translation improved retrieval performance by up to +0.93% points. In contrast, for English-to-Tetun, the inclusion of an example resulted in a performance drop of up to -2.21% points. For Indonesian-to-Tetun, the differences were marginal: a slight performance drop in P@10 and NDCG@10 (up to -0.63% points), while MAP@10 showed a small gain of +0.29% points.

6   Discussion

The effectiveness of CLIR in Tetun varies depending on the translation model and the prompting strategy applied to LLMs. In the zero-shot setting, Google Translate consistently demonstrated stronger retrieval performance overall, particularly for Indonesian-to-Tetun query translation. When paired with the Hiemstra LM, it achieved the highest scores among all zero-shot configurations evaluated. The effectiveness of Google Translate for query translation in CLIR for Tetun aligns with findings from the CLEF 2009 track [4], where its use substantially improved CLIR performance. Likewise, studies on English-to-Chinese CLIR reported retrieval results only marginally lower than monolingual ones when Google Translate was employed for query translation [28].

Under the few-shot configuration, Claude 3.7 Sonnet showed the strongest retrieval performance for all languages, consistent with its strong zero-shot performance in Portuguese-to-Tetun translation, particularly at P@10 and MAP@10. For Portuguese-to-Tetun query translation, few-shot prompting led to a marginal improvement of up to +0.93% points compared to the zero-shot setting. However, for English and Indonesian queries, even when the example was provided, LLM-based translations did not surpass the retrieval performance using Google Translate. These results underscore the effectiveness of Google Translate as a reliable translation tool for CLIR in Tetun under zero-shot settings.

Table 2. Effectiveness of CLIR using zero-shot translated queries compared to the monolingual baseline. Values in **bold** indicate the best CLIR performance for each source language. The baseline, highlighted in orange , indicates the overall best performance across all retrieval metrics.

Translation	Language	Model	P@10	MAP@10	NDCG@10
Baseline	Tetun	DFR BM25	0.8390	0.2804	0.7356
Google Translate	Portuguese - Tetun	BM25	0.5559	0.1659	0.4934
		DFR BM25	0.5576	0.1661	0.4931
		Hiemstra LM	0.5576	0.1706	**0.4914**
	English - Tetun	BM25	0.5712	0.1633	0.4937
		DFR BM25	0.5695	0.1634	0.4907
		Hiemstra LM	**0.5797**	**0.1694**	**0.4971**
	Indonesian - Tetun	BM25	0.6000	0.1861	0.5216
		DFR BM25	0.6017	0.1865	0.5226
		Hiemstra LM	**0.6068**	**0.1893**	**0.5237**
GPT-4.5-preview	Portuguese - Tetun	BM25	0.4864	0.1472	0.4230
		DFR BM25	0.4881	0.1474	0.4235
		Hiemstra LM	0.4983	0.1565	0.4257
	English - Tetun	BM25	0.4966	0.1463	0.4161
		DFR BM25	0.4966	0.1467	0.4155
		Hiemstra LM	0.4847	0.1497	0.4149
	Indonesian - Tetun	BM25	0.5407	0.1646	0.4576
		DFR BM25	0.5424	0.1654	0.4582
		Hiemstra LM	0.5339	0.1614	0.4495
DeepSeek-Chat	Portuguese - Tetun	BM25	0.4407	0.1246	0.3739
		DFR BM25	0.4407	0.1247	0.3734
		Hiemstra LM	0.4441	0.1262	0.3754
	English - Tetun	BM25	0.4373	0.1329	0.3695
		DFR BM25	0.4373	0.1337	0.3686
		Hiemstra LM	0.4407	0.1364	0.3719
	Indonesian - Tetun	BM25	0.5000	0.1490	0.4232
		DFR BM25	0.5000	0.1491	0.4222
		Hiemstra LM	0.4932	0.1439	0.4139
Claude-3.7 Sonnet	Portuguese - Tetun	BM25	0.5475	0.1678	0.4763
		DFR BM25	0.5508	0.1689	0.4774
		Hiemstra LM	**0.5695**	**0.1779**	0.4912
	English - Tetun	BM25	0.5678	0.1571	0.4656
		DFR BM25	0.5627	0.1563	0.4624
		Hiemstra LM	0.5610	0.1625	0.4717
	Indonesian - Tetun	BM25	0.5763	0.1868	0.4910
		DFR BM25	0.5797	0.1879	0.4920
		Hiemstra LM	0.5763	0.1833	0.4890
LLaMA-3.3 70B	Portuguese - Tetun	BM25	0.3831	0.1060	0.3197
		DFR BM25	0.3814	0.1060	0.3185
		Hiemstra LM	0.3729	0.0990	0.3014
	English - Tetun	BM25	0.3508	0.0896	0.2896
		DFR BM25	0.3508	0.0899	0.2887
		Hiemstra LM	0.3525	0.0921	0.2936
	Indonesian - Tetun	BM25	0.3763	0.1149	0.3045
		DFR BM25	0.3763	0.1145	0.3040
		Hiemstra LM	0.3780	0.1139	0.3043

Table 3. Effectiveness of CLIR using few-shot translated queries compared to the monolingual baseline. Values in **bold** indicate the best CLIR performance for each source language. The baseline, highlighted in orange , indicates the overall best performance across all retrieval metrics.

Translation	Language	Model	P@10	MAP@10	NDCG@10
Baseline	Tetun	DFR BM25	0.8390	0.2804	0.7356
GPT-4.5-preview	Portuguese - Tetun	BM25	0.4373	0.1282	0.3755
		DFR BM25	0.4373	0.1283	0.3742
		Hiemstra LM	0.4458	0.1335	0.3775
	English - Tetun	BM25	0.4508	0.1291	0.3696
		DFR BM25	0.4492	0.1287	0.3684
		Hiemstra LM	0.4542	0.1313	0.3738
	Indonesian - Tetun	BM25	0.4847	0.1406	0.4050
		DFR BM25	0.4847	0.1406	0.4050
		Hiemstra LM	0.4627	0.1323	0.3847
DeepSeek-Chat	Portuguese - Tetun	BM25	0.4915	0.1509	0.4253
		DFR BM25	0.4932	0.1513	0.4252
		Hiemstra LM	0.5000	0.1527	0.4321
	English - Tetun	BM25	0.4746	0.1354	0.3921
		DFR BM25	0.4729	0.1353	0.3911
		Hiemstra LM	0.4576	0.1330	0.3850
	Indonesian - Tetun	BM25	0.5237	0.1648	0.4454
		DFR BM25	0.5237	0.1648	0.4443
		Hiemstra LM	0.5220	0.1615	0.4376
Claude-3.7 Sonnet	Portuguese - Tetun	BM25	0.5661	0.1692	0.4987
		DFR BM25	0.5695	0.1713	0.5011
		Hiemstra LM	**0.5797**	**0.1787**	**0.5091**
	English - Tetun	BM25	0.5576	0.1612	0.4702
		DFR BM25	0.5593	0.1628	0.4700
		Hiemstra LM	**0.5661**	**0.1685**	**0.4750**
	Indonesian - Tetun	BM25	0.6034	0.1914	0.5168
		DFR BM25	**0.6051**	**0.1922**	**0.5174**
		Hiemstra LM	0.5949	0.1859	0.5070
LLaMA-3.3 70B	Portuguese - Tetun	BM25	0.3729	0.1096	0.2940
		DFR BM25	0.3729	0.1103	0.2934
		Hiemstra LM	0.3661	0.1068	0.2869
	English - Tetun	BM25	0.3271	0.0769	0.2623
		DFR BM25	0.3271	0.0768	0.2615
		Hiemstra LM	0.3254	0.0779	0.2643
	Indonesian - Tetun	BM25	0.3729	0.1096	0.2940
		DFR BM25	0.3729	0.1103	0.2934
		Hiemstra LM	0.3661	0.1068	0.2869

When examining the relationship between translation quality and retrieval effectiveness, we observed findings consistent with those reported in the literature. For instance, although Google Translate achieved the highest BLEU score for Portuguese-to-Tetun translation (see Table 1), it was outperformed by Claude 3.7 Sonnet in retrieval effectiveness, as shown in Table 2. Similarly, while GPT-4.5-preview achieved the highest BLEU score for English-to-Tetun translation, it yielded lower retrieval performance compared to Google Translate. One possible explanation is that retrieval effectiveness depends not only on translation quality but also on how well the translated queries align with document representations and how effectively the retrieval and ranking models process those queries. Factors such as vocabulary overlap and model-specific ranking behavior may influence retrieval outcomes in ways that BLEU scores do not capture. These findings address RQ1, suggesting that higher translation quality—as measured by BLEU—does not always lead to improved retrieval performance in CLIR. This observation aligns with prior studies by Pecina et al. [21] and Lignos et al. [15], both of which reported similar discrepancies between translation quality and retrieval performance across various domains and language pairs.

When comparing CLIR performance with the monolingual Tetun baselines, addressing RQ2, results remain significantly lower than those achieved by monolingual retrieval. This gap may be explained by the limitations in the translation models' capabilities. Notably, Google Translate only recently added support for Tetun, and the limited number of Tetun documents on the web as of 2023 [10, 14] further constrains the ability of LLMs to process the language effectively.

Limitations and Potential Biases: The volunteer translators are students, and not all have formal training in linguistics, which may affect the overall quality of the human translations. Additionally, no systematic validation of translation quality was conducted, potentially introducing errors or inconsistencies in the translated queries. Another limitation is the short length of the queries (between three and five words), which provides limited context and may hinder accurate translation, particularly in linguistically ambiguous cases. Furthermore, the translators' backgrounds, language preferences, and interpretation styles may introduce bias into how certain terms or phrases are translated across languages.

7   Conclusions and Future Work

This study explored the feasibility and effectiveness of CLIR for Tetun, an under-resourced language, by automatically translating queries from Portuguese, English, and Indonesian using both Google Translate and LLMs. The findings reveal several key insights.

First, despite advances in multilingual technologies, CLIR performance for Tetun remains significantly below that of monolingual retrieval. This highlights the ongoing challenges of supporting LRLs in information access tasks. Second, while LLMs show promise in handling a variety of tasks, including translation, their effectiveness is highly dependent on the source language and their familiarity with or knowledge of the target language. In some cases, traditional machine translation tools like Google Translate prove more reliable, particularly when newly supporting a language like Tetun.

Most critically, our study reveals that translation quality—as measured by standard metrics such as BLEU—does not correlate with retrieval effectiveness. This finding aligns with prior research [15, 21] and suggests the need to move beyond translation-centric metrics when evaluating CLIR systems. Retrieval success depends not only on linguistic translation accuracy but also on how well translated queries align with document representations and the retrieval models.

In future work, we aim to explore more effective CLIR systems for languages like Tetun by going beyond improvements in translation techniques. Our focus will include expanding Tetun's digital footprint and rethinking retrieval strategies to better reflect its linguistic characteristics and resource constraints. We will also employ other translation evaluation metrics, such as ROUGE and METEOR, to more accurately assess translation quality and examine its correlation with retrieval effectiveness.

Acknowledgments. We thank Luisa Carlos, Zeferina da Graça, and Lara da Costa for translating the Tetun queries into English, Portuguese, and Indonesian, respectively. This work is financed by national funds through FCT - Fundação para a Ciência e a Tecnologia, under the support UID/50014/2023 (DOI: 10.54499/UID/50014/2023). Gabriel de Jesus is supported by the Ph.D. studentship grant SFRH/BD/151437/2021, also from FCT (DOI: 10.54499/SFRH/BD/151437/2021).

Disclosure of Interests. The authors have no competing interests to declare that are relevant to the content of this article.

References

1. Adeyemi, M., Oladipo, A., Pradeep, R., Lin, J.: Zero-shot cross-lingual reranking with large language models for low-resource languages. In: Proceedings of the 62nd Annual Meeting of the Association for Computational Linguistics, ACL 2024 - Short Papers, Bangkok, Thailand, 11–16 August 2024, pp. 650–656. Association for Computational Linguistics (2024). https://aclanthology.org/2024.acl-short.59
2. Adeyemi, M., et al.: CIRAL: a test collection for CLIR evaluations in African languages. In: Yang, G.H., Wang, H., Han, S., Hauff, C., Zuccon, G., Zhang, Y. (eds.) Proceedings of the 47th International ACM SIGIR Conference on Research and Development in Information Retrieval, SIGIR 2024, Washington DC, USA, 14–18 July 2024, pp. 293–302. ACM (2024). https://doi.org/10.1145/3626772.3657884
3. Amati, G., van Rijsbergen, C.J.: Probabilistic models of information retrieval based on measuring the divergence from randomness. ACM Trans. Inf. Syst. **20**(4), 357–389 (2002). https://doi.org/10.1145/582415.582416
4. Ferro, N., Peters, C.: CLEF 2009 ad hoc track overview: TEL and persian tasks. In: Peters, C., et al. (eds.) Multilingual Information Access Evaluation I. Text Retrieval Experiments, 10th Workshop of the Cross-Language Evaluation Forum, CLEF 2009, Corfu, Greece, 30 September– 2 October 2009, Revised Selected Papers. Lecture Notes in Computer Science, vol. 6241, pp. 13–35. Springer (2009). https://www.dei.unipd.it/~ferro/papers/2010/CLEF2009Proc-adhoc.pdf

5. He, S.: Prompting chatgpt for translation: a comparative analysis of translation brief and persona prompts. In: Scarton, C., et al. (eds.) Proceedings of the 25th Annual Conference of the European Association for Machine Translation (Volume 1), EAMT 2024, Sheffield, UK, 24–27 June 2024, pp. 316–326. European Association for Machine Translation (EAMT) (2024). https://aclanthology.org/2024.eamt-1.27

6. Instituto Nacional de Estatística Timor-Leste (INETL): Census 2015 priority table population by language (2015). https://inetl-ip.gov.tl/2023/03/09/census-2015-priority-table-population-by-language/. Accessed 17 Mar 2024

7. de Jesus, G.: Text information retrieval in Tetun. In: Kamps, J., et al. (eds.) Advances in Information Retrieval - 45th European Conference on Information Retrieval, ECIR 2023, Dublin, Ireland, 2–6 April 2023, Proceedings, Part III. Lecture Notes in Computer Science, vol. 13982, pp. 429–435. Springer (2023). https://doi.org/10.1007/978-3-031-28241-6_48

8. de Jesus, G.: Text information retrieval in Tetun: a preliminary study. CoRR (2024). https://doi.org/10.48550/ARXIV.2406.07331

9. de Jesus, G., Nunes, S.: Establishing a foundation for Tetun text ad-hoc retrieval: indexing, stemming, retrieval, and ranking. CoRR (2024). https://doi.org/10.48550/ARXIV.2412.11758

10. de Jesus, G., Nunes, S.: Labadain-30k+: a monolingual Tetun document-level audited dataset. In: Melero, M., Sakti, S., Soria, C. (eds.) Proceedings of the 3rd Annual Meeting of the Special Interest Group on Under-resourced Languages @ LREC-COLING 2024, pp. 177–188. ELRA and ICCL, Torino, Italia (2024). https://aclanthology.org/2024.sigul-1.22/

11. de Jesus, G., Nunes, S.: Labadain-30k+: a monolingual Tetun document-level audited dataset [dataset]. INESC TEC (2024). https://doi.org/10.25747/YDWR-N696

12. de Jesus, G., Nunes, S.: Labadain-Avaliadór: A Test Collection for Tetun Ad-hoc Text Retrieval Task [dataset]. INESC TEC (2025). https://doi.org/10.25747/2k6s-e518

13. Koehn, P., et al.: Moses: open source toolkit for statistical machine translation. In: ACL 2007, Proceedings of the 45th Annual Meeting of the Association for Computational Linguistics, 23–30 June 2007, Prague, Czech Republic. The Association for Computational Linguistics (2007). https://aclanthology.org/P07-2045/

14. Kudugunta, S., et al.: MADLAD-400: a multilingual and document-level large audited dataset. In: Oh, A., Naumann, T., Globerson, A., Saenko, K., Hardt, M., Levine, S. (eds.) Advances in Neural Information Processing Systems 36: Annual Conference on Neural Information Processing Systems 2023, NeurIPS 2023, New Orleans, LA, USA, 10–16 December 2023 (2023). http://papers.nips.cc/paper_files/paper/2023/hash/d49042a5d49818711c401d34172f9900-Abstract-Datasets_and_Benchmarks.html

15. Lignos, C., Cohen, D., Lien, Y., Mehta, P., Croft, W.B., Miller, S.: The challenges of optimizing machine translation for low resource cross-language information retrieval. In: Inui, K., Jiang, J., Ng, V., Wan, X. (eds.) Proceedings of the 2019 Conference on Empirical Methods in Natural Language Processing and the 9th International Joint Conference on Natural Language Processing, EMNLP-IJCNLP 2019, Hong Kong, China, 3–7 November 2019, pp. 3495–3500. Association for Computational Linguistics (2019). https://doi.org/10.18653/V1/D19-1353

16. Lin, J., et al.: Simple yet effective neural ranking and reranking baselines for cross-lingual information retrieval. CoRR (2023). https://doi.org/10.48550/ARXIV.2304.01019

17. Macdonald, C., Tonellotto, N.: Declarative experimentation in information retrieval using pyterrier. In: Balog, K., Setty, V., Lioma, C., Liu, Y., Zhang, M., Berberich, K. (eds.) ICTIR 2020: The 2020 ACM SIGIR International Conference on the Theory of Information Retrieval, Virtual Event, Norway, 14–17 September 2020, pp. 161–168. ACM (2020). https://doi.org/10.1145/3409256.3409829

18. Ogundepo, O., Zhang, X., Sun, S., Duh, K., Lin, J.: Africlirmatrix: enabling cross-lingual information retrieval for African languages. In: Goldberg, Y., Kozareva, Z., Zhang, Y. (eds.) Proceedings of the 2022 Conference on Empirical Methods in Natural Language Processing, EMNLP 2022, Abu Dhabi, United Arab Emirates, 7–11 December 2022, pp. 8721–8728. Association for Computational Linguistics (2022). https://doi.org/10.18653/V1/2022.EMNLP-MAIN.597

19. Ounis, I., Amati, G., Plachouras, V., He, B., Macdonald, C., Johnson, D.: Terrier information retrieval platform. In: Losada, D.E., Fernández-Luna, J.M. (eds.) Advances in Information Retrieval, 27th European Conference on IR Research, ECIR 2005, Santiago de Compostela, Spain, 21–23 March 2005, Proceedings. Lecture Notes in Computer Science, vol. 3408, pp. 517–519. Springer (2005). https://doi.org/10.1007/978-3-540-31865-1_37

20. Papineni, K., Roukos, S., Ward, T., Zhu, W.: Bleu: a method for automatic evaluation of machine translation. In: Proceedings of the 40th Annual Meeting of the Association for Computational Linguistics, 6–12 July 2002, Philadelphia, PA, USA, pp. 311–318. ACL (2002). https://doi.org/10.3115/1073083.1073135

21. Pecina, P., et al.: Adaptation of machine translation for multilingual information retrieval in the medical domain. Artif. Intell. Med. **61**(3), 165–185 (2014). https://doi.org/10.1016/J.ARTMED.2014.01.004

22. Robertson, S., Hiemstra, D.: Language models and probability of relevance. In: Proceedings of the Workshop on Language Modeling and Information Retrieval, pp. 21–25. Carnegie Mellon University, United States (2001)

23. Robertson, S.E., Zaragoza, H.: The probabilistic relevance framework: BM25 and beyond. Found. Trends Inf. Retr. **3**(4), 333–389 (2009). https://doi.org/10.1561/1500000019

24. Saleh, S., Pecina, P.: Document translation vs. query translation for cross-lingual information retrieval in the medical domain. In: Proceedings of the 58th Annual Meeting of the Association for Computational Linguistics, ACL 2020, Online, 5–10 July 2020, pp. 6849–6860. Association for Computational Linguistics (2020). https://doi.org/10.18653/V1/2020.ACL-MAIN.613

25. Tang, L., Qin, J., Ye, W., Tan, H., Yang, Z.: Adaptive few-shot prompting for machine translation with pre-trained language models. In: Walsh, T., Shah, J., Kolter, Z. (eds.) AAAI-25, Sponsored by the Association for the Advancement of Artificial Intelligence, 25 February– 4 March 2025, Philadelphia, PA, USA, pp. 25255–25263. AAAI Press (2025). https://doi.org/10.1609/AAAI.V39I24.34712

26. Valentini, F., Kozlowski, D., Larivière, V.: Clirudit: cross-lingual information retrieval of scientific documents (2025). https://arxiv.org/abs/2504.16264

27. Vasconcelos, P.C.B.D., et al.: Constituição anotada da República Democrática de Timor-Leste. Escola de Direito da Universidade do Minho (2011). http://hdl.handle.net/10400.22/4008

28. Wu, D., He, D.: A study of query translation using google machine translation system. In: 2010 IEEE International Conference on Information Retrieval & Knowledge Management (CAMP), pp. 105–110. IEEE (2010). https://doi.org/10.1109/INFRKM.2010.5466911

29. Zhang, R., et al.: Improving low-resource cross-lingual document retrieval by reranking with deep bilingual representations. In: Korhonen, A., Traum, D.R., Màrquez, L. (eds.) Proceedings of the 57th Conference of the Association for Computational Linguistics, ACL 2019, Florence, Italy, 28July–2 August 2019, Volume 1: Long Papers, pp. 3173–3179. Association for Computational Linguistics (2019). https://doi.org/10.18653/V1/P19-1306
30. Zhou, D., Truran, M., Brailsford, T., Wade, V., Ashman, H.: Translation techniques in cross-language information retrieval. ACM Comput. Surv. (CSUR) **45**(1), 1–44 (2012). https://doi.org/10.1145/2379776.2379777

User Behavior in Sports Search: Entity-Centric Query and Click Log Analysis

João Damas⬡ and Sérgio Nunes$^{(\boxtimes)}$⬡

INESC TEC and Faculty of Engineering of the University of Porto,
Rua Dr. Roberto Frias, 4200-465 Porto, Portugal
`ssn@fe.up.pt`

Abstract. Understanding user behavior in search systems is essential for improving retrieval effectiveness and user satisfaction. While prior research has extensively examined general-purpose web search engines, domain-specific contexts—such as sports information—remain comparatively underexplored. In this study, we analyze over 400,000 interaction log entries from a sports-oriented search engine collected over a two-week period. Our analysis combines classic query-level metrics (e.g., frequency distributions, query lengths) with a detailed examination of click behavior, including entropy-based intent variability and a custom query quality scoring model. Compared to established baselines from general and specialized search environments, we observe a high proportion of new and single-term queries, as well as a notable lack of representativeness among top queries. These findings reveal patterns shaped by the event-driven and entity-centric nature of sports content, offering actionable insights for the design of domain-specific retrieval systems.

Keywords: Query log analysis · User behavior · Domain-specific search

1 Introduction

People interact with search systems in various ways, ranging from highly focused searches with well-defined goals to exploratory queries aimed at discovering new information. Understanding how users navigate and engage with search systems is crucial for meeting their expectations. As the Web expanded, analyzing user behavior in search engines became increasingly important due to the diverse needs of a growing user base. Data collected from real user interactions—such as submitted queries and click behavior—offers valuable insights into behavioral patterns and can reveal opportunities for system optimization [8].

Despite being a critical area of research, particularly for informing website optimization strategies and the design of search engines, much of the data collected from user interaction logs remains underutilized. This results in the loss of potentially valuable business insights [9]. Additionally, issues surrounding privacy and confidentiality often prevent the release of public datasets, making it difficult to replicate studies and advance research in this field [1,12].

J. Valente de Oliveira et al. (Eds.): EPIA 2025, LNAI 16122, pp. 276–288, 2026.
https://doi.org/10.1007/978-3-032-05179-0_21

In this study, we analyze two weeks of interactions with a Portuguese sports-specific search engine, comprising over 400,000 log entries. The search engine indexes documents related to various sports entities, including players, managers, teams, and competitions. In addition to recording user search queries, it also captures user interactions with result sets by logging clicks on retrieved documents—providing an analytical perspective that is less commonly explored in prior studies. Given the unique context of this search engine, our primary objective is to assess how user behavior compares not only to general-purpose search engines but also to other domain-specific systems.

To guide our analysis, we focus on the following research questions:

RQ1 How does user search behavior in a sports-specific domain differ from that observed in general-purpose search engines?

RQ2 What distinctive patterns can be identified from click-level interactions in a sports-specific search engine?

The remainder of the paper is structured as follows. Section 2 reviews previous query log analysis studies that serve as benchmarks for our work. Section 3 describes the dataset and the data cleaning and preparation steps. Sections 4 and 5 present our findings at the query and click levels, respectively. Finally, Sect. 6 summarizes the key results and outlines directions for future research.

2   Related Work

Research on query log analysis (QLA) has traditionally focused on general-purpose search engines such as AltaVista, AOL, and Excite [2,14,15]. These studies identified behavioral patterns—such as query length, click distribution, and session length—that continue to serve as useful references across domains. Fewer studies have examined domain-specific QLA. Examples include academic [17], government [4], and expert search systems [6], where user behavior shifts in response to task-specific needs and content structure.

Table 1 summarizes key QLA studies across both general and domain-specific settings, highlighting differences in scope, dataset size, and methodological focus. While prior work has explored a range of contexts, to our knowledge, no study has addressed QLA in the sports domain. Our dataset stands out for its intensity—over 400,000 entries in just two weeks—and for combining query- and click-level analysis in an event-driven, entity-centric environment.

3   Dataset and Preparation

The dataset analyzed comprises user interactions with ZOS's flagship portal, `zerozero.pt`, a Portuguese sports-specific search engine, collected over just over two weeks, from March 5 to March 20, 2020. During this time, tens of thousands of interactions were recorded daily, totaling 400,414 entries. These include both search queries and clicks on results, and are not restricted by subdomain or language—while the platform originated in Portugal, the dataset includes international users and non-Portuguese queries.

Table 1. Comparison of query log analysis (QLA) studies across domains.

Study	Domain	Entries	Period
Silverstein et al. [14]	General (AltaVista)	~1B	6 weeks
Beitzel et al. [3]	General (AOL)	36M	3 months
Chau et al. [4]	Government	1.5M	6 months
Wang et al. [17]	Academic	500K	4 years
Fang et al. [6]	Expert search	80K	1 year
This study	Sports	400K	2 weeks

All logs were recorded directly by zerozero.pt, capturing each submitted query string, timestamp, session ID, clicked URL, entity type (player, team, competition, etc.) and result position. Ranking is performed by an entity-centric relevance model that combines TF-IDF lexical matching with named-entity boosts.

Each entry logs either a query submission or a result click, along with metadata such as timestamps, session identifiers, clicked entity type and position, and user-agent strings. This structure enabled both behavioral and temporal analyses. To ensure data quality, we removed entries generated by bots or crawlers. This was done by matching user-agent strings against known bot signatures [4, 16], complemented by manual inspection. This filtering step excluded 9,215 entries (2.3% of the dataset). We also refined session boundaries, as relying solely on cookie-based identifiers proved insufficient. A 30-min inactivity threshold—commonly used in search log studies [5]—was adopted to delineate sessions. Sessions exceeding 100 queries, which are likely bot-generated, were discarded [14], accounting for 1.1% of the remaining entries.

4 Query Analysis

On this platform, users are shown suggested top results as they type a query and can choose to click on one immediately, bypassing the full results page. Over 57% of log entries correspond to these interactions, which occur on the main page rather than the full results page. Accordingly, we report measurements not only for the complete log but also, when relevant, for this subset—referred to as the *Main Page (MP) Subset*. Table 2 presents general statistics computed at the query level.

4.1 Query Frequency and Uniqueness

Given the short time span over which the dataset was collected, the total number of queries surpasses those reported in other domain-specific search engine studies. The only studies with higher entry counts are the University of Tennessee study by Wang et al. [17], which recorded over 500,000 queries across a four-year period, and the study by Chau et al. [4], which spanned more than six months.

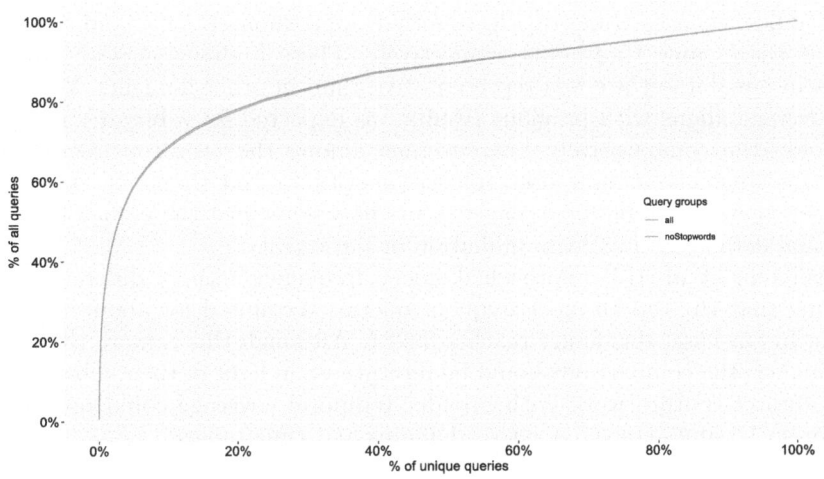

Fig. 1. Query cumulative frequency distribution.

Only about one-fifth of the queries are unique, indicating a degree of overlap in how users express their information needs. This finding aligns with previous studies: Fang et al. [6] and Ribeiro [13] report similar proportions, while Yi et al. [18] observed a uniqueness rate of 25%. Additionally, over 13% of queries appear only once during the collection period.

To further explore this pattern, we analyze the cumulative query frequency distribution to assess how representative the most frequent queries are relative to the entire dataset. Figure 1 presents this distribution. The frequency distribution of queries follows a power law. There are no significant differences between the dataset with and without stop-word filtering; removing stop words results in only a marginal increase in coverage.

4.2 Query Caching and Representativeness

To assess potential caching benefits, we evaluated the cumulative impact of the most frequent queries. Caching the top 0.4% of queries covers 24.58% of all queries. Expanding this to the top 20% increases coverage to 77.68%. Compa-

Table 2. General query level statistics summary.

Metric	Dataset	MP Subset
Number of queries	324,157	221,742
Unique query %	21.63%	19.93%
Never repeated queries %	13.13%	11.82%
Mean characters per query	8.21	6.98
Mean terms per query	1.34	1.17
Mean terms per unique query	1.69	1.38

rable studies, such as Ribeiro [13], reported approximately 50% and 80% coverage at these same thresholds, respectively. These findings suggest that top queries in our dataset are less representative than in other domains. While the 20% coverage aligns with previous results—as expected for a broader inclusion threshold—the comparatively low coverage among the very top queries may reflect the diversity in how users phrase queries to find the same entity. For instance, when searching for a player, users may enter just the name or include additional details such as team affiliation or nationality.

Silverstein et al. [14] approached query frequency from a different angle, reporting that the top 10 most frequent queries accounted for about 1% of all queries. In our case, this figure reaches 3.69%. Although this is more than three times higher, the comparison should be interpreted in light of their substantially larger dataset. Future work with broader temporal coverage could help assess whether such values converge across domains and timeframes.

4.3   Novelty and Temporal Patterns

These observations raise further questions about the frequency of new, unseen queries. Although we lack access to the search engine's full historical logs, we estimated query novelty on a daily basis within our collection period. Specifically, for each day, we computed the ratio of queries that had not been submitted on any prior day to the total number of queries for that day. The results, shown in Fig. 2, reveal a stabilization pattern: after an initial rise, the ratio converges to approximately 22% within three days. The highest observed value beyond this point was 23.56% (on March 18), with daily fluctuations never exceeding two percentage points. For reference, Google reported an average of 15% new queries per day in 2017 [7], suggesting that our dataset exhibits a higher degree of query variability—potentially due to the domain-specific and entity-centric nature of the platform.

4.4   Query Length and Structure

Analyzing query length by number of terms confirms that queries in our dataset are notably short. The average query length is 1.34 terms, increasing to 1.69 when considering only unique queries—indicating that more frequent queries tend to be shorter. This average is lower than those reported in most reference studies. For instance, the AltaVista [14] and Excite [15] datasets reported averages of 2.35 and 2.4 terms per query, respectively, while AOL logs showed an increase from 2.2 [2] to 2.7 [3] over time. In domain-specific contexts, Yi et al. [18] observed an average of over 3 terms per query in both history and psychology databases. Only the INDURE study [6] reported a similarly low average, with 1.96 terms per query. Table 3 presents the full distribution of query lengths by number of terms.

Results show that nearly three-quarters of queries consist of a single term. This suggests that users often search for entities using only their common

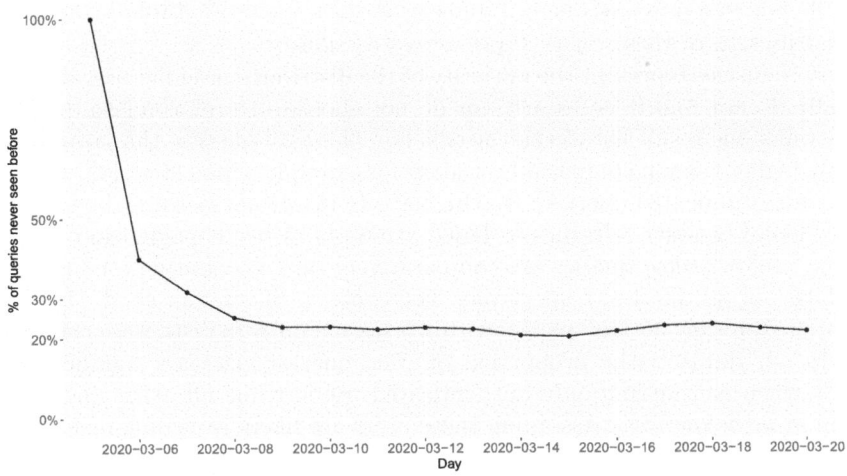

Fig. 2. New searches ratio over a daily basis.

Table 3. Terms per query distribution.   **Table 4.** Query types distribution.

Terms	Frequency	Percentage
1	240,028	74.05%
2	67,198	20.73%
3	11,150	3.44%
4	3,541	1.09%
5	1,283	0.40%
6	457	0.14%
7	258	0.08%
8	100	0.03%
9	45	0.01%
10+	97	0.03%

Type	Frequency	Percentage
Initial	173,468	53.51%
Identical	120,914	37.30%
New	22,191	6.85%
Modified	7,584	2.34%

name(s), rarely providing additional details to refine their queries. For popular entities, a single term is often sufficient—teams and players frequently have well-known names, abbreviations, or nicknames that uniquely identify them. However, in cases where names overlap or the entities are less prominent, this approach may lead to ambiguous or imprecise results.

4.5   Query Reformulation Behavior

It is also informative to examine how users reformulate queries within a search session. We categorize queries into four types: *Initial*, representing the first query in a session; *New*, for queries not previously submitted within the same session; *Identical*, for repeated queries submitted verbatim; and *Modified*, for queries that partially match a previous one but differ in at least one term. Table 4 summarizes the distribution of these query types across sessions.

Initial queries represent the majority of the distribution, indicating that users typically do not find it necessary—or do not choose—to reformulate queries to better tailor the result list to their needs. For *Identical* queries, the proportion is notably higher than in comparable studies; for example, Chau et al. [4] reported a 12.4% rate of repeated queries. This higher rate in our dataset may be explained by accidental browser refreshes or failed attempts at result pagination.

New and *Modified* queries are comparatively rare, accounting for just 6.85% and 2.34% of all queries, respectively. For context, Silverstein et al. [14] found that approximately 35% of queries within a session on AltaVista were completely new. In our dataset, the proportion of *New* queries increases significantly to 21.25% when considering only authenticated users, while all other query types remain at or below 15%. Assuming these users are likely returning or long-term users, this may suggest a more refined search strategy—where ineffective queries are more often abandoned and replaced, rather than reformulated incrementally.

Modified queries follow *New* as the second most frequent reformulation type among authenticated users, suggesting evolving search strategies. In contrast to our findings, other studies have reported a higher occurrence of this type; for instance, Silverstein et al. [14] observed that 10.2% of within-session queries involved term deletion or addition.

Results indicate that users tend to maintain a consistent query length when reformulating, with over half of the reformulations involving term substitution—that is, altering some terms while keeping the overall length unchanged. Additionally, users show a clear preference for specialization through term addition rather than generalization by term deletion. This behavior is expected, as users often begin with broad queries that are easier to formulate and may already yield sufficiently relevant results.

When focusing on authenticated users, a similar pattern emerges: 81.04% of reformulated queries differ by no more than one term. These findings align with prior studies by Ribeiro [13] and Wang et al. [17], both of which observed that users typically modify queries incrementally, often one term at a time. Wang et al. [17] referred to this behavior as reflecting users' "*mental models of Web searching and learning.*" This incremental reformulation pattern appears to be domain-independent and broadly characteristic of user search behavior.

4.6 Temporal Distribution

Given the timestamp associated with each entry, it is possible to analyze query distribution across multiple levels of temporal granularity. We begin by examining the daily distribution over the full data collection period. Figure 3 presents this distribution. On average, 20,260 queries were submitted per day. However, this average reflects two distinct weekly patterns. The first week exhibits activity typical of a regular usage cycle, with daily volumes near the average and noticeable spikes on the weekend—corresponding to the majority of scheduled games. This explains the elevated query counts on March 7th and 8th, which also featured key matches in the Portuguese league. In contrast, March 20th was the least active day overall, with query volume dropping to just over half the daily mean. It is worth noting, however, that the full 24-h periods were not captured on either March 5th or March 20th. As a result, the recorded frequencies for these two days likely underestimate actual activity.

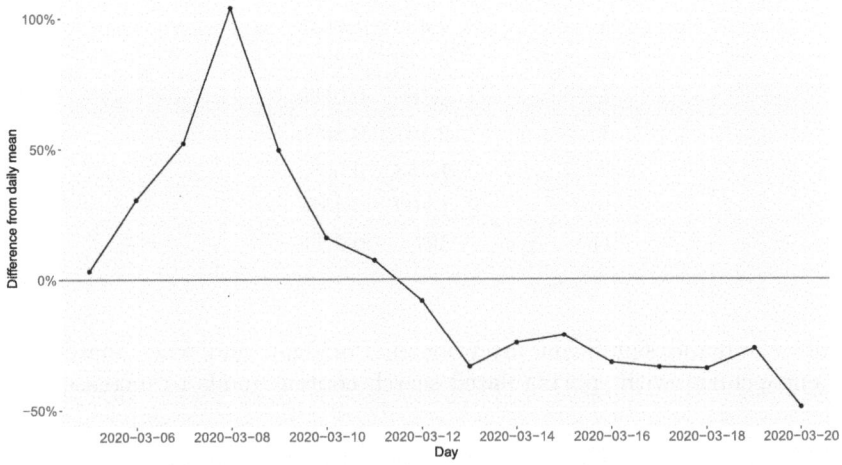

Fig. 3. Daily query distribution (relative difference to mean).

Beginning on March 12th, there is a noticeable decline in query frequency, with most days showing a drop of nearly 25% below the daily average. This reduction coincides with the onset of the COVID-19 pandemic in Portugal, which first recorded confirmed cases in early March. As the situation escalated, the Portuguese Football Federation suspended all competitions on March 12th, with similar measures adopted in other countries around the same time. With professional football on hold, user interest and motivation to perform searches on the platform declined substantially.

By aggregating queries by weekday, we observe—as expected—that the period surrounding the weekend shows the highest activity, aligning with the preferred scheduling of football matches. Sunday stands out with over 20% more queries than the daily average, followed by Thursday in second place. The prominence of Thursday may initially seem surprising, but it is the only weekday that appears three times in the collection period, whereas all others appear only twice, which helps explain the elevated frequency followed by a drop. Under typical conditions, we would expect a gradual rise in activity as the week progresses. This pattern aligns with findings by Beitzel et al. [3] in their analysis of AOL search logs, where activity peaked on Sunday and gradually declined throughout the week, reaching a low on Fridays. Several interpretations are possible. One explanation is a shift in user context over the weekend. Sports—particularly

Table 5. Clicked results ranking distribution.

Result ranking	Clicks	Percentage
1	196,517	72.65%
2	35,187	13.01%
3	13,905	5.14%
4	8,066	2.98%
5	5,359	1.98%
6	3,572	1.32%
7	2,565	0.95%
8	2,161	0.80%
9	1,358	0.50%
10	1,209	0.45%
11+	597	0.22%

football—command significant attention in Portugal, and when matches take place, engagement with sports-related search content tends to increase accordingly.

5 Click Analysis

Our dataset includes not only query entries but also click-through data. For the purpose of click-level analysis, we isolated entries with valid click ranking positions, resulting in a total of 270,496 entries. To better understand user engagement, we explored custom query scoring mechanisms and evaluated ambiguity using entropy-based measurements. These metrics allow us to assess variability in user intent and offer reference points for future research in domain-specific environments.

We began by examining the primary types of entities clicked by users. Players and teams accounted for the majority of clicks, representing 50.2% and 32%, respectively, followed by competitions (7.2%) and managers (2%). Collectively, these four entity types comprised over 90% of all clicks—highlighting the platform's focus on team sports, especially football. Less frequently clicked entities included agents, directors, places, stadiums, and referees. As expected, the majority of clicks occurred on top-ranked results, with users primarily engaging with content on the first page. Table 5 presents the overall distribution of clicks by ranking position.

Top-ranked results account for 72.65% of all clicks. In comparison, Torres et al. [5] reported that adults clicked on the first result approximately 60% of the time, while children did so around 40% of the time. Although our dataset lacks user demographic information, we expect the majority of users to be adults, which aligns our results more closely with those observed for adult populations.

Click distribution also varies by entity type. For players and teams, the top result receives 73.02% and 80.97% of clicks, respectively. In contrast, the share drops to 50.59% for competitions and 63.88% for managers. These differences may reflect ambiguity or familiarity in entity naming for the latter categories.

We further analyzed click behavior across user sessions by examining changes in the rank positions of clicked results. Specifically, we collected the last and maximum clicked rank positions within each session to assess how effectively users refine queries to improve result relevance. Using this information, we calculated the ratio of sessions where the final clicked result ranked higher than earlier ones—indicating a more successful search outcome. In 71.91% of multi-click sessions, users clicked on a higher-ranked result after reformulating their query. When sessions with only one click are included, this figure rises to 79.58%, suggesting that users frequently refine their searches to achieve better results.

Finally, we aimed to rank queries based on criteria related to associated clicks. For that, we first looked at click entropy. Though some users may search using the same query, often the underlying information need varies, i.e. there is different intent. This is common with shorter, less specific queries. With this in mind, Kulkarni et al. [10] propose an analysis on query intent variability by using the concept of entropy. They define the entropy for a query q as:

$$Entropy(q) = - \sum_{u \in P_c(q)} p_c(u|q) \times \log p_c(u|q) \qquad (1)$$

where $P_c(q)$ is the set of entities clicked when searching using query q and $p_c(u|q)$ the click share of entity u for query q. We now replicate this measurement on our analysis.

Table 6 shows the results for query entropy at individual entity level. As expected, queries with higher variability in clicks tend to be shorter, often consisting of a single term. Many of these queries appear incomplete due to the search bar's suggestion mechanism, which displays results after the user types at least three characters. For instance, the query [marc] could refer to [marco], [marcelo], [marcos], or simply the name Marc. The top queries with the highest entropy typically involve personal names, with [diogo] and [nacional] being prime examples—[nacional] could refer to teams (e.g., Nacional da Madeira) or various competitions.

Due to this inherent ambiguity, entropy is not well-suited as a query quality scoring metric. Instead, we turned to click ranking data. However, early attempts to rank queries based on average click position were biased by low-frequency queries associated with high-ranked clicks. To address this, we adapted the traditional TF-IDF weighting scheme [11]. We propose that a query q's score be:

$$Score(q) = \sum_{r \in CR(q)} Freq(q,r) \times \log_{10} \frac{N}{r} \qquad (2)$$

where $CR(q)$ is the set of ranking positions where q led to a click, $Freq(q,r)$ is the amount of times the query led to a click on that position, and N is a scaling factor to favor higher rankings (i.e., better matches). We set N = 930,

Table 6. Top 15 queries with highest entropy at individual entity level.

Query	Entropy	#Entities
luis	3.22	11
pedro	3.14	11
marc	2.99	9
wellington	2.95	9
saulo	2.92	8
cesinha	2.86	8
paulao	2.85	8
jorginho	2.81	9
ward	2.81	7
paraguay	2.77	10
nacional	2.76	13
jose semedo	2.75	7
brasileiro	2.74	10
balde	2.73	7
diogo	2.73	15

Table 7. 10 best scored queries.

Query	Score	#Clicks
sporting	5,141	1,742
flamengo	4,480	1,514
benfica	3,815	1,296
santos	3,682	1,316
braga	3,176	1,087
porto	2,973	1,010
inter	2,568	906
vasco	2,412	814
botafogo	2,397	842
liga	2,374	889

the lowest rank clicked, to favor queries with frequent high-ranking clicks. This adapted formula assigns higher scores to queries that more often lead to clicks on higher-ranked results, while penalizing those associated with lower-ranked clicks. Table 7 presents the top 10 highest-scoring queries according to this metric.

Most of the highest-scoring queries also rank among the most frequently submitted queries on the platform. These are typically single-term queries referring to popular entities or to a small, well-defined set of entities that are easily searchable. Interestingly, some ambiguous queries—such as [liga]—also receive high scores. Although it is unlikely that clicks for such queries consistently land on the top result (given the presence of many competitions with similar names), users still tend to select results appearing near the top of the list. This highlights the influence of click frequency on our scoring formula: even when a query does not consistently lead to clicks on the top result, if the clicked positions are high-ranked and occur frequently, the query can still achieve a strong score.

6   Conclusions

In this study, we analyzed two weeks of user interactions with a sports-specific search engine, focusing on search behavior and click patterns. Our objective was to compare these behaviors with those observed in general-purpose and other domain-specific search environments.

In response to **RQ1**, which examined how user search behavior in a sports-specific domain differs from that in general-purpose search engines, we identified both commonalities and distinctive features. As in general-purpose systems, the frequency distribution of queries follows a power law, with a small number of highly popular queries dominating the volume. However, sports-related queries tend to be shorter—averaging just 1.34 terms—reflecting more focused or entity-driven intents. Additionally, the event-driven nature of sports leads to a high rate of new queries, highlighting the dynamic and time-sensitive nature of user information needs.

Regarding **RQ2**, which addressed the distinctive patterns emerging from click-level data, we observed that users predominantly click on top-ranked results, with most clicks concentrated within the first three positions. Nevertheless, we also found higher click entropy compared to general-purpose engines, indicating more varied user intent. This may be due to the broad range of sports-related entities—such as players, teams, and competitions—which naturally lead to more diverse search behaviors.

Overall, our findings offer actionable insights for developing sports-specific search engines. Improvements in query interpretation and ranking strategies could significantly enhance user experience by better addressing the particularities of this domain. Future work should extend this analysis over longer time spans to capture seasonal patterns and behavior changes linked to major sports events. Comparative studies with other dynamic, entity-rich domains—such as entertainment or finance—could help determine whether the observed behaviors are unique to sports or indicative of broader trends in specialized search.

Acknowledgments. This work is financed by national funds through FCT - Fundação para a Ciência e a Tecnologia, under the support UID/50014/2023 (DOI: https://doi.org/10.54499/UID/50014/2023 10.54499/UID/50014/2023). We gratefully acknowledge the zerozero.pt team at ZOS for their close collaboration and for providing access to the search logs that made this study possible.

Disclosure of Interests. The authors have no competing interests to declare that are relevant to the content of this article.

References

1. Agosti, M., Crivellari, F., Di Nunzio, G.M.: Web log analysis: a review of a decade of studies about information acquisition, inspection and interpretation of user interaction. Data Min. Knowl. Disc. **24**(3), 663–696 (2012). https://doi.org/10.1007/s10618-011-0228-8
2. Beitzel, S.M., Jensen, E.C., Chowdhury, A., Frieder, O., Grossman, D.: Hourly analysis of a very large topically categorized web query log. In: Proceedings of the 27th Annual International ACM SIGIR Conference on Research and Development in Information Retrieval. SIGIR 2004, pp. 321–328. Association for Computing Machinery, New York (2004). https://doi.org/10.1145/1008992.1009048
3. Beitzel, S.M., Jensen, E.C., Chowdhury, A., Frieder, O., Grossman, D.: Temporal analysis of a very large topically categorized web query log. J. Am. Soc. Inform. Sci. Technol. **58**(2), 166–178 (2007)

4. Chau, M., Fang, X., Sheng, O.R.: Analysis of the query logs of a web site search engine. J. Am. Soc. Inform. Sci. Technol. **56**(13), 1363–1376 (2005). https://doi.org/10.1002/asi.20210

5. Duarte Torres, S., Hiemstra, D., Serdyukov, P.: Query log analysis in the context of information retrieval for children. In: Proceedings of the 33rd International ACM SIGIR Conference on Research and Development in Information Retrieval. SIGIR 2010, pp. 847–848. Association for Computing Machinery, New York (2010). https://doi.org/10.1145/1835449.1835646

6. Fang, Y., Somasundaram, N., Si, L., Ko, J., Mathur, A.P.: Analysis of an expert search query log. In: Proceedings of the 34th International ACM SIGIR Conference on Research and Development in Information Retrieval. SIGIR 2011, pp. 1189–1190. Association for Computing Machinery, New York (2011). https://doi.org/10.1145/2009916.2010113

7. Gomes, B.: Our latest quality improvements for search (2017). https://blog.google/products/search/our-latest-quality-improvements-search/. Accessed 25 Apr 2025

8. Jansen, B.J.: Search log analysis: what it is, what's been done, how to do it. Libr. Inf. Sci. Res. **28**(3), 407–432 (2006). https://doi.org/10.1016/j.lisr.2006.06.005

9. Jansen, B.J., Spink, A.: How are we searching the world wide web? A comparison of nine search engine transaction logs. Inf. Process. Manage. **42**(1), 248–263 (2006). https://doi.org/10.1016/j.ipm.2004.10.007, https://linkinghub.elsevier.com/retrieve/pii/S0306457304001396

10. Kulkarni, A., Teevan, J., Svore, K.M., Dumais, S.T.: Understanding temporal query dynamics. In: Proceedings of the Fourth ACM International Conference on Web Search and Data Mining. WSDM 2011, pp. 167–176. Association for Computing Machinery, New York (2011). https://doi.org/10.1145/1935826.1935862

11. Manning, C.D., Raghavan, P., Schütze, H.: Introduction to Information Retrieval. Cambridge University Press, New York (2008)

12. Poblete, B., Spiliopoulou, M., Baeza-Yates, R.: Privacy-preserving query log mining for business confidentiality protection. ACM Trans. Web **4**(3) (2010). https://doi.org/10.1145/1806916.1806919

13. Ribeiro, R.: Characterization of Portuguese Web Searches. Master's thesis, Faculdade de Engenharia da Universidade do Porto (FEUP) (2011)

14. Silverstein, C., Marais, H., Henzinger, M., Moricz, M.: Analysis of a very large web search engine query log. SIGIR Forum **33**(1), 6–12 (1999). https://doi.org/10.1145/331403.331405

15. Spink, A., Jansen, B.J., Wolfram, D., Saracevic, T.: From e-sex to e-commerce: web search changes. Technology **53**(2), 226–234 (2001)

16. Staeding, A.: List of user-agents (spiders, robots, browser). (2011), http://www.user-agents.org/index.shtml, accessed April 2025

17. Wang, P., Berry, M.W., Yang, Y.: Mining longitudinal web queries: trends and patterns. J. Am. Soc. Inf. Sci. Technol. **54**(8), 743–758 (2003). https://doi.org/10.1002/asi.10262, http://doi.wiley.com/10.1002/asi.10262

18. Yi, K., Beheshti, J., Cole, C., Leide, J.E., Large, A.: User search behavior of domain-specific information retrieval systems: an analysis of the query logs from PsycINFO and ABC-Clio's historical abstracts/America: history and life. J. Am. Soc. Inf. Sci. Technol. **57**(9), 1208–1220 (2006). https://doi.org/10.1002/asi.20401, http://doi.wiley.com/10.1002/asi.20401

Multi-agent Retrieval-Augmented Generation for Enhancing Answer Generation and Knowledge Retrieval

Deepak Kumar$^{(\boxtimes)}$ and Bhavesh Jain

Joint Innovation Hub, Fraunhofer ISI, Karlsruhe, Germany
{Deepak.Kumar,bhavesh.mahender.jain}@isi.fraunhofer.de

Abstract. Large language models (LLMs) have shown remarkable capabilities in natural language processing but often exhibit factual inconsistencies when applied to knowledge-intensive tasks, with hallucination rates as high as 30% in open-domain question answering. Retrieval-Augmented Generation (RAG) has emerged as a promising solution by coupling language generation with evidence retrieval. However, conventional RAG systems frequently suffer from noisy document retrieval, limited context coverage, and decreased faithfulness in generated outputs. To address these limitations, this paper introduces a novel architecture, *Multi-Agent Retrieval-Augmented Generation (MA-RAG)*, which decomposes the reasoning process into a set of specialized agents responsible for query reformulation, iterative retrieval refinement, hallucination detection, and answer validation. The modular design enables dynamic coordination and layered decision-making across the retrieval and generation pipeline. We evaluate MA-RAG on three widely used QA benchmarks: SQuAD v1.1, SQuAD v2.0, and HotpotQA, under both realistic large-scale retrieval conditions and idealized filtered settings. System performance is assessed using five retrieval and generation-focused metrics such as context precision, context recall, faithfulness, answer relevancy, and answer correctness, derived from the RAGAS framework. Additionally, we complement this evaluation with span-based metrics including Exact Match (EM), F1, and BLEU scores to capture surface-level overlap and fluency. MA-RAG consistently outperforms both Traditional RAG and Ensemble RAG across all datasets. Compared to Traditional RAG, it achieves up to 29.2% improvement in recall, 25.6% in precision, and 22.7% in correctness. Against Ensemble RAG, gains reach 25.9% in precision, 15.6% in recall, and 7.2% in correctness. On average, MA-RAG improves F1 by over 9% points and BLEU by more than 11%, while nearly doubling EM scores on SQuAD v1.1. These improvements highlight the robustness of the agentic framework under both noisy and clean retrieval environments. The empirical findings suggest MA-RAG thus provides a scalable and interpretable pathway toward building more trustworthy and accurate AI systems for question answering and other knowledge-centric NLP applications.

Keywords: Retrieval-Augmented Generation · Multi-Agent Systems · large Language Models · Query Decomposition · Contextual

© The Author(s), under exclusive license to Springer Nature Switzerland AG 2026
J. Valente de Oliveira et al. (Eds.): EPIA 2025, LNAI 16122, pp. 289–302, 2026.
https://doi.org/10.1007/978-3-032-05179-0_22

Reasoning · Faithful Text Generation · Open-Domain Question
Answering · Hallucination Mitigation · Retrieval Refinement ·
Multi-Hop Reasoning

1   Introduction

Large language models (LLMs) have significantly advanced Natural Language
Processing (NLP), yet they continue to face limitations in factual accuracy.
Hallucinations-confident but unsupported or incorrect outputs-remain prevalent, especially in knowledge-intensive tasks requiring external information for
accurate response generation [1]. Retrieval-Augmented Generation (RAG) has
emerged as a key approach, combining retrieval systems with generative models
to enrich static parametric knowledge with dynamic, external context [2].

Knowledge-intensive tasks, such as open-domain question answering [17] and
domain-specific applications like biomedical or legal question answering [18], benefit from RAG's ability to incorporate relevant documents that cannot be mem-
orized by the model alone. In a typical RAG workflow, documents are retrieved
based on a query and provided to a language model to generate grounded
responses [3].

Despite its utility, traditional RAG systems suffer from notable shortcomings.
Noisy or irrelevant retrieval can reduce answer quality, increase hallucination
rates, and introduce inefficiencies [4]. Furthermore, vague or ill-structured queries
often yield suboptimal retrieval results, emphasizing the need for improved query
reformulation or decomposition [5].

These challenges highlight the importance of more adaptive retrieval-
generation mechanisms-capable of refining queries, filtering relevant context, and
validating generated outputs. A promising direction involves integrating Multi-
Agent Systems (MAS) into RAG pipelines. By leveraging task specialization and
modular reasoning, MAS architectures improve transparency, adaptability, and
control within the generation process [6].

To address these limitations, this paper introduces a Multi-Agent RAG (MA-
RAG) architecture that decomposes the RAG workflow into specialized agents
for query decomposition, iterative retrieval refinement, context validation, and
response generation. This modular approach aims to enhance retrieval precision
and recall, while improving faithfulness, relevancy, and correctness of generated
answers.

The remainder of this paper is structured as follows: Sect. 2 reviews current RAG methodologies and multi-agent advancements. Section 3 details the
datasets used for evaluation. Section 4 presents the MA-RAG architecture and
experimental setup. Section 5 reports empirical findings, comparing MA-RAG
with Traditional and Ensemble RAG systems. Finally, Sect. 6 summarizes the
key results, outlines limitations, and suggests future research directions.

2   State of the Art

Retrieval-Augmented Generation (RAG) has emerged as a solution to the factual limitations of large language models (LLMs) by grounding outputs in external documents. These systems enhance reliability in knowledge-intensive tasks through non-parametric retrieval. However, early RAG models often relied on static top-k retrieval, leading to irrelevant context inclusion, limited adaptability, and suboptimal handling of complex queries.

Recent advancements have explored Agentic Systems as a remedy. These systems emphasize modularity, dynamic reasoning, and specialized agents for distinct subtasks. This section outlines the evolution and limitations of RAG systems (Sect. 2.1), highlights the contributions of agent-based architectures (Sect. 2.2), and introduces tailored evaluation methodologies (Sect. 2.3).

2.1   Evolution and Limitations of Retrieval-Augmented Generation

RAG was developed to improve factual grounding in LLMs by incorporating external documents during generation [2]. Dense Passage Retrieval (DPR) [7] emerged as a foundational method, enabling dense vector-based retrieval in a shared embedding space and outperforming sparse techniques like BM25 in open-domain QA.

Nonetheless, key limitations persist. Dense retrievers often struggle under domain shifts and generalization, where sparse retrievers remain competitive [6]. Hybrid retrieval systems combining sparse and dense methods have increased architectural complexity without fully resolving retrieval challenges [10].

A major issue is static top-k retrieval, which retrieves a fixed number of documents regardless of relevance, often introducing redundant or irrelevant content [8]. This increases hallucination risk and model inefficiency. While reranking with cross-encoders [9] offers improvements, such methods are computationally intensive and still depend on the initial retrieval quality.

Emerging architectures like Self-RAG [8] address these shortcomings by introducing reflective loops to critique and revise outputs. However, they typically lack dynamic query reformulation and remain limited in multi-hop reasoning. Static retrieval paired with noisy documents further exacerbates hallucination risks [11]. Efficiency gains through cache reuse [9] do not address the need for adaptable and interpretable retrieval-generation pipelines.

These issues underscore the need for modular architectures that can support dynamic retrieval, iterative reasoning, and internal validation.

2.2   Agentic RAG Architectures and Their Role in Enhancing RAG

To address RAG limitations, modular multi-agent systems such as MA-RAG have been proposed. Early agent-based models typically relied on a single LLM to manage reasoning, retrieval, and generation without internal specialization. For example, the ReAct framework [13] interleaves reasoning and tool use but lacks component separation and validation steps. As a result, hallucinations remain likely when retrieval is incomplete or reasoning fails.

Other systems like SeeKeR [14] and BlenderBot 2.0 [15] adopt a single-agent design, issuing queries and generating responses without iterative refinement or query adaptation. This static retrieval approach limits performance on complex, multi-hop queries and leads to under-specified outputs in open-domain tasks.

Partially modular systems such as HuggingGPT [16] incorporate a central controller to assign tasks to tools, but lack dynamic inter-agent communication and specialized modules for retrieval verification or hallucination detection. Errors are often propagated without correction due to the absence of internal feedback.

These limitations-monolithic task execution, static retrieval strategies, and minimal internal validation-highlight the need for adaptable, interpretable agentic architectures. MA-RAG addresses these constraints by distributing tasks across specialized agents responsible for decomposition, iterative retrieval, validation, and generation. These agents operate in a coordinated pipeline, enabling dynamic query adjustment, inter-agent feedback, and traceable decision-making. This modular structure improves retrieval relevance and generation faithfulness, while enhancing robustness in noisy and complex scenarios.

2.3   Evaluation Metrics for MA-RAG

As Retrieval-Augmented Generation (RAG) systems grow in complexity, robust and multi-dimensional evaluation becomes essential. Traditional span-based metrics such as Exact Match (EM), F1, and BLEU scores [2] are widely used to assess surface-level correctness by comparing generated answers with references. EM captures strict match, F1 reflects token-level precision and recall, and BLEU evaluates n-gram similarity and fluency. While useful, these metrics often overlook deeper semantic alignment and factual grounding.

To address these limitations, the RAGAS framework [12] supports reference-free evaluation of both retrieval and generation. Faithfulness measures whether generated claims are supported by retrieved evidence, with higher scores indicating fewer hallucinations [11]. Answer relevance evaluates semantic alignment between the query and the generated answer via embedding similarity [12]. When reference answers are available, answer correctness assesses factual accuracy and completeness [12].

For retrieval evaluation, context recall quantifies how comprehensively relevant documents are retrieved, while context precision measures the proportion of retrieved documents that are truly relevant [12]. Higher precision supports cleaner generation by reducing irrelevant content.

Together, these complementary metrics offer a holistic view of system performance. For example, high recall with low faithfulness may indicate ineffective evidence usage, while low precision and poor relevance may point to noisy retrieval. Such insights inform targeted refinements across MA-RAG's modular pipeline.

3   Dataset

To evaluate the performance of the Multi-Agent Retrieval-Augmented Generation (MA-RAG) system, three benchmark question-answering (QA) datasets were used: SQuAD v1.1, SQuAD v2.0, and HotpotQA. These datasets collectively support the evaluation of retrieval precision, context recall, faithfulness, and answer correctness in knowledge-intensive tasks.

SQuAD v1.1 and SQuAD v2.0 contain over 100,000 question-answer pairs derived from 500+ Wikipedia passages. Each question is linked to an answerable span within the context, allowing assessment of the system's ability to retrieve relevant information and generate faithful responses. HotpotQA is a multi-hop QA dataset requiring the aggregation of evidence from multiple documents to answer a single question. It provides a benchmark for evaluating MA-RAG's multi-agent capabilities, including query decomposition, long-context retrieval, and reasoning across multiple sources.

Table 1. Breakdown of Datasets Used for Evaluation

Dataset	Total Q&A Pairs	Q&A Pairs Used for Evaluation
SQuAD v1	107,785	1,000
SQuAD v2	150,000	1,000
HotpotQA	113,000	1,000

For each dataset, the first 1,000 questions were selected to provide a consistent evaluation setting for comparing MA-RAG against Traditional and Ensemble RAG baselines (Table 1). Table 2 further highlights that both SQuAD datasets predominantly consist of fact-seeking queries beginning with "what," "which," "how," or "who," with relatively few reasoning-oriented or structurally ambiguous questions.

Table 2. Top Three Question Types (First 1,000 Samples)

Dataset	Top Type	Second Type	Third Type
SQuAD v1.1	what (39.8%)	which (17.3%)	how (15.1%)
SQuAD v2.0	what (43.6%)	who (15.3%)	which (13.1%)
HotpotQA	what (35.6%)	which (26.9%)	who (19.3%)

4   Methodology

This study introduces a novel Multi-Agent Retrieval-Augmented Generation (MA-RAG) architecture aimed at enhancing retrieval precision, generative accuracy, and response faithfulness in knowledge-intensive NLP tasks. The system adopts a modular agent-based framework built using LangChain for inter-agent orchestration and ChromaDB as a persistent vector store for indexing and retrieval.

To evaluate MA-RAG, two baseline architectures-Traditional RAG and Ensemble RAG-are implemented as described in Sect. 4.1. These serve as comparative references for assessing retrieval performance and answer quality under standard and hybrid retrieval setups. The detailed design of the proposed MA-RAG architecture, including agent roles and workflow, is discussed in Sect. 4.2.

4.1 Baseline Architectures for Comparative Analysis

To contextualize MA-RAG's performance, two baseline systems are used: Traditional RAG and Ensemble RAG. These reflect single-strategy and hybrid retrieval mechanisms.

The Traditional RAG architecture operates via a two-stage pipeline. Documents are embedded as high-dimensional vectors and stored in a vector index. Upon query input, the top-k most similar documents are retrieved using dense similarity search and passed to a Large Language Model (LLM) for answer generation (Fig. 1).

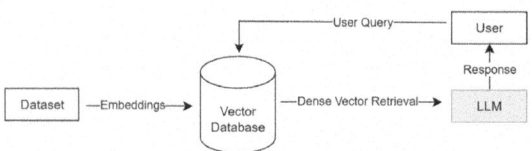

Fig. 1. Traditional RAG Architecture

The Ensemble RAG variant combines dense semantic retrieval with sparse BM25-based keyword matching. Results from both methods are merged and reranked by relevance. The top passages are fed to the LLM, increasing recall and improving answer quality where both lexical and semantic signals are important (Fig. 2).

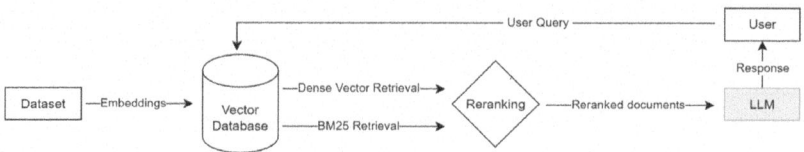

Fig. 2. Ensemble RAG Architecture

4.2 Proposed Architecture: Multi-Agent RAG (MA-RAG)

The MA-RAG architecture (Fig. 3) introduces a modular, agent-inspired design to enhance retrieval precision and answer faithfulness in knowledge-intensive tasks. Unlike conventional ensemble RAG setups, MA-RAG leverages a pipeline of specialized components, each acting as a focused LLM-driven module coordinated through a deterministic workflow implemented via LangChain's State-Graph framework.

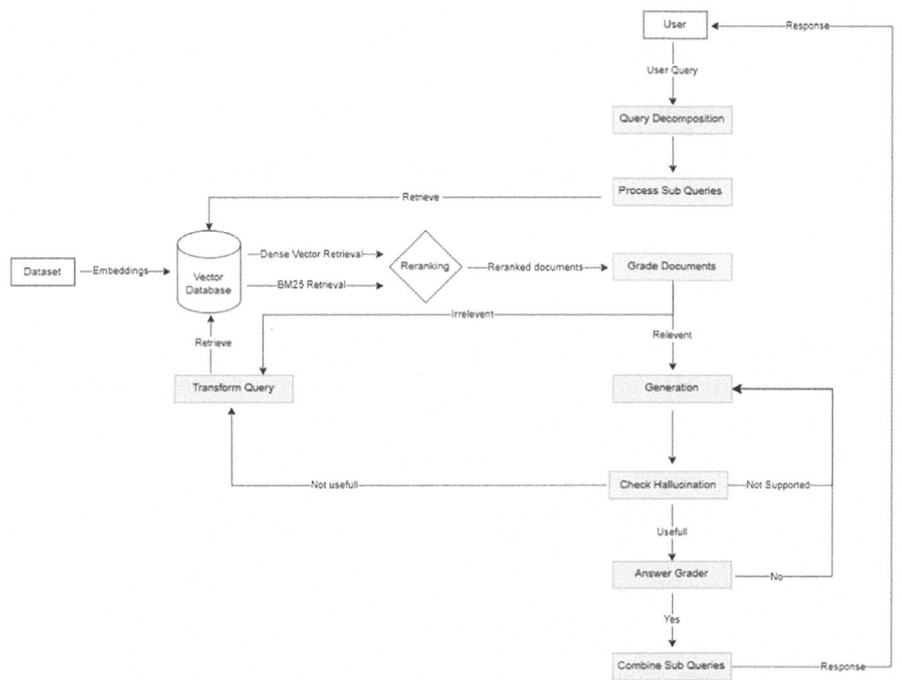

Fig. 3. Multi-Agent RAG (MA-RAG) Architecture

The pipeline begins with a Query Decomposition Agent, which reformulates the input question into multiple sub-queries to improve coverage and retrieval diversity. These are processed by a hybrid retrieval module that combines BM25 keyword search and dense vector retrieval, with weighted merging to balance semantic relevance and lexical overlap. Retrieved documents are then filtered by a Document Grading Agent, which assesses their relevance to the sub-queries.

In cases where no high-quality context is found, a Query Rewriting Agent iteratively reformulates the sub-query and re-triggers the retrieval cycle, supporting up to 25 iterations. Once relevant passages are identified, a Generate Agent produces candidate answers constrained to retrieved evidence.

The system integrates a multi-stage Hallucination Detection Agent, which performs three-way classification: *useful* (strongly grounded), *not useful* (weak support), and *not supported* (hallucinated). Responses labeled not useful trigger further retrieval, while hallucinated ones initiate re-generation. Only useful responses proceed to an Answer Grader Agent for final relevance validation.

Validated sub-answers are aggregated into a unified output. If no reliable information is available, the system returns a fallback response indicating the absence of sufficient evidence.

Implementation Details.   MA-RAG is implemented in Python using LangChain and LangGraph for workflow control. All agents rely on the GPT-4o-mini model accessed via the Azure OpenAI API. The retrieval module uses ChromaDB for vector search with `sentence-transformers/paraphrase-mpnet-base-v2` embeddings and combines top-5 BM25 and top-7 dense retrieval results using a 0.4/0.6 weighting strategy. Each agent's behavior is governed by static, task-specific prompts designed for transparency, modularity, and performance consistency.

5   Experiment and Results

To evaluate the performance of the proposed Multi-Agent Retrieval-Augmented Generation (MA-RAG) architecture, experiments were conducted using three benchmark QA datasets: SQuAD v1.1, SQuAD v2.0, and HotpotQA. MA-RAG was compared to two baseline models: traditional RAG and ensemble RAG, under two distinct retrieval conditions to investigate how knowledge base scale and noise impact system performance.

5.1   Experimental Setup

Two experimental configurations were established. In Experiment One, models retrieved information from an unfiltered, large-scale knowledge base: 107,785 passages for SQuAD v1.1, 150,000 for SQuAD v2.0, and 113,000 for HotpotQA. This setup reflected realistic, high-noise retrieval environments where relevant content is embedded within large volumes of unrelated information.

Experiment Two utilized a constrained and noise-free retrieval setting. Only the passages directly associated with answers for the first 1,000 questions were included in the indexed document set. This configuration enabled the isolation of retrieval and generation performance under ideal conditions (Table 3).

System performance was evaluated using five core RAGAS metrics: Mean Context Precision (MCP), Mean Context Recall (MCR), Mean Faithfulness (MF), Mean Answer Relevancy (MAR), and Mean Answer Correctness (MAC). These capture retrieval relevance and generative factuality, as detailed in Sect. 2.3.

To complement these, span-based overlap metrics—Exact Match (EM), F1, and BLEU-were also computed, offering additional insight into span-level answer fidelity and surface-form fluency without requiring extra annotations.

Table 3. Datasets and Evaluation Statistics for Experiment One and Two

Dataset	Source Documents (Exp. 1)	Source Documents (Exp. 2)	Q&A Pairs (Both)
SQuAD v1	107,785	1,000	1,000
SQuAD v2	150,000	1,000	1,000
HotpotQA	113,000	1,000	1,000

5.2 Span-Based Metric Results

In addition to RAGAS-derived metrics, Exact Match (EM), F1, and BLEU scores were computed to further evaluate answer quality across all three QA datasets. These metrics provide complementary insight into span-level correctness (EM), token-level semantic overlap (F1), and surface-form fluency (BLEU).

The results, summarized in Table 4, demonstrate that MA-RAG consistently outperforms both Traditional RAG and Ensemble RAG across all datasets.

Table 4. Span-Based Evaluation Results for Experiment One (EM, F1, BLEU)

Dataset	Classifier	EM (%)	F1 (%)	BLEU (%)
HotpotQA	MA-RAG	**11.09**	**74.22**	**53.15**
	Traditional RAG	7.20	64.57	41.93
	Ensemble RAG	7.20	69.15	44.63
SQuAD v1.1	MA-RAG	**17.30**	**72.06**	**50.66**
	Traditional RAG	9.80	56.90	35.57
	Ensemble RAG	9.80	60.54	37.32
SQuAD v2.0	MA-RAG	**13.20**	**67.99**	**46.03**
	Traditional RAG	9.80	53.57	33.06
	Ensemble RAG	9.30	55.58	33.63
Average	MA-RAG	**13.86**	**71.42**	**49.95**
	Traditional RAG	8.93	58.35	36.85
	Ensemble RAG	8.77	61.76	38.53

The largest gains were observed on SQuAD v1.1 and HotpotQA. On SQuAD v1.1, MA-RAG nearly doubled the EM score compared to Ensemble RAG, with significant improvements in F1 (+11.5%) and BLEU (+13.3%). On HotpotQA, where multi-hop reasoning is critical, MA-RAG achieved +3.89% higher EM, +5.07% higher F1, and +8.52% higher BLEU than Ensemble RAG.

5.3 Experiment One: Full Knowledge Base Retrieval

To evaluate system performance under large-scale, noisy retrieval conditions, Experiment One employed full document collections for HotpotQA, SQuAD v1.1, and SQuAD v2.0. Results across all evaluation metrics and model configurations are presented in Table 5, providing dataset-specific insights.

Table 5. Dataset-wise and Average Results for Experiment One (Full Knowledge Base)

Dataset	Classifier	MCP	MCR	MF	MAR	MAC
HotpotQA	MA-RAG	**0.836**	**0.837**	**0.796**	**0.722**	**0.842**
	Traditional RAG	0.657	0.667	0.551	0.485	0.566
	Ensemble RAG	0.665	0.828	0.755	0.692	0.803
SQuAD v1.1	MA-RAG	**0.816**	**0.700**	**0.803**	**0.781**	**0.840**
	Traditional RAG	0.646	0.555	0.764	0.707	0.766
	Ensemble RAG	0.651	0.583	0.790	0.748	0.809
SQuAD v2.0	MA-RAG	**0.828**	**0.676**	**0.802**	**0.768**	**0.837**
	Traditional RAG	0.670	0.491	0.736	0.659	0.721
	Ensemble RAG	0.678	0.505	0.772	0.675	0.739
Average	MA-RAG	**0.8262**	**0.7376**	**0.8003**	**0.7567**	**0.8396**
	Traditional RAG	0.6577	0.5708	0.6838	0.6167	0.6842
	Ensemble RAG	0.6646	0.6383	0.7724	0.7048	0.7835

For a consolidated view, average scores across datasets are reported in Table 5. These results facilitate system-level benchmarking across varied QA settings.

MA-RAG consistently outperformed both baselines across all metrics. In retrieval, it achieved the highest mean context precision (0.826) and recall (0.738), compared to Ensemble RAG (0.665 MCP, 0.638 MCR) and Traditional RAG (0.658 MCP, 0.571 MCR). Superior answer generation was also observed, with MA-RAG reaching 0.800 in faithfulness, 0.757 in answer relevance, and 0.840 in correctness. These results highlight MA-RAG's robustness under noisy retrieval, supported by its agent-based decomposition and document filtering mechanisms.

5.4   Experiment Two: Constrained Knowledge Base Retrieval

Experiment Two evaluated model performance using a constrained knowledge base containing only answer-supporting documents, minimizing retrieval noise. Dataset-specific and average scores across datasets results are reported in Table 6

MA-RAG achieved the highest scores across all datasets and metrics. In HotpotQA, it recorded an MCP of 0.895 and MAC of 0.860, substantially outperforming both baselines. The averaged results in Table 6 confirm its leading performance, with notable margins in faithfulness (0.843) and correctness (0.863).

Interestingly, Traditional RAG slightly outperformed Ensemble RAG in MCP (0.700 vs. 0.690), suggesting reduced benefit from reranking when retrieval is

Table 6. Dataset-wise and Average Results for Experiment Two (Constrained Knowledge Base)

Dataset	Classifier	MCP	MCR	MF	MAR	MAC
HotpotQA	MA-RAG	**0.895**	**0.858**	**0.844**	**0.749**	**0.860**
	Traditional RAG	0.591	0.822	0.821	0.700	0.803
	Ensemble RAG	0.616	0.835	0.823	0.743	0.852
SQuAD v1.1	MA-RAG	**0.844**	**0.716**	**0.826**	**0.808**	**0.870**
	Traditional RAG	0.688	0.628	0.797	0.727	0.791
	Ensemble RAG	0.692	0.624	0.769	0.735	0.802
SQuAD v2.0	MA-RAG	**0.868**	**0.732**	**0.860**	**0.796**	**0.860**
	Traditional RAG	0.821	0.515	0.661	0.604	0.659
	Ensemble RAG	0.762	0.626	0.766	0.748	0.820
Average	MA-RAG	**0.8690**	**0.7686**	**0.8434**	**0.7808**	**0.8634**
	Traditional RAG	0.6999	0.6552	0.7596	0.6768	0.7510
	Ensemble RAG	0.6901	0.6949	0.7859	0.7417	0.8246

noise-free. Overall, MA-RAG's consistent superiority across metrics underscores its adaptability and effectiveness in clean retrieval conditions.

5.5   Cross-Experiment Comparison

To examine the influence of retrieval scale on model performance, a cross-experiment comparison was conducted using results from Experiment One (full retrieval) and Experiment Two (constrained retrieval). For each model—Traditional RAG, Ensemble RAG, and MA-RAG—the relative change in performance was computed by measuring the percentage difference between the two settings, based on the average values reported in Tables 5 and 6. This comparison provides a normalized view of how retrieval context impacts key evaluation metrics.

Table 7. Percentage Improvement from Experiment One to Experiment Two

Model	MCP	MCR	MF	MAR	MAC
MA-RAG	+5.18%	+4.20%	+5.39%	+3.19%	+2.83%
Ensemble RAG	+3.84%	+8.88%	+1.75%	+5.24%	+5.24%
Traditional RAG	**+6.42%**	**+14.80%**	**+11.09%**	**+9.76%**	**+9.76%**

The results, summarized in Table 7, reveal that Traditional RAG benefited the most from the constrained setting. A +14.80% increase in mean context recall and +9.76% gain in answer correctness indicate its reliance on clean, targeted retrieval. Ensemble RAG showed moderate improvements, most notably in context recall (+8.88%) and answer relevancy (+5.24%), reflecting the partial noise mitigation offered by its reranking component.

MA-RAG also experienced consistent gains across all metrics, despite already strong baseline performance under noisy retrieval. Its +5.18% improvement in mean context precision and +5.39% in faithfulness further highlight its robustness and adaptability across retrieval conditions.

5.6   Comparative Performance Analysis

The performance gains of MA-RAG were evaluated relative to two baselines: Ensemble RAG and Traditional RAG. Improvements were derived from average results in Experiment One (Table 5) and Experiment Two (Table 6) and are presented in Table 8 as percentage deltas across five key evaluation metrics.

Against Ensemble RAG, MA-RAG achieved notable gains, including up to +25.92% in mean context precision and +7.16% in answer correctness. Relative to Traditional RAG, the improvements were more pronounced, reaching +29.24% in mean context recall and +22.71% in answer correctness under the large-scale retrieval setting of Experiment One. These results demonstrate MA-RAG's effectiveness in both retrieval quality and generation faithfulness.

Table 8. Percentage Performance Gains of MA-RAG Compared to Baselines

Exp.	Baseline	MCP	MCR	MF	MAR	MAC
Exp. 1	Ensemble RAG	+24.32%	+15.57%	+3.61%	+7.37%	+7.16%
	Traditional RAG	+25.62%	+29.24%	+17.03%	+22.70%	+22.71%
Exp. 2	Ensemble RAG	+25.92%	+10.61%	+7.32%	+5.28%	+4.70%
	Traditional RAG	+24.16%	+17.30%	+11.03%	+15.36%	+14.96%

6   Conclusion and Outlook

This study introduced MA-RAG, a novel Multi-Agent Retrieval-Augmented Generation architecture designed to improve retrieval accuracy and response faithfulness in knowledge-intensive NLP tasks. By integrating specialized agents for query decomposition, retrieval refinement, hallucination detection, and answer validation, MA-RAG consistently outperformed Traditional and Ensemble RAG baselines across multiple datasets and retrieval scenarios. As shown in Tables 5 and 6, notable gains were achieved in context recall, precision, and answer correctness, particularly in large-scale or noisy environments. These results highlight the effectiveness of agent-based orchestration in enhancing both factual grounding and retrieval relevance.

While the results are promising, the evaluation was limited to 1,000 samples per dataset. Future work should extend testing to full datasets and incorporate benchmarks such as Natural Questions or BioASQ to assess domain generalizability. Further enhancements may focus on reducing runtime overhead through adaptive thresholds, parallel agent execution, or learned scheduling. Additionally, expanding MA-RAG to support multi-modal inputs, integrated explainability, and intelligent agent coordination mechanisms could further strengthen its applicability in real-world, high-stakes domains.

Disclosure of Interests. The authors are research associates, and this work was funded and supported by the Joint Innovation Hub Heilbronn, research group of Fraunhofer Institute for Systems and Innovation Research ISI.

References

1. Ji, Z., et al.: Survey of hallucination in natural language generation. ACM Comput. Surv. **55**(12), 1–38 (2023)
2. Lewis, P., et al.: Retrieval-augmented generation for knowledge-intensive NLP tasks. arXiv preprint arXiv:2005.11401 (2020)
3. Chen, Y., et al.: Improving retrieval-augmented generation through multi-agent reinforcement learning. arXiv preprint arXiv:2501.15228 (2025)
4. Barnett, S., Kurniawan, S., Thudumu, S., Brannelly, Z., Abdelrazek, M.: Seven failure points when engineering a retrieval augmented generation system. arXiv preprint arXiv:2401.05856 (2024)
5. Besen, S.: The limitations and advantages of retrieval augmented generation. https://medium.com/data-science/the-limitations-and-advantages-of-retrieval-augmented-generation-rag. Accessed 04 May 2025
6. Ligteringen, J.: Everything wrong with retrieval-augmented generation. https://www.leximancer.com/blog/everything-wrong-with-retrieval-augmented-generation. Accessed 04 May 2025
7. Karpukhin, V., et al.: Dense passage retrieval for open-domain question answering. In: EMNLP 2020, pp. 6769–6781 (2020)
8. Asai, A., Wu, Z., Wang, Y., Sil, A., Hajishirzi, H.: Self-RAG: learning to retrieve, generate, and critique through self-reflection. arXiv preprint arXiv:2310.11511 (2023)
9. An, Y., Cheng, Y., Park, S.J., Jiang, J.: HyperRAG: enhancing quality-efficiency tradeoffs in retrieval-augmented generation with Reranker KV-cache reuse. arXiv preprint arXiv:2504.02921 (2025)
10. Zhang, Y., Sun, R., Chen, Y., Pfister, T., Zhang, R., Arik, S.Ö.: Chain of agents: large language models collaborating on long-context tasks. In: NeurIPS 2024, vol. 37 (2024)
11. Zhang, W., Zhang, J.: Hallucination mitigation for retrieval-augmented large language models: a review. Mathematics **13**(5), 856 (2025). https://doi.org/10.3390/math13050856
12. Rajagopal, S., et al.: RAGAS: evaluation of retrieval-augmented generation with reference-free metrics. arXiv preprint arXiv:2309.16521 (2023)
13. Yao, S., et al.: ReAct: synergizing reasoning and acting in language models. In: ICLR 2023 (2023)

14. Shuster, K., Komeili, M., Adolphs, L., Roller, S., Szlam, A., Weston, J.: Language models that seek for knowledge: modular search & generation for dialogue and prompt completion. In: Findings of ACL (2022)
15. Komeili, M.: Internet-augmented dialogue generation. arXiv preprint arXiv:2107.07566 (2021)
16. Shen, Y., Song, K., Tan, X., Li, D., Lu, W., Zhuang, Y.: HuggingGPT: solving AI tasks with ChatGPT and its friends in hugging face. In: NeurIPS 2023 (2023)
17. Joshi, M., Choi, E., Weld, D., Zettlemoyer, L.: TriviaQA: a large scale distantly supervised challenge dataset for reading comprehension. In: ACL (2017)
18. Soni, S., Yadav, V., Singh, S.: RAG-based biomedical question answering using clinical notes. In: EMNLP Workshop on HealthNLP (2022)

A Quantitative Evaluation of Natural Language Retrieval Methods for OpenAPI Specifications

Shankar Mathew Palamootil$^{(\boxtimes)}$ (ID) and Jacomine Grobler (ID)

Department of Industrial Engineering, Stellenbosch University,
Stellenbosch, South Africa
23687436@sun.ac.za

Abstract. Effective schema-based data generation fundamentally depends on utilising the correct schema. Consequently, the ability to accurately retrieve the schema most relevant to specific user requirements constitutes a critical area of research. This paper investigates three research questions: 1) What is the most effective mechanism for retrieving structured data? 2) How do different representations of this structured data influence retrieval performance? 3) Can a selective reranking approach improve efficiency without substantially compromising effectiveness? To address these questions, this work introduces *NL-to-OpenAPI*, a novel dataset pairing natural language queries with corresponding OpenAPI specifications. The queries are specifically designed to evaluate both keyword-based and semantic retrieval approaches. Additionally, a novel selective reranking method is proposed that uses a z-score threshold to estimate retrieval confidence, enabling a trade-off between computational efficiency and retrieval effectiveness.

Keywords: Structured data · Natural language retrieval · OpenAPI specification

1 Introduction

Generating structured data from *natural language* (NL) input—while conforming to a specific schema—is critical in many real-world data capture scenarios. Traditional approaches often rely on static questionnaires, manual annotation, or complex parsing techniques, each with its own limitations. Recently, *large language models* (LLMs) have demonstrated strong capabilities in understanding and executing tasks based on NL, opening new avenues for schema-conforming data generation. This has led to a growing interest in leveraging LLMs to directly translate NL input into structured, schema-compliant data.

The transformation of NL into structured data hinges on accurately identifying key entities in the input and mapping them to a corresponding schema. LLMs are in-context learners [10] and thus, the quality and relevance of information provided within the prompt significantly influence the LLM's output.

© The Author(s), under exclusive license to Springer Nature Switzerland AG 2026
J. Valente de Oliveira et al. (Eds.): EPIA 2025, LNAI 16122, pp. 303–315, 2026.
https://doi.org/10.1007/978-3-032-05179-0_23

More relevant examples or context generally lead to more accurate, grounded, and fitting responses. LLMs also struggle to recall information when the volume within the prompt context window increases [11]. These limitations underscore the importance of providing concise yet highly relevant information to effectively guide the LLM in completing its designated task.

As a result, NL-based retrieval has emerged as an active area of research, with the goal of enhancing LLM performance by dynamically providing query-relevant context at inference time [12]. Most benchmark datasets [5] focus on the retrieval of unstructured natural language documents, largely overlooking the retrieval of structured data—despite its widespread use in real-world applications. Prior work has explored translating natural language into structured query languages [13,14] but these efforts primarily target data querying rather than the retrieval of structured schemas. While existing techniques perform well in unstructured text retrieval or structured query execution, there is a clear lack of research and evaluation concerning the retrieval of structured *Javascript object notation* (JSON) documents using natural language.

This gap is addressed in the present work through the introduction of a new benchmark dataset focused on JSON schema retrieval. The dataset consists NL queries related to *application programming interface* (API) creation and their corresponding *OpenAPI specifications* (OAS), a standard structured form of data that defines the API. *State-of-the-art* (SOTA) retrieval methods are then evaluated on this task, highlighting the unique challenges associated with retrieving structured JSON documents.

The findings indicate that a dense retriever was the most effective single-pass mechanism, achieving a **10.3% improvement in the *normalised discounted cumulative gain at rank 10* (nDCG@10) over the lexical baseline, *best matching 25* (BM25)**, albeit being approximately 2.37 orders of magnitude slower. Regarding data representation, **LLM generated summaries of OAS documents yielded the most significant retrieval improvements**. Finally, the selective two-stage reranking approach, combining BM25 with the dense retriever *inf-retriever-v1-1.5b* , achieved a modest **1.9% increase in nDCG@10**. This method was 1.78 orders of magnitude slower than standalone BM25 but roughly four times faster than using the dense retriever exclusively.

The key contributions of this paper are therefore threefold: (1) the introduction of a novel NL-to-OpenAPI dataset for evaluating retrieval on structured data; (2) an empirical evaluation and critical analysis of SOTA retrieval methods on this dataset; and (3) the proposal of a novel selective reranking approach.

2   Relevant Theory

This section defines the notion of structured data in the context of this research (Sect. 2.1) and provides an overview of the SOTA retrieval methodologies evaluated (Sect. 2.2).

2.1   Structured Data

An API contract functions as a formal blueprint outlining the API's structure, available endpoints (data query points), data models (inputs and outputs), authentication methods, and expected behaviours. While various conventions exist for defining API contracts, the OAS [9] has emerged as the dominant, widely adopted standard. This standardisation promotes the reusability of API definitions and facilitates seamless integration across diverse platforms. Ideally, through the API contract, all the necessary information required to recreate or understand the API implementation can be found. These OAS documents are typically serialised as JSON or *Yet another markup language* (YAML) formats. Owing to their highly structured and exhaustive nature, they are susceptible to failure if even minor syntactic or structural errors are introduced. The ability to automatically retrieve and interpret relevant segments of an OAS in response to a NL query presents significant opportunities for downstream applications in LLMs. Such capabilities could enhance tasks such as API-centric question answering or enable the generation of API infrastructure by allowing users to replicate or adapt the design of existing specifications for their own systems. As such, the OAS constitutes the structured data component analysed in the study. An example of an OAS is given in Listing 1.

```
1   {
2     "openapi": "3.0.0",
3     "info": {
4       "title": "Simple Weather API",
5       "description": "API that returns the current weather for a city."},
6     "paths": {"/weather": {"get": {
7         "summary": "Get weather by city",
8         "parameters": [
9           {
10            "name": "city",
11            "in": "query",
12            "required": true,
13            "description": "City name",
14            "schema": {"type": "string"}
15          }],}}}}
```

Listing 1. Simple OpenAPI JSON snippet

2.2   Retrieval Mechanisms

This study evaluates and compares five distinct retrieval methodologies for retrieving relevant OAS documents based on natural language queries. These include: sparse retrieval, dense retrieval, hybrid retrieval and a novel selective reranking approach. In the context of this work, the term 'document' refers specifically to an OAS within the corpus, while the 'query' denotes the user's natural language input used to find the relevant OAS.

Sparse retrieval techniques represent documents and queries as high-dimensional sparse vectors. These vectors are termed 'sparse' because they are primarily composed of zero entries, with non-zero values corresponding only to the terms present in the document or query relative to the entire vocabulary. This term-based representation is relatively interpretable, as the dimensions directly correspond to words. Crucially, it enables the use of an inverted index: a data structure that maps each term (word) to a list of all documents containing that term. Consequently, when searching for documents relevant to a query, the system only needs to consider the documents associated with the terms present in the query, drastically reducing the search space compared to examining every document in the corpus.

Two specific sparse retrieval algorithms are employed in this paper. The first one is Okapi BM25 [8]. It calculates a relevance score for a document with respect to a query by aggregating scores for individual query terms. This scoring considers three primary factors, namely how often a query term appears in the candidate document, how infrequent the query term appears in other documents and adjusting the score to account for candidate document length–reducing the potential bias exerted by longer documents. BM25 remains a robust and widely used baseline retrieval algorithm; its reliance on surface-level keyword matching, though, limits its effectiveness in semantically rich use cases—that is, scenarios where relevant documents may use different vocabulary or phrasing than the query. In such cases, meaningful matches depend on understanding underlying concepts or synonyms rather than exact term overlap, leading BM25 to frequently miss relevant results due to vocabulary mismatch.

Contemporary sparse retrieval models address the inefficacy of BM25 in semantic contexts by integrating vocabulary expansion mechanisms that enhance the model's ability to capture latent semantic relationships. One such approach is the *sparse lexical and expansion model* (SPLADE) [7]. The framework employs a transformer-based language model to generate embeddings that capture the semantic meaning of documents and queries. These embeddings are then processed through a linear projection layer that projects them into sparse representations consisting of the most representative words from the output vocabulary. These sparse representations can be indexed and retrieved efficiently using traditional inverted indices, enabling SPLADE to combine the semantic capabilities of deep language models with the speed and interpretability of sparse retrieval. SPLADE or more specifically SPLADE-v3 [6] is the current SOTA model in the field of neural sparse retrieval.

Dense retrieval methods represent documents and queries as dense, multi-dimensional vectors within a shared latent space, aiming to capture semantic meaning rather than relying solely on lexical overlap. The core principle is that documents and queries encoded into this space should be located close to each other if they are semantically similar. Retrieval usually involves calculating the vector similarity (commonly using cosine similarity or dot product) between the query vector and the document vector. This approach is effective but can be slow. Unlike sparse retrieval methods that leverage inverted indices for efficiency, this dense approach typically requires comparing the query vector to every document in the corpus. Given the variety of available dense retrieval models, specific criteria were established for selecting an appropriate model for this study. This criteria is presented in Table 1.

Applying these criteria on the *massive text embedding benchmark leaderboard* (MTEB) [4], the *inf-retriever-v1-1.5b*[1] model (DIR) was selected as the most suitable dense retriever for this study. It is a variant of *gte-Qwen2-1.5B-instruct* that was fine-tuned for retrieval tasks.

Table 1. Evaluation criteria for dense retrieval model

Criteria	Description
Availability	The model should be open source.
Size	The model should be less than three billion parameters.
Context length	To prevent truncation of the largest OAS (approximately 6,000 tokens), the model should support an input context length of at least 7,000 tokens.
Performance	Models demonstrating stronger generalisation to unseen data are prioritised, as they are more likely to perform effectively on the novel NL-to-OpenAPI dataset.

Hybrid retrievers incorporate both dense and sparse retrieval techniques. Although this approach sounds similar to neural sparse retrievers (SPLADE), they differ in how they incorporate the different techniques together. Whereas some neural sparse retrievers, like SPLADE, use dense embeddings to produce a single, semantically-informed sparse representation suitable for inverted index retrieval, common hybrid retrieval strategies typically involve running a traditional sparse retriever (e.g., BM25) and a dense retriever independently. The final relevance ranking is then produced by fusing the results from these two separate systems, for example, by combining their scores. The SOTA hybrid retriever that is incorporated in this paper is the *Salient phrase aware retriever* (SPAR) [3].

The established BEIR (benchmarking information retrieval) benchmark [5] was used to provide a preliminary validation for the selected retrieval models and to verify the correctness of the implementation. BEIR is particularly relevant as it provides a heterogeneous suite of datasets designed to evaluate generalisation capabilities of retrieval models across diverse tasks and domains outside of their training dataset (zero-shot). The rationale for using BEIR was that models demonstrating strong zero-shot performance on its varied tasks are more likely to generalise effectively to the novel dataset (introduced in this paper). However, given the extensive nature of the full BEIR suite, preliminary validation

---

[1] https://huggingface.co/infly/inf-retriever-v1-1.5b.

adopted a pragmatic approach: Where available, published BEIR performance results from original papers or associated leaderboards were used as reference points for the selected models. In cases where such results were unavailable or required verification on specific subsets, limited experiments were conducted using a comparatively smaller subset of the BEIR collection. The results of this benchmark are provided in Table 2. The BEIR benchmark, and subsequent experiments, were conducted on a system equipped with a *13th Gen Intel® Core^{TM} i7-13850HX* processor, 32 GB of RAM, and an *NVIDIA RTX 3500 Ada Generation* laptop GPU.

Table 2. *The normalised discounted cumulative gain*(nDCG@k) [1] *for zero-shot performance on the BEIR benchmark. All scores denote the percentage nDCG@10 scores. The best scores are given in* **bold**. *The star* (*) *dictates that the scores were computed by the author.*

Model (→)	Lexical	Neural sparse		Dense		Hybrid
Dataset (↓)	BM25	docT5query	SPLADE	GenQ	DIR *	SPAR
TRE-COVID	0.656	0.713	**0.748**	0.619	0.696	0.630
NFCorpus	0.325	0.328	**0.357**	0.319	0.350	0.337
FiQA-2018	0.236	0.291	0.374	0.374	**0.481**	0.341
ArguAna	0.315	0.349	0.509	0.493	**0.570**	0.459
Quora	0.789	0.802	0.863	0.814	**0.893**	0.875
SCIDOCS	0.158	0.162	0.156	0.158	**0.228**	0.169
SciFact	0.665	0.675	0.682	0.710	**0.788**	0.695

3   Selective Reranking

Two-stage reranking is a common strategy that balances retrieval effectiveness and computational efficiency by first retrieving a candidate set using a lightweight method (e.g., BM25), then applying a more accurate but computationally intensive reranker to refine results. However, unconditional reranking can introduce unnecessary overhead or even degrade performance. To address these shortcomings, this study proposes a selective reranking approach that applies the second-stage retriever only when the first-stage results indicate low confidence. Confidence is quantified using a z-score threshold applied to the variance of BM25's top-k scores, based on the assumption that low variance signals uncertainty in the ranking. Specifically, when the z-score of the top retrieved document falls below a predefined threshold, this indicates that the document scores are similar, contrasting with scenarios where the top document significantly outperforms others. When the z-score of the top document is below the threshold, the top-k documents and their corresponding queries are passed to the reranker, which reorders this smaller subset based on query-document relevance. While edge cases may exist where all documents are equally good or poor, these scenarios have limited impact on the quality of the top-ranked document, as reranking will yield comparably good or poor results respectively. This method enables targeted use of reranking, optimising both performance and efficiency. The methodology of this selective reranker is presented in Fig. 1.

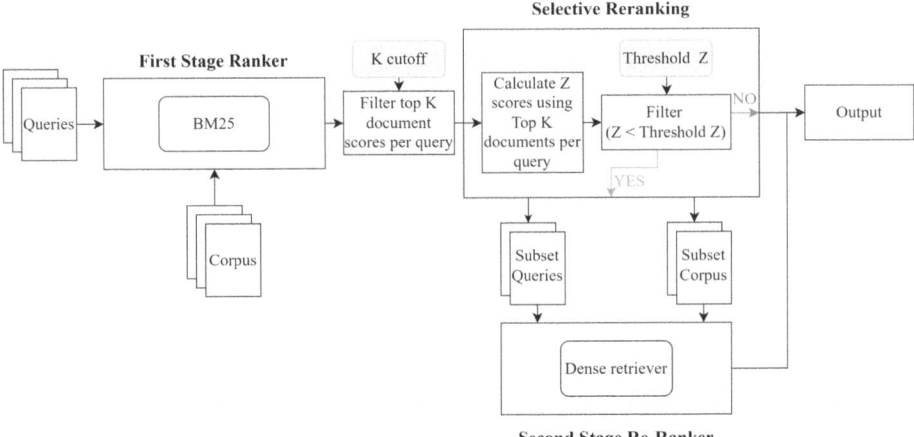

Fig. 1. A flow diagram illustrating the operation of the selective reranking process. Yellow blocks denote tunable hyperparameters within the pipeline. (Color figure online)

4   NL-to-OpenAPI Dataset Creation

The dataset simulates a common scenario where a user formulates a query in NL describing desired data, functionality, and the goal is to retrieve the most relevant OAS that fulfils this need. The source for the OAS documents was APIs.guru[2], a large public directory of API definitions. To create a manageable yet diverse collection, the following selection criteria were implemented:

– Specifications were initially filtered based on size, i.e. the 200 shortest definitions, determined by number of declared paths, were selected to favour more focused APIs.
– From this pool, specifications were chosen randomly to promote diversity.
– To prevent over-representation from single providers, a maximum of five specifications were included per originating application (e.g., different versions or components of the same core service).
– To prevent memory issues, specifications were also capped at 10000 tokens.

---

[2] https://apis.guru/.

This process resulted in a final corpus containing 198 unique OAS documents.

NL queries for each selected OAS were generated synthetically using an LLM, specifically Meta-llama-3.1-8B[3]. Utilising LLMs for synthetic data generation is an increasingly common approach, particularly where manual data creation is resource-intensive, as LLMs can generate diverse, human-like linguistic variations [2]. A temperature of 0.5 was used when generating queries. This parameter controls the randomness of the model's output—lower values make responses more focused and deterministic, while higher values produce more varied but less predictable results. Inspired by observations from Thakur et al. [5] suggesting that some benchmark datasets might inadvertently favour keyword-based retrieval methods like BM25, the aim was to create query sets that could evaluate both lexical and semantic retrieval capabilities. Therefore, two distinct sets of queries were generated:

– **The lexical query set** consisted of the initial, specific questions generated by the LLM, designed to have significant keyword overlap with the corresponding OAS content.
– **The semantic query set** was created by processing the 'lexical set' queries through a second LLM pass. For this pass, the LLM was specifically instructed to introduce noise within the question by paraphrasing the query, increasing ambiguity, and using synonyms. The objective was to generate queries requiring deeper semantic understanding, reducing reliance on direct keyword matching.

This dual-set approach allowed for a more nuanced evaluation of retrieval model robustness. The final dataset comprised five lexical and five semantic queries per specification. The combination of these queries resulted in 1980 query-specification pairs. Table 3 provides an example of each respective query type. The dataset and the queries used in this research are available on Github[4].

Table 3. Examples of Lexical and Semantic Queries

Query Type	Example Query	Description
Lexical Query	IP geolocation API providing current location data via a GET request to '/v1/' requiring an 'api_key' query parameter.	Unique words like GET, '/v1/' and 'api_key' assist in lexical matching.
Semantic Query	Find an API that provides current location data based on IP address.	Unique words are removed but intent of lexical query is preserved.

---

[3] https://huggingface.co/meta-llama/Llama-3.1-8B.
[4] https://github.com/shankarmpgit/Nl-to-OpenAPI.git.

5   Experiment

For the experimental evaluation, the selected retrieval mechanisms were benchmarked on the novel NL-to-OpenAPI dataset.

5.1   Results

The results provided in Table 4 alluded to Dense retrieval (DIR model) being the highest performing method of retrieval on structured data compared to the other methods. It boasted an average 10.3% over the BM25 baseline. The most consistent model, judged by the difference between the semantic and lexical scores was the SPLADE model.

Table 4. Zero-shot performance on the NL-to-OpenAPI dataset, evaluated using normalised discounted cumulative gain (nDCG@10) [1], Recall@10, and inference time. Results are reported for both the lexical and semantic subsets, along with the mean performance. All nDCG and recall values are expressed as percentages. Total runtime (in seconds) reflects the end-to-end execution time for the benchmark. Best results are shown in **bold**, with second-best results <u>underlined</u>.

Metric (→)	nDCG@10			Recall@10		Runtime (s)		
Model (↓)	Lexical	Semantic	Mean	Lexical	Semantic	Lexical	Semantic	Mean
BM25	0.944	0.753	0.821	<u>0.980</u>	0.852	**7.295**	**7.106**	**7.201**
SPLADE	0.736	0.710	0.727	0.839	0.820	<u>13.08</u>	<u>12.67</u>	<u>12.88</u>
SPAR	0.830	0.753	0.768	0.913	<u>0.880</u>	23.05	23.17	23.11
DIR	**0.963**	**0.910**	**0.924**	**0.991**	**0.979**	1150.0	2131.0	1641.0
BM25 + DIR	<u>0.947</u>	<u>0.772</u>	<u>0.860</u>	<u>0.980</u>	0.854	466.2	391.5	428.9

As illustrated in Fig. 2, further experiments explored the impact of different OAS representations on retrieval performance. In addition to using the raw specifications, three alternative document formats were evaluated. The first, *LLM Summary*, consisted of concise descriptions of each application's purpose and functionality, generated by a Large Language Model based on the content of the corresponding OAS. The second, *No Punctuation*, involved removing all punctuation (such as JSON braces, commas, and colons) from the specifications, preserving only the sequential textual content. The third, *Concatenated Descriptions*, was created by extracting and concatenating all textual descriptions from the specification along with the path to each description within the JSON structure.

The results indicate that BM25 and DIR demonstrated relative robustness across these varied representations. Notably, when utilising the LLM-generated summaries as the document representation, BM25's performance improved by approximately eight percent. A more substantial impact was observed with

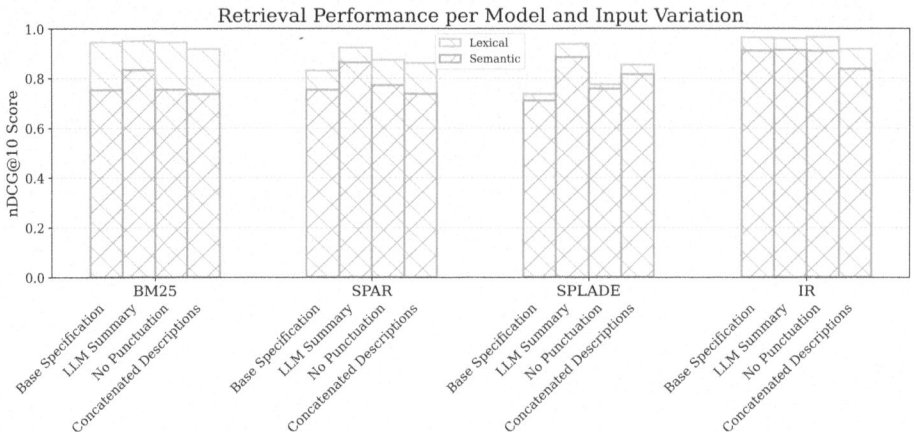

Fig. 2. Bar chart illustrating the overlapping retrieval performance (nDCG@10) of various retrieval techniques across different representations of the OAS.

SPLADE, which achieved an average performance increase of 18.8% when retrieving from the LLM-generated summaries.

The initial results of the novel selective reranking methodology are presented in the "BM25 + DIR" row of Table 4. A modest increase of 1.9% in nDCG@10 was achieved using a z-threshold of 1.3 with k = 4 for the first-stage retrieval. These hyperparameter values were determined through systematic experimentation across multiple z-threshold and k configurations. The associated runtime for this selective approach was approximately 1.78 orders of magnitude slower than standalone BM25, yet roughly four times faster (representing about a quarter of the runtime) than using the DIR for a full dense retrieval pass.

5.2 Discussion

Research Question 1: Based on the findings of this study, dense retrieval (DIR) emerges as the most effective mechanism for retrieving structured data. This result is consistent with performance trends observed on a smaller subset of the BEIR benchmark. However, a key point of divergence lies in the relative performance of BM25: while it ranks among the weakest performers across most BEIR tasks, it achieves the third-best performance on the NL-to-OpenAPI dataset. This discrepancy may be attributed to the nature of OAS documents, which tend to use simple, object-centric language with limited lexical variation. Such characteristics reduce the need for semantic matching and make traditional lexical retrievers like BM25 more competitive in this context. The runtime of the DIR model is about 2.37 orders of magnitude slower than that of the BM25 retriever. This disparity highlights a significant challenge for scalability, particularly in latency-sensitive applications adding to the competitiveness of the BM25 algorithm in single pass applications. While the initial encoding of a document corpus by a dense retriever can often be performed offline as a one-time pre-processing step, the query encoding and subsequent similarity search across document embeddings still contribute to online latency.

Research Question 2: The results obtained in Fig. 2 suggest that, overall, the LLM-generated summary representation yielded the most consistent benefits across the tested retrieval models. The condensation of information should intuitively perform better as unimportant information is discarded creating more succinct embeddings but the improvement of the BM25 algorithm was surprising. This improvement might be attributed to an increased lexical overlap between the LLM-generated queries (used in the main experiment) and these LLM-generated summaries, even if both were independently created.

Research Question 3: Although a modest improvement of 1.9% in nDCG@10 was observed, particularly unremarkable considering the increased computational cost over standalone BM25, the concept of selective reranking remains a promising, under-researched avenue for balancing retrieval performance and efficiency. In the context of this benchmark, where the document set is relatively small and each document is uniformly represented across the query space, the benefits of reranking are limited, as there is little room to reduce the number of document encodings without affecting relevance. However, in scenarios involving large corpora with many unrelated or less relevant documents, selective reranking could offer substantial efficiency gains by selectively focusing computation on the most promising candidates.

6   Conclusion

In conclusion, a novel NL-to-OpenAPI dataset designed to evaluate retrieval performance on structured data is introduced. It is used to benchmark state-of-the-art retrieval models on structured OAS data retrieval. Initial results find that dense retrieval (DIR) achieved the highest accuracy overall albeit being magnitudes slower than BM25. The dataset is also used to offer informed insights into the representation of OAS documents to enhance retrieval outcomes. Notably, generating LLM-based summaries of OAS documents led to performance improvements across most retrieval methodologies. Finally, a new selective reranking approach was proposed and its effectiveness was empirically validated on the NL-to-OpenAPI dataset. The results find a small improvement in accuracy over the BM25 algorithm but a four times speed increase compared to DIR.

Future research directions include incorporating real-world user queries to enhance the ecological validity of the benchmark. While this study focused on shorter specifications with limited API paths, evaluating model performance on longer and more complex OAS documents could offer deeper insights—particularly into whether increased document length reduces the effectiveness of dense retrieval due to higher computational costs. In addition, exploring more compact, structured representations of OAS documents or applying query expansion techniques may further boost retrieval performance. Finally, investigating alternative model architectures, including smaller transformer models or different architectural designs, could yield improved performance-efficiency trade-offs that better suit resource-constrained environments.

Acknowledgements. This work was funded by an industry partner that requested to remain anonymous. The sponsor had no involvement in study design, data collection and analysis, decision to publish, or preparation of the manuscript.

Disclosure of Interests. The authors do not have any competing interests to declare that are relevant to the content of this study.

References

1. Wang, Y., Wang, L., Li, Y., He, D., Liu, T.: A theoretical analysis of NDCG type ranking measures. In: Shalev-Shwartz, S., Steinwart, I. (eds.) Proceedings of the 26th Annual Conference on Learning Theory, Proceedings of Machine Learning Research, vol. 30, pp. 25–54. PMLR, Princeton (2013)
2. Nadas, M., Diosan, L., Tomescu, A.: Synthetic data generation using large language models: advances in text and code. *arXiv preprint*arXiv:2503.14023 (2025)
3. Chen, X., et al.: Salient phrase aware dense retrieval: can a dense retriever imitate a sparse one? In: Goldberg, Y., Kozareva, Z., Zhang, Y. (eds.) Findings of the Association for Computational Linguistics: EMNLP 2022, pp. 250–262. Association for Computational Linguistics, Abu Dhab (2022). https://doi.org/10.18653/v1/2022.findings-emnlp.19
4. Muennighoff, N., Tazi, N., Magne, L., Reimers, N.: MTEB: massive text embedding benchmark. *arXiv preprint*arXiv:2210.07316 (2022). https://doi.org/10.48550/ARXIV.2210.07316
5. Thakur, N., Reimers, N., Rücklé, A., Srivastava, A., Gurevych, I.: BEIR: a heterogeneous benchmark for zero-shot evaluation of information retrieval models. In: Thirty-fifth Conference on Neural Information Processing Systems Datasets and Benchmarks Track (Round 2) (2021)
6. Lassance, C., Déjean, H., Formal, T., Clinchant, S.: SPLADE-v3: New baselines for SPLADE. *arXiv preprint*arXiv:2403.06789 (2024)
7. Formal, T., Piwowarski, B., Clinchant, S.: SPLADE: sparse lexical and expansion model for first stage ranking. In: Proceedings of the 44th International ACM SIGIR Conference on Research and Development in Information Retrieval, pp. 2288–2292. ACM, New York (2021). https://doi.org/10.1145/3404835.3463098
8. Robertson, S., Walker, S., Hancock-Beaulieu, M.: Okapi BM25: a non-binary model - best matching estimate to 25 years. In: Proceedings of the 20th Annual International ACM SIGIR Conference on Research and Development in Information Retrieval, pp. 357–360. ACM, Philadelphia (1997). https://doi.org/10.1145/258525.258578
9. OpenAPI Initiative (OAI): OpenAPI Specification. Version 3.0.3 (2020). https://spec.openapis.org/oas/v3.0.3.html. Accessed 18 Apr 2025
10. Wei, J., et al.: Emergent abilities of large language models. *arXiv preprint*arXiv:2206.07682 (2022)

11. Liu, N.F., et al.: Lost in the middle: how language models use long contexts. Trans. Assoc. Comput. Linguist. **12**, 157–173 (2024)
12. Borgeaud, S., et al.: Improving language models by retrieving from trillions of tokens. In: Chaudhuri, K., Jegelka, S., Song, L., Szepesvari, C., Niu, G., Sabato, S. (eds.) Proceedings of the 39th International Conference on Machine Learning (ICML 2022), PMLR, vol. 162, pp. 2206–2240 (2022). https://proceedings.mlr.press/v162/borgeaud22a.html
13. Kesarwani, M., et al.: GraphQL query generation: a large training and benchmarking dataset. In: Proceedings of the 2024 Conference on Empirical Methods in Natural Language Processing: Industry Track, pp. 1595–1607 (2024)
14. Kim, H., So, B.-H., Han, W.-S., Lee, H.: Natural language to SQL: where are we today? Proc. VLDB Endow. **13**(10), 1737–1750 (2020). https://doi.org/10.14778/3401960.3401970

Authorship Verification of the Caesarian Corpus Using Siamese BERT

Brandon Li[1]([✉])[ID], David Nizovsky[2], Anna Leonenko[3],
Tingying Helen Zeng[4][ID], and Mikhail Shalaginov[5][ID]

[1] Belmont Hill School, Belmont, MA 02478, USA
brandonli319@gmail.com
[2] Vanderbilt University, Nashville, TN 37235, USA
[3] Citibank, New York, NY 10013, USA
[4] Academy for Advanced Research and Development, Cambridge, MA 02142, USA
[5] Massachusetts Institute of Technology, Cambridge, MA 02139, USA

Abstract. The question of Caesarian authorship of *De Bello Alexandrino*, *De Bello Africo*, and *De Bello Hispaniensi* has puzzled classical scholars for millennia. Although these three texts have traditionally been attributed to Caesar, stylistic differences between these texts and the rest of Caesar's corpus have resulted in doubts as to their true authorship. Prior computational studies on the authorship of these texts have involved traditional stylometric feature-based analysis and methods from the field of distributional semantics. However, with the advent of the transformer architecture in 2017, more sophisticated approaches to authorship verification have since emerged. This study builds upon previous results by employing the state-of-the-art transformer-based model Siamese BERT to investigate the authorship of *De Bello Alexandrino*, *De Bello Africo*, and *De Bello Hispaniensi*. As a secondary goal, this study also evaluates the effectiveness of Siamese BERT in conducting authorship analysis in Latin, thus assessing its potential for language-agnostic application. Following training on an open-source dataset provided by Vainio et al. (2019), the model achieved a 95.5% accuracy on the validation dataset. The model was further validated through cross-comparison of each text in Caesar's *De Bello Gallico* corpus, successfully identifying Book VIII as an outlier with regards to authorship. Finally, following authorship verification of the unknown texts using the model, results suggest that *De Bello Alexandrino* and *De Bello Africo* may have been written by Caesar, whereas *De Bello Hispaniensi* definitively was not written by Caesar. These findings offer new insight into a two-millennium-old mystery of authorship and contribute meaningfully to the historical interpretations about these texts. Furthermore, the results demonstrate that Siamese BERT is effective in authorship analysis of Latin, indicating its broader applicability across languages.

Keywords: Authorship Verification · Natural Language Processing · Digital Classics · Digital Humanities · Siamese BERT · Julius Caesar

© The Author(s), under exclusive license to Springer Nature Switzerland AG 2026
J. Valente de Oliveira et al. (Eds.): EPIA 2025, LNAI 16122, pp. 316–325, 2026.
https://doi.org/10.1007/978-3-032-05179-0_24

1   Introduction

The texts *De Bello Alexandrino*, *De Bello Africo*, and *De Bello Hispaniensi* recount Gaius Julius Caesar's conquests in Egypt, Africa, and Spain, respectively, and have traditionally been included in the collection of Caesar's works. However, since antiquity, classical scholars have questioned their authenticity due to stylistic differences between these texts and those that have been confirmed to be authored by the Roman general himself. This paper uses the state-of-the-art Siamese BERT model architecture to address this two-millennium-old mystery of authorship verification.

The fields of authorship attribution and verification have important applications. Techniques in the field have been used in forensic linguistics to contribute evidence in court, helping to convict the guilty and protect the innocent. One famous example of this is Ted Kaczynski, the Unabomber, who was convicted after his manifesto was attributed to him through stylometric techniques [7]. Authorship attribution and verification have also been used to analyze authorship claims about historical texts. Knowledge of such authorship is important for the historical record, as it provides useful context for the document in question, which enriches its understanding and interpretation. Authorship studies of historical texts have been done most famously with Shakespeare, whose works have been the subject of many computational studies over the years [13].

The corpus of texts with undisputed Caesarian authorship consists of Books I through III of De Bello Civili and Books I through VII of *De Bello Gallico* [5]. Book VIII of *De Bello Gallico*, which completes the set, is known to have been authored by Aulus Hirtius, a military officer serving under Caesar. This has led some scholars to question the degree to which Hirtius was responsible for authoring the rest of Caesar's corpus: Alfred Klotz argued in 1910 that Hirtius also authored *De Bello Alexandrino* due to stylistic similarities between it and Book VIII of *De Bello Gallico* [6].

A distinction should be made between authorship attribution and authorship verification. Authorship attribution attempts to classify a text into a closed set of potential authors, where the true author of the text is guaranteed to be within the set. In contrast, authorship verification is a binary classification task that attempts to determine whether a document was authored by a given author or not [9]. Since it is difficult to determine whether the true author of *De Bello Alexandrino*, *De Bello Africo*, and *De Bello Hispaniensi* is actually in the set of potential authors or not, this paper focuses on the authorship verification task instead of the authorship attribution task, seeking to determine whether these three documents were authored by Caesar or not.

Traditionally, stylometric feature-based analysis has been used to perform authorship verification in the Latin language. Stylometry, defined as "the statistical analysis of variations in literary style between one writer or genre and another," involves the comparison of "features" between texts. Such features can be lexical, syntactic, semantic, or n-gram-based, and encode a text's stylistic qualities that are unique to an author's writing style [4]. Feature-based comparison methods were used by Kestemont et al. (2016) to classify *De Bello*

Table 1. Prior authorship work on the Caesarian corpus

Study	Texts analyzed	Technique used
Klotz (1910)	*Alexandrino*	Manual stylometry
Kestemont et al. (2016)	All three	Computational stylometry
Zhang et al. (2018)	All three	Distributional semantics

Alexandrino, *De Bello Africo*, and *De Bello Hispaniensi*. The paper concluded that Caesar wrote the first 21 chapters of *De Bello Alexandrino*, Hirtius wrote the remaining chapters of *De Bello Alexandrino*, and that *De Bello Africo* and *De Bello Hispaniensi* were written by two distinct but non-Caesarian authors [5].

More recently, methods from the field of distributional semantics have also been used for this authorship verification task. In Zhang et al. (2018), which also evaluated the claim that Caesar authored the three texts in question, Random Indexing and Latent Dirichlet Allocation were used to generate a vector to represent each document [14]. This study concluded that all three of *De Bello Alexandrino*, *De Bello Africo*, and *De Bello Hispaniensi* were not written by Caesar (Table 1).

However, the advent of the transformer architecture in deep learning in 2017 has allowed for the development of more sophisticated authorship verification approaches. In contrast to previous models, these transformer-based approaches can capture deeply embedded semantic information while minimizing the need for manual feature engineering. Reimers and Gurevych (2019) first introduced the Siamese BERT network as an improvement upon Google's BERT model in semantic textual similarity tasks [8]. Tyo et al. (2021) then adapted the Siamese BERT architecture to the task of authorship verification by introducing a dense layer, which was used to extract the unique markers of authorship from the semantic output vectors of BERT [10]. The Siamese BERT architecture was found to be state-of-the-art in the English language for the authorship verification task by Tyo et al. (2022) [11]. However, Siamese BERT has not yet been tested for Latin, a language in which authorship verification provides a vital historical tool. To our knowledge, this is the first study to apply the Siamese BERT architecture to authorship analysis of Latin text.

Thus, this study provides two key contributions. First, it reevaluates the authorship of *De Bello Alexandrino*, *De Bello Africo*, and *De Bello Hispaniensi* using the state-of-the-art Siamese BERT model. Second, it assesses the versatility of the Siamese BERT architecture in conducting authorship verification across different languages.

2   Methods

2.1   Siamese BERT Architecture

To test the authorship of the texts in question, we train a Siamese BERT model modified to process Latin text instead of English text. The architecture of the model is shown in Fig. 1.

Following preprocessing and tokenization, the two texts x_1 and x_2 are each converted by the BERT model into their respective outputs of dimensionality $n \times 768$, with n representing the number of input tokens. To conduct authorship analysis of Latin text, we use a BERT model specifically trained on the Latin language provided by Bamman and Burns (2020) [1]. A mean pooling layer then averages out each $n \times 768$ BERT representation into a one-dimensional tensor of size 768, resulting in two document vectors y_1 and y_2 which encapsulate the semantic information of x_1 and x_2 respectively. The unique essence of each author's writing style is ultimately determined by feeding BERT outputs y_1 and y_2 through a feedforward neural network. This FNN consists of an input layer of size 768, a hidden layer of size 512, and an output layer of size 256, using the ReLu activation function. The final tensors z_1 and z_2 from this output layer encode stylistic representations of the texts x_1 and x_2. These two "style" tensors are ultimately compared with a distance metric to produce an output in the range $[0, 1]$ representing the degree of authorship similarity between x_1 and x_2. In this study, four different distance metrics are tested: cosine similarity, Euclidean distance, Manhattan distance, and dot distance. Ultimately, high similarity implies same authorship, and low similarity implies different authorship.

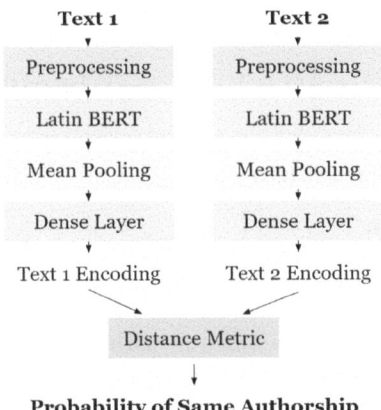

Fig. 1. Siamese BERT model architecture.

2.2   Dataset and Training

We use a publicly available corpus of Latin text compiled by Vainio et al. (2019). The corpus consists of 572 Latin documents and 42 authors, totaling 31,063,901 words. Texts from the original dataset were retrieved from The Latin Library and Bibliotheca Augustana [12]. For preprocessing, the data was converted back from CONLL-U to normal text format using Python's conllu library, enabling the BERT model to accept it as input. The text was tokenized with each word representing a token.

The dataset consisted of 4576 input pairs of 512 consecutive tokens, which were randomly sampled from the corpus. An even split between same-author pairs and different-author pairs was used throughout training. 512 tokens is the maximum input length of BERT, and training in this manner was most logical.

The model was trained for 10 epochs, with each epoch consisting of the same 4576 input pairs. Although the weights of the BERT model itself were frozen, a contrastive loss function was used to train the dense layer of the model. As shown in Eq. 1, contrastive loss, introduced by Hadsell et al. (2006), minimizes distances between semantically similar embeddings and maximizes distances between semantically different embeddings [3]. $L(W, Y, \boldsymbol{X}_1, \boldsymbol{X}_2)$ is the loss computed for a pair of inputs $\boldsymbol{X}_1$ and $\boldsymbol{X}_2$. W represents the weights of the dense layer, Y represents the binary label indicating whether the pair is of same or different authorship, D_W represents the distance between the embedded representations of $\boldsymbol{X}_1$ and $\boldsymbol{X}_2$, and m is the margin that defines the minimum required distance between dissimilar pairs. Contrastive loss has traditionally been used in authorship verification tasks with Siamese networks to optimize model performance [10]. Prior to training, all parameters in the dense layer were randomized.

$$L(W, Y, \boldsymbol{X}_1, \boldsymbol{X}_2) = \frac{1}{2}(1 - Y)D_W^2 + \frac{1}{2}Y\left\{\max(0, m - D_W)\right\}^2 \qquad (1)$$

3   Results and Discussion

3.1   Model Validation

To evaluate the strength of our model in classifying full-length texts, we construct a test dataset consisting of 90 pairs of full-length historical documents. This dataset consists of 45 pairs of documents, with both having been authored by Caesar, and 45 pairs of documents, with one authored by Caesar and the other authored by a different person.

To compare the authorship similarity of two full-length documents, methods from Tyo et al. (2022) were once again used. First, texts were chunked into groups of 512 tokens. Then, the model generated a similarity value for the first pair of 512 tokens of each text, a value for the second pair of 512 tokens, and continued until either of the texts had exhausted their chunks. The remaining unpaired portion of the text with a great number of words was truncated. The final similarity between the documents was the average of all similarities. This

Table 2. Model performance using cosine, manhattan, euclidean, and dot metrics.

	Accuracy	F1	Precision	Recall
Cosine	95.5%	0.957	93.6%	97.8%
Manhattan	82.2%	0.846	74.5%	97.8%
Euclidean	84.4%	0.857	75.0%	100%
Dot	55.6%	0.692	52.9%	100%

approach, which was used to analyze full-length documents in the validation dataset, allowed the entire document to be considered and avoided the problem of truncating full texts due to the short input maximum of BERT [11].

Throughout training, the model was periodically assessed on the validation dataset to evaluate training progress, and the cosine accuracy of the model on the validation dataset following each epoch is shown in Fig. 2. Throughout training, model accuracy on the validation dataset improved, saturating at 95.5%. Accuracy, precision, recall, and F1 metrics were taken across four distance metrics: cosine, manhattan, euclidean, and dot. The model worked best overall using the cosine distance metric, achieving a cosine accuracy of 95.5% and a cosine F1 score of 0.957. Final model results are provided in Table 2.

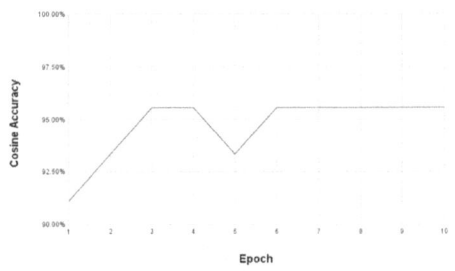

Fig. 2. Model validation throughout training.

3.2   Analysis of *De Bello Gallico*

To further demonstrate the validity of the model, we use the model to cross-compare each of the 8 books in *De Bello Gallico*, with results shown in Table 3. Larger numbers indicate higher similarities, with 1.0 being the maximum possible similarity used for identical vectors. The Siamese BERT architecture successfully differentiates Book 8, written by Aulus Hirtius, from the rest of the books in the set, written by Caesar. It accomplishes this with a noticeably lower average cosine similarity (0.405) between Book 8 and the rest of the books in the set.

Table 3. Cross comparison of all books in the *De Bello Gallico* set

	Book 1	Book 2	Book 3	Book 4	Book 5	Book 6	Book 7	Book 8
Book 1	–	0.449	0.525	0.496	0.472	0.483	0.451	0.266
Book 2		–	0.465	0.450	0.504	0.437	0.450	0.427
Book 3			–	0.496	0.492	0.451	0.525	0.540
Book 4				–	0.514	0.465	0.521	0.441
Book 5					–	0.496	0.499	0.350
Book 6						–	0.482	0.443
Book 7							–	0.366
Book 8								–
Mean	0.449	0.455	0.499	0.483	0.475	0.465	0.471	0.405

For further validation of the model's classification capabilities, we performed a Student's t-test on the cosine similarity scores between each pair of books in *De Bello Gallico*. The results revealed statistically significant differences ($p <$ 0.05) between Book VIII and each of Books IIIâĂŞVII, while Books IâĂŞVII showed no significant differences among themselves.

3.3 Classification of *De Bello Alexandrino*, *De Bello Africo*, and *De Bello Hispaniensi*

We finally turn to the task of authorship verification of *De Bello Alexandrino*, *De Bello Africo*, and *De Bello Hispaniensi*. Using our trained model, we cross-compared these three texts with *De Bello Civili*, *De Bello Gallico* excluding Book 8, and *De Bello Gallico* Book 8. Results are shown in Table 4. On average, each book in this set contains 8209.07 words. Comparisons between two volumes averaged out the set of similarities between all possible distinct pairs comparing a text of one volume and a text of another volume.

De Bello Civili and *De Bello Gallico* show relatively high cosine similarity, as expected, due to their confirmed Caesarian authorship. *De Bello Gallico* VIII shows lower relative cosine similarity, demonstrating its known authorship by Hirtius. *De Bello Alexandrino* also shows relatively high cosine similarity with De Bello Civili and *De Bello Gallico*, indicating potential Caesarian authorship. The same can be said for *De Bello Africo*, which shows high cosine similarity with the texts of known Caesarian authorship. However, *De Bello Hispaniensi* was the exception, showing low cosine similarity with all other texts in question.

To further validate model findings, we conducted a Student's t-test comparing stylistic similarity scores across Caesar's known works and the three disputed texts. Table 5 shows that *De Bello Gallico* VIII differs significantly ($p <$ 0.05) from both *De Bello Civili* and *De Bello Gallico*, reinforcing its known non-Caesarian authorship. In contrast, *De Bello Alexandrino* shows no statistically significant difference from Caesar's confirmed works ($p = 0.99$), aligning with

Table 4. Cross comparison of texts associated with the Caesarian corpus

	Civili	Gallico	Gallico VIII	Alexandrino	Africo	Hispaniensi
Civili	–	0.471	0.389	0.488	0.481	0.358
Gallico		–	0.405	0.459	0.470	0.376
Gallico VIII			–	0.355	0.336	0.365
Alexandrino				–	0.483	0.395
Africo					–	0.382
Hispaniensi						–
Mean	0.437	0.436	0.37	0.436	0.430	0.375

the model's classification of *Alexandrino* as likely authentic. *De Bello Africo* also exhibits no significant differences from the Caesarian corpus ($p > 0.7$), supporting the conclusion of same authorship. However, *De Bello Hispaniensi* shows near-significant divergence from *Civili* and *Gallico* ($p = 0.058$), while showing no difference from *Gallico* VIII ($p = 0.896$), suggesting that *Hispaniensi* was likely authored by someone distinct from Caesar. These findings provide statistical support for the model's conclusions and bolster the argument for varied authorship within the Caesarian corpus.

4   Conclusion

In this study, we demonstrated the effectiveness of the Siamese BERT architecture in performing authorship verification on Latin text, with the trained model achieving a 95.5% accuracy on the validation dataset. This demonstrates the versatility of the Siamese BERT architecture in classifying texts across multiple languages. We further validated the model by showing how the model could detect stylistic disparities between Book VIII of *De Bello Gallico* and the rest of the books in the *De Bello Gallico* set. Finally, we used the model to classify three texts with disputed Caesarian authorship: *De Bello Alexandrino*, *De Bello Africo*, and *De Bello Hispaniensi*, suggesting that *De Bello Alexandrino* and *De Bello Africo* were written by Caesar and that *De Bello Hispaniensi* was not. It should be noted that this study contradicts Zhang et al. (2018) and Kestemont et al. (2016), who both found that all three texts were definitively not authored by Caesar [5,14]. In this way, this paper builds upon previous results using new transformer-based authorship verification methods.

While this study demonstrates the effectiveness of Siamese BERT for Latin authorship verification, several limitations remain. First, although we performed basic word-level tokenization, we did not explore Latin-specific tokenization strategies, which may better capture the morphological richness of the language. Second, the use of random sampling to generate training pairs may have introduced limited overlap between training and evaluation data, which could affect model generalization. Third, we did not conduct a detailed error analysis of model predictions, such as examining false positives or negatives, or investigating how the model handles stylistic drift over time within an author's corpus. Finally, while our approach achieves strong performance, it was not compared against traditional stylometric baselines or hybrid models that combine neural embeddings with handcrafted features—both of which may offer complementary insights and warrant future investigation.

There are several areas in which future research could potentially be conducted. The Siamese BERT architecture could be tested in more languages to further ascertain how its effectiveness is dependent on the qualities and structure of a given language. Furthermore, Siamese BERT and other classifying architectures could help ascertain the authorship of other documents from the classical era with unknown or uncertain authorship. Additionally, although this study employed a relatively basic preprocessing pipeline consisting solely of word tokenization, future work could test preprocessing pipelines tailored more specifically to the Latin language. This could be beneficial, and algorithmic consideration of the complexity of Latin noun, verb, and adjective endings may improve the ability of the BERT model to develop a sound representation of the text. In addition, future work could explore stricter train-test data separation to avoid even minor overlaps caused by random sampling, as well as include formal benchmarking against traditional stylometric baselines or hybrid approaches combining transformer models with hand-engineered features. A more granular error analysis—such as evaluating false positives and false negatives or tracking how the model handles stylistic drift over time—may also provide greater interpretability and insight into model behavior. Furthermore, although the model functions well with 95.5% accuracy, the algorithmic nature of its decision-making process remains relatively black-box. Future studies may focus on interpretability, shedding light on how the Siamese BERT architecture ultimately detects same or different authorship.

Finally, the application of new transformer models may result in improved performance and interpretability. Among these include new large language models such as ChatGPT and DeepSeek in recent years, as well as Google's T5 large language model series. New techniques such as SimCSE (Gao et al. 2021), which uses dropout noise to mitigate representation collapse in sentence embeddings, may also improve model performance [2].

Acknowledgements. This research was conducted as part of the InnoBridge Institute research program in Cambridge, Massachusetts, USA, and was supported in part by InnoBridge Institute's Future Scholars Grant and Alumni Innovation Grant. We would like to thank the anonymous reviewers for their constructive feedback and valuable suggestions, as well as Dr. Xiaoying Jin for her assistance with the statistical analysis of results.

Disclosure of Interests. The authors have no competing interests to declare that are relevant to the content of this article.

References

1. Bamman, D., Burns, P.J.: Latin bert: a contextual language model for classical philology (2020). arXiv preprint
2. Gao, T., Yao, X., Chen, D.: Simcse: simple contrastive learning of sentence embeddings (2021). arXiv preprint
3. Hadsell, R., Chopra, S., LeCun, Y.: Dimensionality reduction by learning an invariant mapping. In: 2006 IEEE Computer Society Conference on Computer Vision and Pattern Recognition (CVPR), vol. 2, pp. 1735–1742. IEEE (2006)
4. He, X., Lashkari, A.H., Vombatkere, N., Sharma, D.P.: Authorship attribution methods, challenges, and future research directions: a comprehensive survey. Information **15**(3) (2024)
5. Kestemont, M., Stover, J., Koppel, M., Karsdorp, F., Daelemans, W.: Authenticating the writings of Julius Caesar. Expert Syst. Appl. **63**, 86–96 (2016)
6. Klotz, A.: Cäsarstudien. B.G. Teubner, Leipzig (1910)
7. Kreuz, R.J.: How the unabomber's unique linguistic fingerprints led to his capture (2023). https://theconversation.com/how-the-unabombers-unique-linguistic-fingerprints-led-to-his-capture-207681. Accessed 05 Sept 2024
8. Reimers, N., Gurevych, I.: Sentence-bert: sentence embeddings using siamese bert-networks (2019). arXiv preprint
9. Stamatatos, E.: Authorship verification: a review of recent advances. Res. Comput. Sci. **123**, 9–25 (2016)
10. Tyo, J., Dhingra, B., Lipton, Z.C.: Siamese bert for authorship verification. In: Working Notes of CLEF 2021 - Conference and Labs of the Evaluation Forum, pp. 2169–2177. Bucharest, Romania (2021)
11. Tyo, J., Dhingra, B., Lipton, Z.C.: On the state of the art in authorship attribution and authorship verification (2022). arXiv preprint
12. Vainio, R., et al.: Reconsidering authorship in the ciceronian corpus through computational authorship attribution. Ciceroniana On Line **3**(1), 15–48 (2019). https://doi.org/10.13135/2532-5353/3518
13. Vickers, B.: Review: Shakespeare and authorship studies in the twenty-first century. Shakespear. Q. **62**(1), 106–142 (2011)
14. Zhang, O., McGill, S., Cohen, T.: Did Gaius Julius Caesar write de bello Hispaniensi: a computational study of Latin classics. Hum. IT **14**(1), 28–58 (2018)

CrioleSet: A New Corpus for Cape Verdean Creole, Towards Robust Machine Translation

Roberto Carlos Medina[1,2], Fernando Batista[1,2(✉)], and Estanislau Lima[3]

[1] ISCTE – Instituto Universitário de Lisboa, Lisbon, Portugal
`fernando.batista@iscte-iul.pt`
[2] INESC-ID Lisboa, Lisbon, Portugal
[3] UTA - Atlantic Technical University, Mindelo, Cabo Verde
`https://www.iscte-iul.pt/`, `https://inesc-id.pt/`,
`https://uta.cv/`

Abstract. This paper presents CrioleSet, a new parallel corpus designed to facilitate neural machine translation (NMT) for Cape Verdean Creole (CVC), a low-resource language spoken by the majority of Cape Verdeans. Comprising over 6,000 translation pairs in English, Portuguese, French, and CVC, the dataset addresses the scarcity of annotated resources for CVC, which is further challenged by dialectal variation across the archipelago. We trained and evaluated three neural network architectures LSTM, GRU with gated attention (GAtt), and Transformer—base to perform English-CVC translation tasks. Experimental results demonstrate that the Transformer-base models significantly outperforms the others, achieving the highest BLEU and METEOR scores and the lowest TER, reflecting better translation quality and robustness. This confirms that attention-based architectures can effectively handle low-resource translation, even with relatively modest datasets. The work underscores the potential of focused data curation and deep learning to advance NLP resources for underrepresented languages. Future work includes expanding the dataset to encompass more dialects and refining models for broader NLP tasks in CVC, thereby contributing to linguistic inclusivity and cross-cultural communication.

Keywords: Machine Translation · Natural Language Processing · Deep Learning · dataset

1 Introduction

Although Portuguese is still the nation's official language, the vast majority of Cape Verdeans speak CVC as their mother tongue. In terms of computational linguistic resources, CVC has received little attention despite being an essential part of Cape Verdean culture and everyday communication. Standardization and language processing tasks are especially difficult because each of the nine inhabited islands in the archipelago has developed its own variant of CVC.

© The Author(s), under exclusive license to Springer Nature Switzerland AG 2026
J. Valente de Oliveira et al. (Eds.): EPIA 2025, LNAI 16122, pp. 326–338, 2026.
https://doi.org/10.1007/978-3-032-05179-0_25

Given the expanding tourism industry of the nation, more than 819,999 hotel guests were recorded in 2019 [1], most of them from English, French, and Portuguese speaking nations, language barriers between residents and tourists can make communication difficult. Systems that can translate between CVC and other commonly spoken languages are becoming more and more necessary because many Cape Verdeans do not speak English, or other languages, fluently. Additionally training professional translators is expensive and time consuming, automated solutions are a desirable substitute.

Recent developments in machine translation and natural language processing (NLP), especially with regard to Deep Learning (DL) techniques, have greatly improved the quality of translation systems [2,3]. However, these models usually need extensive annotated datasets, which low-resource languages like CVC frequently lack. For NLP to be more inclusive and to benefit underrepresented languages, this gap must be closed.

A study on the creation of DL-based models for automatic translation between English and CVC is presented in this paper. As part of this work, a custom dataset called CrioleSet was created, which contains over 6,000 translation pairs in English, Portuguese, French, and CVC. We assess and contrast three neural architectures for translation: Transformer [3], GAtt (GRU-Gated Attention) [4,5], and LSTM [6].

The development of NLP resources for CVC is hindered by several key challenges. These include limited annotated datasets, the lack of a standardized orthography, and the presence of multiple dialects that complicate linguistic analysis [7]. Additionally, as a low-resource language, CVC faces difficulties in leveraging existing NLP technologies, which are predominantly designed for high-resource languages like English, Spanish, and Portuguese [8,9].

Low-resource languages often struggle with data scarcity, making it difficult to train robust NLP models [10]. Transfer learning and multilingual models, such as mBERT [11,12], offer potential solutions, but their effectiveness in languages with significant linguistic variation remains an open question. Furthermore, the absence of computational tools tailored for CVC limits applications in essential NLP tasks such as machine translation [13], named entity recognition [14], and sentiment analysis [15].

The main contributions of this paper are as follows: (1) We present CrioleSet, a carefully selected parallel dataset that consists of more than 6,000 translation pairs in English, Portuguese, French, and CVC; (2) We implement and compare three DL-based MT models: LSTM, GAtt, and Transformer; (3) We evaluate the models using common metrics (BLEU, METEOR, TER) and show that the Transformer model achieves the highest performance; and (4) We show that, by creating targeted datasets and adapting DL, it is possible to develop machine translation systems for underrepresented languages.

2   Related Work

This section outlines key developments in NLP and MT for low-resource languages and reviews deep learning-based translation models relevant to this study.

2.1   NLP and MT for Low-Resource Language

Due in large part to the availability of deep learning architectures and large-scale datasets, NLP has advanced significantly over the last ten years. However, high-resource languages like English, Chinese, and French have disproportionately benefited from this advancement, with large language datasets [16,17]. The dearth of standardized orthographies, linguistic tools, and annotated corpora for low-resource languages like CVC limits NLP research in these languages.

Three methods are usually used in efforts to develop NLP resources for under-represented languages: data augmentation, transfer learning, and manual corpus creation [18]. Notably, transfer learning has demonstrated encouraging outcomes in tasks like machine translation and part-of-speech tagging for morphologically complex or non-standardized languages [19].

2.2   Deep Learning in Machine Translation

Rule-based systems gave way to statistical machine translation (SMT) and, more recently, NMT in the evolution of machine translation [20]. Translation performance underwent a sea change with the introduction of encoder-decoder architectures utilizing Recurrent Neural Networks (RNNs), such as LSTM [6] and GRU [4,21]. This was especially true when combined with attention mechanisms [3,5].

RNN-based systems have limitations when it comes to modeling long-range dependencies, despite their benefits. The Transformer architecture [3], which is based solely on self-attention mechanisms and has since emerged as the state-of-the-art in NMT tasks, was introduced to address this shortcoming.

According to recent comparative studies, the Transformer performs better than RNN-based models in terms of training efficiency and translation quality, especially when applied to larger datasets [16]. Its performance on small, low-resource datasets, like those for Creole languages, is still understudied, though, and this paper attempts to address that.

3   The CrioleSet Dataset

The creation of CrioleSet, a parallel corpus of sentences in English and CVC as well as other languages, is a key element of this work. It was created to facilitate NMT tasks. The dataset was created from scratch using a combination of manual translation, semi-automatic alignment, and carefully selected content from both spoken and written sources because there was no publicly accessible corpus before this work.

3.1 Language Overview

Spoken throughout the nine inhabited islands of Cape Verde, CVC is a Creole language with a Portuguese foundation. Every island has its own variant with lexical, phonological, and syntactic differences, such as São Vicente's Sanpadjudu or Santiago's Badiu. Despite their differences, native speakers can still understand each other. However, natural language processing is hampered by the coexistence of several dialects and the absence of a standard orthography.

Text samples from the São Vicente and Santo Antão variants were used to create the dataset for this study in an effort to maintain common linguistic traits and guarantee cross-dialect comprehensibility.

3.2 Data Collection and Preprocessing

The CrioleSet dataset, presented in the scope of this article, includes translation pairs between CVC and three languages: Portuguese, English, and French. In addition to translating a few English phrases from the Multi30K [17] dataset, Creole sentences were also gathered from actual message exchanges between the author and other people (with permission from about 20 people).

The languages were chosen strategically: French because of a similarly high rate of tourists from France ($\approx$ 10.4% in 2019 [1]); English because of its international status and the high influx of UK tourists to Cape Verde ($\approx$ 24% in 2019 [1]); and Portuguese because it is the linguistic foundation of Creole.

Translations were done sequentially from Creole to Portuguese, English, and French after sentence validation and any necessary corrections. Examples of translations for all four languages are shown in Table 1, and token distributions are displayed in Table 2. More than 6,000 sentence pairs make up the final dataset, which is divided into **6,000 for training**, **222 for validation**, and **183 for testing**.

Table 1. Paired examples of translation of dataset CrioleSet

Sentence	Cape Verdean Creole	Portuguese	English	French
S1	Algo xtronhê tite contsê ei.	Algo estranho está acontecendo aqui.	Something weird's going on here.	Quelque chose de bizarre se passe ici.
S2	M te otxá ke bô ê mut exigente.	Eu acho que você é muito exigente.	I think you're too picky.	Je pense que tu es trop pointilleux.
S3	M percebê ke m tava te precisa de ajuda.	Eu percebi que precisava de ajuda.	I realized I needed help.	J'ai réalisé que j'avais besoin d'aide.

Table 2. Number of tokens per language in the CreoleSet dataset

Language	Number of Tokens
Cape Verdean Creole	5154
Portuguese	5251
English	4135
French	4810

4   Methodology

4.1   Model Architectures

Three distinct neural models, namely LSTM, GAtt, and Transformer-based, that are frequently employed in sequence-to-sequence (seq2seq) translation tasks were put into practice and assessed. All of the models are encoder-decoder based and were modified to work with token embeddings and variable-length sequences. An example of seq2seq models architecture can be seen in Fig. 1 [22].

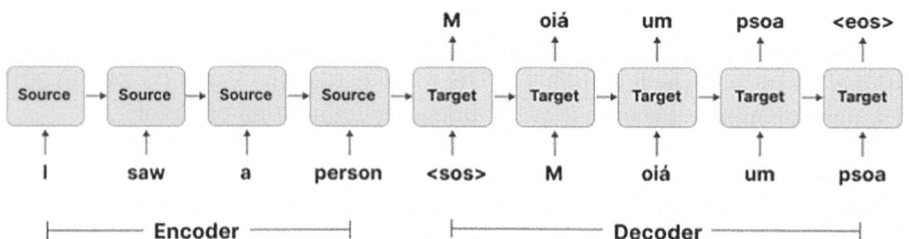

Fig. 1. Basic Sequence-by-Sequence Model.

LSTM. Long Short-Term Memory (LSTM) model, [6] is a type of RNN capable of capturing long-range dependencies in sequential data. The encoder reads the input CVC sentence and generates a fixed-length context vector, which the decoder uses to produce the corresponding English sentence token by token, using the sequence-to-sequence architecture on Fig. 1.

GAtt (GRU-Gated Attention). The GAtt model integrates Gated Recurrent Units (GRU) [4] with an attention mechanism [5]. GRUs offer simpler computation than LSTMs, while attention helps focus on relevant parts of the input sequence at each decoding step, improving translation quality.

Transformer. The Transformer model [3] eliminates recurrence entirely and uses multi-head self-attention and feedforward networks. Its parallelizable architecture accelerates training and yields state-of-the-art performance in translation tasks. We use a 4-layer Transformer with positional encoding.

Three standard metrics are used to evaluate the translation quality: BLEU, which measures n-gram precision with a brevity penalty [23]; METEOR, which accounts for stemming, synonymy, and word order [24]; and TER, which calculates the minimum number of edits needed to match the reference translation [25].

4.2   Training Configuration

All models were trained using the same train-validation-test split of the Criole-Set dataset. The models were trained using gradient clipping set to 1, batch size of 10, and learning rate of $3e^{-4}$. 256-dimensional embedding layers were used in all models. The Transformer used 256 hidden units, compared to 1024 in the LSTM and GAtt models. Eight attention heads, four encoder and decoder layers, and 512-dimensional encoder embeddings were added to the Transformer's configuration. During training, dropout was used, with a value of 0.5 for GAtt and LSTM and 0.3 for all models. Training was monitored by early stopping. The Transformer had 260 training epochs, GAtt had 230, and LSTM had 160. In Table 3, we can see more information about models training.

Moving forward, finding, for example, GAtt$_{(cv-en)}$ means that a GAtt model was trained to translate from CVC to English, and GAtt$_{(en-cv)}$ the other way around.

Table 3. Model training data

Model	Number of trainable parameters	Number of training epochs	Training time (minutes)
GAtt$_{(cv-en)}$	16,472,222	250	80
GAtt$_{(en-cv)}$		220	65
LSTM$_{(cv-en)}$	29,133,470	156	45
LSTM$_{(en-cv)}$		156	45
Transformer$_{(cv-en)}$	6,722,772	150	70
Transformer$_{(en-cv)}$		250	118

5   Results and Discussion

As already mentioned, in Table 3, for each model (GAtt, LSTM and Transformer) two different models are trained to perform machine translation tasks from CVC to English (cv-en), and from English to CVC (en-cv). Therefore, for each of these trained models there are results regarding their training parameters, in Table 4 you can see the results of all these models where it is possible to see that the Transformer models, Transformer$_{(cv-en)}$ and Transformer$_{(en-cv)}$, are the models that present the best results over the others, and the models that obtained the worst results were the LSTM models, LSTM$_{(cv-en)}$ and LSTM$_{(en-cv)}$. Although the Transformer models (Transformer$_{(cv-en)}$ and Transformer$_{(en-cv)}$) do not attain the highest validation accuracy during training, we can see in Fig. 2 that they perform better than the others in the final testing phase, yielding the best results throughout.

Table 4. Accuracy and Loss Model training and validation measures

Model	Accuracy		Loss	
	Training	Validation	Training	Validation
LSTM$_{(cv-en)}$	72.96%	72.68%	16.11%	9.33%
LSTM$_{(en-cv)}$	71.15%	72.02%	20.97%	10.91%
GAtt$_{(cv-en)}$	74.58%	74.74%	15.85%	8.00%
GAtt$_{(en-cv)}$	72.92%	74.02%	19.96%	9.83%
Transformer$_{(cv-en)}$	**44.51%**	**84.21%**	**11.12%**	**3.50%**
Transformer$_{(en-cv)}$	**44.81%**	**83.57%**	**12.17%**	**4.20%**

5.1   Quantitative Results

All models were evaluated using BLEU, METEOR, and TER on the held-out test set. As shown in Table 5, the Transformer model consistently outperformed both LSTM and GAtt across all metrics in both translation directions (cv-en and en-cv).

Table 5. Metrics

Model	BLUE	METEOR	TER
LSTM$_{(cv-en)}$	34.95%	66.43%	51.95%
LSTM$_{(en-cv)}$	31.49%	68.83%	50.95%
GAtt$_{(cv-en)}$	37.27%	73.69%	30.02%
GAtt$_{(en-cv)}$	32.44%	71.38%	32.70%
Transformer$_{(cv-en)}$	**41.63%**	**75.53%**	**27.01%**
Transformer$_{(en-cv)}$	**36.72%**	**73.80%**	**31.01%**

The Transformer achieved the highest BLEU scores (Transformer$_{(cv-en)}$: 41.2%; Transformer$_{(en-cv)}$: 39.8%), indicating stronger n-gram overlap with the reference translations. It also scored highest in METEOR and lowest in TER, confirming its superior performance in terms of semantic accuracy and edit efficiency.

These results support the robustness of the Transformer architecture, even in low-resource settings when regularization and early stopping are applied effectively.

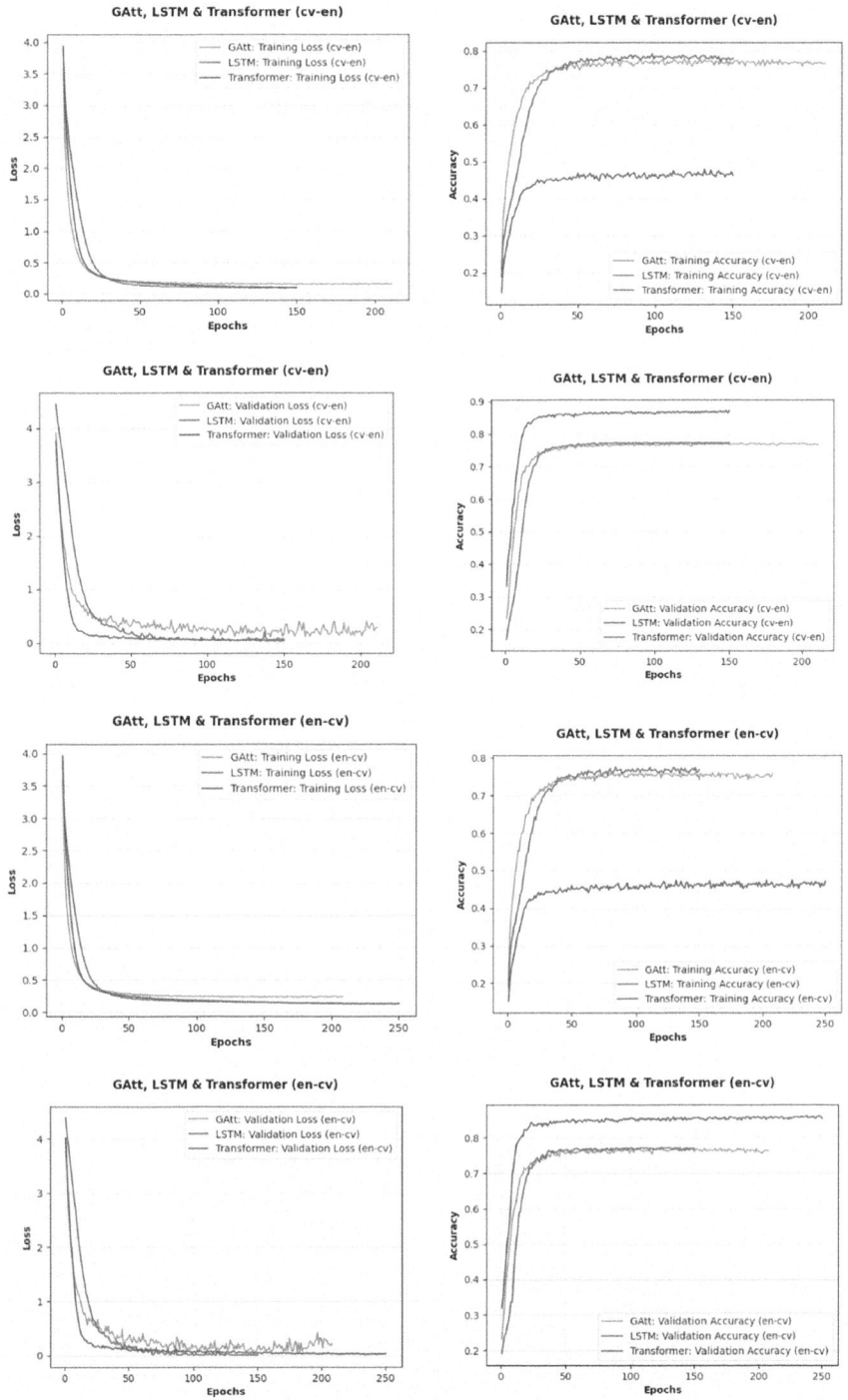

Fig. 2. Models accuracy and loos during training and evaluation in both directions (cv-en and en-cv).

5.2   Comparative Analysis

Although LSTM and GAtt models showed decent performance, they were notably less stable during training. The LSTM model exhibited higher variance in both training and validation losses, especially in the $\text{LSTM}_{\text{(en-cv)}}$ direction. GAtt provided marginal improvements over plain GRUs by incorporating attention but was still limited in generalization capability.

Using the self-attention mechanism allows the Transformer to better capture global dependencies, which is particularly useful for languages like CVC that exhibit flexible word order and variation in morphology. Its faster convergence and lower overfitting risk made it more suitable for the CrioleSet's modest scale.

5.3   Qualitative Examples

Selected translation outputs demonstrate the Transformer's superiority not only in metrics but also in fluency and context preservation. Below are representative samples translated by each model (Table 6).

Table 6. Model Translations examples

Example (CVC)	System	Translation (EN)
M te bem fca casa, pe pode relaxá.	Reference	I'm going to stay at home, so I can relax
	Transformer	I'll stay home, to relax
	GAtt	I stay at the house
	LSTM	I'm in a house
Talvez porkê nhe irmá ê advogada, agoh um kris ser também	Reference	Maybe because my sister is a lawyer, now I want to be too
	Transformer	Maybe because my sister is a lawyer, now I wanted to be too
	GAtt	Maybe why lawyer, I want too
	LSTM	The and it is to. The I be was the of, and want
Kel casal antig sentá lód a lód	Reference	The old couple sat side by side
	Transformer	Kel casal antig tava sentód lód a lód
	GAtt	<unk><unk><unk><unk><unk><unk>
	LSTM	different

As seen above, the Transformer model produces contextually fluent translations, even when vocabulary or syntax diverge from English norms. Meanwhile, the LSTM model often generates overly literal or ambiguous phrases.

In the reverse direction (en-cv), similar trends were observed. The Transformer captured idiomatic expressions more naturally, while LSTM and GAtt models tended toward phrase-level literalism.

These results demonstrate that while all three architectures are viable for low-resource translation, Transformer models offer a clear advantage in both reliability and translation quality when applied with modest-sized but well-curated datasets like CrioleSet.

6   Limitations

Although this study demonstrates the feasibility of developing NMT systems for CVC, several limitations must be acknowledged. These are primarily related to the scope of the dataset, dialectal diversity, model robustness, and resource constraints.

Just over 6,000 sentence pairs make up CrioleSet, which is sufficient for a proof of concept but insufficient for training neural translation models that can recognize intricate syntactic and semantic patterns. The rich morphosyntactic diversity of CVC dialects is not fully reflected in the dataset, despite its careful linguistic curation. Performance may suffer on underrepresented or unseen variants since CVC differs greatly among islands in vocabulary, grammar, and phonology, and the models were not specifically trained to identify or adjust to these dialectal differences.

The trained models, especially Transformers and GAtt, demonstrate strong learning within the scope of the data set, but it is not clear how well they generalize to other contexts or genres. Informal or poetic language, domain-specific vocabulary (e.g., legal, medical), and idiomatic expressions are likely to pose challenges. Moreover, the absence of a standardized orthography introduces additional ambiguity in the tokenization and embedding processes.

7   Conclusion and Future Work

This paper presents a new corpus for Cape Verdean Creole and presents a deep learning-based approach to the bidirectional machine translation between CVC and English. Addresses the critical lack of computational resources and tools for this underrepresented language. The CrioleSet parallel corpus, comprises more than 6,000 sentence pairs, and was created to support model training and evaluation.

Three neural models, LSTM, GAtt, and Transformer-based, were implemented and compared using standard evaluation metrics (BLEU, METEOR, TER). The Transformer model significantly outperformed the others, producing more fluent and semantically accurate translations. These results confirm that even with limited training data, deep learning techniques, especially attention-based architectures, can effectively handle the translation needs of low-resource languages.

Beyond technical achievements, this work demonstrates that meaningful progress in NLP for Creole languages is possible with focused data curation, modest computational resources, and adaptation of state-of-the-art models.

The following steps include adding more dialects from different Cape Verdean islands and diverse sources to the CrioleSet dataset, training with more sophisticated state-of-the-art models, and integrating a wider variety of NLP tasks like named entity recognition and classification. As a first step toward improving NLP for CVC, the objective is to offer more comprehensive linguistic resources and tools.

The development of CrioleSet and the implementation of deep learning–based translation models mark a significant step toward addressing the systemic lack of resources for underrepresented languages in NLP. Cape Verdean Creole, like many African and Creole languages [15, 26], has historically been excluded from mainstream computational linguistic research due to its low resource status, dialectal variation, and lack of standardized orthography.

The methodologies developed here can be extended to other low-resource settings, offering a replicable path toward language preservation, cross-cultural communication, and democratization of NLP technology.

Acknowledgments. This work was supported by national funds through FCT, Fundação para a Ciência e a Tecnologia, under project UIDB/50021/2020 (DOI: 10.54499/ UIDB/50021/2020).

Competing Interests. The authors have no competing interests to declare that are relevant to the content of this article.

References

1. INE. Cape Verde statistical yearbook 2019 – tourism. Instituto Nacional de Estatística (2019). Accessed 24 May 2025
2. Deng, L.: Deep learning: methods and applications. Found. Trends® Signal Process. **7**(3–4), 197–387 (2014)
3. Vaswani, A., et al.: Attention is all you need. In: Advances in Neural Information Processing Systems, vol. 30 (2017)
4. Cho, K., et al.: Learning phrase representations using RNN encoder-decoder for statistical machine translation. In: Proceedings of the EMNLP 2014, pp. 1724–1734 (2014)
5. Bahdanau, D., Cho, K., Bengio, Y.: Neural machine translation by jointly learning to align and translate. arXiv preprint arXiv:1409.0473 (2014)
6. Hochreiter, S., Schmidhuber, J.: Long short-term memory. Neural Comput. **9**(8), 1735–1780 (1997)
7. Abdul-Nabi, R., Obeidat, R., Bsoul, A.: A survey on machine translation of low-resource Arabic dialects. In: 2024 15th International Conference on Information and Communication Systems (ICICS), pp. 1–6 (2024)
8. Joshi, P., Santy, S., Budhiraja, A., Bali, K., Choudhury, M.: The state and fate of linguistic diversity and inclusion in the NLP world. In: Proceedings of ACL 2020. Association for Computational Linguistics (2020)

9. Blasi, D., Anastasopoulos, A., Neubig, G.: Systematic inequalities in language technology performance across the world's languages. In: Proceedings of ACL 2022 (Volume 1: Long Papers), pp. 5486–5505. Association for Computational Linguistics (2022)

10. Adelani, D.I., et al.: The effect of domain and diacritics in Yoruba–English neural machine translation. In: Duh, K., Guzmán, F. (eds.) Proceedings of Machine Translation Summit XVIII: Research Track, pp. 61–75, Virtual. Association for Machine Translation in the Americas (2021)

11. Devlin, J., Chang, M.-W., Lee, K., Toutanova, K.: BERT: pre-training of deep bidirectional transformers for language understanding. In: Burstein, J., Doran, C., Solorio, T. (eds.) Proceedings of NAACL 2019: HLT, Minneapolis, Minnesota, vol. 1, pp. 4171–4186. Association for Computational Linguistics (2019)

12. Conneau, A., et al.: Unsupervised cross-lingual representation learning at scale. In: Proceedings of ACL 2020, pp. 8440–8451. Association for Computational Linguistics (2020)

13. Sennrich, R., Haddow, B., Birch, A.: Neural machine translation of rare words with subword units. In: Erk, K., Smith, N.A. (eds.) Proceedings of ACL 2016, Berlin, Germany, pp. 1715–1725. Association for Computational Linguistics (2016)

14. Xei, T., Li, Q., Zhang, Y., Liu, Z., Wang, H.: Self-improving for zero-shot named entity recognition with large language models. In: Proceedings of NAACL 2024: HLT (Volume 2: Short Papers), pp. 583–593. Association for Computational Linguistics (2024)

15. Raychawdhary, N., Das, A., Bhattacharya, S., Dozier, G., Seals, C.D.: Enhancing sentiment analysis in Amharic: leveraging transformer-based language model for low-resource African languages. In: SoutheastCon 2024, pp. 50–55 (2024)

16. Barrault, L., et al.: Findings of the 2020 conference on machine translation (WMT20). In: Proceedings of the Fifth Conference on Machine Translation, pp. 1–55 (2020)

17. Elliott, D., Frank, S., Sima'an, K., Specia, L.: Multi30K: multilingual English-German image descriptions. In: Proceedings of the 5th Workshop on Vision and Language, pp. 70–74 (2016)

18. Anastasopoulos, A., Neubig, G.: Pushing the limits of low-resource morphological inflection. In: Proceedings of ACL 2019, pp. 2942–2952 (2019)

19. Adams, O., Neubig, G., Cohn, T., Bird, S.: Cross-lingual word embeddings for low-resource language modeling. In: Proceedings of the 55th Annual Meeting of the ACL (Volume 1: Long Papers), pp. 1100–1111 (2017)

20. Bojar, O., et al.: Findings of the 2014 workshop on statistical machine translation. In: Proceedings of the Ninth Workshop on Statistical Machine Translation, pp. 12–58 (2014)

21. Cho, K., van Merriënboer, B., Bahdanau, D., Bengio, Y.: On the properties of neural machine translation: encoder-decoder approaches. In: Proceedings of SSST-8, Eighth Workshop on Syntax, Semantics and Structure in Statistical Translation, pp. 103–111 (2014)

22. Russell, S.J., Norvig, P.: Artificial Intelligence: A Modern Approach. Pearson (2020)

23. Papineni, K., Roukos, S., Ward, T., Zhu, W.-J.: BLEU: a method for automatic evaluation of machine translation. In: Proceedings of ACL 2022, pp. 311–318 (2002)

24. Banerjee, S., Lavie, A.: METEOR: an automatic metric for MT evaluation with improved correlation with human judgments. In: Proceedings ACL 2005, pp. 65–72 (2005)

25. Snover, M., Dorr, B., Schwartz, R., Micciulla, L., Makhoul, J.: A study of translation edit rate with targeted human annotation. In: Proceedings of the 7th Conference of the Association for Machine Translation in the Americas: Technical Papers, pp. 223–231 (2006)
26. Raychawdhary, N., Das, A., Bhattacharya, S., Dozier, G., Seals, C.D.: Optimizing multilingual sentiment analysis in low-resource languages with adaptive pretraining and strategic language selection. In: 2024 IEEE 3rd International Conference on Computing and Machine Intelligence (ICMI), pp. 1–5 (2024)

ExpliCIT-QA: Explainable Code-Based Image Table Question Answering

Maximiliano Hormazábal Lagos[1,2]([✉]) [ID], Álvaro Bueno Sáez[2] [ID],
Pedro Alonso Doval[2] [ID], Jorge Alcalde Vesteiro[2] [ID],
and Héctor Cerezo-Costas[2] [ID]

[1] Computer Vision Center, Universitat Autònoma de Barcelona, Barcelona, Spain
mhormazabal@cvc.uab.es
[2] Gradiant, Vigo, Galicia, Spain
{abueno,palonso,jalcalde,hcerezo}@gradiant.org

Abstract. We present ExpliCIT-QA, a system that extends our previous MRT approach for tabular question answering into a multimodal pipeline capable of handling complex table images and providing explainable answers. ExpliCIT-QA follows a modular design, consisting of: (1) Multimodal Table Understanding, which uses a Chain-of-Thought approach to extract and transform content from table images; (2) Language-based Reasoning, where a step-by-step explanation in natural language is generated to solve the problem; (3) Automatic Code Generation, where Python/Pandas scripts are created based on the reasoning steps, with feedback for handling errors; (4) Code Execution to compute the final answer; and (5) Natural Language Explanation that describes how the answer was computed. The system is built for transparency and auditability: all intermediate outputs, parsed tables, reasoning steps, generated code, and final answers are available for inspection. This strategy works towards closing the explainability gap in end-to-end TableVQA systems. We evaluated ExpliCIT-QA on the TableVQA-Bench benchmark, comparing it with existing baselines. We demonstrated improvements in interpretability and transparency, which open the door for applications in sensitive domains like finance and healthcare where auditing results are critical. Code available at https://github.com/maxhormazabal/ExpliCIT.

Keywords: Visual Question Answering · Tabular Data · Explainability · Chain-of-Thought Reasoning

1 Introduction

Real-world documents often contain important information in tables, which are frequently embedded as images in PDF's. Tables may use complex layouts (with merged cells, multi-row headers, or irregular schemas). Question Answering over Tabular Data (TableQA) has seen progress when tables are provided in structured text in a stable row and column distribution. However, the complex visual

J. Valente de Oliveira et al. (Eds.): EPIA 2025, LNAI 16122, pp. 339–351, 2026.
https://doi.org/10.1007/978-3-032-05179-0_26

tables on real documents usually have more uncommon structures with columns that overlap, multiple tables in one, etc. This scenarios still remains challenging in Visual Question Answering over Table Images (TableVQA). Vision-Language Models (VLLMs) like GPT-4V [22] have demonstrated an impressive ability to directly interpret table images and answer questions, achieving the highest accuracy on benchmarks like TableVQA-Bench [13]. However, these end-to-end models act as black boxes: they do not reliably reveal how the answer was obtained or which table cells were used, and their internal reasoning is hidden and often ambiguous. In high-stakes domains like finance or healthcare, such lack of transparency is problematic, as users need to trust and verify the answer derivation [14,18].

That is why explainability in current TableVQA systems is an open gap to explore in both classical pipelines and end-to-end VLLMs to offer different levels of traceability in their decision process. This can be done by explaining predictions from end-to-end models by the understanding of their attention maps [3,20] and also by delegating the final decision to a simpler model or procedure that can be easily explainable or even interpretable. Recent work has begun addressing this gap with proposals like Plan-of-SQLs (POS) [19], which decomposes table queries into interpretable sub-queries (SQL statements) to explain the reasoning. Their approach allowed verification of answers, without sacrificing accuracy on text-table QA. TRH2TQA for table images performs first detailed table recognition and then feeds the structured data to a QA model [11].

We propose ExpliCIT-QA, an extension of our Maximizing Recovery from Tables (MRT) [9] to deal with complex table images in a multi-step VLLMs and Large Language Models (LLMs) to offer a natural language explanation based of how the answer was calculated. The key idea is to convert and transfer this tabular data pipeline to the task of visual question answering on complex table images by a series of transparent sub-tasks: (1) re-interpret a table image with a complex layout to transform it into serialized table data by Chain-of-Thought (CoT) reasoning (2) obtain and structure a step-by-step explanation of how to calculate the answer to the question, (3) translate the reasoning into executable python code, (4) compute the answer with that code and (5) get a final explanation and description of the actual step carried out to get the answer which can be examined by users.

This work makes the following contributions:

- **ExpliCIT-QA**: A novel pipeline that extends MRT approach for visual question answering for table images by integrating VLM and LLM reasoning.
- **Explainability and Traceability**: We highlight the importance of transparency in TableVQA. Our system provides human-readable CoT explanations and runnable code for every answer, addressing the ambiguity of end-to-end model explanations
- **Evaluation on TableVQA-Bench**: We present experiments on the TableVQA-Bench dataset, comparing ExpliCIT-QA with baselines.

This paper is organized as follows. Section 2 reviews related work in TableQA, TableVQA, CoT, and program-aided reasoning. Section 3 details the ExpliCIT-

QA system design. Section 4 presents experimental results and comparisons. Section 5 offers discussions on accuracy vs. interpretability and future improvements, and Sect. 6 concludes the paper.

2   Related Work

2.1   Question Answering over Tabular Data

Traditional Table QA assumes a structured table as input in order to read table content directly. Recent large-scale datasets such as WikiTableQuestions [21], WikiSQL [29] and TabFact [4] have driven progress in textual table QA. In particular, LLMs fine-tuned for table tasks [8,28] and prompt-based methods [15] have achieved high accuracy. However, as we mentioned above, these solutions often struggle with traceability and explanations.

2.2   Table Visual Question Answering

Visual Table QA (TableVQA) extends this challenge where the table is given as an image, requiring visual understanding. Early attempts decomposed this into pipeline stages: detect table region, perform OCR, and then apply a textual QA model. Such pipelines were interpretable but prone to OCR errors and required significant engineering for each format. End-to-end deep models [4,10,12,21,30] have been proposed to directly answer from document images without explicit structure extraction but internal workings remain opaque.

VLLMs struggle with complex tables unless multiple vision queries are allowed. For instance, TableVQA-Bench [13] results showed that GPT-4V had 54.5% accuracy with a vision-language only approach whereas its performance increase to 60.7% when separating the inference process in two steps with multimodal Table Structure Reconstruction followed by a LLM based inference. But it still underperformed when compared to an LLM that was given an equivalent text-input of the table itself.

While these strategies have shown progress in the task of TableVQA, they mostly rely on black box models that do not favor explainability and provide an opportunity to improve reliability by explicitly extracting table structure first, and then reasoning over it. Pipeline approaches for document QA that combine multiple deep learning modules are more transparent and monitored [11,19,23,25].

2.3   Chain-of-Thought Reasoning

CoT encourages LLMs to "think aloud" and produce intermediate reasoning steps [24]. It has been shown to improve performance on arithmetic, logical, and multi-hop reasoning tasks, by breaking problems into manageable steps [16, 17]. Current state-of-the-art models can operate in a thorough reasoning mode, performing self-consistency checks and detailed step-by-step derivations, at the cost of some latency [6,27]. Strategies such as [7] suggest that thinking can be done in the form of patches or latent knowledge, however, the standard is still to think in the form of text. This means that CoT can also be partially applied to VLLMs in the textual step of the generation that is to be used for interpretation of visual elements and their spatial distribution.

2.4   Code-Based Answering

A way to ensure faithful reasoning is to delegate problem solving (in this case answering the question) to a simpler and interpretable model or algorithm based on the LLM output. Most of the table data solutions opt to generate executable code as the intermediate reasoning step showing that this process can yield more reliable and explainable results. This approach follows the Program-aided Language Models (PAL) [5] paradigm where the LLM's job is to produce a correct program that a computer can execute to get the answer.

The code serves as a formal specification of the reasoning eliminating ambiguity and arithmetic mistakes by delegating those to a Python/SQL interpreter system. The results of the system can be easily monitored, being able to generate explanations of how the output was computed and providing traceability as well. Furthermore, they do not need to process all the table structure at once, as some of the end-to-end solutions do, thus sidestepping problems related to context window size with large tables.

3   Methodology

Our system consists of five main modules that operate sequentially: (1) Multimodal Table Understanding, (2) Language-based Reasoning based on CoT, (3) Automatic Code Generation with error feedback, (4) Code Execution and (5) Natural Language Explanation. Figure 1 conceptually illustrates the pipeline. All intermediate steps such as extracted table, model propmts, reasoning, code and explanation are available as auditable outputs, allowing to manually verify the traceability of the process.

Given an input consisting of a table image and a natural language question, the following steps are performed:

3.1   Multi-modal Table Understanding

The table image is processed to extract its content along with the table structure. This extraction is not a simple parsing process because the target data are tables with a complex layout usually composed of multiple sub-tables joined together for enterprise reports. A simple parsing process is not always going to be able to be easily translated into a tabular data format like *csv*. We employ Qwen-2.5-VL [1] for this task because of its powerful document understanding capabilities.

We decompose this step into two substeps. First we use the VLLM spatial reasoning to generate a CoT of the 'to-do inner steps' and considerations to transform this complex layout into a stable two-dimensional tabular data that

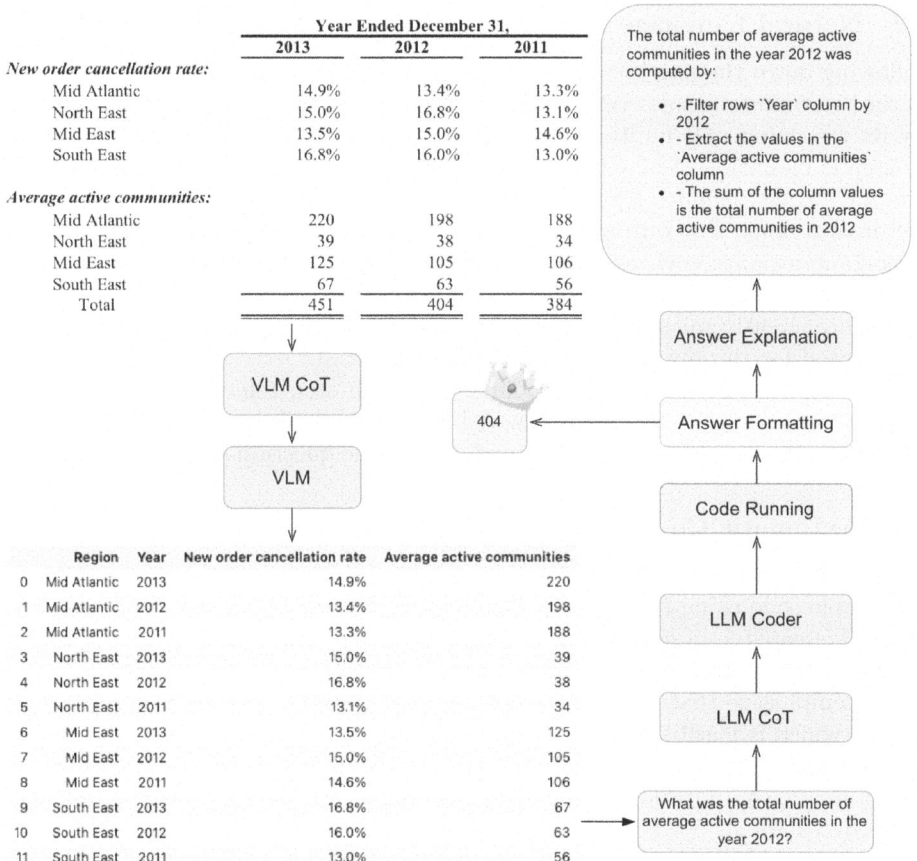

Fig. 1. ExpliCIT-QA: (1) Multimodal understanding: a vision model generates a visual reasoning to extract and structure the tabular content of a complex layout table image; (2) Natural language reasoning: an LLM produces a human-readable step-by-step describing the logic of the answer; (3) Automatic code generation: the steps are translated into executable code; (4) Code execution: the script is run deterministically on the extracted table to compute the answer; and (5) Final answer and explanation: how each operation in the code resulted in the result is synthesized in natural language.

can be parsed into a formal structure. Secondly, we use the 'to-do list' generated on step one to use the model to generate a *csv* like data with the information of the table. This often involves replicating and redundant data in order to reduce the dimensionality of the table and make it more easily manageable.

This structured table can be directly verified by humans (or in the worst case scenario another VLLM acting as a judge) against the image, ensuring no critical data was lost or misread.

3.2   Natural Language Instructions with Chain-of-Thought

Following down the pipeline the question and the extracted table data are given to the reasoning module. We use the recently released Qwen 3 [26] LLM known for its reasoning and multi-step problem solving abilities. We produce a step-by-step explanation of how to get the answer to a question using the table. The prompt format includes a sample of the table, the column name, the question, and instructions. The output is not only the steps in natural language but also important insights such as columns to be used and values to be filtered. We implemented helper functions that hat employ fuzzy search in case categorical values are slightly mismatched during any part of the pipeline. Real names are substituted for those wrongly generated by the LLM.

This CoT steps are human-readable and each step references specific table content or operations. Having the model articulate the logic helps with the validation that the model has correctly understood the question and table structure.

3.3   Automatic Code Generation

Once we have the reasoning steps, the next module converts these steps into an executable code using Python and Pandas as a dataframe library. We found that Qwen 3 is capable of generating correct Pandas code for most cases, especially in cases like this where tables were transformed to two-dimension format.

We emphasize that our code is not hand-written: the system generates it on the fly, which is feasible thanks to the reasoning trace as a guide. It also means the final answer is not just whatever the LLM guesses, but is the output of a deterministic computation, eliminating occasional arithmetic or logical mistakes made by LLMs.

Similar to the fuzzy search helper functions, we have an stock of pre-made helper functions for data management that can be referenced by the model in this code generation process and have more accurate results.

3.4   Code Execution and Error Feedback

Generated code is executed in a Python environment with the DataFrame from step (1) available. It has a *max_tries* parameter set to 3 in order to give the coder module the opportunity to solve possible errors by checking the error and re-generating the code with feedback.

As we mentioned, in the code-generation step the executor has access to the helper functions and can re-use them to avoid common mistakes when they have to build them from scratch. Those function definitions are included in the prompt in this step along the question and natural language instructions. Once the code runs without exceptions, we obtain the final answer to the question.

3.5   Explanation Step

Finally, once the answer is obtained, a natural language explanation is elaborated based entirely on the code that has been executed to compute the answer. To some extent the same explanation could be reused as a step-by-step description of how to get the answer, however, it is not strictly necessary that the code is always fully linked to the explanation, so we have decided to use a previously trained model to extract the code steps used in a python script[1] this brings us closer to the explanation being linked to the arithmetic and logical processes used to compute and obtain the answer.

The step-by-step behavior of ExpliCIT-QA, we present a complete example taken from the *FinTabNetQA* subset of the TableVQA-Bench benchmark.

Question: *What was the net sales for North America in the year 2013?*

3.5.1   Visual Understanding

Following the example the Table 1 shows the actual tabular data extracted for the image Fig. 2 which contains a complex financial layout with merged cells and multi-row headers. The system produces a visual reasoning trace that decomposes the layout into a normalized CSV format with the following columns: Year, Region, Net Sales, YoY % Growth, YoY % Growth (ex FX), and Net Sales Mix.

	Year Ended December 31,		
	2013	2012	2011
Net Sales:			
North America	$ 44,517	$ 34,813	$ 26,705
International	29,935	26,280	21,372
Consolidated	$ 74,452	$ 61,093	$ 48,077
Year-over-year Percentage Growth:			
North America	28%	30%	43%
International	14	23	38
Consolidated	22	27	41
Year-over-year Percentage Growth, excluding effect of exchange rates:			
North America	28%	30%	43%
International	19	27	31
Consolidated	24	29	37
Net Sales Mix:			
North America	60%	57%	56%
International	40	43	44
Consolidated	100%	100%	100%

Fig. 2. Example of image which belongs to the FinTabNetQA subdataset on the TableVQA-Bench.

3.5.2   Natural Language Reasoning

The extracted table and the question are processed by Qwen 3, which generates the following CoT:

---

[1] huggingface.co/sagard21/python-code-explainer.

Table 1. Output example of the resulting csv like tabular data after Table Understanding process.

Year	Region	Net Sales	YoY % Growth	YoY % Growth (ex FX)	Net Sales Mix
2011	North America	$26,705	43%	43%	56%
2011	International	$21,372	38%	31%	44%
2012	North America	$34,813	30%	30%	57%
2012	International	$26,280	23%	27%	43%
2013	North America	$44,517	28%	28%	60%
2013	International	$29,935	14%	19%	40%

1. Filter the table to include only rows where the `Region` column is equal to "North America" and the `Year` column is equal to 2013.
2. Verify that the `Net Sales` column contains a numeric value for the filtered row.
3. Retrieve the value from the `Net Sales` column for the filtered row.
4. Ensure that no additional calculations or transformations are applied to the `Net Sales` value.
5. Return the retrieved `Net Sales` value as the final answer.

3.5.3 Automatic Code Generation, Execution and Feedback

The reasoning is automatically translated into executable Pandas code that is executed within a controlled Python environment with error recovery mechanisms (up to 3 retries).

```python
import pandas as pd

def parse_dataframe(df: pd.DataFrame) -> str:
    # <<< MAIN LOGIC IMPLEMENTATION START >>>
    # Step 1: Filter the DataFrame for 'North America' in 2013
    filtered_df = df[
    (df['Region'] == 'North America') & (df['Year'] == 2013)
    ]

    # Step 2: Verify that the 'Net Sales'
    # column contains a numeric value
    if not filtered_df.empty
    and pd.api.types.is_numeric_dtype(filtered_df['Net Sales']):
        # Step 3: Retrieve the 'Net Sales' value
        net_sales_value = filtered_df['Net Sales'].values[0]
        # Step 4: Assign to result and cast to string
        result = str(net_sales_value)
    else:
        result = ""
```

```
# <<< MAIN LOGIC IMPLEMENTATION END >>>

return result
```

3.5.4 Final Explanation

A natural language explanation is generated based on the actual procedure to compute the answer:

The net sales for North America in the year 2013 were calculated by filtering the table for that year and region, verifying the numeric value in the 'Net Sales' column, and extracting the result.

3.5.5 Result

- Ground truth: $44,517
- Model output: 44517

Although numerically correct, the output differs in format, which highlights the importance of normalization strategies for exact-match evaluation.

4 Experimentation

Our evaluation is conducted on the TableVQA-Bench dataset [13], which consolidates several sub-datasets (VWTQ, VWTQ-Syn, VTabFact, and FinTabNetQA) targeting different table-centric reasoning capabilities in visual contexts. Each instance in the benchmark consists of a table image and a natural language question. Each domain represents different structural and contextual challenges in table images, ranging from synthetic layouts to financial reports.

The pipeline evaluation consisted of two main stages: Table Understanding (TU) and Question Answering, which uses language-based reasoning and code execution to compute the final answer. For the visual table understanding, both the layout-aware CoT and cell extraction were performed using Qwen 2.5-VL 8B, a vision-language model known for robust multimodal understanding. For the language reasoning stage we have tested three configurations of the ExpliCIT-QA reasoning engine, using Qwen 3 at different parameter scales (4B, 8B, and 14B). Each version was responsible for generating the reasoning trace and executable Python code required to compute the answer based on the extracted table data.

Table 2 presents the results of our pipeline on the four sub-datasets, comparing three Qwen 3 configurations. For context, we include scores from the benchmark TableVQA-Bench paper where models use a similar two-stage pipeline to parse visual tables and then apply an LLM for question answering.

The accuracy values across different Qwen 3 configurations remain comparable, showing only marginal variation. While our system does not yet reach the performance of top-tier vision-to-text pipelines like GPT-4V/GPT-4 or GeminiProV/GeminiPro, it maintains a competitive accuracy level given its primary

Table 2. Accuracy comparison on TableVQA-Bench sub-datasets. Our results (Qwen-based pipeline) are compared to the state-of-the-art two-stage pipeline (GPT-4V → GPT-4).

Model	VWTQ	VWTQ-Syn	VTabFact	FinTabNetQA	Avg.
GPT-4V + GPT-4 [13]	**45.2**	**55.6**	**78.0**	**95.2**	**60.7**
Gemini-ProV + Gemini-Pro [13]	34.8	40.4	71.0	75.6	48.6
T.U pipeline + Qwen3-4B	35.99	44.97	2.68	29.76	27.69
T.U pipeline + Qwen3-8B	38.85	53.02	2.23	31.22	30.27
T.U pipeline + Qwen3-14B	42.99	49.66	4.91	29.76	31.50

design goal: maximizing explainability. The models used in our experimentation are much smaller than current state of the art models. Our strategy has very promising results and is model agnostic. Hence different models could be tested depending on the hardware limitations. Notably, our structured reasoning and executable code path enable interpretability on answer computation, a feature lacking in most end-to-end models.

We observe significantly higher accuracy on VWTQ and VWTQ-Syn across all Qwen configurations, which aligns with their simpler, Wikipedia-style structure and well-distributed QA design. For FinTabNetQA this subset contains financial tables with multi-row headers and merged cells. Despite using CoT for layout reconstruction, these structures remain challenging and prone to misinterpretation. In contrast, VTabFact suggests that fact verification tasks, especially those requiring semantic alignment rather than numeric computation, are less compatible with our current code-based reasoning approach.

Our current pipeline prioritizes transparency and step-wise auditability over raw performance. As a result, while the accuracy lags behind state-of-the-art LLM-backed vision QA systems, it provides a unique benefit in terms of trustworthiness, making it a promising direction for applications in regulated or high-stakes domains. We discuss these trade-offs and future optimization strategies for this system.

5 Discussion

Experiments on TableVQA-Bench reveal both positive aspects and areas for improvement that are worth examining closely. First, the performance gap between tables extracted directly from Wikipedia (VWTQ) and those generated synthetically (VWTQ-Syn) suggests that the models still rely on source-specific clues rather than on a deep understanding of the tabular structure. While for 14B configurations average accuracies close to 49% are achieved in VWTQ-Syn, in FinTabNetQA these fall in several cases below 30%. This dependence on graphical elements (colors, margins, fonts) shows that generalization outside the original domain is still limited.

The drastic drop in accuracy in VTabFact, where it does not exceed 4,9%, reinforces the hypothesis that the main point of improvement of this system is the Table Understanding phase and that currently mechanisms to deal with irregular layouts such as multilevel headers, merged cells and footnotes cause recurrent errors in cell identification and cross-information aggregation.

Another critical point is the overall accuracy metric beyond this benchmarking. In many QA systems the accuracy metric is applied in an exact-match logic. While this is a clear and simple way to evaluate, it does not differentiate between formatting errors. It is true that this benchmarking proposes to use looser versions of accuracy (called *relieved accuracy*) that use parsing and normalization processes to decide if the answers are correct or not, however, these are introduced in a customized way to each split of the dataset and this can lead to fundamental interpretation errors. An open gap is to extend the use of more general metrics such as Average Normalized Levenshtein Similarity (ANLS) proposed in the ICDAR 2019 [2] Competition which also offers opportunities for improvement but can mean a more general comparison and not so directed to the specific dataset to evaluate QA systems.

6   Conclusions and Future Work

ExpliCIT-QA demonstrates that the combination of multimodal vision, reasoning, and code execution is viable for Visual Table QA, offering traceability and arithmetic error reduction. The accuracy gap in complex tables is a major constraint to extending its application in real environments with diverse formats, so improving the understanding of the more complex structures in table images is vital to improving this approach.

Future work will include different approaches to understand and simplify information from tables with distributions that include various dimensions of analysis, merged cells, complex layouts and others. This may involve subprocessing and normalization and denormalization in order to arrive at a simpler representation using a code-based approach that is in itself much more explainable and verifiable than end-to-end black-box methods. It is also a priority to be able to measure the internal coherence of the CoT and the fidelity of the generated explanations so that the final explanation makes even more sense and to dispense with extra code explanation processes by having a verifiable correlation between the steps to be followed and the executed code.

Other interesting avenues to explore are intermediate representations such as graphs to facilitate image conversion to coherent data structures. Evaluate hybrid methods combining neural networks with symbolic rules to better handle the variety of layouts.

The real lever for improvement will lie in strengthening the multimodal understanding of heterogeneous tabular structures and in diversifying the evaluation criteria to reflect not only accuracy, but also robustness and explanatory coherence. These efforts will help reduce latency, increase flexibility in the face of new table formats and layouts and close the gap with purely performance-oriented systems.

Disclosure of Interests. This work was carried out by employees of Gradiant (Vigo, Spain) and a student from the Universitat Autònoma de Barcelona (UAB) as part of the UAB PhD program. The participation of the UAB student was supported by the National Agency for Research and Development (ANID)/Scholarship Program/BECAS CHILE/2024-72240209, Government of Chile.

References

1. Bai, S., et al.: Qwen2. 5-vl technical report. arXiv preprint arXiv:2502.13923 (2025)
2. Biten, A.F., et al.: ICDAR 2019 competition on scene text visual question answering. CoRR abs/1907.00490 (2019). http://arxiv.org/abs/1907.00490
3. Braşoveanu, A.M., Andonie, R.: Visualizing and explaining language models. In: Integrating Artificial Intelligence and Visualization for Visual Knowledge Discovery, pp. 213–237. Springer, Cham (2022)
4. Chen, W., et al.: Tabfact: a large-scale dataset for table-based fact verification. CoRR abs/1909.02164 (2019). http://arxiv.org/abs/1909.02164
5. Gao, L., et al.: Pal: program-aided language models (2023). https://arxiv.org/abs/2211.10435
6. Guo, D., et al.: Deepseek-r1: incentivizing reasoning capability in LLMs via reinforcement learning. arXiv preprint arXiv:2501.12948 (2025)
7. Hao, S., et al.: Training large language models to reason in a continuous latent space (2024). https://arxiv.org/abs/2412.06769
8. Herzig, J., Nowak, P.K., Müller, T., Piccinno, F., Eisenschlos, J.M.: TAPAS: weakly supervised table parsing via pre-training. CoRR abs/2004.02349 (2020). https://arxiv.org/abs/2004.02349
9. Hormázabal-Lagos, M., Saez, Á.B., Cerezo-Costas, H., Doval, P.A., Vesteiro, J.A.: MRT at SemEval-2025 task 8: maximizing recovery from tables with multiple steps. In: Proceedings of the 19th International Workshop on Semantic Evaluation (SemEval-2025). Association for Computational Linguistics, Vienna, Austria (2025)
10. Hu, A., et al.: mplug-docowl2: high-resolution compressing for OCR-free multi-page document understanding (2024). https://arxiv.org/abs/2409.03420
11. Jirachanchaisiri, P., Ly, N.T., Takasu, A.: TRH2TQA: table recognition with hierarchical relationships to table question-answering on business table images. In: 2025 IEEE/CVF Winter Conference on Applications of Computer Vision (WACV), pp. 8844–8852. IEEE Computer Society, Los Alamitos, CA, USA (2025). https://doi.org/10.1109/WACV61041.2025.00857. https://doi.ieeecomputersociety.org/10.1109/WACV61041.2025.00857
12. Kim, G., et al.: Donut: document understanding transformer without OCR. CoRR abs/2111.15664 (2021). https://arxiv.org/abs/2111.15664
13. Kim, Y., Yim, M., Song, K.Y.: Tablevqa-bench: a visual question answering benchmark on multiple table domains (2024). https://arxiv.org/abs/2404.19205
14. Lakkaraju, K., Jones, S.E., Vuruma, S.K.R., Pallagani, V., Muppasani, B.C., Srivastava, B.: LLMs for financial advisement: a fairness and efficacy study in personal decision making. In: Proceedings of the Fourth ACM International Conference on AI in Finance, pp. 100–107 (2023)

15. Lan, Y., Li, X., Liu, X., Li, Y., Qin, W., Qian, W.: Improving zero-shot visual question answering via large language models with reasoning question prompts. In: Proceedings of the 31st ACM International Conference on Multimedia, pp. 4389–4400 (2023)
16. Li, J., Li, G., Li, Y., Jin, Z.: Structured chain-of-thought prompting for code generation. ACM Trans. Softw. Eng. Methodol. **34**(2), 1–23 (2025)
17. Mitra, C., Huang, B., Darrell, T., Herzig, R.: Compositional chain-of-thought prompting for large multimodal models. In: Proceedings of the IEEE/CVF Conference on Computer Vision and Pattern Recognition, pp. 14420–14431 (2024)
18. Nazi, Z.A., Peng, W.: Large language models in healthcare and medical domain: a review. In: Informatics, vol. 11, p. 57. MDPI (2024)
19. Nguyen, G., Brugere, I., Sharma, S., Kariyappa, S., Nguyen, A.T., Lecue, F.: Interpretable LLM-based table question answering (2025). https://arxiv.org/abs/2412.12386
20. Park, D.H., et al.: Multimodal explanations: justifying decisions and pointing to the evidence. In: Proceedings of the IEEE Conference on Computer Vision and Pattern Recognition, pp. 8779–8788 (2018)
21. Pasupat, P., Liang, P.: Compositional semantic parsing on semi-structured tables. CoRR abs/1508.00305 (2015). http://arxiv.org/abs/1508.00305
22. Team, O.: GPT-4 technical report (2024). https://arxiv.org/abs/2303.08774
23. Wang, Z., et al.: Chain-of-table: evolving tables in the reasoning chain for table understanding (2024). https://arxiv.org/abs/2401.04398
24. Wei, J., et al.: Chain-of-thought prompting elicits reasoning in large language models. In: Advances in Neural Information Processing Systems, vol. 35, pp. 24824–24837 (2022)
25. Wu, Z., Feng, Y.: Protrix: building models for planning and reasoning over tables with sentence context (2025). https://arxiv.org/abs/2403.02177
26. Yang, A., et al.: Qwen3 technical report (2025). https://arxiv.org/abs/2505.09388
27. Yang, A., et al.: Qwen3 technical report. arXiv preprint arXiv:2505.09388 (2025)
28. Yin, P., Neubig, G., Yih, W., Riedel, S.: Tabert: Pretraining for joint understanding of textual and tabular data. CoRR abs/2005.08314 (2020). https://arxiv.org/abs/2005.08314
29. Zhong, V., Xiong, C., Socher, R.: Seq2sql: generating structured queries from natural language using reinforcement learning. CoRR abs/1709.00103 (2017). http://arxiv.org/abs/1709.00103
30. Zhong, X., ShafieiBavani, E., Jimeno-Yepes, A.: Image-based table recognition: data, model, and evaluation. CoRR abs/1911.10683 (2019). http://arxiv.org/abs/1911.10683

Ambient Intelligence and Affective Environments (AmIA)

Lightweight Tree Ensembles with Optimized Features for Five-Class Sleep Apnea Stratification

Vasco Silva[✉][iD], Goreti Marreiros[iD], and Luís Conceição[✉][iD]

GECAD/LASI, ISEP, Polytechnic of Porto, Porto, Portugal
{vapcs,mgt,msc}@isep.ipp.pt

Abstract. Wrist-worn photoplethysmography (PPG) and tri-axial accelerometry, already standard in many consumer wearables, open the door to home-based assessment of sleep-disordered breathing. Using the public DREAMT corpus with overnight polysomnography ground truth, this study examined whether these two signals alone can separate the five clinically recognized breathing states: normal, hypopnea, obstructive, central and mixed apneas. After basic cleaning and quality checks, statistical, spectral and motion features were extracted from each recording and several lightweight machine-learning models were evaluated. Tree ensembles outperformed other approaches: Random Forest and Light-GBM achieved balanced accuracy of 62% and Cohen's κ of ≈ 0.53 on an independent test set. Both models attained high recall above 70% for central apneas and normal breathing, moderate recall near 60% for obstructive apneas and hypopneas, and lower recall for mixed events, mirroring challenges reported in earlier studies. These findings demonstrate that commodity-grade PPG combined with accelerometry can already support practical five-class screening, laying the groundwork for explainable wrist-based tools capable of bringing full-phenotype sleep breathing monitoring into everyday life.

Keywords: Sleep apnea classification · Photoplethysmography · Accelerometry · Multi-class machine learning · Wearable sensors

1 Introduction

Obstructive sleep apnea (OSA) already affects nearly one billion adults aged 30–69 years worldwide [2]. Despite its high prevalence, obstructive sleep apnea is frequently overlooked, as only 2% of affected women and 4% of affected men are diagnosed clinically [16]. A major driver of under-diagnosis is the reliance on attended overnight polysomnography (PSG), a multichannel test that is costly, labor-intensive, and capacity-limited [12].

Home-based wearables that can deliver richer information than the usual binary classification output are therefore a clear public health need. Two low-power sensors already embedded in consumer devices meet the practical requirements for widespread screening [14]. Photoplethysmography (PPG) captures

J. Valente de Oliveira et al. (Eds.): EPIA 2025, LNAI 16122, pp. 355–367, 2026.
https://doi.org/10.1007/978-3-032-05179-0_27

pulse-wave amplitudes and variability, which are modulated by intrathoracic-pressure swings and autonomic arousals during disordered breathing, while tri-axial accelerometers (ACC) sense subtle thoraco-abdominal effort and posture. Mainstream wearables such as the Apple Watch, Fitbit Sense, and Oura Ring already embed both an optical PPG sensor and a triaxial accelerometer. In a 61-participant, polysomnography-controlled pilot study, inertial signals from the Apple Watch alone identified moderate-to-severe OSA with 100% sensitivity and 90% specificity, but the cohort was small and the algorithm could not differentiate event types, highlighting the need for richer PPG-based features [4]. A prototype home-testing system has shown that fusing PPG with ACC can separate obstructive from central events in unsupervised recordings [10]. Remote monitoring extends this idea by coupling wearable sensors with cloud-based dashboards so clinicians can follow patients continuously at home. Comparable remote monitoring platforms have already shown clear clinical value and strong patient adherence in the management of other chronic disorders [6].

Machine-learning (ML) models built on these signals reach impressive performance for binary OSA detection, a 2024 systematic review reports a pooled accuracy of 0.87 [1], but their effectiveness drops once finer stratification is attempted. The few multiclass examples to date either limit themselves to three categories (normal/apnea/hypopnea) using LSTM on PPG only [7], or focus on distinguishing central from obstructive apnea with finger PPG ensembles [11]. Even the recent multimodal Vision-Transformer that combines PPG with respiratory flow and effort handles ≤4 classes and depends on channels absent from commodity wearables [8]. Although several studies have shown that photoplethysmography (sometimes coupled with wrist accelerometry) can do more than simple yes/no screening, most still stop at binary OSA detection, or, when they venture into three or four class problems, they typically add extra channels such as nasal airflow or thoracic belts or rely on large deep-learning architectures.

This study is carried out under the REMO (Remote Monitoring for Active and Independent Ageing) project, which develops unobtrusive, continuous monitoring and personalized coaching solutions for older adults. Within this framework, wrist-level PPG + ACC, sensors that are already available in most consumer-grade wrist-worn devices, alone can drive lightweight ML models, which are particularly important due to the memory and processing constraints of deployment on wearable devices, capable of distinguishing all five sleep-disordered breathing event types without any additional channels. It should be noted that this work represents an initial phase of the REMO project. A subsequent stage will involve the collection of real-world data from users in home settings. This will allow the proposed pipeline to be evaluated under more heterogeneous conditions, thereby enhancing its external validity and practical applicability.

2   Related Work

Recent efforts in PPG-based detection of sleep-disordered breathing have shifted beyond simple thresholding, though many still rely on binary classification frameworks. Jiang *et al.* trained a one-dimensional convolutional neural network to distinguish between normal and sleep apnea cases using overnight PPG recordings from 59 individuals (20 healthy, 39 with sleep apnea syndrome). Their model achieved over 90% classification accuracy and demonstrated moderate robustness to noise, but the strictly binary setup and small sample size limit its applicability to more nuanced clinical scenarios [5].

Similarly, Bozkurt *et al.* developed an embedded system based on a binary support vector machine classifier trained on 16 selected features derived from PPG and heart rate variability (HRV). Their system reached up to 95% accuracy in distinguishing apnea from non-apnea recordings. While the lightweight design is promising for real-time use, the model's dependence on hand-crafted features and binary output constrains its utility for detailed phenotyping [3].

Hybrid sensor platforms do help untangle event subtypes, but current implementations remain limited. Lazazzera *et al.* mounted a reflective PPG probe plus a tri-axial accelerometer on the fingertip of 96 in-lab subjects and used a two-stage pipeline: a rule-based detector first marked candidate apnea/hypopnea epochs (75% balanced accuracy), after which a random-forest model labeled each event as obstructive apnea, central apnea, obstructive hypopnea, or central hypopnea. Their obstructive-vs-central split reached 92.6% accuracy, and the four-way classification reached about 83%, yet the work still (i) omitted mixed events, (ii) depended on SpO_2 triggers rather than an end-to-end model, (iii) used only four classes, and (iv) was validated on a small, highly imbalanced dataset, so the broader question of whether a single, lightweight model can distinguish *all five* clinically relevant phenotypes from wrist-level PPG and ACC remains unanswered [9].

Targeted phenotyping has also been attempted: Massie *et al.* trained an ensemble of decision trees on PPG from 266 PSG nights and could flag central sleep apnea with 81% sensitivity and 99% specificity at cAHI ≥ 10 events $\cdot$ h^{-1} [11].

Severity grading poses another challenge. Papini *et al.* used wrist-worn reflective PPG, together with the co-located accelerometer, to place recordings into the four standard AHI strata; their deep network achieved a weighted Cohen's κ of 0.51 and ROC-AUCs of 0.84–0.86 across mild, moderate, and severe categories, substantially lower than binary figures reported on the same data [13].

The literature shows a clear pattern: binary PPG-based screening achieves high accuracy, but performance degrades as the number of classes increases. To date, no work has addressed all five clinically relevant event types using only wrist-level PPG and accelerometry with lightweight, easily deployable models. Table 1 summarises the principal studies that inform this assessment.

Table 1. Representative studies on sleep-apnea classification using PPG or PPG + ACC signals

Study	Classes	Class Focus	Signals	Approach	Key Metrics
Jiang *et al.*, 2023	2	Sleep apnea, Normal	PPG	1D-CNN	Accuracy > 90%
Bozkurt *et al.*, 2019	2	OSA, Normal	PPG	SVM	Accuracy = 95%
Lazazzera *et al.*, 2021	4	OSA, CSA, OH, CH	PPG + ACC	Rule-based + Random Forest	Epoch acc = 75%
Massie *et al.*, 2023	2	OSA, CSA	PPG	Tree ensemble	Sens = 81%; Spec = 99%
Papini *et al.*, 2020	4	AHI severity	PPG + ACC	CNN	Cohen's κ 0.51

3   Methodology

This section presents the steps taken to ingest, clean, and structure the DREAMT dataset before applying machine learning models. Figure 1 illustrates the complete workflow. Each stage is described in detail in its subsection.

3.1   Materials

This study uses the public DREAMT corpus (*Dataset for Real-time sleep-stage EstimAtion using Multisensor wearable Technology*) [15]. The release provides one full-night PSG-controlled record for each of 100 adults (54% male; mean age 56.2 ± 16.6 y; BMI 33.7 ± 8.6 kg m^{-2}), spanning healthy to severe sleep-disordered breathing. During the study every participant also wore an Empatica E4 wristband that streams infrared PPG at 64 Hz and tri-axial ACC at 32 Hz. Each subject's data are supplied in a single `.csv` file containing the raw sensor channels and 30 s technician labels, which are, sleep stage, obstructive apnea, central apnea, mixed apnea, hypopnea, or normal breathing—scored according to the 2023 AASM rules.

Collection was approved by the Duke IRB (Pro00108961) and written consent was obtained and all files were anonymized before release, so no further ethical clearance is required.

3.2   Dataset Reading

This section explains how the nightly CSV files supplied by the DREAMT repository were converted into a uniform collection of fixed-length, labeled segments that could be passed directly to the machine-learning pipeline shown in Fig. 2. Each file contains the wrist photoplethysmography signal sampled at sixty-four hertz, tri-axial accelerometry, instantaneous heart rate, inter-beat intervals, and four event counters exported from clinical scoring. On loading, channels unrelated to cardiorespiratory analysis, such as skin temperature and electrodermal

Reading (1)

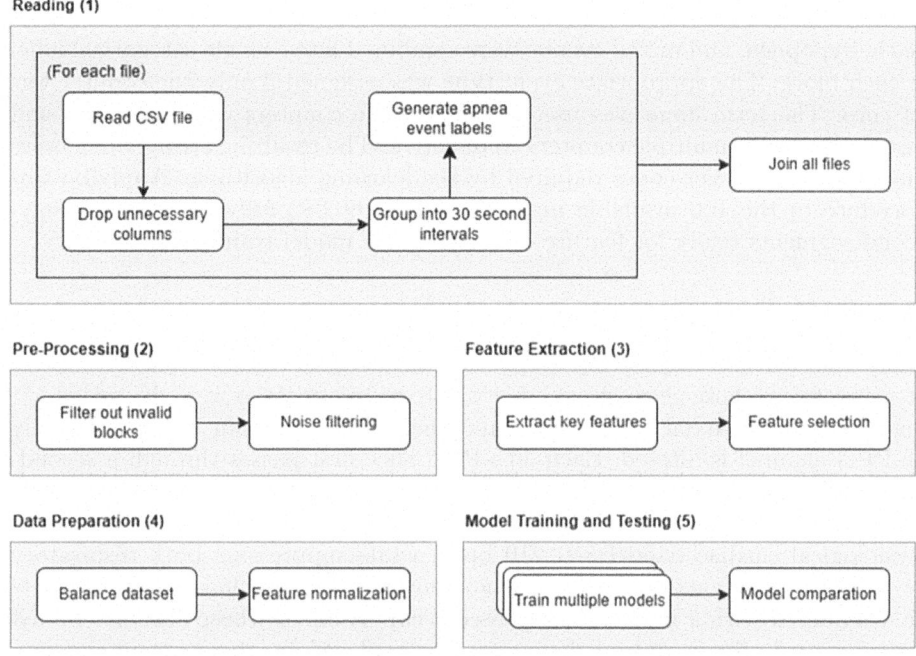

Pre-Processing (2)

Feature Extraction (3)

Data Preparation (4)

Model Training and Testing (5)

Fig. 1. Methodology followed for data processing and model training.

activity, were discarded, keeping only the variables required for the present study. Timestamps were expressed as seconds from lights-off, and the stream was split into consecutive thirty-second blocks, the standard epoch length used in sleep scoring. Every block retained the full vector of photoplethysmography samples, the matching accelerometer vectors, the mean heart rate, and the list of inter-beat intervals that fell within the thirty-second window.

Read CSV	CSV file					
Split into 30s intervals	30s	30s	30s	30s	30s	30s
Read Apnea Labels	None	Obstructive|Central	None	Hypopnea	Mixed	Obstructive
Apnea Labels simplified	None	Mixed	None	Hypopnea	Mixed	Obstructive

Fig. 2. Data reading and simplification process.

The four event counters provided by DREAMT, obstructive apnea, central apnea, hypopnea, and mixed events, were combined into a single categorical label for each block. The appropriate event type was assigned if only one counter was not zero. The term `None` was used if none of the counters were non-zero, and `Mixed` was used if multiple counters were active. The resulting string labels were converted into integer codes required by the learning algorithms. Applying this procedure to the 100 available nights produced 60,082 fully annotated thirty-second segments ready for feature extraction and model training.

3.3   Dataset Pre-processing

Before any feature engineering step, the raw streams were screened for basic integrity: rows whose sleep-stage label was `Missing` or `Wake` were discarded. At this point, the tri-axial ACC values and the IBI lists remain unchanged; only the PPG channel is filtered. Each 30 s PPG slice first passes through a second-order high-pass filter with a 0.15 Hz cut-off to remove slow baseline wander, followed by a fourth-order Butterworth band-pass (0.7–8 Hz) that retains the physiological cardiac band ($\approx$40–210 bpm) while suppressing both respiratory low-frequency content and high-frequency sensor noise. Residual motion artefacts are attenuated with a median-based z-score clip: samples whose absolute robust z-score exceeds five standard deviations are replaced by the segment median, and the whole trace is lightly smoothed with a 3-sample median filter. Segments that still exhibit abnormal variance or a flat-line waveform after cleaning are rejected.

Figure 3 illustrates the effect of the procedure on a representative 30 s interval: the large displacement spike visible in the raw trace (panel a) is completely removed, baseline drift is eliminated, and the underlying pulsatile morphology emerges clearly in the processed signal (panel b). Windows that satisfy these quality criteria are forwarded to the feature extraction block described in Sect. 3.4.

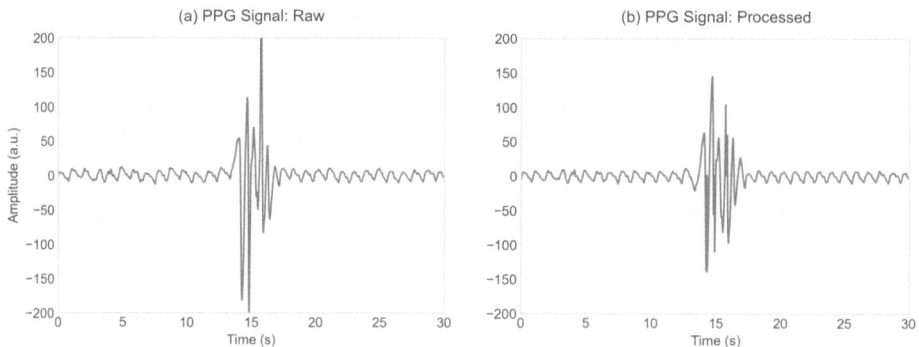

Fig. 3. Example wrist-PPG window before (a) and after (b) the cleaning cascade.

3.4 Feature Extraction

Table 2 lists the 22 pulse–wave variables, which capture basic statistics, morphology, spectral content, beat timing, shape/complexity, and a fast signal–quality proxy (SNR). IBI-derived heart-rate–variability markers (Table 3) characterize autonomic tone in both the time and non-linear domains, while the 10 ACC descriptors (Table 4) quantify the intensity and orientation of gross body motion. Together, the three blocks form a 42-dimensional feature space sufficient for the five-class sleep apnea classifier.

Retaining every dimension, however, inflates model complexity and risks overfitting, so a data-driven pruning stage is applied. Feature relevance was examined from four complementary angles. Mutual information and ANOVA F tests supplied two independent univariate rankings, and features that stayed near the bottom of both were marked as weak. A principal component analysis highlighted variables with negligible loadings, while a Pearson correlation map revealed pairs that were almost perfectly redundant. Any signal that met these low-value criteria was removed from the pool. Two features were discarded in this way: the `ppg_mean` and `ppg_peak_freq`. The screening left a clean set of 40 variables for model fitting.

Beyond reducing dimensionality and improving generalisation, this selection step also facilitates future application of Explainable AI techniques. By restricting the model to a compact and non-redundant feature set, post hoc attribution methods such as SHAP or LIME can generate clearer and more interpretable explanations. This is particularly valuable in multiclass classification settings, where understanding the relative importance of each feature for different output classes supports both transparency and clinical validation.

3.5 Data Preparation

All 40 pruned features and the five class labels underwent the following steps before model fitting:

1. **Stratified split.** The full dataset of 60,082 thirty-second segments was randomly partitioned into an 80% development set (48,066 samples) and a 20% hold-out set (12,016 samples), preserving the original class proportions for Wake, Obstructive, Central, Hypopnea, and Mixed events.
2. **Class balancing.** On the development set, each minority class was first oversampled via SMOTE up to twice the size of the smallest class, then all five classes were undersampled to exactly 1,328 samples each, yielding 6,640 training examples. The hold-out set was lightly under-sampled (without SMOTE) to 166 examples per class, yielding 830 test samples, ensuring no synthetic data appears at evaluation. Although this balanced configuration enables fair comparison across classes, it does not represent true clinical prevalence, which will be addressed in future validations using naturally imbalanced real-world data collected in the next phase of the REMO project.

Table 2. PPG-based features (22 per window)

Group	Feature	Brief description
Descriptive	ppg_mean, ppg_median, ppg_std, ppg_mad, ppg_iqr	Classical location and spread measures
Morphology	ppg_rise_time, ppg_decay_time, ppg_slope	Global rise, fall, and trend of the pulse wave
Cardiac power	ppg_band_pow, ppg_peak_freq	Welch power (0.7–4 Hz) and its peak frequency
Time–frequency	ppg_cwt_energy, ppg_fft_energy	Energy from Gaussian-CWT map and half-sided FFT
Beat timing	ppg_hr_bpm, ppg_rr_mean	Heart-rate and mean RR interval from detected peaks
Shape/complexity	ppg_skewness, ppg_kurtosis, hjorth_activity, hjorth_mobility, hjorth_complexity	Higher-order moments and Hjorth parameters
Quality/Resp.	ppg_snr_db, kurt_ratio, resp_amp_mean, resp_amp_std	Fast SNR proxy, kurtosis ratio, and respiratory-band envelope statistics

3. **Feature scaling.** A Min–Max scaler was fitted on the development features (mapping each to [0,1]) and then applied unchanged to both the development and hold-out sets.

After these steps, the models are trained on a 6640×40 feature matrix and evaluated on an 830×40 hold-out matrix, each perfectly balanced across the five apnea categories.

3.6   Model Training and Testing

Hyperparameters were tuned through either an exhaustive grid or a 200-draw random search, depending on computational cost and model complexity, always wrapped in stratified k-fold cross-validation to avoid optimistic bias. Table 5 lists every classifier investigated and the corresponding ranges explored during the search procedure.

Table 3. IBI-based features (10 per window)

Group	Feature	Brief description
Time-domain HRV	ibis_mean, ibis_std, sdnn, ibis_rmssd, rmssd, ibis_pnn50	Mean, spread and short-term variability of successive intervals.
Poincaré	ibis_sd1, ibis_sd2	Short and long axis spread of the Poincaré plot.
Complexity	ibis_sampen	Sample entropy (irregularity) of the IBI series.
Spectral power	ibis_total_power	Integrated 0.003–0.4 Hz power of the HRV spectrum.

Table 4. Accelerometer features (10 per window)

Group	Feature	Brief description
Axis statistics	acc_{x,y,z}_mean, acc_{x,y,z}_std	Mean and standard deviation for each axis.
Axis energy	acc_{x,y,z}_energy	Sum of squared samples per axis (movement intensity).
Composite	acc_mag_mean	Mean vector magnitude (overall motion).

Table 5. Hyper-parameter grids/ranges explored for each candidate model

Model	Parameter	Values tested
Decision Tree	criterion	{gini, entropy}
	max_depth	{None, 5, 10}
	min_samples_split	{2, 5, 10}
Random Forest	n_estimators	200 . . . 1500 (14 values)
	max_depth	{5, 15, 25, ..., 95}
	min_samples_split	{2, 5, 10, 20}
	min_samples_leaf	{1, 2, 4, 8}
	criterion	{gini, entropy, log_loss}
XGBoost	n_estimators	{100, 150, 200}
	max_depth	{None, 5, 10}
	min_samples_split	{2, 5, 10}
k-Nearest Neighbours	n_neighbors	{3, 5, 7}
	weights	{uniform, distance}
	metric	{euclidean, manhattan}
AdaBoost	n_estimators	{50, 100, 150}
	learning_rate	{0.01, 0.1, 1.0}
LightGBM	n_estimators	200 . . . 1500 (14 values)
	max_depth	{5, 15, 25, ..., 95}
	learning_rate	0.001 . . . 0.30 (30 values)
	num_leaves	{20...140, step 10}
	min_child_samples	{5...95, step 10}

4   Results and Discussion

Table 6 summarizes overall accuracy and Cohen's κ for each classifier on the hold-out test set.

Table 6. Overall test accuracy and Cohen's Kappa by model

Model	Accuracy (%)	Cohen's Kappa
Decision Tree	45.06	0.313
AdaBoost	42.53	0.282
KNN	56.51	0.456
XGBoost	59.76	0.497
LightGBM	**61.81**	**0.523**
Random Forest	**62.05**	**0.526**

Table 7 reports per-class precision, recall and F_1-score for the two top models. Both Random Forest and LightGBM excel at detecting *Central* and *Mixed* events, while performance is weakest on *Hypopnea*.

Table 7. Per-class metrics for Random Forest and LightGBM (support = 166 each)

Class	Random Forest			LightGBM			Support
	Prec	Rec	F_1	Prec	Rec	F_1	(n)
Central	0.70	0.73	0.71	0.68	0.73	0.71	166
Hypopnea	0.63	0.58	0.61	0.61	0.60	0.61	166
Mixed	0.67	0.41	0.51	0.66	0.37	0.47	166
None	0.64	0.68	0.66	0.64	0.69	0.66	166
Obstructive	0.52	0.70	0.59	0.54	0.70	0.61	166

Tree-based ensembles delivered the strongest overall performance in our five-class apnea task. Random Forest achieved a balanced accuracy of 62.05% and Cohen's κ of 0.526, with LightGBM trailing only slightly at 61.81% balanced accuracy and Cohen's Kappa = 0.523. A closer look at per-category metrics shows why. Both Random Forest and LightGBM correctly identify central apneas in roughly 73% of cases (precision $\approx$ 0.70), and normal breathing segments with about 68–69% recall (precision $\approx$ 0.64). Obstructive apneas are likewise well flagged (70% recall), though precision dips into 50%, reflecting a few false alarms. Hypopneas prove more subtle: recall hovers around 58–60% and precision around 61–63%, signifying moderate sensitivity to these milder events. The most challenging category remains mixed-type events, where recall falls to 41%

for Random Forest and just 37% for LightGBM, despite a precision of roughly 66%, indicating that many true mixed events slip through undetected. These patterns mirror the underlying feature space: pure central and normal segments exhibit large, characteristic swings in pulse rate and motion that our statistical, spectral, and accelerometer descriptors capture effectively, whereas mixed events combine elements of both and blur those signatures.

In summary, gradient-boosted and bagged trees deliver the strongest performance across all five apnea phenotypes, achieving a balanced accuracy of approximately 62%, which provides a solid foundation for further advancements. Improving detection of mixed and hypopneic events, where recall remains below 60%, will likely require adding new sensors or temporal modeling to resolve their more nuanced PPG/ACC patterns. Nonetheless, our results demonstrate that lightweight, wrist-level feature sets can already deliver promising multi-class screening performance.

5   Conclusion and Future Work

The proposed approach demonstrates that a concise set of wrist-level features extracted from PPG and accelerometer signals can enable five-class sleep apnea classification with competitive performance. Tree-based ensembles, Random Forest and LightGBM, achieved balanced accuracies above 61% and Cohen's κ coefficients around 0.53 on hold-out data. Both models exhibited strong sensitivity for central apneas and normal breathing (recall above 70%), moderate detection of obstructive apneas and hypopneas (recall near 60%), and revealed mixed-type events as the most difficult category (recall below 45%). These findings confirm that lightweight statistical, spectral, and motion descriptors capture the majority of discriminative information in wrist-level recordings. By reliably distinguishing wake, central apnea, obstructive apnea, hypopnea, and mixed-type events from a single wrist device, this work brings five-class sleep apnea screening within effortless daily reach.

Future work, in line with REMO's goal of delivering adaptable monitoring and coaching systems that foster active and independent aging, will (i) enrich the pulse and motion feature set with time–frequency and non-linear descriptors to sharpen mixed-event recognition, (ii) test temporal deep networks and sequence-to-sequence models for continuous night-to-night monitoring at home, (iii) embed explainable-AI modules so clinicians and users can visualize the signal cues that drive each decision, a component that is already under development and may help elucidate, for example, the relative importance of each feature in predicting specific event classes, and (iv) validate the full pipeline on larger, more diverse ambulatory cohorts, ensuring robust deployment in aging-in-place scenarios, as the REMO project progresses to a subsequent phase.

Acknowledgments. This research work was developed under the project REMO (ITEA-2023-23005-REMO), funded by the European Regional Development Fund (ERDF) within the project number COMPETE2030-FEDER-01233000, and funded by National Funds through the Portuguese FCT—Fundação para a Ciência e a Tecnologia under the R&D Units Project Scope, UIDB/00760/2020 https://doi.org/10.54499/UIDB/00760/2020.

Disclosure of Interests. The authors have no competing interests to declare that are relevant to the content of this article.

References

1. Abd-alrazaq, A., et al.: Detection of sleep apnea using wearable AI: systematic review and meta-analysis. J. Med. Internet Res. **26**, e58187 (2024). https://doi.org/10.2196/58187. https://www.jmir.org/2024/1/e58187
2. Benjafield, A.V., et al.: Estimation of the global prevalence and burden of obstructive sleep apnoea: a literature-based analysis. Lancet Respir. Med. **7**(8), 687–698 (2019). https://doi.org/10.1016/S2213-2600(19)30198-5
3. Bozkurt, M.R., Uçar, M.K., Bozkurt, F., Bilgin, C.: In obstructive sleep apnea patients, automatic determination of respiratory arrests by photoplethysmography signal and heart rate variability. Australas. Phys. Eng. Sci. Med. **42**(4), 959–979 (2019). https://doi.org/10.1007/s13246-019-00796-9
4. Hayano, J., Adachi, M., Murakami, Y., Sasaki, F., Yuda, E.: Detection of sleep apnea using only inertial measurement unit signals from apple watch: a pilot-study with machine learning approach. Sleep Breathing **29**(1), 91 (2025). https://doi.org/10.1007/s11325-025-03255-w, epub 2025 Feb 1
5. Jiang, X., Ren, Y., Wu, H., Li, Y., Liu, F.: Convolutional neural network based on photoplethysmography signals for sleep apnea syndrome detection. Front. Neurosci. **17** (2023). https://doi.org/10.3389/fnins.2023.1222715
6. Souza, J., et al.: A remote monitoring platform for the management of lower limb vascular diseases. Stud. Health Technol. Inform. **302**, 1013–1014 (2023). https://doi.org/10.3233/SHTI230330. https://ebooks.iospress.nl/doi/10.3233/SHTI230330
7. Kang, C.H., Erdenebayar, U., Park, J.U., Lee, K.J.: Multi-class classification of sleep apnea/hypopnea events based on long short-term memory using a photoplethysmography signal. J. Med. Syst. **44**(1), 14 (2019). https://doi.org/10.1007/s10916-019-1485-0, epub 2019 Dec 6
8. Kazemi, K., Azimi, I., Khine, M., Khayat, R.N., Rahmani, A.M., Liljeberg, P.: Multimodal sleep stage and sleep apnea classification using vision transformer: a multitask explainable learning approach (2025). https://arxiv.org/abs/2502.17486
9. Lazazzera, R., et al.: Detection and classification of sleep apnea and hypopnea using PPG and SPO$_2$ signals. IEEE Trans. Biomed. Eng. **68**(5), 1496–1506 (2021). https://doi.org/10.1109/TBME.2020.3028041
10. Manoni, A., et al.: A new wearable system for home sleep apnea testing, screening, and classification. Sensors (Basel, Switzerland) **20**(24), 7014 (2020). https://doi.org/10.3390/s20247014, epub 2020 Dec 8
11. Massie, F., Vits, S., Khachatryan, A., Van Pee, B., Verbraecken, J., Bergmann, J.: Central sleep apnea detection by means of finger photoplethysmography. IEEE J. Transl. Eng. Health Med. **11**, 126–136 (2023). https://doi.org/10.1109/JTEHM.2023.3236393, epub 2023 Jan 12

12. Natsky, A.N., Vakulin, A., Coetzer, C.L.C., McEvoy, R.D., Adams, R.J., Kaambwa, B.: Economic evaluation of diagnostic sleep studies for obstructive sleep apnoea: a systematic review protocol. System. Rev. **10**(1), 104 (2021). https://doi.org/10.1186/s13643-021-01651-3, epub 2021 Apr 9

13. Papini, G.B., Fonseca, P., van Gilst, M.M., Bergmans, J.W., Vullings, R., Overeem, S.: Wearable monitoring of sleep-disordered breathing: estimation of the apnea-hypopnea index using wrist-worn reflective photoplethysmography. Sci. Rep. **10**, 13512 (2020). https://doi.org/10.1038/s41598-020-69935-7, epub 2020 Aug 11

14. Vulcan, R.S., André, S., Bruyneel, M.: Photoplethysmography in normal and pathological sleep. Sensors (Basel, Switzerland) **21** (2021). https://doi.org/10.3390/s21092928

15. Wang, K., Yang, J., Shetty, A., Dunn, J.: DREAMT: dataset for real-time sleep stage estimation using multisensor wearable technology. PhysioNet, version 2.1.0 (2025). https://doi.org/10.13026/7r9r-7r24

16. Young, T., Palta, M., Dempsey, J., Skatrud, J., Weber, S., Badr, S.: The occurrence of sleep-disordered breathing among middle-aged adults. N. Engl. J. Med. **328**(17), 1230–1235 (1993). https://doi.org/10.1056/NEJM199304293281704

Framework for Adaptive and Creative Learning Based on Generative Artificial Intelligence in Higher Education

Juan M. Núñez V.[1]($\boxtimes$) ⓘ, Leonardo Saavedra Munar[2,3] ⓘ,
Claudia L. Arias Sánchez[2] ⓘ, Valentina López Vargas[2] ⓘ,
and Fernando De la Prieta[1] ⓘ

[1] BISITE Research Group, University of Salamanca, Salamanca, Spain
jmnunez@usal.es
[2] Universidad Autónoma de Occidente, Cali, Colombia
[3] Universidad Politécnica de Cataluña, Barcelona, Spain

Abstract. Generative artificial intelligence (GenAI) is redefining higher education by enabling adaptive and creative learning environments. This study presents a framework applied in a pilot course on Algorithms and Programming, which combines automated skill diagnostics, team formation through classification algorithms (K Nearest Neighbors), content personalization, and continuous feedback based on large language models (LLMs), implemented through the MAKE platform. The results show a significant improvement in learning efficiency and quality: GenAI-assisted teams reduced delivery times by up to 50% in key stages, and 80% achieved functional prototypes, compared to 45% in the control group. Additionally, the adaptive environment fostered creativity by supporting ideation, autonomy, and personalized exploration. This model demonstrates how GenAI can transform teaching in technical fields such as engineering by combining academic performance with creative development. The study also addresses challenges related to technological equity, data protection, and the need for teacher training to ensure ethical and effective implementation. The proposed framework represents a strong pathway toward more personalized, innovative, and student-centered education.

Keywords: Higher Education · Gen AI · Engineering Education · Steam+AI

1 Introduction

Artificial Intelligence (AI) is transforming higher education by enabling real-time adaptive learning systems tailored to individual needs [1]. These tools analyze cognitive profiles, performance, and learning styles with a sophistication that previously required manual input [2]. While offering personalized learning experiences, challenges remain in data privacy, scalability, and ethical use [3,4].

© The Author(s), under exclusive license to Springer Nature Switzerland AG 2026
J. Valente de Oliveira et al. (Eds.): EPIA 2025, LNAI 16122, pp. 368–381, 2026.
https://doi.org/10.1007/978-3-032-05179-0_28

AI-driven systems now support dynamic learner models that adapt through real-time feedback, enhancing outcomes in complex fields such as engineering [5]. By detecting learning styles and traits, they deliver targeted content and timely feedback, boosting engagement and performance [6]. However, concerns persist regarding bias, the accuracy of automated assessments, and overreliance on technology [7].

Pedagogically, AI-driven adaptive learning empowers educators to design student-centered curricula by offering customized interventions that support self-directed and autonomous learning [8]. In an era where traditional teaching methods often struggle to address the diverse learning needs of learners, the ability to dynamically adapt content is essential in fostering critical thinking, problem solving, and lifelong learning skills [9]. At the societal level, graduates who experience these innovative educational approaches are better prepared to engage in complex problem solving and contribute to a rapidly evolving knowledge economy [10]. Therefore, higher education institutions bear the responsibility of integrating AI-based adaptive learning systems not only to enhance instructional effectiveness, but also to ensure equitable access to quality education in an interconnected world [11]. Based on the above, this article reviews the state-of-the-art in AI-enabled adaptive learning systems in higher education, with a special focus on engineering programs. The review synthesizes findings from 4 key studies, examining both the technological innovations and the pedagogical implications of adaptive learning. The findings indicate that while these systems offer substantial benefits in terms of personalization and participation, challenges related to system design, scalability, and ethical data management must be addressed [12–14]. Furthermore, the integration of learning analytics plays a critical role in the continuous refinement of adaptive strategies, helping optimize learning outcomes [15, 16]. Finally, cluster-based analyses reveal emerging trends and thematic groupings that underscore the ongoing evolution and future potential of adaptive learning technologies [10, 17, 18]. This paper comprises the following sections: Introduction, Background, Research Methodology, Analysis of Results, Experimental Case, Discussion, Conclusions, and References.

2   Background

Adaptive learning marks a paradigm shift in education by using AI and machine learning to personalize instruction based on individual needs, preferences, and progress. This approach has been shown to boost engagement and academic performance, with literature reviews highlighting its wide application across diverse educational contexts [1, 17]. A key strength of adaptive learning is its ability to incorporate personal traits—such as learning styles, cognitive profiles, and metacognitive skills—into dynamic learner models. Traditional static methods are being replaced by AI-driven techniques that update learner profiles in real time [13, 17]. Automatic detection of learning styles has become essential, allowing systems to tailor content, feedback, and pacing more effectively [12, 16]. The effectiveness of adaptive learning remains debated. While many studies report better outcomes than traditional methods [4,11], challenges such as scalability, data privacy, and ethical use of learner data persist [4,10]. Learning analytics support these systems by enabling real-time performance monitoring and data-driven instructional adjustments [6]. Adaptive learning is not only enhancing individual learning experiences but also advancing broader educational goals. In fields such as engineering and computer science, AI-driven adaptive systems have been effectively used to promote deeper learning and better prepare students for professional challenges [8,14]. Theoretical frameworks have evolved, with some scholars viewing adaptive learning as "structure learning in time," where systems update internal models to guide personalized instruction [12]. Research has also identified performance metrics—such as accuracy and error patterns—as indicators of adaptive learning outcomes [15], while cluster analyses reveal diverse approaches and emerging trends [18]. Collectively, these studies highlight both the transformative potential and the challenges of fully integrating adaptive learning into higher education.

3   Research Methodology

This study conducted a systematic literature review based on the guidelines in [19] and the PRISMA framework [20], focusing on GenAI-based adaptive learning in higher education, especially in engineering. It examined effectiveness compared to traditional methods, current implementation strategies, and reported outcomes. The methodology included defining research questions, establishing inclusion/exclusion criteria, and designing search protocols.

3.1   Research Questions

Table 1 outlines the research questions that frame the scope of this systematic review.

3.2   Information Resources and Search Strategies

Search protocols were designed to locate articles and book chapters across selected databases relevant to GenAI and its role in adaptive learning within higher education and engineering. These protocols targeted sources aligned with the study's research questions. Table 2 outlines the main search terms used.

3.3   Inclusion and Exclusion Criteria

To guide the selection and classification of articles for the systematic review, a series of inclusion and exclusion criteria was established. Table 3 outlines these criteria.

Table 1. Research questions and their motivation

Code	Research Question Statement	Motivation
RQ1	How does the effectiveness of adaptive learning based on generative artificial intelligence compare with traditional educational approaches?	To evaluate the potential advantages and limitations of integrating GenAI in adaptive learning, providing insights into its efficacy relative to conventional methods in higher education
RQ2	What are the current strategies for adaptive learning using generative artificial intelligence tools in engineering programs?	To identify and understand innovative practices within engineering education that leverage GenAI for adaptive learning
RQ3	What outcomes or benefits have been reported from implementing adaptive learning mediated by generative artificial intelligence in engineering programs?	To assess the impact and advantages of GenAI-mediated adaptive learning on educational outcomes in engineering, supporting evidence-based decision-making for curriculum design and technology integration

3.4 Data Recovery

An Excel template was used to organize the retrieved data, ensuring efficient management and collaboration during the review. After applying the search protocols and inclusion/exclusion criteria, results were grouped by database. For each article, key details were recorded: (a) search protocol, (b) title, (c) authors, (d) year, (e) source type, (f) abstract, (g) DOI/ISBN/ISSN, and (h) a brief analysis. The review, conducted between January and February 2025, initially retrieved **85** results; after filtering, **4** relevant documents were identified. Table 4 presents a summary of the findings.

3.5 Results Analysis

Reference [21] highlights the role of generative AI in adaptive learning, particularly for content creation and personalized learning paths. Building on this, [22] and [23] propose adaptive models that use AI to enhance personalization and engagement, with potential for broader application in higher education. Student perspectives are addressed in [24], which reports increased motivation and learning efficiency with GenAI, while also noting concerns around privacy and algorithmic bias. The study calls for student-centered approaches and teacher training. Practical implementations are seen in [25] and [26], where GenAI tools—such as GPT-based roleplay and the PMTutor chatbot—improve engagement, critical thinking, and self-assessed competence in engineering education, despite some usability issues.

In biomedical education, [27] demonstrates how GenAI supports adaptive content and hands-on learning, while also raising ethical concerns. Reference [28] explores the

Table 2. Databases and search sentences

Databases	Sentences
ScienceDirect	("generative artificial intelligence" OR GenAI) AND ("adaptive learning" OR "adaptive curriculum") AND (engineering) AND (effective OR benefit OR strategy OR challenge)
Spinger	("generative artificial intelligence" OR GenAI) AND ("adaptive learning" OR "adaptive curriculum") AND (engineering) AND (effective OR benefit OR strategy OR challenge)
IEEE	("adaptive learning" AND ("generative AI" OR "generative artificial intelligence" OR "GenAI") AND ("engineering" OR "engineering education" OR "engineering programs"))

Table 3. Inclusion and exclusion criteria

Code	Inclusion Criteria	Code	Exclusion Criteria
IC1	Studies exploring adaptive learning specifically in the context of engineering programs.	EC1	The document is not available for download
IC2	Studies written between 2022 and 2025.	EC2	Published before 2022
IC3	English language.	EC3	GenAI in education is not the main focus
IC4	Primary research (papers, conference papers, books).	EC4	Not in English
		EC5	Not primary research (report)

integration of large language models (LLMs) in education, focusing on advanced prompt engineering techniques—such as few-shot prompting, ReAct, and chain-of-thought— that improve the adaptability and performance of educational systems. Finally, [29] reviews AI adoption in African higher education, showing widespread use in teaching, research, and self-directed learning.

4   Experimental Case

The experimental case was designed following the principles outlined by authors such as Baig, M.I. [4], who emphasize the role of generative artificial intelligence (GenAI) in creating personalized learning paths and adaptive educational content. In alignment with these ideas, the AI-4EDU framework operationalizes several key concepts identified in the literature, including adaptive personalization, GenAI-mediated creativity, and team formation based on learning profiles, as explored in references [22,23], and

Table 4. Search results and relevant documents by database

Database	Search Results	Relevant Documents
ScienceDirect	30	1
Spinger	34	1
IEEE	21	

[26]. Building on these foundations, an experiment was conducted with students from the Algorithmics and Programming course, where GenAI agents were integrated into a structured six-step learning model to personalize and enhance the educational experience. This methodology responds directly to gaps identified in the systematic review, particularly the lack of practical implementation models in higher education and the need for strategies that foster student motivation, reduce response times, and increase the overall efficiency of learning processes.

The results of the pilot study demonstrated the positive impact of AI-driven personalized learning. Through the feedback generated by the MAKE platform, students were able to clearly identify both their strengths and areas for improvement, which contributed to a greater awareness of their learning progress. Figure 1 presents the proposed framework for skill-based adaptive learning.

Framework for Adaptive Learning Using GenAI

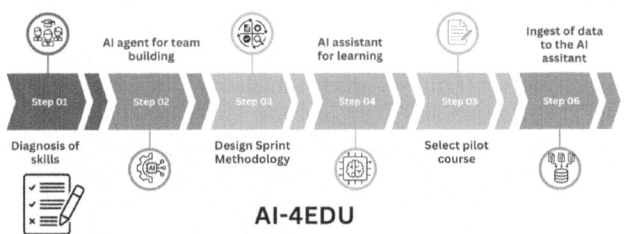

Fig. 1. Proposed framework for adaptive learning based on AI agents.

The framework for adaptive learning with GenAI proposed by AI-4EDU is based on a structured sequence of six steps that integrate artificial intelligence agents to personalize and optimize educational processes in higher education. It begins with a skills diagnosis (Step 1), where individual student competencies are identified. Then, using an AI agent, work teams are formed (Step 2), followed by the application of Design Sprint methodologies (Step 3) to co-create educational solutions. In Step 4, an AI assistant is incorporated to support learning by adjusting resources and content to the student's profile. Next, a pilot course is selected (Step 5) to implement the system, and finally, data is ingested into the AI assistant (Step 6), enabling continuous feedback and dynamic adaptation. This approach aims to promote more efficient, autonomous, and personalized learning experiences, consistent with current trends in GenAI-enhanced education, as evidenced by the outcomes observed in the pilot.

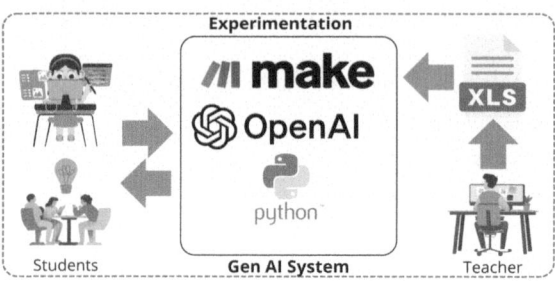

Fig. 2. Inclusive text to audio system.

4.1   Population Characterization

The study involved two distinct groups of students enrolled in the Algorithmics and Programming course. The control group, which followed a traditional learning approach without AI support, consisted of 25 students—21 men (84%) and 4 women (16%). In contrast, the experimental group, which implemented a structured six-stage GenAI-supported learning framework, included 30 students—20 men (66.7%) and 10 women (33.3%). This distribution reflects a more gender-balanced composition in the experimental group, potentially contributing to more diverse collaboration dynamics and learning experiences.

To evaluate the academic impact of the intervention, a descriptive analysis was performed on the final course grades for each group. The results revealed a notable improvement in the experimental group, with a mean score of 4.260 compared to 3.312 in the control group—an increase of approximately 28.6%. Additionally, the experimental group showed higher centrality in scores (median = 4.250; mode = 4.800), reduced dispersion (standard deviation = 0.558), and lower variance (0.311), suggesting a more homogeneous and consistent learning performance. Minimum and maximum values also improved in the experimental group, indicating that both the lowest and highest performing students achieved better outcomes with the support of GenAI tools.

Figure 2 illustrates the GenAI system that facilitates personalized learning by linking teachers and students through a continuous feedback loop. Educators input performance data (e.g., grades or qualitative feedback) into a spreadsheet, which is then processed using tools such as Make, OpenAI, and Python. The system analyzes the inputs and generates individualized recommendations, supporting both individual and group learning. Furthermore, Fig. 3 depicts an AI-powered mechanism for identifying students' skill profiles and forming development teams. Students complete an assessment form, generating data that is classified into profiles (Clarify, Ideate, Develop, Implement) using algorithms such as K-Nearest Neighbors. Based on these profiles, the system assembles balanced teams to enhance collaboration and improve project outcomes.

Figure 4 presents a comparative analysis of the average delivery times across different stages of a project, distinguishing between those developed with the support of artificial intelligence (AI) tools and those without. The results show a significant reduction in delivery times when AI systems were integrated throughout the development process. In the Review stage, the average time decreased from 4.58 to 3.16 days with the use of AI. In the Problematization phase, it dropped from 4.92 to 3.01 days. During Ideation, the time was reduced from 4.61 to 2.82 days, while the Prototyping stage

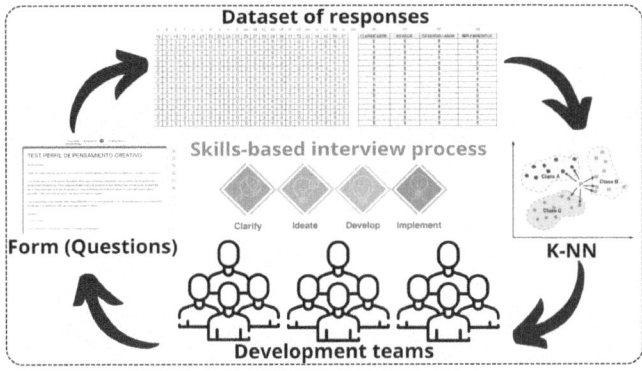

Fig. 3. Skills identification process.

showed the most notable improvement, decreasing from 5.36 to 2.86 days. Finally, in the Validation stage, the delivery time was reduced from 5.15 to 2.78 days. These findings suggest that the integration of generative AI tools significantly enhances process efficiency, accelerating each phase of the design and development cycle. These results are consistent with findings by Li et al. [21], who highlight how generative AI contributes to adaptive learning by enabling personalized instruction and optimizing educational pathways. Likewise, Iza et al. [22] report that AI-enhanced adaptive learning improves understanding and performance, especially in complex domains such as science education. These insights support the evidence presented here regarding increased project efficiency and reduced completion time through the integration of GenAI tools.

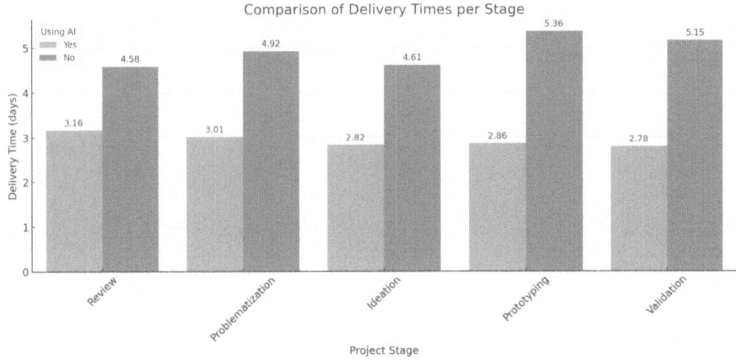

Fig. 4. Comparision of delivery time per stage.

Figure 5 shows that AI-assisted projects (yellow line) exhibit an upward trend from the Review stage through to Prototyping, reaching their highest point in week 11 with a score close to 4.6. Although a slight decline is observed during the Validation stage (week 15), performance remains above 4.0, indicating consistency in quality.

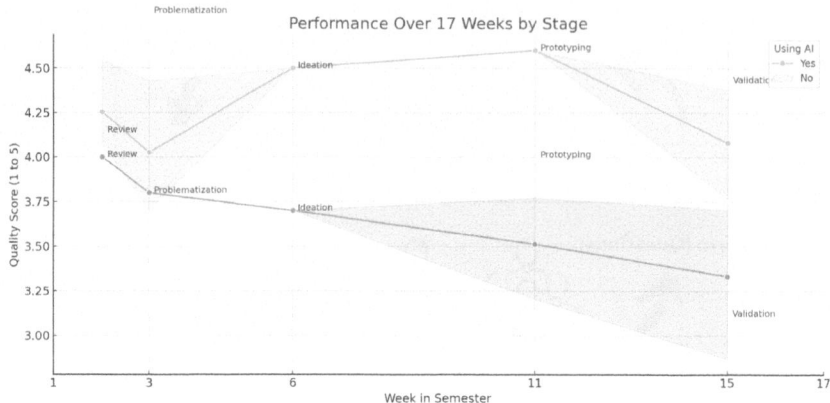

Fig. 5. 17-week performance by stage. (Color figure online)

In contrast, projects without AI support (orange line) display a continuous downward trend over time. After starting at around 4.0 during the Review stage, performance gradually drops to 3.3 by the Validation stage, highlighting a sustained decline in work quality as the semester progresses.

This trend aligns with the arguments made by Chen et al. [26], who found that continuous personalized feedback through AI-driven systems contributes to sustained learner engagement and outcome quality. The consistency observed in AI-supported projects may thus be attributed to such dynamic and responsive learning environments.

Figure 6 compares prototype outcomes between teams using the AI-4EDU system (yellow) and those without it (orange). Teams supported by AI-4EDU achieved functional beta versions in 80% of cases, showing notable progress in development and functionality. In contrast, non-AI teams mostly produced lower-level outputs: 45% reached an alpha version, while 65% delivered only high-fidelity prototypes lacking advanced functionality.

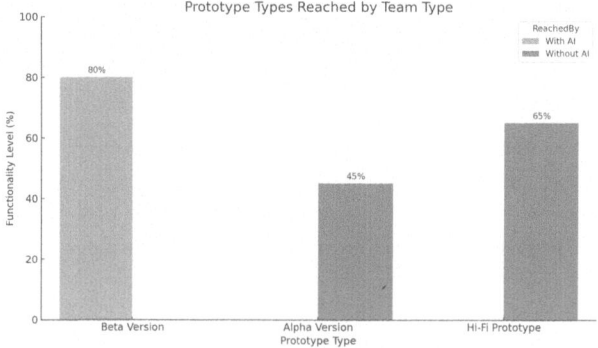

Fig. 6. Prototyping results. (Color figure online)

The results of the pilot study demonstrate a substantial improvement not only in learning efficiency but also in students' creative capacity, stimulated by the integration of generative artificial intelligence (GenAI) tools. This creativity was particularly evident during the ideation and prototyping phases, where AI-assisted teams were able to develop more functional and sophisticated solutions compared to those without such support. The significant reduction in delivery times during these stages, as shown in Fig. 4, suggests that GenAI systems not only optimize processes but also free up cognitive resources, enabling students to focus on innovation and divergent thinking.

This finding aligns with studies such as those by Honig et al., where scenario simulation through role-play with GPT fostered critical and creative thinking in engineering contexts. Similarly, Chen et al. demonstrated how educational chatbots with adaptive features promoted creative self-efficacy in solving complex problems. In the present study, team formation based on skill profiles (Clarify, Ideate, Develop, Implement) also encouraged a rich collaborative dynamic, in which the diversity of approaches nurtured the generation of original ideas.

The creative dimension is further enhanced by the use of tools that allow real-time personalization of content and pedagogical strategies, which encourages the exploration of original solutions and the design of more sophisticated products. Through the continuous support of intelligent agents and dynamic feedback systems, students experience a more autonomous, experimental, and exploratory learning environment—an essential condition for the development of creative competencies.

It is worth highlighting that the sustained performance throughout the semester, particularly during the more advanced stages of the project, reflects an environment that not only fosters productivity but also creative resilience—understood as the ability to maintain high levels of innovation under pressure or over extended periods. However, the integration of GenAI in creative processes also raises important questions. One of the main risks is the potential for technological dependency, which could limit original authorship if a critical awareness of these tools is not developed. In this regard, it is essential to train educators not only in the technical use of AI, but also in strategies that promote genuine creativity in their students, avoiding the over-automation of ideas. Finally, while creativity is enhanced in technologically advanced contexts, it also requires a pedagogical environment that values, assesses, and promotes it as a crosscutting competency. In this study, the framework proposed by AI4EDU, based on skills diagnostics, agile methodologies, and continuous feedback, provides a practical and scalable example of how AI-mediated creative learning can be systematized in higher education.

5   Discussion

The implementation of GenAI-based adaptive learning in higher education reveals a multidimensional impact that extends beyond improvements in academic performance. The pilot study demonstrates that the integration of generative artificial intelligence not only accelerates development cycles but also enhances students' capacity for creative problem-solving and collaborative engagement. These findings are consistent with previous literature highlighting the dual role of GenAI in both optimizing content delivery and fostering innovative thinking environments [21, 22, 25].

The significant reductions in delivery times observed across all project stages underscore the efficiency gains made possible by GenAI-mediated workflows. As shown in Fig. 4, stages such as Ideation and Prototyping benefited from an over 40% decrease in average completion time, suggesting that generative systems alleviate procedural burdens, thereby enabling students to allocate more cognitive effort to higher-order tasks. This aligns with prior studies that associate GenAI with enhanced learner agency and performance in complex tasks [24,26]. Moreover, the sustained performance levels and higher quality outcomes achieved by AI-assisted teams Fig. 5 and Fig. 6 suggest that the framework not only supports short-term productivity but also contributes to long-term engagement and quality maintenance. These results validate claims from recent research indicating that adaptive learning environments, when powered by real-time feedback and learner profiling, can maintain consistent academic rigor over extended periods [6,13,14].

The creative dimension also emerges as a benefit of this approach. The use of design sprint methodologies, dynamic feedback loops, and AI-generated recommendations appears to have facilitated a more autonomous and exploratory learning experience, particularly in the ideation stages. The integration of skill-based team formation Fig. 3 enhanced collaborative diversity, further promoting creative thinking, an effect echoed in Honig et al.'s findings on GPT-driven role-play scenarios in engineering education [25].

However, despite these promising outcomes, the study also brings to light several concerns that must be addressed to ensure sustainable implementation. The risk of technological dependency, for example, may undermine the development of original authorship and critical judgment if not mitigated through proper pedagogical design. As highlighted in [4] and [27], educators must be trained not only in the operational aspects of GenAI tools but also in cultivating environments that balance automation with creative autonomy.

Ethical concerns about data privacy and algorithmic bias remain critical. Although the current framework showed success in a controlled environment, broader institutional adoption requires clear governance protocols, as highlighted in recent literature on AI in education [3,10,28]. Ensuring transparency in data usage, equitable access to technology, and inclusivity in instructional design is essential for GenAI-supported adaptive learning to achieve its transformative potential without reinforcing existing educational inequalities.

The AI-4EDU framework is a scalable and replicable model that integrates generative technologies into adaptive learning ecosystems. It provides diagnostics, personalized feedback, and agile pedagogy to transform education, especially in engineering. Its ongoing improvement and ethical implementation require interdisciplinary collaboration between educators and policymakers.

6 Conclusions

The use of GenAI enables the adaptation of teaching content and methodologies to meet the individual needs of students, significantly improving motivation, academic performance, and autonomous learning in higher education programs, especially in fields like engineering.

The framework proposed by AI-4EDU, which includes skill assessment, team formation, agile methodologies, and continuous feedback, has proven effective in personalizing and optimizing educational processes, as demonstrated by the experimental case with programming students.

Despite its benefits, the implementation of adaptive systems with GenAI in education faces significant challenges, such as technological dependency, data privacy, equitable access, and the need for teacher training to ensure responsible and effective use of these technologies.

The incorporation of generative artificial intelligence in educational environments offers the potential to achieve unprecedented levels of personalized learning. Through models capable of dynamically adapting to students' individual needs, learning styles, and paces, new opportunities arise to enhance knowledge retention, intrinsic motivation, and educational equity.

Generative AI offers transformative potential for learning but poses ethical, privacy, authorship, and bias challenges. Its implementation must be guided by strong governance policies to ensure responsible, inclusive, and transparent use. Fostering a critical and ethical digital culture is key to its sustainable integration in higher education.

Acknowledgments. This research is part of the International Chair Project on Trustworthy Artificial Intelligence and Demographic Challenge within the National Strategy for Artificial Intelligence (ENIA), in the framework of the European Recovery, Transformation and Resilience Plan. Reference: TSI-100933-2023-0001. This project is funded by the Secretary of State for Digitalization and Artificial Intelligence and by the European Union (Next Generation).

Disclosure of Interests. The authors have no competing interests to declare that are relevant to the content of this article.

References

1. Ezzaim, A., Dahbi, A., Haidine, A., Aqqal, A.: AI-based adaptive learning: a systematic mapping of the literature. J. Univ. Comput. Sci. **29**(10), 1161 (2023)
2. Cortese, A.: Metacognitive resources for adaptive learning. Neurosci. Res. **178**, 10–19 (2022)
3. Ifenthaler, D., Yau, J.Y.-K.: Utilising learning analytics to support study success in higher education: a systematic review. Educ. Tech. Res. Dev. **68**(4), 1961–1990 (2020). https://doi.org/10.1007/s11423-020-09788-z
4. Baig, M.I., Yadegaridehkordi, E.: Factors influencing academic staff satisfaction and continuous usage of generative artificial intelligence (genai) in higher education. Int. J. Educ. Technol. High. Educ. **22**(1), 5 (2025)
5. Verdu, E., Regueras, L.M., Verdu, M.J., De Castro, J.P., Pérez, M.: Is adaptive learning effective? A review of the research. **7**, 710–715 (2008)
6. Mavroudi, A., Giannakos, M., Krogstie, J.: Supporting adaptive learning pathways through the use of learning analytics: developments, challenges and future opportunities. Interact. Learn. Environ. **26**(2), 206–220 (2018)
7. Strielkowski, W., Grebennikova, V., Lisovskiy, A., Rakhimova, G., Vasileva, T.: AI-driven adaptive learning for sustainable educational transformation. Sustain. Dev. (2024)

8. Barbosa, P.L.S., Carmo, R.A.F.d., Gomes, J.P., Viana, W.: Adaptive learning in computer science education: a scoping review. Educ. Inf. Technol. **29**(8), 9139–9188 (2024)
9. Apoki, U.C., Al-Chalabi, H.K.M., Crisan, G.C.: From digital learning resources to adaptive learning objects: an overview, pp. 18–32 (2019)
10. Kabudi, T., Pappas, I., Olsen, D.H.: Ai-enabled adaptive learning systems: a systematic mapping of the literature. Comput. Educ. Artif. Intell. **2**, 100017 (2021)
11. Martin, F., Chen, Y., Moore, R.L., Westine, C.D.: Systematic review of adaptive learning research designs, context, strategies, and technologies from 2009 to 2018. Educ. Tech. Res. Dev. **68**(4), 1903–1929 (2020). https://doi.org/10.1007/s11423-020-09793-2
12. Linda, Q.Y., Wilson, R.C., Nassar, M.R.: Adaptive learning is structure learning in time. Neurosci. Biobehav. Rev. **128**, 270–281 (2021)
13. Essa, S.G., Celik, T., Human-Hendricks, N.E.: Personalized adaptive learning technologies based on machine learning techniques to identify learning styles: a systematic literature review. IEEE Access **11**, 48392–48409 (2023)
14. Gligorea, I., Cioca, M., Oancea, R., Gorski, A.T., Gorski, H., Tudorache, P.: Adaptive learning using artificial intelligence in e-learning: a literature review. Educ. Sci. **13**(12), 1216 (2023)
15. dos Santos Sachete, A., Gomes, R.S., Canto Filho, A.B., de Lima, J.V.: Indicadores de aprendizaje adaptativo en entornos virtuales de aprendizaje: Revisión sistemática de la literatura. Revista Latinoamericana de Tecnología Educativa-RELATEC **23**(2), 69–87 (2024)
16. Normadhi, N.B.A., Shuib, L., Nasir, H.N.M., Bimba, A., Idris, N., Balakrishnan, V.: Identification of personal traits in adaptive learning environment: systematic literature review. Comput. Educ. **130**, 168–190 (2019)
17. Ezzaim, A., Dahbi, A., Aqqal, A., Haidine, A.: AI-based learning style detection in adaptive learning systems: a systematic literature review. J. Comput. Educ. 1–39 (2024)
18. Fadieieva, L.O.: Adaptive learning: a cluster-based literature review (2011–2022). Educ. Technol. Q. **2023**(3), 319–366 (2023)
19. Keele, S., et al.: Guidelines for performing systematic literature reviews in software engineering (2007)
20. Page, M.J., et al.: The PRISMA 2020 statement: an updated guideline for reporting systematic reviews. BMJ **372** (2021)
21. Li, H., et al.: Bringing generative AI to adaptive learning in education. arXiv preprint arXiv:2402.14601 (2024)
22. Iza, C.A., Crespo, M.V.Y., Jaramillo, G.F.U., Lucín, M.A.V., et al.: Aprendizaje adaptativo mediante inteligencia artificial en la enseñanza de las ciencias naturales. Reincisol. **3**(6), 4443–4456 (2024)
23. Lhafra, F.Z., Abdoun, O.: A comparative study of learning style model using machine learning for an adaptive e-learning. Multimed. Tools Appl. 1–20 (2025)
24. Wang, X., Xu, X., Zhang, Y., Hao, S., Jie, W.: Exploring the impact of artificial intelligence application in personalized learning environments: thematic analysis of undergraduates' perceptions in china. Humanities Soc. Sci. Commun. **11**(1), 1–10 (2024)
25. Honig, C.D., Desu, A., Franklin, J.: GenAI in the classroom: customized GPT roleplay for process safety education. Educ. Chem. Eng. **49**, 55–66 (2024)
26. Chen, D.L., Aaltonen, K., Lampela, H., Kujala, J.: The design and implementation of an educational chatbot with personalized adaptive learning features for project management training. Technol. Knowl. Learn. 1–26 (2024)

27. Khojah, R., Werth, A., Broadhead, K.W., Dobrucki, L.W., Geiger, C., Ruben-stein, D.A.: Integrating generative artificial intelligence tools and competencies in biomedical engineering education. Biomed. Eng. Educ. 1–17 (2025)
28. Chondamrongkul, N., Hristov, G., Temdee, P.: Addressing technical challenges in large language model-driven educational software system. IEEE Access (2025)
29. Falebita, O.S., Kok, P.J.: Strategic goals for artificial intelligence integration among stem academics and undergraduates in African higher education: a systematic review. Discover Educ. **3**(1), 151 (2024)

Enabling Context-Aware Sarcasm Detection in Ambient Intelligence Through Local LLMs

Adelino Gala[1,2]([✉]) [iD], Manuel Rodrigues[1] [iD], Francisco S. Marcondes[1] [iD], and Paulo Novais[1] [iD]

[1] ALGORITMI Research Centre/LASI, University of Minho, Braga, Portugal
{manuel.rodrigues,francisco.marcondes}@algoritmi.uminho.pt,
pjon@di.uminho.pt
[2] Science and Technology Department, Portucalense University, Porto, Portugal
adelino.gala@mail.upt.pt

Abstract. Sarcasm detection, a challenge in sentiment analysis crucial for Ambient Intelligence (AmI), faces hurdles with cloud LLMs due to privacy, cost, and accessibility. This paper evaluates locally runnable LLMs for detecting author-intended sarcasm using the iSarcasm dataset. Our evaluation of Gemma, Phi, Mistral, and Qwen variants shows Qwen (qwen3:30B) achieves the highest F1-score of 0.507 for sarcasm. These LLMs demonstrate improved performance over traditional methods (average F1-score $\approx$ 0.332), though their performance currently trails human annotation (F1-score of 0.616). Despite this difference, our findings highlight their significant potential for on-premise, privacy-preserving sentiment analysis in AmI, paving the way for more responsive and context-aware human-computer interaction.

Keywords: Large Language Models (LLM) · Natural Language Processing (NLP) · Sentiment analysis · Sarcasm detection

1 Introduction

Sentiment analysis, a key Natural Language Processing (NLP) area, extracts subjective information from text for applications like opinion mining [16] and social media monitoring. Figurative language, especially sarcasm, where the intended meaning opposes literal interpretation, complicates the accurate judgment of sentiments. Sarcasm is prevalent on the Internet and its detection is vital to understanding the true sentiment of users. The iSarcasm dataset, for instance, specifically targets author-intended sarcasm in online discourse [15].

Large Language Models (LLMs) have advanced NLP by computing context and nuance [7,9]. Most known LLMs are proprietary and cloud based. However, recent developments also offer capable LLMs for local deployment [2,13,20,21]. These local LLMs provide benefits in data privacy, cost, customization, and offline access. However, their efficacy in complex tasks like sarcasm detection, particularly against larger or specialized models, needs more investigation.

J. Valente de Oliveira et al. (Eds.): EPIA 2025, LNAI 16122, pp. 382–394, 2026.
https://doi.org/10.1007/978-3-032-05179-0_29

This paper evaluates selected locally runnable LLMs for sarcasm detection using the iSarcasm dataset [15]. We use a direct prompting strategy to assess baseline capabilities. Objectives are:

1. Benchmark open-source Qwen, Mistral, Phi, and Gemma on iSarcasm.
2. Analyze their strengths/weaknesses in identifying sarcasm with our prompt.
3. Offer insights for practitioners considering local LLMs for sentiment analysis involving sarcasm.

Our study focuses on the practical utility of these models with a defined prompt, reflecting common usage scenarios.

The remainder of this paper is organized as follows. Section 2 reviews the related work on sarcasm detection, from classical methods to the use of Large Language Models. Section 3 details our methodology, including the selected local LLMs, the iSarcasm dataset, and the few-shot prompting strategy used for evaluation. In Sect. 4, we present the quantitative and qualitative results of our experiments. Section 5 discusses the implications of these findings in the context of prior benchmarks and outlines the study's limitations. Finally, Sect. 6 concludes the paper and proposes directions for future research.

2 Related Work

Within Natural Language Processing, sarcasm detection presents a considerable challenge, closely linked to sentiment analysis. While Zhang [24] recently provided an evaluation of machine learning, deep learning, and large language models using the iSarcasmEval dataset and its distinct experimental framework, our work shifts the focus to the iSarcasm dataset.

2.1 Lexicon-Based and Classical Machine Learning Methods

Lexicon-based methods [4,12] struggle with sarcasm as it often uses positive words for negative sentiment, requiring context beyond lexical polarity [11]. Classical machine learning (e.g., SVMs [8], Naïve Bayes [14]) rely on engineered features (n-grams, bag of words) [18] and tend to perform better for specific trained domains, struggling to generalize. Deep learning (LSTMs [10], CNNs [19]) learns features automatically but can falter with sarcasm needing extensive world knowledge.

2.2 Large Language Models for Sarcasm Detection

Transformer-based LLMs [22] like BERT [9] and GPT variants [7] have advanced NLP by capturing complex language nuances. Fine-tuning large models on sarcasm-specific datasets often yields good performance for perceived datasets [17]. The iSarcasm dataset [15] was introduced to provide a more robust benchmark for intended sarcasm, revealing that even advanced models found it challenging. This highlighted the difference between perceived and intended sarcasm.

Most research has focused on extensively trained or fine-tuned models based on large annotated dataset [3,5]. The performance of smaller, locally runnable LLMs with direct prompting on challenging datasets like iSarcasm is less explored. These local models are vital for privacy-centric or offline and cost effective applications [6]. This study contributes to understanding their few-shot capabilities in this domain.

3 Methodology

This section outlines the methodology employed for evaluating the sarcasm detection capabilities of selected local Large Language Models (LLMs) using the iSarcasm dataset. It details the specific models tested, the dataset characteristics, the prompting strategy, and the metrics used for performance assessment.

3.1 Selected Local LLMs

Open-source LLMs for local deployment were chosen based on their reported capabilities, parameter size, and availability:

– Phi (phi4:latest) [2]
– Mistral (mistral-small3.1:latest) [13]
– Gemma (gemma3:27b-it-qat) [20]
– Qwen (qwen3:30B) [23]

We used the Ollama framework and Python scripts for the tests. The Models quantization are: (GGUF Q4). The models were run on a local machine with 90 GB memory RAM.

3.2 Dataset: iSarcasm

We utilized the *iSarcasm dataset* [15]. This dataset is specifically designed to address the challenge of sarcasm detection by focusing on intended sarcasm, where the authors of the text self-annotate their posts as sarcastic. This approach contrasts with datasets labeled by third-party annotators, which may reflect perceived sarcasm and be subject to socio-cultural biases or ambiguity.

The iSarcasm dataset contains 4,484 English tweets, each labeled by its author as "sarcastic" or "non-sarcastic". Approximately 20% of the tweets are sarcastic (777 sarcastic, 3,707 non_sarcastic). Sarcastic tweets are further categorized into types of sarcastic speech: sarcasm, irony, satire, understatement, overstatement, or rhetorical question, providing a finer granularity for analysis (though this study focuses on binary sarcasm detection).

The creators of the data sets argue that its focus on authorial intent makes it a challenging benchmark, as evidenced by the lower performance of the state-of-the-art models compared to other data sets [15]. We used the complete data set provided for evaluation. The data includes tweet IDs, sarcasm labels, and sarcasm types.

3.3 Prompting Strategy

To assess the LLMs, we used the following few-shot prompt. This prompt was designed to elicit a binary classification of sarcasm with stable-format results. And also a brief rationale from the model.

Your Task: Analyze the provided "TEXT TO ANALYZE" for sarcasm.

TEXT TO ANALYZE:
"{input_text}"

CRITICAL OUTPUT FORMATTING INSTRUCTIONS:
You MUST output EXACTLY two lines in the following format. Do NOT add any other headers,
text, or formatting.

PREDICTION: [SINGLE DIGIT: 0 for Non−Sarcastic, 1 for Sarcastic]
RATIONALE: [Your brief explanation for the classification. Limit to 1−2 concise
    sentences.]

Example of YOUR EXACT output for a sarcastic text:
PREDICTION: 1
RATIONALE: The speaker is likely being ironic, as spilling coffee is generally not a
    positive event.

Example of YOUR EXACT output for a non−sarcastic text:
PREDICTION: 0
RATIONALE: This statement appears to be a literal and straightforward
    observation about the weather.

Now, analyze the "TEXT TO ANALYZE" above and provide your output strictly
    following this two−line format.

For the quantitative evaluation presented in this paper, the model's output was parsed to extract the single digit ('0' or '1') from the PREDICTION: line. The RATIONALE: provided by the models was recorded and utilized for qualitative analysis and error inspection, though it did not directly factor into the primary classification metrics reported. The placeholder "input_text" was replaced with the actual text from the iSarcasm dataset for each evaluation instance.

3.4 Evaluation Metrics

Standard classification metrics were used: Accuracy, Precision (sarcastic class), Recall (sarcastic class), and F1-Score (sarcastic class, crucial for imbalanced datasets). A confusion matrix will also aid error analysis.

4 LLM Quantitative Evaluation Results

This section presents the quantitative and qualitative results.

4.1   Quantitative Results

Table 1 shows the performance of the evaluated local Large Language Models on the iSarcasm test set.

Table 1. Sarcasm Detection Performance (Author-Intended Sarcasm)

Model	Accuracy	Precision	Recall	F1-Score
Gemma (gemma3:27b-it-qat)	0.457	0.312	0.969	0.472
Phi (phi4:latest)	0.421	0.306	0.980	0.466
Mistral (mistral-small3.1:latest)	0.391	0.286	0.958	0.441
Qwen (qwen3:30B)	**0.572**	0.356	0.880	0.507
ManualLabelling	—	**0.550**	0.701	**0.616**
Results from Oprea & Magdy (2020) [15]:				
ManualLabelling	—	**0.550**	0.701	**0.616**
LSTM	—	0.217	0.747	0.336
Att-LSTM	—	0.260	0.436	0.325
CNN	—	0.261	0.563	0.356
SIARN	—	0.219	0.782	0.342
MIARN	—	0.236	0.793	0.364
3CNN	—	0.250	0.333	0.286
Dense-LSTM	—	0.375	0.276	0.318

Note: LLM results are from prompted evaluations on the author-intended sarcasm set of the iSarcasm dataset. Results for models from LSTM to Dense-LSTM, and ManualLabelling, are sourced from [15]; accuracy was not reported for these in the original paper. "Manual Labelling" reflects performance using perceived sarcasm labels by human annotators.

The evaluation on the iSarcasm dataset reveals varied performance across the tested Large Language Models for detecting author-intended sarcasm. Qwen (qwen3:30B), with its thinking mode on, emerged as the strongest performer, achieving the highest overall accuracy of 0.572 and the best F1-score for the sarcastic class at 0.507. It also registered the highest precision for sarcastic instances (0.356) while maintaining a high recall of 0.880. Following Qwen, Gemma (gemma3:27b-it-qat) delivered an F1-score of 0.472 with an overall accuracy of 0.457. Phi (phi4:latest) and Mistral (mistral-small3.1:latest) recorded F1-scores of 0.466 and 0.441, and overall accuracies of 0.421 and 0.391, respectively.

A prominent trend across all models is a significantly higher recall for the sarcastic class (ranging from 0.880 to 0.980) compared to their precision scores (ranging from 0.286 to 0.356). This indicates that while the models are adept at identifying a large portion of actual sarcastic instances, they also exhibit a tendency to incorrectly label many non-sarcastic instances as sarcastic, although with less tendency in the Qwen case. The overall accuracy and F1-scores, generally hovering around or below the 0.5 mark, underscore the challenging nature of this specific sarcasm detection task for LLMs in a few-shot setting.

4.2 Qualitative Analysis and Error Examples

To complement the quantitative results, a qualitative analysis of the models' predictions was conducted. This involved examining the confusion matrices to understand error distributions and reviewing specific misclassified instances to identify common patterns.

The Run Summary for Qwen (qwen3:30B) reported 3466 successfully parsed predictions. The confusion matrix for Qwen (Q) 1482 misclassified examples overall. Other models matrices like Gemma (G), Phi (P), and Mistral (M) also had a significant number of misclassifications: 1882, 1839, and 2110 respectively, though Phi's total evaluated samples were slightly fewer at 3176, suggesting that the phi4 model struggle in generating formatted results.

The confusion matrix for Qwen (Q) reveals a key trend also seen in other models (G, M and P): a high number of True Positives for the sarcastic class (762 correctly identified sarcastic instances) and a relatively low number of False Negatives for this class (104 sarcastic instances missed). This contributes to the high recall for sarcasm (0.880). However, there's a high number of False Positives: 1378 non-sarcastic instances were incorrectly classified as sarcastic. This significantly impacts the precision (0.356) for the sarcastic class. The model correctly identified 1222 non-sarcastic instances.

Consider the following confusion matrices,

$$G = \begin{array}{c} \\ N \\ S \end{array}\begin{array}{cc} N & S \\ \left[745 \right. & 1855 \\ \left. 27 \right. & 840 \end{array}], M = \begin{array}{c} \\ N \\ S \end{array}\begin{array}{cc} N & S \\ \left[526 \right. & 2074 \\ \left. 36 \right. & 831 \end{array}], P = \begin{array}{c} \\ N \\ S \end{array}\begin{array}{cc} N & S \\ \left[533 \right. & 1823 \\ \left. 16 \right. & 804 \end{array}], Q = \begin{array}{c} \\ N \\ S \end{array}\begin{array}{cc} N & S \\ \left[1222 \right. & 1378 \\ \left. 104 \right. & 762 \end{array}]$$

in all of them, N stands for non-sarcastic and S for sarcastic. Rows represent actual labels; columns show predicted ones.

Examining specific misclassifications provides further information:

False Negatives (Sarcastic Text Classified as Non-Sarcastic): This was a less common error type where the model failed to detect the author's intended sarcasm, often due to the subtlety of the sarcasm or the model's tendency towards literal interpretation.

– **Gemma (gemma3:27b-it-qat) - Dataset Index: 154**

> Text: @sonofsama1 @Santandave1 you're trash
> Ground Truth: 1 (Sarcastic), Predicted: 0 (Non−Sarcastic)
> LLM Rationale: This is a direct insult with no indicators of irony or playful intent
> ; it appears to be a genuine negative assessment.

Observation: The model struggles to differentiate a direct insult intended sarcastically from a genuinely literal insult without more contextual cues. Mistral also misclassified this example similarly.

- **Mistral (mistral-small3.1:latest) - Dataset Index: 7**

> Text: someone hit me w a horse tranquilizer istg ive been in a pool of sweat for 6 hours and i havent slept im so tired but i love my friend so much and oh my fucking god i cant rn
> Ground Truth: 1 (Sarcastic), Predicted: 0 (Non—Sarcastic)
> LLM Rationale: The text expresses genuine frustration and exhaustion, indicating a sincere emotional state rather than sarcasm.

Observation: The model interprets intense emotional expression and hyperbole literally, missing the sarcastic intent. Qwen also misclassified this example similarly.

False Positives (Non-Sarcastic Text classified as Sarcastic): These high counts indicated in the confusion matrix that models often over interpreted cues, misread strong emotions, or were overly sensitive to phrasing that can sometimes be associated with sarcasm, even when used literally.

- **Phi (phi4:latest) - Dataset Index: 868**

> Text: life is so much better with a heating blanket
> Ground Truth: 0 (Non—Sarcastic), Predicted: 1 (Sarcastic)
> LLM Rationale: 'The statement likely uses irony, as it suggests that life is significantly improved by something as simple as a heating blanket, which may imply dissatisfaction with current conditions.'

Observation: The model interprets a simple statement of comfort as sarcastic, perhaps due to the perceived triviality of a heating blanket significantly improving life, reading dissatisfaction where none might be intended.

- **Qwen (qwen3:30B) - Dataset Index: 876**

> Text: Why do I have a doctorate and miss the restaurant industry SO MUCH
> Ground Truth: 0 (Non—Sarcastic), Predicted: 1 (Sarcastic)
> LLM Rationale: The juxtaposition of holding a doctorate with intensely missing the restaurant industry creates an ironic contrast, suggesting the speaker might be humorously exaggerating their nostalgia or expressing dissatisfaction with their current academic path.

Observation: The model interprets the strong emotion ("SO MUCH") and the contrast between a high academic achievement and a less prestigious industry as ironic, when the author might be expressing a genuine, albeit perhaps wistful, sentiment.

The prevalence of False Positives across all models underscores the challenge of distinguishing genuine strong statements or figurative language from actual sarcastic intent using the current prompting strategy without more nuanced contextual understanding or specific fine-tuning.

Error Patterns: A primary challenge stems from the nature of "intended sarcasm" in the iSarcasm dataset. The author's intent is not always transparent from the text alone and often relies on unstated context, shared knowledge between the author and their audience, or subtle linguistic cues that current LLMs struggle to consistently interpret without explicit fine-tuning on such nuances. The "Rephrase" provided in the misclassified examples often clarifies the sarcastic intent, but this meta-information is unavailable to the LLM during prediction.

The few-shot prompt used, with its specific examples, likely guided the models to look for certain patterns of sarcasm (e.g., overt contradiction) or non-sarcasm (e.g., very literal statements). More nuanced sarcasm, or statements that could be literal in one context but sarcastic in another, were frequently misjudged. The models' rationales often indicate a default to literal interpretation when clear ironic markers are absent. For example, Qwen's rationale for misclassifying "Text: I never thought I'd say this, but I have become one of those people who like bounty bars". (Ground Truth: Sarcastic, Predicted: Non-Sarcastic) was: "The statement expresses a genuine personal preference change without ironic or contradictory language".

The high recall for the sarcastic class across most models, coupled with low precision, suggests that the models are "trigger-happy" in labeling text as sarcastic if there's even a slight hint of negativity, strong emotion, or unusual phrasing. This leads to correctly identifying many sarcastic instances but also sweeping in many non-sarcastic ones. Qwen, while being the best performer, still exhibits this trend, albeit to a lesser extent than models like Mistral or Phi in terms of overall balance.

5   Discussion

To contextualize the performance of the local Large Language Models evaluated in this study, it is important to consider the benchmarks established in the original iSarcasm paper by Oprea and Magdy (2020) [15].

Their research highlighted the significant challenge of detecting author-intended sarcasm, as opposed to sarcasm perceived by third-party annotators. For the author-intended sarcasm labels, traditional machine learning and deep learning models of that time exhibited notable difficulties. For instance, a standard LSTM achieved a Precision of 0.217, Recall of 0.747, and an F1-score of 0.336, while a more advanced MIARN model showed a Precision of 0.236, a high Recall of 0.793, but still a modest F1-score of 0.364.

These models often struggled with Precision, indicating a higher number of false positives, and achieving relatively high Recall in some cases, suggesting they identified a good portion of actual sarcastic instances, but at the cost of misclassifying many non-sarcastic ones. It is also worth mentioning the Dense-LSTM result with Precision 0.375, Recall 0.276 and F1 0.318, showing higher precision, albeit with much lower recall and F-score. In contrast, when using sarcasm labels based on third-party annotators' perception (termed "Manual-Labelling"), the performance was markedly better with a Precision of 0.550, Recall of 0.701, and an F1-score of 0.616 [15].

In a review contrasting various sarcasm detection methods, including RNNs and BERT-based models, and experimenting with data augmentation, [1] found mutation-based augmentation superior, achieving an F1-sarcastic of 0.414 with their best ensemble system. These differences underscore the unique difficulty posed by the author-intended annotations within the iSarcasm dataset. The generally lower Precision and F1-scores from these earlier models on intended sarcasm provide a critical baseline against which we can now discuss the capabilities and limitations of the local LLMs investigated in our work.

In our experiments with local Large Language Models on the iSarcasm dataset, we observed a range of performances in detecting author-intended sarcasm. The Qwen (qwen3:30B) model, with its think mode on, demonstrated the strongest performance, achieving an F1-sarcastic score of 0.507, with a Precision of 0.356 and a Recall of 0.880. Following Qwen, the gemma3:27b-it-qat model achieved an F1-sarcastic score of 0.472 (Precision: 0.312, Recall: 0.969). The phi4:latest model yielded an F1-sarcastic score of 0.466 (Precision: 0.306, Recall: 0.980), and the mistral-small3.1:latest model produced an F1-sarcastic score of 0.441 (Precision: 0.286, Recall: 0.958). Given that Qwen (qwen3:30B) outperformed the other local models, the subsequent discussion will focus on its results in comparison to established benchmarks.

Our evaluation of the local Qwen (qwen3:30B) model on the iSarcasm dataset demonstrates a notable advancement over these established benchmarks for author-intended sarcasm. The Qwen model achieved an F1-score for the sarcastic class of 0.507, coupled with a strong Recall of 0.880 and a Precision of 0.356. This F1-score significantly surpasses the 0.364 F1-score of the MIARN model and the 0.414 F1-score reported by Abaskohi et al. (2022) [1] for their ensemble system.

While Qwen's Precision of 0.356 is slightly lower than the Dense-LSTM's 0.375, its Recall (0.880) is substantially higher than MIARN's 0.793 or LSTM's 0.747. This indicates a robust ability to identify a large proportion of sarcastic instances. The superior F1-score achieved by Qwen, driven by a better balance of precision and high recall compared to the other tested LLMs and many previous benchmarks, suggests it offers a more effective few-shot solution for this challenging task. While the model, like its predecessors, still grapples with false positives, its capacity to capture a significant amount of sarcastic intent while achieving the highest F1-score among the evaluated LLMs marks it as the most promising approach in this study for author-intended sarcasm detection using the employed prompting strategy.

The qualitative analysis of misclassifications describe the challenges these local LLMs face with author-intended sarcasm. A dominant pattern, as exemplified by Qwen (qwen3:30B) and mirrored across other models, is the struggle with False Positives—incorrectly labeling non-sarcastic text as sarcastic. This often occurred when models over-interpreted strong emotional language, emphatic phrasing, or common expressions that can have dual literal and ironic meanings (e.g., Qwen flagging Why do I have a doctorate and miss the restaurant industry SO MUCH as sarcastic due to the perceived ironic contrast).

The high recall for sarcasm, while positive in capturing many true sarcastic instances, seems to come at the cost of this lower precision, suggesting the models are, to an extent, "trigger-happy". Conversely, False Negatives arose when sarcasm was subtle, highly contextual, or lacked overt contradictory cues that the few-shot prompt might have primed the models to expect. For instance, models took positive statements with emojis at face value (e.g., Started watching house of cards...good choice) or interpreted direct insults as literal rather than sarcastically intended, as seen with Gemma misclassifying @sonofsama1 @Santandave1 you're trash.

This reliance on literal interpretation when clear ironic markers are absent, combined with a sensitivity to potentially ambiguous emotional cues, contributes significantly to the performance characteristics observed, where identifying nuanced authorial intent remains a hurdle even for the best-performing local models like Qwen. The nature of the iSarcasm dataset, with its reliance on author self-annotation, means that some sarcastic intent might be opaque without external context, a challenge that few-shot prompting alone may not fully overcome.

Limitations: This study's findings are subject to several limitations. The evaluation was conducted using only a specific set of local LLM models and their particular versions available at the time of testing; performance may differ with newer or alternative models that may be released. A single few-shot prompting strategy was employed, and results could vary with different models.

The findings are specific to the iSarcasm dataset, which focuses on author-intended sarcasm in English tweets, and may not generalize to other datasets, languages, or sarcasm expressed in different domains or forms, although LLMs tend to perform better than machine learning and deep learning models in generalization scenarios. Highlight that iSarcasm may be the most difficult published dataset focusing on sarcasm to be tested.

Furthermore, the study primarily focused on binary sarcasm classification (sarcastic vs. non-sarcastic) and did not delve into the finer-grained sarcasm types within iSarcasm. The inherent imbalance of the dataset (fewer sarcastic instances) also presents a challenge that influences metric interpretation, particularly precision and recall.

Implications for Practitioners: For tasks involving author-intended sarcasm detection like that in iSarcasm, local LLMs such as Qwen (qwen3:30B) can establish a useful baseline (F1-sarcastic: 0.507) with few-shot prompting, outperforming some older benchmarks. A key consideration is the typical trade-off observed: high recall (e.g., Qwen's 0.880) at the cost of modest precision (Qwen's 0.356), meaning models identify most sarcastic instances but also produce many false positives.

Practitioners should:

- **Align model choice with error tolerance:** Prioritize high recall if missing sarcasm is critical; seek precision improvements if false alarms are problematic. Qwen (qwen3:30B) offered the best balance in our study.
- **Refine prompts and few-shot examples:** The initial prompt is a baseline; iterative prompt engineering and optimizing few-shot examples can enhance performance.
- **Consider fine-tuning for demanding applications:** To significantly improve accuracy on challenging datasets like iSarcasm, fine-tuning local LLMs on relevant data is likely necessary.
- **Validate on target data:** Always test and validate rigorously on the specific application data, as iSarcasm performance may not generalize directly.

While local LLMs provide accessibility and privacy, achieving high-fidelity sarcasm detection for nuanced, author-intended sarcasm will likely require careful model selection, advanced prompting, or fine-tuning.

6   Conclusion and Future Work

This paper evaluated local LLMs (Qwen, Mistral, Phi, and Gemma variants) for sarcasm detection using the iSarcasm dataset and a defined few-shot prompting strategy. Our findings indicate that these LLMs exhibit varied but promising capabilities for detecting author-intended sarcasm, a notoriously challenging task. Models like Qwen (qwen3:30B), which achieved an F1-sarcastic score of 0.507, demonstrated a notable grasp of sarcasm, surpassing several earlier benchmarks and other tested local LLMs. However, the task remains difficult, as evidenced by modest precision scores across models, highlighting a tendency towards false positives despite high recall. While the performance of these locally deployed models with straightforward prompting may not yet match that of larger, extensively fine-tuned, or cloud-based systems, their inherent benefits in terms of accessibility, cost-effectiveness, and data privacy are significant for many applications.

Future work in this area could productively explore:

- Evaluating a broader range of local LLMs and their evolving versions on the iSarcasm dataset to track progress in the field.
- Systematically analyzing the impact of prompt engineering, including variations in prompt structure, the number and quality of few-shot examples, and techniques like chain-of-thought reasoning, on sarcasm detection performance.
- Conducting fine-tuning experiments with these local LLMs on the iSarcasm dataset (or similar author-intended sarcasm datasets) and comparing these results against the few-shot prompting baseline established in this study.
- Performing a deeper qualitative and quantitative error analysis, potentially correlating misclassifications with the specific sarcasm types delineated within the iSarcasm dataset (e.g., irony, satire, understatement) to understand model weaknesses better.

– Benchmarking the computational efficiency of these local models (e.g., inference speed, memory usage) against their sarcasm detection performance to provide a more holistic view for practical deployment.
– Investigating the models' understanding of context and common-sense reasoning, which are crucial for robust sarcasm detection, perhaps by designing targeted adversarial examples and testing other datasets.

As local LLMs continue to evolve and become more powerful, their contribution to nuanced NLP tasks like the detection of author-intended sarcasm is expected to grow, offering practical solutions for a wider range of users and scenarios.

Acknowledgments. This work has been supported through the FCT project 2024.07 420.IACDC, https://doi.org/10.54499/2024.07420.IACDC.

Disclosure of Interests. The authors have no competing interests to declare that are relevant to the content of this article.

References

1. Abaskohi, A., Rasouli, A., Zeraati, T., Bahrak, B.: Utnlp at semeval-2022 task 6: a comparative analysis of sarcasm detection using generative-based and mutation-based data augmentation. arXiv preprint arXiv:2204.08198 (2022)
2. Abdin, M., et al.: Phi-4 technical report. arXiv preprint arXiv:2412.08905 (2024)
3. Atmojo, W.T., Rustad, S., Syukur, A., Andono, P.N.: A bibliometric analysis of sarcasm detection. In: 2023 International Seminar on Application for Technology of Information and Communication (iSemantic), pp. 417–422. IEEE (2023)
4. Baccianella, S., Esuli, A., Sebastiani, F.: SentiWordNet 3.0: an enhanced lexical resource for sentiment analysis and opinion mining. In: Proceedings of the Seventh International Conference on Language Resources and Evaluation (LREC 2010), pp. 2200–2204. European Language Resources Association (ELRA), Valletta, Malta (2010)
5. Băroiu, A.C.: Trăusan-Matu,: automatic sarcasm detection: systematic literature review. Information **13**(8), 399 (2022)
6. Bommasani, R., et al.: On the opportunities and risks of foundation models. arXiv preprint arXiv:2108.07258 (2021)
7. Brown, T., et al.: Language models are few-shot learners. Adv. Neural. Inf. Process. Syst. **33**, 1877–1901 (2020)
8. Cortes, C., Vapnik, V.: Support-vector networks. Mach. Learn. **20**(3), 273–297 (1995)
9. Devlin, J., Chang, M.W., Lee, K., Toutanova, K.: Bert: pre-training of deep bidirectional transformers for language understanding. arXiv preprint arXiv:1810.04805 (2018)
10. Hochreiter, S., Schmidhuber, J.: Long short-term memory. Neural Comput. **9**(8), 1735–1780 (1997)
11. Hung, C., Chen, S.J.: Word sense disambiguation based sentiment lexicons for sentiment classification. Knowl.-Based Syst. **110**, 224–232 (2016)

12. Hutto, C., Gilbert, E.: Vader: a parsimonious rule-based model for sentiment analysis of social media text. In: Proceedings of the Eighth International AAAI Conference on Weblogs and Social Media (ICWSM), vol. 8, pp. 216–225 (2014)
13. Jiang, A.Q., et al.: Mistral 7b. arXiv preprint arXiv:2310.06825 (2023)
14. McCallum, A., Nigam, K.: A comparison of event models for Naive Bayes text classification. In: AAAI-98 Workshop on Learning for Text Categorization, pp. 41–48. Madison, Wisconsin (1998)
15. Oprea, S., Magdy, W.: iSarcasm: a dataset of intended sarcasm. In: Proceedings of the 58th Annual Meeting of the Association for Computational Linguistics (ACL), pp. 4017–4023. Association for Computational Linguistics, Online (2020). https://www.aclweb.org/anthology/2020.acl-main.371
16. Pang, B., Lee, L.: Opinion mining and sentiment analysis. Found. Trends® Inf. Retrieval 2(1–2), 1–135 (2008)
17. Potamias, R.A., Siolas, G., Stafylopatis, A.: Transformer-based conditional layers for sarcasm detection. In: Proceedings of the 28th International Conference on Computational Linguistics (COLING), pp. 420–430. International Committee on Computational Linguistics, Barcelona (Online) (2020)
18. Sebastiani, F.: Machine learning in automated text categorization. ACM Comput. Surv. (CSUR) 34(1), 1–47 (2002)
19. Tang, D., Qin, B., Liu, T.: Document modeling with gated recurrent neural network for sentiment classification. In: Proceedings of the 2015 Conference on Empirical Methods in Natural Language Processing (EMNLP), pp. 1422–1432. Association for Computational Linguistics, Lisbon (2015)
20. Team, G., et al.: Gemma 3 technical report. arXiv preprint arXiv:2503.19786 (2025)
21. Touvron, H., et al.: Llama 2: open foundation and fine-tuned chat models. arXiv preprint arXiv:2307.09288 (2023)
22. Wolf, T., et al.: Transformers: state-of-the-art natural language processing. In: Proceedings of the 2020 Conference on Empirical Methods in Natural Language Processing: System Demonstrations, pp. 38–45. Association for Computational Linguistics (2020)
23. Yang, A., et al.: Qwen3 technical report. arXiv preprint arXiv:2505.09388 (2025)
24. Zhang, Y., Zou, C., Lian, Z., Tiwari, P., Qin, J.: Towards evaluating large language models on sarcasm understanding. arXiv e-prints pp. arXiv–2408 (2024)

An Explainable Deep Learning Architecture for the Detection of Gastrointestinal Lesions in Colonoscopy Images

Hugo Pereira[1] (ID), Diogo Martinho[1,2](✉) (ID), and Goreti Marreiros[1,2] (ID)

[1] GECAD – Research Group on Intelligent Engineering and Computing for Advanced Innovation and Development, ISEP, Polytechnic of Porto, Rua DR. António Bernardino de Almeida, 4249-015 Porto, Portugal
{hsdrp,dep,mgt}@isep.ipp.pt
[2] LASI, School of Engineering, University of Minho, Campus Azurém, 4800-058 Guimarães, Portugal

Abstract. Gastrointestinal diseases have a growing impact on public health, often requiring timely and accurate diagnosis to prevent complications and improve patient outcomes. In this context, artificial intelligence (AI) has emerged as a promising tool to support clinicians in image-based diagnosis. This study presents the design and evaluation of an explainable deep learning system for the automatic detection and classification of gastrointestinal anomalies in colonoscopy images. Using transfer learning and convolutional neural networks, the proposed architecture incorporates a fine-tuned ResNet18 model alongside explainable AI (XAI) methods to ensure both high diagnostic performance and model transparency. The system was trained and validated using the Kvasir dataset, a clinically annotated collection of endoscopic images covering multiple gastrointestinal conditions. Experimental results show that the use of transfer learning significantly improved classification outcomes, with F1-scores exceeding 0.90 for several key categories. A web-based interface was also developed to facilitate clinical adoption, providing visual explanation tools such as heatmaps. These allow healthcare professionals to understand the basis of each prediction, promoting trust and supporting informed decision-making. Overall, the system contributes to more accurate, interpretable, and efficient diagnostic processes in the field of gastrointestinal healthcare.

Keywords: Gastrointestinal Diagnosis · Colonoscopy · Deep Learning · Transfer Learning · Explainable AI · Medical Image Classification · Clinical Decision Support

1 Introduction

Gastrointestinal diseases have become increasingly prevalent worldwide, largely due to modern lifestyle factors such as poor diet, physical inactivity, and tobacco use. These conditions not only increase the risk of developing colorectal cancer and inflammatory bowel disease (IBD) [1] but also significantly affect patients' quality of life, often

J. Valente de Oliveira et al. (Eds.): EPIA 2025, LNAI 16122, pp. 395–406, 2026.
https://doi.org/10.1007/978-3-032-05179-0_30

leading to chronic pain, nutritional limitations, psychological distress, and long-term dependency on medical care. The adoption of Western dietary patterns, characterized by high consumption of red and processed meats and low intake of fiber, further exacerbates this risk [2].

Colonoscopy remains the gold standard for the detection and diagnosis of colorectal neoplasia, offering high sensitivity for identifying polyps and early-stage lesions. However, its effectiveness is significantly influenced by the endoscopist's expertise, leading to variability in detection rates and potential omission of lesions, particularly those that are small or have atypical appearances [3]. Additionally, the procedure requires extensive bowel preparation and carries risks such as bleeding, perforation, and patient discomfort [4]. Explainable AI enables intelligent healthcare environments by supporting adaptive, data-driven decision-making that improves patient care.

At the same time, the growing presence of artificial intelligence (AI) in healthcare, particularly through deep learning and emerging generative models, is reshaping diagnostic practices. These technologies are increasingly used to support clinical decision-making, offering enhanced accuracy, automation, and interpretability. In this context, computer vision and deep learning techniques have emerged as promising tools to support medical diagnostics. Convolutional neural networks (CNNs) have demonstrated strong performance in medical image analysis, with successful applications in the real-time detection of polyps during colonoscopy procedures [5, 6]. These technologies can help standardize interpretation and increase diagnostic accuracy, assisting healthcare professionals in identifying suspicious lesions and deciding when biopsies are necessary [7].

Among the most relevant approaches, image segmentation models play a crucial role by enabling the precise localization and delineation of anatomical structures. The development of architectures such as U-Net has significantly advanced this field, allowing for the accurate highlighting of relevant regions in endoscopic images and facilitating the differentiation between benign and malignant tissue [8]. Extensions and variants of U-Net, including attention-based U-Nets and residual U-Nets, further refine performance by focusing on context-aware features and better handling of complex textures.

In parallel, classification models, often based on architectures like ResNet and Inception, are widely adopted for lesion characterization [9]. These models benefit from transfer learning strategies, which leverage pre-trained networks on large-scale datasets to improve performance in medical contexts where annotated data are scarce. Combining segmentation and classification approaches into unified or cascaded frameworks enhances the diagnostic pipeline, for instance, using segmentation outputs to guide or refine classification decisions.

Together, these integrated approaches, combining segmentation, classification, and transfer learning, contribute to more robust, interpretable, and generalizable AI-based diagnostic systems for gastrointestinal image analysis [10].

This paper proposes an AI-based architecture for the detection and tracking of gastrointestinal diseases from colonoscopy images. By combining CNNs with advanced segmentation models, the aim is to develop an intelligent system that complements medical analysis, reducing human error and improving screening efficiency. This approach may contribute to earlier and more accurate diagnoses, reduce unnecessary biopsies, and support more effective clinical decision-making, particularly in high-demand gastroen-terology settings. The paper is structured into four main sections: a review of the relevant literature, the presentation of the proposed architecture, initial experimental results, and final conclusions.

2   Literature Review

In recent years, artificial intelligence (AI) has demonstrated substantial potential in the field of medical imaging, particularly in gastrointestinal (GI) diagnostics. The increasing application of deep learning techniques has driven the development of automated systems for the detection, segmentation, and classification of lesions in colonoscopy images, contributing to earlier and more consistent diagnoses.

2.1   AI Techniques and Model Architectures

The most commonly used models include convolutional neural networks (CNNs), trans-formers, and hybrid architectures, applied to tasks such as polyp detection, lesion segmentation, and cancer classification [11, 12]. Innovative approaches involve CNN-transformer combinations for improved feature extraction, as well as weakly-supervised learning methods that enable segmentation with limited annotated data [13]. To address challenges related to data scarcity and variability, techniques such as active learning (e.g., INP and CCQ) [14], domain adaptation [15], and meta-learning have also been explored.

Polyp detection remains a major focus, with models like YOLOv5 [16], self-learning methods [17], and transformer-based approaches [18] achieving promising results. In segmentation tasks, advanced architectures such as DeepLabv3 + (with ResNet-101), GI-Net, and UNet ++ have demonstrated strong performance [11, 19, 20]. In par-allel, privacy-aware frameworks such as TEFAL and LEFAL [14], along with recent transformer-CNN hybrids like MixFormNet, Swin Transformer, and SAM [16, 21], aim to balance accuracy with clinical adaptability.

2.2   Datasets and Performance Evaluation

High-quality datasets are fundamental for training and validating AI models in GI diagnostics. Publicly available datasets such as Kvasir-SEG, CVC-ClinicDB, and the Medical Segmentation Decathlon are widely used [19], along with histopathological datasets like NCT-CRC-HE-100K and LC25000 [15]. In some cases, researchers rely on institution-specific or manually annotated datasets to address domain-specific needs [14].

Regarding performance, many models report Dice Similarity Coefficients (DSC) and mean Intersection over Union (mIoU) values exceeding 90% on benchmark datasets [22]. CNN-based classifiers often outperform earlier architectures like VGG16 and AlexNet [20], while transfer learning and data augmentation remain key strategies for improving model generalization and robustness [14, 15].

Despite these advances, challenges remain in ensuring consistent performance across diverse clinical settings. Several studies report performance degradation when AI models are applied to data from different imaging devices, patient populations, or clinical environments not represented in the training set. Moreover, models often struggle to maintain accuracy in detecting subtle or atypical lesions, and their performance can be compromised by image artifacts such as poor lighting, motion blur, or inadequate bowel preparation. These limitations highlight the need for more robust generalization strategies and domain adaptation techniques to improve model reliability in real-world scenarios. Additionally, the successful integration of AI tools into clinical workflows depends on the active involvement of medical professionals and the resolution of concerns related to trust, interpretability, and usability. The literature reveals a clear shift toward clinically supportive AI systems that complement medical expertise, particularly in colorectal cancer screening contexts [20, 21].

3 Proposed Architecture

The architecture developed in this project is designed to support the detection and classification of gastrointestinal anomalies in endoscopic images through a robust, explainable, and clinically adaptable artificial intelligence system. The central objective is to increase diagnostic precision in the identification of lesions such as colorectal polyps, while reducing the variability associated with human interpretation and optimizing the time required for analysis and decision-making.

The system follows a modular pipeline composed of five key components:

1. **Image Acquisition and Preprocessing:** Endoscopic images are standardized through resizing, normalization, and segmentation. Data augmentation (e.g., rotation, flipping, Gaussian noise) increases variability and model robustness.
2. **Model Training:** The model is trained in Python using TensorFlow and PyTorch, with labeled data from the Kvasir dataset. Transfer learning accelerates convergence and enhances generalization.
3. **Hybrid CNN Model:** The core architecture, HybridResEffDenseCNN, combines ResNet50 (feature depth), EfficientNet-B0 (efficiency), and DenseNet121 (feature reuse), improving detection of subtle GI patterns.
4. **Explainability Module:** Grad-CAM, Integrated Gradients, and Occlusion Analysis generate visual explanations, helping clinicians interpret model predictions with greater confidence.
5. **Web-Based Application:** A FastAPI and Tailwind CSS web interface delivers real-time predictions, confidence scores, and visual heatmaps, supporting clinical decision-making in an accessible format.

A visual representation of this workflow is shown in Fig. 1, which illustrates the interaction between components from image acquisition to explainability and user feedback. This design promotes clinical usability, system traceability, and integration into diagnostic routines. Modular architecture enables seamless integration, creating intelligent environments where data flows between imaging, AI, and clinical decision-making.

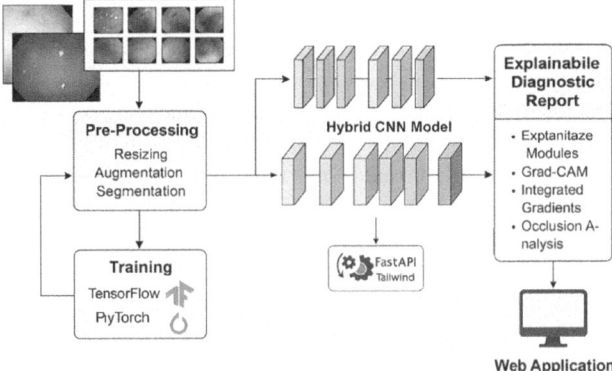

Fig. 1. Overview of the proposed AI-based diagnostic system

3.1 Core Model and Implementation

At the core of the system lies a hybrid convolutional neural network (CNN) model, termed HybridResEffDenseCNN, which combines three pre-trained architectures: ResNet50, EfficientNet-B0, and DenseNet121. Each model contributes unique strengths: ResNet50 captures deep hierarchical features by learning at multiple levels of abstraction, from edges to complex semantic patterns, enabling the system to distinguish subtle anomalies in gastrointestinal images—a capability shown to be essential in medical image analysis [23]. EfficientNet-B0 ensures computational efficiency by scaling model dimensions in a balanced way, while DenseNet121 enhances feature propagation and reuse through dense connectivity, resulting in improved performance and generalization.

To overcome limitations posed by small medical datasets, the model employs transfer learning, where convolutional layers are initialized with weights pre-trained on large-scale datasets. Only the final classifier layers are retrained for the specific classification task. This strategy significantly improves training efficiency and generalization to new clinical samples [24].

The system was developed using Python, with TensorFlow, PyTorch, and OpenCV frameworks. Implementation was carried out in Visual Studio Code and executed on Google Colab to take advantage of GPU acceleration for model training and inference.

The model was trained on the Kvasir dataset [25], a publicly available and clinically validated collection of annotated endoscopic images developed by the Cancer Registry of Norway in collaboration with Vestre Viken Health Trust. The Kvasir dataset used in this study contains approximately 8,000 labeled endoscopic images spanning eight distinct classes. These include anatomical landmarks, pathological conditions such as polyps, esophagitis, and ulcerative colitis, as well as images related to polyp removal procedures. All images were subjected to a preprocessing pipeline that included resizing to 224 × 224 pixels, normalization based on ImageNet standards, and data augmentation techniques such as rotation, horizontal flipping, and the application of Gaussian noise to increase data diversity and enhance model robustness. Additionally, segmentation of regions of interest was performed to reduce the influence of irrelevant content and improve model focus.

To ensure trust and usability in clinical environments, the architecture incorporates explainable AI (XAI) components. Grad-CAM, Integrated Gradients, occlusion maps, and uncertainty visualization modules are embedded into the system to generate visual explanations for each classification. These techniques allow physicians to identify the specific image regions that influenced the model's decision, reinforcing transparency and interpretability, key factors for real-world adoption [26]. Furthermore, fairness and bias detection tools are included to monitor potential disparities in model performance across demographic groups. Future development will include a detailed subgroup analysis (e.g., age, gender, population origin) to assess and mitigate any systematic bias, ensuring equitable performance in diverse clinical contexts.

Regarding deployment, the system was implemented as a secure, scalable web application. The backend was developed using FastAPI, while the frontend leverages Tailwind CSS to provide a responsive and intuitive interface. Upon image upload, the system performs automatic analysis and displays a visual report, including predicted class labels, confidence scores, and interpretability heatmaps. All patient data is anonymized, encrypted, and handled in accordance with GDPR and medical data protection guidelines. Multi-factor authentication and role-based access controls are employed to guarantee secure use.

By integrating advanced deep learning models, explainability mechanisms, and privacy-by-design principles, this architecture offers a practical and clinically viable solution for enhancing the early detection and monitoring of gastrointestinal diseases.

4 Experimentation

The initial experimental phase aimed to validate the feasibility of developing a reliable deep learning-based system for classifying gastrointestinal anomalies in colonoscopy images. The system was designed not only to assist clinicians in early detection but also to ensure transparent and interpretable decision-making through the integration of Explainable Artificial Intelligence (XAI) and Transfer Learning techniques.

As a first step, an exploratory data analysis (EDA) of the Kvasir dataset was conducted. The dataset, comprising 4000 images equally distributed across eight classes, presented substantial variability in resolution and visual characteristics. To ensure consistency, all images were resized to 224 × 224 pixels. Data augmentation techniques such as image rotation, horizontal flipping, and brightness adjustment were employed to increase dataset diversity and reduce overfitting. Additional preprocessing included grayscale conversion, edge detection with intensity thresholds, and artifact removal, enhancing relevant image features and suppressing noise.

The dataset was divided into training (70%), validation (15%), and test (15%) sets, maintaining class balance across all partitions. A simple CNN model was initially trained without data augmentation or transfer learning to establish a baseline. The results, shown in Table 1, demonstrate the limitations of this approach.

Table 1. Evaluation Metrics for Baseline CNN

Class	Precision	Recall	F1-Score	Support
Dyed-lifted-polyps	47%	28%	35%	75
Dyed-resection-margins	43%	8%	13%	75
Esophagitis	0%	0%	0%	75
Normal-cecum	0%	0%	0%	75
Normal-pylorus	0%	0%	0%	75
Normal-z-line	0%	0%	0%	75
Polyps	0%	0%	0%	75
Ulcerative-colitis	14%	100%	24%	75

The ROC curve (Fig. 2) displays the classification performance across all diagnostic categories in the test set. Most classes achieve high AUC values, including normal-pylorus (AUC = 0.93) and esophagitis (AUC = 0.92), indicating strong discriminative power. In contrast, polyps (AUC = 0.68) and normal-cecum (AUC = 0.77) show relatively lower AUCs, suggesting potential overlap with other categories. Overall, the model demonstrates reliable classification ability, with most curves significantly above the random baseline (Table 2).

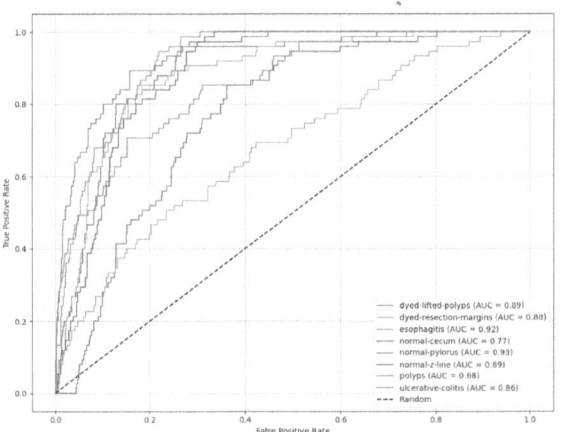

Fig. 2. Roc Curve per category

Table 2. Performance Metrics for Baseline CNN

Category	Precision	Recall	F1-Score	Support
Macro avg	13%	17%	17%	600
Weighted avg	13%	17%	9%	600
Total Accuracy	–	–	9%	600

The performance was unsatisfactory, with several classes showing near-zero scores. Notably, ulcerative-colitis showed high recall but low precision, while critical classes like polyps and normal-pylorus underperformed, indicating poor generalization.

To address this, a second experiment was conducted using transfer learning with a pre-trained ResNet18 model, fine-tuned on the Kvasir dataset. This approach involved replacing the classifier layer while retaining the pretrained convolutional layers. Compared to the initial model, which was trained from scratch, this method yielded significant improvements in both precision and recall across most classes, as detailed in Table 3. The fine-tuned model demonstrated better feature extraction and generalization, particularly in challenging classes, confirming the benefits of leveraging pretrained knowledge in medical image analysis.

Table 3. Evaluation Metrics for ResNet18 with Transfer Learning

Class	Precision	Recall	F1-Score	Support
Dyed-lifted-polyps	84%	81%	82%	75
Dyed-resection-margins	82%	93%	88%	75
Esophagitis	78%	76%	77%	75
Normal-cecum	99%	91%	94%	75
Normal-pylorus	99%	89%	94%	75
Normal-z-line	70%	95%	81%	75
Polyps	98%	67%	79%	75
Ulcerative-colitis	75%	80%	77%	75

This ROC curve (Fig. 3) illustrates the performance of a highly accurate model, achieving near-perfect classification for several diagnostic categories. Normal-cecum, normal-pylorus, and dyed-resection-margins all reached an AUC of 1.00, indicating flawless discrimination. Even the lowest AUC, observed for esophagitis (0.95), reflects excellent predictive performance. The curves align closely with the top-left corner, confirming strong class separation (Table 4).

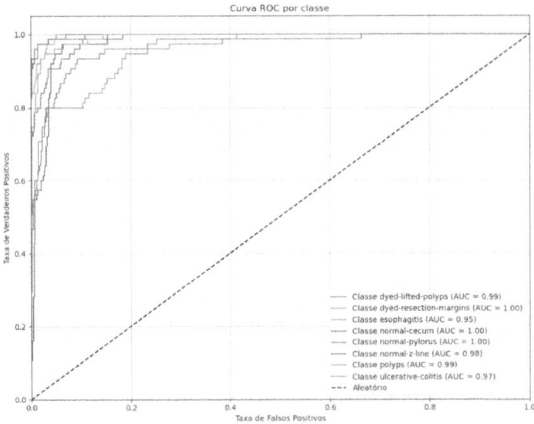

Fig. 3. Roc Curve per category

Table 4. Performance Metrics for ResNet18 with Transfer Learning

Category	Precision	Recall	F1-Score	Support
Macro avg	86%	84%	84%	600
Weighted avg	86%	84%	84%	600
Total Accuracy		–	84%	600

These results reflect a robust improvement across all metrics and classes, particularly for *normal-pylorus*, *ulcerative-colitis*, and *polyps*. The F1-score for *polyps* rose from 0.27 to 0.84, demonstrating the effectiveness of using pretrained models for medical image classification. Moreover, macro and weighted averages for precision, recall, and F1-score exceeded 85%, supporting the model's overall consistency and balance.

This experimentation confirms that transfer learning not only improves performance but also contributes to faster training and reduced computational cost. Since the model is initialized with pre-trained weights, it requires fewer epochs to converge compared to models trained from scratch, resulting in a more efficient training process. These outcomes support the feasibility of developing a reliable clinical decision support tool for gastrointestinal disease detection, setting a solid foundation for further refinements. Although the model achieved high average metrics, certain classes such as polyps and esophagitis still presented occasional misclassifications. These errors often involved visually ambiguous cases or poor image quality, highlighting areas for improvement in feature extraction or segmentation preprocessing. Compared to the baseline CNN trained from scratch, the ResNet18-based model achieved an average F1-score gain of +67 percentage points (from 17% to 84%), demonstrating a significant improvement in classification effectiveness across all classes.

Despite the promising results, it is important to note that the model was exclusively trained and validated using the Kvasir dataset. This reliance on a single data source may limit its generalizability to other clinical scenarios, devices, or patient populations. Additionally, the current study does not include a comparison with Vision Transformer architectures, which have shown state-of-the-art performance in recent medical imaging tasks. Future benchmarking against these models could offer further insights into architectural trade-offs.

5 Conclusion

This work proposed and evaluated a deep learning-based system for the automatic detection and classification of gastrointestinal anomalies in colonoscopy images, with a particular focus on transparency, efficiency, and clinical relevance. Combining convolutional neural networks, transfer learning, and explainable artificial intelligence (XAI), the system was designed to assist medical professionals in the early identification of relevant pathological patterns, while reducing diagnostic variability and supporting informed decision-making. One current limitation of this study is the exclusive use of static images. Colonoscopy procedures are inherently temporal, and dynamic features captured in video sequences are crucial for accurate lesion detection and clinical decision-making. Future work should address this by incorporating real-time video analysis capabilities.

Initial experimentation confirmed the limitations of traditional CNNs trained from scratch, which showed low performance across several classes. However, the application of transfer learning using the pre-trained ResNet18 architecture significantly improved classification metrics across all categories, achieving F1-scores above 0.90 for multiple classes, including *ulcerative-colitis* and *normal-pylorus*. The marked improvement in performance for critical categories such as *polyps* demonstrated the effectiveness of pretrained features for medical image tasks, particularly in datasets with limited size and high intra-class variability.

In addition to performance gains, the integration of XAI methods such as Grad-CAM and Integrated Gradients ensures that the model's predictions can be interpreted by clinicians, promoting greater confidence in its adoption. The system's design also prioritized scalability, security, and compliance with data protection regulations, ensuring its viability for integration into real-world clinical environments. Explainability and real-time processing underpin intelligent medical environments, adapting to evolving clinical needs.

The central objective is to increase diagnostic precision in the identification of lesions such as colorectal polyps, while reducing the variability associated with human interpretation and optimizing the time required for analysis and decision-making. Since the system is designed to support clinical workflows, future work will focus on evaluating its usability, acceptability, and perceived value among medical professionals and healthcare teams, a critical step for effective integration in real-world environments. To date, the system has not yet been tested with practicing clinicians, and real-world user testing will be essential to assess its practical impact and clinical utility. Further development will explore the integration of temporal information from colonoscopy video sequences, the validation of the system on external clinical datasets from different institutions to ensure robustness, the application of ensemble learning strategies combining CNNs with transformer-based models, and the adoption of multimodal approaches that incorporate both image data and structured clinical metadata. The explainable AI (XAI) components will be refined iteratively based on expert feedback, ensuring that visual explanations are both accurate and clinically meaningful. Hybrid deep learning models are key to intelligent environments connecting automated analysis with human-centered clinical workflows.

The goal is to deliver a robust, interpretable, and deployable solution that enhances diagnostic accuracy in gastrointestinal healthcare and contributes to earlier and more efficient disease detection.

Acknowledgments. This research was supported by the PROFIT project - Procedure Optimization and Data-driven Operational Efficiency in Healthcare Environments (ITEA 22021), funded by the European Regional Development Fund (ERDF) through the COMPETE 2030 Programme, project number COMPETE30-FEDER-00376900, and by national funds from the Portuguese Foundation for Science and Technology (FCT), under the R&D Units Project Scope UIDB/00760/2020 and UIDP/00760/2020. More information is available at: https://itea4.org/pro ject/profit.html.

Disclosure of Interests.   The authors declare no competing interests relevant to the content of this article.

References

1. Wu, T., Cheng, H., Zhuang, J., Liu, X., Ouyang, Z., Qian, R.: Risk factors for inflammatory bowel disease: an umbrella review. Front. Cell. Infect. Microbiol. **14** (2025). https://doi.org/10.3389/fcimb.2024.1410506
2. Wu, Y., Li, Y., Giovannucci, E.: Potential impact of time trend of lifestyle risk factors on burden of major gastrointestinal cancers in China. Gastroenterology **161**(6), 1830–1841 (2021). https://doi.org/10.1053/j.gastro.2021.08.006
3. Rex, D.K., et al.: Quality indicators for colonoscopy. Gastrointest. Endosc. **100**(3), 352–381(2024). https://doi.org/10.1016/j.gie.2024.04.2905
4. Lv, X.-H., Lu, Q., Wang, Z.-J., Wang, Z., Yang, J.-L.: Colonoscopy-related adverse events in the 21st century: an updated systematic review and meta-analysis. Off. J. Am. Coll. Gastroenterol. ACG (2022). https://doi.org/10.14309/ajg.0000000000003429
5. Clinical evaluation of a real-time artificial intelligence-based polyp detection system: a US multi-center pilot study. Sci. Rep. https://www.nature.com/articles/s41598-022-10597-y. Acedido: 13 de maio de 2025
6. CAD-AIDED COLONOSCOPY AND ADVANCED ADENOMas – NCI. https://www.can cer.gov/news-events/cancer-currents-blog/2023/colonoscopy-cad-artificial-intelligence Acedido: 13 de maio de 2025
7. Samarasena, J., Yang, D., Berzin, T.M.: AGA clinical practice update on the role of artificial intelligence in colon polyp diagnosis and management: commentary. Gastroenterol. **165**(6), 1568–1573 (2023). https://doi.org/10.1053/j.gastro.2023.07.010
8. Isensee, F., Jaeger, P.F., Kohl, S.A.A., Petersen, J., Maier-Hein, K.H.: nnU-Net: a self-configuring method for deep learning-based biomedical image segmentation. Nat. Methods **18**(2), 203–211 (2021). https://doi.org/10.1038/s41592-020-01008-z
9. Urban, G., et al.: Deep learning localizes and identifies polyps in real time with 96% accuracy in screening colonoscopy. Gastroenterol. **155**(4), 1069–1078 (2018). https://doi.org/10.1053/j.gastro.2018.06.037

10. Khalili Fakhrabadi, A., Shahbazzadeh, M.J., Jalali, N., Eslami, M.: A hybrid inception-dilated-ResNet architecture for deep learning-based prediction of COVID-19 severity. Sci. Rep. **15**(1), 6490 (2025). https://doi.org/10.1038/s41598-025-91322-3

11. Harb, S., et al.: Accurate colon segmentation using 2D convolutional neural networks with 3D contextual information. In: 2024 IEEE International Conference on Image Processing (ICIP), pp. 3212–3218 (2024). https://doi.org/10.1109/ICIP51287.2024.10647313

12. Vidyullatha, P., Thanh Hung, B., Chakrabarti, P.: An adaptive deep convolution neural network for high pixel image segmentation and classification. In: 2023 International Conference on Innovative Data Communication Technologies and Application (ICIDCA), pp. 247–253. IEEE, Uttarakhand, India (2023). https://doi.org/10.1109/ICIDCA56705.2023.10100246

13. Belharbi, S., Rony, J., Dolz, J., Ayed, I.B., Mccaffrey, L., Granger, E.: Deep interpretable classification and weakly-supervised segmentation of histology images via max-min uncertainty. IEEE Trans. Med. Imaging **41**(3), 702–714 (2022). https://doi.org/10.1109/TMI.2021.3123461

14. Hu, W., et al.: Learning from incorrectness: active learning with negative pre-training and curriculum querying for histological tissue classification. IEEE Trans. Med. Imaging **43**(2), 625–637 (2024). https://doi.org/10.1109/TMI.2023.3313509

15. Oliveira, H., Gama, P.H.T., Bloch, I., Jr, R.M.C.: Meta-learners for few-shot weakly-supervised medical image segmentation. 11 de maio de 2023. arXiv: arXiv:2305.06912

16. Chen, C., Dou, Q., Chen, H., Qin, J., Heng, P.-A.: Synergistic image and feature adaptation: towards cross-modality domain adaptation for medical image segmentation. 18 de junho de 2019. arXiv: arXiv:1901.08211

17. TP, R., Kumar, J., Balasundaram, S.R.: DeepCPD: deep learning with vision transformer for colorectal polyp detection. Multimed. Tools Appl. **83**, 1–24 (2024). https://doi.org/10.1007/s11042-024-18607-z

18. Zhang, R., et al.: AG-CRC: anatomy-guided colorectal cancer segmentation in CT with Imperfect Anatomical Knowledge. 1 de dezembro de 2023. arXiv: arXiv:2310.04677

19. Singh, D., Somani, A. Horsch, A., Prasad, D.K.: Counterfactual explainable gastrointestinal and colonoscopy image segmentation. In: 2022 IEEE 19th International Symposium on Biomedical Imaging (ISBI), pp. 1–5 (2022). https://doi.org/10.1109/ISBI52829.2022.9761664

20. Chen, C., Dou, Q., Chen, H., Qin, J., Heng, P.A.: Unsupervised bidirectional cross-modality adaptation via deeply synergistic image and feature alignment for medical image segmentation. 6 de fevereiro de 2020. arXiv: arXiv:2002.02255

21. Yan, W., et al.: The domain shift problem of medical image segmentation and vendor-adaptation by Unet-GAN. 30 de outubro de 2019. arXiv: arXiv:1910.13681

22. Wang, Y., Deng, Z.: A deep learning method for colon polyp segmentation with better universality. In: 2023 IEEE International Conference on Medical Artificial Intelligence (MedAI), pp. 355–365. IEEE, Beijing, China (2023). https://doi.org/10.1109/MedAI59581.2023.00054

23. Litjens, G., et al.: A survey on deep learning in medical image analysis. Med. Image Anal. **42**, 60–88 (2017). https://doi.org/10.1016/j.media.2017.07.005

24. Raghu, M., Unterthiner, T., Kornblith, S., Zhang, C., Dosovitskiy, A.: Do vision transformers see like convolutional neural networks? 3 de março de 2022. arXiv: arXiv:2108.08810

25. Pogorelov, K., et al.: KVASIR: a multi-class image dataset for computer aided gastrointestinal disease detection. In: Proceedings of the 8th ACM on Multimedia Systems Conference, pp. 164–169. ACM, Taipei Taiwan (2017). https://doi.org/10.1145/3083187.3083212

26. Suara, S., Jha, A., Sinha, P., Sekh, A.A.: Is Grad-CAM explainable in medical images? vol. 2009, pp. 124–135 (2024). https://doi.org/10.1007/978-3-031-58181-6_11

Challenges of AI in Healthcare Projects

Liepa Bikulciene[1,2](✉) ⓘ and Egle Butkeviciute[1] ⓘ

[1] Kaunas University of Technology, K. Donelaičio St. 73, 44249 Kaunas, Lithuania
{liepa.bikulciene,egle.butkeviciute}@ktu.lt
[2] Vilnius University Kaunas Faculty, Muitinės St. 8, 44280 Kaunas, Lithuania

Abstract. Artificial Intelligence (AI) is increasingly applied in healthcare, but projects often encounter formidable technical and practical challenges. This article examines these challenges through the lens of three international scientific projects – CareWare, Inno4health and REMO – which implemented or will implement AI for wearable systems, health monitoring and rehabilitation. Key technical obstacles are identified in AI modelling as data quality, sensor integration, interoperability, and system validation. AI models in healthcare must contend with limited and heterogeneous datasets, high variability in physiological signals, and the need for interpretability and personalization. Data quality issues – such as sensor noise, missing data, and inconsistent data collection – can undermine model reliability. Integrating multiple sensors and ensuring interoperability between devices and health information systems remain difficult due to a lack of common standards. Validation of AI-driven systems is also challenging, requiring rigorous clinical evaluation and compliance with strict regulations to ensure safety and effectiveness. Specific technical barriers observed in project development (e.g., noisy wearable device signals, variability in vital signs, limitations of cognitive feedback systems and real-time analytics for remote care) are highlighted with examples from the projects. The article concludes recommendations for future development and research, emphasizing improvements in data quality standards, better sensor and system interoperability, robust validation frameworks in healthcare.

Keywords: AI in data analysis · Bio-signal analysis · Physical and mental health evaluation

1 Introduction

AI technologies hold great promises to improve healthcare delivery and outcomes, from predictive diagnostics to personalized treatment and remote patient monitoring [1]. However, the implementation of AI in real-world healthcare projects has proven to be complex, with many initiatives facing significant technical and organizational hurdles. Effective deployment of AI in healthcare relies on numerous factors – high-quality and available data, interpretability of models, ethical and bias considerations, appropriate model complexity, scalability, integration with existing systems, user acceptance, and regulatory compliance [2]. These factors are intertwined, and deficiencies in any of them can impede AI adoption. Indeed, experience has shown an "inconvenient truth" that

J. Valente de Oliveira et al. (Eds.): EPIA 2025, LNAI 16122, pp. 407–419, 2026.
https://doi.org/10.1007/978-3-032-05179-0_31

many AI solutions struggle to translate from controlled research settings into practical clinical use [3].

This article discusses the challenges of AI in healthcare projects, drawing on experiences from three applied research projects: CareWare, Inno4Health and REMO. The CareWare project (2014–2017) aimed to create a wearable device for personal health and wellness monitoring, drawing on innovations in body area networks, wearable sensors, electronic textiles, and physiological signal analysis. The Inno4Health project (2019–2022) developed an individualized continuous health monitoring system for athletes, integrating psychophysiological sensors and cognitive training tools to optimize athletic training. The REMO project (started 2025) focuses on a remote monitoring system for spinal disorder rehabilitation, utilizing wearable sensors (such as electromyography (EMG) and heart rate monitors) to provide biofeedback and ensure patients perform exercises correctly in clinics and at home. These projects, including domains of wearable health technology, sports medicine and tele-rehabilitation, encountered many of the common technical challenges that beset AI in healthcare.

In the following sections, key technical challenges are examined in detail: challenges in developing and deploying AI models for healthcare; issues of data quality and variability (especially from wearable and sensor data); and the problems of validating AI systems and ensuring they meet clinical and regulatory standards. Within each area, specific examples are highlighted – such as the impact of signal noise in wearable devices, variability in physiological data streams, limitations observed in cognitive feedback systems, and the need for real-time analytics in remote care.

2   AI Modeling Challenges in Healthcare

Developing AI models for healthcare applications presents unique difficulties compared to other domains. Medical data are typically complex, high-dimensional, and often limited in quantity or diversity for a given task. Models must handle a variety of data types (e.g. sensor time-series, images, clinical text) and patient-specific heterogeneity [4]. One fundamental challenge is obtaining sufficient high-quality data to train reliable models. Unlike domains such as online services, healthcare data are fragmented among institutions and strict privacy rules limit data sharing, resulting in relatively small or specific data sets for model training. Moreover, the data that is available may not fully represent the patient population or conditions of interest, leading to models that perform well in research settings but generalize poorly in real-world clinical environments. Ensuring that AI models are trained on representatives, bias-free datasets is critical. Otherwise, algorithmic bias can emerge, and the model systematically underperforms for certain demographic or clinical subgroups, posing safety risks. Identifying and mitigating such bias is an ongoing concern in medical AI development [5].

Another modeling challenge is the variability and complexity of physiological data. Human biology is dynamic and patient conditions vary widely; thus, AI models must cope with significant intra- and inter-patient variability [6]. Creating models that are both general enough to scale and flexible enough to personalize remains a difficult balance. Personalization of AI models is often needed – algorithms may require calibration or adaptation for everyone to account for baseline differences in signals like heart rate or

EMG. This need for personalization increases development complexity, as models might have to incorporate patient-specific parameters or employ online learning.

Additionally, explainability and interpretability are important modeling considerations in healthcare. Clinicians and patients are more likely to trust and adopt an AI system if its reasoning can be understood or validated. Many powerful AI techniques (e.g. deep learning neural networks) operate as "black boxes," making it hard to explain their predictions [7]. Lack of interpretability can be a barrier to clinical acceptance (a part of the broader user adaptation challenge). Researchers are exploring interpretable AI or hybrid models (combining data-driven and knowledge-based approaches) to address this but achieving high accuracy while maintaining transparency is challenging. Indeed, effective AI in healthcare demands not only high performance, but also reliability and safety guarantees.

2.1 Data Quality and Variability Issues

Ensuring high-quality data is often problematic in practice. Healthcare datasets frequently contain noise, errors, or inconsistencies that can degrade model performance. This is especially true for data collected from wearable sensors and IoT devices [8], which play a central role in modern health monitoring projects. Wearable sensor data are inherently noisy because they are recorded during real-life activities and outside controlled environments. Wearable sensor noise generally falls into two categories: motion-induced noise (caused by movement, e.g. accelerometer disturbances or electrode shifts on the skin) and sensor-intrinsic noise (stemming from the sensor hardware, such as thermal noise in electronic components). Motion-induced artifacts are common in devices monitoring body movement or respiration, whereas intrinsic noise might result from temperature effects in resistive sensors or drift in capacitive sensors. A significant engineering effort is needed to filter or compensate for such noise (using techniques like signal filtering, calibration, or sensor fusion) to extract reliable features for AI analysis.

Beyond noise, variability in data collection practices and sensor types poses a major quality challenge. The same health metric can be measured by different devices in different ways, yielding incompatible data.

Missing data and contextual data gaps further undermine quality. In real deployments, it is common to encounter periods where sensors were not worn (non-wear time) or data were not recorded due to technical issues (battery failure, loss of connectivity). These gaps mean AI systems must handle incomplete time series. Moreover, contextual information about how data were collected is often lacking [9]. Projects have learned that incorporating context (via patient diaries, activity logs, or intelligent inference of activity from sensor data) is important for maintaining data fidelity.

Addressing data quality and variability is a multifaceted challenge. Standard signal processing methods (filtering, smoothing) are routinely applied to reduce noise. More sophisticated approaches include sensor fusion (combining multiple sensors to cross-verify data) and machine learning methods that learn to distinguish signal from noise. Calibration procedures are used to align different sensors. For instance, a new wearable might be calibrated against a gold-standard hospital device for a short period [10].

2.2 Sensor Integration and Interoperability

Healthcare AI projects often involve multiple sensors and devices that must work simultaneously, producing an integrated view of the patient's state. Achieving seamless sensor integration and system interoperability is a major technical hurdle. Integration refers to bringing together data from disparate sensors (wearables, ambient monitors, medical devices) into a cohesive platform, while interoperability extends to the ability of different systems and software to exchange and use information effectively [11]. In practice, many wearable or medical devices operate in separately, each with proprietary data formats, communication protocols, and interfaces. This lack of compatibility complicates efforts like the CareWare project's goal of an integrated wearable health solution.

Compatibility is not just a technical issue of data formats; it also involves communication protocols and system architectures. Wearable sensors commonly use wireless protocols (Bluetooth Low Energy, Wi-Fi, etc.) to transmit data. Ensuring reliable connectivity for multiple devices simultaneously (e.g., a patient wearing an ECG patch, a blood pressure cuff, and a smartwatch) can be difficult. Data loss during wireless transmission is a known problem. Projects like REMO, which rely on sensors to communicate exercise performance to a cloud system in real time, must design for intermittent connectivity or implement buffering to prevent data gaps. Moreover, different devices might not easily communicate with each other or a central hub unless they follow standard communication protocols. Body area networks (BAN) have been proposed to network multiple sensors on a person, but ensuring interoperability often requires adhering to standards [12].

In summary, sensor integration and interoperability challenges encompass technical issues (data formats, protocols, network reliability) and broader systemic issues (lack of standards, multi-device coordination). Overcoming these challenges is essential for AI systems to leverage the full spectrum of patient data. Projects often spend considerable effort on middleware and standardization tasks – work that is invisible to end-users but critical to making the technology function as a unified whole. The experience from projects like CareWare strongly indicates that improving interoperability (through standards and modular system designs) is a key enabler for future AI-driven healthcare solutions.

2.3 Real-Time Analytics for Remote Care

Many AI in healthcare applications involve remote monitoring and feedback in real time – for example, continuously observing a patient's vital signs to detect emergencies, or providing immediate corrective feedback during an exercise [11]. Real-time analytics introduces another set of challenges related to latency, computational resources, and system reliability. In remote care scenarios such as REMO's home-based spinal rehabilitation, the system must analyze incoming sensor streams on the fly to give patients and clinicians prompt insights (e.g., detecting if an exercise is done incorrectly so that the patient can be alerted or coached instantly). Implementing such real-time capabilities requires a robust infrastructure: data must be transmitted with minimal delay, processed either on-device or on a server nearly instantly, and results returned or displayed to users in a human-friendly form without noticeable lag.

One major challenge is ensuring sufficient computing power and efficient algorithms to handle data streams in real time. High-frequency sensor data (like a multi-channel EMG sampled at hundreds of Hz) can produce a large data volume that needs continuous processing [13]. If using cloud-based AI analysis, as many telehealth solutions do, the system depends on network bandwidth and server responsiveness. Network latency or outages can disrupt the real-time loop. One recommendation from experts is to leverage cloud computing advancements to gain the needed computing power for real-time decision support. Cloud platforms can scale resources to perform heavy computations quickly. However, relying on clouds means the network connection becomes a point of failure.

Real-time systems also must be highly reliable and fault tolerant. If an AI-driven remote monitoring system crashes or freezes, the consequences could be serious (missing a critical event or giving false reassurance). Ensuring uptime and handling exceptions (such as data spikes, sensor errors) are thus part of the challenge. Techniques like watchdog timers, redundant sensors (if one fails, another can cover), and fail-safe modes (if AI is unsure, escalate to human review) are employed to make real-time healthcare AI safer [14]. For example, in Inno4health's athlete monitoring, if the system could not process incoming ECG data fast enough due to any glitch, it was designed to default to a safe state (e.g., pause the training session or revert to a simpler feedback mode) rather than continue with potentially invalid outputs.

2.4   System Validation and Regulatory Hurdles

Before AI systems can be trusted and widely deployed in healthcare, they must undergo rigorous validation to ensure they are safe, effective, and reliable. System validation is a broad process that includes technical validation, clinical validation, and meeting regulatory standards for medical devices or software. This is an area where many AI healthcare projects face significant challenges, as evidenced by the slower-than-expected translation of research prototypes into clinical practice.

A core difficulty is designing validation studies that truly assess the AI in real-world conditions [15]. AI models often show impressive performance on retrospective test datasets or in controlled pilot studies. However, these may not capture the full complexity of clinical reality. For instance, an AI that analyzes vital signs to predict heart failure might be trained on hospital in-patient data. Recognizing this, experts emphasize conducting prospective trials and "translational" research, i.e. deploying the AI in live settings under monitoring to observe its performance. Such studies are costly and time-consuming. Projects usually includes pilot testing phases with end-users (patients or athletes) to validate system functionality and usefulness. Even on a small scale, these pilots revealed unexpected issues.

From a regulatory standpoint, many AI healthcare systems qualify as medical devices (especially if they provide diagnoses, predictions about health, or recommendations for treatment). Regulatory agencies have stringent requirements for evidence of safety and efficacy [16]. Traditional medical device validation involves multi-phase clinical trials and documentation of risk management, quality control, etc. AI software introduces new regulatory questions – for example, how to handle an AI that continuously learns from new data (a "learning" algorithm could change over time, so the certified state could drift). Currently, regulations often require locking down the algorithm before approval; any change can trigger a need for re-approval. This poses a challenge for AI projects: they must plan for a validation cycle where the AI is frozen and tested thoroughly. In fast-moving AI research, this can feel antithetical to the iterative improvement process. Nonetheless, for high-risk applications, it is necessary. The EU's Medical Device Regulation (MDR) and proposed AI Act are moving towards clear guidelines specifically for AI-based medical devices, emphasizing risk management and post-market surveillance to catch any performance degradation or biases that appear after deployment.

Ethical and privacy considerations are another broad implication. AI in healthcare deals with sensitive personal data and often makes decisions that could significantly affect patient lives. Ensuring ethical use involves addressing issues like data privacy, informed consent, algorithmic fairness, and transparency [17]. Data must be handled in compliance with privacy regulations which may dictate how data is stored, shared, and anonymized. For projects like REMO that collect personal health data remotely, robust encryption and secure data management practices are essential to protect patient confidentiality.

The user adaptation aspect or how end-users (clinicians, nurses, patients) accept and adapt to AI tools is crucial for success. Even a perfectly engineered system can fail if users do not trust it or find it burdensome to use. Studies of clinician adoption of AI cite barriers such as lack of trust, fear of technology replacing jobs, and insufficient training on AI systems [18]. Projects should involve end-users early through co-design, making sure the AI tool fits into existing workflows rather than disrupts them. Training programs can help explain what it does and doesn't do, its limitations, and how to interpret outputs. When users understand the tool, their trust increases.

3   Results and Examples of AI Use in Projects

3.1   General Workflow and Data Analysis

Healthcare applications usually are not focused on specific diagnosis and are more related to monitoring daily life activities. The AI based application implementation process contains four main steps: data collection, data pre-processing, decision making, user interface development. In Fig. 1. Steps of general workflow. of analysis process consisting of four steps is presented.

Probably the hardest part is data gathering. The devices for bio-signals recordings need to be selected carefully. Two main aspects need to be considered: devices should be user friendly and wearable (in most cases replicable electrodes only are used in laboratory conditions); devices should provide access to the raw data (many devices provide only pre-processed data where some important information might be lost).

In most cases, together with bio signal recordings various activities and tests are being performed, such as cognitive abilities evaluations tests or physical exercises. Some other important information is gathered using questionnaires or self-assessment tasks. Furthermore, many additional devices are being used during experiments such as video cameras or virtual reality glasses. All the data and its variety depend on a specific task and further investigation into the most important features is usually required.

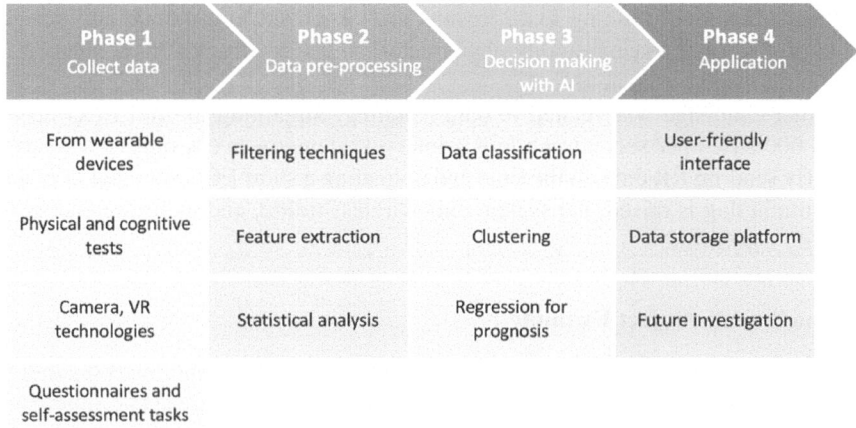

Fig. 1. Steps of general workflow.

3.2 Careware Project Example

In the Careware project the focus was on smart wearable sport and health solutions. The initial data of ECG signals were recorded using a Cardioscout device, which was attached to the special T-shirts. The goal was to prepare a recommendation system for choosing different intensity levels in training. This application is prepared for professional athletes that want to reach the best results with the highest intensity level minimizing possible damage to heart activity [1]. The general steps of process are presented in Fig. 2.

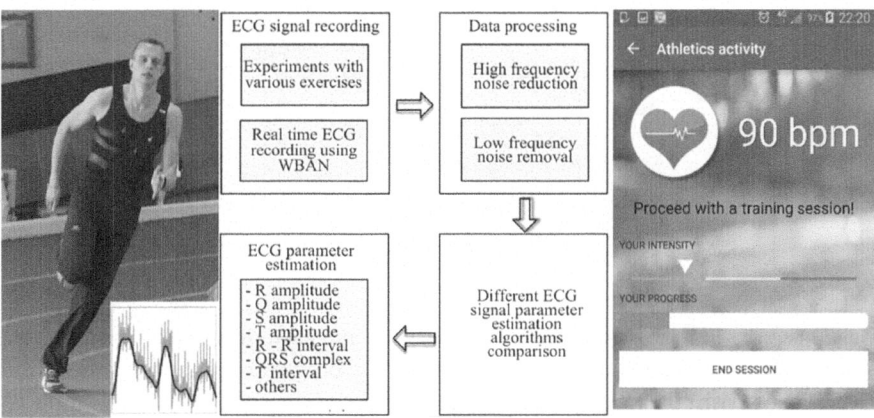

Fig. 2. Steps and results of the project.

The biggest challenge here was data quality and sensors development, because ECG signals were collected in movement. Using silver-nylon textile electrodes, the prototype reached R-peak detection sensitivity above 90% at rest and above 70% during motion after 1 000 reuse cycles. A trained prediction model combines the ECG stream with the athlete's historical training load. Results are visualized in a mobile app designed for both professional coaches and hobby athletes, so that feedback ("slow down", "add recovery") is available instantly.

Another challenge was related to data handling. Streaming the full ECG needs ~ 2 000–4 000 bytes per second, while RR-interval telemetry needs only 2–4 bytes per second. By sending RR data all the time and uploading a short ECG segment only when an arrhythmia flag is raised, the system cuts wireless traffic, and therefore energy use, by roughly 2 000-fold.

3.3 Inno4health Project Example

"Inno4health" project focused on improving cognitive abilities and analysis about its relationship with decision making abilities in professional sports area. The anticipation, concentration, decision-making, attention transfer tests were performed. Gathered data together with heart rate variability was used as initial data. As a result, the individualized training plan was prepared that was based on cluster analysis. The research showed that this platform improved mental abilities of sportsmen [10]. The general steps of workflow are presented in Fig. 3.

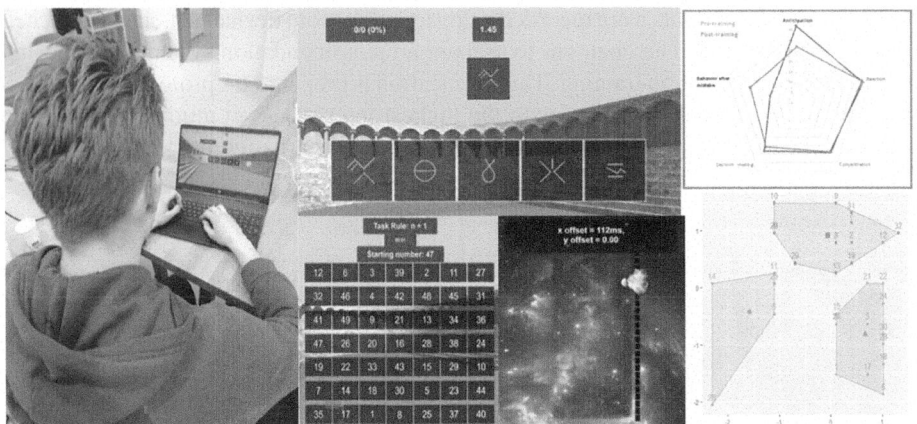

Fig. 3. Steps and results of the project.

The biggest challenge here was data collection and system with VR creation. Then another step was to create a training model based on prognosis methods and individual physical insights. In the system three different tasks were implemented for initial and post training evaluation as well as for training. The concentration task evaluates reaction time, concentration with and without stimulus. The main idea of this task is to compare one (separate) figure with 5 others listed below and respectively press (or select) a button if there is a match or not. The attention transfer task was selected for memory, reaction time, attention peculiarities, and concentration evaluation. The task consists of two parts consistently followed by each other during the whole task. The anticipation task is made for the evaluation of mental skills such as decision-making, anticipation, reaction time and focus. The purpose of this task is to capture the accuracy of the prediction in space and time.

During the pilot > 60 users, including 37 elite athletes, completed a "check-up" consisting of three screen-based tests (concentration, attention shifting, anticipation) while wearing a Polar HR sensor. Unsupervised k-means clustering on the combined HRV test features split the cohort into two clear profiles: higher-performance (~0.88 correct answers, ~0.98 reaction time, and ~12.3 HRV index), at-risk (~0.77 correct answers, ~1.42 reaction time, and ~ 9.1 HRV index). A rules engine turns the cluster label and baseline scores into a one-month micro-training plan (3 × week, 10 min per session). Plans adapt weekly using the new HRV trend and test results. The same logic is used to build SCORM packages for VR delivery, which early experiments show improves engagement.

Results showed that the cognitive task results had a statistically significant improvement after 4 weeks training for almost all users, a mean change of 7% in concentration, 9% in attention transfer, and 11% in anticipation task. AI based cluster analysis was performed, and it is possible to see different types of possible training results, with allow psychologists to have initial plan for training and only add specialized individual plan of different types of sportsmen's.

3.4 Future Investigation in REMO Project

European countries, driven by advanced healthcare infrastructure, have increasingly adopted multidisciplinary approaches to spinal disorders. Treatments range from surgery to physiotherapy, often accompanied by pain management techniques. Research also suggests the importance of early intervention and active rehabilitation for optimal recovery [19]. In the REMO project one of use cases addresses patients undergoing spinal disorders and/or back pain rehabilitation with individually customized parameters of the physiological load of the applied rehabilitation, such as exercise duration, performance speed, amplitude, etc. Individualization with biofeedback will ensure that the patient has correctly performed rehabilitation exercises that activate the right muscle parts and achieve the optimal fatigue effect leading to the required rehabilitation result.

After back-pain rehab, only ≈ 10% of patients keep doing their prescribed exercises at home, and as many as 1 in 5 are re-hospitalised within 12 months across Europe [20]. REMO tackles both issues by coupling low-cost EMG + HR wearables with cloud AI that scores every repetition and flags technique errors in real time (see Table 1).

The system will be designed to be used in rehabilitation clinics. It will allow training patients to properly activate muscles during prescribed treating exercises. Beyond supporting rehabilitation in clinics, will be proposed facilitating a seamless transition for patients to continue exercises at home using sensors and telemonitoring software. Utilization of the latest, remote, low-cost sensors for EMG (electromyogram) and HR (heart rate) monitoring, patient education, and communication with patients adopted and new developed software (app) with usage of AI models for evaluation of exercising quality based on sensors data.

It seems that in this case it will be challenged to collect and preprocess data, but also AI algorithms and data interoperability can be very specific. It is planned to use

Table 1. Quantitative baseline and goals

Metric	Today (baseline)	2026 goal	Why it matters
Home-exercise continuity	10% of discharged patients complete their program	$\geq$ 50% under automated quality supervision	Increases functional recovery
12-month re-admission	Up to 20% of spinal-disorder patients re-hospitalized	Cut to $\leq$ 10%	Fewer episodes mean lower cost and pain

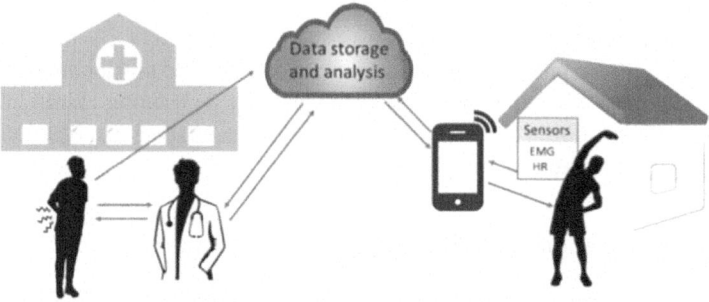

Fig. 4. Scheme of the use case.

clusters and prognosis for patients' data and hope that it will make less kinesitherapy doctor workload and help for patients feel better.

4   Discussion, Conclusions and Recommendations

Healthcare projects integrating AI face a multifaceted array of challenges, from technical hurdles in data and modeling to issues of interoperability, validation, and user acceptance. Real-world project experiences underscore that success requires not just clever algorithms, but also robust data engineering, system integration, extensive validation, and attention to ethical and human-centric design. The road from AI concept to deployed healthcare solutions is complex, but the lessons learned points out the way to better practices. Besides, project execution time is quite short, and it leads to bigger challenges than in long time living healthcare systems.

The following key recommendations are:

- Improve data quality and context: Invest in methodologies and tools for enhancing data quality at the source. This includes developing better noise reduction techniques for wearable sensors, consistent calibration procedures, and capturing contextual metadata with sensor readings. Research into adaptive filtering and machine learning techniques to distinguish signal from noise should be continued. Additionally, establishing local and global data quality standards (as suggested in recent literature) will help ensure that AI models train on and receive reliable data.
- Adopt standardization and interoperability frameworks: Future projects should build on and contribute to emerging standards for data formats and device communication. Collaboration with standards organizations and participation in interoperability consortia (such as open wearable initiatives) will accelerate this progress.
- Focus on robust, real-time capable AI algorithms: Continued research is needed on AI algorithms that are not only accurate but also computationally efficient and robust in real-time settings. Simulation studies and stress-testing of AI systems under various real-world scenarios (e.g., sensor dropouts, extreme patient conditions) should become a standard part of development.
- Strengthen validation and evaluation protocols: it is recommended that AI healthcare projects integrate validation planning into their development lifecycle. Partnerships between technologists and clinical researchers can facilitate rigorous clinical evaluation.

Looking ahead, three practical moves can help any mid-size clinic turn these prototype systems into day-to-day tools. First, train your models separately, so each hospital, health center or research institute keeps data on-site and only shares the learned weights. Recent reviews show this gives almost the same accuracy as centralized training without the privacy issues [21]. Second, run small, quantized versions of the models on the wearable or phone itself. 2024 edge-AI studies report roughly 40–50% lower network traffic and faster alerts for patient monitoring [22]. Third, line up early with the new rules, such as use the "Good Machine-Learning Practice" principles and check that each use-case fits the EU AI Act's "high-risk" category. If your data is still too small, you can increase it with privacy-safe synthetic images generated by modern diffusion models (they keep diagnostic detail and have hit AUC scores up to 0.99 in recent tests) [23]. Taken together, these steps tackle the three biggest problems: data sharing, real-time performance, and regulation without burdening busy care teams with new jargon or complex workflows.

Moving forward, the hope is that by addressing these challenges and implementing such recommendations, AI systems in healthcare will mature from experimental pilots to reliable, widely adopted tools that truly benefit clients' (patients or sportsmen's) care and outcomes. The collective experience of projects like CareWare, Inno4health and REMO highlights all the difficulties and the potential rewards of AI in medicine.

Acknowledgments. The activities of the project "Remote Patient - targeted Health Monitoring to Reduce Workload (REMO)" were financed by European Union funds and co-financing funds, the funding institution is the Research Council of Lithuania.

Disclosure of Interests. Authors have no conflict of interest to declare.

References

1. Bajwa, J., Munir, U., Nori, A., Williams, B.: Artificial intelligence in healthcare: transforming the practice of medicine. Futur. Healthc. J. **8**(2), e188–e194 (2021). https://doi.org/10.7861/fhj.2021-0095
2. Bertl, M., et al.: Challenges for AI in healthcare systems, pp. 165–186 (2025)
3. Kelly, C.J., Karthikesalingam, A., Suleyman, M., Corrado, G., King, D.: Key challenges for delivering clinical impact with artificial intelligence. BMC Med. **17**(1), 195 (2019). https://doi.org/10.1186/s12916-019-1426-2
4. Canali, S., Schiaffonati, V., Aliverti, A.: Challenges and recommendations for wearable devices in digital health: Data quality, interoperability, health equity, fairness. PLOS Digit. Heal. **1**(10), e0000104 (2022). https://doi.org/10.1371/journal.pdig.0000104
5. Panch, T., Mattie, H., Celi, L.A.: The 'inconvenient truth' about AI in healthcare. NPJ Digit. Med. **2**(1), 77 (2019). https://doi.org/10.1038/s41746-019-0155-4
6. Tachkov, K., et al.: Barriers to use artificial intelligence methodologies in health technology assessment in central and East European Countries. Front. Public Heal. **10** (2022). https://doi.org/10.3389/fpubh.2022.921226
7. Sendak, M.P., D'Arcy, J., Kashyap, S.: A path for translation of machine learning products into healthcare delivery. EMJ Innov. (2020). https://doi.org/10.33590/emjinnov/19-00172
8. Heikenfeld, J., et al.: Wearable sensors: modalities, challenges, and prospects. Lab Chip **18**(2), 217–248 (2018). https://doi.org/10.1039/C7LC00914C
9. Vijayan, V., Connolly, J.P., Condell, J., McKelvey, N., Gardiner, P.: Review of wearable devices and data collection considerations for connected health. Sensors **21**(16), 5589 (2021). https://doi.org/10.3390/s21165589
10. Butkevičiūtė, E., Bikulčienė, L., Žvironienė, A.: Physiological state evaluation in working environment using expert system and random forest machine learning algorithm. Healthcare **11**(2), 220 (2023). https://doi.org/10.3390/healthcare11020220
11. Ramadan, O.M.E., Alruwaili, M.M., Alruwaili, A.N., Elsehrawy, M.G., Alanazi, S.: Facilitators and barriers to AI adoption in nursing practice: a qualitative study of registered nurses' perspectives. BMC Nurs. **23**(1), 891 (2024). https://doi.org/10.1186/s12912-024-02571-y
12. Zhang, F., Lian, Y.: QRS detection based on multiscale mathematical morphology for wearable ECG devices in body area networks. IEEE Trans. Biomed. Circuits Syst. **3**(4), 220–228 (2009). https://doi.org/10.1109/TBCAS.2009.2020093
13. Butkevičiūtė, E., Bikulčienė, L., Blažauskas, T., Žemaitytė, A.: Cognitive checkup and mental training platform for elite athletes. Balt. J. Mod. Comput. **11**(2) (2023). https://doi.org/10.22364/bjmc.2023.11.2.03
14. Van Der Donckt, J., et al.: Mitigating data quality challenges in ambulatory wrist-worn wearable monitoring through analytical and practical approaches. Sci. Rep. **14**(1), 17545 (2024). https://doi.org/10.1038/s41598-024-67767-3
15. Quinn, T.P., Senadeera, M., Jacobs, S., Coghlan, S., Le, V.: Trust and medical AI: the challenges we face and the expertise needed to overcome them. J. Am. Med. Informatics Assoc. **28**(4), 890–894 (2021). https://doi.org/10.1093/jamia/ocaa268
16. Shrivastava, A., Jain, U., Al-Farouni, M., Kumar, Y., Anandhi, R.J., Bhavana, M.: Proposed framework for modifications to artificial intelligence/machine learning (Ai/Ml)-based software as a medical device (SAMD). In: 2024 7th International Conference on Contemporary Computing and Informatics (IC3I), pp. 1755–1763 (2024). https://doi.org/10.1109/IC3I61595.2024.10829073
17. Hickman, E., Petrin, M.: Trustworthy AI and corporate governance: The EU's ethics guidelines for trustworthy artificial intelligence from a company law perspective. Eur. Bus. Organ. Law Rev. **22**(4), 593–625 (2021). https://doi.org/10.1007/s40804-021-00224-0

18. Topol, E.J.: High-performance medicine: the convergence of human and artificial intelligence. Nat. Med. **25**(1), 44–56 (2019). https://doi.org/10.1038/s41591-018-0300-7

19. Friedman, G.N., et al.: Multidisciplinary approaches to complication reduction in complex spine surgery: a systematic review. Spine J. **20**, 1248–1260 (2020). https://doi.org/10.1016/j.spinee.2020.04.008

20. Anar, S.Ö.: The effectiveness of home-based exercise programs for low back pain patients. J. Phys. Ther. Sci. **28**(10), 2727–2730 (2016). https://doi.org/10.1589/jpts.28.2727

21. Teo, Z.L., et al.: Federated machine learning in healthcare: A systematic review on clinical applications and technical architecture. Cell Rep. Med. **5**(2), 101419 (2024). https://doi.org/10.1016/j.xcrm.2024.101419

22. 2024 State of Edge AI Report. https://dateurope.com/wp-content/uploads/2024/05/2024ST AGEOFEDGEAIREPORT.pdf. Accessed 10 July 2025]

23. Hosseini, A., Serag, A.: Is synthetic data generation effective in maintaining clinical biomarkers? Investigating diffusion models across diverse imaging modalities. Front. Artif. Intell. **7** (2024). https://doi.org/10.3389/frai.2024.1454441

Thermal Impact on Vegetable Growth: Case Study in Lettuce Production

Juan M. Núñez V.$^{(\boxtimes)}$ [ID], Claudia Helena Ramírez-Soler[ID],
Sofania M. Rojas-Landacay[ID], Sebastián López Flórez[ID],
and Fernando De la Prieta[ID]

BISITE Research Group, University of Salamanca, Salamanca, Spain
jmnunez@usal.es
https://bisite.usal.es/es

Abstract. This article addresses the challenge of climate change in agriculture, focusing on the optimization of lettuce production through bio-inspired algorithms supported by an Internet of Things (IoT) architecture. The study underscores the sensitivity of lettuce to thermal stress and proposes a decision-making system that recommends optimal temperature ranges to maximize yield. It highlights the need to maintain optimal environmental temperatures for efficient growth. This research reveals a marked negative correlation between lettuce yield and variables such as evapotranspiration and soil temperature, through data analysis from two regions in Colombia. As a solution, the use of bio-inspired algorithms is proposed to create agricultural recommendation systems capable of identifying temperature ranges that maximize yield. The methodology employs Internet of Things technologies for data collection, and the proposed models include statistical techniques and bio-inspired algorithms, experimentally tested to refine crop management strategies in the face of adverse climatic conditions. The study emphasizes the urgency of implementing adaptive strategies to sustain agricultural productivity and ensure food security in the face of climate volatility.

Keywords: Climate change · Bio-inspired algorithms · Thermal stress

1 Introduction

Climate change is intrinsically linked to the increase in temperatures and the occurrence of more extreme weather events, such as intense or prolonged rainfall. Climate change will increase the number and severity of heatwaves and is expected to negatively impact crop yields. This climatic alteration directly impacts the interactions among crops, pests, pathogens, and weeds, exacerbating various trends. Among these are the decline of pollinating insects, the growing scarcity of water, the increase in tropospheric ozone concentrations, and the rise in atmospheric carbon dioxide (CO_2) concentrations, which play a significant role in this changing landscape and the reduction of photosynthesis as temperatures increase [1,2]. The influence of climate change on agriculture is a matter

© The Author(s), under exclusive license to Springer Nature Switzerland AG 2026
J. Valente de Oliveira et al. (Eds.): EPIA 2025, LNAI 16122, pp. 420–432, 2026.
https://doi.org/10.1007/978-3-032-05179-0_32

of growing concern, where high environmental temperatures play a critical role. This increase in both atmospheric and soil temperatures not only increases the atmospheric demand for water, leading to an intensification of evapotranspiration processes, but also directly affects vegetable yields [3,4]. This phenomenon can particularly have a negative impact on the growth and development of vegetables, which, according to Keatinge et al. [5], show different levels of sensitivity to fluctuations in diurnal air temperature and soil temperature. In this context of climate variability and emerging natural phenomena, the combination of increased temperature and water scarcity has become a significant obstacle to irrigation and food production, as noted by Felipe et al. [6]. Since irrigation is a key factor for plant growth and productivity, as highlighted by Guimarães et al. [7], it is imperative to develop strategies to mitigate these challenges. The relationship between climate change and agriculture has been widely studied, emphasizing how extreme temperature fluctuations can significantly alter crop yields. Siebert et al. [8] underline the need to integrate the impact of irrigation in our assessments of climate change, particularly in terms of thermal stress in agriculture. Irrigation presents itself as a partially effective strategy to counteract the negative consequences of high temperatures on crops [9,10].

In this context, the main objective of this study is to design and validate a decision-making system for lettuce production optimization using bio-inspired algorithms (Genetic Algorithm (GA), Simulated Annealing (SA), and Artificial Bee Colony (ABC)), supported by a four-layer IoT architecture for real-time data collection and analysis. This approach enables the identification of optimal environmental conditions that maximize crop yield under changing climate scenarios.

In the case of lettuce cultivation, it is classified as a vegetable sensitive to high temperatures and water deficits. Various studies have indicated a range of optimal temperatures for the vegetative growth of lettuce, demonstrating variations in the thermal environmental requirements of this species. Jenni et al. [11] point out that the ideal average ambient temperature ranges between 7 and 24 °C. The FAO [12] specifies a narrower range of 15 to 20 °C as the most favorable. Ahmed et al. [1] propose that the optimal interval is even higher, ranging between 22 and 25 °C, highlighting the importance of this thermal band for efficient control of CO_2 uptake, essential for photosynthesis and biomass generation. Yamori et al. [4] add that the ambient temperature should not exceed 30 °C to avoid compromising the growth and development of the plant, also emphasizing the need for frequent irrigation. Felipe et al. [6] complement this information by highlighting the importance of an appropriate irrigation schedule, especially because the part of the plant that is harvested is the leafy area, underscoring the relevance of maintaining specific environmental and management conditions to optimize lettuce yield. High temperatures and the resulting water demand can have an adverse impact on the growth, development, and yield of lettuce plants in various regions where it is cultivated. Climate variability and rising temperatures are exacerbating the challenges faced by farmers in producing sensitive crops like lettuce in Colombia [13]. This situation poses significant risks to food security in Colombia, where vegetables play a crucial role in the diet of the population [14]. The main contributions of this paper are Generate georeferenced recommendation systems for optimal ranges using bioinspired algorithms for decision-making. Generating results and analyses on the impact of temperatures on yield can contribute to improving crop models and Comparison of evolutionary optimization models developed under irrigation treatments in different conditions or zones, which include temperature variations, potentially leading to resource optimization. The structure of this paper is organized as follows: Sect. 2 provides a literature review pertinent to the study, encompassing various case studies and predictive and recommendation techniques applicable to agriculture. Section 3 details the materials and methods, outlining the methodology implemented for this project, along with the tools utilized for data collection and validation within the IoT architecture. Section 4 presents the experimental process and the outcomes derived from the predictive and recommendation algorithm. Section 5 discusses the conclusions.

2   Related Works

As climate change continues to impact weather patterns and increase the frequency of extreme weather events, it is crucial to understand and address the specific risks faced by vegetable crops, such as lettuce, in order to ensure the food and nutritional security of populations. Various crop model studies predict substantial yield reductions in lettuce at elevated temperatures [4,15,16]. In this scenario, predictive models and artificial intelligence (AI) emerge as key tools to anticipate and mitigate the adverse effects of climate change on agriculture. Utilizing vast amounts of climatic and agronomic data, AI-based predictive models can analyze how temperature variations affect growth and production, allowing farmers to adapt their cultivation practices in real time. These models can not only forecast crop yields under different climatic scenarios but also suggest optimal irrigation and management strategies that minimize losses and maximize production, despite the uncertainty introduced by climate change [4].

In this context, artificial intelligence (AI) emerges as a promising tool to overcome some of these challenges. Since its initial conception by Alan Turing in 1950, through the resurgence of interest in deep learning in 2006, AI has evolved to become a fundamental pillar in both academia and industry [17]. This evolution suggests an untapped potential in the application of AI algorithms to develop predictive models that can anticipate the performance of crops like lettuce under extreme climatic conditions. These models could not only offer a more accurate and efficient alternative for irrigation management but also help to formulate more adaptive and resilient agricultural strategies to climate change.

One of the algorithms used in the field of agriculture is the GA, which is a type of optimization algorithm based on the processes of biological evolution and natural selection. As Goldberg [18] notes, these algorithms are based on the idea that a population of solutions can evolve towards optimal solutions through the application of genetic operators such as selection, crossover, and mutation. In the field of agriculture, there are studies where GA are applied to address limitations in water availability, plant stress, and variability in irrigation systems, among others [19–21].

On the other hand, linear regression is a statistical technique used to model the relationship between one or more independent (predictor) variables and a dependent (target) variable. The goal is to find the best line or plane that fits the observed data, minimizing the sum of the squared errors between the actual observations and the model's predictions [22]. In the field of agriculture, linear regressions are used to relate variables such as climate, soil, among others, to the production or growth of a plant species. Edreira et al. [23] used linear regression to test the relationship between climatic variables such as temperature and solar radiation on maize grain yield under thermal stress. They found that heat stress had a negative effect on biomass production, which was related to variations in radiation use efficiency and the amount of light captured by the crop. Gobin [24] points out that models are needed to understand how climate affects crops. She conducted a study in Belgium using the regional crop model REGCROP [25] and linear regressions to examine the behavior of changing bioclimatic patterns in relation to each sensitive growth phase of six crops (winter wheat, sugar beet, winter oilseed rape, winter barley, potatoes, and corn) and their yield with the residuals from the linear regression analysis. Indeed, they found that vapor pressure deficit is the best predictor of the yields of the target crops. Additionally, Liu et al. [26] analyzed how wheat growth parameters respond to heat stress using wheat crop growth models and simple linear regression. They examined grain filling duration, total aerial biomass at maturity, grain yield, grain number and size, as well as grain nitrogen concentration. The regression slopes between the observed or simulated growth parameters of wheat and heat stress were evaluated, resulting in a decline in all variables except for grain protein content. Another algorithm used in the agricultural field is the Artificial Bee Colony (ABC) algorithm, an optimization technique inspired by the intelligent behavior of honey bees in searching for food sources. This algorithm is based on the processes of searching and exploiting food sources by three groups of bees: scouts, foragers, and onlookers. Each of these bees plays a crucial role in locating the best solutions during the optimization process. The primary goal of the ABC is to find the optimal solution to complex problems by simulating the cooperative and adaptive behavior of bee colonies. This approach is grounded on principles of collective intelligence and evolutionary algorithms, allowing it to address nonlinear and high-dimensional optimization problems common in various areas of research and industrial application [27]. In the context of agriculture, the ABC has proven to be a valuable tool, especially for optimal water resource management in irrigation systems. For instance, in Roeva's study [28], the ABC was used to develop a simulation-optimization model for the joint operation of reservoirs and ponds to maximize annual returns in a multi-crop irrigation system [29]. SA is an algorithm aimed at finding the optimal solution in complex optimization problems, based on the process of annealing metals, mimicking the physical process by which a material is heated and then cooled slowly to reach a state of minimum energy. It performs a random walk through a solution space, accepting more profitable new estimates while allowing less profitable configurations to avoid getting stuck in local optima [30]. In some agricultural studies, annealing algorithms such as SA have been used to calibrate crop and groundwater simulation models, as well as to optimize large-scale simulation models of realistic agricultural systems. Although they have proven effective in other disciplines, their application in agricultural and resource economics has been limited [31].

3 Materials and Methods

The methodology used for this research is based on user-centered design with a focus on the IoT. Initially, a list of context requirements is compiled, which includes identifying the seed to be cultivated, the area, and other agricultural practices such as irrigation systems. This refers to the empathy and problem definition process. This is followed by a design and implementation process for an IoT architecture tailored to the actual conditions of the context, thus ensuring a robust data capture and cleaning process. Finally, a comparative analysis is proposed between regression-based and bio-inspired models. Figure 1 shows the methodological process implemented.

METHODOLOGY BASED ON DESIGN THINKING

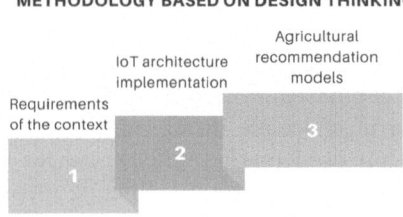

Fig. 1. Research methodology.

3.1 Technical Requirements of the Context and the Crop

The present work was conducted in Calima and El Poblado, two municipalities located in the Valle del Cauca department, Colombia. Calima had an average daytime temperature of 20.99 °C and an average relative humidity of 72.52%.

Lettuce seeds of the curly green variety were used, which were sown in 294-cell trays with a substrate composed of soil and California red worm humus in a 4:1 ratio. After 7 days, the seedlings were transplanted to field conditions in soils characterized by high organic matter and nitrogen content, neutral pH, high to medium fertility, clayey texture, and low electrical conductivity. They were planted in plots with a total area of $100\,m^2$, at a spacing of $0.20\,m$ between plants. Six planting cycles were conducted throughout the year.

The lettuce seedlings were transplanted into $100\,\mathrm{m}^2$ plots ($10\,\mathrm{m}\times10\,\mathrm{m}$), using a drip irrigation system in Calima and a sprinkler system in El Poblado. Each system operated at a flow rate of 200 Liters of water over 30 min, with adjustments based on ambient temperature conditions.

3.2 IoT Architecture Implementation

This article presents the development and implementation of a four-layer IoT architecture aimed at environmental and soil monitoring, utilizing a sampling methodology every 30 min during daytime periods. The sensors used, including the DS18B20 for temperature measurements, are integrated into an environment characterized by intermittent connectivity, using technologies such as Wi-Fi and the MQTT protocol to ensure efficient and reliable data transmission. At the processing level, the capabilities of ESP32 and Raspberry Pi 4 devices are used in environments with restricted connectivity. Based on this, the use of local microservices is necessary to process the information and generate recommendation systems based on bio-inspired algorithms. The objective of layer three (3) is to ensure that transmitted data is processed through microservices designed to operate locally. This reduces latency and enhances data analysis efficiency, enabling the generation of automatic recommendations and real-time alerts for resource management and response to extreme conditions. Finally, the last layer provides a dashboard that presents the data and analysis in an understandable way, allowing users to make informed decisions based on updated and accurate data. Figure 2 shows the implemented IoT architecture.

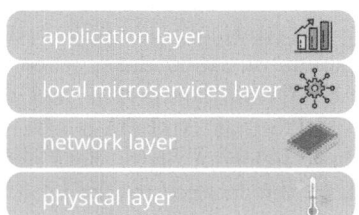

Fig. 2. Proposed IoT architecture.

3.3 Agricultural Recommendation Models

For the development of recommendation systems based on optimization algorithms, it is necessary to choose the models to be used. Based on the state of the art and the opportunities for improvement in the implementation of bio-inspired algorithms focused on agriculture, it is decided to implement such algorithms, such as genetic, SA, and artificial bee colony, for the maximization of a cost function. This cost function was found through the application of a linear regression, where the output factor is productivity.

4   Experiments and Results

To evaluate the various bio-inspired models planned for implementation, two experimental series of lettuce cultivation were conducted. Each series was repeated six times over the course of a year, maintaining uniform conditions in terms of cultivation, seed type, irrigation system, and applied agricultural techniques. The implemented scenario is shown in Fig. 3. The SHT71 and DS18B20 temperature sensors were used, as well as a stack of IoT technologies, such as the MQTT protocol and the ubidots cloud platform.

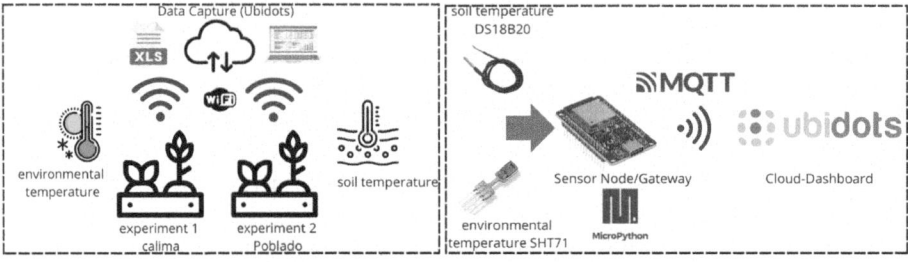

Fig. 3. Experimental scenario and technology stack.

4.1   Exploratory Data Analysis (EDA)

Using the pandas, Numpy and Matplolib libraries, a data cleaning process was performed, for a total amount of 34560 data, where in some cases null and duplicate data were cleaned. All data is stored in the Ubidots platform, therefore its registration is done in Excel format. An EDA has been conducted with the aim of understanding the intrinsic behavior of the data and obtaining a descriptive summary of it. Using Python, the detailed results have been obtained as follows. Table 1 shows the data captured for each experiment and repetition. Table 2 and Table 3 show the respective EDA.

The inclusion of percentiles (25th, 50th, and 75th) in Tables 2 and 3 provides a more nuanced understanding of the data distribution beyond the mean and standard deviation. Percentiles are particularly useful for identifying the central tendency and variability in non-normally distributed datasets, which are common in agricultural environments due to climatic fluctuations. The 25th percentile indicates the lower bound of typical values, the 50th percentile (median) shows the central value, and the 75th percentile marks the upper range of typical observations. These statistical descriptors help identify thresholds and trends that may not be visible from the mean alone and are valuable for calibrating the optimization models and setting recommendation limits for temperature and yield management.

Table 1. Original data for each scenario

| | Calima Darien | | | Poblado | | |
	ET	ST	Yield (pounds)	ET	ST	Yield (pounds)
1	17.12	19.55	41	28.34	28.01	23
2	18.33	22.01	38	31.35	30.48	13
3	20.32	22.97	35	30.58	29.51	16
4	23.22	24.95	32	24.39	25.52	27
5	17.15	18.51	42	26.50	27.02	24
6	20.27	22.98	36	28.36	27.02	24

Table 2. EDA Calima

Statistic	ET	ST	Yield (pounds)
Mean	19.401667	21.828333	37.333333
Standard Deviation	2.349531	2.392057	3.777124
Minimum	17.120000	18.510000	32.000000
25% Percentile	17.445000	20.165000	35.250000
50% Percentile	19.300000	22.490000	37.000000
75% Percentile	20.307500	22.977500	40.250000
Maximum	23.220000	24.950000	42.000000

Table 3. EDA Poblado

Statistic	ET	ST	Yield (pounds)
Mean	28.253333	27.926667	21.166667
Standard Deviation	2.569869	1.814912	5.419102
Minimum	24.390000	25.520000	13.000000
25% Percentile	26.960000	27.020000	17.750000
50% Percentile	28.350000	27.515000	23.500000
75% Percentile	30.025000	29.135000	24.000000
Maximum	31.350000	30.480000	27.000000

The correlation analysis reveals a strong positive correlation between evapotranspiration (ET) and soil temperature (ST) ($r = 0.94$), indicating environmental interdependence. More importantly, both variables exhibit a strong negative correlation with lettuce yield: ET ($r \approx -0.92$ to -0.97) and ST ($r \approx -0.98$ to -0.99), confirming that higher temperatures and water loss are consistently associated with decreased production.

4.2 Bio-Inspired Optimization Models

For the successful implementation of bio-inspired algorithms aimed at agriculture, it is first necessary to define the cost function in order to find the optimal ranges that maximize the function. By applying a multiple linear regression model, a quantitative correlation has been established between the ambient temperature (ET) and the soil temperature (ST) with agricultural productivity. This analysis has allowed for the estimation of regression coefficients that quantify the unitary impact of each independent variable on the dependent variable, productivity, measured as yield in pounds (Yield). The Eq. (1) corresponds to the Calima experiment, and Eq. (2) Poblado.

$$Yield = 70.8316 - 0.6522 \times ET - 0.9549 \times ST \tag{1}$$

$$Yield = 106.3147 + 0.3770 \times ET - 3.4304 \times ST \tag{2}$$

In the following Table 4, the optimal ranges recommended by the regression and their estimated production can be appreciated.

Table 4. Optimal Ranges through Linear Regression

Calima		Poblado	
ET	ST	ET	ST
17.12	18.51	31.25	25.52
Estimated Yield: 41.99		Estimated Yield: 32.61	

Figure 4 shows a distribution of the data according to productivity; it can be seen that in the green zones, a high productivity of lettuce is expected, so the environmental and soil temperature values should be kept below 20 °C. In the red zone, there are values indicating low productivity with their respective temperature values above 25 °C.

A simulation is conducted to evaluate the potential impact of climate change on crop yields in two locations, Calima Darien and Poblado (see Fig. 5). A 10% increase in Evapotranspiration (ET) and Soil Temperature (ST) due to climate change is assumed. The resulting graphs allow visualizing the direct comparison between current and projected yields under the simulated climate change scenario. The difference between the blue and red dots provides a visual representation of the impact of climate change on crop yields according to the model used. The analysis of the influence of climate change on agricultural production is vital to anticipate future challenges, develop effective responses, and ensure the resilience of food systems and ecosystems against climate disruptions. Figure 5 shows the impact of climate change with a 10% increase, which is a factor projected for 2050 according to the FAO. Subsequently, bio-inspired models are implemented in GA, SA, and bee colony. GA are implemented using the

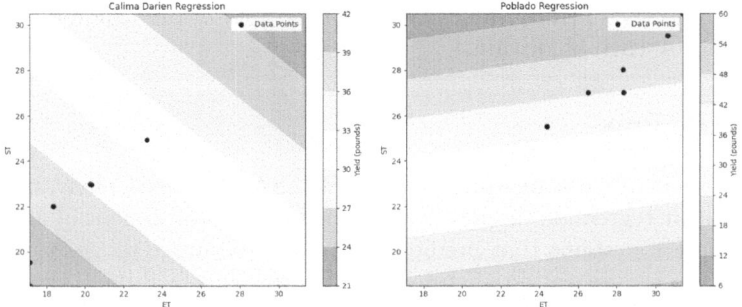

Fig. 4. Distribution of the data according to productivity.

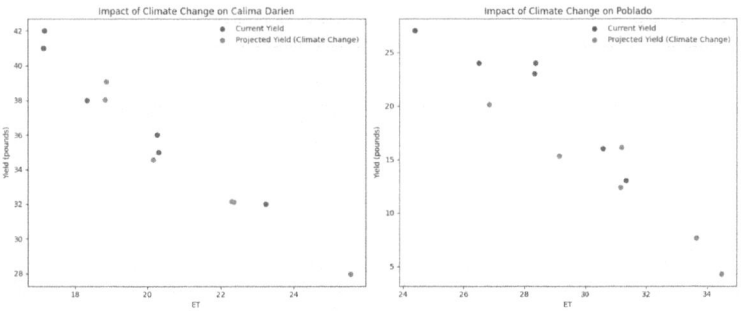

Fig. 5. Projected impact of climate change.

Table 5. Agricultural Recommendation System Based on Bio-Inspired Algorithms

Model	Experiment	ET	ST	Estimated Yield (pounds)
	Calima	17.12	18.51	41.99
Linear Regression	Poblado	31.25	25.52	32.61
	Calima	17.11	18.05	42.55
Genetic Algorithm	Poblado	32.04	25.08	31.25
	Calima	17.12	15.51	41.19
Simulated Annealing	Poblado	31.35	25.52	30.58
	Calima	19.15	18.22	40.93
Bee Colony Algorithm	Poblado	29.38	25.85	39.88

PyGAD library, SA uses scipy, and for the bee colony, the random and numpy libraries are used. Each algorithm acts as a recommendation system, thus providing the optimal ranges for ambient temperature and soil temperature, as well as an estimate of productivity. Each algorithm uses the linear regression cost function to find the optimal values for maximization. Table 5 shows the optimal ranges found by each algorithm.

5   Conclusions

The use of bio-inspired algorithms, such as GA, SA, and Bee Colony, in conjunction with linear regression models, has enabled the establishment of agricultural recommendation systems that predict optimal temperature ranges to maximize lettuce yield. The integration of an IoT architecture has facilitated the collection and processing of essential environmental data for this purpose. Experimental results support the usefulness of these bio-inspired models in informed decision-making, which can potentially improve resource use efficiency and counteract the negative effects of the temperature increase projected for 2050, according to the FAO, ensuring the sustainability of lettuce production under changing climatic conditions.

The study reveals a significant negative correlation between lettuce yield and environmental factors such as evapotranspiration and soil temperature, with correlation values of r = −0.92 and r = −0.98, respectively. These findings suggest that an increase in evapotranspiration and soil temperature is associated with a decrease in yield. Based on this, decisions are made to improve the irrigation planning system and thus achieve the temperatures given by the agricultural recommendation system.

Acknowledgments. This research is part of the International Chair Project on Trustworthy Artificial Intelligence and Demographic Challenge within the National Strategy for Artificial Intelligence (ENIA), in the framework of the European Recovery, Transformation and Resilience Plan. Reference: TSI-100933-2023-0001. This project is funded by the Secretary of State for Digitalization and Artificial Intelligence and by the European Union (Next Generation).

Disclosure of Interests. The authors have no competing interests to declare that are relevant to the content of this article.

References

1. Ahmed, H.A., Yu-Xin, T., Qi-Chang, Y.: Optimal control of environmental conditions affecting lettuce plant growth in a controlled environment with artificial lighting: A review. S. Afr. J. Bot. **130**, 75–89 (2020)
2. Rotundo, J.L., Tang, T., Messina, C.: Response of maize photosynthesis to high temperature: implications for modeling the impact of global warming. Plant Physiol. Biochem. **141**, 202–205 (2019)
3. Ogunkanmi, L., MacCarthy, D.S., Adiku, S.G.: Impact of extreme temperature and soil water stress on the growth and yield of soybean (glycine max (l.) merrill). Agriculture **12**(1), 43 (2021)
4. Yamori, N., Levine, C.P., Mattson, N.S., Yamori, W.: Optimum root zone temperature of photosynthesis and plant growth depends on air temperature in lettuce plants. Plant Mol. Biol. **110**(4), 385–395 (2022)

5. Keatinge, J., Ledesma, D., Keatinge, F., Hughes, J.: Projecting annual air temperature changes to 2025 and beyond: implications for vegetable production worldwide. J. Agric. Sci. **152**(1), 38–57 (2014)
6. Felipe, A.J.B., Bareng, J.L.R.: Growth and yield assessment of lettuce (lactuca sativa l.): an economic feasibility and performance evaluation of capillary wick irrigation system. Plant Sci. Today **9**(1), 62–69 (2022)
7. Guimarães, C.M., et al.: Agronomic performance of lettuce cultivars submitted to different irrigation depths. Plos One **14**(12), e0224264 (2019)
8. Siebert, S., Webber, H., Zhao, G., Ewert, F.: Heat stress is overestimated in climate impact studies for irrigated agriculture. Environ. Res. Lett. **12**(5), 054023 (2017)
9. Vogel, E., et al.: The effects of climate extremes on global agricultural yields. Environ. Res. Lett. **14**(5), 054010 (2019)
10. Karam, F., Mounzer, O., Sarkis, F., Lahoud, R.: Yield and nitrogen recovery of lettuce under different irrigation regimes. J. Appl. Hort. **4**(2), 70–76 (2002)
11. Jenni, S., Truco, M.J., Michelmore, R.W.: Quantitative trait loci associated with tipburn, heat stress-induced physiological disorders, and maturity traits in crisphead lettuce. Theor. Appl. Genet. **126**, 3065–3079 (2013)
12. FAO: Climate change fans spread of pests and threatens plants and crops, new FAO study (2021)
13. Ramirez-Villegas, J., Salazar, M., Jarvis, A., Navarro-Racines, C.E.: A way forward on adaptation to climate change in Colombian agriculture: perspectives towards 2050. Clim. Change **115**, 611–628 (2012)
14. Jarma Orozco, A., Cardona Ayala, C., Araméndiz Tatis, H.: Efecto del cambio climático sobre la fisiología de las plantas cultivadas: una revisión. Rev. UDCA Actualidad Divulgación Científica **15**(1), 63–76 (2012)
15. Lorenz, H., Wiebe, H.: Effect of temperature on photosynthesis of lettuce adapted to different light and temperature conditions. Sci. Hortic. **13**(2), 115–123 (1980)
16. Sage, R.F., Kubien, D.S.: The temperature response of C3 and C4 photosynthesis. Plant Cell Environ. **30**(9), 1086–1106 (2007)
17. Morandín-Ahuerma, F.: ¿ what is artificial intelligence? (2022)
18. MGoldberg, D.E., H.J.: Genetic algorithms and machine learning. Mach. Learn. (1988)
19. Ines, A.V., Honda, K., Gupta, A.D., Droogers, P., Clemente, R.S.: Combining remote sensing-simulation modeling and genetic algorithm optimization to explore water management options in irrigated agriculture. Agric. Water Manag. **83**(3), 221–232 (2006)
20. Roy, S.K., De, D.: Genetic algorithm based internet of precision agricultural things (IopaT) for agriculture 4.0. Internet Things **18**, 100201 (2022)
21. Sadati, S.K., Speelman, S., Sabouhi, M., Gitizadeh, M., Ghahraman, B.: Optimal irrigation water allocation using a genetic algorithm under various weather conditions. Water **6**(10), 3068–3084 (2014)
22. Middela, M.S., Ramadurai, G.: Modelling urban freight generation using linear regression and proportional odds logit models. Transp. Policy **148**, 145–153 (2024)
23. Edreira, J.I.R., Otegui, M.E.: Heat stress in temperate and tropical maize hybrids: differences in crop growth, biomass partitioning and reserves use. Field Crop. Res. **130**, 87–98 (2012)
24. Gobin, A.: Impact of heat and drought stress on arable crop production in Belgium. Nat. Hazard. **12**(6), 1911–1922 (2012)
25. Gobin, A.: Modelling climate impacts on crop yields in Belgium. Climate Res. **44**(1), 55–68 (2010)

26. Liu, B., Asseng, S., Liu, L., Tang, L., Cao, W., Zhu, Y.: Testing the responses of four wheat crop models to heat stress at anthesis and grain filling. Glob. Change Biol. **22**(5), 1890–1903 (2016)

27. Kerr, A., Dialesandro, J., Steenwerth, K., Lopez-Brody, N., Elias, E.: Vulnerability of California specialty crops to projected mid-century temperature changes. Clim. Change **148**, 419–436 (2018)

28. Roeva, O., Zoteva, D., Castillo, O.: Joint set-up of parameters in genetic algorithms and the artificial bee colony algorithm: an approach for cultivation process modelling. Soft. Comput. **25**, 2015–2038 (2021)

29. Sathish, C., Srinivasan, K., et al.: An artificial bee colony algorithm for efficient optimized data aggregation to agricultural IoT devices application. J. Appl. Sci. Eng. **24**(6), 927–935 (2021)

30. Santé-Riveira, I., Boullón-Magán, M., Crecente-Maseda, R., Miranda-Barrós, D.: Algorithm based on simulated annealing for land-use allocation. Comput. Geosci. **34**(3), 259–268 (2008)

31. Dong, Y., Zhao, C., Yang, G., Chen, L., Wang, J., Feng, H.: Integrating a very fast simulated annealing optimization algorithm for crop leaf area index variational assimilation. Math. Comput. Model. **58**(3–4), 877–885 (2013)

AI and Creativity (AIC)

Text Rewriting with Transformers for Humor Generation in Portuguese

André Moreira$^{(\boxtimes)}$, Marcio Lima Inácio, and Hugo Gonçalo Oliveira

CISUC/LASI – Centre for Informatics and Systems of the University of Coimbra,
Department of Informatics Engineering, University of Coimbra, Polo II,
Pinhal de Marrocos, 3030-290 Coimbra, Portugal
`andremoreira@student.dei.uc.pt`, `{mlinacio,hroliv}@dei.uc.pt`

Abstract. Humor Generation has been tackled by Artificial Intelligence for a long time, but remains a challenge, in particular for less-resourced languages. We explore Humor Generation in Portuguese through the task of rewriting a text to make it funny, taking advantage of data available for Portuguese and of transformers, which were: (i) fine-tuned for the task (T5); (ii) used as the mutation operator and fitness function (BERT) of a Genetic Algorithm that evolves text; (iii) prompted for the task (via instruction-tuned LLMs). Given the subjectivity of Humor, funniness of the produced text and its relation to the input was scored by human judges. Results reveal that the only approaches that produce potentially funny text most of the time are those based on prompting LLMs, which suggests that the complexity of humor is better targeted with larger models, even if not specifically trained for the task.

Keywords: Humor Generation · Large Language Models · Natural Language Generation · Transformers · Genetic Algorithms · Portuguese

1 Introduction

Humor plays a relevant role in human communication, ranging from its presence in many social interactions to contributing to our overall well-being [26]. So much that it is often referred to as a measure of human intelligence and a means of expressing emotion [12]. Although creating Humor appears natural for humans, it poses significant challenges for Artificial Intelligence (AI), due to the necessary interplay of semantics, pragmatics, as well as the cultural background.

Before the emergence of deep learning, most Humor Generation systems were template-based [1]. They were able to deliver Humor but lacked flexibility and struggled with context adaptation. Advances such as evolutionary algorithms [32] and deep neural networks [24], including transformers [10], allowed for more dynamic and human-like Humor Generation. However, this remains a complex task, facing limitations such as cultural references, the adaptation to sensitive audiences, or the lack of data for specific languages. These challenges illustrate that, while remaining complex, ongoing advancements are steadily leading AI closer to human-like Humor.

© The Author(s), under exclusive license to Springer Nature Switzerland AG 2026
J. Valente de Oliveira et al. (Eds.): EPIA 2025, LNAI 16122, pp. 435–447, 2026.
https://doi.org/10.1007/978-3-032-05179-0_33

Our main objective is to contribute to the task of Humor Generation, focusing on the Portuguese language. Inspired by recent work and current technologies, we tackle the task of rewriting a text into a funny one with the following approaches: (i) fine-tuning a T5 transformer [22]; (ii) adapting a genetic algorithm (GA) that uses a masked language model (MLM) [32] for mutation and another transformer for computing fitness; (iii) prompting general-purpose instruction-tuned large language models (LLMs), both in a zero- and a few-shot scenario. The work involved adapting the previous to Portuguese and, towards useful conclusions, assessing their results based on human opinions.

Our findings indicate that instruction-tuned LLMs generate funnier texts, which are also more related to the input. On the other hand, the fine-tuned model failed to produce funny text, suggesting that, achieving Humor is complex, and the size of the LLMs is more relevant than specific training.

The main contributions of this work are: (i) the adaptation of three distinct methods for Humor Generation in Portuguese, taking advantage of existing corpora [14], pretrained language models [5,7,11,21], and a framework for Humor Generation based on a GA [32]; (ii) the study of the previous adaptations, previously unexplored for Portuguese, which highlighted their strengths and weaknesses; and (iii) the exploration of LLMs as a Humor judge, employed as the fitness function of our GA.

In the remainder of the paper, we: introduce some background and related work on Humor Generation; present our task and describe the explored approaches; explain how they were adapted to Portuguese; describe the performed experimentation and discuss the obtained results, to finally conclude.

2   Background

The study of Humor Generation in the scope of AI started back in the 1990s, with systems like the Light Bulb Joke Generator [23] and JAPE [2], which produced jokes based on handcrafted templates. A range of template-based systems exists, varying in their input and how templates are filled. They may generate humorous text given one or more seed words [2,16,20,23,25], or an acronym and its meaning [29]. Towards the humor effect, more information can be obtained from an external source of knowledge, such as lexica, semantic networks, or n-gram counts, constrained by the input. Other works combine the previous sources with statistical methods and have longer expressions as input. A seed word can be extracted from this input [6], or specific words can be replaced by others with a similar sound and specific features (e.g., taboo) [27,31]. Even though the latter start with a longer context, humor results from heavily-constrained replacements, which limit the range of inputs for which these systems actually work, as well as their adaptability to any context.

The introduction of neural networks marked a shift of paradigm. Early models, based on long-short-term memory (LSTM) networks, aimed to learn humorous patterns directly from data. Notable examples include the generation of jokes [24] and puns [33] by training LSTMs on humor specific datasets, allowing the model to understand linguistic patterns found in humorous texts.

More recent advances rely on transformers, which combine the use of large amounts of training data and self-attention mechanisms to generate humor by understanding language patterns and contextual information. Examples include fine-tuning a T5 model [19], or guiding LLMs like GPT-3 [4] and ChatGPT 3.5 [10] through prompting. GALMET [32] combines GAs with transformers for evolving real headlines into satirical ones. In each generation, a word in the headline can be replaced with the help of a BERT MLM, while the fitness of each individual is computed by a RoBERTa model fine-tuned for scoring funniness.

Specifically for Portuguese, work on Humor Generation is reduced, but still covers formats like memes [8], generated for a given context, considering a range of textual features; short texts [18], resulting from adapting a given context and computing analogy; or riddles [9] fed by a semantic network, or, more recently, by a LLM [13]. This still leaves out many approaches, including GAs and several relying on transformers.

3   Text Rewriting for Humor Generation

In the scope of Humor Generation, we tackle the task of creating Humor for a given input. Instead of merely generating a (random) joke, producing one that has strong connections with a given context can be more challenging, but enables a more coherent adaptation to any situation, thus contributing to engagement.

Specifically, given a short text in Portuguese, our goal is to generate a new funny related text. This can be, and is often, done by editing the original text. Figure 1 summarizes the task with a real example.

Fig. 1. Running example of the tackled task.

Towards our goal, we selected a range of text rewriting approaches, previously unexplored for generating Humor in Portuguese. The first is a supervised approach, where a pretrained encoder-decoder transformer model like T5 [22] is fine-tuned for our task. For this, pairs of humorous and non-humorous texts with minimal differences are necessary.

Since rewriting is related to evolving text, the second set of approaches explores evolutionary computation through GALMET [32]. Initial population results from duplicating the input text several times and is evolved by crossover (i.e., creating new texts with parts of existing texts) and mutation (i.e., creating new texts by adding/removing tokens, or by replacing them) operators. To keep the funniest texts after each generation, every text is assessed by a fitness function that computes the Humor potential (e.g., a Humor classifier), while favoring texts with fewer edits, according to the Levenshtein distance.

The third set of approaches follows the current paradigm of prompting instruction-tuned LLMs, exploiting their flexibility. Here, the focus is on the prompt, which must instruct the model to transform the input text into a funny one, possibly providing additional tips or examples of the task (i.e., few-shot).

4 Humor Generation in Portuguese

The selected Humor Generation approaches were adapted to Portuguese, with different settings resulting in a total of 9 tested instantiations. This section identifies exploited models and their settings.

4.1 Fine Tuning

PTT5-v2 [21] is a T5 model pretrained for Portuguese, which we fine-tuned in the task of rewriting a short text into a funny one. For this, we instructed the model using the prefix "`Humor:`", in order to identify the task. This fine-tuning was possible thanks to PUNTUGUESE [14], a corpus that pairs short humorous texts in Portuguese (target), produced by comedians, and their non-humorous version (input), manually produced by human volunteers, through minimal edits.[1] Table 1 illustrates the contents of PUNTUGUESE with two pairs.

Table 1. Two puns and their non-humorous version from Puntuguese.

No-pun	Pun
Porque é que o poste caiu? Vento forte	Porque é que o poste caiu? Tinha alta tensão
Um homem matou uma ovelha e agora foi preso. Está na cadeia	Um lobo matou uma ovelha e agora foi preso. Está na cadeia alimentar

To select the best hyper-parameters for fine-tuning in the PUNTUGUESE dataset, we used Weights & Biases[2] for a Bayesian Search, minimizing the loss on the dataset's designated validation split. The optimized values are: 50 training epochs and a learning rate of 1×10^{-3}. For more frequent monitoring of the training progress, we employed a step-based evaluation strategy, which evaluated the model every 100 training steps rather than after each epoch.

---

[1] PUNTUGUESE is available at https://huggingface.co/datasets/Superar/Puntuguese.
[2] https://wandb.ai.

4.2   Genetic Algorithm

The original implementation of GALMET is publicly available[3] and prepared for evolving English headlines. Its adaptation to Portuguese required changing the models used for mutation and for computing the fitness.

Mutations may result from three different operations: (i) addition of token; (ii) deletion of token; or (iii) substitution of token. Adaptation of the latter required an MLM for Portuguese, leading us to BERTimbau-Base (aka "bert-base-portuguese-cased") [28], based on the BERT architecture. Like other MLMs, given a sequence of text with a masked token ([MASK]), the pretrained BERT suggests suitable replacements for this token, considering context.

When we observed that the masked tokens could be parts of words (sub-words), and that this could lead to strange outputs, we decided to make an additional change in the substitution operator, and force it to always select complete words. Specifically, for any selected token, if it is part of a longer word, a single mask replaces all tokens belonging to this word. This is possible because, in BERTimbau's tokenizer, sub-words start with "##".

The original fitness function of GALMET considers the Levenshtein distance between each individual and the input text, and a funniness score, given by a RoBERTa model fine-tuned for this specific purpose. Since we are not aware of data available for training such a model in Portuguese (i.e., text with funniness ratings), we considered two alternatives for computing the fitness of each individual in Portuguese. One was again based on BERTimbau Base, fine-tuned in the PUNTUGUESE corpus for pun recognition. This model achieved the best performance in classifying text as punning or not [14] and is publicly available[4]. Although the model is not trained for scoring jokes, we used the softmax score as an approximation to how close the classified text would be to a pun.

The second fitness function follows the more and more popular LLM-as-judge [17] paradigm, and is based on prompting a quantized version of Llama 3.3-70B [11] for scoring how funny a given text is, using the system prompt in Table 2, with temperature set to 0.

Table 2. System prompt used for humor evaluation.

> You are a Humor evaluator. Your task is to rate the funniness of a given text from 0 to 1, where 0 means 'not funny at all' and 1 means 'extremely funny'. Return just a number between 0.00 and 0.99, nothing else.

The best hyper-parameters for running GALMET (depicted in Table 3) were selected, among a set of 50 randomly chosen options, by maximizing the average fitness in our experiments.

---

[3] https://github.com/twinters/galmet.
[4] https://huggingface.co/Superar/pun-recognition-pt.

Table 3. Hyper-parameters selected for GALMET.

Hyper-parameter	Value	Hyper-parameter	Value
Crossover Probability	0.3418	Elite Duplicates	5
Total Mutation Probability	0.8476	Mutate Token Probability	0.8071
Population Size	500	Add Token Probability	0.0648
Number of Generations	30	Remove Token Probability	0.0990
Goal Fitness	0.99	Number of Mutations	3
Max Edit Distance	8	Human Check	False
Max Elites	4		

4.3   Instruction-Tuned LLMs

Llama 3.3 (70B) [11], Gemma 3 (27B) [7], and Llama distilled from DeepSeek-R1 (70B) [5], all used in a 4-bit quantized version through Ollama[5], were explored for Humor Generation in Portuguese. Each model was provided with the same system prompt (Table 4) in two different settings: (i) zero-shot; and (ii) 10-shot. The prompt was in Portuguese and included: a short definition of joke; an instruction for assigning the role of a comedian to the model, followed by an explanation of the task; and some additional rules. The user prompt included the input text and, only for the 10-shot, ten examples randomly selected collected from PUNTUGUESE, presented as shown in Table 4. Temperature was set to 0.7.

Table 4. System and user prompts for generating a joke from an input.

System prompt
Uma piada é uma exibição de Humor em que as palavras são usadas dentro de uma estrutura narrativa específica e bem definida para fazer as pessoas rirem e geralmente não devem ser levadas a sério
Você é um comediante português com um talento excepcional para criar piadas inteligentes e criativas. Sua missão é transformar um texto comum em uma versão bem-humorada, incorporando trocadilhos ou jogos de palavras sempre que possível. Mantenha o conteúdo original o mais intacto possível, alterando apenas o necessário para gerar Humor
REGRAS:
– Não explique a piada nem comente o resultado
– Responda apenas com o texto modificado, já com as piadas incorporadas
– Seja criativo, mas preserve a estrutura e o contexto do texto original
– Adicione sempre conteudo para gerar Humor, focando na criação de piadas
User prompt
Transforma o seguinte texto numa piada: "[TEXT]" {Exemplos: [EXAMPLE_1] [EXAMPLE_2] ...}*

---

[5] https://ollama.ai/.

5   Experimentation

To reach conclusions on the suitability of each approach, they were tested with the top headlines in Google News for Brazil and Portugal on January 30th, 2025. For each country, we selected 15 headlines—five from each of the following categories: Science and Technology, Entertainment, Sports—totaling 30 texts, with some examples in Table 5. These were treated as a benchmark, allowing us to measure the performance of each approach for identical inputs.

Table 5. Example of headlines.

ID	Headline
H01	Juventus-Benfica, 0–2 Os destaques do Benfica: Um, dois, três... tantos Florentinos
H02	Não gostou, mas usou! Vânia Sá veste polémico vestido de Inês Morais após discussões sem fim
H03	Falámos com José Condessa. Eis o que esperar do futuro de 'Rabo de Peixe'
H04	E assim foi o terceiro episódio de "A Herança"
H05	A Apple não quer mais os iPhones ficando sem internet
H06	Vodafone realiza primeira videochamada espacial do mundo com smartphone
H07	Champions League sorteia nesta sexta-feira os cruzamentos dos playoffs e oitavas de final. Confira os times e o chaveamento

5.1   Evaluation Protocols

Given the subjectivity of Humor, we conducted a human evaluation with 19 native speakers of European Portuguese (ages 19–60). Each participant evaluated the results for 3–4 headlines, with every generated text evaluated by two different judges. The headline was followed by the generated texts, in a random order, and two aspects were to be scored, using a 3-point scale: Funniness, i.e., how funny the text was—(1) Not funny at all, (2) A bit funny, (3) Funny; and Relation, i.e., how semantically-related the text is to the original headline—(1) Not related at all, (2) A bit related (iii) Related.

5.2   Results

Figures 2 and 3 present the distribution of the ratings for funniness and relation, respectively. Table 6 complements the previous with the median scores, the consensus, computed with the Tastle-Wierman formula [30], which was designed specifically for Likert-scale evaluations and the Krippendorff's alpha values [15]. While the latter tells us if the evaluators agreed with each other overall, the Tastle-Wierman consensus tells us how close their answers are to each other. Together, they help us understand not just whether people gave similar ratings, but also how focused or spread out those ratings were. Table 7 illustrates the output of the system with the funniest results by each approach.

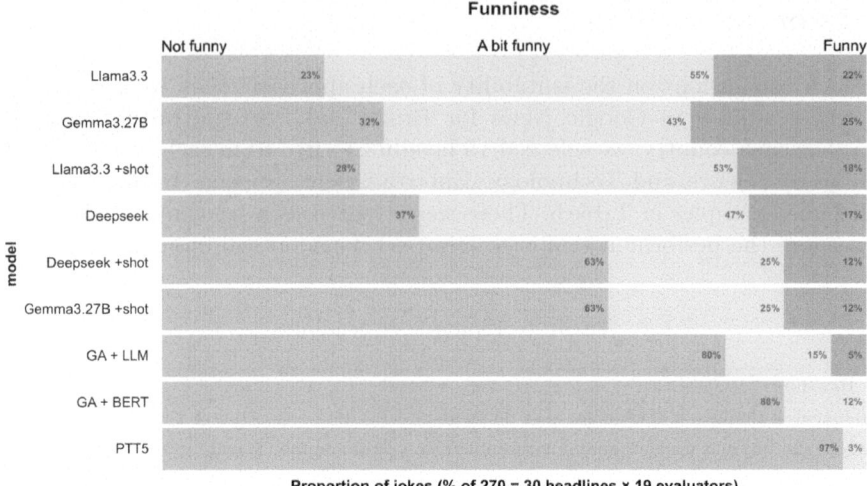

Fig. 2. Funniness ratings distribution.

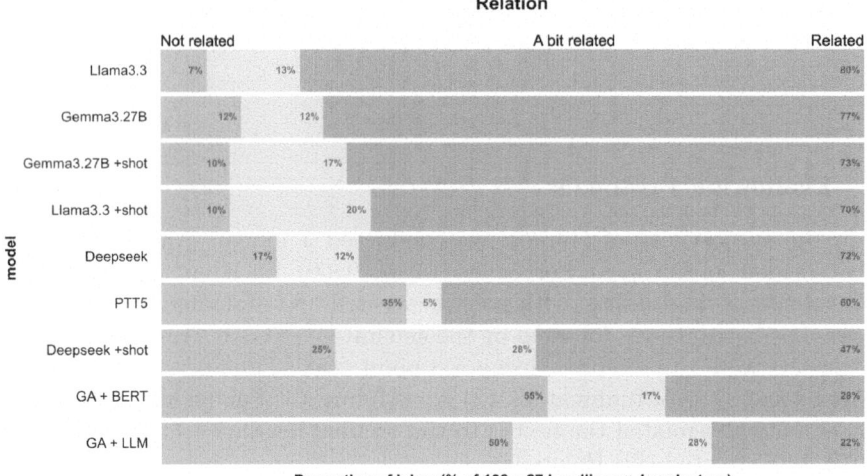

Fig. 3. Relation ratings distribution.

Figure 2 shows that, despite targeting Humor Generation, and according to human opinions, all the approaches still produce many non-humorous texts. Nevertheless, some approaches produce a majority of texts that are at least a bit funny, whereas the worst ones completely fail to do so. The highest proportion of funny texts (18–25%) is obtained with the instruction-tuned LLMs, in a zero-shot scenario, and Llama in 10-shot. These are the approaches that tend to generate fewer texts that are not funny at all, with Llama 3.3 being the model where this proportion is lower (23%). Llama 3.3 is also the model with the highest proportion of texts that are semantically related to the input (as seen in Fig. 3), and one for which the participants agreed relatively more on their assessment. This suggests that Llama 3.3 is the most suitable for our task.

Curiously, the inclusion of examples in the prompts did not help, as the zero-shot approaches were all preferable to 10-shot with the same models. In fact, seeing examples does not seem to help, as the worse results (97% not funny) were obtained with the fine-tuned T5, which frequently produced outputs identical to the original headlines. This suggests that, despite the data available in PUNTUGUESE ($\approx$4,000 training examples), PTT5 was not able to learn the specific task of rewriting a text into its humorous version, likely due to the low variation in the dataset, where humorous texts usually differ by only one or two tokens from the non-humorous. This small variation might not be enough for the model to learn how to transform the text. When assessing the relation to the input, consensus, as depicted in Table 6, was particularly low (0.09), further suggesting difficulty in evaluating the generated text. However, this is contrasted by a moderate Krippendorff's alpha ($\alpha = 0.57$), indicating that the users still showed some agreement in their relation judgments despite the low consensus score. In other words, while users differed in their exact ratings, they generally agreed on which outputs were more or less related to the original input.

The generating texts related to the input was more successful, but this becomes less relevant to our objectives when Humor is not present. In this aspect, only the GA-based approaches failed to produce more than 50% of their texts that were even slightly related to the input. Some examples are shown in Table 7, where the output can be considered humorous but often unrelated to the main topic. Even when it comes to Humor, the GA-based fell behind our expectations, being only slightly better than PTT5. Using an LLM as the fitness function seems like a better option than using the pun classifier, but low proportion of funny texts makes it hard to make stronger conclusions.

Table 6. Evaluation scores per model. Med = median (1–3); Cons = consensus (Tastle-Wierman, 0–1); α = Krippendorff's alpha for inter-annotator agreement.

Model	Fun. (Med)	Fun. (Cons)	Rel. (Med)	Rel. (Cons)	Fun. (α)	Rel. (α)
PTT5	1.0	**0.79**	**3.0**	0.09	**0.49**	**0.57**
GA + BERT	1.0	0.48	1.0	0.19	−0.01	0.19
GA + LLM	1.0	0.59	2.0	0.30	0.11	0.18
Deepseek	**2.0**	0.44	**3.0**	0.32	0.05	0.21
Deepseek +shot	1.0	0.40	2.0	0.28	0.06	0.26
Gemma3.27B	**2.0**	0.42	**3.0**	0.43	0.27	0.33
Gemma3.27B +shot	1.0	0.40	**3.0**	0.45	0.20	0.31
LLaMA3.3	**2.0**	0.54	**3.0**	**0.55**	0.19	0.40
LLaMA3.3 +shot	**2.0**	0.50	**3.0**	0.44	0.27	0.24

Table 7. Best jokes generated by each model, based on human evaluation. Average scores for funniness and relation are included.

ID	Model	Generated Joke	Fun. (Avg.)	Rel. (Avg.)
H01	PTT5	Juventus-Benfica, 0–2 Os destaques do Benfica: Um, dois, três... tantos Florentinos	1.5	2.0
H02	GA + BERT	Não gostou, mas usou!ânia Sá veste polémico vestido de modo Fis discussõescu fim	1.5	2.5
H03	GA + LLM	Falámos com José Condesssa. E o que esperar do ministro? ' Rabo de Pee?	2.5	2.5
H04	DeepSeek	E assim foi o terceiro episódio de "A Herança", onde os herdeiros descobriram que a única coisa que realmente herdaram foram as dívidas do pai e as sardas da mãe. Quem diria que a herança mais valiosa seria o problema de escolher entre pagar ou tapar!	3.0	3.0
H05	DeepSeek +shot	A Apple não quer mais os iPhones ficando sem iMãe.	2.0	1.5
H06	Gemma3.27B	Champions League sorteia nesta sexta-feira os cruzamentos dos playoffs e oitavas de final. Preparem os amendoins e as pipocas, porque o sorteio promete ser de "chaves" altas! Dizem que alguns clubes já estão a treinar a sorte, para não ficarem "às oito" nas oitavas. Confiram os times e o chaveamento, e lembrem-se: no futebol, como na vida, nem sempre a gente "chuta" para o gol certo!	2.0	2.0
H07	Gemma3.27B +shot	Vodafone realiza primeira videochamada espacial do mundo com smartphone... Parece que a cobertura finalmente chegou às estrelas, agora até o ET pode reclamar da fatura!	2.5	3.0
H08	Llama3.3	Champions League sorteia nesta sexta-feira os cruzamentos dos playoffs e oitavas de final, ou como alguns jogadores chamam, 'o começo do fim da sua carreira se você não ganhar'. Confira os times e o chaveamento, mas não se preocupe se você não entender, é como tentar ler um mapa para encontrar o caminho para a final... sem GPS, nem Messi para te ajudar!	3.0	3.0
H09	Llama3.3 +shot	Juventus-Benfica, 0–2. Os destaques do Benfica? Bem, foi um show de 'flores'... ou melhor, Florentinos! Parecia que a Juventus estava em 'flor' de desalinho, enquanto o Benfica estava 'semeando' gols por toda parte!	2.5	3.0

By analyzing the consensus and agreement for all models, we can understand the subjectivity of Humor, highlighting that human evaluators each had an inherent personal nature of what they considered funny. We also point out that consensus for relation scores is exceptionally low, with correspondingly low alpha values showing that even determining how related a joke is to its non-humorous counterpart involves some subjectivity, especially when dealing with texts close to a nonsensical interpretation.

6   Conclusion

In this paper, we explored various approaches for rewriting Portuguese short texts in a funny way, where transformers were: (i) fine-tuned; (ii) used for mutating and scoring individuals in a genetic algorithm; (iii) instructed through a prompt. Text by each approach for a set of headlines were assessed by humans, considering two criteria: funniness and relation of the text to the headline.

Results suggest that the funniest outputs are generated by prompting larger general-purpose models. This is different from classification tasks, where it is generally preferable to have a smaller but specialized fine-tuned model [3]. However, rewriting a textual input as humorous involves minimal and subtle edits, which can be challenging to learn. For better dealing with this task, general-purpose LLMs are probably taking advantage of the higher amount of data that they have seen during pretraining, in various formats, registers, and languages. However, it is important to note that these results are for our implemented approaches and, it is possible that a more heavily fine-tuned model or a more complex genetic algorithm could reach similar or even superior results to the LLMs tested in this paper.

Despite the pioneering results for Humor Generation in Portuguese, as well as the interesting findings, this work has limitations. First, the results were obtained through a single run, when both the LLMs and the GA are inherently stochastic, meaning that a single run may not fully capture the potential and variability of these approaches. Second, the runtime of the GA-based method is significantly higher than for the LLM-based approaches (about 55 min *vs* about 2 min), which affects its practicality and real-world use.[6] Another limitation is related to our use of MLMs for Portuguese, which include subword vocabularies due to tokenizer constraints, therefore compromising the quality of generated mutations. Lastly, the involvement of human evaluators introduces subjectivity, a limitation that may lead to inconsistencies in the results, since human opinions may vary.

All of our code and data will be made publicly available upon acceptance of the paper. Future improvements may result from experimenting with other models, especially larger and non-quantized ones. This would include fine-tuning transformers beyond PTT5; prompting other LLMs, for text rewriting or for the fitness function of the GA; or testing other MLMs for the mutation operator.

Acknowledgments. This work was supported by the Portuguese Recovery and Resilience Plan through project C645008882-00000055, Center for Responsible AI; and by national funds through FCT – Foundation for Science and Technology, I.P. (grant number UI/BD/153496/2022), within the scope of the project CISUC (UIDB/00326/2025 and UIDP/00326/2025).

---

[6] All experiments were performed in a Intel(R) Xeon(R) Silver 4310 CPU @ 2.10 GHz, 12 cores, 2 threads per core, 256 GB RAM, with the LLMs running in a NVIDIA RTX A6000 GPU, with 48 GB vRAM.

Disclosure of Interests. The authors have no competing interests to declare that are relevant to the content of this article.

References

1. Amin, M., Burghardt, M.: A survey on approaches to computational humor generation. In: Proceedings of the 4th Joint SIGHUM Workshop on Computational Linguistics for Cultural Heritage, Social Sciences, Humanities and Literature, pp. 29–41. International Committee on Computational Linguistics, Online (2020)
2. Binsted, K., Ritchie, G.: An implemented model of punning riddles. University of Edinburgh, Department of Artificial Intelligence (1994)
3. Bucher, M.J.J., Martini, M.: Fine-tuned 'small' LLMs (still) significantly outperform zero-shot generative AI models in text classification. arXiv preprint arXiv:2406.08660 (2024)
4. Chen, Y., Shi, B., Si, M.: Prompt to GPT-3: step-by-step thinking instructions for humor generation. arXiv preprint arXiv:2306.13195 (2023)
5. DeepSeek-AI: DeepSeek-R1: incentivizing reasoning capability in LLMs via reinforcement learning (2025). https://arxiv.org/abs/2501.12948
6. Dybala, P., Ptaszynski, M., Higuchi, S., Rzepka, R., Araki, K.: Humor prevails! - implementing a joke generator into a conversational system. In: Wobcke, W., Zhang, M. (eds.) AI 2008. LNCS (LNAI), vol. 5360, pp. 214–225. Springer, Heidelberg (2008). https://doi.org/10.1007/978-3-540-89378-3_21
7. Gemma Team: Gemma 3 technical report. arXiv preprint arXiv:2503.19786 (2025)
8. Gonçalo Oliveira, H., Costa, D., Pinto, A.: One does not simply produce funny memes! – explorations on the automatic generation of Internet humor. In: Proceedings of the 7th International Conference on Computational Creativity, ICCC 2016, Paris, France, pp. 238–245 (2016)
9. Gonçalo Oliveira, H., Rodrigues, R.: Exploring lexical-semantic knowledge in the generation of novel riddles in Portuguese. In: Proceedings of the 3rd Workshop on Computational Creativity in Natural Language Generation (CC-NLG), pp. 17–25 (2018)
10. Gorenz, D., Schwarz, N.: How funny is ChatGPT? A comparison of human- and A.I.-produced jokes. PLoS One **19**(7), e0305364 (2024)
11. Grattafiori, A., Dubey, A., Jauhri, A., et al.: The LLaMA 3 herd of models. arXiv preprint arXiv:2407.21783 (2024)
12. Hurley, M.M., Dennett, D.C., Adams, R.B.: Inside Jokes: Using Humor to Reverse-Engineer the Mind. The MIT Press (2011)
13. Inácio, M.L., Gonçalo Oliveira, H.: Generation of punning riddles in Portuguese with prompt chaining. In: Proceedings of the 15th International Conference on Computational Creativity. ICCC, ACC, Jönköping, Sweden (2024)
14. Inácio, M.L., et al.: Puntuguese: a corpus of puns in Portuguese with micro-edits. In: Proceedings of the 2024 Joint International Conference on Computational Linguistics, Language Resources and Evaluation (LREC-COLING 2024), pp. 13332–13343. ELRA and ICCL, Torino (2024)
15. Krippendorff, K.: Bivariate agreement coefficients for reliability of data. Sociol. Methodol. **2**, 139–150 (1970)
16. Labutov, I., Lipson, H.: Humor as circuits in semantic networks. In: Proceedings of the 50th Annual Meeting of the Association for Computational Linguistics (Volume 2: Short Papers), pp. 150–155 (2012)

17. Li, H., et al.: LLMs-as-judges: a comprehensive survey on LLM-based evaluation methods. arXiv preprint arXiv:2412.05579 (2024)
18. Mendes, R., Gonçalo Oliveira, H.: Amplifying the range of news stories with creativity: Methods and their evaluation, in Portuguese. In: Proceedings of the 13th International Conference on Natural Language Generation, pp. 252–262 (2020)
19. Mittal, A., Tian, Y., Peng, N.: AmbiPun: Generating humorous puns with ambiguous context. In: Proc. 2022 Conference of the North American Chapter of the Association for Computational Linguistics: Human Language Technologies, pp. 1053–1062. ACL, Seattle (2022)
20. Petrović, S., Matthews, D.: Unsupervised joke generation from big data. In: Proceedings of the 51st annual meeting of the association for computational linguistics (volume 2: Short papers), pp. 228–232 (2013)
21. Piau, M., Lotufo, R., Nogueira, R.: ptt5-v2: a closer look at continued pretraining of T5 models for the Portuguese language. In: Paes, A., Verri, F.A.N. (eds.) BRACIS 2024. LNCS, vol. 15413, pp. 324–338. Springer, Cham (2024). https://doi.org/10.1007/978-3-031-79032-4_23
22. Raffel, C., et al.: Exploring the limits of transfer learning with a unified text-to-text Transformer. J. Mach. Learn. Res. 21(140), 1–67 (2020)
23. Raskin, J.D., Attardo, S.: Non-literalness and non-bona-fide in language: An approach to formal and computational treatments of humor. Pragmat. Cogn. 2(1), 31–69 (1994)
24. Ren, H., Yang, Q.: Neural joke generation. Technical report, Stanford University (2017). Final Project Reports of Course CS224n
25. Ritchie, G., Manurung, R., Pain, H., Waller, A., Black, R., O'Mara, D.: A practical application of computational humour. In: Proceedings of the 4th International Joint Conference on Computational Creativity, London, UK, pp. 91–98 (2007)
26. Savage, B.M., Lujan, H.L., Thipparthi, R.R., DiCarlo, S.E.: Humor, laughter, learning, and health! A brief review. Adv. Physiol. Educ. 41(3), 341–347 (2017)
27. Sjöbergh, J., Araki, K.: A complete and modestly funny system for generating and performing Japanese stand-up comedy. In: Coling 2008: Companion volume: Posters, pp. 111–114 (2008)
28. Souza, F., Nogueira, R., Lotufo, R.: BERTimbau: pretrained BERT models for Brazilian Portuguese. In: 9th Brazilian Conference on Intelligent Systems, BRACIS, Rio Grande do Sul, Brazil (2020)
29. Stock, O., Strapparava, C.: HAHAcronym: a computational humor system. In: Proceedings of the ACL Interactive Poster and Demonstration Sessions, pp. 113–116. ACL, Ann Arbor (2005)
30. Tastle, W.J., Wierman, M.J.: Consensus and dissention: a measure of ordinal dispersion. Int. J. Approximate Reasoning 45(3), 531–545 (2007)
31. Valitutti, A., Doucet, A., Toivanen, J.M., Toivonen, H.: Computational generation and dissection of lexical replacement humor. Nat. Lang. Eng. 22(5), 727–749 (2016)
32. Winters, T., Delobelle, P.: Survival of the wittiest: evolving satire with language models. In: Proceedings of the 12th International Conference on Computational Creativity (ICCC 2021), pp. 82–86. ACC) (2021)
33. Yu, Z., Tan, J., Wan, X.: A neural approach to pun generation. In: Proceedings of the 56th Annual Meeting of the Association for Computational Linguistics (Volume 1: Long Papers), pp. 1650–1660. ACL (2018)

Artificial Intelligence in Power and Energy Systems (AIPES)

Reinforcement Learning for Real-Time Price Prediction in Energy Systems

David Araújo⬛, Gabriel Santos$^{(\boxtimes)}$ ⬛, Brígida Teixeira⬛, Pedro Faria⬛,
and Zita Vale⬛

GECAD - Research Group on Intelligent Engineering and Computing for Advanced Innovation
and Development, LASI - Intelligent Systems Associate Laboratory, ISEP, Polytechnic of Porto,
Rua Dr. António Bernardino de Almeida, 4249-015 Porto, Portugal
{ddsaa,gjs,bccta,pnf,zav}@isep.ipp.pt

Abstract. The integration of renewable energy sources into modern electricity
systems introduces high uncertainty, making energy related forecasts increasingly
complex. This paper proposes a framework to forecast Iberian day-ahead market clearing prices using multiple forecasting techniques, from pure statistical to
machine learning models. A reinforcement learning approach dynamically selects
the best forecasting model for each negotiation period. The methodology was validated using market price data from Portugal and Spain. All models underwent
sensitivity analysis to determine optimal parameters and were cyclically retrained
to incorporate new data patterns. The case study focuses on the first half of 2024,
during which the reinforcement learning model continuously adapted based on
real prices and model predictions, identifying the most suitable approach at each
iteration. The models used in the study include Ridge Regression, Stochastic Gradient Descent, Random Forest, Extreme Gradient Boost, Deep Neural Network,
and Long Short-Term Memory. Results showed that the proposed method outperforms individual models, achieving performance improvements ranging from
7.27% to 88.38% compared to using any of the models alone.

Keywords: Day-Ahead Market · Machine Learning · Market Clearing Price
Forecasting · Reinforcement Learning · Statistical models

1 Introduction

The increasing complexity of modern energy systems, combined with the introduction
of renewable energy sources (RES), such as solar and wind, requires intelligent, effective and adaptive energy management, as these are sensitive to weather conditions [1].
Renewable energy is essential for sustainability, but it presents challenges due to its variability and unpredictability, complicating price forecasting and grid stability. Climate
change is a global concern that affects natural systems and their development, threaten-
ing the availability of renewable resources [2]. Therefore, defining optimal operations
in energy projects is complex and requires clear methodologies.

With the emerging evolution of Artificial Intelligence (AI), it can be very beneficial
in helping to anticipate events in the power and energy systems (PES) field, such as

J. Valente de Oliveira et al. (Eds.): EPIA 2025, LNAI 16122, pp. 451–463, 2026.
https://doi.org/10.1007/978-3-032-05179-0_34

helping to predict electricity prices. To this end, several machine learning (ML) and statistical models are capable of analysing and indicating the best prediction for a given target of a data set [3].

ML models handle large data sets, identifying hidden patterns and trends, offering greater adaptability and performance in dynamic environments. The applicability of statistical and ML technologies is fundamental to predict electricity consumption, generation or price. The study presented by Lipu *et al.* [4], indicates that intelligent automation using ML may result in substantial savings.

Predictive modelling can be approached using different methodologies, depending on the nature of the problem and the characteristics of the data. Statistical models rely on mathematical formulations to interpret relationships between variables, based on historical data [5]. One of the most widely used types of statistical models is regression, which is specifically designed to predict more complex continuous variables. Regression is a statistical methodology that was developed to predict continuous variables. There are several types of regression, such as: simple or multiple linear and non-linear and polynomial.

However, in dynamic environments, where data is not constant, simply choosing a single model may not be enough to guarantee the best results. It is necessary to address more flexible methodologies that can deal with data variability. To optimize selection and prediction, Reinforcement Learning (RL) has emerged as a promising technique. RL allows systems to learn and adapt through interaction with their environment, using feedback mechanisms to optimize decision-making over time [6]. In the context of energy systems, RL can be used to dynamically select prediction models, optimizing energy consumption by adjusting to user preferences, leading to cost reduction, thus promoting sustainability [7]. This work proposes a novel framework integrating ML-based models with RL to predict daily market prices in the Iberian market.

The remaining of the manuscript is organized as follows. The Related Work section addresses existing work, identifying the gap addressed by this work. The Methodology section exposes the system´s architecture and operation. The Case Study section characterizes and presents the used data along with an overview of the execution process. The Results and Discussion section details and analysis the achieved results. Finally, the Conclusions section presents the main reflections.

2   Related Work

The integration of RES and energy storage in smart grids (SG) is increasingly common as it is beneficial for the environment [8]. The use of ML methods in the scope of SG, for forecasting distinct data, has proven to be very useful and relevant in recent years, with a reduction in energy consumption of between 20% and 40%, including a reduction in the execution and response times [9].

A study by Pinto *et al.* [10] compared three forecasting models for short-term electrical load forecasting. The models analysed were Gradient Boosted Regression Trees, Random Forest (RF), and AdaBoost. By exploring the correlation of variables, they concluded that there was a significant improvement in forecasting, responding to the challenges of highly dynamic energy systems.

A study by Teixeira *et al.* [11] evaluated the impact of forecasting methods on wholesale electricity market participation, highlighting that model selection based solely on accuracy can overlook the economic effects of prediction errors. Using a simulation model applied to the Iberian market, the authors analysed how price forecasting deviations affect trading outcomes. They proposed a RL approach to select forecasting models based on both prediction performance and economic impact, showing that even small errors can significantly affect profitability.

In a study focused on forecasting electricity prices, for daily and intraday markets at the Iberian level, statistical models were used [12]. Historical data from the Iberian market, were used. This dataset includes features such as date, period, wind and solar power generation, load, among others. Gradient Boosting Trees (GBT) and Linear Quantile (LQ) were the models used in this study.

An RL model was implemented for the adaptive control of energy consumption forecasting in building contexts [13]. The results showed an increase in forecast accuracy and flexibility in adapting to various energy usage scenarios. A study carried out by Pinto *et al.* [14], uses RL to select the best trading strategy in electricity markets.

Most existing solutions do not use a sufficient variety of prediction models. This ends up being a limitation, as including more models and integrating them with RL for continuous learning has proven beneficial, improving prediction results [15]. This work proposes a novel framework combining ML-based algorithms with RL to forecast day-ahead market clearing prices in the scope of the Iberian electricity market. It comprises 6 statistical and ML-based regression models and a reward function to determine the best forecasting model at each time. Table 1 overviews existing adaptive selection techniques.

Table 1. Overview of existing adaptive selection techniques and the proposed framework.

Study	Application Domain	Adaptive selection
[10]	Short-term load forecast	N/A
[11]	Day-ahead market price forecast	Selection based on prediction performance and economic impact
[12]	Day-ahead and Intraday markets price forecast	N/A
[13]	Building consumption forecasting	Selection based on prediction performance
[14]	Electricity markets trading strategies	Selection based on best trading strategy

From Table 1, there are already a few works using RL to improve forecast accuracy. Although the work [11] is also applied to day-ahead market price forecasting, it differs in the way the selection is made by RL, as it not considers a balance between the current and previous rewards. The next section presents the methodology of the proposed framework, describing its architecture and operation.

3 Methodology

The proposed framework integrates ML-based models with RL to support players in electricity markets by predicting the most probable market clearing price for a given transaction period. Figure 1 represents the conceptual diagram of the proposed tool.

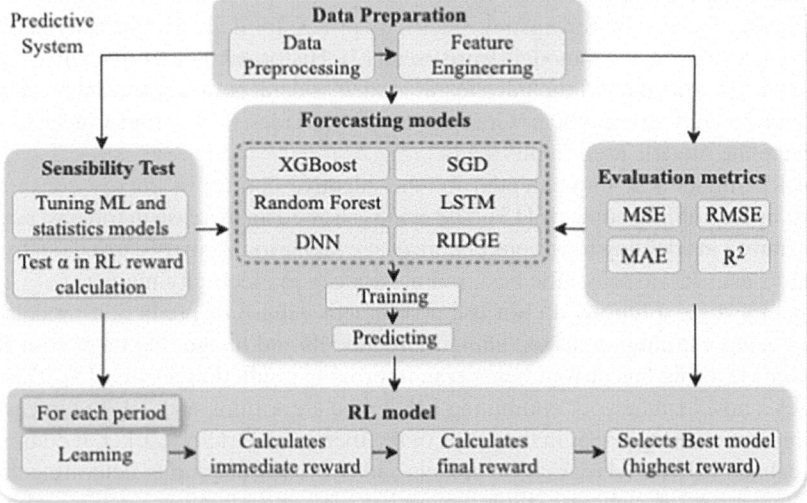

Fig. 1. Conceptual model diagram.

The tool execution starts with the Data Preparation. Data preprocessing is carried out, obtaining publicly available data from the Iberian market operator (OMIE) and system operators (i.e., REE – Red Eléctrica de España, REN – Redes Energéticas Nacionais). This data is normalized, possible missing data are computed and included, and data standardization is performed. In Feature Engineering, categorical variables are transformed into several binary columns using One-hot encoding [16], which enables the model to understand each category as a separate and independent feature.

Advanced ML and statistical models were selected and deployed as Forecasting models. Currently, it includes 6 forecasting models from Scikit-learn [17] and Tensor-Flow [18] libraries, of which two are pure statistical models, namely Ridge Regression (RR) and Stochastic Gradient Descent (SGD), two are ML models, more precisely RF and XGBoost, and finally, and the last two are deep learning (DL) models, specifically DNN and LSTM. These methods are subjected to Sensitivity Test to find the best parameterization for a specific data set using Grid Search [19].

An RL technique is used, which aims to obtain the best forecasting model at each moment. To do this, the RL model selects the most suitable model for each period of each day, through an individual and cumulative reward. The central basis of the method is the Mean Squared Error (MSE) Evaluation metric, which is used for forecasting models. The RL model process starts by calculating the MSE for each predicted value. The MSE values of each model are normalized and adjusted to a range from 0 to 1, thus ensuring scale equivalence and preventing excess values. The reward for each instant is calculated for each model using Eq. (1):

$$Immediate\ reward = 1 - \frac{(MSE_i) - min(MSE_i)}{max(MSE_i) - min(MSE_i)} \tag{1}$$

Equation (1) normalizes the reward across all models, assigning the highest reward to the model that achieved the lowest MSE. At the end of each period i, the calculated reward is added to the individual rewards of each model. If there is no reward history, then the instant reward will be the first reward. If there is already a history, the reward is updated as shown in Eq. (2):

$$Final\ reward = \frac{\alpha * immediate\ reward}{(1 - \alpha) * previous\ reward} \tag{2}$$

In Eq. (2) α is a decision factor, since it prioritizes historical or instant reward. For example, if α is equal to 50%, the final reward will have a balance between the immediate reward and the previous reward. If the α is greater than 50%, the immediate reward is prioritized. On the other hand, if α is less than 50%, priority will be given to the historical reward. The RL model calculates the reward of each model per period. Therefore, the RL model selects the Forecasting model with the higher reward.

Once the best parameterization of the statistical and ML models has been found using an automated ML mechanism, a Sensitivity Test is performed on the RL model to test various percentage values of α. For the sensitivity test, four model evaluation techniques were used to optimize the parameterization of each model, and to evaluate each model's outcomes: MSE, RMSE, MAE and Coefficient of determination (R^2). MSE calculates the squared error between the predicted value and the actual value, penalizing large errors. RMSE calculates the root of the MSE value, reflecting the average deviations between the predicted and actual values. MAE calculates the mean absolute error but is less sensitive to outliers. The MSE, RMSE, and MAE metrics indicate whether the model has good performance when their values are closer to zero, whereas the opposite happens with the R^2 technique, indicating the proportion of the data variance explained by the model. The configuration with the best results will be selected as the optimal one.

4   Case Study

The objective of this case study is to predict electricity market prices, more specifically in the Iberian day-ahead market, aiming to support its players with valuable predictions. To demonstrate the applicability and benefit of the proposed tool, data from REN [20], REE [21] and OMIE [22] were used, ranging from January to June 2024. Each data record is characterized by its timeframe, comprising the year, month, day, day of the week and the hourly period. Table 2 presents the features extracted from REN and REE data, identifying the total electricity volume generated and consumed in Portugal and Spain, respectively. REN provides this data at a 15-min interval, whereas REE only makes available the daily total volumes. In the case of REN data, 15-min periods are grouped into hourly periods. On the other hand, REE data is used as is for each hourly period of the day without any type of disaggregation. REN and REE data are made publicly available at 1:00 a.m., Central European Time (CET), of the following day.

Table 2. Features extracted from REN and REE data.

Feature	Description	Country
E-act-wind-pt-(d,h)	Total volume of wind energy produced PT	Portugal
E-act-wind-es-(d,h)	Total volume of wind energy produced ES	Spain
E-act-solar-pt-(d,h)	Total volume of photovoltaic energy produced PT	Portugal
E-act-solar-es-(d,h)	Total volume of photovoltaic energy produced ES	Spain
E-act-hydro-pt-(d,h)	Total volume of hydro energy produced PT	Portugal
E-act-hydro-es-(d,h)	Total volume of hydro energy produced ES	Spain
E-act-nuclear-es-(d,h)	Total volume of nuclear energy produced ES	Spain
E-act-load-pt-(d,h)	Total volume of energy consumed PT	Portugal
E-act-load-es-(d,h)	Total volume of energy consumed ES	Spain

Table 3, in turn, displays the features obtained from OMIE's day-ahead result data. These features identify the total energy volume traded in the day-ahead market for each of the previous unit types (i.e., wind, photovoltaic, hydro, nuclear and load), and the market clearing price for each country. OMIE's day-ahead data is made publicly available every day at 2 p.m. CET.

Table 3. Features extracted from OMIE data.

Feature	Description	Country
E-dam-wind-pt-(d,h)	Total volume of wind energy traded PT	Portugal
E-dam-wind-es-(d,h)	Total volume of wind energy traded ES	Spain
E-dam-solar-pt-(d,h)	Total volume of photovoltaic energy traded PT	Portugal
E-dam-solar-es-(d,h)	Total volume of photovoltaic energy traded ES	Spain
E-dam-hydro-pt-(d,h)	Total volume of hydro energy traded PT	Portugal
E-dam-hydro-es-(d,h)	Total volume of hydro energy traded ES	Spain
E-dam-nuclear-es-(d,h)	Total volume of nuclear energy traded ES	Spain
E-dam-load-pt-(d,h)	Total volume of load energy traded PT	Portugal
E-dam-load-es-(d,h)	Total volume of load energy traded ES	Spain
mcp-pt-(d,h)	Market clearing price PT	Portugal
mcp-es-(d,h)	Market clearing price ES	Spain

Each feature introduced in Table 2 and Table 3 comprises data for a given 'day' and 'hourly period' (d,h). To these features are also added analogous features for the same hourly period (h) of the previous three days (i.e., d-1,h; d-2,h; d-3,h), except for the total volumes of energy consumed, the total volumes of load energy traded, and the market clearing price in Portugal and Spain. For the load energy related features, four extra features are added, namely, a feature for the same measurement at the same hourly period of the previous day (d-1,h); two features for the adjacent periods of the previous feature (i.e., d-1,h-1; d-1,h + 1); and a feature for the same measurement at the same hourly period one week earlier (d-7,h). To each market clearing price feature, five new features are included. The first four features are similar to the ones introduced for the load energy features, while the fifth feature is for the same measurement at the same hourly period two weeks earlier (d-14,h). Thus, this study comprises a total of 93 features, being the target feature the market clearing price of Portugal for the following day (i.e., mcp-pt-(d,h)).

All forecasting models have been through a sensitive test to optimize their parameterization. To this end, after the data preparation step, each of these models has been trained with data from January 2024. Subsequently, the RL model was trained using data from February 2024, where each forecasting model has been used to predict the respective market clearing prices. Finally, the March 2024 data was used to test the performance of the RL model. Figure 2 illustrates this timeline, showing the data periods used for training and testing during the sensitivity test.

Fig. 2. Overview of the data split for the sensitivity test.

The sensitivity test of the RL model was performed with three α percentages (see Eq. (2)), namely, 20%, 50%, and 80%. In all tests, the RL model stood out as the best prediction model in relation to the remaining forecasting models, having the best performance with $\alpha = 20\%$. It means that, when the RL model computes the reward for each forecasting model, a weight of 20% is given to the immediate reward, prioritizing the accumulated reward with a weight of 80%. Thus, for the final test, i.e., the prediction of the Iberian market clearing prices for June 2024, α is set to 20%.

For the final evaluation, the forecasting models were trained with data from January 2024 to March 2024, the RL model was trained with data from April 2024 to May 2024, and the testing of the RL model was performed with data from June 2024 as depicted in Fig. 3. It should be noted that, during the training and testing phases of the RL model in the final test, each forecasting model is retrained after each execution month.

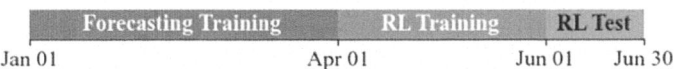

Fig. 3. Overview of the data used in the final evaluation.

The following section presents the evaluation results for each model in the prediction of the Iberian day-ahead market clearing prices for June 2024. The case study was run on a Windows 11 Pro machine equipped with an Intel Core i5 processor (13th Gen), 16 GB of RAM and an integrated Intel Iris Xe Graphics card.

5   Results and Discussion

To evaluate the different models' results, the MSE, RMSE, MAE and R^2 error metrics were considered. Table 4 presents the error values of each metric per forecasting model for the prediction of the Iberian market clearing prices for June 2024.

Table 4. Forecasting results evaluation.

Model	MSE	RMSE	MAE	R^2
RL	50,8164	7,1286	3,1479	0,9755
XGBoost	54,5114	7,3832	3,5470	0,9630
RF	73,9264	8,5980	5,2631	0,9498
RR	76,2892	8,7344	5,0942	0,9482
LSTM	218,535	14,9075	12,1127	0,9032
DNN	255,926	15,4391	19,7845	0,8970
SGD	356,997	16,8374	20,1983	0,8613

As demonstrated in Table 4, the RL model outperformed the remaining forecasting models, according to the evaluation metrics, with the lowest MSE, RMSE, and MAE error values, and the highest R^2 value. It is also demonstrated the proximity of the RL model predictions to the real value throughout the month of June, with an average difference of approximately 3.15 EUR/MWh (see MAE column). Thus, highlighting the model's perception of possible uncertainties and deviations from the real market price. To identify how the proposed RL model performs when large deviations from the actual value occur, the RMSE metric is used to select the worst day and the best day. Figure 4 represents the value of the RMSE throughout the month of June.

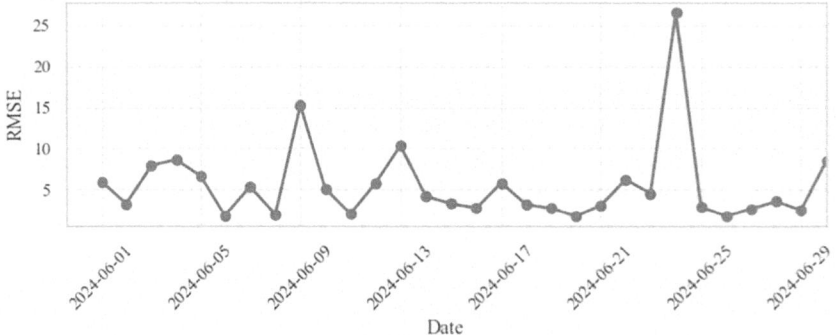

Fig. 4. RMSE throughout June.

According to Fig. 4, the RMSE values remain generally low throughout June, with most days showing values below 10 EUR/MWh. This suggests that the forecasting models selected by the RL model maintained a good level of accuracy over time, reflecting consistent performance. In particular, the worst day was June 24th, with an RMSE value of approximately 26.45 EUR/MWh, and the best day was June 20th with an RMSE around 1.77 EUR/MWh. Figure 5 shows the prediction model selection ratio.

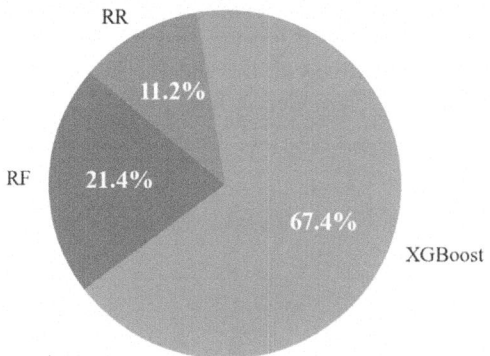

Fig. 5. Percentage of forecasting model selection by RL.

According to Fig. 5, the most selected forecasting model was XGBoost, being selected 67.4% of the times. RF follows, having been selected 21.4% of the times, and RR comes in third place being selected 11.2% of the times. The LSTM, DNN and SGD models were not selected for June 2024. These results highlight not only the stability of the forecasting process but also the effectiveness of the reward computation used by the proposed RL model.

Analysing the results of the best and worst days identified above, Fig. 6 displays a comparison between the values predicted by each model and the actual market clearing price value on June 24th, 2024.

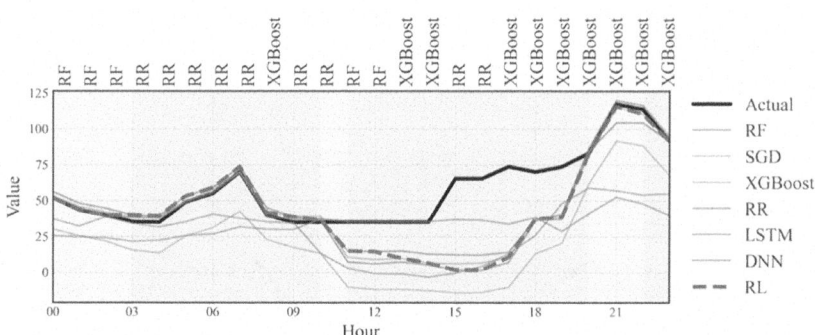

Fig. 6. Predicted values vs actual market clearing price on June 24th, 2024.

By Analysing Fig. 6, the most frequently selected forecasting model on June 24th was XGBoost, chosen in 41.7% of the periods, followed by RR with 37.5%, and RF with 20.8%. Although on the worst day the RL did not always select the best-performing model (periods in red), in many cases the chosen model was among those with the lowest forecast error. This is reasonable given that multiple models often produce very similar results. Furthermore, since the RL model bases its decisions on accumulated rewards, it tends to favour models with consistently good historical performance, even if they are not the best in every individual day. This can be seen in the periods between 10:00h and 20:00h, where price forecasts exhibited greater variation, and the RL model selected a model that did not adapt as effectively to the specific behaviour of the day. Figure 7 shows the reward evolution of each model on June 24th, 2024.

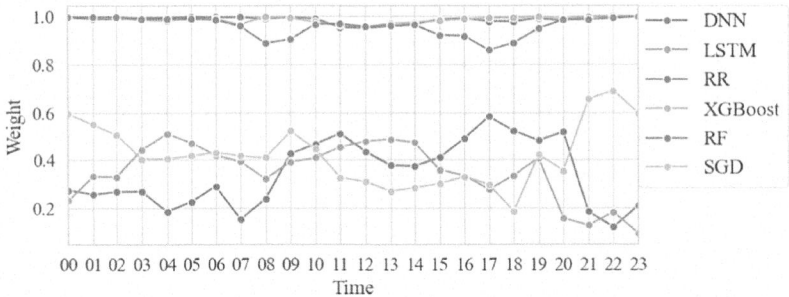

Fig. 7. Evolution of rewards for June 24th, 2024.

As shown in Fig. 7, the rewards of RR, RF, and XGBoost models were consistently close to the maximum value throughout the day. Although the LSTM model was the best option between 10 a.m. and 8 p.m. (Fig. 6), it was never selected. It's weight never exceeded 0.5 due to the cumulative reward computation (Eq. (2)).

Figure 8 introduces the comparison between the values predicted by each model and the actual market clearing price value on June 20th, 2024. On this day the most frequently selected forecasting model was XGBoost, chosen in 66.7% of the periods. RF was selected 25.0% of the time, and RR only 8.3%. The results also show a strong preference for XGBoost, especially in the second half of the day, where it was almost exclusively selected.

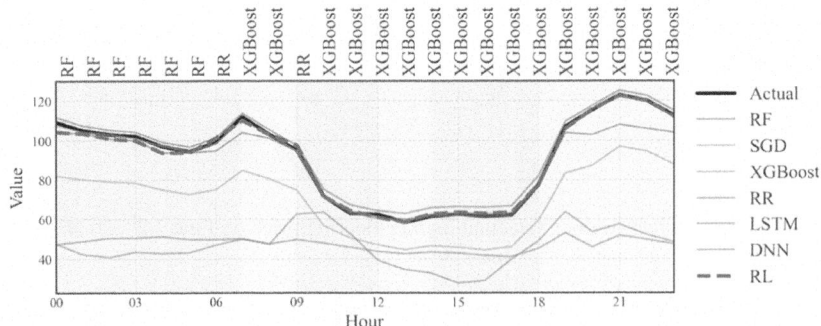

Fig. 8. Predicted values vs actual market clearing price on June 20th, 2024.

The predictions made by the RL model closely follow the actual values, as shown in Fig. 8. This indicates that the RL model effectively adapted its model selection strategy to maintain forecasting accuracy throughout the day. The consistent performance across different periods suggests that the RL model was able to identify and reinforce the use of forecasting models with more reliable historical performance under similar conditions, particularly XGBoost in this case. The competitiveness among models and the dynamic nature of their performance can be further understood by observing the evolution of the reward values assigned to each forecasting model, as illustrated in Fig. 9.

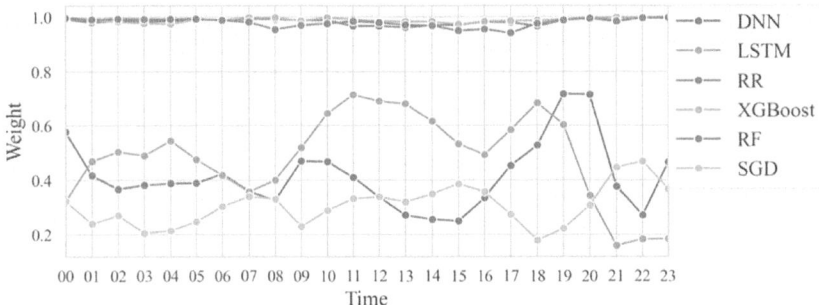

Fig. 9. Evolution of rewards for June 20th, 2024.

As illustrated in Fig. 9, the reward values of XGBoost, RF, and RR models are very close, being always one of these models selected by the RL algorithm. SGD, LSTM, and DNN, in turn, are never selected by RL as their rewards are never the best, at each moment.

6   Conclusions

The increasing use of RES in modern PES and the advent of the concept of SG bring new challenges to be addressed. In the energy sector, there is a lack of exploration of the integration of multiple forecasting methods with RL techniques. To address this issue, this work proposes a novel framework integrating several statistical and ML models with RL to select the best model at each iteration.

The proposed model has been trained and tested with real day-ahead market data gathered from the Iberian market and system operators. Sensitive tests were performed to identify the optimal parameterization of each model, and after, the proposed framework has been tested with the prediction of the Iberian day-ahead market clearing prices. Results demonstrate that the RL model can select and propose predictions very close to the actual market clearing price, with a monthly average MAE of approximately 3.15 EUR/MWh. Combining RL with forecasting models improved overall forecasting results compared to using each model independently. Thus, emphasising the potential of combining RL with ML to support decision-making within the PES sector.

Acknowledgments. This work was funded by GECAD research center supported by FCT (UIDB/00760/2020, doi: https://doi.org/10.54499/UIDB/00760/2020). Brígida Teixeira received funding from FCT, namely 2020.08174.BD, DOI: https://doi.org/10.54499/2020.08174.BD. Pedro Faria received funding from FCT, namely CEECIND/02109/2021 CIND, DOI: https://doi.org/10.54499/2021.01423.CEECIND/CP1652/CT0002.

Disclosure of Interests. The authors have no competing interests to declare.

References

1. Kotzur, L., et al.: A modeler's guide to handle complexity in energy systems optimization. Adv. Appl. Energy **4**, 100063 (2021). https://doi.org/10.1016/j.adapen.2021.100063
2. Fidalgo, J.N., de São José, D., Silva, C.: Impact of climate changes on the portuguese energy generation mix. In: 2019 16th International Conference on the European Energy Market (EEM), set, pp. 1–6 (2019). https://doi.org/10.1109/EEM.2019.8916539
3. Ahmad, T., Madonski, R., Zhang, D., Huang, C., Mujeeb, A.: Data-driven probabilistic machine learning in sustainable smart energy/smart energy systems: key developments, challenges, and future research opportunities in the context of smart grid paradigm. Renew. Sustain. Energy Rev. **160**, 112128 (2022). https://doi.org/10.1016/j.rser.2022.112128
4. Lipu, M.S.H., et al.: Artificial intelligence based hybrid forecasting approaches for wind power generation: progress, challenges and prospects. IEEE Access **9**, 102460–102489 (2021). https://doi.org/10.1109/ACCESS.2021.3097102
5. Mishra, N., Silakari, D.S.: Predictive analytics: a survey, trends, applications, oppurtunities & challenges, vol. 3 (2012)
6. Radhamani, R., Karthick, S., Kishore Kumar, S., Gokulraj, M.: Deployment of an IoT-integrated home energy management system employing deep reinforcement learning. In: 2024 2nd International Conference on Artificial Intelligence and Machine Learning Applications Theme: Healthcare and Internet of Things (AIMLA), pp. 1–4 (2024). https://doi.org/10.1109/AIMLA59606.2024.10531519
7. Calegari, R., Ciatto, G., Mascardi, V., Omicini, A.: Logic-based technologies for multi-agent systems: a systematic literature review. Auton. Agents Multi-Agent Syst. **35**(1), 1 (2020). https://doi.org/10.1007/s10458-020-09478-3
8. Kwangkaew, A., Racharak, T., Charoenlarpnopparut, C.: Toward forecast techniques in optimal sizing of energy storage system with volatile energy sources for hybrid renewable energy system. In: 2020 International Conference on Smart Grids and Energy Systems (SGES), pp. 390–395 (2020). https://doi.org/10.1109/SGES51519.2020.00075
9. Kotsiopoulos, T., Sarigiannidis, P., Ioannidis, D., Tzovaras, D.: Machine learning and deep learning in smart manufacturing: the smart grid paradigm. Comput. Sci. Rev. **40**, 100341 (2021). https://doi.org/10.1016/j.cosrev.2020.100341
10. Pinto, T., Praça, I., Vale, Z., Silva, J.: Ensemble learning for electricity consumption forecasting in office buildings. Neurocomputing **423**, 747–755 (2021). https://doi.org/10.1016/j.neucom.2020.02.124
11. Teixeira, B., Faia, R., Pinto, T., Vale, Z.: Study of forecasting methods' impact in wholesale electricity market participation. In: Mehmood, R., (eds.) Distributed Computing and Artificial Intelligence, Special Sessions I, 20th International Conference, pp. 267–276. Springer Nature Switzerland, Cham (2023). https://doi.org/10.1007/978-3-031-38318-2_27
12. Andrade, J.R., Filipe, J., Reis, M., Bessa, R.J.: Probabilistic price forecasting for day-ahead and intraday markets: beyond the statistical model. Sustainability **9**(11), 11 (2017). https://doi.org/10.3390/su9111990
13. Ramos, D., Faria, P., Gomes, L., Vale, Z.: A contextual reinforcement learning approach for electricity consumption forecasting in buildings. IEEE Access **10**, 61366–61374 (2022). https://doi.org/10.1109/ACCESS.2022.3180754

14. Pinto, T., Vale, Z., Sousa, T.M., Praça, I., Santos, G., Morais, H.: Adaptive learning in agents behaviour: a framework for electricity markets simulation. Integr. Comput.-Aided Eng. **21**(4), 399–415 (2014). https://doi.org/10.3233/ICA-140477
15. Ibrahim, M.S., Dong, W., Yang, Q.: Machine learning driven smart electric power systems: Current trends and new perspectives. Appl. Energy **272**, 115237 (2020). https://doi.org/10.1016/j.apenergy.2020.115237
16. Gnat, S.: Impact of categorical variables encoding on property mass valuation. Procedia Comput. Sci. **192**, 3542–3550 (2021). https://doi.org/10.1016/j.procs.2021.09.127
17. Pedregosa, F., et al.: Scikit-learn: machine learning in python. Mach. Learn. PYTHON
18. Abadi, M., et al.: TensorFlow: large-scale machine learning on heterogeneous distributed systems. 16 de março de 2016. arXiv: arXiv:1603.04467
19. Alibrahim, H., Ludwig, S.A.: Hyperparameter optimization: comparing genetic algorithm against grid search and Bayesian optimization. In: 2021 IEEE Congress on Evolutionary Computation (CEC), pp. 1551–1559 (2021). https://doi.org/10.1109/CEC45853.2021.9504761
20. REN Data Hub». Acedido: 29 de maio de 2025. [Online]. Disponível em: https://datahub.ren.pt/pt/
21. Redeia, «Todate», Red Eléctrica. Acedido: 29 de maio de 2025. [Online]. Disponível em: https://www.ree.es/en/date/todate
22. Preço do mercado diário I OMIE». Acedido: 29 de maio de 2025. [Online]. Disponível em: https://www.omie.es/pt/market-results/daily/daily-market/day-ahead-price

Optimizing Quay Crane Operations Considering Energy Consumption

João Pedro Rebelo de Almeida(✉)(iD), Adrian Carrillo-Galvez(iD),
John Peñaloza Morán(iD), Tiago André Soares(iD),
and Zenaida Sobral Mourão(iD)

INESC TEC, Faculty of Engineering, University of Porto, Rua Dr. Roberto Frias,
4200-465 Porto, Portugal
joao.almeida@inesctec.pt

Abstract. Seaport cranes operate continuously and consume large amounts of energy while aiming to minimise containerships' berthing time. Although previous studies have contributed to addressing the crane scheduling problem, most have focused exclusively on loading time, often overlooking the aspect of energy consumption. Furthermore, crane activity is typically modelled in a simplified manner—commonly assuming a fixed cycle duration or constant energy usage when handling a container—without accounting for the impact of variable container masses. In this study, an energy-aware quay crane scheduling formulation for container terminals is proposed, highlighting the importance of integrating an energy model into the scheduling problem. The optimisation problem is formulated as a Mixed Integer Linear Programming (MILP) model. The objective is to minimise total energy costs by reordering the sequence in which containers are handled, while respecting precedence constraints defined by the ship's stowage plan. Two solution methods—a MILP approach solved using CPLEX and a genetic algorithm (GA)—are compared. The results indicate that, for larger containerships, the genetic algorithm provides a more efficient solution method. Moreover, incorporating detailed energy consumption models for electric cranes may significantly reduce energy costs during containership handling operations.

Keywords: Energy cost · Genetic Algorithm · Mixed Integer Linear Programming · Quay crane scheduling · Seaport

1 Introduction

In the coming years, seaports will undergo a significant electrification process. In this new reality, obtaining accurate electricity load forecasting of the port's assets and establishing energy management models is crucial for reducing costs and ensuring a stable energy supply [9, 15]. Within container terminals, operational efficiency largely depends on cargo handling equipment, which, as highlighted in [11], can account for the majority of electricity consumption. Quay cranes operate at the shoreline, where they are responsible for the loading and unloading of each of the containerships' bays, hence influencing the berthing time [20]. These cranes must reach the top of vessels, requiring heavier construction and higher operating velocities. However, basic cycle phases remain identical: hoist up/down and trolley and gantry movements - lateral movements with or without a container, along the shore in the latter case [14]. Therefore, fully understanding and modelling crane performance is fundamental to improving key terminal performance indicators, such as vessel turnaround time.

There is a wide range of literature concerning cranes. Regarding their modelling and sizing, some studies adopt a more technical approach, as seen in [5,14], which focus on hybrid rubber-tyred gantry (RTG) cranes. These works analyse the complete operational cycle and dimension the crane based on its technical and mechanical specifications. However, these models typically simplify operations by assuming a fixed base load cycle, constant container mass, and often exclude gantry movements - factors that significantly affect energy consumption. In [18], the authors develop a detailed model of crane behaviour, though it focuses on load-handling trajectories rather than the full operational cycle. A second line of research focuses on energy management systems (EMS) tailored to crane operations. Some studies [2,8] explore EMS strategies that integrate storage systems to reduce peak loads and improve energy use. Others, such as [1], include dynamic electricity pricing to optimise crane energy consumption. Despite these advances, most models simplify crane behaviour using average consumption values and rarely incorporate detailed operational dynamics like container mass variability. For instance, in [8], a fixed consumption of 6.5 kWh/move is considered for each container. Finally, a third group of studies addresses the crane scheduling problem itself. Various optimization techniques — such as ant colony systems and other heuristic and metaheuristic methods - have been employed to minimize berthing time [3,13,17]. Although some papers incorporate energy-related aspects, they often focus only on yard cranes or, again, assume constant energy consumption [6,7,16]. Other works focus more broadly on energy efficiency without explicitly targeting cost minimisation [22]. In general, there remains a gap in the literature for an integrated model that couples detailed crane energy consumption, taking into account container weight, with crane scheduling and real-time electricity cost optimisation.

In this paper, a detailed energy model is integrated into an optimisation problem to solve the scheduling problem, with consideration of key factors as the vessels' stowage plans restrictions and other practical operation rules. The optimisation model aims to minimise the total energy costs while determining the optimal container handling sequence, taking into account the variability of container masses and electricity prices. By aligning container handling sequences with periods of lower energy cost, terminals can achieve more efficient and sustainable operations. Thus, the integration of a detailed crane energy model into a quay crane scheduling problem is proven important, with better accuracy. Two approaches are compared for this purpose - a Mixed Integer Linear Programming (MILP) problem solved with CPLEX and a genetic algorithm (GA).

The rest of the paper is organised as follows. In Sect. 2, the energy modelling is presented, and in Sect. 3, the description and formulation of the optimisation problem are shown. In Sect. 4, the results are compared and discussed. Finally, Sect. 5 gives a conclusion and a direction for future research.

2   Cranes Energy Modelling

This section presents the mathematical formulation of a crane cycle's energy consumption, highlighting the influence of container mass and other key parameters. A base cycle example is provided to illustrate the model's inputs and underlying assumptions.

The base cycle of the model is derived from mathematical expressions, drawing from previous works such as [14, 18, 21]. The main differences between crane cycle phases - hoist, trolley, or gantry - lie in the forces acting on the crane. The power consumed in each movement (P_{ideal}) is calculated using the product of the resultant force (F) and the velocity (v) of the movement, see Eq. (1). For the hoisting phase, the calculation must also include the drum inertia.

$$P_{ideal} = F_{\text{total}} \cdot v \tag{1}$$

The power consumption at each instant (P_{motor}) accounts for the combined efficiency of the gearbox (η_{GB}), inverter (η_{inv}), and motor (η_{motor}).

$$P_{\text{motor}} = \frac{\frac{P_{ideal}}{\eta_{\text{GB}}} + \omega \cdot J \cdot \alpha}{\eta_{\text{inv}} \cdot \eta_{\text{motor}}} \tag{2}$$

The balance of forces varies depending on whether the crane performs a horizontal movement (using trolley, see Eq. (3) or gantry motors, see Eq. (4)) or a vertical movement (see Eq. (5)).

$$\text{(Trolley)} \quad F_{\text{total}} = F_{\text{air resistance}} + F_{\text{rolling}} + m \cdot a \tag{3}$$

$$\text{(Gantry)} \quad F_{\text{total}} = F_{\text{rolling}} + m \cdot a \tag{4}$$

$$\text{(Hoist)} \quad F_{\text{total}} = F_{\text{friction}} + m \cdot g + m \cdot a \tag{5}$$

A crane's vertical movement is governed by the interaction of three main forces: the frictional force (F_{friction}), the gravitational force, and the inertial force due to acceleration. The gravitational force is calculated as the product of the container's mass m and the gravitational acceleration g, while the acceleration force is given by ma, where a is the vertical acceleration. These forces, where mass plays an important role, act together to determine the power requirements during upward or downward hoisting. In horizontal movements, different forces must be considered. Alongside the acceleration force, the rolling resistance (F_{rolling}) accounts for energy losses due to wheel friction, and air resistance ($F_{\text{air resistance}}$) acts on the trolley as it moves along the girder.

Throughout each movement phase—whether vertical or horizontal—the values of velocity and mass depend on the direction (upward/downward or forward/backwards) and whether the crane is handling a container or moving

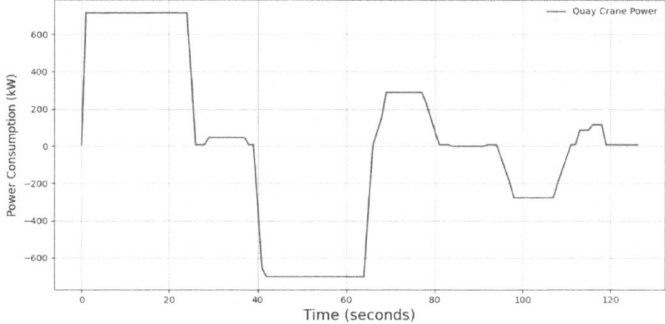

Fig. 1. Quay crane estimated load cycle.

empty. These varying conditions influence the resulting forces and, ultimately, the crane's energy consumption. For a detailed mathematical description of the energy consumption associated with each crane movement, the reader is referred to [14,18,21]. Figure 1 illustrates an example of an estimated load cycle, considering the inputs of Table 1 and certain assumptions, which simplify the model calculations. In general, a constant cycle duration is assumed, regardless of operator skill or container weight. Idle power consumption is treated as a fixed value, and crane movement parameters—such as velocity and acceleration time—are also fixed. Movements are considered non-simultaneous.

Table 1. Crane inputs to the simulation model.

Parameters		Value	Unit	REF
Cycle Length		112	s	[10]
Container Mass		40	ton	–
Spreader Mass		10	ton	–
Crane Mass		1280	ton	[4]
Velocity	Hoist w/ Load	1.25	m/s	[12]
	Hoist w/ No Load	2.50	m/s	[12]
	Trolley	3.50	m/s	[12]
	Gantry	0.75	m/s	[12]
Acceleration Time	Hoist w/ Load	2	s	[10]
	Hoist w/ No Load	4	s	[10]
	Trolley	4	s	[19]
	Gantry	4	s	[19]
Efficiency	Inverter	98		[14]
	Motor	96		[14]
	Gearbox	92		[14]
Drum Radius		0.4	m	–
Idle Power		7000	W	[14]
Gear Ratio	Hoist	30	–	–
	Trolley	15	–	–
	Gantry	25	–	–

The different phases of the cycle and their impact on energy consumption are clearly visible. Hoisting operations demand the highest power peaks, while trolley and gantry movements require significantly less energy. As expected, the crane consumes more energy while carrying a container—operation phase which lasts until around the second 67—compared to when it is empty. As shown, in the uncommon case of handling a 40-ton container, power peaks can reach up to 700 kW. It is important to note that the energy consumption profile varies significantly. Therefore, assuming an average consumption per move neglects the inherent variability in crane energy usage and may result in significant underestimation or overestimation of the total energy consumed.

3   Quay Cranes Energy Aware Scheduling

This section presents an optimisation model for a quay crane scheduling problem, with a specific focus on minimising the total energy costs of container handling operations. The model integrates a detailed representation of crane energy consumption—explicitly accounting for container weight variability—with real-time electricity price fluctuations. By reordering the sequence in which containers are unloaded, the model aims to identify the most cost-efficient handling schedule. This results in a combinatorial optimisation problem, where the challenge lies in determining the optimal sequence among all feasible container handling orders.

To better illustrate the optimisation problem, Fig. 2 presents a simplified example involving the handling of five containers, distributed across two stacks in a containership bay. Each container has a different weight, and precedence constraints must be considered (e.g., container 2A can only be moved after container 1A). By comparing the total energy cost of all valid sequences, while accounting for electricity price variations throughout the day, the model identifies the optimal solution, i.e., the sequence that results in the lowest overall

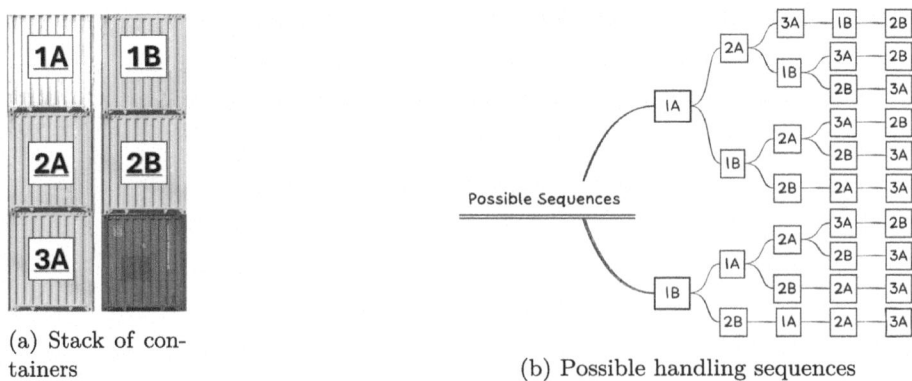

(a) Stack of containers

(b) Possible handling sequences

Fig. 2. Optimisation problem: (a) stack of containers, and (b) possible handling sequences.

energy cost among the ten possible sequences, see Fig. 2b. For simplicity, the model considers a single quay crane operating in a single bay (excluding gantry movements), unloading one container at a time, and assumes that ship stability remains unaffected. Future work will focus on relaxing these assumptions. Nevertheless, some constraints can be readily incorporated into the model—for example, by expanding the definition of set P in constraint (13). The optimisation model presented follows the methodology presented in Fig. 3.

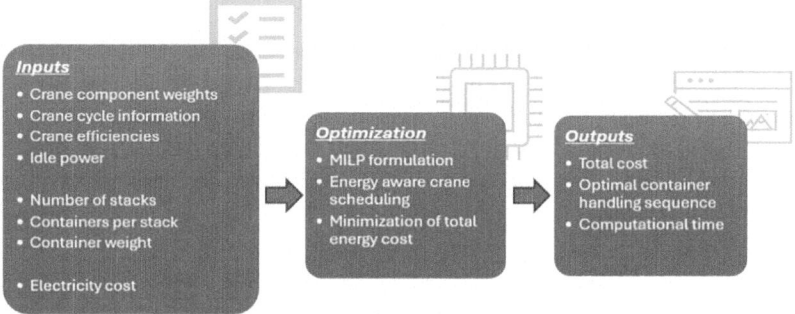

Fig. 3. Diagram of the proposed model.

3.1 Mathematical Formulation

The objective function, shown in Eq. (6), captures both the energy costs associated with moving the crane's spreader from the position of container i in the containership's bay to the next position j, and the energy costs of unloading container i from the vessel to the quay. The cost associated with handling each container is calculated based on the crane's instantaneous power at each simulated time step, as defined by Eqs.(1)–(5). During each second of the load cycle, a specific type of motion—hoisting, trolley, or gantry—is assigned to every moment, determining the corresponding forces balance and power consumption and, consequently, the energy cost. As a result, the container's weight directly influences the energy calculations at every time step of the model.

$$
\min \sum_{\substack{i \in C_n \\ j \in C_n \\ i \neq j}} \frac{P_{QC_{i,t_{sc}}} \cdot \Delta t}{3600} \cdot dist_{i,j} \cdot x_{ij} \cdot CE_{u[i] \cdot Cycle + t_{sc}}
$$

$$
+ \sum_{j \in Orders} \sum_{\substack{t \in \{0,...,Cycle\} \\ t \neq t_{sc}}} \sum_{i \in C_n} \frac{P_{QC_{i,t}} \cdot \Delta t}{3600} \cdot CE_{u[i] \cdot Cycle + t} \cdot y_{ij}
$$

(6)

In this formulation, $P_{QC_{i,t}}$ is the power demanded by the crane at time t when moving container i. Although the detailed definition of P_{QC} is not provided here due to space limitations, it follows a piecewise linear function, as illustrated in Fig. 1. In this case, each breakpoint is determined based on the different submovements the crane can perform during a complete handling cycle. C_n represents the complete set of containers, which are organised in vertical stacks, and the set of handling positions is denoted by $Orders = \{0, 1, ..., |C_n| - 1\}$. The variable $Cycle$ denotes the set of crane operation cycles, which are modelled as discrete time steps, and Δt is the time interval, fixed at 1 s. The parameter m_i corresponds to the weight of container i, while CE_t represents the cost of electrical energy at each time step t, expressed in €/kWh. The total time horizon over which the energy costs are evaluated is defined as T. The moment in time when the crane moves from one container to the next one is indicated by t_{sc}, and $dist_{ij}$ quantifies the moved distance. Finally, among decision variables, $y_{i,t}$ is a binary variable that equals 1 if container i is removed during time step t, and 0 otherwise, while x_{ij} is also a binary variable that equals 1 if container j is handled immediately after container i, and 0 otherwise. The objective function is submitted to the following constraints to ensure feasible and realistic crane operation schedules:

$$x_{ii} = 0 \quad \forall i \in C_n \tag{7}$$

$$\sum_{\substack{j \in C_n \\ j \neq i}} x_{ij} \leq 1 \quad \forall i \in C_n \tag{8}$$

$$\sum_{\substack{i \in C_n \\ j \neq i}} x_{ij} \leq 1 \quad \forall j \in C_n \tag{9}$$

$$\sum_{i \in C_n} \left(1 - \sum_{\substack{j \in C_n \\ j \neq i}} x_{ij} \right) = 1 \tag{10}$$

$$\sum_{j \in C_n} \left(1 - \sum_{\substack{i \in C_n \\ j \neq i}} x_{ij} \right) = 1 \tag{11}$$

$$u_i - u_j + |C_n| \cdot x_{ij} \leq |C_n| - 1 \quad \forall i, j \in C_n, \ i \neq j \tag{12}$$

$$u_i + 1 \leq u_j \quad \forall (i, j) \in P \tag{13}$$

$$\sum_{j \in Orders} y_{ij} = 1 \quad \forall i \in C_n \tag{14}$$

$$u_i = \sum_{j \in Orders} j \cdot y_{ij} \quad \forall i \in C_n \tag{15}$$

In here, the set P contains pairs (i, j) indicating vertical precedence relationships. Among the decision variables, $u_i \in Orders$ represents the position of container i in the overall handling sequence. A unique time attribution is guaranteed for each movement in Eq. (7). Each container can have at most one successor and one predecessor, defined by Eqs. (8) and (9), forming a valid handling sequence. There must be exactly one initial container without a predecessor (Eq. (10)) and one final container without a successor (Eq. (11)). The formation of partial cycles or subtours is prevented in Eq. (12), while Eq. (13) guarantees that vertical precedence is respected, meaning a container cannot be moved before those stacked above it. Finally, Eq. (14) ensures a unique position in the handling sequence for each container, while Eq. (15) ensures consistency between position and binary decision variables.

4   Results and Discussion

In this section, we evaluate the integration of detailed crane energy modelling into scheduling optimisation. To this end, both a small test system with a randomly generated set of containers and a larger, more realistic use case are analysed. To solve the complex MILP formulation, a genetic algorithm is proposed and its performance is compared with that of an exact method using CPLEX. The optimal solutions obtained from both approaches are then compared to a reference handling sequence, in which containers are moved following a standard vertical downward order, a common practice in terminals. The small test system consists of 3 stacks with 6 containers each; while the larger case is inspired by the unloading process of a mega ship, representing one bay with 19 stacks of 6 containers. Both the container masses and the electricity cost function are inspired in data from the Port of Sines, Portugal.

The CPLEX solver returns a solution with zero gap, whereas, in the genetic algorithm, to ensure a fair comparison, every test was done with the same population size and identical stopping criteria. The size of the population and the elite, the probability of the mutation and the maximum number of iterations were fixed to, respectively, 500, 30% of the population size, 0.4 and 3000. Ten simulations for each test system were performed to improve the statistical robustness of the results. Each solution is encoded as an ordered list of containers, where the position of each element indicates its removal order, as shown in Fig. 4.

Fig. 4. Example of the encoding of a solution.

The results are presented in Table 2. For the small system, the solutions obtained using CPLEX and the GA are similar, with both achieving acceptable CPU times, as shown below.

Table 2. Comparison of the results with different solving methods and the reference handling sequence.

Test System	Method	Run Time [s]	Total Energy Costs [€]
Small System (3×6)	REF	–	9.96
	CPLEX	38.0	9.47 (-5%)
	GA	2.56	9.47 (-5%)
Large System (19×6)	REF	–	151
	CPLEX	–	–
	GA	420	129 ± 1 (-15%)

In the case of the large system, consisting of one bay with 114 containers, CPLEX was unable to provide a solution within a 4-hour time limit, and the execution was subsequently interrupted. In contrast, the genetic algorithm successfully solved the problem to optimality within a few minutes. This highlights the critical importance of incorporating artificial intelligence-based tools, such as metaheuristic algorithms, for efficiently solving the complex optimisation problem proposed in this work.

Figure 5 illustrates the convergence path toward the optimal solution for the case with the largest number of containers. As one can observe, no significant improvement is achieved after 2000 iterations.

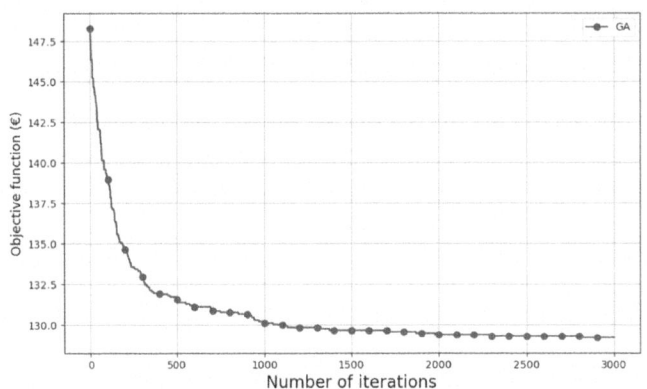

Fig. 5. Convergence graph of the large system optimisation.

Unlike the reference handling sequence, the optimal solution effectively accounts for the impact of variable container masses on the crane's energy demand, as well as fluctuations in energy prices. As shown in Fig. 6a, during periods of lower electricity prices, the optimal solution prioritises handling heavier containers, whereas lighter containers are moved when prices are higher. This results in a 5% and 15% reduction in total energy costs, in the small and large system cases, respectively.

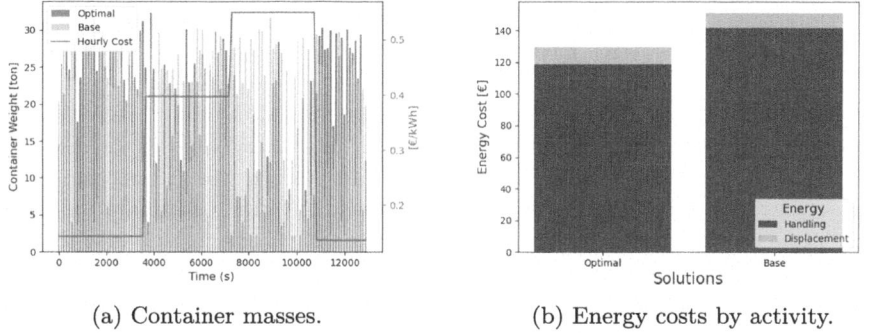

(a) Container masses.   (b) Energy costs by activity.

Fig. 6. Energy cost analysis: (a) cost-driven handling sequence adaptation, and (b) breakdown by activity.

Although displacement energy is considered in the optimisation process and may increase in some cases—such as when it is more efficient to handle a lighter container located farther away than a heavier one nearby—it remains relatively minor. As illustrated in Fig. 6b, the energy required for container handling far outweighs that of crane displacements, making the latter nearly negligible (around 0.11% of the total energy consumed). As expected, the optimal handling sequence results in significantly lower total energy costs compared to the base scenario.

One must also note that the influence of mass on the results is evident in Table 3. For instance, a light container of 5 tons represents only a consumption of 1.1 kWh/move, while one heavy container of 40 tons represents a consumption of almost seven times more energy. This shows the importance of not assuming an average value of energy consumption per move.

Table 3. Comparison of the energy consumption values using a detailed energy model and an average value.

Container	Weight [ton]	Energy Consumption per Cycle [kWh/move]
3A	31	5.8
1A	40	7.4
3B	17	3.3
6B	5	1.1

Finally, it is important to highlight that the results presented herein reflect the operation of a single quay crane handling containers from one bay of a containership. In real-world scenarios, however, the scale is significantly larger—both in terms of the number of cranes and the volume of containers handled—resulting in much greater potential for operational savings.

5   Conclusions and Future Work

This work developed a detailed crane energy consumption model and integrated it into a scheduling optimisation framework for quay crane operations. By incorporating container mass variability and real-time electricity prices, the energy-aware quay crane scheduling formulation proposed is valid and, in fact, minimises costs, while enhancing the accuracy and realism of energy cost estimations. For solving the MILP formulation, a genetic algorithm is proposed.

Results demonstrate that the genetic algorithm offers an efficient solution method, particularly for larger problem instances. The incorporation of a detailed energy consumption model for electric cranes reduces energy costs significantly during containership handling operations when compared to traditional sequential handling, showing the importance of the integration of an energy model in this type of problems.

As future work, the proposed model can be extended to address more complex operations, including multiple quay cranes, bays, and eventually yard cranes. The model can be extended to a real port with multiple quay cranes by adjusting the objective function and constraints, based on crane independence and physical limitations to avoid interference. Furthermore, applying this model in quay crane allocation problems could provide additional insights into energy-efficient terminal management.

Acknowledgments. This work is co-financed by Component 5 - Capitalization and Business Innovation, integrated in the Resilience Dimension of the Recovery and Resilience Plan within the scope of the Recovery and Resilience Mechanism (MRR) of the European Union (EU), framed in the Next Generation EU, for the period 2021–2026, within project NEXUS, with reference 53.

Disclosure of Interests. The authors have no competing interests to declare that are relevant to the content of this article.

References

1. Alasali, F., Haben, S., Becerra, V., Holderbaum, W.: Optimal energy management and MPC strategies for electrified RTG cranes with energy storage systems. Energies **10**(10), 1598 (2017). https://doi.org/10.3390/en10101598, https://www.mdpi.com/1996-1073/10/10/1598
2. Alasali, F., Haben, S., Holderbaum, W.: Energy management systems for a network of electrified cranes with energy storage. Int. J. Electr. Power Energy Syst. **106**, 210–222 (2019). https://doi.org/10.1016/j.ijepes.2018.10.001, https://www.sciencedirect.com/science/article/pii/S0142061518315631

3. Azza, L., El merouani, M., Medouri, A.: Ant colony system for solving Quay crane scheduling problem in container terminal. In: 2014 International Conference on Logistics Operations Management, pp. 176–180 (2014). https://doi.org/10.1109/GOL.2014.6887437, https://ieeexplore.ieee.org/document/6887437/authors

4. Bartošek, A., Marek, O.: Quay cranes in container terminals. Trans. Transp. Sci. **6**(1), 9–18 (2013). https://doi.org/10.2478/v10158-012-0027-y, http://tots.upol.cz/doi/10.2478/v10158-012-0027-y.html

5. Bolonne, S., Chandima, D.: Modeling and simulation of an electrome-chanical system for a hybrid rubber tire gantry crane. In: 2018 2nd International Conference on Electrical Engineering (EECon), pp. 14–20 (2018). https://doi.org/10.1109/EECon.2018.8540991, https://ieeexplore.ieee.org/document/8540991/?arnumber=8540991

6. Chargui, K., Zouadi, T., Sreedharan, V.R.: Berth and quay crane allocation and scheduling problem with renewable energy uncertainty: a robust exact decomposi-tion. Comput. Oper. Res. **156**, 106251 (2023). https://doi.org/10.1016/j.cor.2023.106251, https://www.sciencedirect.com/science/article/pii/S0305054823001156

7. He, J., Huang, Y., Yan, W.: Yard crane scheduling in a container terminal for the trade-off between efficiency and energy consumption. Adv. Eng. Inform. **29**(1), 59–75 (2015). https://doi.org/10.1016/j.aei.2014.09.003, https://www.sciencedirect.com/science/article/pii/S1474034614000901

8. Iris, Ç., Lam, J.S.L.: Optimal energy management and operations planning in seaports with smart grid while harnessing renewable energy under uncer-tainty. Omega **103**, 102445 (2021). https://doi.org/10.1016/j.omega.2021.102445, https://linkinghub.elsevier.com/retrieve/pii/S0305048321000542

9. Kanellos, F.D., Volanis, E.S.M., Hatziargyriou, N.D.: Power management method for large ports with multi-agent systems. IEEE Trans. Smart Grid **10**(2), 1259–1268 (2019). https://doi.org/10.1109/TSG.2017.2762001, https://ieeexplore.ieee.org/document/8064731

10. Kermani, M., Parise, G., Chavdarian, B., Martirano, L.: Ultracapacitors for port crane applications: sizing and techno-economic analysis. Energies **13**(8), 2091 (2020). https://doi.org/10.3390/en13082091, https://www.mdpi.com/1996-1073/13/8/2091

11. Kim, G., Lee, G., An, S., Lee, J.: Forecasting future electric power consumption in Busan New Port using a deep learning model. Asian J. Shipp. Logist. **39**(2), 78–93 (2023). https://doi.org/10.1016/j.ajsl.2023.04.001, https://www.sciencedirect.com/science/article/pii/S2092521223000184

12. Konecranes: Ship-to-shore crane (STS) technical datasheet (2024). https://www.konecranes.com/system/files/2024-04/7593_sts_monobox_technical_doc_v2.pdf. Accessed 15 May 2025

13. Montemanni, R., Smith, D., Rizzoli, A., Gambardella, L.: Sequential ordering problems for crane scheduling in port terminals. Int. J. Simul. Process Mod-ell. **5**(4), 348 (2009). https://doi.org/10.1504/IJSPM.2009.032597, http://www.inderscience.com/link.php?id=32597

14. Niu, W., et al.: Sizing of energy system of a hybrid lithium battery RTG crane. IEEE Trans. Power Electron. **32**(10), 7837–7844 (2017). https://doi.org/10.1109/TPEL.2016.2632202

15. Sadiq, M., et al.: Future greener seaports: a review of new infrastruc-ture, challenges, and energy efficiency measures. IEEE Access **9**, 75568–75587 (2021). https://doi.org/10.1109/ACCESS.2021.3081430, https://ieeexplore.ieee.org/document/9433559

16. Sha, M., et al.: Scheduling optimization of yard cranes with minimal energy consumption at container terminals. Comput. Industr. Eng. **113**, 704–713 (2017). https://doi.org/10.1016/j.cie.2016.03.022, https://linkinghub.elsevier.com/retrieve/pii/S036083521630095X

17. Skaf, A., Lamrous, S., Hammoudan, Z., Manier, M.A.: Solving methods for the quay crane scheduling problem at port of Tripoli-Lebanon. RAIRO - Oper. Res. **55**(1), 115–133 (2021). https://doi.org/10.1051/ro/2020135, https://www.rairo-ro.org/10.1051/ro/2020135

18. Takalani, R.L.E., Masisi, L.: Development of an optimal port crane trajectory for reduced energy consumption. Energies **16**(20), 7172 (2023). https://doi.org/10.3390/en16207172, https://www.mdpi.com/1996-1073/16/20/7172

19. Vlahopoulos, D., Bouhouras, A.S.: Solution for RTG crane power supply with the use of a hybrid energy storage system based on literature review. Sustain. Energy Technol. Assess. **52**, 102351 (2022). https://doi.org/10.1016/j.seta.2022.102351, https://www.sciencedirect.com/science/article/pii/S2213138822004039

20. Yang, K.H.: The influence of the quay crane traveling time for the quay crane scheduling problem. In: Proceedings of the International MultiConference of Engineers and Computer Scientists (IMECS), pp. 1298–1301 (2012). https://www.iaeng.org/publication/IMECS2012/IMECS2012_pp1298-1301.pdf

21. Zhao, N., Schofield, N., Niu, W., Suntharalingam, P., Zhang, Y.: Hybrid power-train for port crane energy recovery. In: 2014 IEEE Conference and Expo Transportation Electrification Asia-Pacific (ITEC Asia-Pacific), pp. 1–6 (2014). https://doi.org/10.1109/ITEC-AP.2014.6941043, https://ieeexplore.ieee.org/document/6941043

22. Zhao, N., Fu, Z., Sun, Y., Pu, X., Luo, L.: Digital-twin driven energy-efficient multi-crane scheduling and crane number selection in workshops. J. Clean. Prod. **336**, 130175 (2022). https://doi.org/10.1016/j.jclepro.2021.130175, https://www.sciencedirect.com/science/article/pii/S0959652621043407

Dynamic Retraining Framework for Reliable Energy Forecasting in Smart Buildings

Letícia Gomes, Brigida Teixeira$^{(\boxtimes)}$, and Zita Vale

GECAD - Research Group on Intelligent Engineering and Computing for Advanced
Innovation and Development, LASI - Intelligent Systems Associate Laboratory,
Polytechnic of Porto, Porto, Portugal
{lmccg,bct,zav}@isep.ipp.pt

Abstract. In dynamic building environments, machine learning models
used for energy management often suffer from performance degradation
due to seasonality and evolving user behavior. This paper presents an
adaptive retraining strategy that combines model performance evaluation with explainability-driven analysis to detect behavioral drift. By
monitoring prediction accuracy and feature importance consistency, the
system identifies when models require updating and classifies the urgency
of retraining into three priority levels. Scheduling decisions are guided by
contextual factors, such as energy consumption patterns and renewable
energy availability, enabling timely retraining that supports continuous
adaptation and aligns with green computing principles by minimizing
both environmental and computational impacts. To validate the proposed strategy, a case study was conducted in a real smart office building environment. Experimental results show that the adaptive retraining strategy consistently outperforms a non-retrained baseline, reducing
Weighted Absolute Percentage Error (WAPE), Symmetric Mean Absolute Percentage Error (SMAPE), and Root Mean Squared Percentage
Error (RMSPE) by up to 5%. These improvements reflect enhanced predictive accuracy and robustness under shifting consumption patterns.

Keywords: Energy Efficiency · Explainable AI (XAI) · Machine
Learning (ML) · Model Retraining · Smart Buildings

1 Introduction

In recent decades, there has been a growing interest in developing intelligent,
automated systems aimed at enhancing user comfort and improving the interaction between occupants and their environments, particularly in residential and
commercial buildings [6]. As they are among the largest consumers of energy
worldwide, optimizing building usage while maintaining user comfort has become
a key research priority [5]. In this context, intelligent energy management systems that adapt to user preferences and dynamic environmental conditions are

J. Valente de Oliveira et al. (Eds.): EPIA 2025, LNAI 16122, pp. 477–490, 2026.
https://doi.org/10.1007/978-3-032-05179-0_36

essential. However, end-users often lack the expertise to manage energy resources efficiently, resulting in suboptimal comfort and higher operational costs [8], and highlighting the need for systems capable of autonomously learning and adapting to evolving usage patterns and operational contexts within buildings [11].

Machine Learning (ML) models have increasingly been applied to support energy management in buildings, offering capabilities such as demand forecasting, anomaly detection, and energy optimization [4,18]. Despite their success, these models tend to degrade over time, particularly when influenced by seasonal fluctuations or changes in building usage patterns [2]. To preserve predictive accuracy and system performance, periodic retraining becomes necessary. However, retraining incurs computational and energy costs, making it essential to define not only when retraining should occur, but also how to perform it efficiently.

Prior work has investigated retraining strategies using drift detection methods, error thresholds, and fixed update intervals [13,17]. These approaches often rely on static assumptions, which may overlook the complexity of real-world conditions. Despite these efforts, the majority of retraining strategies in smart buildings remain isolated in scope, focusing either on error-based thresholds or offline and posterior SHapley Additive exPlanations (SHAP) analysis, without integrating both into a real-time system [7,16]. Moreover, most approaches are tested in controlled or synthetic environments, and few address the need for retraining prioritization under operational constraints, and depend exclusively on traditional error metrics as drift signals [1], neglecting the potential of explainability-based indicators. To the best of our knowledge, no existing work explores the dynamic combination of forecasting error and explainability deviations to guide context-aware retraining within a live smart building deployment.

This paper addresses that gap by proposing an integrated, dual-trigger framework designed for practical, scalable implementation, introducing a hybrid retraining framework that combines forecasting error metrics with deviations in feature relevance patterns captured via SHAP values. The dual-trigger strategy enables early detection of model misalignment and supports the scheduling of retraining during periods of low energy demand or high renewable availability, reducing operational disruptions. Unlike conventional methods, which are limited to offline validation, our framework is designed for continuous deployment in real-world smart building environments, where timely adaptation directly improves energy efficiency and occupants' comfort.

Furthermore, to minimize resource usage and environmental impact, the proposed approach incorporates principles of green computing, aiming to reduce the computational overhead associated with retraining processes [10,14]. Retraining actions are prioritized based on the severity of performance degradation and the potential cost-benefit for the user, ensuring that model updates occur at the most advantageous times, maintaining predictive accuracy while optimizing energy consumption and system efficiency. The result is a robust, adaptive, and context-aware energy management system that can evolve in response to changing user behavior and environmental conditions.

The remainder of this paper is organized as follows: After the introductory section, Sect. 2 details the retraining methodology based on model performance and explainability indicators. Section 3 describes the case study. Section 4 discusses results and evaluates the approach. Section 5 concludes and suggests future work.

2   Methodology

The proposed methodology outlines a robust and adaptive strategy to maintain the accuracy and reliability of ML models deployed in smart building energy management systems. These models are inherently prone to performance degradation over time due to factors such as seasonality, occupancy variability, and other dynamic environmental conditions. To maintain consistent performance, the system continuously monitors model behavior in real-time, using both forecasting error metrics and explainability-based indicators to detect degradation and determine whether retraining is necessary. Retraining decisions are guided by a prioritization and scheduling scheme following green computing principles.

The system operates through two independent processes: one for generating predictions and another for monitoring and scheduling retraining. The monitoring service queries the database periodically, every 15 min, to identify models eligible for retraining based on timestamp constraints and priority levels.

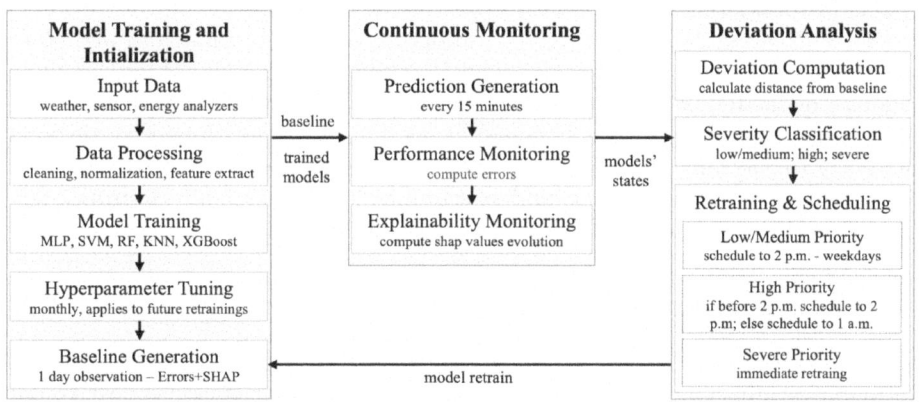

Fig. 1. Retrain model conceptual diagram.

The retraining logic consists of a structured sequence of steps, as illustrated in Fig. 1. Once a new model is trained and deployed, it enters an initial observation phase, during which its performance is systematically evaluated within a specified time window. During this stage, the system collects data on both forecasting accuracy and feature importance (via SHAP values) to characterize the model's behavior under normal operating conditions. The aim is to establish statistical reference baselines, specifically, the mean and standard deviation of key indicators, that will later be used to detect deviations indicative of performance drift. Following this phase, the model transitions into continuous monitoring for the remainder of its lifecycle. At each evaluation point, error metrics and SHAP-based attributions are compared to their respective baselines. When a significant deviation is identified, a severity level is assigned to guide retraining decisions. Model updates are executed using pre-tuned hyperparameters to reduce computational overhead and maintain system stability. Additionally, a hyperparameter optimization routine is scheduled monthly, leveraging one year of historical data to ensure that seasonally adjusted model configurations are optimized. The following subsections describe the key components of the proposed methodology.

2.1 Observation Phase

After training and deployment, the model enters a 96-period observation phase, during which its performance is systematically monitored every 15 min. Throughout this phase, the system collects data on both predictive accuracy and feature importance, the latter derived from explainability techniques such as SHAP. These indicators describe the model's behavior under normal operating conditions. The primary goal of this phase is to establish a statistical baseline, capturing the mean and standard deviation of forecasting errors and feature attribution scores. These baselines serve as reference points for detecting future deviations that signal performance degradation or behavioral drift.

The ML models currently used in the system are Artificial Neural Networks (ANN), K-Nearest Neighbors (KNN), Support Vector Machines (SVM), Random Forests (RF), and eXtreme Gradient Boosting (XGBoost). For each of these models, a dedicated baseline is built, capturing its individual behavior and internal dynamics. This separation is essential, as different algorithms may respond differently to the same input data. Maintaining model-specific baselines ensures that all subsequent monitoring and retraining decisions remain appropriately tailored to the characteristics of the deployed model.

2.2 Continuous Evaluation Process

Once the initial observation phase is complete, the model transitions into a continuous evaluation mode. Every 15 min, the system assesses its most recent behavior by comparing both forecasting errors and feature attribution values against the corresponding baselines established during the observation period. To ensure that both predictions and real values are available at the time of evaluation, error metrics are computed based on forecasts issued two time steps earlier, corresponding to a 30-minute delay. This design allows the actual observed values to be known and can be reliably compared to the earlier forecast.

The monitoring process runs on a separate service that accesses the same database as the forecasting service. Every 15 min, it evaluates model predictions by calculating performance metrics and SHAP values, comparing them to the baseline. If the model's behavior is within acceptable bounds, the new prediction is integrated into the baseline. Otherwise, the severity of the deviation is computed, and the retraining request is stored and prioritized.

Model performance is quantified using three core error metrics: Weighted Absolute Percentage Error (WAPE), Symmetric Mean Absolute Percentage Error (SMAPE), and Root Mean Squared Percentage Error (RMSPE). Absolute Error (AE) is also computed to assess the accuracy of individual forecasts. These metrics are recalculated at each evaluation point to measure deviation from expected behavior. WAPE provides a normalized measure of overall deviation, SMAPE is robust to near-zero values, and RMSPE emphasizes larger errors that may have a greater impact on system stability and user comfort. The AE captures the raw magnitude of individual forecast deviations.

Concurrently with error assessment, the system computes SHAP values to evaluate each input feature's contribution to the forecast. These values offer an interpretable, model-agnostic explanation of the internal decision-making process. By comparing current SHAP values to their historical baselines, the system detects shifts in feature relevance that may signal changes in occupant behavior, sensor anomalies, or environmental conditions. Notably, even when traditional error metrics remain within acceptable bounds, significant deviations in SHAP values can indicate latent behavioral drift, justifying proactive retraining. This dual-layer evaluation enhances the system's ability to deliver resilient, context-aware forecasting over time, combining predictive accuracy and explainability.

2.3   Deviation Analysis

To determine whether a model has drifted from expected behavior, the system performs a deviation analysis by comparing recent predictions against a reference set of historical outputs, referred to as the base set. This process is applied to both the model's predictive accuracy and the relative importance of input features, as quantified by SHAP values. It first evaluates SMAPE, WAPE, and RMSPE. If any exceed 25%, it classifies the retraining urgency as severe, and retrain immediately. If not, for each input feature, the system computes the mean SHAP value across all instances in the base set, capturing the typical contribution of that feature to the model's output under normal conditions. In parallel, the standard deviation is calculated to capture the natural variability in feature influence. Given a feature f, where $SHAP_j^{(f)}$ denotes the SHAP value at instance j, the mean and standard deviation are defined as shown in Eqs. 1 and 2, respectively.

$$\mu_{SHAP}^{(f)} = \frac{1}{n} \sum_{j=1}^{n} SHAP_j^{(f)} \tag{1}$$

$$\sigma_{SHAP}^{(f)} = \sqrt{\frac{1}{n} \sum_{j=1}^{n} \left(SHAP_j^{(f)} - \mu_{SHAP}^{(f)} \right)^2} \tag{2}$$

Based on these statistics, the system defines an acceptable operating range for each feature. A new SHAP value is expected to fall within an interval centered around the mean and scaled by a configurable deviation factor. Specifically, any SHAP value lying outside this range is flagged as a deviation. The sensitivity of this detection is controlled by a parameter k, representing the number of standard deviations tolerated from the mean, typically set to 1, 2, or 3, depending on the desired strictness of the monitoring policy (Eq. 3).

$$\mu_{SHAP}^{(f)} = \pm k \cdot \sigma_{SHAP}^{(f)} \tag{3}$$

A similar process is applied to the evaluation of prediction errors, where the system computes both the mean and standard deviation of historical errors in the base set, using AE metric. Let E_j represent the prediction error at time instance j. The average prediction error is given by Eq. 4, and its standard deviation is defined in Eq. 5. As with SHAP values, a new error measurement is flagged as a deviation if it lies outside the permissible interval specified in Eq. 6.

$$\mu_{Error} = \frac{1}{n} \sum_{j=1}^{n} E_j \tag{4}$$

$$\sigma_{Error} = \sqrt{\frac{1}{n} \sum_{j=1}^{n} (E_j - \mu_{Error})^2} \tag{5}$$

$$\mu_{Error} = \pm k \cdot \sigma_{Error} \tag{6}$$

By combining analyses of predictive performance and model explainability, the system obtains a comprehensive view of the model's behavioral integrity. This dual perspective enables the detection of subtle changes that may not be captured by error metrics alone. For instance, a model may continue to deliver seemingly accurate forecasts while progressively shifting its reliance toward features that were previously less influential, potentially indicating changes in data distribution or system dynamics.

Each identified deviation is subsequently classified according to its severity, based on the extent to which it surpasses the acceptable range. This classification informs the urgency of the retraining decision and is defined as follows:

– Low/Medium severity: deviation falls within one standard deviation from the mean (i.e., $k = 1$);
– High severity: deviation lies between one and two standard deviations from the mean ($1 < k \leq 2$);
– Severe: deviation exceeds three standard deviations from the mean ($k > 3$), indicating a major behavioral shift that could compromise model reliability.

This categorization based on severity levels directly informs the retraining priority mechanism described in the following section.

2.4   Retraining Execution and Scheduling Strategy

When retraining is triggered, the system determines its urgency based on the detected deviation severity, as previously described. This classification governs both the timing of retraining and its scheduling relative to other ongoing tasks.

The scheduling mechanism queries the database to identify models eligible for retraining at each moment. The assignment is made based on predefined rules: severe deviations are sent for immediate retraining, high-severity deviations are scheduled for times of high renewable generation (e.g., 14:00) or low demand (e.g., 01:00), and low/medium severity retraining tasks are scheduled for off-peak hours during the workweek or extended through weekends if needed.

Retraining is executed using the most recently optimized hyperparameters for the respective model, avoiding the computational overhead of tuning during every retraining cycle. To maintain long-term adaptability, a complete hyperparameter tuning process is conducted monthly using one year of historical data sampled at 15-min intervals. The resulting configurations are stored and reused until the next tuning cycle.

The retraining dataset includes one year of data preceding the trigger point, capturing both recent patterns and seasonal variations. Retraining is performed using the same model class originally deployed, preserving consistency in learned behavior and system expectations.

Retraining tasks are scheduled by priority, reflecting the deviation severity:

- Low/Medium priority: These cases reflect mild deviations and are handled during off-peak periods, such as times of high renewable generation or reduced building occupancy. A limit is imposed on the number of concurrent low-priority retraining operations to prevent resource contention. If a task remains unexecuted for multiple days, its priority is elevated.
- High priority: Represents noticeable but manageable performance degradation. Retraining is scheduled promptly, either within the current operational window or during nighttime when energy consumption is at its lowest. High-priority tasks take precedence over lower-priority ones in the queue.
- Severe priority: Denotes significant deviation that may compromise model reliability. Retraining is executed immediately, skipping scheduling constraints.

The scheduling mechanism is designed to align with the building's operational profile and energy availability. By deferring lower-priority tasks to off-peak hours and leveraging renewable resources when available, the system ensures efficient retraining while adhering to green computing principles.

3   Case Study

To validate the proposed retraining framework in a real-world context, a case study was conducted in an operational smart building equipped with an energy forecasting system. The objective was to determine whether the monitoring and adaptation strategy, based on performance metrics and model XAI results, could effectively sustain forecasting accuracy in a dynamic environment influenced by both behavioral and environmental variability.

The study focused on a specific zone within the building, consisting of three interconnected office rooms. The forecasting task involved predicting the total electricity consumption for this area, using input features that captured patterns of use and contextual factors. These features included data from lighting, sockets, and air conditioning systems, obtained from multiple sensors installed in the buildings, monitoring the environmental conditions affecting energy usage. To implement the proposed framework, the system was developed in Python 3.12, using scikit-learn [12], XGBoost [3], SHAP [9], and the PEAK framework [15], a MAS development platform built on top of SPADE that leverages the XMPP protocol to support distributed, asynchronous communication among agents.

In this study, forecasts were generated using the XGBoost algorithm, chosen for its balance of predictive accuracy and computational efficiency in time-sensitive applications. Hyperparameter tuning for the initial deployment was performed via grid search with cross-validation. The selected configuration, used as a baseline for both retrained and non-retrained model versions, included a learning rate of 0.1, tree depth of 5, and subsampling rate of 0.6. These parameters were then retained and updated during tuning cycles described in Sect. 2.

Model training was performed using historical data from January 1 to October 31, 2023. The evaluation period spanned from November 1 to 14, during which the system assessed model performance at 15-minute intervals, following its continuous monitoring protocol.

Forecast accuracy was evaluated using the primary metrics defined in the methodology: WAPE, SMAPE, and RMSPE. Retraining was initiated when any of these metrics exceeded a 25% threshold, or when significant deviations were detected in the contribution patterns of input features, as indicated by SHAP values. Combining performance and explainability evaluation enabled the detection of both clear degradation and subtle behavioral shifts.

Retraining processes were scheduled according to the severity and priority classification, as described earlier. High and severe deviations triggered immediate or near-term retraining. At the same time, low-priority cases were deferred to off-peak hours, typically when energy demand was lower or renewable availability was higher, ensuring that model maintenance is aligned with the building's operational profile, energy efficiency, and sustainability.

4   Results and Discussion

The proposed adaptive forecasting approach was evaluated over a two-week period, from November 1 to November 14, 2023. During this time, the system operated under real conditions within a smart building environment, continuously generating and assessing energy consumption predictions every 15 min. The primary objective was to determine whether the retraining strategy, guided by performance thresholds and feature relevance monitoring, could sustain predictive accuracy despite potential behavioral and environmental changes.

Figure 2 illustrates the actual and predicted energy consumption over the evaluation period. The vertical lines mark the timestamps at which model retraining was triggered. These retrainings were initiated either because forecasting error metrics exceeded predefined thresholds or due to abnormal variations in input feature importance patterns, as determined by SHAP values.

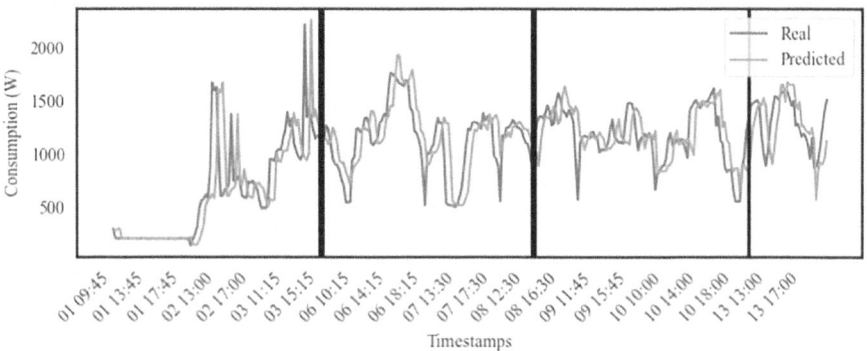

Fig. 2. Real and predicted electricity consumption between November 1st and November 14th, 2023.

Table 1 details the triggering conditions for each retraining event to contextualize the decisions. For each instance, it specifies the trigger type (whether due to forecast error or SHAP deviation), the value that led to the retraining decision, and the corresponding threshold or range that was exceeded. All retrainings were classified as severe priority, reflecting the magnitude of the detected deviations.

Table 1. Retraining events and triggering conditions during the evaluation period.

Date	Trigger Type	Triggered Value	Threshold	Retraining Level
3rd, 15:15	Error	29.31%	Max accepted: 25%	Severe priority
8th, 13:15	SHAP	10.73	[1.00 − 1.21]	Severe priority
13th, 10:15	SHAP	148.75	[−36.78 − 124.12]	Severe priority

A closer analysis of Fig. 2, in conjunction with Table 1, reveals how the model responded to distinct types of performance degradation. The retraining mechanism was activated three times, each under different triggering conditions. The first retraining, on November 3rd, was due to the WAPE reaching 29.31%, exceeding the maximum acceptable limit of 25%. This scenario represents a clear case of performance deterioration, where the model's output diverged from observed consumption to an extent that was quantitatively verifiable.

In contrast, the retrainings on November 8th and 13th were triggered based on explainability signals, specifically, deviations in SHAP value distributions. In both cases, the triggered SHAP values fell outside the expected empirical interval, defined as $\mu \pm 2\sigma$. On November 8th, the SHAP value reached 10.73, far above the upper bound of [1.00, 1.21]. On November 13th, the SHAP deviation reached 148.75, exceeding the threshold of [−36.78, 124.12]. These deviations indicate that the model had begun to rely disproportionately on specific input features, suggesting a drift from the behavior learned during training.

Notably, in both SHAP-triggered cases, forecasting errors remained within acceptable limits at the time of retraining. This demonstrates the complementary role of SHAP-based monitoring: while traditional error metrics signal observable performance loss, SHAP deviations enable the early detection of latent behavioral shifts. By capturing changes in the model's internal logic, the retraining mechanism was able to act preemptively, preventing further performance deterioration and ensuring the model's long-term reliability.

Figure 3 and Fig. 4 present the temporal evolution of SMAPE and WAPE, respectively, comparing the proposed strategy to a non-retraining baseline.

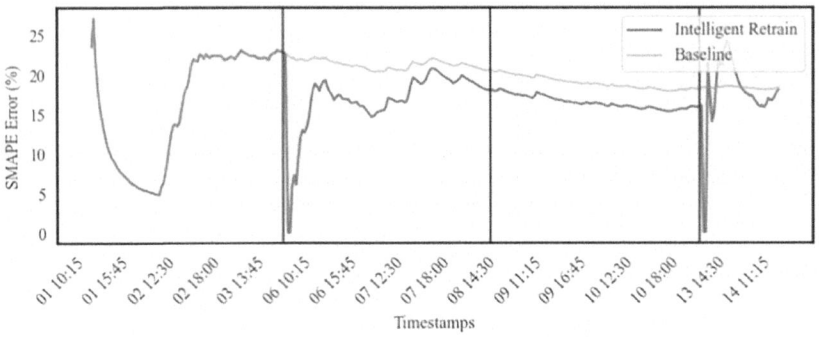

Fig. 3. SMAPE over time with and without retraining.

Figure 3 shows that the SMAPE associated with the non-retrained model increases progressively throughout the evaluation period, indicating a continuous degradation in predictive accuracy. In contrast, the retrained model displays a pattern characterized by localized error peaks followed by rapid correction, reflecting the positive impact of retraining on maintaining model alignment with the data distribution. A similar pattern can be seen in Fig. 4, where WAPE for the non-adaptive model rises steadily, whereas the retrained model maintains consistently lower and more stable error levels. A reduction in WAPE follows each retraining event, further validating the effectiveness of the adaptation strategy in mitigating performance drift.

To complement the temporal analysis, Table 2 presents a detailed comparison of forecasting performance for each evaluation slot, contrasting the retrained model against the static baseline. Each slot corresponds to the period between

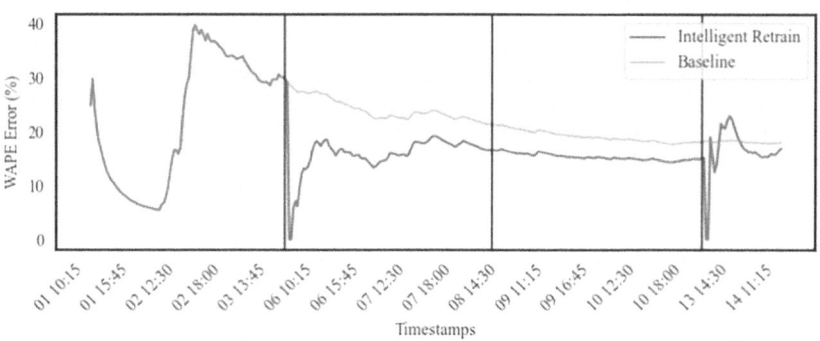

Fig. 4. WAPE over time with and without retraining.

two retraining events (or until the end of the evaluation window, in the final case). The metrics considered are WAPE, SMAPE, and RMSPE, which collectively offer insight into absolute accuracy, symmetric error behavior, and sensitivity to large deviations, respectively.

Table 2. Forecasting performance per slot, comparing retrained and baseline models.

Slot	Model	WAPE %	SMAPE %	RMSPE %
V_0	Retraining	29.31	22.63	18.19
	Baseline	29.31	22.63	18.19
V_1	Retraining	16.58	18.07	15.72
	Baseline	21.23	20.40	17.10
V_2	Retraining	13.55	14.12	14.84
	Baseline	18.24	18.41	16.47
V_3	Retraining	16.86	18.06	16.22
	Baseline	18.02	18.35	16.44

In slot V_0, both models present identical values, as retraining was triggered only at the end of the interval and had no effect on preceding forecasts. From V_1 onward, however, the retrained models consistently outperform the static base-lines across all metrics. In V_1, retraining yields a noticeable improvement in WAPE and SMAPE, along with a reduction in RMSPE from 17.10% to 15.72%, indicating better management of error variance. In slot V_2, the retrained model achieves further gains, with RMSPE reduced by 1.63% compared to the baseline, reflecting increased alignment with recent consumption dynamics. Both models exhibit similar performance in the final slot, V_3, though the retrained version maintains a slight advantage. These results reinforce the benefit of incorporating adaptive retraining, particularly in environments with shifting usage patterns or evolving feature relevance.

While the system demonstrates robust performance, its current deployment is limited to a single smart building with pre-processed and well-synchronized data sources. In real-world scenarios, issues such as sensor noise, data latency, and missing values may compromise evaluation reliability. Although the architecture can accommodate these, future work should validate resilience in noisier, multi-building contexts. Additionally, although the retraining strategy has yielded promising results with XGBoost, extending its application to models like MLP, KNN, SVM, and RF will further support generalizability.

5   Conclusions

This work presented an adaptive retraining framework for short-term energy forecasting in smart buildings, combining performance-based triggers with explainability indicators from SHAP values. The system was evaluated using real consumption data from a smart office building. The proposed strategy integrates retraining decisions based on both forecasting errors and internal shifts in feature relevance, enabling timely interventions before major performance degradation occurs. SHAP-based triggers proved especially valuable in detecting latent model drift, complementing traditional error-based monitoring.

Contributions include a retraining scheduler aligned with energy efficiency principles, the integration of explainability into decision-making processes, and a multi-model evaluation setup. Although the current deployment focuses on a single building zone and a relatively short time window, the architecture is flexible and designed for broader applications.

These results represent an initial exploration of dual-trigger retraining in real-world smart building scenarios. While the strategy enhances predictive accuracy, the retraining frequency directly affects energy consumption and computational cost. Since there is no universally optimal frequency, the framework incorporates mitigation mechanisms, such as prioritization rules and minimum intervals between retraining events, to balance performance with efficiency.

Future work will focus on continuous deployment and the application of the framework to a broader set of ML models (e.g., MLP, KNN, RF), each with tailored monitoring and tuning strategies to ensure scalability and robustness.

Acknowledgments. This work was funded by GECAD research center supported by FCT (UIDB/00760/2020, doi:10.54499/UIDB/00760/2020). Brígida Teixeira received funding from FCT, namely 2020.08174.BD, DOI: 10.54499/2020.08174.BD.

Disclosure of Interests. The authors declare that they have no competing interests.

References

1. Azeem, A., et al.: Mitigating concept drift challenges in evolving smart grids: an adaptive ensemble LSTM for enhanced load forecasting. Energy Rep. **13**, 1369–1383 (2025). https://doi.org/10.1016/j.egyr.2024.12.078
2. Bayram, F., Ahmed, B.S., Kassler, A.: From concept drift to model degradation: an overview on performance-aware drift detectors. Knowl.-Based Syst. **245**, 108632 (2022). https://doi.org/10.1016/j.knosys.2022.108632
3. Chen, T., Guestrin, C.: XGBoost: a scalable tree boosting system. In: Proceedings of the 22nd ACM SIGKDD International Conference on Knowledge Discovery and Data Mining, pp. 785–794 (2016). https://doi.org/10.1145/2939672.2939785
4. Costa, R., Silva, R., Faia, R., Gomes, L., Faria, P., Vale, Z.: Empowering energy management in smart buildings: a comprehensive study on distributed energy storage systems for Sustainable consumption. Energy Build. **324**, 114953 (2024). https://doi.org/10.1016/j.enbuild.2024.114953
5. Faia, R., Faria, P., Vale, Z.: Optimal energy management with discomfort calculation in residential buildings considering load shifting and home battery storage system. Sustain. Energy Grids Netw. **41**, 101624 (2025). https://doi.org/10.1016/j.segan.2025.101624
6. Gailhofer, P., et al.: The role of artificial intelligence in the European green deal (2021). https://doi.org/10.13140/RG.2.2.26789.22244
7. González-Briones, A., et al.: Evolution of building energy management systems for greater sustainability through explainable artificial intelligence models. Eng. Appl. Artif. Intell. **147**, 110324 (2025). https://doi.org/10.1016/j.engappai.2025.110324
8. Lazdins, R., Mutule, A., Zalostiba, D.: PV energy communities–challenges and barriers from a consumer perspective: a literature review. Energies **14**(1616), 4873 (2021). https://doi.org/10.3390/en14164873
9. Lundberg, S.M., Lee, S.I.: A unified approach to interpreting model predictions. In: Guyon, I., Luxburg, U.V., Bengio, S., Wallach, H., Fergus, R., Vishwanathan, S., Garnett, R. (eds.) Advances in Neural Information Processing Systems, vol. 30, pp. 4768–4777. Curran Associates, Inc. (2017)
10. Mahadevan, A., Mathioudakis, M.: Cost-aware retraining for machine learning. Knowl.-Based Syst. **293**, 111610 (2024). https://doi.org/10.1016/j.knosys.2024.111610
11. Ng, K., Chen, C.H., Lee, C., Jiao, J., Yang, Z.X.: A systematic literature review on intelligent automation: aligning concepts from theory, practice, and future perspectives. Adv. Eng. Inform. **47**, 101246 (2021). https://doi.org/10.1016/j.aei.2021.101246
12. Pedregosa, F., et al.: Scikit-learn: machine learning in Python. J. Mach. Learn. Res. **12**, 2825–2830 (2011)
13. Pham, T.M.T., Premkumar, K., Naili, M., Yang, J.: Time to retrain? Detecting concept drifts in machine learning systems (2024). https://doi.org/10.48550/arXiv.2410.09190
14. Ramos, D., Faria, P., Gomes, L., Vale, Z.: Energy forecast in buildings addressing computation consumption in a green computing approach, pp. 1–6 (2022). https://doi.org/10.1109/EEEIC/ICPSEurope54979.2022.9854723
15. Ribeiro, B., Dias, D., Gomes, L., Vale, Z.: PEAK: python-based framework for heterogeneous agent communities. SoftwareX **30**, 102190 (2025). https://doi.org/10.1016/j.softx.2025.102190

16. Saranya, A., Subhashini, R.: A systematic review of explainable artificial intelligence models and applications: recent developments and future trends. Decis. Anal. J. **7**, 100230 (2023). https://doi.org/10.1016/j.dajour.2023.100230
17. Teixeira, B., Valina, L., Pinto, T., Reis, A., Barroso, J., Vale, Z.: Exploring clustering to improve interpretability in complex energy forecasting models. In: 2024 International Conference on Smart Energy Systems and Technologies (SEST), pp. 1–6 (2024). https://doi.org/10.1109/SEST61601.2024.10694413
18. Yao, Z., et al.: Machine learning for a sustainable energy future. Nat. Rev. Mater. **8**(3), 202–215 (2023). https://doi.org/10.1038/s41578-022-00490-5

Fuzzy Data Analysis and Applications (FDA)

EvoNFuzz: A New Evolutionary Neuro-Fuzzy Network with Genetic Programming-Based Learning

Glender Brás[1]([⊠]) [iD], Alisson Marques Silva[1] [iD], and Elizabeth F. Wanner[1,2] [iD]

[1] Federal Center of Technological Education of Minas Gerais, Belo Horizonte, Brazil
glenderbras@gmail.com, {alisson,efwanner}@cefetmg.br
[2] Aston University, Birmingham, UK

Abstract. This paper presents EvoNFuzz, a novel Evolutionary Neuro-Fuzzy Network that integrates functional fuzzy rules with a hybrid learning approach combining Multi-Gene Genetic Programming (MGGP) and gradient-based optimization. Unlike traditional Takagi-Sugeno models, EvoNFuzz employs polynomial-based consequents, evolved via MGGP, to more effectively capture complex non-linear relationships in data. Additionally, EvoNFuzz incorporates rule weights akin to those in neural networks, allowing it to assign varying degrees of importance to each fuzzy rule. The membership functions are determined using the K-Means clustering algorithm. A Gradient-based learning algorithm adjusts the rule weights and the membership functions. The performance of EvoNFuzz is rigorously tested against alternative models on non-linear regression tasks. The computational results demonstrate that EvoNFuzz consistently outperforms or matches the performance of alternative models.

Keywords: neuro-fuzzy network · genetic programming · regression

1 Introduction

Evolutionary Fuzzy Systems (EFS) combine evolutionary algorithms with fuzzy logic to improve adaptability and performance, particularly in scenarios that require continuous rule updates [5]. Neuro-fuzzy networks combine the ability to handle uncertainty and imprecision of fuzzy systems with the learning and generalization capabilities of neural networks [15]. A key advantage of these networks is their ability to dynamically adjust parameters in response to changing operational conditions, without modifying the underlying rule base [3].

Genetic Programming (GP) is an evolutionary technique based on representation tree structures, well-suited for modeling mathematical expressions and symbolic regression [12,14]. Its flexibility allows for the evolution of fuzzy rule structures as mathematical expressions, enabling the generation of polynomial fuzzy rules [9]. These rules extend classical Takagi-Sugeno models [16], using polynomial functions in the consequents to better capture complex non-linear relationships [10,17].

J. Valente de Oliveira et al. (Eds.): EPIA 2025, LNAI 16122, pp. 493–505, 2026.
https://doi.org/10.1007/978-3-032-05179-0_37

Several studies have investigated evolutionary techniques to enhance learning in fuzzy systems. While GA remains the most commonly employed method in this field, GP has increasing interest due to its flexibility and powerful rule-evolution capabilities. For instance, in [8], various strategies for leveraging GP in parameter tuning, rule learning, and defining membership functions in fuzzy systems are discussed. A GP-based model for generating trading fuzzy rules was introduced in [11], while an automatic synthesis method for fuzzy systems using GP was also developed by [8].

More recent studies continue to demonstrate the flexibility and adaptability of GP in modeling fuzzy systems. For example, [18] introduced a fuzzy regression model based on Multi-Gene Genetic Programming (MGGP) for customer satisfaction analysis derived from online reviews. In another study, [10] employed GP to tackle high-dimensional data in fuzzy system modeling. GP's adaptability has also been applied to various practical domains. For instance, an adaptive neuro-fuzzy network utilizing GP for welding forecasting was developed in [2], while a GP-based model for diet optimization was presented in [4]. Additionally, [13] showcased GP's ability to explore robust search spaces, enabling the discovery of global optima even in scenarios with numerous local optima.

In this context, this work introduces a novel evolutionary neuro-fuzzy network, dubbed EvoNFuzz, which employs MGGP for learning. EvoNFuzz is a polynomial model employing functional rules with Gaussian antecedents and polynomial consequents. Unlike many existing neuro-fuzzy models that lack a rule weight structure akin to neural networks and focus solely on tuning parameters for antecedents and consequents, EvoNFuzz integrates rule weights, significantly enhancing its flexibility and learning capacity.

Moreover, while many models using functional rules depend on predefined function formats, which constrain adaptability, the proposed approach allows for dynamic rule evolution. By representing rules as mathematical expressions defined through MGGP, EvoNFuzz can better capture complex relationships, making it more robust and adaptable in diverse applications. The proposed model brings some significant novelties: (i) EvoNFuzz incorporates functional rules with associated rule weights, aligning its structure more closely with neural networks, (ii) it employs Multi-Gene Genetic Programming to model the consequent functions while utilizing a gradient-based backpropagation algorithm to fine-tune the parameters of both the membership functions and rule weights, (iii) as a functional polynomial model with polynomial consequents, EvoNFuzz effectively captures mathematical relationships between variables, excelling in modeling complex non-linear interactions, (iv) the output is computed in a simplified manner, mirroring the computational logic of neural networks for improved efficiency.

The remainder of this work is organized as follows. Section 2 details the structure and learning process of the proposed model. Section 3 describes the computational experiments conducted to validate its performance. Finally, Sect. 4 provides the conclusions, final remarks, and potential directions for future research.

2   EvoNFuzz - Evolutionary Neuro-Fuzzy Network

This section introduces the proposed Evolutionary Neuro-Fuzzy Network (EvoN-Fuzz). First, we describe the architecture of the EvoNFuzz predictor, highlighting its main components and structural design. Next, we explain the learning procedure used to build the structure and update its components and parameters.

2.1   Network Structure

The EvoNFuzz structure comprises three layers, each playing a crucial role in the inference process, as detailed below.

Fuzzification Layer (L^1). The first layer is responsible for fuzzifying the input variables. Each node in this layer applies a Gaussian membership function to an input value. The output of each node in this layer (L_{ij}^1) reflects the degree of membership μ of each variable x_i to each membership function A_{ij}:

$$L_{ij}^1 = \mu_{A_{ij}}(x_i), \tag{1}$$

in which i is index of input variables, j is index of the membership function, x is the current data sample described as $[x_1^t \cdots x_i^t \cdots x_m^t]^T$, t is the current step and m is the dimension of the input space. The time index t is omitted to avoid overnotation. The EvonNFuzz uses Gaussian membership functions and its activation degree $\mu_{A_{ij}}(x_i)$ is given by:

$$\mu_{A_{ij}}(x_i) = exp\left(-\frac{1}{2}\left(\frac{x_i - c_{ij}}{s_{ij}}\right)^2\right), \tag{2}$$

where c_{ij} e s_{ij} are the center and spread of the membership function j related to input variable i, respectively.

Rule Layer (L^2). This layer encapsulates the functional IF-THEN rules. The antecedents, derived from fuzzified input variables passed from the previous layer, are combined using compositional logical operators such as AND and OR. The consequents are represented by a mathematical function $f(\bullet)$ designed using MGGP.

Assume an EvoNFuzz model with three input variables x_1, x_2, and x_3, in which the domain of each input variable is partitioned into five membership functions: $(A_{11} \cdots A_{1i} \cdots A_{15})$ for x_1, $(A_{21} \cdots A_{2i} \cdots A_{25})$ for x_2, and similarly for x_3. The EvoNFuzz fuzzy rules are of the following form:

R_1:

$$\overbrace{x_1 \text{ is } A_{12}}^{L_{12}^1 = \mu_{A_{12}}(x_1)} \quad \overbrace{x_2 \text{ is } A_{23}}^{L_{23}^1 = \mu_{A_{23}}(x_2)} \quad \overbrace{x_3 \text{ is } A_{35}}^{L_{35}^1 = \mu_{A_{35}}(x_3)}$$

If x_1 is A_{12} **AND** x_2 is A_{23} **AND** x_3 is A_{35}

Then $Y_1 = (2x_1 + 5x_3)/(x_2 x_1)$.

R_k:

$$\overbrace{x_1 \text{ is } A_{24}}^{L_{24}^1 = \mu_{A_{24}}(x_1)} \quad \overbrace{x_3 \text{ is } A_{31}}^{L_{31}^1 = \mu_{A_{31}}(x_3)}$$

If x_1 is A_{24} **OR** x_3 is A_{31}

Then $Y_k = x_3(5x_1/2) + ((x_1 - x_3)2x_1)$.

in which R represents a fuzzy rule, k indexes the rules, and Y denotes the polynomial consequent $f(\bullet)$. We can see in the given example that a fuzzy rule is composed of one or more input variables, each associated with exactly one membership function. The rule's antecedent is constructed using a single fuzzy operator, such as a t-norm (e.g., AND) or an s-norm (e.g., OR). The antecedent firing degree D is determined using the *min* operation for AND rules. For the example presented above for R_1, it is computed as follows:

$$D_k = min(L_{12}^1, L_{23}^1, L_{35}^1),$$ (3)

and using *max* for OR rules. For instance, for R_k, it is obtained by:

$$D_k = max(L_{24}^1, L_{31}^1).$$ (4)

Then, the output of each of the activated rules[1], i.e., the output of each node for the Second Layer L_k^2, is computed by the antecedent firing degree D_k multiplied by its respective consequent Y_k. More specifically:

$$L_k^2 = D_k Y_k,$$ (5)

where k is the rule's index.

Output Layer L^3. The third and final layer computes the EvoNFuzz's output by aggregating the rules. The model output $\hat{y}$ is achieved through the sum of the rule outputs (L^2) multiplied by corresponding rule weights (w), divided by the sum of the weights. The rule weights connect this layer with the previous one and indicate the importance of each rule in the rule base, as well as its contribution to the final output. The network's output is given by:

$$\hat{y} = L^3 = \frac{\sum_{k=1}^z L_k^2 w_k}{\sum_{k=1}^z w_k}.$$ (6)

where z is the number of activated rules and k is the rule's index.

2.2 Learning Process

The learning process of EvoNFuzz occurs in two phases: unsupervised and supervised. In the unsupervised phase, the focus is on partitioning the universe of discourse into fuzzy sets and determining the membership functions for Layer 1 of the network. This phase can be executed using clustering algorithms, allowing the network to autonomously adapt to the input data and thereby reducing the initial error at the start of training. Moreover, defining membership functions tailored to the input data helps guide the learning algorithm toward more promising regions of the search space early in the process. This, in turn, reduces the number of steps required for convergence and enhances the model's accuracy.

---

[1] Activated rule is one whose antecedent firing degree is greater than zero.

The supervised phase addresses two key tasks: rule extraction and parameter updating. Rule extraction employs an MGGP method to model the rules that form Layer 2. Meanwhile, a Gradient-based algorithm is used to update the network's parameters. This update involves adjusting both the membership functions in Layer 1 and the rule weights linking the rules in Layer 2 to Layer 3. This process is carried out in an integrated manner; that is, for each generation of the genetic programming algorithm, l gradient steps are performed for each individual, as each individual has its own set of parameters. l is a defined algorithm's parameter. Thus, the gradient method helps improve the individual's performance with each generation. This process will be illustrated later in Algorithm 1.

Definition of Membership Functions. The definition of membership functions can be accomplished either through expert knowledge or automated techniques such as clustering algorithms. In this work, the K-Means clustering algorithm [7], combined with the elbow method [6], is employed in EvoNFuzz to optimize the network's adaptation to the input data. K-Means is an iterative algorithm that partitions data into k clusters, aiming to minimize the sum of squared distances between data points and their corresponding cluster centroids. The elbow method is used to determine the optimal number of clusters, as K-Means requires the number of clusters, k, to be specified as an input parameter. The elbow method involves plotting the sum of squared errors (SSE) for different values of k. The "elbow" of the resulting curve, where the rate of SSE decrease begins to level off, indicates the ideal number of clusters. This technique helps avoid both under- and over-segmentation of the data, resulting in more accurate and well-defined membership functions for the network.

Subsequently, each cluster generated by K-Means is mapped to a fuzzy set, with the centroid $(\bar{c}_{ij})$ of each cluster assigned to the center (c_{ij}) of the membership function j for input variable i. The spread (s_{ij}) of the membership function is proportional to the density of the cluster, specifically the number of elements it contains, as indicated by the label vector $(labels)$. This vector identifies which cluster each input belongs to. Thus, s is a value ranging from 0 to 1, representing the percentage of elements classified within that cluster, as shown by:

$$s_{ij} = \frac{n_j}{N}, \tag{7}$$

where n_j is the number of elements classified with label j and N is the number of samples. For example, if all elements belong to a single group, the spread will be 1.0; if only half of the elements belong, the spread will be 0.5. This approach simplifies the initial definition of membership functions, providing a foundation for further adjustments during the supervised phase.

Rule Extraction. Following the supervised phase, an MGGP method is used to construct the rule base. This approach models individuals as collections of representation trees, allowing multiple rules to be encapsulated within a single individual. This flexibility enhances the model's ability to represent complex relationships and supports more comprehensive rule extraction.

In the proposed model, each individual represents a complete rule base for the network. The individual is structured as a multi-tree, where each tree corresponds to a consequent function associated with an antecedent. As discussed earlier in this section, each consequent function is multiplied by the activation degree of its antecedent. The functions are constructed using basic operations, such as addition, subtraction, multiplication, and division, alongside input variables and numerical constants. Additionally, the user must set the minimum and maximum number of rules per individual in the initial population.

The initial population is generated randomly. First, the variables to be included in the rules are selected, and for each chosen variable, a fuzzy set is assigned to form the rule's antecedent. Next, a logical operator (AND or OR) is randomly chosen to complete the rule's antecedent. To define the consequents, a random representation tree (which represents a mathematical function for a polynomial fuzzy rule) is generated, and a random weight between 0 and 1 is assigned. It is important to note that all these decisions in the initial population are made randomly.

After generating the individuals, their performance must be evaluated using a fitness measure. This process involves calculating the network output estimated by each individual, comparing it to the expected output, and then applying an error metric to assess the discrepancy between them. In this case, the Mean Squared Error (MSE) is used as the fitness measure, obtained by:

$$MSE = \frac{\sum_{t=1}^{N}(y^t - \hat{y}^t)^2}{N},$$ (8)

where y^t is the desired output at time t, $\hat{y}^t$ the network output, and N the number of samples.

The new population is generated using genetic operators, including crossover, mutation, and natural selection, with an elitist approach to ensure that the best individual is preserved across generations. In MGGP, crossover and mutation can occur at low or high levels. In this study, both operations were performed at a high level, which means that entire rules are changed during both crossover and mutation. This ensures that both crossover and mutation swap entire rules without impacting the structure of specific parts in the rules. The tournament method was used for selection, applied to both parent selection and the formation of the new population. Additionally, the elitism operator is applied before the selection process, ensuring that the best individual from the previous generation is retained and replicated in the new population. The crossover and mutation operations are illustrated in Figs. 1 and 2.

Adjusting of Parameters. At each generation, the network parameters must be adjusted for each individual. This adjustment is performed using a gradient-based method, where a specified number of gradient epochs, l, is executed for each generation in the GP process. In this study, three gradient epochs were used

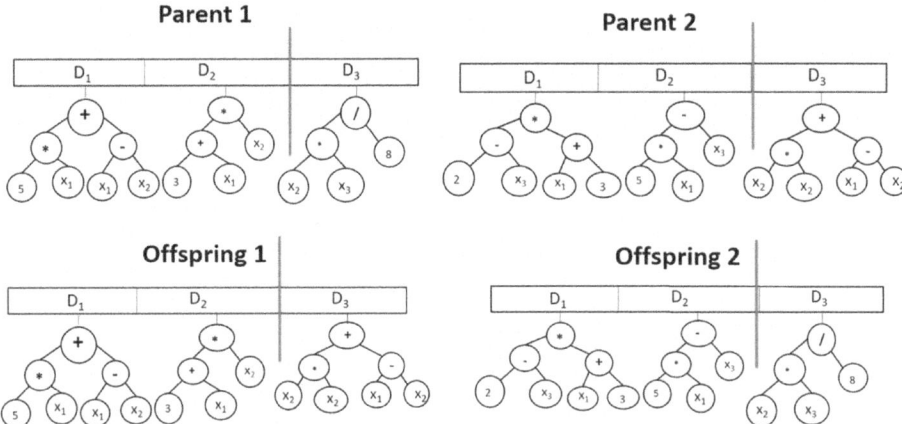

Fig. 1. Crossover in EvoNFuzz.

per generation to accelerate convergence and prevent premature convergence of the algorithm. The parameter adjustments are made according to the following equations:

$$c_{ij} = c_{ij} - \alpha \left(y - \hat{y} \right) dw_k \, dc_{ij}, \tag{9}$$

$$s_{ij} = s_{ij} - \alpha \left(y - \hat{y} \right) dw_k \, ds_{ij}, \tag{10}$$

$$w_k = w_k - \alpha \left(y - \hat{y} \right) x_i, \tag{11}$$

in which α is the learning rate, k indexes the rule, y is the desired output, $\hat{y}$ is the network output and, dw_{ij}, dc_{ij} and ds_{ij} are obtained respectively by:

$$dw_{ij} = \frac{\mu_{A_{ij}}}{\sum_{j=1}^{m_i} \mu_{A_{ij}}}, \tag{12}$$

$$dc_{ij} = \mu_{A_{ij}} \frac{x_i - c_{ij}}{(c_{ij})^2}, \tag{13}$$

$$ds_{ij} = \mu_{A_{ij}} \frac{x_i - s_{ij}}{(s_{ij})^2}. \tag{14}$$

Learning Algorithm. The complete learning algorithm is summarized in Algorithm 1.

3   Computational Experiments

The performance of EvoNFuzz is evaluated using datasets from non-linear regression tasks extracted from the UCI Machine Learning Repository[2]. Table 1 summarizes the datasets. A comparative analysis is performed between EvoNFuzz

---

[2] https://archive.ics.uci.edu/ml/index.php.

Before Mutation

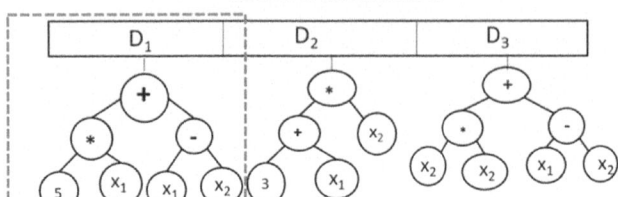

After mutation

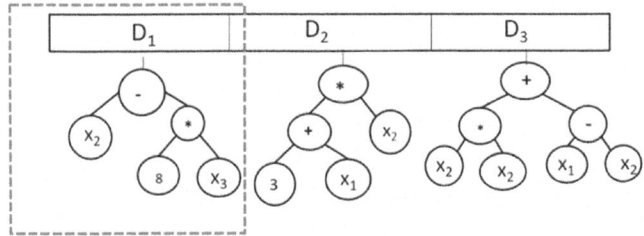

Fig. 2. Mutation in EvoNFuzz.

and five alternative models: AdaBoost (AB), Decision Tree (DT), Gradient Boosting (GB), Multi-Layer Perceptron (MLP), and Random Forest (RF).

Table 1. Datasets' summary, in which N: number os samples; m: number of attributes; X_{rng}: range of input values; Y_{rng}: range of output values; X_{std} = standard deviation of inputs values; Y_{std}: standard deviation of output values.

Dataset	N	m	X_{rng}	Y_{rng}	X_{std}	Y_{std}
Auto-MPG	391	7	(1.0, 5140.0)	(9.0, 46.6)	143.0794	7.8033
CCPP	9567	4	(1.81, 1033.3)	(420.26, 495.76)	10.1747	17.0658
Real Estate	413	6	(0.0, 6488.021)	(7.6, 117.5)	212.8847	13.6230
Concrete	1029	8	(0.0, 1145.0)	(2.33, 82.6)	62.8739	16.6569

The datasets were divided into two subsets: 80% of the samples were used to determine the optimal hyperparameters and train the models, while the remaining 20% were reserved for performance evaluation. The hyperparameters of the alternative models were fine-tuned using a grid search method [1]. In contrast, for EvoNFuzz, the hyperparameters were not fine-tuned, aiming to evaluate whether its learning process is sufficiently generic and efficient to achieve strong performance, even with the simplified initial network configuration. However, some preliminary tests were conducted to select a satisfactory configuration based on

Algorithm 1. EvoNFuzz Learning Algorithm.

Input x^t, y^t, g, $size\_pop$, tx_c, tx_m,
Output $\hat{y}_t$
Apply inputs to K-Means with the elbow method
Set membership functions center $c_{ij} \leftarrow \bar{c}_{ij}$
Compute membership functions spread s_{ij} (7)
//Generate initial popularion
for $i = 1 : size\_pop$ **do**
  Set randomly a number of rules n_r
  for $k = 1 : n\_r$ **do**
    Set randomly the variables that will compose the rule
    Set randomly one fuzzy set per chosen variable
    Set randomly an operator AND or OR
    $Y(k) \leftarrow$ generate random tree to the consequent
    $w(k) \leftarrow$ random weight

  end
  for $t = 1 : N$ **do**
    Compute L_{ij}^1 (1)
    Compute D_k (3) and (4)
    Compute L_k^2 (5)
    Compute $\hat{y}_t$ (6)

  end
  Compute fitness function (8)

end
//Generations
for $ger = 1 : g$ **do**
  for $i = 1 : size\_pop$ **do**
    for $epoch = 1 : l$ **do**
      for $t = 1 : N$ **do**
        Compute dw_{ij} (12), dc_{ij} (13), and ds_{ij} (14)
        Update c_{ij} (9) and s_{ij} (10)
        Update $w(k)$ (11)   with $k = 1...z$, $i = 1..n$
        Compute L_{ij}^1 (1)
        Compute D_k (3) and (4)
        Compute L_k^2 (5)
        Compute $\hat{y}_t$

      end
    end
    Compute fitness function (8)

  end
  Apply Elitism
  for $individual = 2 : size\_pop$ **do**
    Parent1 $\leftarrow$ TournamentSelection(CurrentPulation,Trn)
    Parent2 $\leftarrow$ TournamentSelection(CurrentPulation,Trn)
    Offspring1 $\leftarrow$ Crossover(Parent1,Parent2)
    Offspring2 $\leftarrow$ Crossover(Parent2,Parent1)
    Offspring1 $\leftarrow$ Mutation(Offspring1)
    Offspring2 $\leftarrow$ Mutation(Offspring2)

  end
  Compute fitness function (8)
  Select new population by tournament

end

---

insights from the literature on evolutionary computation. Table 2 summarizes the hyperparameters and their values used for fine-tuning the alternative models, along with the fixed hyperparameters employed in EvoNFuzz.

Table 2. Tested values in the grid search.

Model	Hyperparameter	Values
DT	*max_depth*	$None, 10, 20, 30$
	min_samples_split	$2, 10, 20$
RF	*n_estimators*	$100, 150, 200$
	max_depth	$None, 10, 20$
	min_samples_split	$2, 5, 10$
AB	*n_estimators*	$50, 100, 200$
	learning_rate	$0.01, 0.1, 1$
GB	*n_estimators*	$100, 200$
	learning_rate	$0.01, 0.1$
	max_depth	$3, 5, 10$
MLP	*hidden_layer*	$(100, 50), (50, 50), (100, 100)$
	activation	*tanh, relu*
	solver	*adam*
	alpha	$0.0001, 0.001, 0.01$
	learning_rate	*constant, adaptive*
EvoNFuzz	*population_size*	50
	generations	100
	gradient_epochs	3 per generation
	crossover_rate	0.7
	mutation_rate	0.1
	min_rules_individual	3 in initial population
	max_rules_individual	10 in initial population
	selection_method	*binary_tournament*

The models are evaluated based on the average RMSE and standard deviation across 30 runs for each dataset. A Boxplot Diagram is also used to analyze the statistical differences between EvoNFuzz and the alternative models. If the boxes do not overlap, it indicates a statistical difference between the models. However, when the boxes of two models overlap, a hypothesis test is needed to determine if there is a significant difference. To assess this, a one-sided pairwise T-test is conducted between EvoNFuzz and each alternative model, with a significance level of $p = 0.05$.

Table 3 presents the model's RMSE and standard deviation (St. Dev.), with the best performance highlighted in bold. The results indicate that EvoNFuzz outperforms the alternative models on 3 to 4 datasets (Auto-MPG, CCPP, and Real Estate). For the Concrete dataset, EvoNFuzz achieves the second-best result, with Gradient Boosting yielding the lowest RMSE.

Figure 3 presents the boxplot comparisons. The boxplots show that EvoNFuzz is statistically superior to the alternative models on the Auto-MPG, CCPP, and

Table 3. Model's performance by RMSE.

Datset	EvoNFuzz	DT	RF	AB	GB	MLP
Auto-MPG - RMSE	**2.42**	3.36	2.73	3.03	2.83	3.76
	0.16	0.27	0.25	0.20	0.24	0.44
CCPP - RMSE	**3.12**	4.14	3.37	4.80	3.32	6.03
	0.31	0.09	0.09	0.09	0.09	3.71
Real Estate - RMSE	**5.59**	9.11	7.42	1.31	7.79	8.48
	0.30	1.55	1.40	1.34	1.34	1.21
Concrete - RMSE	4.91	6.94	5.05	7.58	**4.68**	7.13
	0.20	0.62	0.35	0.35	0.36	0.55

Real Estate datasets. However, for the Concrete dataset, a T-test was conducted to compare EvoNFuzz against Random Forest and Gradient Boosting. For the Gradient Boosting comparison, the T-test returned a p-value of 0.004, indicating that Gradient Boosting is statistically superior to EvoNFuzz. In contrast, the T-test for Random Forest yielded a p-value of 0.028, indicating a statistically significant difference. Despite this, EvoNFuzz has a lower RMSE, indicating that it is statistically superior to Random Forest, even though the results are very close.

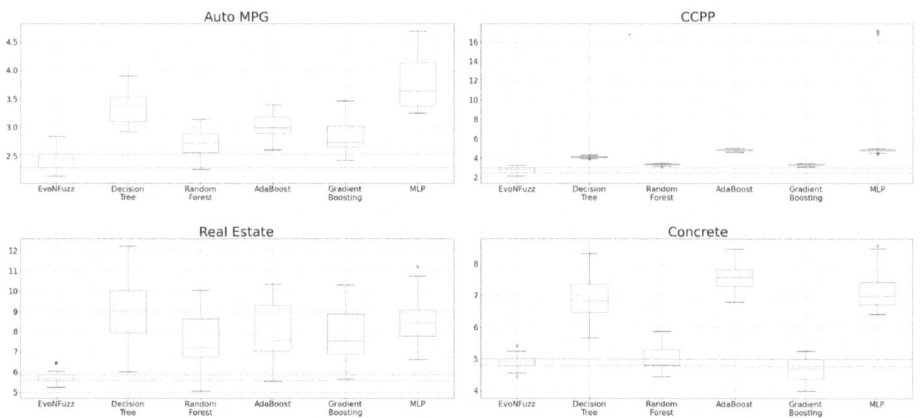

Fig. 3. Boxplot of EvoNFuzz for all datasets.

As an example of rules generated by the GP proposed method, the following illustrates a rule base designed by EvoNFuzz for the CCPP dataset with 5 rules:

$\mathbf{R_1}$: **If** x_1 is A_{11} OR x_2 is A_{23} OR x_3 is A_{33} **Then** $Y_1 = 2x_3 + x_2$.

$\mathbf{R_2}$: **If** x_1 is A_{14} AND x_2 is A_{23} AND x_3 is A_{32} AND x_4 is A_{32} **Then** $Y_1 = 2$.

$\mathbf{R_3}$: **If** x_1 is A_{12} OR x_2 is A_{21} OR x_3 is A_{32} OR x_4 is A_{32} **Then** $Y_1 = 17 + 2x_4$.

$\mathbf{R_4}$: **If** x_1 is A_{13} OR x_2 is A_{23} OR x_3 is A_{33} OR x_4 is A_{32} **Then** $Y_1 = 7x_4 - 9$.

$\mathbf{R_5}$: **If** x_1 is A_{13} AND x_2 is A_{22} AND x_3 is A_{31} AND x_4 is A_{34} **Then** $Y_1 = 7x_2 + x_3$.

Due to the high level of crossover and mutation operators, the depth of the trees does not increase significantly, thereby avoiding excessive growth of rules. This strategy enables the creation of a rule base with simple rules, as illustrated in the example. It can be observed that the antecedent of rule 1 does not contain all input variables, and rule 2 is a constant (zero-order) rule, showing the capacity of the MGGP in creating different types and formats of rules. It is also interesting to see that the consequent is not necessarily composed of all input variables involved in the antecedent.

4   Final Considerations

This work introduces a novel Evolutionary Neuro-Fuzzy network, EvoNFuzz, which utilizes polynomial rules and is driven by Multi-Gene Genetic Programming (MGGP) for learning. MGGP proved effective in extracting multiple polynomial rules for the rule base. The incorporation of rule weights into the consequents, similar to neural networks, and the hybridization with backpropagation techniques enhances the learning and generalization capabilities of the model.

Experiments demonstrated the efficiency of EvoNFuzz in addressing generic non-linear regression problems. The EvoNFuzz was consistently superior to or similar to five alternative models from the literature. Notably, the proposed model did not undergo parameter refinement like the alternative models, highlighting that the learning algorithm is effective for autonomous modeling of Neuro-Fuzzy networks. It is important to note that, like a hybrid and evolutionary model, the complexity can increase significantly as the number of variables increases. Therefore, given the experiments conducted, EvoNFuzz is considered ideal for problems that do not have a large number of input variables.

Future work can explore various directions, including the use of other T-norms and S-norms in fuzzy operations and evolving them into multi-gene individuals, as well as techniques for reducing the search space and eliminating redundancies in the rule base. Additionally, the applicability of EvoNFuzz to classification problems can be evaluated.

Acknowledgments. The authors acknowledge CAPES, Brazilian Ministry of Education, code 001. Alisson Silva gratefully acknowledges the Fundação de Amparo à Pesquisa do Estado de Minas Gerais (FAPEMIG) for Grant APQ-03224-24.

Disclosure of Interests. The authors declare have no competing interests to declare that are relevant to the content of this article.

References

1. Bischl, B., et al.: Hyperparameter optimization: foundations, algorithms, best practices, and open challenges. Wiley Int. Rev. Data Mining Knowl. Discov. (2023)
2. Chatterjee, S., Mahapatra, S.S., Lamberti, L., et al.: Prediction of welding responses using AI approach: adaptive neuro-fuzzy inference system and genetic programming. J. Braz. Soc. Mech. Sci. Eng. (2022)
3. Cox, E.: Adaptive fuzzy systems. IEEE Spectrum 27–31 (1993)
4. El Moutaouakil, K., et al.: Hybrid firefly genetic algorithm and integral fuzzy quadratic programming to an optimal moroccan diet. Math. Model. Comput. 338–350 (2023)
5. Fernandez, A., Herrera, F., Cordon, O., del Jesus, M.J., Marcelloni, F.: Evolutionary fuzzy systems for explainable artificial intelligence: why, when, what for, and where to? IEEE Comput. Int. Mag. 69–81 (2019)
6. Humaira, H., Rasyidah, R.: Determining the appropiate cluster number using elbow method for k-means algorithm. In: Proceedings of the 2nd Workshop on Multidisciplinary and Applications (WMA) 2018, 24-25 January 2018, Padang, Indonesia (2020)
7. Ikotun, A.M., Ezugwu, A.E., Abualigah, L., Abuhaija, B., Heming, J.: K-means clustering algorithms: a comprehensive review, variants analysis, and advances in the era of big data. Inf. Sci. **622**, 178–210 (2023)
8. Koshiyama, A.S., Tanscheit, R., Vellasco, M.M.: Automatic synthesis of fuzzy systems: an evolutionary overview with a genetic programming perspective. Wiley Int. Rev. Data Mining Knowl. Discov. (2019)
9. Lam, H.K.: Polynomial fuzzy-model-based control systems: stability analysis via piecewise-linear membership functions. IEEE Trans. Fuzzy Syst. (2011)
10. Mamaghani, A.S., Pedrycz, W.: Genetic-programming-based architecture of fuzzy modeling: towards coping with high-dimensional data. IEEE Trans. Fuzzy Syst. (2020)
11. Michell, K., Kristjanpoller, W.: Strongly-typed genetic programming and fuzzy inference system: an embedded approach to model and generate trading rules. Appl. Soft Comput. (2020)
12. Miranda Filho, R., Lacerda, A., Pappa, G.L.: Explaining symbolic regression predictions. In: IEEE Congress on Evolutionary Computation (CEC), pp. 1–8 (2020)
13. Pietropolli, G., Menara, G., Mauro, C., et al.: A genetic programming based heuristic to simplify rugged landscapes exploration. Emerg. Sci. J. (2023)
14. Poli, R., Koza, J.: Genetic programming. In: Search Methodologies: Introductory Tutorials in Optimization and Decision Support Techniques. Springer (2013)
15. Shihabudheen, K., Pillai, G.: Recent advances in neuro-fuzzy system. Know.-Based Syst. 136–162 (2018)
16. Takagi, T., Sugeno, M.: Fuzzy identification of systems and its applications to modeling and control. IEEE Trans. Syst. Man Cybern. (1985)
17. Tanaka, K., Ohtake, H., Wang, H.O.: Guaranteed cost control of polynomial fuzzy systems via a sum of squares approach. IEEE Trans. Syst. Man Cybern. 561–567 (2008)
18. Yakubu, H., Kwong, C.K., Lee, C.K.M.: A multigene genetic programming-based fuzzy regression approach for modelling customer satisfaction based on online reviews. Soft. Comput. **25**(7), 5395–5410 (2021). https://doi.org/10.1007/s00500-020-05538-8

Author Index

J. Valente de Oliveira et al. (Eds.): EPIA 2025, LNAI 16122, pp. 507–510, 2026.
https://doi.org/10.1007/978-3-032-05179-0

510   Author Index

Sousa, Inês   I-81
Sousa, Ricardo   I-243
Souza Pacheco Júnior, José Carlos   I-452
Spallone, Roberta   I-109
Stolper, Inesa   II-134
Stork, Lise   I-26

T
Teixeira, Brígida   II-451
Teixeira, Brigida   II-477
Tikhonova, Olha   I-188
Toribio, M. Carmen   I-426
Torres, Luis H. M.   I-375
Trofimenko, Irina   I-15

V
Vagnoni, Simone   I-492
Valach, Ondřej   II-205
Vale, Zita   II-451, II-477
Valente de Oliveira, José   II-163
Vargas, Valentina López   II-368
Veloso, Bruno   II-232

W
Wanner, Elizabeth F.   II-493

Z
Zeng, Tingying Helen   II-316
Zhai, Xiaoshui   II-83

The manufacturer's authorised representative in the EU is Springer
Nature Customer Service Centre GmbH, Europaplatz 3, 69115 Heidelberg,
Germany. If you have any concerns regarding our products, please
contact ProductSafety@springernature.com

Printed and bound by CPI Group (UK) Ltd, Croydon, CR0 4YY
29/04/2026
02099511-0009